*Mt. Edith Cavell in Jasper National Park, Alberta, Canada, dusted with the first snow of September. The mountain was named for a British nurse who was executed by the Germans in World War I.*

# Funk & Wagnalls
# New Encyclopedia

## VOLUME 1

### A to AMERICAN ELK

LEON L. BRAM
**Vice-President and Editorial Director**

**Funk & Wagnalls Corporation**

Publishers since 1876

# FOREWORD

This splendid edition of Funk & Wagnalls New Encyclopedia holds a special meaning for me. It carries forward the high ideals of my grandfather, Dr. Isaac K. Funk—ideals which he and his founding partner, Dr. Adam W. Wagnalls, established well over a century ago.

In 1875, my grandfather founded I.K. Funk & Co., a small publishing firm in New York City. Two years later, he was joined by Dr. Wagnalls and together they launched Funk & Wagnalls, dedicating their company to producing informative publications of quality and value. In the following years, their long list of distinguished reference and educational books and periodicals grew to include the Funk & Wagnalls dictionaries, the magazine *The Literary Digest*, and thousands of other publications.

It was in 1912 that the Funk & Wagnalls Standard Encyclopedia was first published. The objectives of the encyclopedia were clearly stated from the very beginning: to publish a useful, accessible set—intelligible to both students and adults—one that would encompass the broadest range of knowledge, and that all families could afford. Needless to say, that first edition was an immediate success. Now, decades later, with a new name and many times revised and expanded to accommodate the growth of information, Funk & Wagnalls New Encyclopedia still holds fast to those same objectives.

Just as readers did in 1912, today's readers—whether students or adults—will find in this encyclopedia the facts, history, and theory they need to help them grasp both specific topics and broad categories of knowledge. Detailed information is given on an enormous range of subjects, and readers with little or no background on a topic are provided with a maximum amount of enlightening material. Underscoring the content, the style of presentation stresses clarity, objectivity, balance, and unbiased expression throughout the set.

A wonderful improvement on the first edition are the colorful and practical illustrations and graphics that support so many of the topics in Funk & Wagnalls New Encyclopedia. The finely detailed maps, intriguing photographs, and specially commissioned charts and graphs—most in brilliant color—highlight key points of information throughout the 25,000 articles in the set and energize the unique frontmatter in Volume 1. This edition of Funk & Wagnalls New Encyclopedia is an example of encyclopedia publishing at its finest, and will add distinction to the homes, schools, and libraries of the United States and Canada.

The hundreds of dedicated editors, scholars, and consultants who revise and update Funk & Wagnalls New Encyclopedia are a far cry from the handful who put together that first edition so many years ago. Yet, they share the same time-honored ideals in planning, writing, editing, and illustrating a set of books that carry a generations-old name in which quality, practicality, and value are still the hallmarks.

Peter V. K. Funk
Author & Educator

# INFORMATION AND THE FUTURE

In today's world the ability to manipulate and interpret information is a key to individual and organizational success. The editors, consultants, and contributors who continually revise and improve Funk & Wagnalls New Encyclopedia do so in the expectation that readers will use the information within the encyclopedia's pages to achieve success—whether in school, business, or other endeavors. To meet the informational needs of today and tomorrow, the encyclopedia's professional staff and hundreds of outside experts must continually improve and refine the process of reviewing, selecting, organizing, and presenting new and revised information with every new printing.

In the past, encyclopedias could confidently be said to contain within their pages the then-current state of the arts and sciences, politics and philosophies, and other activities and interests of humankind. Changes affecting their contents were relatively few in the short term. Revision, replacement, or addition of articles was a matter of noting the extent of change in a particular subject, compiling such changes in many subjects over a period of time—perhaps decades—and then assembling a staff and auxiliary experts to bring the work up to date.

Today's world is far different. In all areas of human activity and interest, change is constant, vast, and swift moving. Although the task of the encyclopedia has not changed, the means by which that task is accomplished have altered dramatically. No longer can it be claimed that an encyclopedia, whatever its size or reputation, can incorporate within its articles, illustrations, or supplements all the knowledge that its intended audience wants or needs to know. Nor, for that matter, can any other information resource—whether paper, film, or electronic—make such a claim. And if such a goal were somehow to be attained by an archive not yet imagined, the velocity of change would make the claim of achievement obsolete by the time it was uttered. The flood of knowledge unleashed during the recent decades of this century has far outstripped the capacity of any human-made reservoir of information storage and retrieval to contain it.

An encyclopedia serving the homes and students of the U.S. and Canada—as does Funk & Wagnalls New Encyclopedia—must be carefully planned to cope with this vast outpouring. The organization and selection of information in all major areas of knowledge and activity—the arts and humanities, science, technology, history, the social sciences, sports and hobbies, philosophy and religion—must create a network of articles interrelated in such a way that no area is omitted or inadvertently isolated. Each article must concentrate resources of space, text, and graphics where they are most useful to the audience. The various information-finding devices are essential supporting networks to the articles. The index and internal cross-references ensure that all the information in the articles is accessible to the reader and that information need not be repeated in several places, occupying valuable space. The bibliography cross-references lead the reader from those articles most likely to create a desire for further research to the reading lists in the bibliography, where the reader will find appropriate sources of additional information. In the complexity of these various systems, constructed of many small units that combine in several levels of increasingly complex organization, the encyclopedia may usefully be compared to a living creature.

An encyclopedia for modern audiences must not only be a product of careful planning, it must be maintained after completion as an ongoing enterprise. As facts and fads change, as people and empires grow and then die, as new knowledge is discovered and old knowledge discredited, the encyclopedia must also change. In this respect—the constancy of change and the need for internal changes to meet changes in the outside world—the similarity between an encyclopedia and a living organism is even more striking.

Thus, the Funk & Wagnalls editorial staff, together with its expert consultants and contributors, constantly reviews the currents of change. Updates, additions, and revisions are made at every printing of the encyclopedia. Not only are specific facts within articles, or entire articles, subject to change, but so are major systems. The life sciences, for example, were subjected to thorough revision when basic changes were made in the scientific classification of all living organisms. The information-finding devices may also be altered to meet new requirements. As a case in point, a complete system of bibliography cross-references was added to the set in the early 1980s to facilitate the growing need to link specific articles to one or more specific reading lists. The standards and elements of style and format are subject to revision, as well. From printing to printing, grammar, syntax, and vocabulary are continually revised to make the language more meaningful to the broadest possible range of people in the English-reading audience. Writing that is directed toward one level of educational attainment and away from another, to one gender rather than both, to some socioeconomic, ethnic, or language groups rather than all, is eliminated wherever it is found. And the changes in graphics—the use of more full-color illustrations, new typographic standards, new formats combining text, art, and maps—are perhaps the most dramatic of all. They reflect the increasing reliance at all levels of society on the visual display of communications for an ever-widening network of purposes and users.

The creative effort that resulted in the publication of Funk & Wagnalls New Encyclopedia in 1971 and has guided the subsequent program of revision and improvement—indeed, that continues even as these words are being read—has created a work of high quality and broad utility. As the value of the information it presents increases, so will the intensity of the editorial commitment increase. Whether used for quick reference, research and school work, background reading, or browsing, Funk & Wagnalls New Encyclopedia provides easy access to essential information, guidance for further study, and the authority, accuracy, and currency expected of a product bearing the distinguished Funk & Wagnalls imprint.

The Editors

# THE COURSE OF HUMAN SOCIETY

## *INTRODUCTION*

Let us make two clear and significant distinctions concerning human beings and society. The first is between kinship and civilization, as the primary organizing principles of human society. The second is between balance and imbalance, as the primary orientations of human personality within society.

**Kinship** means that *all* one's loyalties are to kin, relatives, and not to strangers. Duties are to parents, grandparents, aunts, uncles, spouses, cousins, and these duties are reciprocal. Everyday life is lived face-to-face with kin. Pleasures are shared with them. What modern persons call politics, economics, and even culture are subsumed within kinship and can be derived from it.

**Civilization** means that most of one's loyalties are not to kin but to persons, typically strangers, who are positioned higher in some hierarchy by a mechanism other than kinship. Authority flows

---

*In kinship-based cultures, the elders continually educate and pass on their knowledge to the children, by demonstration, story-telling, as seen here, and other means.*

downward, and obedience upward, in political, economic, and other social hierarchies: Any one person will be obedient to persons higher in the hierarchy and, in turn, will expect obedience from persons lower. Kinship loyalties are often sacrificed to the demands of superiors in the hierarchy.

**Balance** means that two large clusters of mental activity are equal, each functioning fully. One cluster is based on the act of making distinctions —for example, creating hierarchies and valuing precision and orderliness in human affairs. The second cluster is based on dissolving distinctions. In contrast to the first, this cluster dissolves hierarchies and values richness of experience and complexity as opposed to narrowness of focus and precision. A balanced person can do everything in both clusters, responding appropriately to differences in his or her environment.

*The opening of the British Parliament by the reigning monarch and her consort demonstrates by costume, placement, and ceremony the hierarchical structure in a civilized society.*

**Imbalance** describes the dominance of the distinction-making cluster, with a corresponding weakening of the distinction-dissolving cluster. Imbalanced persons possess a smaller repertory of responses to different environments and thus often respond to change inappropriately. Most important, the weakening of their capacity to dissolve distinctions between themselves and others means that imbalanced persons are less able to identify with other people and thus more able to injure them.

If the two distinctions are combined, the four fundamental modes of human society are obtained:

Balanced kinship—the mode of the hunting and gathering family groups of primitive and tribal cultures, both ancient and contemporary.

Imbalanced kinship—the aggressive, often horse-mounted, tribal confederations exemplified by the Mongols before they became an empire.

Balanced civilization—historically important, but nonexistent today.

Imbalanced civilization—the dominant mode of contemporary nations and most other political and economic organizations.

# 200,000 To 10,000 Years Ago

Before 200,000 years ago, several ancestral forms of modern humans lived on the planet. Then, somewhere about 200,000 years ago, a few genetically modern women and men appeared in Africa. For tens of thousands of years afterward, premodern humans lived alongside modern humans *(Homo sapiens)*, until genetic convergence occurred about 35,000 years ago. Since then, there has been one, and only one, kind of human being *(Homo sapiens sapiens)*. Any visible variations among humans have become meaningless—except where imbalanced civilizations have arbitrarily assigned meaning to differences.

In all of the various studies of the human condition, hardly any question has stimulated controversy and engaged emotion as heatedly

as this: What were human beings like over the lengthy period of prehistoric time that they, our ancestors, lived? If humans were typically violent for almost a quarter of a million years, then it may be concluded that human nature must be inherently violent—and that axiom has far-reaching consequences in all human activity, from child rearing to politics. The presumption of human violence as inherent and pervasive would require society to exert tight control over every aspect of the life of individual human beings, most especially, of children and the education of children, in order to maintain amity. If, however, humans were typically peaceful over that span of time, then the axiom will be a different one, and the consequences will be of an entirely different kind.

Ample evidence supports the hypothesis that human beings from about 200,000 to 10,000 years ago lived largely in balanced kinship, the first mode describing the human condition, with pockets here and there of imbalanced kinship, the second mode. The kinship part is

certain. The balanced, rather than imbalanced, aspect is strongly suggested by **(1)** evidence of continuous ritual and symbolism that depend on dissolving distinctions, **(2)** the absence of evidence pointing to distinction-making institutions familiar to civilization, and **(3)** what some anthropologists have called the elaborate and unmistakable "amity syndrome," responsible for a peaceful way of life.

Balanced kinship did not end 10,000 years ago. There developed, rather, a new relationship between humans and the earth—one that seems, in fact, to have intensified balanced kinship for thousands of years.

*Early modern humans, the Cro-Magnons, who are seen here hunting reindeer, lived largely in balanced kinship.*

# 10,000 TO 6000 YEARS AGO

The period between 200,000 and 35,000 years ago saw two biological milestones in human history: Modern humans appeared, and all other kinds of humans eventually disappeared. Then, about 10,000 years ago, a cultural milestone—the birth of agriculture—changed human life. Previously all humans had depended on earth's natural supply for food. They foraged, gathered, and hunted. In most settings, such a life seems not to have required extended effort to find food. There was plenty of time for the complex human interchanges of balanced kinship. Distinction-making capacities were employed to assert the numerous relationships, rights, and obligations of kinship. At the same time, distinction-dissolving capacities were put to ritual purposes—humans "becoming" the animals in

*This gathering of Kwakiutl Indians represents a pre-urban hunting and fishing society typical of all humans before the 10th millennium BC. The double-headed eagle mask (inset), a Kwakiutl totem, is a sign of a kinship-based society.*

*As humans began to settle near crop fields and animal pastures, such Mayan temple cities as El Mirador (above) flourished. This development, as well as the statue (right) of a Toltec warrior from a pyramid at Tula, were indications of civilization in Mesoamerica.*

their environment, for example. This life, relying on what the earth grew and going about daily activities supported by kinship and symbolism, was by far the longest lasting of all human ways to live.

Then, about 10,000 to 6000 years ago, the method of food acquisition changed. Humans began to plant food and raise animals, depending less on the earth's natural provisions. Those peoples who adopted this mode of life settled down—they needed to remain near their fields and pastures. They increased in numbers, but kinship and ritual still remained the primary realities of their life. Now, however, the home of balanced kinship included the pre-urban village as well as the forest and grassland.

The village would ultimately develop into the city, and a major division of humanity that is still a part of human culture would come into being—the distinction between "primitive" and "civilized." The peoples of imbalanced civilizations have assumed superiority to and dominance over "primitive" balanced-kinship peoples based on technical, economic, and bureaucratic accomplishments. Balanced kinship societies never spent their intellectual and emotional force on such matters. Their energies went elsewhere, to kinship and ritual. Nevertheless, the accomplishments of balanced kinship societies have not prevented their almost total elimination in the last 6000 years.

The deepest of all cultural changes in human history occurred in what Westerners call the Middle East about 6000 years ago: Imbalanced civilization came into the world. A new human being, the city person, or, in the countryside, the city-controlled person, appeared for the first time. The most succinct way to describe the history of the last 6000 years—the history of the entire biosphere, so consequential for all other forms of life did the new kind of person become—is to say that it is the story of the inexorable spread, usually by violent means, of imbalanced civilization. Today it is virtually the only mode of human life on earth.

The first cities (imbalanced civilizations) appeared in Mesopotamia (present-day Iraq). Archaeological findings at the biblical city of Jericho allow a date as early as about 9000 BC. The essence of the Mesopotamian cities, and most subsequent cities and the countrysides they controlled, was the destruction of balanced kinship. Cities replaced balanced kinship with hierarchies: hierarchical political bureaucracies wielding coercive power, and hierarchical economic institutions gradually giving themselves over to competition for wealth. The city was the most aggressive social organism in history, not only destroying balanced kinship but introducing armies into the world, for the purpose of destroying other cities.

About 4000 years ago, imbalanced-kinship peoples began to make their presence felt. They were based on the Eurasian steppe, and lived by herding rather than gathering or farming. These clans, tribes, and confederations were as violently expansionist as imbalanced civilizations. For 3500 years these two aggressive social orders would be at each other's throats—with control of much of Central and Western Asia and Eastern Europe passing back and forth between them—until the more inventive imbalanced civilization perfected the rifle and began, literally, to shoot imbalanced kinship to death, about 500 years ago.

*The scene of Scythian warriors (left) represents a typical imbalanced-kinship society. The vulture goddess necklace (above) is a symbol of the beauty and delicacy of culture and art achieved during the height of Egyptian civilization.*

At this point, balanced kinship was effectively gone in Eurasia, and imbalanced civilization was fighting imbalanced kinship. One mode of human society remains to be described: balanced civilization.

Imbalanced civilization, first found on the Persian Gulf, destroyed balanced kinship and substituted its own institutions, point by point, for those it eliminated. By contrast, balanced civilization, arising on the Nile in Africa a few centuries after the first imbalanced civilization, preserved a number of balanced-kinship institutions, adding its own institutions to them. Thus, Egypt, on the Nile, was a balanced cumulative culture, keeping its past; Sumer, on the Persian Gulf, was an imbalanced displacement culture, destroying its past as it went.

A few civilizations, therefore, in western Eurasia—Egyptian, the first; the Minoan, on the island of Crete, perhaps stimulated by Egypt; and the Indus Valley, in South Asia—were actually at one and the same time balanced-kinship and balanced-civilization societies. They were remarkable for their symbolic, ritual lives and for their

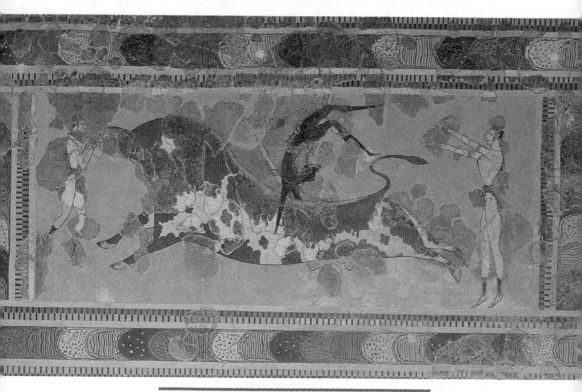

*"The Toreador Fresco" (c. 1500 BC), a large and dynamic
Cretan mural, shows the ritual Minoan game of bull leaping.*

*The Mongols waged war (13th cent. AD) on Europe and held dominance in much of Eurasia. Genghis Kahn, the founder of their empire, is depicted here ambushing Chinese warriors.*

monumental, hierarchically organized achievements. Suggestively, Egypt and the Minoans resisted the founding of cities for centuries.

For different reasons, involving both natural disasters and raids by imbalanced-kinship peoples, this type of balanced-civilization society disappeared about 3500 years ago. At almost exactly the same time, a modified balanced civilization began its career to the east, on the other side of Eurasia. China, slowly coming into being, would reach a thousand-year cultural plateau in the modern era.

Imbalanced civilization remained dominant, however. By 2000 years ago, several major subvarieties of imbalanced civilization had acquired their shapes. The foundations of the Western subvariety had been laid by the earlier Greek and Hebrew cultures, and they were now being synthesized and spread over a large area by a Roman empire that would soon become a Christian Roman empire. Similarly, the modern Indian and Middle Eastern subvarieties were becoming mature imbalanced civilizations.

# 2000 To 1000 Years Ago

The Western subvariety of imbalanced civilization was slow to mature. The Hebrews, at about the mid-2d millennium BC, provided an enduring model of religion founded on transcendent monotheism. Ancient Greece, between the 8th and the 5th centuries BC, produced an equally enduring model of urbanity, intellectuality, and aesthetic creation, all brilliantly imbalanced. These sacred and secular traditions were confined to small areas until elements of both were absorbed into a large empire circling the Mediterranean—Rome.

Another transcendent, monotheistic religion, Christianity, with roots in the Hebrew tradition, was adopted as the state religion of the Roman Empire more than 1600 years ago. The Christian Roman Empire was very soon shattered into small, economically autonomous

*The Italian bankers' exchange is an example of early economic activity which led to the emergence of European civilizations and to their domination of much of the world.*

pieces by imbalanced-kinship warrior clans. A fragmented Christian, classical, imbalanced civilization then became interwoven with the imbalanced-kinship cultures of Europe. That amalgam became the complex and unstable foundation of the modern West.

Islam, a third transcendent, monotheistic religion, incorporating both Hebrew and Christian traditions, created a renaissance in the ancient Middle Eastern imbalanced civilization about 1300 years ago. The Islamic religious invigoration of the Middle East matured spectacularly. Within a century of its founding, Islam stood as one of the major powers of the world. Its high culture, like its military success, was suffused with religiosity, and achieved an eminence surpassing that of the proto-West in Europe.

A thousand years ago, then: **(1)** A great, modified balanced civilization existed in East Asia. China was several centuries into a millennium of considerable stability—simultaneously the most populous and most urban, most agricultural and most industrial, and, by many standards, the most culturally developed civilization in the world. To the west of China, on the Eurasian steppe **(2)**, imbalanced-kinship peoples were continuing to harass all existing civilizations, balanced and imbalanced. Along the long southern edge of the steppe, the **(3)** Indian and **(4)** Muslim imbalanced civilizations conducted their affairs energetically. On the western edge of the steppe, **(5)** Western civilization, that quilt of Greek and Hebrew, Roman and Christian, and imbalanced-kinship institutions, lay quiet, soon to experience a military, political, and economic takeoff of unprecedented proportions. What **(6)** balanced kinship remained lay in the southern hemisphere, particularly in Africa and in the Americas.

---

*This carpet of Islamic design, made from Tehran silk and wool, was used for religious purposes.*

# 1000 YEARS AGO TO THE PRESENT

The drama of the last thousand years is that of Western coalescence and of Western impingement on all other societies, kinship-ordered and civilized. It is also the drama of the dominance of imbalance.

Shortly after the turn of the present millennium, the West began its phenomenal career in commerce. Wealth grew, and moved to the center of Western values. All the skills of distinction making became honed even finer than in Rome. More and more emphasis was put onto the deritualized cluster of distinction-making competencies. Particular instances of this increase in emphasis came to be labeled the "Renaissance," when art was at stake, and the "Reformation," in the case of religion. Less and less importance was given to the symbolic, ritualized cluster of distinction-dissolving competencies. The resulting weakening of ability to identify with other human beings contributed to the violence of Western conduct, on a large and small scale. Finally, a series of scientific and technological breakthroughs, products of the now white-hot distinction-making cluster, armed the West, sometimes literally, sometimes figuratively, in a largely successful effort to remake all other world civilizations, including the Chinese, in its own image.

And what of imbalanced kinship? On a worldwide scale, the Western rifle destroyed the mounted warrior clan confederations. The demands, however, of imbalanced civilization—the removal of family members to the factory, the elimination of agricultural and other rural extended families, and the changing aspirations of individuals within imbalanced societies—have profoundly affected the family itself. That basic human institution, the major constituent of balanced kinship in all societies, has in the modern world become in many places imbalanced—dysfunctional, unsupportive of its members, even violent.

As the 21st century approaches, the great technical and organizational accomplishments of imbalanced civilization promise much, but humanity's ability to destroy itself and all life on the planet through weaponry, pollution, and other means presents an obvious challenge. Perhaps the benefits of balance at all levels of human society—from the nuclear family to the international organizations of nations—can somehow be reintroduced. The process may start with the family, but wherever it may begin, its purpose would be to ensure that our children—the citizens of the 21st century—will know better how to live together in the society of the next millennium.

Marvin Bram
Professor, Department of History
Hobart and William Smith Colleges

The education of our children for leading healthy and productive lives, as seen in this substance-abuse discussion, is a necessary goal to ensure the future of humanity.

As advances continue to be made in technology, a priority for humanity is the protection of the earth from the damaging results of these advances, such as pollution.

# FOR FURTHER STUDY

Funk & Wagnalls New Encyclopedia contains many articles that will increase your understanding of the preceding essay. They include:

| | |
|---|---|
| Anthropology | Human |
| Archaeology | Human Evolution |
| Civilization | Patriarchy |
| Clan | Sociology |
| Ethnology | Totemism |
| Family | Tribe |
| Gens | Warfare |

For a listing of important figures in the study of human society, see the listings under the entry ANTHROPOLOGY in the Volume 29 Index.

To find listings of books and publications that will further increase your knowledge, use the bibliography cross-references at the ends of many articles. They lead to the numbered reading lists in the Bibliography section of Volume 28, pp. 184-448.

The following feature, "The TimeScope™ of Human Society," contains numerous cross-references to articles on specific nations, peoples, individuals, and other topics related to the history of human society.

---

# ART AND PHOTO CREDITS

# THE TIMESCOPE™ OF HUMAN SOCIETY

The following 34 pages contain a special-purpose timeline of the history of human society. The 17 two-page spreads cover the period 200,000 BC to the present. Each spread details the progress of human society in a specific span of years. In the fifth spread, pp. 32-33, the span is 4000 BC to 2500 BC.

Each page is divided into two columns; each spread is divided into four columns representing parts of the span. The tinted date type blocks at the left of each column show the starting date of that part of the span—4000 BC, 3500 BC, 3000 BC, and 2700 BC in the fifth spread. The ending date of the fourth part of the span is the starting date of the next spread, 2500 BC.

The different tints in the four date type blocks are used in the small squares, or icons, set at the head of each caption. The tint of the icon indicates which span part, or column, the caption and the illustration relate to.

The paragraphs printed across the bottom of each spread provide the necessarily brief narrative of the history of society. But each paragraph has one or more cross-references to related articles in the encyclopedia, and these articles, in turn, have numerous cross-references to other articles and to books and publications in the Volume 28 Bibliography, pp. 184-448.

---

*Paleolithic hand axes chipped from flint nodules, found in London.*

*Neanderthal man, a member of Homo sapiens or, by a recent theory, another type of human altogether, lived in parts of Europe and the Middle East between 100,000 and 35,000 years ago.*

*Cro-Magnon man, a more recent member of Homo sapiens, flourished in southern Europe.*

## 200,000 BC □ □ □ □

## 100,000 BC □ □ □ □

The human species, *Homo sapiens*, develops out of populations of prehuman species *Homo erectus*, traced to African origins. According to this theory, which is based on analysis of human DNA, all other populations of *Homo sapiens* —all people—are descended from early human beings who migrated from Africa to other areas of the earth. SEE: EVOLUTION: THE SYNTHETIC THEORY; HUMAN EVOLUTION; PALEONTOLOGY.

The Neanderthals coexist with *Homo sapiens sapiens* (the most recent modern humans) for tens of thousands of years; often classified as *Homo sapiens neanderthalensis*, they were thought to be in a direct line of human evolution, but their disappearance from the fossil record around 35,000 years ago seems to contradict this theory. SEE: ANTHROPOLOGY: EVOLUTION OF HUMANS.

■ Skull of the saber-toothed tiger, an extinct genus of the cat family that lived during the Ice Age.

■ Acheulean hand axe, a crude tool dating from about 200,000 BC.

☐ Acheulean fossilized wood cleaver, which may be evidence of hunting and meat eating.

**60,000 BC**

First humans reach the northern region of the continental landmass that is presently known as Australia. They probably came from Melanesia. Their long journey by sea between the coastlines of the two areas during this period of the Ice Age involved the first presumed use of boats, probably of simple design, by humans. SEE: AUSTRALIA: AUSTRALIAN ABORIGINES; HUMAN EVOLUTION.

**50,000 BC**

During an Ice Age lowering of the sea, a land bridge joins Siberia and Alaska. This was the probable route of the first migration of prehistoric peoples from Asia to North America, which might have occurred 10,000 or 20,000 years before the generally accepted dating of about 30,000 years ago. SEE: AMERICAN INDIANS: EARLIEST MIGRATIONS; ARCHAEOLOGY: THE AMERICAS; NORTH AMERICA: HISTORY.

*Background: Elephants on African plain, Kenya.*

■ The technical ability used in making this notched stone spearhead contributed to the evolutionary success of humans.

■ Cro-Magnon cave dwellers left impressive cave paintings in Lascaux in southern France.

■ Folsom point and arrowhead tool used by North American hunters.

■ Spearpoint carved by native Americans during the Stone Age.

■ "Venus of Willendorf," a late Paleolithic limestone statuette found in Austria.

## 35,000 BC ☐ ☐ ☐ ☐    28,000 BC ☐ ☐ ☐ ☐ ☐

Neanderthals disappear from the fossil record. Modern *Homo sapiens sapiens* is now the only human form inhabiting the earth. SEE: HUMAN EVOLUTION.

Cro-Magnons in southern Europe and humans elsewhere in the world develop the arts of stone carving and cave and rock painting, some of which are still preserved. SEE CAVE DWELLERS; CRO-MAGNON; PALEOLITHIC ART.

The lithic (stone) age, the earliest stage of human life in the New World, begins around this time (although older dates have been suggested). The earliest migrants from Asia in North America hunt big game—mammoth, giant elk, giant sloth, and other animals. Several waves of migration occur. Nomadic populations eventually reach South America. SEE: ARCHAEOLOGY: THE AMERICAS.

■ *The dog, considered to be the first domesticated animal, was a hunter partner for humans. Its direct ancestor is believed to be the wolf.*

■ *Paleolithic hunters crossing the Bering land bridge between present-day Siberia and Alaska.*

**20,000 BC** □ □ □ □ **13,000 BC** □ □ □ □ □

Humans are now present on all habitable continents. Archaeological discoveries of incised bone fragments (in southern France) from this period are interpreted as records of phases of the moon—the first form of writing. Grinding of wild grass seeds by stones is indicated in southern Egypt. SEE: AFRICA: HISTORY; ASIA: HISTORY; EUROPE: HISTORY; NORTH AMERICA: HISTORY; SOUTH AMERICA: HISTORY; WRITING.

Last glaciation of Ice Age ends. Bering Sea covers land bridge between Siberia and Alaska. SEE: ICE AGES.

Earliest pottery from the Jōmon period, about 10,500 BC, made in southern Japan (Fukui Cave). Storage vessels and cult figurines—dōgu—were decorated with characteristic cord markings. SEE: ARCHAEOLOGY: OTHER ASIAN COUNTRIES; POTTERY.

*Background: Glacier in the Bering Strait.*

□ *Australian aborigine mask, representative of the striking body decorations and elaborate headdresses worn on ritual occasions.*

□ *Harpoons of bone, ivory, and deer antler, made during the late Paleolithic period.*

□ *Venus figure of a standing woman, from a shrine at Çatal Hüyük in Anatolian Turkey.*

## 10,000 BC □ □ □ □

Copper tools and ornaments are made from raw metal nuggets in southeastern Europe and western Asia. SEE: METALWORK; ASIA MINOR.

Southern tip of South America is reached by migratory peoples; western hemisphere is fully inhabited. SEE: AMERICAN INDIANS: SOUTH AMERICA.

## 9000 BC □ □ □ □

Earliest settlements appear in Fertile Crescent, notably Jericho, and in Anatolia, where Çatal Hüyük becomes major trading center. SEE: JERICHO; ARCHAEOLOGY: OTHER MIDDLE EASTERN AREAS.

First domestication of sheep in northern Mesopotamia. SEE: AGRICULTURE: HISTORY; SHEEP.

■ *Painted bowls of Sialk Ware from northern Mesopotamia.*

■ *Animal domestication, shown by this sheepherder and two sheep, signifies the beginning of agriculture.*

■ *Deer carved and incised on a bone sickle handle, from el-Wad cave, at Mount Carmel, Israel.*

## 8000 BC

Aborigines reach southernmost Australia. SEE: AUSTRALIA: AUSTRALIAN ABORIGINES.

First crop—squash—is cultivated in Mexico. SEE: MEXICO: HISTORY.

Crop raising—wheat, barley, and beans—extends throughout Fertile Crescent. SEE: CROP FARMING.

## 7000 BC

Crop and livestock farming extends throughout area of eastern Europe and western Mediterranean, and from Anatolia to Pakistan. SEE: AGRICULTURE.

Farmers and herders thrive in pre-desertified Saharan region; settlers leave rock and cave painting record. SEE: AFRICAN ART AND ARCHITECTURE.

*Background: Saharan rock painting from Tassili.*

□ *Ornamental objects, such as this necklace, show the sophistication of prehistoric city dwellers.*

□ *"The Ancestor," a sandstone figure from the modern-day Balkans, the site of intense early Neolithic development.*

□ *Neolithic ruins, Tall as-Sultān, on the site of ancient Jericho.*

□ *Showing little wear, this flint and bone knife from Çatal Hüyük was probably used in religious rites.*

| 6000 BC | □ □ □ □ | 5500 BC | □ □ □ □ |

Agricultural settlements spread throughout Aegean area; farmers grow wheat, barley, grapes, olives; raise livestock. SEE: AEGEAN CIVILIZATION.

Painted, fired pottery develops in Middle East. SEE: POTTERY: WESTERN POTTERY.

Farming spreads northward in Europe as far as Poland and the Low Countries. SEE: EUROPE: HISTORY.

Farming communities in Indus Valley grow wheat and barley; raise sheep, cattle, and goats. SEE: INDUS VALLEY CIVILIZATION.

Cultivation of rice begins in eastern China. SEE: RICE.

Irrigation systems are used in Egypt, increasing food production. SEE: IRRIGATION.

■ Egyptian fresco depicting a shadoof, which was used for lifting water from streams to higher-lying fields.

■ Finely crafted utensils reflect the advanced culture of Çatal Hüyük.

■ Indus Valley vessels with cattle designs reflect an agricultural civilization.

## 5000 BC ■ ■ ■ ■ 4500 BC ■ ■ ■ ■

Chinese agriculture develops in Huang He (Yellow River) Valley. SEE: CHINA: HISTORY; HUANG HE.

Earliest villages in Europe develop in Thessaly, on Aegean coast. SEE: EUROPE: HISTORY.

First megaliths (stone monuments) erected in northern Europe. SEE: MEGALITHIC MONUMENTS.

Preurban communities in Mesopotamia increase in size and number. A combination temple and trading center is built in Eridu. SEE: SUMER; RELIGION.

Annealing and smelting of copper spreads throughout Middle East and agricultural Europe. SEE: METALWORK.

Horse is domesticated in what is now Ukraine. SEE: AGRICULTURE: HISTORY.

Background: The ancient city of Irbil, Iraq.

■ *Golden cups reflect wealth of the Sumerian city-state of Ur.*

■ *Egyptian funeral rites, dating from 4th millennium BC, reach heights with elaborate sarcophagus of King Tutankhamen.*

**4000 BC** □ □ □ □ **3500 BC** ■ ■ ■ ■

Ancient Egyptians settle on fertile land along Nile River. SEE: EGYPT: HISTORY; ARCHAEOLOGY.

Ubaidian people establish first urban settlements in Sumer. SEE: MESOPOTAMIA; SUMER.

Prehistoric Yang-shao culture flourishes in Huang He (Yellow River) Valley. SEE: YANG-SHAO CULTURE.

Upper (southern) and Lower (northern) Egypt unite to form first great kingdom. Cities begin to arise; Old Kingdom pharaohs rule from Memphis, the capital. SEE: MEMPHIS (Egypt).

Sumerians expand trade. Powerful city-states—Uruk, Eridu, Lagash, Ur, Kish—emerge. SEE: MESOPOTAMIAN ART AND ARCHITECTURE; SUMERIAN LITERATURE; SUMERIAN RELIGION; UR.

■ Fragment of Babylonian cuneiform tablet recounts deeds attributed to Gilgamesh, king of Sumerian city-state of Uruk.

■ The tumblebug, a scarab, was sacred to the ancient Egyptians; a symbol of immortality, it was represented in gold and jeweled pectorals like this one from the tomb of Tutankhamen (14th cent. BC).

■ Decorated sound box of a lyre from Ur, 2600 BC, showing a king and his officers (top) and other scenes at a victory feast.

■ A Sumerian gaming board shows wild animals of the region.

| 3000 BC | | | | | 2700 BC | | | | |
|---|---|---|---|---|---|---|---|---|---|

Bronze Age begins in area of Greece and in the Aegean. SEE: AEGEAN CIVILIZATION; BRONZE AGE.

Minoans, on Crete, establish flourishing civilization; trade with Egypt. SEE: CRETE; KNOSSOS; MINOAN CULTURE.

Troy and other cities arise along the coasts of Asia Minor and eastern Mediterranean. SEE: ASIA MINOR; TROY.

Under 4th Dynasty rulers, Egyptian civilization reaches peaks in sciences, engineering, and arts. SEE: EGYPTIAN ART AND ARCHITECTURE; PYRAMIDS.

Gilgamesh rules prosperous Uruk. SEE: GILGAMESH EPIC; SUMER.

Kurgan (barrow) culture brings Indo-European languages to Black Sea area. SEE: INDO-EUROPEAN LANGUAGES.

Background: The Pyramids at Giza, Egypt.

■ *Portrait of an Akkadian ruler, from Nineveh, about 2300–2000 BC, emphasizing the dignity of the Akkadian kings, the Semitic conquerors of Sumer.*

■ *Buffalo seals from Mohenjo-daro, used by merchants to label their goods by impressing them on clay tags.*

■ *Statuette of Gudea, ruler of Lagash, a prominent city in Mesopotamia during the Neo-Sumerian period, in which the art of portraiture was revived.*

## 2500 BC

Earliest known civilization in southwest Asia—the Harappan—covers extensive area in Indus River Valley. SEE: INDUS VALLEY CIVILIZATION.

Indo-Aryans invade Indian subcontinent, displace Dravidian tribes living there. SEE: INDIA: PREHISTORY.

Desertification of Sahara begins; agriculture declines. SEE: SAHARA.

## 2400 BC

Sumer is conquered by Akkadians, and new Empire of Sumer and Akkad lasts about a century before being laid waste by invading Gutians. SEE: MESOPOTAMIA: EARLY MESOPOTAMIAN STATES; SUMER.

In Indus Valley, Bronze Age cities develop and prosper, trading cotton and textiles with Mesopotamia. Artisans produce distinctive pottery, other works. SEE: ASIA: INDIAN CIVILIZATIONS; MOHENJO-DARO.

□ *Elegantly crafted gold crown excavated from the Sumerian city of Uruk.*

□ *Golden head of a bull, the Sumerian symbol of strength and fertility, affixed to a lyre.*

□ *Statue of a monkey, the product of the skillful and inventive artists of ancient Sumer.*

## 2200 BC

Egypt declines as pharaohs lose power to regional rulers, who vie for control of kingdom. SEE: EGYPT: THE OLD KINGDOM.

The 3rd Dynasty of Ur begins with the rule of Ur-Nammu, who revives Empire of Sumer and Akkad. SEE: UR.

Indo-European-speaking tribes invade Greece and Cyclades Islands. SEE: ACHAEANS; GREECE; MYCENAE.

## 2100 BC

As Middle Kingdom period begins, Egypt is reunified by Theban kings, who foster cultural, artistic renaissance. Thebes remains Egyptian capital for centuries. SEE: THEBES (EGYPT).

Ziggurat of Nanna and other great temples are built in Ur. City grows wealthy, remains powerful until Elamites conquer it, about 2000 BC. SEE: SUMERIAN RELIGION; ZIGGURAT.

*Background: Site of the city of Mohenjo-daro.*

■ *The Minoans worshiped nature and often portrayed their appreciation in such artwork as this dolphin fresco from the palace at Knossos.*

■ *The specialized artisans of the Shang dynasty in China produced elaborate ceremonial wine vessels.*

■ *Libation vessel carved in the shape of a bull's head, which had special religious significance for the Minoans.*

## 2000 BC

Lung-shan culture emerges in northern China, where farmers live in settlements with complex social and economic organization. SEE: LUNG-SHAN CULTURE.

According to biblical account, Judaism is founded by Abraham, who migrates from Ur to Palestine. SEE: ABRAHAM; UR.

Hittites, Indo-European-speaking people, invade Anatolia. SEE: HITTITES.

## 1800 BC

Hammurabi becomes ruler of Babylonia in 1792 BC and extends his empire over all Mesopotamia. He establishes earliest known legal code. SEE: BABYLONIA; HAMMURABI; HAMMURABI, CODE OF

First major Chinese civilization—the Shang dynasty—is founded c. 1766 BC, will remain in power for over 700 years. SEE: ARCHAEOLOGY: CHINA; CHINESE ART AND ARCHITECTURE.

■ *The brilliance of Minoan culture is reflected in this libation jug from a tomb at Knossos.*

■ *Detail from a fresco at Knossos demonstrates the mastery of Minoans, among the earliest creators in this medium.*

■ *This block of black diorite depicts Hammurabi receiving the Code of Hammurabi from the sun god, Shamash.*

■ *Minoan storage jar embodies Cretan meticulousness and innovation.*

## 1700 BC

Harappan civilization disintegrates as great cities are abandoned. SEE: INDUS VALLEY CIVILIZATION.

The Hyksos, invaders from Palestine, conquer Egypt, found 15th Dynasty. SEE: EGYPT: HISTORY; HYKSOS.

Hittites grow powerful, eventually dominate Asia Minor and become rivals of Egypt. SEE: ASIA MINOR.

## 1600 BC

Egypt is reunited under pharaohs of the 18th Dynasty, who found New Kingdom, achieve great power and wealth. SEE: EGYPTIAN ART AND ARCHITECTURE.

Kassites conquer Babylon and rejuvenate Babylonian empire. SEE: KASSITES.

Minoan civilization dominates Aegean area, reaching height c. 1600 BC. SEE: CRETE; MINOAN CULTURE.

· *Background: Stones and lintels of Stonehenge.*

■ *Mycenaean stemmed pottery goblet, dating from about 1400–1300 BC, decorated with stylized cuttlefish.*

■ *Ornamented gold cup dating from 1500 BC, found in a tomb at Vaphio in Laconia, Greece.*

■ *Bust of Queen Nefertiti depicts the shift from the stiff, expressionless tradition of Egyptian art to the natural and lifelike.*

■ *The gods Osiris, Nephthys, and Isis are depicted in this detail, c. 1250 BC, from the Egyptian Book of the Dead.*

## 1500 BC □ □ □ □

## 1300 BC □ □ □ □ □

The Olmec establish first major Mesoamerican civilization at San Lorenzo and other sites (modern Vera Cruz and Tabasco states) in Mexico. SEE: OLMEC; PRE-COLUMBIAN ART AND ARCHITECTURE: MESOAMERICAN AREA.

Aryans migrating from Central Asia destroy remaining Indus Valley cities, later settle Ganges Valley in northeast India. SEE: ASIA: HISTORY.

Mycenaeans complete their takeover of the Minoans and soon assert their political and cultural dominance over the Aegean area. SEE: MINOAN CULTURE; MYCENAE.

Moses leads Israelites out of Egypt, according to the Bible, and receives tablets inscribed with the Ten Commandments from God on Mt. Sinai. SEE: JUDAISM; MOSES; TEN COMMANDMENTS.

☐ A colossal stone head carved by the Olmec people, who were the first in the Americas to use stone architecturally and sculpturally.

■ One of the two seated statues of the Egyptian ruler Amenhotep III from the 18th Dynasty, known as the Colossi of Memnon.

■ The so-called gold death mask of Agamemnon, son of Atreus, from the height of Mycenaean civilization.

## 1200 BC

Under Joshua, Israelites conquer Jericho and settle western Palestine. SEE: BIBLICAL ARCHAEOLOGY.

Greeks lay siege to Troy, in Asia Minor, eventually capture and burn the city. SEE: ATREUS, HOUSE OF; TROJAN WAR; TROY.

Sea Peoples from Aegean conquer Hittite Empire but are defeated in attempt to invade Egypt. SEE: HITTITES; EGYPT: HISTORY.

## 1100 BC

After death of Ramses III, Egypt begins centuries of decline. SEE: RAMSES III.

Phoenician cities, free of Egyptian rule, become dominant maritime power in Mediterranean. SEE: PHOENICIA.

Iron Age is brought to Greece by Dorian invaders. Three major ethnic confederacies—Doric, Aeolian, and Ionic—are established. SEE: GREECE: HISTORY.

Background: "Procession of the Trojan Horse."

☐ *Bull from the Babylonian palace of Nebuchadnezzar II, the Chaldean king who controlled almost all of Mesopotamia.*

☐ *Ritual wine vessel of the Chou dynasty reflects the artistic sophistication of the Chinese.*

☐ *Statue of the Chinese philosopher Confucius, whose practical and ethical teachings exerted a powerful influence on China.*

## 1000 BC ☐ ☐ ☐ ☐  800 BC ☐ ☐ ☐ ☐

Solomon succeeds David as king of Israel, builds Temple at Jerusalem, and extends nation's power. After his death, kingdom divides and declines. SEE: JEWS; SOLOMON.

Chou dynasty expands borders of China, rules feudal society through local over-lords. SEE: CHINA: HISTORY.

Phoenicians found Carthage, great city and port near modern Tunis. SEE: CARTHAGE.

Assyrians dominate Middle East from southern Anatolia to Persian Gulf. They destroy Israel and deport many Jews, who become "lost tribes." SEE: ASSYRIA.

Greek city-states grow in importance, with Athens and Sparta predominant. *Iliad* and *Odyssey* are composed. SEE: HOMER.

According to tradition, Rome is founded in 753 BC. SEE: ROME; ROMULUS.

The Ishtar Gate, decorated with brick reliefs of dragons and bulls, was located in the Babylonian capital, Babylon.

Stone sculpture of a winged bull with the head of a bearded man, which guarded the gate of an Assyrian palace.

The Cushites, who controlled part of Egypt in the 8th century BC, crafted this gold pectoral of the winged goddess Isis.

## 700 BC        600 BC

Etruscans reach height of power, ruling Italy from the Alps to the Tiber, including city of Rome. SEE: ETRUSCAN CIVILIZATION.

First coins are minted by Lydians in Asia Minor. SEE: COINS AND COIN COLLECTING.

Assyrian Empire declines as its capital, Nineveh, is sacked. Babylonia later flourishes under Chaldean king, Nebuchadnezzar. SEE: NINEVEH; NEBUCHADNEZZAR II.

Cyrus the Great establishes Persia as preeminent world power. SEE: PERSIA.

In Asia, two great movements are born. Siddhartha Gautama (the Buddha) experiences his Great Enlightenment in India. Chinese philosopher Confucius begins teaching. SEE: BUDDHA; CONFUCIUS.

Romans abolish monarchy, found republic, 509 BC. SEE: ROME, HISTORY OF.

*Background: Persepolis, a capital of Persia.*

■ Portrayal of "Virgin and Child" by Master della Fasce testifies to the emergence of Christianity.

■ Silver rhyton associated with the cult of the Greek god Dionysus, whose popularity rose during the Hellenistic age.

□ Ruins of the temple of Aphaia, built on Aegina, Greece, prior to its conquest by Athens.

■ This Scythian gold vessel reflects a rich culture characterized by fine metalwork and a brilliant art style.

## 500 BC

Persians driven from Greece by 480 BC, and golden age of Athens begins, c. 460 BC. SEE: DELIAN LEAGUE; PERICLES.

Alexander the Great unifies Greece, conquers Persia, and extends his empire from Egypt to India. SEE: HELLENISTIC AGE.

Alexander dies, 323 BC; his empire breaks up, and Ptolemy I establishes dynasty in Egypt. SEE: PTOLEMAIC DYNASTY.

## 300 BC

Rome gains control of Italian peninsula, c. 265 BC, begins war with Carthage to control Mediterranean. SEE: PUNIC WARS.

Asoka, greatest of the Maurya dynasty, rules India; Buddhism becomes dominant religion of empire. SEE: INDIA: HISTORY.

First Ch'in emperor of China, Shih Huang Ti, unites country, builds Great Wall (completed c. 204 BC). SEE: GREAT WALL.

■ The "Nike of Samothráki,"
or "Winged Victory" is considered
one of the finest Hellenistic
sculptures.

□ Alexander the Great
portrayed on a silver
coin.

■ Bas-relief stone figure
of Buddha, seated in the
traditional cross-legged
meditative pose.

## 200 BC

Han dynasty rules China, establishes
Confucianism as official ideology.
SEE: CHINA: HISTORY; CONFUCIANISM.

Rome expands power in Mediterranean,
destroying Carthage and subjugating
Greece. SEE: ROME, HISTORY OF

In India Buddhism declines as Brahmanism
becomes dominant under powerful Sunga
dynasty. SEE: BRAHMA; HINDUISM.

## 100 BC

Romans capture Jerusalem, 63 BC,
rule Egypt after death of Cleopatra.
Octavian becomes first emperor of
Rome, 27 BC. SEE: AUGUSTUS.

Parthian empire grows to rival Roman
power in central Asia. SEE: PARTHIA.

Jesus Christ is born in Palestine between
8 and 4 BC. SEE: CHRISTIANITY; JESUS CHRIST;
MESSIAH.

Background: The Great Wall of China.

□ To commemorate Titus's capture and destruction of Jerusalem, his brother Domitian erected the Arch of Titus in Rome.

□ Mural from the temple of Quetzalcoatl in Teotihuacán, the first urban Mesoamerican civilization.

■ Sardonyx portrayal of a Roman emperor in battle.

## 1 AD □ □ □ □

Jesus Christ is crucified; Christianity begins in Palestine and throughout Roman Empire. SEE: CHRISTIANITY: HISTORY.

Jews' revolt against Roman rule is crushed; they are exiled, and period of persecution begins. SEE: JEWS: SUBJECT JUDEA; PALESTINE.

Buddhism is introduced into China from Central Asia and into Southeast Asia. SEE: BUDDHISM; MISSIONARY MOVEMENTS.

## 100 AD □ □ □ □

Roman Empire reaches its greatest extent, stretching from the British Isles to the Caspian Sea. SEE: HADRIAN; TRAJAN.

Teotihuacán, earliest city in western hemisphere, is built by unknown civilization. SEE: PRE-COLUMBIAN ART AND ARCHITECTURE.

Han dynasty in China loses power; empire breaks apart. Buddhism and Taoism overshadow Confucianism. SEE: CHINA: HISTORY.

■ Clay heads from the tomb of Jing Di, the 5th emperor of China's Han dynasty.

■ Roman silver bowl depicts barbarians paying homage to the conquering Romans.

■ Statue of Buddha in Datong, China, reflects the profound influence of Buddhism in Chinese cultural life.

■ Depiction of the baptism of Clovis I, founder of the Merovingian dynasty and head of the Salian Franks.

## 300 AD  □ □ □ □ □

## 400 AD  □ □ □ □ □

Constantine the Great is first Christian emperor of Rome. He grants legal status to church, rebuilds Byzantium as his capital. SEE: BYZANTINE EMPIRE.

Gupta dynasty comes to power in India, expands empire. Hinduism has revival. SEE: INDIA: GUPTA EMPIRE.

Mayan culture spreads across Meso-america. SEE: MAYA.

Attila, king of the Huns, conquers area between Black and Mediterranean seas, invades Europe. SEE: ATTILA; HUNS.

Western Roman Empire falls to barbarians, who sack Rome in 410 and 455. SEE: GOTHS; ROMULUS AUGUSTULUS.

Clovis I, king of the Franks, converts to Christianity, establishes rule in Gaul and part of Germany. SEE: CLOVIS I; FRANKS.

Background: The Colosseum in Rome.

Replica of a helmet found on the 7th-century Saxon ship excavated at Sutton Hoo, England.

El Castillo, the large pyramid at Chichén Itzá, the most important Mayan city, in Yucatán, Mexico.

## 500 AD

Justinian becomes Byzantine emperor; extends rule to North Africa and Italy, promulgates Justinian Code of civil law. SEE: JUSTINIAN I.

Buddhism spreads to Japan, is proclaimed state religion in 593. SEE: JAPAN: THE IMPERIAL CLAN.

Under Gregory the Great, papacy becomes political force. SEE: PAPACY.

## 600 AD

Muhammad launches his mission in Arabia; his followers spread Islam through conquest of Near East, North Africa, and (by 719) Spain. SEE: ISLAM; MUHAMMAD.

Muslim advance into Europe is halted near Poitiers, France, in 732. SEE: CHARLES MARTEL.

Last great Hindu king, Harsha, rules India. SEE: INDIA: GUPTA EMPIRE.

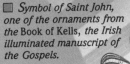

☐ Symbol of Saint John, one of the ornaments from the Book of Kells, the Irish illuminated manuscript of the Gospels.

☐ Page from the Koran, the sacred scripture of Islam containing Muhammad's revelations, with its Arabic text enlarged above.

☐ Figure of Justinian I, a detail from a Byzantine mosaic in the Church of San Vitale, in Ravenna, Italy.

## 800 AD    900 AD

Charlemagne, king of the Franks, is proclaimed Roman emperor by Pope Leo III. SEE: HOLY ROMAN EMPIRE.

Russian Empire is founded by Rurik, who unites warring Eastern Slavs. SEE: RUSSIA: THE HOUSE OF RURIK.

Persecution of Buddhists begins in China, 845, as T'ang dynasty declines. SEE: CHINA: THE T'ANG DYNASTY.

Toltec empire expands in Valley of Mexico. Mayans thrive in Yucatán. SEE: AMERICAN INDIANS: MESOAMERICA.

Era of Islamic power and cultural achievement begins to fade as Abbasid dynasty loses power and Byzantine Empire revives. SEE: CALIPHATE.

Medieval Ghana, West Africa, reaches its zenith. SEE: GHANA, KINGDOM OF

Background: Mosque in Córdoba, Spain.

■ *The brilliant rose window from Chartres, epitome of French Gothic cathedrals.*

■ *An unknown artist's depiction of Genghis Khan, whose Mongol empire stretched from China to Russia.*

□ *French manuscript illustration of the embarkation from Naples of the Chevaliers du Saint-Esprit on a Crusade.*

## 1000 AD

Conquest of Jerusalem by Seljuk Turks leads to First Crusade. SEE: CRUSADES.

New movement, Neo-Confucianism, takes hold in China. SEE: CHINESE PHILOSOPHY.

After battle of Hastings, 1066, Normans rule England. SEE: WILLIAM I (ENGLAND).

Schism divides Christianity. SEE: ORTHODOX CHURCH; ROMAN CATHOLIC CHURCH.

## 1100 AD

Vikings end seacoast raids, settle in Normandy and England. SEE: VIKINGS.

Shoguns (military chiefs) take control of Japan. SEE: JAPAN: EARLY SHOGUNS.

Muslim rule spreads through India. SEE: INDIA: MUSLIM AND MONGOL INVASIONS.

Angkor Wat, magnificent temple complex, is built in Cambodia. SEE: ANGKOR.

■ *Viking achievements included objects of art and craftsmanship, such as this silver pendant.*

■ *The Vikings depicted their heroes on their coins.*

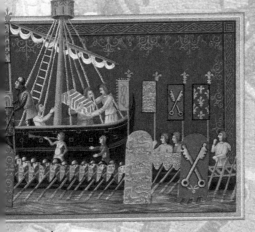

■ *Wearing armor and carrying a white banner, Joan of Arc led the French to a momentous victory over the English.*

## 1200 AD ■ ■ ■ ■ 1400 AD ■ ■ ■ ■ ■

English nobles force king to sign Magna Charta, first royal decree recognizing rights of subjects. SEE: MAGNA CHARTA.

Genghis Khan leads Mongols in conquering vast empire, including most of western and eastern Asia. SEE: MONGOL EMPIRE.

Mameluke dynasty brings prosperity to Egypt; repels invasions of Mongols and Crusaders. SEE: EGYPT: THE MAMELUKES.

Two voyages change the world. Christopher Columbus sails across Atlantic, links Europe and Americas. Vasco da Gama sails around Africa to India. SEE: COLUMBUS, CHRISTOPHER; GAMA, VASCO DA.

Joan of Arc leads French in defeating English invaders. SEE: HUNDRED YEARS' WAR.

Spanish drive last Muslims from Iberia. SEE: SPAIN: THE CHRISTIAN EMPIRE.

*Background: The Normans advance at Hastings.*

◼ *Christopher Columbus, shown in an engraving by Theodor de Bry, led European exploration of the Americas.*

◼ *The marble* Pietà *by Michelangelo exemplifies the innovation and monumentality of High Renaissance sculpture.*

◼ *16th-century plaque of Benin chiefs wearing pangolin skin.*

## 1500 AD ☐ ☐ ☐ ☐ 1550 AD ☐ ☐ ☐ ☐

Leonardo da Vinci, Michelangelo, other artists produce greatest works. SEE: RENAISSANCE ART AND ARCHITECTURE.

Spain begins to colonize Central and South America, conquering Aztecs in Mexico, Incas in Peru. SEE: CORTÉS, HERNÁN; PIZARRO, FRANCISCO.

Luther initiates Reformation in Germany. SEE: REFORMATION; PROTESTANTISM.

England enters era of literary brilliance, political success; navy defeats Spanish Armada. SEE: ELIZABETH I.

Ottoman Empire reaches peak, stretching from Arabia to Hungary. SEE: TURKEY: RISE OF THE OTTOMANS.

Akbar, Muslim emperor, forges ties with Hindus to build vast empire. SEE: INDIA: THE MUGHAL EMPIRE.

TERRA AUSTRALIS

■ *Indian goldsmiths in Colombia created elegant jewelry and other beautiful objects, such as this gold and copper pectoral.*

■ *Saint Basil's Cathedral in Moscow, built during the reign of Ivan the Terrible to commemorate the conquest of Kazan.*

■ *A doubleheaded serpent, an important Aztec symbol, done in turquoise mosaic.*

## 1600 AD

## 1700 AD

Manchus seize control of China, rule for next three centuries. SEE: CHINA: THE MANCHU, OR CH'ING, DYNASTY.

Peace of Westphalia ends Thirty Years' War, weakens Habsburg control of Holy Roman Empire. SEE: THIRTY YEARS' WAR.

First settlers arrive in Virginia, 1607; in Québec, 1608. SEE: NORTH AMERICA: FRENCH AND ENGLISH COLONIZATION.

Burgeoning slave trade brings millions of African laborers to colonial plantations. SEE: BLACKS IN THE AMERICAS; SLAVERY.

Peter I establishes Russian Empire, expands borders, encourages scientific and cultural development. SEE: PETER THE GREAT.

Under Frederick the Great, Prussia becomes major military power and cultural center. SEE: FREDERICK II (PRUSSIA).

*Background: Willem J. Blaeu's world map, 1635.*

■ *Scenes from* The Triumph of Steam and Electricity, *a commemoration of Queen Victoria's diamond jubilee in 1897.*

■ *Drum from the period of the French Revolution, decorated with revolutionary flags and watchwords.*

| 1750 AD | 1820 AD |
|---|---|

Spread of industrialization begins in England. SEE: INDUSTRIAL REVOLUTION.

American colonies win independence, form new nation. SEE: AMERICAN REVOLUTION; WASHINGTON, GEORGE.

French overthrow monarchy; Napoleon seizes power, conquers vast empire, meets defeat, 1815. SEE: FRANCE: HISTORY; FRENCH REVOLUTION; NAPOLEONIC WARS.

Latin American colonies gain independence from Spain. SEE: BOLÍVAR, SIMÓN; SOUTH AMERICA: WARS OF INDEPENDENCE.

Greece gains autonomy from Ottomans. SEE: EASTERN QUESTION.

Revolution in China fails, but Manchu rule is weakened; foreign governments expand "spheres of influence." SEE: CHINA: TAIPING REBELLION; IMPERIALISM.

■ Artist's depiction of Japan's decisive triumph over China in the 1894–95 Sino-Japanese War.

■ Portrayal of Simón Bolívar, the principal leader in the struggle for South American independence from Spain.

■ Hayter's portrait of Queen Victoria, the British monarch who reigned for 63 years.

## 1860 AD ■ ■ ■ ■ 1880 AD ■ ■ ■ ■

U.S. Civil War ends in victory for Union forces. SEE: CIVIL WAR, AMERICAN.

Canada is united as a dominion under British Crown. SEE: CANADA.

British consolidate rule over India; Victoria is crowned empress. SEE: VICTORIA.

Emperor Meiji opens Japan to Western influence, industrialization. SEE: MEIJI.

Most of Africa is divided among European powers. SEE: AFRICA: EUROPEAN POLITICS; SOUTH AFRICA: HISTORY; BOER WAR.

Japan defeats China in war, gains new power and territory. SEE: JAPAN: RESTORATION OF IMPERIAL RULE.

U.S. wins Spanish-American War, becomes world power. SEE: UNITED STATES OF AMERICA: FOREIGN AFFAIRS (1865–1920).

Background: Beginning of the U.S. Constitution.

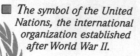
■ *The symbol of the United Nations, the international organization established after World War II.*

■ *The popularity of motion pictures and movie stars increases with the development of sound films.*

*Marlene Dietrich*

*Charlie Chaplin*

*Greta Garbo*

*Maurice Chevalier*

*Bette Davis*

## 1900 AD ☐ ☐ ☐ ☐ 1914 AD ☐ ☐ ☐ ☐

Chinese overthrow Manchu dynasty, establish republic. SEE: SUN YAT-SEN.

Wright brothers in first flight; Einstein, Planck publish revolutionary theories. SEE: AVIATION; PHYSICS: MODERN PHYSICS.

Australia becomes a commonwealth, New Zealand and South Africa, dominions. SEE: AUSTRALIA; NEW ZEALAND; SOUTH AFRICA.

Serbian nationalist assassinates heir to Austrian throne; Europe's hostile camps plunge into war. SEE: WORLD WAR I.

Czarist regime in Russia collapses. Bolsheviks defeat rivals, set up Communist government. SEE: RUSSIAN REVOLUTION.

Allies, joined by United States in 1917, defeat Central Powers. Germany and Austria lose empires. SEE: VERSAILLES, TREATY OF.

■ The China Clipper, a "flying boat" designed for transpacific service, made its first flight in 1935.

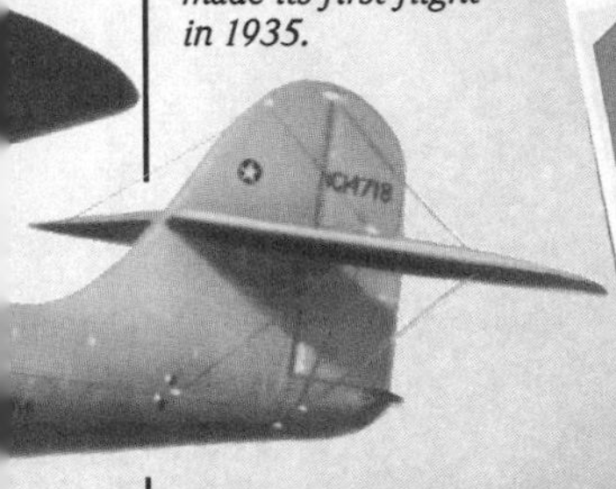

■ During World War I, the United States used recruiting posters to encourage enlistment.

**JOIN THE AIR SERVICE and SERVE in FRANCE**

**DO IT NOW**

**WORK PROMOTES CONFIDENCE**

■ Depression poster heralds U.S. government's program to provide jobs for millions of unemployed workers.

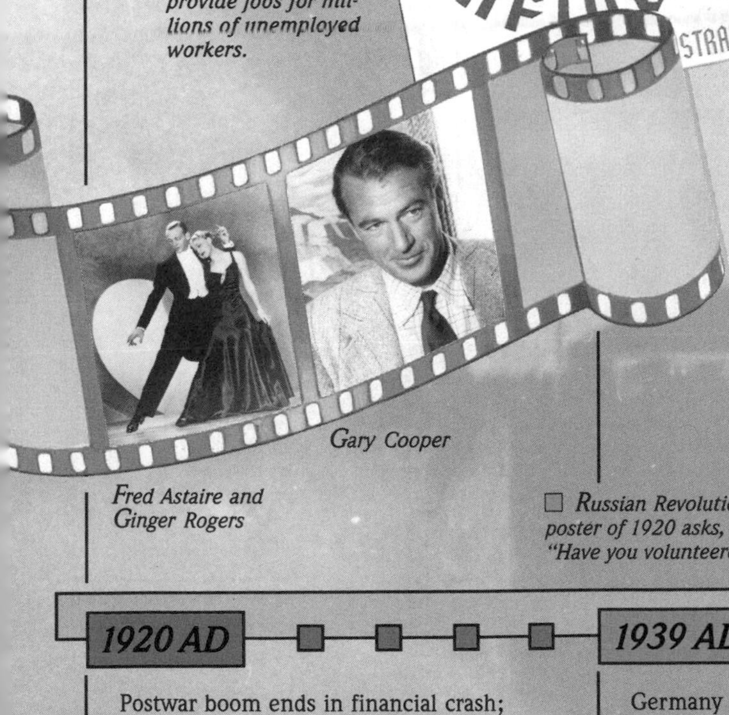

STRATION

**ТЫ**

Gary Cooper

Fred Astaire and Ginger Rogers

☐ Russian Revolution poster of 1920 asks, "Have you volunteered?"

**ЗАПИСАЛСЯ ДОБРОВОЛЬЦЕМ?**

## 1920 AD ☐ ☐ ☐ ☐ 1939 AD ☐ ☐ ☐ ☐ ☐

Postwar boom ends in financial crash; Great Depression follows. SEE: UNITED STATES OF AMERICA: ROARING TWENTIES.

Radio, motion pictures create worldwide communications network. SEE: RADIO, HISTORY; MOTION PICTURES, HISTORY OF.

Japan invades China; dictators triumph in Europe. SEE: HITLER, ADOLF; JAPAN: HISTORY; STALIN, JOSEPH; TOTALITARIANISM.

Germany begins war in Europe, 1939; United States joins Allies, 1941, after Japan attacks Hawaii. In 1945, Germans surrender, and war in Pacific ends after U.S. drops atomic bombs on Japan. SEE: NUCLEAR WEAPONS; WORLD WAR II.

In aftermath of war, United Nations is founded, and Communist regimes take power in China and Eastern Europe. SEE: COLD WAR; UNITED NATIONS.

*Background: Bombing of St. Paul's Cathedral.*

☐ *In the 1980s, the space shuttle became the major space program of the United States.*

☐ *Jawaharlal Nehru, India's first prime minister, shown on the eve of Indian independence from Great Britain.*

☐ *During the reign of Queen Elizabeth II, seen here in Nigeria, much of Great Britain's colonial empire was dismantled.*

☐ *The development of the microchip revolutionized the computer industry by making the devices smaller, faster, cheaper, and more reliable.*

☐ *Boris Yeltsin, the first popularly elected president in Russian history and the dominant figure in the former Soviet republics.*

## 1950 AD ☐ ☐ ☐ ☐ ## 1957 AD ☐ ☐ ☐ ☐

Western Europe, aided by U.S., recovers from war devastation and forms NATO alliance. SEE: EUROPEAN RECOVERY PROGRAM; NORTH ATLANTIC TREATY ORGANIZATION.

UN/U.S. fight North Korean invaders of South Korea. SEE: KOREAN WAR.

Colonial empires recede as African, Asian nations begin to gain autonomy. SEE: COLONIES AND COLONIALISM.

Space Age begins. USSR puts satellite in orbit (1957), U.S. puts man on moon (1969). SEE: SPACE EXPLORATION.

European Economic Community (Common Market) is founded. SEE: EUROPEAN UNION.

U.S. defense of South Vietnam turns into major war; U.S. withdraws, 1973, North Vietnam prevails. SEE: VIETNAM WAR.

■ When Communist rule unraveled in East Germany, the Berlin Wall was opened and East and West Germany reunited.

■ Jordan's King Hussein and Prime Minister Yitzhak Rabin of Israel shake hands to mark 1994 peace pact between the two nations, as U.S. President Bill Clinton applauds.

■ The Ginza, Tokyo's bustling shopping and amusement center, exemplifies Japan's economic vitality.

## 1975 AD ■ ■ ■ ■ 1989 AD TO THE PRESENT ■

Japan, West Germany, emerge as economic powers to rival U.S. SEE: GERMANY, WEST: ECONOMY; JAPAN: ECONOMY.

Computers come of age, revolutionize both business and personal life. SEE: COMPUTER; MICROPROCESSOR.

First AIDS case is identified, deadly virus spreads worldwide. SEE: ACQUIRED IMMUNE DEFICIENCY SYNDROME.

East, West Germany reunite, 1990. Soviet bloc in turmoil as USSR renounces Communism, breaks up, 1991. SEE: EUROPE: COLLAPSE OF COMMUNISM.

First world conference on environment meets in Rio de Janeiro, Brazil, in June 1992. SEE: ENVIRONMENT; POLLUTION.

UN sends peacekeeping forces to Balkans, Somalia. SEE: UNITED NATIONS.

*Background: Audience for the Pope at the Vatican.*

# EDITORIAL STAFF

**DIRECTOR OF EDITORIAL PRODUCTION**   Andrea J. Pitluk

**COPY CHIEF**
Eileen O'Reilly

**PRODUCTION EDITOR**
Carol Wheelan

**SENIOR COPY EDITOR**
Ileana Parvulescu

**COPY EDITORS AND PROOFREADERS**
Peggy Dorris
Anne M. Pulido

**COPY EDITING STAFF**
Barbara A. Devine
Charlotte R. Gross
Suzanne Gruber
Dean Stuart Holmes
Judith K. Johnson
Eleanor Mikucki
Gail Anne Mulligan
Lois R. Papp
Frank A. Petruzalek
Stephanie Salomon
Winifred vanRoden
Deborah D. Walker

**DESKTOP PUBLISHING ASSOCIATE**
Melissa Janssens

**DESKTOP PUBLISHING ASSISTANT**
Hana Shaki

**SENIOR INDEX EDITOR**   Sheila A. Morgan-Smith

**ASSOCIATE INDEX EDITOR**
Charles Paul May

**INDEX CONSULTANT**
Barbara M. Preschel

**CONTRIBUTING INDEX EDITORS**
Jerry Ralya
Gwen Sloan
Dorothy Thomas
Mary F. Tomaselli

**CONTRIBUTING INDEXERS**
Hilda Feinberg
Gerry Flanzraich
Judith B. Katz
Karen Hegge Simmons
Dianne E. Wheeler

**SENIOR DESIGN ARTIST**
Amy Scerbo

**GRAPHIC DESIGNER**
Maggie Jarvis

**CONTRIBUTING ARTIST**
Clifton Line

**CONTRIBUTING LAYOUT ARTISTS**
Herbert Ascher
Peter Kluge
Dennis Thomas
Wendy Wage-Matto

**PICTURE EDITOR**
Kirchoff Wohlberg, Inc.

**CONTRIBUTING PICTURE EDITORS**
Donna Dennis
Todd LaRoche
John Schultz

# GUIDE TO FUNK & WAGNALLS NEW ENCYCLOPEDIA

Funk & Wagnalls New Encyclopedia consists of 29 volumes. Volumes 1–27 and the first half of volume 28 contain some 25,000 articles in alphabetical order. The bibliography and listing of consultants and contributors constitute the last half of volume 28. Volume 29 is the index.

The reader's access to information in Funk & Wagnalls New Encyclopedia will be enhanced by reading the front matter (pp. 3–64) of volume 1. The foreword (p. 5) presents an educator's view of this encyclopedia. The preface (pp. 6–7), titled "Information and the Future," is a statement from the editors concerning the goals and purposes of Funk & Wagnalls New Encyclopedia. The essay

"The Course of Human Society" and "The TimeScope™ of Human Society" (pp. 8–57) follow. Editorial staff listings are on pp. 58–59, and selected abbreviations used in the text of this encyclopedia are listed on p. 64. The Funk & Wagnall's MapScope™, describing the encyclopedia's map program, is on pp. 6a–p, in volume 2.

At the end of volume 28 are listed the experts who acted as subject area consultants (pp. 448–455); bibliography consultant-contributors are listed on p. 456. Article contributors are listed on pp. 457–468. Preceding each person's name is a set of initials, which appears at the end of an article that was written or reviewed by this person.

## ALPHABETICAL ARRANGEMENT

Articles in Funk & Wagnalls New Encyclopedia are entered in letter-by-letter alphabetical order by title. If titles are identical to the comma, they are alphabetized according to what follows the comma.

ANDERSON (South Carolina)
ANDERSON, Carl David
ANDERSON, Marian
ANDERSON, Maxwell
ANDERSONVILLE PRISON

Spaces between words, diacritic marks, hyphens, apostrophes, articles, prepositions, conjunctions, titles such as Sir and Baron, and portions of persons' names enclosed in parentheses are ignored for purposes of alphabetization.

D'AUBIGNÉ, Jean Henri Merle
DAUBIGNY, Charles François
DAUDET, (Louis Marie) Alphonse
DAUGAVPILS
DAUGHTERS OF THE AMERICAN REVOLUTION, NATIONAL SOCIETY OF THE

FRENCH, Daniel Chester
FRENCH HORN
FRENCH INDIA
FRENCH AND INDIAN WAR
FRENCH LANGUAGE
FRENCH LITERATURE

Identical titles are alphabetized in the order of person, place, thing.

ELDER (person)
ELDER (tree)
IOWA (state)
IOWA (river)
PARIS (mythological character)
PARIS (France)

Identical place-names are alphabetized by the larger political unit of which each is a component.

ALBANY (Georgia)
ALBANY (New York)
ALBANY (Oregon)

Saints, popes, and kings of the same name are entered in that order. Popes of the same name are in numerical order; kings of the same name are in numerical order alphabetically by country.

JOHN I, Saint
JOHN II (pope)
JOHN VIII (pope)
JOHN X (pope)
JOHN I (king of Castile and León)
JOHN (king of England)
JOHN II (king of France)
JOHN I (king of Portugal)
JOHN II (king of Portugal)
JOHN II (king of Sweden)

Names beginning with Mac and Mc are all entered as if written Mac.

McCULLERS, Carson
MacDIARMID, Hugh
MacDONALD, (James) Ramsay
McGRAW, John Joseph
McKAY, Claude
MACKAY, John William

The abbreviation St. is alphabetized as if spelled out.

SAINT ANDREWS
ST. ANDREWS, UNIVERSITY OF
SAINT BERNARD, GREAT
ST. CATHERINES
SAINT CHARLES

## ARTICLE STRUCTURE

Article Title. Persons are entered under the name by which they are popularly known, last name first. If they are known by initials or by only a portion of their name, the rest of the name (except for middle names) is in parentheses.

ELIOT, T(homas) S(tearns)
BOGART, Humphrey DeForest
WILSON, (Thomas) Woodrow

Persons known by their nicknames, pseudonyms, or professional names are entered accordingly. Their real names follow.

RUTH, Babe, real name GEORGE HERMAN RUTH
ELIOT, George, pseudonym of MARY ANN EVANS
GRANT, Cary, professional name of ALEXANDER ARCHIBALD LEACH

Persons who are known by only one of their names or by a part of their name are so entered. The full name follows.

DURANT, Will, full name WILLIAM JAMES DURANT
VERGIL, full name PUBLIUS VERGILIUS MARO

Persons whose names include a title of nobility are entered as they are popularly known, whether by family name or peerage.

EDEN, (Robert) Anthony, 1st Earl of Avon
CHESTERFIELD, Philip Dormer Stanhope, 4th Earl of

The life and work of members of some families are intertwined. In such cases the most important individuals are entered under the family name; each is discussed within the article and the full name is in boldface type when first mentioned.

AMATI, family of celebrated Italian violin makers of Cremona.
Andrea Amati (c. 1520–78), founder of the Cremona school of violin makers. His model was a small violin with high back and belly, amber varnish, and a clear although weak tone.
Antonio Amati (c. 1550–c. 1638) and Girolamo Amati (c. 1556–c. 1630), sons of Andrea Amati. They worked together and followed their father's style. Girolamo also developed a larger violin with an altered sound hole. . . .

Place-names include political units, such as cities, states, and countries, and physical features, such as mountains, rivers, and islands. When a geographic entity is known by more than one name, the alternate is also given.

LEGHORN or LIVORNO

Former names, ancient names, and foreign equivalents follow.

THAILAND, formerly SIAM
TICINO (anc. Ticinus)
AACHEN (Fr. Aix-la-Chapelle)

Things include all subjects except persons and places. When the name of a thing is more than one word, it is entered in inverted order according to the most significant word.

**BASEBALL HALL OF FAME AND MUSEUM, NATIONAL**
**FOOTBALL, AMERICAN**
**FORESTS, NATIONAL AND STATE**

Terms with more than one meaning are treated in separate articles; an identifying phrase follows the article title.

**METER,** in mathematics . . .
**METER,** in music . . .
**METER,** in poetry . . .

**Opening Sentence.** Following a person's name are life dates (in parentheses), the person's nationality and profession, and place of birth. Longer biographies also include a statement of the person's historical significance. A geographic entity is identified by political unit or description and is located by boundaries. Terms denoting things are in general followed by a definition. In some cases the article title is followed by a period, and the opening sentence introduces the topic.

**Subheads.** Longer articles are divided into sections by subheads that indicate a change from one aspect of a subject to another. Articles may be arranged chronologically, geographically, or topically. Subheads are set in four kinds of special type, indicating level of specificity, and articles may contain one, two, three, or four levels. Below, in order from most general to most specific, are examples of subheads from the article AFRICA.

HISTORY
*THE ERA OF EUROPEAN COLONIALISM*
**West Africa.**
*Slave trade.*

**Cross-references.** Cross-references are devices that guide the reader to information located elsewhere in the encyclopedia. These devices usually direct the reader from a general article on a subject to a more specific article on that subject. Funk & Wagnalls New Encyclopedia uses five types of cross-references: main-entry cross-references, q.v., *See, See also,* and For additional information on . . . see . . . .

A main-entry cross-reference indicates that information on the topic indicated by the entry term is located under another title.

**DECOMPRESSION SICKNESS.** *See* BENDS.

The abbreviation (q.v.) stands for Latin *quod vide,* meaning "which see." Its position following a word or a term signals that the word or term is itself the title of an article in this encyclopedia.

A *See* reference either within a sentence in parentheses or at the end of a paragraph or an article directs the reader to an article or articles that provide further information on the topic under discussion. A *See also* reference directs the reader to an article that provides information on related topics.

Within an article persons are identified by nationality and profession unless they are universally well known, such as, for example, George Washington and Julius Caesar. Life dates follow the name of any persons on whom this encyclopedia does not have an article, unless such dates are unavailable. The reader is reminded of this by the use of the following statement at the end of long articles such as countries or discipline surveys.

> For additional information on historical figures, see biographies of those whose names are not followed by dates.

**Signature.** Initials at the end of an article are those of the writer or reviewer and are keyed to the list of contributors beginning on page 457 of volume 28.

**Bibliography Cross-reference.** At the end of many articles is a cross-reference that leads the reader to a list of pertinent bibliographic materials in volume 28.

> For further information on this topic, see the Bibliography in volume 28, section 859.

> For further information on this person, see the section Biographies in the Bibliography in volume 28.

See the Preface and Guide to the Bibliography (vol. 28, pp. 186–87) for a complete description of the bibliography and a discussion on how to use it. The midvolume front matter to the bibliography also contains the essays "How to Use the Library" (pp. 190–94) and "How to Write a Term Paper" (pp. 195–97). The reading lists that constitute the major part of the bibliography begin on page 205.

## GRAPHIC AIDS

In addition to some 25,000 articles, Funk & Wagnalls New Encyclopedia contains illustrations (both in color and in black and white), maps, indexes to the maps, charts, tables, and special two-page graphics accompanying articles on U.S. states and Canadian provinces. All illustrations have captions and, when appropriate, credit lines. The hundreds of maps and map indexes in the encyclopedia are produced by GeoSystems Global Corporation, and are designed to show the most important places in each area in clear, easy-to-read type. Graphics appear where they will be of most value to the reader; in addition, references to accompanying graphics appear in the text. Diagrams illustrate many technical and scientific articles. Other illustrations either help explain the topic or extend the text of an article.

## INDEX

Volume 29 of Funk & Wagnalls New Encyclopedia is the index. Using the same letter-by-letter alphabetical approach as the encyclopedia, the index contains some 130,000 entries. For a full description of its format and a discussion of how to use it, see Guide to the Index (vol. 29, pp. 6–8).

## STYLE

**Abbreviations and Diacritic Marks.** A selected list of abbreviations used in the encyclopedia appears on page 64 of volume 1 and on page 6 of volumes 2–28. An expanded list of abbreviations accompanies the article ABBREVIATIONS AND ACRONYMS in vol. 1. A diacritic mark is a sign placed over, under, through, or after a letter to indicate a special sound or value for the letter to which it is attached. Those frequently used in this encyclopedia are shown and explained in the article DIACRITIC MARK.

**Transliteration.** Words of a foreign language written in a non-Roman alphabet, such as Arabic, Russian, and Chinese, must be transliterated for use in a work written in English; that is, letters of the English alphabet must be substituted for the non-Roman characters. In this encyclopedia commonly accepted systems of transliteration have been used for all languages using non-Roman alphabets. The most recent system to be standardized and widely adopted is Pinyin, the Chinese phonetic alphabet. Its use was authorized by the State Council of the People's Republic of China beginning Jan. 1, 1979. It was based on standard Peking (*Pinyin*: Beijing) pronunciation of Mandarin, the official Chinese language. In this encyclopedia Pinyin is used for all Chinese names and terms except names of ancient places and historical persons, historical and classical terms (for example, *I Ching*), and the following place-names: Inner Mongolia and Tibet. The modified Wade-Giles system is used for names that are not transliterated in Pinyin; in addition, the Wade-Giles romanization is given as one of the alternative spellings for each article title in Pinyin. Following local usage, Wade-Giles is used for transliterating the names of people and places in Taiwan (Republic of China).

**Use of the Metric System.** For units of measurement, except those of historic record, the metric is given first followed by the customary in parentheses.

30.3 million sq km (11.7 million sq mi)

Temperature is given first in degrees Celsius and then in degrees Fahrenheit in parentheses.

20° C (68° F)

For further information on the metric system, see the articles CGS SYSTEM; INTERNATIONAL SYSTEM OF UNITS; METRIC SYSTEM; WEIGHTS AND MEASURES.

**Typography.** Funk & Wagnalls New Encyclopedia employs various typographical devices to distinguish among its many components. All article titles are in **boldface** type, a darker type characterized by thick heavy lines. Cross-references are set in a combination of *italics* and LARGE and SMALL capital letters. The body, or text, of an article is set in lightface, as is this sentence. RUNNING HEADS are printed in large capital letters at the top of the page. The running head on the left-hand page is the first article title on that page; the running head on the right-hand page is the last article title on that page. Running heads in an article that covers several pages repeat the article title.

# SELECTED ABBREVIATIONS USED IN TEXT*

| | | | | | |
|---|---|---|---|---|---|
| AC | alternating current | F | Fahrenheit | Nor. | Norwegian |
| AD | *anno Domini* (Lat., "in the year of the Lord") | Finn. | Finnish | O.E. | Old English |
| | | fl. | flourished | O.Fr. | Old French |
| | | FM | frequency modulation | O.H.G. | Old High German |
| alt. | altitude | | | O.N. | Old Norse |
| AM | *ante meridiem* (Lat., "before noon") | Fr. | French | Op. | *Opus* (Lat., "work") |
| | | ft | foot, feet | oz | ounce(s) |
| | | g | gram(s) | Pers. | Persian |
| AM | amplitude modulation | gal | gallon(s) | PM | *post meridiem* (Lat., "after noon") |
| | | Ger. | German | | |
| amu | atomic mass unit(s) | GeV | billion electron volts | Pol. | Polish |
| Arab. | Arabic | | | pop. | population |
| Arm. | Armenian | Gr. | Greek | Port. | Portuguese |
| A.S. | Anglo-Saxon | ha | hectare(s) | q.v. | *quod vide* (Lat., "which see") |
| ASSR | Autonomous Soviet Socialist Republic | Heb. | Hebrew | | |
| | | hp | horsepower | r. | reigned |
| atm. | atmosphere | hr | hour | R. | River |
| at.no. | atomic number | Hung. | Hungarian | repr. | reprinted |
| at.wt. | atomic weight | Hz | hertz or cycle(s) per second | rev. | revised |
| b. | born | | | Rom. | Romanian |
| BC | before Christ | Icel. | Icelandic | Rus. | Russian |
| b.p. | boiling point | i.e. | *id est* (Lat., "that is") | S | south; southern |
| Btu | British Thermal Unit | | | sec. | second(s); secant |
| | | in | inch(es) | SFSR | Soviet Federated Socialist Republic |
| bu | bushel(s) | inc. | incorporated | | |
| Bulg. | Bulgarian | Ital. | Italian | Skt. | Sanskrit |
| C | Celsius | Jap. | Japanese | Span. | Spanish |
| c. | *circa* (Lat., "about") | K | Kelvin | sp.gr. | specific gravity |
| cent. | century | kg | kilogram(s) | sq | square |
| Chin. | Chinese | km | kilometer(s) | sq km | square kilometer(s) |
| cm | centimeter(s) | kw | kilowatt(s) | sq mi | square mile(s) |
| Co. | Company, County | kwh | kilowatt hour(s) | SSR | Soviet Socialist Republic |
| cu | cubic | Lat. | Latin | | |
| d. | died | lat | latitude | St. | Saint, Street |
| Dan. | Danish | lb | pound(s) | Sum. | Sumerian |
| DC | direct current | long | longitude | Swed. | Swedish |
| Du. | Dutch | m | meter(s) | trans. | translated, translation, translator(s) |
| E | east; eastern | mass no. | mass number | | |
| ed. | edited, edition, editors | MeV | million electron volts | | |
| | | | | Turk. | Turkish |
| e.g. | *exempli gratia* (Lat., "for example") | mg | milligram(s) | Ukr. | Ukrainian |
| | | mi | mile(s) | UN | United Nations |
| | | min | minute(s) | U.S. | United States |
| Egypt. | Egyptian | ml | milliliter(s) | USSR | Union of Soviet Socialist Republics |
| Eng. | English | mm | millimeter(s) | | |
| est. | established; estimated | m.p. | melting point | v. | versus; verse |
| | | mph | miles per hour | Ved. | Vedic |
| et al. | *et alii* (Lat., "and others") | Mt(s). | Mount, Mountain(s) | vol. | Volume(s) |
| | | | | W | west; western |
| EV | electron volt(s) | N | north; northern | yd | yard(s) |

*For a more extensive listing, see ABBREVIATIONS AND ACRONYMS. Charts of pertinent abbreviations also accompany the articles DEGREE, ACADEMIC; ELEMENTS, CHEMICAL; MATHEMATICAL SYMBOLS; and WEIGHTS AND MEASURES.

**A,** first letter and first vowel of the English alphabet and most alphabets of the Indo-European languages. The **A** shape apparently originated in an Egyptian hieroglyph of an eagle (*ahom*) in cursive hieratic writing. The Phoenicians renamed the letter *aleph* ("ox"), from a fancied resemblance to the head and horns of that animal. In the earliest Greek alphabet, *aleph* became the letter *alpha;* in turn, this became the Roman *A*, the form and general value of which were passed on to the peoples who later adopted the Roman alphabet. At present the sound of the *a* in "late" (long *a*) is the name of the letter in English. The English *a* may indicate many other sounds, as in "bat" (short *a*), "care," and "sofa." Modifications of its sound appear also in other modern languages.

**AACHEN,** (Fr. *Aix-la-Chapelle*), city, W central Germany, in North Rhine-Westphalia, near Belgium and the Netherlands. Aachen is known for its excellent mineral springs and has been a health resort since the 1st century AD. The city is an important railroad junction and industrial center. The major manufactures include machinery, processed food, railroad equipment, and textiles. Noteworthy structures include the town hall, built in 1353 on the ruins of Charlemagne's palace, and the cathedral (the chancel of which was built in the 13th–14th cent.), which contains Charlemagne's tomb.

The city is rich in historical associations and is thought to be the birthplace of Charlemagne. During his reign (800–14), Charlemagne made the city a center of Carolingian culture and had his palace and cathedral erected in Aachen. It was the coronation site for Holy Roman emperors from 936 until 1562, when the site was moved to Frankfurt am Main. During the French Revolution Aachen was occupied by the French and in 1801 was formally ceded to France. After the defeat of Napoleon in 1815, Aachen was acquired by Prussia. The city was badly damaged in World War II. Pop. (1992 est.) 244,442.

**AAIÚN, EL-,** also el-Aiúm, town, principal urban center of Western Sahara (formerly the overseas Province of Spanish Sahara), near the Atlantic Ocean. The town is an artificially constructed oasis, where grains and vegetables are grown by irrigation. Phosphate deposits have been discovered to the S. El-Aaiún is the site of a museum of Saharan culture. The modern town was built in 1938 to serve as the administrative center of Spanish Sahara. It remained under Spanish control until Dec. 11, 1975, when it was occupied by Moroccan troops; the last of the Spanish forces withdrew on Dec. 20. The town's name is also spelled Laayounne or Layoun. Pop. (1982 est.) 93,875.

**AAKJAER, Jeppe** (1866–1930), Danish writer. A leading regional and social-protest author of Jutland, he is read today as a lyric poet rather than

*The cathedral at Aachen.* O. Troisfontaines–Shostal/Superstock

*The Gullichsen house, Villa Mairea, Pori, Finland, illustrates Alvar Aalto's use of different tones of wood to bring warmth and beauty to a home.*

as a novelist. The novel *Vredens børn, et tyendes saga* (Children of Wrath: A Hired Man's Saga, 1904) helped bring some small improvements for rural workers. *Rugens sange* (Songs of the Rye, 1906) is his best-known work. He became known as the Danish Burns because his work somewhat resembles that of the Scottish poet Robert Burns.

**AALST** (Fr. *Alost*), city, W central Belgium, in East Flanders Province, on the Dender R. Manufactures include textiles, beer, footwear, and machinery. The city hall (begun early 13th cent.) and the Gothic Church of Saint Martin (begun late 15th cent.) are notable landmarks. Aalst was founded by the 9th century. It was ruled by France during 1667–1706 and was occupied by Germany in World Wars I and II. Pop. (1993 est.) 76,514.

**AALTO, (Hugo) Alvar Henrik** (1898–1976), Finnish architect, one of the 20th century's foremost architects and designers, who combined in his buildings and furnishings clear functionalism with uncommon grace and warmth.

Aalto was born Feb. 3, 1898, in Kuortane, and graduated (1921) from the Helsinki Polytechnic School. His first buildings to gain wide acclaim were a newspaper office and plant (1927–30) in Turku, notable for the use of tapered columns to support the pressroom roof, and the superbly sited Paimio Tuberculosis Sanatorium (1929–33), in which the patients' building provides, along with the most advanced hospital technology, such amenities as sunlit balconies with a fine view. For this and for many other buildings, Aalto and his first wife, Aino Marsio (1894–1949), also designed all furnishings and fittings, often entirely of laminated wood. In 1935 they founded Artek, a firm that continues to produce innovative furnishings.

Aalto's international reputation grew with his Finnish Pavilion for the 1937 Paris Exposition; the understated luxury of Villa Mairea (1938–39), built for a wealthy patron; and his innovative Finnish Pavilion for the 1939 New York World's Fair, with interior walls of undulating glass and molded wood. In 1940, Aalto was invited to the U.S. as a visiting professor at the Massachusetts Institute of Technology, where he remained for eight years, and designed Baker House (1947), a striking serpentine-plan dormitory on the Charles River.

Aalto returned to Finland in 1948 to head the planning office set up to rebuild that country following the devastation of World War II. For Säynätsalo, an island village, he created (1950–52) a civic center of brick and timber units set on a high terrace. Of Aalto's many buildings in Helsinki, the most impressive is Finlandia House (1967–75), the city's lakeside cultural center. Aalto died May 11, 1976, in Helsinki.

**AAR.** See AARE.

**AARDVARK** (Afrik., "earth pig"), common name for a burrowing, ant-eating mammal, *Orycteropus afer*, constituting the order Tubulidentata. The aardvark is found throughout much of Africa, from the southern part of Egypt to the Cape of Good Hope. A nocturnal animal, it lives in burrows and feeds entirely on ants and termites.

The aardvark is up to 2 m (6 ft) long, including the fleshy, tapering tail, which it uses to throw earth backward when it burrows. It has an arched back, a tubular snout, and large, upright ears. The aardvark uses its specialized, chisel-shaped claws to break open the hard clay of termite nests; then it uses its sticky tongue to capture the insects in the nest. Unlike the animals known as anteaters, which are toothless, the aardvark has 20 cylindrical, rootless teeth that grow continually throughout its lifetime.

The female gives birth to a single offspring, which digs its own burrow at the age of six months. Although timid, the aardvark will fight when it cannot flee or burrow to safety; lying on its back, it defends itself with its powerful claws.

**AARDWOLF,** common name for a carnivorous quadruped, *Proteles cristatus*, of southern and eastern Africa, usually placed with the hyena (q.v.) in the family Hyaenidae. Unlike the hyena,

*African aardvark,* Orycteropus afer

N. Myers–Bruce Coleman, Inc.

which has only four toes on its forefeet, the aardwolf has five; for this reason it sometimes is placed in a family of its own, Protelidae. The aardwolf stands about 51 cm (about 20 in) high at the shoulder, is about 76 cm (about 2.5 ft) long, and is covered with long, coarse hair. It is light buff in color, with an orange tint and dark brown bands. At night it leaves its burrow, traveling singly or in a troop, to forage for carrion and insects, especially termites. When attacked, the aardwolf erects its mane, achieving a formidable appearance, and ejects a foul-smelling fluid from its anal gland. Having weak jaws and small teeth, however, it is unable to fight off such enemies as the dog. Toward December the female aardwolf finds a burrow and bears a litter of two to four young.

**AARE,** also Aar (anc. *Obringa*), major river, central and N Switzerland. The source of the Aare is in Bern Canton. After flowing through the Brienzersee and Thunersee, the river joins the Rhine R. near the town of Waldshut, Germany. The main tributaries are the Reuss and Limmat rivers. It is about 280 km (about 175 mi) long and is navigable from the mouth to the town of Thun, Switzerland.

**AARON,** first Jewish high priest and traditional founder of the Hebrew priesthood. According to the Old Testament Book of Exodus, Aaron was the older brother of Moses and a direct descendant of the tribe of Levi. When Moses declined the mission of delivering the Children of Israel from Egyptian bondage, because he was "slow of speech," Aaron was appointed his minister and spokesman (see Exod. 4:10–15). He delivered the message of Jehovah to the Israelites and to the court of the pharaoh, confirming the words of the message by wonderful signs (see Exod. 4–12). With Moses, Aaron led the Israelites out of Egypt, and in the battle against the Amalekites (see Exod. 17), Hur and Aaron held up the hands of Moses while he prayed for victory. Aaron was specially chosen for the office of priest, which was to be hereditary in his family (see Exod. 28), and was formally consecrated. At Mount Sinai, when Moses and Joshua ascended the mount to receive the stone tablets containing the Law, Aaron and Hur were left in charge of the Israelites. The people, dismayed at Moses' long absence on the mountain, cried out for a god to worship, and Aaron made them a golden calf (see Exod. 32:1–24); he thereby incurred the anger of Jehovah and was pardoned only through the intercession of Moses. For their doubts (see Num. 20), Moses and Aaron were forbidden to enter the promised land; Aaron died on Mount Hor, and his office was given to his son Eleazar.

**AARON, Hank,** full name HENRY L. AARON (1934–   ), American baseball player, born in Mobile, Ala. Aaron, a right fielder, played for the Milwaukee Braves (after 1966, the Atlanta Braves) from 1954 to 1974, when he was traded to the Milwaukee Brewers. On April 8, 1974, while still with the Braves, he hit his 715th home run, topping the previous all-time record of 714, owned by Babe Ruth since the 1930s. When Aaron retired after the 1976 season, he held many all-time career batting records, including most home runs (755), total bases (6856), extra-base hits (1477), runs batted in (2297), and times at bat (12,364). Aaron was elected to the Baseball Hall of Fame in 1982.

Hank Aaron                                    Focus on Sports

**ABA,** large town, SE Nigeria, Imo State, on the Aba R. Aba is served by a railroad and is a road center as well. Originally a small village adjacent to a British military camp, the town has become an important trade center, particularly for palm oil and kernels; the processing of cola nuts is also important. Manufactures include textiles, soap, pharmaceuticals, shoes, beer, and mineral water. Pop. (1990 est.) 257,300.

**ABACA.** *See* MANILA HEMP.

**ABACUS,** instrument used in performing arithmetic calculations. It consists essentially of a tablet or frame bearing parallel wires or grooves on which counters or beads are moved. In the modern abacus, each wire or groove represents one place in the system of notation (that is, units, tens, hundreds, thousands); each bears two groups of counters, one of five counters, each representing one unit, and one of two counters, each representing five units.

Many early civilizations used the abacus. In ancient Rome it was a sand-covered wax tablet, marked table, or grooved table or tablet. In China and Japan, where it is still used, the abacus is a frame with beads strung on parallel wires. A simplified abacus, used in medieval England, consisted of a tablet ruled into spaces representing the positions of counters such as buttons or stones. The checkered tablecloth, from which the term *exchequer* was derived, was originally a calculating device.

**ABADAN,** city, SW Iran, Khuzestan Province, on Abadan Island, in the Shatt al-Arab, near the head of the Persian Gulf. It is a major petroleum-refining and petroleum-shipping center. Crude oil is pumped to the city from oil fields that lie to the N. Abadan has an international airport and is the seat of Abadan Institute of Technology (1939). The site was ceded to Iran by Turkey in 1847. Oil was discovered in the vicinity in 1908, and in 1913 Abadan was selected as the site of a pipeline terminus refinery. During the Iran-Iraq war the city was virtually destroyed by shelling, and recovery has been slow. The 1991 census did not cover Abadan; unofficial estimates place the population at less than half the 1976 figure of 296,081.

**ABALONE,** common name for any marine snail (q.v.) of the family Haliotidae, found on rocks near the shores of warm seas except the western Atlantic Ocean. They feed on seaweed. Their flattened, ovoid shells, sometimes 30 cm (about 1 ft) long, are used to make ornate objects (*see* MOTHER-OF-PEARL). The thick muscle, or foot, with which it attaches itself to a rock, is edible. The flesh can be served fresh, but is usually dried. The red abalone, *Haliotis refescens*, is found in large numbers off the California coast.

**ABANDONMENT.** For the abandonment of goods, *see* DERELICT; SALVAGE. For the desertion of children, *see* PARENT AND CHILD. For abandonment as grounds for altering the marriage relationship, *see* DESERTION; DIVORCE; HUSBAND AND WIFE; SEPARATION.

**ABATEMENT,** in law, form of defense or plea that ends an action in law or equity on grounds that a technical error of fact prevents continuation of the action (*see* LAW). When used in an action in law, the proceeding is ended, and the plaintiff must institute a new suit to pursue the case. In equity, the action may be undertaken again after correction of the error of fact. Abatement, when

*Abalone shells*    Top: © 1987 Mark E. Gibson–The Stock Market
Bottom: © E. R. Degginger–Bruce Coleman, Inc.

applied in contracts, debts, legacies, customs, duties, and taxes, means a reduction in the payable sum. Applied to nuisances, abatement signifies removal of the cause.

**ABBADIDS,** dynasty of so-called party kings (Span. *reyes de taifas*) of Seville, noted for the cultural brilliance of their court. In power from 1023 to 1091, the dynasty included three succeeding rulers, the first of whom was Abbad ibn Muhammad (r. 1023–42), a qadi (magistrate) who governed behind the screen of a puppet caliph. That pretense was dropped by his son, Abbad al-Mutadid (r. 1042–68), who reigned openly and conquered several adjacent petty kingdoms. Himself a poet, he was also a patron of the arts and kept a lavish court. In this, however, he was outdone by his son, Abbad al-Mutamid (1040–95), who, as Abbad III (r. 1068–91), made Seville the outstanding center of Muslim culture. Having added Córdoba to his realm early in his reign, al-Mutamid later sought help from the Almoravids against Alfonso I of Castile, who was spearheading the Christian reconquest of Spain; thus reinforced, he defeated Alfonso in 1086. In 1091,

however, his former allies returned to Seville uninvited and deposed him. Al-Mutamid died destitute in Morocco four years later.

**ABBAS,** full name AL-ABBAS IBN AL-MUTTALIB (566?–653), paternal uncle of the Prophet Muhammad and of the fourth caliph, Ali. A rich merchant of Mecca, Abbas initially fought against the new religion, but he was converted in 629. Thereafter he staunchly supported Islam with both money and arms, and he accompanied his nephew on his march on Mecca in 630. Abbas was the forebear of the Abbasid dynasty of caliphs.

**ABBAS I,** full name ABBAS HILMI (1813–54), pasha of Egypt (1849–54), grandson of the pasha Muhammad Ali. In 1848, on the death of his uncle Ibrahim Pasha, Abbas became regent of Egypt. He was created pasha in the following year. Most of the domestic reforms accomplished by Muhammad Ali were undone during the reign of Abbas, who was murdered by his slaves.

**ABBAS II,** full name ABBAS HILMI PASHA (1874–1944), last khedive (Turkish viceroy) of Egypt. He succeeded his father Muhammad Tawfik Pasha (1852–92) to the throne of Egypt in 1892. During the early years of his reign he opposed British interference in Egyptian affairs. After 1900, however, he was compelled to cooperate with progressive measures instituted by the British resident at Cairo. During his reign Egypt reconquered the Sudan (1898); the railway to Khartoum, Sudan, was completed (1899), as was the first Aswan Dam (1902). Abbas II supported the Ottoman Turks in World War I and was deposed in 1914, when Great Britain established a protectorate over Egypt.

**ABBAS I,** sometimes called Abbas the Great (1571–1629), Safavid shah of Iran (1588–1629). He began his rule by ceding lands to the Uzbeks and the Ottomans in order to gain time to establish a standing army. Beginning in 1588, however, Abbas won back all the ceded territory, and by 1623 he ruled over an empire extending from the Tigris to the Indus River. A superb administrator, Abbas also encouraged commerce and industry. He maintained a lavish court and was a patron of the arts, which flourished during his reign as never before. A zealous builder, Abbas also rebuilt Esfahan, which he made his capital; many of the city's most splendid edifices date from his time.

**ABBAS, Ferhat** (1899–1985), Algerian leader in the struggle for independence, born in Taher, and educated as a pharmacist. A political moderate disillusioned with French policy, he advocated Algerian self-determination and independence and was intermittently jailed for his political activities. In 1956 he joined the Cairo-based National Liberation Front (NLF), then waging a war of independence against the French, and from 1958 to 1961 he headed its government in exile. After independence (1962), Abbas soon quarreled with the more radical NLF leadership and was put under house arrest (1964–65). He then retired from public life.

**ABBASIDS.** *See* CALIPHATE.

**ABBESS,** woman who is superior of a convent in certain religious orders. An abbess has administrative jurisdiction equivalent to that of the abbot of a monastery but does not exercise the rights and duties of the priesthood. The title dates from the 6th century. Most of the original secular privileges of the position, such as membership in the king's council and rank of nobility equivalent to that of temporal peers, were abolished in the 16th century, at the time of the Reformation.

**ABBEY,** self-sufficient monastic house ruled by an abbot or an abbess.

**ABBEY THEATRE,** repertory-theater company and the auditorium in which it performs, in Dublin, Ireland. Founded to present native plays about native subjects, the company later expanded its repertory to include classical drama, including that of Shakespeare, and contemporary works by dramatists of continental Europe.

The Abbey Theatre is a product of the Irish cultural revival that began late in the 19th century. The revival was initiated largely by the Irish poet and dramatist William Butler Yeats, who urged Irish writers to draw their inspiration directly from Irish life and traditions rather than from English and European sources. In 1899 Yeats helped to establish the Irish Literary Theatre, reorganized in 1902 as the Irish National Theatre Society. With financial assistance provided by the English theater manager Annie Elizabeth Fredericka Horniman (1860–1937), the Irish National Theatre Society established in 1904 the repertory company that became known as the Abbey Theatre, which, since 1924, has received an annual government subsidy. The new group introduced realistic and poetic elements into the Irish theater and soon gained a popular following. Notable Irish dramatists whose works were presented at various times included Yeats, John Millington Synge, Lady Isabella Augusta Gregory , Æ (George William Russell), Padraic Colum, St. John Greer Ervine (1883–1971), and Sean O'Casey. Among the favorite plays of Abbey audiences were *Cathleen ni Houlihan* (1902) by Yeats, *Riders to the Sea* (1904) and *Playboy of the Western World* (1907) by Synge, and *Juno and the Paycock* (1924) and *The Plough and the Stars* (1926) by O'Casey. The

quality of the presentations declined after the death of Yeats in 1939. In 1951 the Abbey auditorium was severely damaged by fire, and the company moved to the Queen's Theatre. On July 18, 1966, the completely new, 628-seat Abbey Theatre was opened on the site of its predecessor. Beneath the Abbey foyer is the Peacock Theatre, used for experimental productions and for performances by students enrolled in the Abbey School of Acting.    E.B.

*See also* IRISH LITERATURE.

**ABBOT** (Aram. *abba,* "father"), in certain religious orders, the head of a monastery or abbey elected (sometimes for life) by the members of the order. Regarded as the father of his community, the abbot has the authority to enforce observance of the rules of the order and to administer the goods of the monastery. Until the beginning of the 10th century, the head of every monastery was called abbot, but many of the orders founded after that time rejected the title. The Carthusians, Dominicans, Carmelites, and Augustinians called the superior prepositor, or prior; the Franciscans, *custos,* or guardian. During the Middle Ages many chief abbeys were under the influence of lay rulers who sought control of monastic wealth. The members of the royal household received grants of abbeys as their maintenance, and monarchs kept the richest for themselves. In the Orthodox church the superiors of monasteries are called hegumens or archimandrites.

**ABBOTT, Berenice** (1898–1991), American photographer, famous for her magnificent documentation of New York City and for her pioneering camera work in the physical sciences. Born in Springfield, Ohio, Abbott studied sculpture in New York City and Paris before turning to photography in the mid-1920s at the suggestion of the American surrealist Man Ray. Through Ray she also encountered the great Parisian photographer Eugène Atget just before his death in 1927 and worked tirelessly to spread his fame. Returning to the U.S. in 1929, Abbott resolved to record New York City with a camera in the manner that Atget had recorded Paris; the result was her epic *Changing New York* (1939). From the 1940s to the '60s Abbott explored such natural phenomena as magnetism with a camera.

**ABBOTT, George** (1887–1995), American playwright, producer, director, and actor, born in Forestville, N.Y., and educated at the University of Rochester and Harvard University. He became an actor in 1913 but turned increasingly to writing, producing, and directing, both in film and theater. From 1928 to 1958 he worked on 11 films including *All Quiet on the Western Front* (1930). His

Sir John Joseph Caldwell Abbott during his brief tenure as prime minister of Canada.

PA-33933/Public Archives, Canada

greatest success, however, was on Broadway where he was involved in more than 120 productions. Abbott directed and produced the comedies *Boy Meets Girl* (1935) and *Kiss and Tell* (1943) and the musicals *Pal Joey* (1940), *On the Town* (1944), *Call Me Madam* (1950), *Wonderful Town* (1953), and *A Funny Thing Happened on the Way to the Forum* (1962). He wrote and directed the musicals *The Boys from Syracuse* (1938; adapted from Shakespeare's *Comedy of Errors*), *Where's Charley?* (1948), and *New Girl in Town* (1957). He was coauthor and director of the comedy *Three Men on a Horse* (1935) and the musicals *The Pajama Game* (1954), *Damn Yankees* (1955), and *Fiorello!* (1959; Pulitzer Prize, 1960).

**ABBOTT, Grace** (1878–1939), American social worker, born in Grand Island, Nebr., and educated at the universities of Nebraska and Chicago. Devoted to the cause of child welfare, she taught high school until 1907, worked with various philanthropic organizations in Chicago, and was director of the Child Labor Division of the U.S. Children's Bureau from 1921 to 1934. In this capacity she promoted legislation to regulate

child labor and directed studies of related problems, including delinquency and child neglect. From 1934 to 1939 she was professor of public welfare at the School of Social Service Administration of the University of Chicago. Among her books are *The Immigrant and the Community* (1917) and *The Child and the State* (2 vol., 1938).

**ABBOTT, Sir John Joseph Caldwell** (1821–93), Canadian lawyer, educator, and statesman, who served briefly as prime minister (1891–92).

Born in Saint Andrews, Lower Canada (now Québec), on March 12, 1821, Abbott graduated from McGill University, Montréal, studied for the bar, and began his practice in 1847. He was elected to the Legislative Assembly of the united Province of Canada in 1857 and served there and in the House of Commons until 1874, when he was involved with other Conservatives in an election-financing scandal and lost his seat. In 1880 he was voted back into the House, and was appointed to the Senate in 1887. After service in the cabinet as minister without portfolio, he was chosen prime minister in 1891, but ill health soon forced him to resign. He was knighted in 1892. An expert in commercial law, Abbott was dean of the law faculty of McGill (1855–80).

**ABBREVIATIONS AND ACRONYMS,** letter or group of letters used in writing, printing, and speech to represent a word or phrase in shortened form. Abbreviations are used to save space and time. The most common are arbitrary signs or initial letters for the words themselves.

Shortened word forms have been in use since antiquity, and many current abbreviations have come from Latin. Most of the arts and sciences use symbols as abbreviations; they are universally understood. Although no specific rule governs the formation of abbreviations, certain kinds have become standard. The most common are (1) first and last letters, for example, Pa. for Pennsylvania; (2) key identifying letters, for example, apt. for apartment; (3) syllables, for example, anon. for anonymous; (4) initials, as with titles or long names, for example, OAS for Organization of American States.

A word formed from the initials or from the elements of a compound term is called an acronym and is usually spelled without periods, such as NATO for North Atlantic Treaty Organization. An organization may adopt a name so that the acronym indicates the nature of the organization, for example, WAVES, which comes from Women Accepted for Volunteer Emergency Service.

See the accompanying selective list of commonly used abbreviations. For college and university degrees, *see* DEGREE, ACADEMIC.

*See also* INTERNATIONAL SYSTEM OF UNITS.

# A

Å  angstrom
AA  Alcoholics Anonymous
AAA  American Automobile Association
AAAS  American Association for the Advancement of Science
AAU  Amateur Athletic Union
AC  alternating current
ACLU  American Civil Liberties Union
ACTH  adrenocorticotropic hormone
AD  *anno Domini* (Lat., "in the year of the Lord")
ADA  American Dental Association; Americans for Democratic Action
Adm.  Admiral
AEC  Atomic Energy Commission
AFB  Air Force Base
AFL  American Federation of Labor
AFL-CIO  American Federation of Labor and Congress of Industrial Organizations
AFM  American Federation of Musicians
Afrik.  Afrikaans
AFT  American Federation of Teachers
AIA  American Institute of Architects
AIC  American Institute of Chemists
AID  Agency for International Development
AIDS  acquired immune deficiency syndrome
AIP  American Institute of Physics
AK  Alaska
aka  also known as
AKC  American Kennel Club
Ala., AL  Alabama
ALA  American Library Association
alt.  altitude
Alta.  Alberta
AM  *ante meridiem* (Lat., "before noon")
AM  amplitude modulation
AMA  American Medical Association
amp  ampere(s)
amu  atomic mass unit(s)
AMVETS  American Veterans of World War II, Korea, and Vietnam
ANC  African National Congress
anc.  ancient
anon.  anonymous
ANPA  American Newspaper Publishers Association
antilog  antilogarithm
AP  American plan; Associated Press
APB  all points bulletin
APO  Army Post Office
Apr.  April
apt.  apartment
Arab.  Arabic
Aram.  Aramaic
Ariz., AZ  Arizona
Ark., AR  Arkansas
Arm.  Armenian
A.S.  Anglo-Saxon
ASAP  as soon as possible
ASCAP  American Society of Composers, Authors and Publishers
ASCE  American Society of Civil Engineers
ASEAN  Association of Southeast Asian Nations
ASME  American Society of Mechanical Engineers
ASPCA  American Society for the Prevention of Cruelty to Animals
assoc.  associate; association
ASSR  Autonomous Soviet Socialist Republic
asst.  assistant
atm  atmosphere
at.no.  atomic number
atty.  attorney
at.wt.  atomic weight
A.U.  atomic unit(s)
Aug.  August
AVC  American Veterans Committee
avdp.  avoirdupois (Fr., *avoir de pois*), unit of weight
Ave.  avenue
avg.  average
AWOL  absent without leave

# B

b.  born
BBC  British Broadcasting Corporation
bbl  barrel(s)
BC  before Christ
B.C.  British Columbia
BCE  before the Common Era
bd ft  board foot, board feet
bf  boldface
Blvd.  boulevard
bor.  borough
b.p.  boiling point
BPOE  Benevolent and Protective Order of Elks
Brig.  Brigadier
bro.  brother(s)
Btu  British thermal unit(s)
bu  bushel
Bulg.  Bulgarian

# C

C  Celsius
c.  circa (Lat., "about")
cal  calorie(s)
Cal  large calorie(s)
Calif., CA  California
CAP  Civil Air Patrol
Capt.  Captain
CARE  Cooperative for American Relief Everywhere
CBC  Canadian Broadcasting Corporation
CC  closed-captioned
cc  cubic centimeter(s)
CCC  Civilian Conservation Corps; Commodity Credit Corporation
cd  candela (Lat., "candle"), unit of luminous intensity
CD  certificate of deposit; compact disk
CDC  Centers for Disease Control and Prevention
CE  Common Era
cent.  century
cf.  compare
cgs  centimeter-gram-second
Chin.  Chinese
1 Chron.  1 Chronicles
2 Chron.  2 Chronicles
CIA  Central Intelligence Agency
CIO  Congress of Industrial Organizations
cm  centimeter(s)
CO  Colorado, Commanding Officer
Co.  Company, County
c/o  care of
COD  cash on delivery
Col.  Colonel; Colossians
Colo., CO  Colorado
Comdr.  Commander
comp.  compiled, compiler
Conn., CT  Connecticut
1 Cor.  1 Corinthians
2 Cor.  2 Corinthians
CORE  Congress of Racial Equality
Corp.  Corporation
cos  cosine
cot  cotangent
coul  coulomb(s)
CPA  certified public accountant
Cpl.  Corporal
CPO  Chief Petty Officer
csc  cosecant
CST  Central Standard Time
cu  cubic

# D

d.  died
DA  District Attorney
Dan.  Daniel; Danish

DAR  Daughters of the American Revolution
dB  decibel(s)
DC  direct current
D.C., DC  District of Columbia
DDT  dichlorodiphenyltrichloroethane
Dec.  December
Del., DE  Delaware
dept.  department
Deut.  Deuteronomy
dr.  dram(s)
diam.  diameter
dim.  dimension; diminuendo
DNA  deoxyribonucleic acid
DOA  dead on arrival
DP  displaced person
Dr.  doctor; Drive (street address)
DST  daylight saving time
D.T.'s  delirium tremens
Du.  Dutch

# E

E  East
ea.  each
Eccl.  Ecclesiastes
ed.  edited, edition, editor(s)
e.g.  *exempli gratia* (Lat., "for example")
Egypt.  Egyptian
EKG  electrocardiogram
encl.  enclosure
Eng.  English
enl.  enlarged
EP  European plan
EPA  Environmental Protection Agency
Eph.  Ephesians
ERA  earned run average; Equal Rights Amendment
ESP  extrasensory perception
Esq.  Esquire
EST  Eastern standard time
est.  established; estimated
et al.  *et alii* (Lat., "and others")
etc.  *et cetera* (Lat., "and so forth")
EU  European Union
eV  electron volts
Exod.  Exodus
Ezek.  Ezekiel

# F

F  Fahrenheit
FAA  Federal Aviation Administration
fac.  facsimile (Lat., *fac simile* "make similar")
FAO  Food and Agriculture Organization
FBI  Federal Bureau of Investigation
FCC  Federal Communications Commission
FDA  Food and Drug Administration
FDIC  Federal Deposit Insurance Corporation
Feb.  February
fem.  feminine
FDA  Food and Drug Administration
ff.  following
FHA  Federal Housing Administration
FICA  Federal Insurance Contribution Act
fig.  figure
Finn.  Finnish
fl.  flourished
Fla., FL  Florida
fl oz  fluid ounce(s)
FM  frequency modulation
FOB  free on board
Fr.  French
Fri.  Friday
FSLIC  Federal Savings and Loan Insurance Corporation
ft  foot, feet
FTC  Federal Trade Commission
ft-lb  foot-pound(s)
FYI  for your information

# G

G gauss
g gram(s)
Ga., GA Georgia
Gal. Galatians
gal gallon(s)
GATT General Agreement on Tariffs and Trade
GDP gross domestic product
Gen. General; Genesis
Ger. German
GeV billion electron volts
GHz gigahertz
GMT Greenwich mean time
GNP gross national product
GOP Grand Old Party (Republican party)
Gov. Governor
govt. government
GPO General Post Office; Government Printing Office
Gr. Greek
gr grain(s)

# H

ha hectare
Hab. Habbakuk
Hag. Haggai
Heb. Hebrew; Hebrews
HI Hawaii
HMS His (Her) Majesty's Ship (Service)
Hon. the Honorable
Hos. Hosea
hp horsepower
hr hour(s)
ht. height
HUD Department of Housing and Urban Development
Hung. Hungarian
hwy. highway
Hz hertz or cycle(s) per second

# I

IA Iowa
ibid. *ibidem* (Lat., "in the same place")
ICBM intercontinental ballistic missile
ICC Interstate Commerce Commission
Icel. Icelandic
ID Idaho; identification
i.e. *id est* (Lat., "that is")
IGY International Geophysical Year
Ill., IL Illinois
ILGWU International Ladies' Garment Workers' Union
in inch(es)
inc. incorporated
Ind., IN Indiana
IOU I owe you
IQ intelligence quotient
IRA individual retirement account; Irish Republican Army
IRS Internal Revenue Service
Isa. Isaiah
Ital. Italian
ital. italic (print)
ITU International Telecommunications Union; International Typographical Union
IWW Industrial Workers of the World

# J

J joule(s)
Jan. January
Jap. Japanese
Jer. Jeremiah
Josh. Joshua
J.P. Justice of the Peace
Jr. Junior
Judg. Judges

# K

K Kelvin; kilobyte(s); strikeout
Kans., KS Kansas
kc kilocycle(s)
kg kilogram(s)
kg m kilogram meter(s)
KKK Ku Klux Klan
kl kiloliter(s)
km kilometer(s)
km/hr kilometers per hour
KO knockout
KP kitchen police
kw kilowatt(s)
kwh kilowatt hour(s)
Ky., KY Kentucky

# L

l liter(s)
La., LA Louisiana
Lam. Lamentations
Lat. Latin
lat latitude
lb *libra* (pound), *librae* (pounds)
Lev. Leviticus
Lith. Lithuanian
loc. cit. *loco citato* (Lat., "in the place cited")
log logarithm
long longitude
LP long-playing record
LSD lysergic acid diethylamide
Lt. Lieutenant
Ltd. Limited

# M

m meter(s)
Maj. Major
Mal. Malachi
Man. Manitoba
MAP modified American plan
Mar. March
masc. masculine
Mass., MA Massachusetts
mass no. mass number
Matt. Matthew
M.C. master of ceremonies
Md., MD Maryland
ME Maine
M.E. Middle English
MeV million electron volts
Mex. Mexican
mg milligram(s)
M.H.G. Middle High German
mi mile(s)
MIA missing in action
Mic. Micah
Mich., MI Michigan
min minute(s)
Minn., MN Minnesota
misc. miscellaneous
Miss., MS Mississippi
mks meter-kilogram-second
ml milliliter(s)
mm millimeter(s)
Mo., MO Missouri
Mon. Monday
Mont., MT Montana
MP Military Police
m.p. melting point
mph miles per hour
MRI magnetic resonance imaging
MS, MSS manuscript(s)
MSG monosodium glutamate
MST Mountain standard time
Mt., Mts. mount, mountain, mountains

# N

N north; Newton(s)
*N* normal (unit of measure)
NAACP National Association for the Advancement of Colored People
NAFTA North American Free Trade Agreement
Nah. Nahum
NASA National Aeronautics and Space Administration
NASDAQ National Association of Securities Dealers Automated Quotations
NATO North Atlantic Treaty Organization
N.B. New Brunswick; *nota bene* (Lat., "mark well")
NBA National Basketball Association
N.C., NC North Carolina
NCAA National Collegiate Athletic Association
NCO noncommissioned officer
N.Dak., ND North Dakota
NE northeast
NEA National Education Association
Nebr., NE Nebraska
Neh. Nehemiah
Nev., NV Nevada
New Lat. New Latin
NFL National Football League
Nfld. Newfoundland
N.H., NH New Hampshire
NHL National Hockey League
NIH National Institutes of Health
N.J., NJ New Jersey
NLRB National Labor Relations Board
N.Mex., NM New Mexico
Nor. Norwegian
Nov. November
NRA National Rifle Association
N.S. Nova Scotia
NSF National Science Foundation
N.T. New Testament
Num. Numbers
NW northwest
NWT Northwest Territories
N.Y., NY New York
NYSE New York Stock Exchange

# O

OAS Organization of American States
OAU Organization of African Unity
Obad. Obadiah
O.B.E. Officer of the Order of the British Empire
OCS Officer Candidates School
Oct. October
O.E. Old English
OECD Organization for Economic Cooperation and Development
OED Oxford English Dictionary
O.Fr. Old French
OH Ohio
O.H.G. Old High German
Okla., OK Oklahoma
O.N. Old Norse
Ont. Ontario
op. *opus* (work)
op. cit. *opere citato* (Lat., "in the work cited")
OPEC Organization of Petroleum Exporting Countries
Oreg., OR Oregon
O.T. Old Testament
oz ounce(s)

# P

p., pp. page, pages
Pa., PA Pennsylvania
PAC political action committee
P.E.I. Prince Edward Island
Pers. Persian
1 Pet. 1 Peter
2 Pet. 2 Peter
PFC Private First Class
PGA Professional Golfers' Association
Phil. Philippians
Philem. Philemon
Pl. place
pl. plural

# ABBREVIATIONS AND ACRONYMS

PLO   Palestine Liberation Organization
PM   *post meridiem* (after noon)
PO   Petty Officer
Pol.   Polish
pop.   population
Port.   Portuguese
POW   prisoner of war
PR   Puerto Rico
Prof.   professor
pro tem   *pro tempore* (Lat., "for the time being")
Prov.   Proverbs
P.S.   *post scriptum* (Lat., "postscript"); Public School
Ps., Pss.   Psalm(s)
PST   Pacific standard time
pt   pint(s)
pt.   part(s)
PTA   Parent-Teacher Association
pub.   published; publisher
Pvt.   Private

# Q

qt   quart(s)
Que.   Québec
q.v.   *quod vide* (Lat., "which see"); plural, qq.v.

# R

R   Roentgen
R.   River
RAF   Royal Air Force (Britain)
RAM   random-access memory
RBI   run(s) batted in
RCAF   Royal Canadian Air Force
RCMP   Royal Canadian Mounted Police
Rd.   road
RDA   recommended daily allowance
REA   Rural Electrification Administration
R and D   Research and Development
repr.   reprinted
Rev.   Revelation; Reverend
rev.   revised
RFD   Rural Free Delivery
Rh factor   Rhesus factor
R.I., RI   Rhode Island
R.N.   Registered Nurse
RNA   ribonucleic acid
Rom.   Romanian; Romans
ROM   read-only memory
ROTC   Reserve Officers Training Corps
rpm   revolution(s) per minute
RR   railroad
RSVP   *répondez s'il vous plaît* (Fr., "please reply")
Rus.   Russian

# S

S   south
SAC   Strategic Air Command
1 Sam.   1 Samuel
2 Sam.   2 Samuel
Sask.   Saskatchewan
Sat.   Saturday
S.C., SC   South Carolina
SCLC   Southern Christian Leadership Conference
S.Dak. SD   South Dakota
SE   southeast
SEC   Securities and Exchange Commission
sec   second(s); secant
sect.   section

Sept.   September
SFSR   Soviet Federated Socialist Republic
Sgt.   Sergeant
sin   sine
sing.   singular
S.J.   Society of Jesus
Skt.   Sanskrit
Span.   Spanish
SPCA   Society for the Prevention of Cruelty to Animals
SPCC   Society for the Prevention of Cruelty to Children
spec.   specialist
sp.gr.   specific gravity
sq   square
sq km   square kilometer(s)
sq mi   square mile(s)
Sr.   Senior
SRO   standing room only
SS   ship; steamship
SSR   Soviet Socialist Republic
SST   supersonic transport
St.   Saint; Street
STD   sexually transmitted disease
Ste.   Sainte
STP   standard temperature and pressure
Sun.   Sunday
SW   southwest
Swed.   Swedish

# T

tan   tangent
TB   tuberculosis
tbsp.   tablespoon
temp.   temperature
Tenn., TN   Tennessee
Tex., TX   Texas
1 Thess.   1 Thessalonians
2 Thess.   2 Thessalonians
Thurs.   Thursday
1 Tim.   1 Timothy
2 Tim.   2 Timothy
TKO   technical knockout
TNT   trinitrotoluene, trinitrolvol
trans.   translated, translation, translator(s)
tsp.   teaspoon
Tues.   Tuesday
Turk.   Turkish
TV   television
TVA   Tennessee Valley Authority

# U

UAW   United Auto Workers
UFO   unidentified flying object
UHF   ultrahigh frequency
U.K.   United Kingdom
Ukr.   Ukrainian
UN   United Nations
UNESCO   United Nations Educational, Scientific, and Cultural Organization
UNICEF   United Nations Children's Fund
UPI   United Press International
U.S.   United States
USA   United States Army
USAF   United States Air Force
USCG   United States Coast Guard
USMC   United States Marine Corps
USN   United States Navy
USO   United Service Organizations
USS   United States Ship
USSR   Union of Soviet Socialist Republics
UT   universal time, Utah

# V

V   volt(s)
v.   versus, verse

V.A.   Veterans Administration, Department of Veterans Affairs
Va., VA   Virginia
VAT   value-added tax
VCR   videocassette recorder
VD   venereal disease
Ved.   Vedic
VFW   Veterans of Foreign Wars
VHF   very high frequency
VI   Virgin Islands
VIP   very important person
vol.   volume(s)
Vt., VT   Vermont

# W

W   watt(s); west
WAC   Women's Army Corps
Wash., WA   Washington
WAVES   Women Accepted for Voluntary Emergency Service
WCTU   Women's Christian Temperance Union
Wed.   Wednesday
WHO   World Health Organization
Wis., WI   Wisconsin
wt   weight
W.Va., WV   West Virginia
Wyo., WY   Wyoming

# X

x   an unknown quantity
Xmas   Christmas

# Y

yd   yard(s)
YMCA   Young Men's Christian Association
YMHA   Young Men's Hebrew Association
YT   Yukon Territory
YWCA   Young Women's Christian Association
YWHA   Young Women's Hebrew Association

# Z

Zech.   Zechariah
Zeph.   Zephaniah
ZIP   Zoning Improvement Program

**ABC POWERS,** early 20th-century term for Argentina, Brazil, and Chile. Beginning in 1899, these nations, striving to maintain peace in South and Central America and to achieve common action and policy on problems concerning all Latin American countries, concluded a series of treaties that provided for arbitration of disputes and mutual assistance against aggression. The respective alliances were primarily directed against certain policies of the U.S., particularly those implicit in the Monroe Doctrine. Shortly before the outbreak of World War I, the alliances assumed the character of an entente cordiale. Treaties providing for such an entente were drafted and signed in 1915 but were never ratified. One of the most important accomplishments of the ABC Powers was the mediation in 1914 of a serious dispute between the U.S. and Mexico arising from the refusal of the U.S. to recognize Gen. Victoriano Huerta as president of Mexico.

**ABD AL-HAMID I** (1725–09), Ottoman sultan of Turkey (1774–89), son of Ahmed III (1673–1736). He succeeded to the throne on the death of his brother Mustafa III (1717–74) and left his mark on Turkey as one of the strongest reformers of the 18th century. He was, however, drawn into a disastrous war (1787–92) against Russia and Austria.

**ABD AL-HAMID II** (1842–1918), Ottoman sultan of Turkey (1876–1909), son of Abd al-Madjid I (1823–61). He succeeded his brother Murad V (1840–1904), who had been declared insane. In reprisal against Turkish misrule in the Balkans, Russia declared war against Turkey in the second year of Abd al-Hamid's reign. He suffered disastrous military reverses and, by the terms of the Treaty of San Stefano in 1878, was deprived of most of his European territorial possessions. Massacres of Armenians occurred in Turkey during 1895 and 1896, but Abd al-Hamid refused to intervene, despite international protests. Internal dissatisfaction with his despotic rule led to the development of the powerful revolutionary organization known as the Young Turks. In 1909 Abd al-Hamid II was deposed and exiled.

**ABD-AR-RAHMAN** (d. 732), Arab soldier and emir of Spain (731–32). He became governor of southern France in 721. In 732, when the growth of Frankish power menaced the Muslim position in Spain, he led an army across the Pyrenees Mountains into the dominions of the Franks. His army met the Franks, led by Charles Martel, near Tours, France, later that year. The battle was indecisive, but the Muslims turned back after Abd-ar-Rahman fell.

**ABD-AR-RAHMAN I** (731–88), first Umayyad emir of Spain (756–88). Having narrowly escaped the massacre (750) of the Umayyads in Damascus, Abd-ar-Rahman wandered through North Africa until 755. With the backing of Umayyad sympathizers in Spain and in Ceuta, North Africa, he then intervened between feuding Muslims in Spain, captured Córdoba in 756, and was recognized as emir. His realm, however, was not pacified until the defeat of Charlemagne's army at Roncesvalles in 778. Abd-ar-Rahman rebuilt the great mosque (now cathedral) of Córdoba.

**ABD-AR-RAHMAN III** (889–961), eighth Umayyad ruler of Spain (912–61). Succeeding to an emirate diminished by provincial governors who acted like independent rulers, Abd-ar-Rahman at once set out to reassert Umayyad authority over all his territories; he recaptured Toledo, the last of the wayward cities, in 932. In the meantime, however, he had built up a navy unmatched anywhere in the world at the time and had wrested part of Morocco from the Fatimids. He also inflicted several defeats on the Christian kingdoms of León and Navarre, checking their expansion; by 929 he felt confident enough to assume the title of caliph.

Abd-ar-Rahman's greatest legacy was the transformation of Córdoba, which in splendor rivaled Baghdad and Constantinople, into the greatest cultural center in the Western world, a distinction it held for some 200 years.

**ABD-EL-KRIM** (1880?–1963), leader of the Riffians, an Arab tribe of Morocco. In 1921 he led his tribe against a Spanish military post in Er Rif, Morocco, capturing it and massacring 16,000 soldiers. By 1924 the Spanish were forced to retreat to their holdings along the coast of Morocco. Meanwhile, France laid claim to territory in southern Er Rif. The following year a French force under Marshal Henri Philippe Pétain and a Spanish army began operations against the Riffians. Hard fighting continued for a year, but finally the combined armies defeated the forces of Abd-el-Krim. He was exiled to the French island of Réunion from 1926 to 1947, when he was granted permission to live in southern France. He left the ship carrying him to France and, accepting an offer of protection from the king of Egypt, became a resident of that country. After 1948 he was a leader of the North African nationalist opposition to European rule.

**ABDERA,** city of ancient Thrace, near the mouth of the Néstos River, diagonally opposite the island of Thásos. It was founded by colonists from the ancient Ionian city of Clazomenae in the 7th century BC. The Greek philosophers Democritus and Protagoras were born here.

**ABDICATION,** relinquishment of office by a sovereign or other ruler. In modern times, sover-

*King Edward VIII (later the duke of Windsor) of Great Britain in Enzesfield Castle in Austria shortly after his abdication in 1936.*                                     **UPI**

eigns have abdicated for many different reasons.

Queen Christina of Sweden relinquished her crown in 1654 because she was weary of the cares of office. Ill health caused the abdication of the Holy Roman emperor Charles V in 1558 and of King Philip V of Spain in 1724. Louis Bonaparte, appointed (1806) king of Holland by Napoleon, abdicated in 1810 in protest because his brother treated Holland as merely a province of France. King Charles Emmanuel IV of Sardinia (1751–1819) was compelled by the French government to abdicate in 1802; his successor, King Victor Emmanuel I, abdicated in 1821 in the face of a popular uprising against his regime. Foreign force compelled the abdications of the Polish kings Augustus II the Strong (1670–1733, deposed 1704, abdicated 1706), Stanislas I Leszczyński (1735), and Stanislas II Augustus (1795) and of Charles IV of Spain (1808). Napoleon also was forced to abdicate by allied foreign powers, both in 1814 and, after his return, in 1815.

Insurrections often have forced abdications, including those of Richard II of England (1399), Mary, queen of Scots (1567), Charles X of France (1830), Louis Philippe of France (1848), Ferdinand I of Austria (1848), Louis I of Bavaria (1848), King Charles Albert of Sardinia-Piedmont (1798–1849, abdicated 1849), King Amadeus of Spain (1845–90, abdicated 1873), Prince Alexander I of Bulgaria (1857–93, abdicated 1886), King Milan of Serbia (1854–1901, abdicated 1889), Manuel II of

Portugal (1910), and Nicholas II of Russia (1917).

The defeat of the Central Powers in World War I resulted (1918) in a number of abdications, including those of William II of Germany, Charles I of Austria-Hungary, Louis III of Bavaria (1845–1921), King Frederick Augustus III of Saxony (1865–1932), and William II of Württemberg. Several more abdications occurred between World War I and World War II. King Constantine I of Greece was forced to abdicate twice: by foreign and domestic political pressure in 1917, during World War I, and, after his recall, again in 1922 as a consequence of the Greek defeat in the Turkish War. King Prajadhipok (1893–1941) of Siam (now Thailand) abdicated in 1935 because of bad health. King Edward VIII of Great Britain (later duke of Windsor) abdicated in 1936 because the government opposed his marriage plans.

In 1940, during World War II, Germany forced King Carol II of Romania to abdicate. The Iranian ruler Riza Shah Pahlavi was allegedly an Axis sympathizer, so when Great Britain and the USSR occupied key areas of Iran in 1941 he abdicated in favor of his son. King Victor Emmanuel III of Italy abdicated in 1946 in favor of his son, Humbert II (1904–83). The Italians, however, voted to make Italy a republic, and Humbert was deposed in 1947. King Michael of Romania (1921–   ) abdicated in 1947 under the pressure of Romanian Communists.

Queen Wilhelmina of the Netherlands abdicated in 1948 because of ill health. Left-wing political pressures forced King Leopold III of Belgium to abdicate in 1951. King Faruk I of Egypt had to abdicate in 1952 after a military coup d'état. King Norodom Sihanouk chose to abdicate the throne of Cambodia in 1955 in protest against internal opposition to his pro-Western policies. Queen Juliana of the Netherlands abdicated in 1980 at the age of 71.

**ABDOMEN,** lower of the two cavities into which the diaphragm divides the human body, or the region of the body containing this cavity. It is subdivided into two parts, the abdomen proper and the pelvis, or basin. The abdomen proper contains organs of digestion, such as the liver, pancreas, stomach, small and large intestines, and the spleen and kidneys. The pelvis contains the sigmoid flexure, the rectum, the urinary bladder, and the internal organs of the reproductive system. The term *abdomen* also refers to the posterior section of insects and other arthropods.

**ABDUCTION.** *See* KIDNAPPING.

**ABDUL-JABBAR, Kareem** (1947–   ), American professional basketball player. Originally named Ferdinand Lewis Alcindor, Jr., he was born in New York City. He was educated at the University of California at Los Angeles, where he led the university's basketball team to three National Collegiate Athletic Association championships (1967–69). While a student he converted to the Black Muslim faith and changed his name in 1971. From 1969 to 1975 he played center for the Milwaukee Bucks of the National Basketball Association (NBA) and led his team to the NBA championship in 1970–71. In 1975 the 7-ft, $1\frac{3}{8}$-in. player was traded to the Los Angeles Lakers; he led that team to five NBA championships. When he retired in 1989, he was the all-time NBA leader in points (38,387) and games played (1,560), and he had been named most valuable player six times.

**ABDULLAH IBN HUSEIN** (1882–1951), king of Jordan (1946–51). The son of King Husein ibn Ali (1856–1931) of Hejaz (al-Hijaz), he was born in Mecca but educated in İstanbul, Turkey, where he was active in Arab circles; later he represented Mecca in the Ottoman legislature. During World War I, however, he and his father sided with the Allies and in 1916 led an Arab revolt against the Ottomans. Abdullah became the nominal ruler (emir) of the British mandate of Transjordan in 1921, and when the mandate ended in 1926, he proclaimed himself king.

In May 1948, immediately after the creation of Israel, King Abdullah, pressured by other Arab countries, led his British-trained army against the new state, capturing a large area of its territory. After the armistice in 1949, Jordan—as the kingdom was renamed—retained control of this area, now called the West Bank (q.v); it was officially part of Jordan from 1950 to 1967. Violently opposed by Palestinian Arabs, who suspected him of collusion with Israel, he was assassinated by one of them on July 20, 1951.

**ABDUL RAHMAN, Tunku** (1903–90), first prime minister of the Federation of Malaya (1957–63) and of Malaysia (1963–70). Son of the sultan of Kedah, he was born in Alor Setar and was educated in Malaya, Thailand, and England. As head of the United Malay National Organization, he became chief minister of Malaya after an election victory in 1955, and when Malaya attained sovereignty in 1957, the tunku (prince) became its prime minister. Later, he was the principal architect of the alliance of Malaya with Singapore, Sarawak, and Sabah, which in 1963 resulted in the creation of Malaysia. Abdul Rahman steered the federation through its first difficult years.

**ABÉCHÉ,** town, central Chad. A major trade center, with road traffic E to Sudan and caravans N to Libya, the town trades in livestock, dried fish, hides and skins, gum arabic, dates, salt, and indigo, and it is noted for the weaving of textiles. Abéché is in a sheep-raising and farming area and has a meat-packing plant. It is the site of a college. The town was the capital of an independent sultanate in the 16th century and of the Wadai kingdom in the 19th century; it was a notorious slave-trading center for about 300 years. The name of the town is sometimes spelled Abeshr or Abéchér. Pop. (1992 est.) 89,000.

*Kareem Abdul-Jabbar pushing up his skyhook shot.* **Focus on Sports**

**ABEL,** in the Old Testament Book of Genesis, the second son of Adam and Eve and the brother of Cain. Abel was a shepherd, and his older brother, Cain, cultivated the land. Both made an offering to God: Abel offered the firstborn of his flock, and Cain gave some fruits of his harvest. When Cain's offering was rejected, he became jealous and killed his brother (see Gen. 4:2–16). This story is thought by many theologians to illustrate early nomadic tribal beliefs that filtered down into religious thought. Animal herding, the principal occupation of many nomads, was considered more pleasing to their gods than agriculture; hence, Abel's sacrifice was accepted, but Cain's was not (see Heb. 11:4, 12:24).

**ABEL, Niels Henrik** (1802–29), Norwegian mathematician, who was the first to demonstrate conclusively the impossibility of solving by the elementary processes of algebra general equations of any degree higher than the fourth. Abel was born on Finnøya Island, Rogaland Co. After study at the University of Christiania (now Oslo), he spent two years in Paris and Berlin and in 1828 was made instructor at the university and military school in Christiania. His chief contributions were to the theory of functions, of which he was a founder. An important class of transcendental functions is known as Abelian, after their discoverer, as are Abelian equations, groups, and bodies. The binomial theorem had been formulated by Sir Isaac Newton and the Swiss mathematician Leonhard Euler, but Abel gave it a more comprehensive generalization, including the cases of irrational and imaginary exponents.

**ABELARD, Peter** (1079–1142?), French philosopher and theologian, whose fame as a teacher made him one of the most celebrated figures of the 12th century.

Born in Le Pallet, Brittany, Abelard left home to study at Loches with the French nominalist philosopher Roscelin and later in Paris with the French realist philosopher William of Champeaux (c. 1070–1121). Critical of his masters, Abelard began to teach at Melun, at Corbeil, and in 1108 at Paris. He soon gained fame throughout Europe as a teacher and original thinker. In 1117 he became tutor to Héloïse (c. 1098–1164), the niece of Fulbert (fl. 1070–1120), a canon of Notre-Dame in Paris.

Héloïse and Abelard fell in love, and she gave birth to a son whom they named Astrolabe (fl. 1118–50). At Abelard's insistence they were married secretly, since he had not yet received major orders. Abelard persuaded Héloïse to take holy vows at the Benedictine Abbey of Saint-Argenteuil. Her uncle Fulbert, at first enraged by the relationship between Héloïse and Abelard and later

*Peter Abelard, as portrayed in a 19th-century French etching.* **The Granger Collection**

somewhat placated by their marriage, finally decided that Abelard had abandoned Héloïse at the abbey and had him emasculated. Abelard, too, retired to a religious retreat at the Abbey of Saint-Denis-en-France, in Paris.

Abelard's first published work, a treatise on the Trinity (1121), was condemned and ordered burned by a Roman Catholic council that met at Soissons in the same year. Forced by criticism to leave St.-Denis-en-France, Abelard founded a chapel and oratory, called the Paraclete, at Nogent-sur-Seine. In 1125 he was elected abbot of the monastery at Saint-Gildas-de-Rhuis. Héloïse, who meanwhile had become prioress at Argenteuil, was called to the Paraclete as abbess of the convent established there. At St.-Gildas, Abelard wrote his autobiographical *Historia Calamitatum* (History of Misfortunes, 1132). At this time the famous exchange of letters with Héloïse began; these letters have become classics of romantic correspondence. In 1140 St. Bernard of Clairvaux, an eminent French ecclesiastic who thought Abelard's influence dangerous, prevailed upon a Roman Catholic council in session at Sens, and upon Pope Innocent II (r. 1130–43), to condemn Abelard for his skeptical, rationalistic writings and teaching. On his way to Rome to appeal the condemnation, Abelard accepted the hospitality of Peter the Venerable (1092?–1156), abbot of the

Abbey of Cluny, remaining there for many months. Abelard died at a Clunist priory near Chalon-sur-Saône. His body was taken to the Paraclete; when Héloïse died in 1164 she was buried beside him. In 1817 both bodies were moved to a single tomb in the cemetery of Père Lachaise in Paris.

The romantic appeal of the life of Abelard often overshadows the importance of his thought. In the emphasis he placed on dialectical discussion, Abelard followed the 9th-century philosopher and theologian Johannes Scotus Erigena, and he foreshadowed the Italian Scholastic philosopher Thomas Aquinas. Abelard's important dialectical thesis that truth must be attained by carefully weighing all sides of any issue is presented in *Sic et Non* (Thus and Otherwise, 1123?). He also foreshadowed the later theological reliance on the works of Aristotle, rather than on those of Plato.

Abelard reacted strongly against the theories of extreme realism, denying that universals have an independent existence outside the mind. According to Abelard, a universal is a functional word expressing the combined image of that word's common associations within the mind. This position is not nominalism, because Abelard adds that the associations from which the image is formed and to which a universal name is given have a certain likeness, or common nature. His theory is a definite step toward the moderate realism of Aquinas, but it lacks an explanation of how ideas are formed. In the development of ethics, Abelard's great contribution was to maintain that an act is to be judged by the intention of the doer.

In addition to the writings mentioned, Abelard wrote many works in Latin on ethics, theology, and dialectics, as well as poetry and hymns.

**ABEOKUTA,** town, SW Nigeria, capital of Ogun State. It is connected to Lagos by rail and serves as the shipping center for an area in which cacao, palm kernels, and palm oil are produced. Hand-woven fabrics are dyed in local factories. Abeokuta is inhabited largely by the Yoruba people. Pop. (1990 est.) 367,900.

**ABERDEEN,** city, administrative center of Grampian Region, NE Scotland, on the North Sea at the mouths of the Dee and Don rivers. Aberdeen is the third largest city in Scotland and the principal industrial center of N Scotland. It is also an important seaport and the country's largest fishing port. Aberdeen's harbor facilities were improved in the 1970s, and the city has become the major service center for the North Sea petroleum industry. Manufactures include chemicals, machinery, textiles, and paper. Aberdeen is a tourist resort known for its sandy beaches; it is popularly known as the Granite City because many of its buildings are constructed of local granite, the chief export. Points of interest include the Cathedral of Saint Machar (begun 15th cent.) and the University of Aberdeen, formed in 1860 by the merger of the Roman Catholic King's College (1495) and the Protestant Marischal College (1593). The city also has several museums and colleges of agriculture and technology. Aberdeen was made a royal burgh in 1159. In 1337 the town and its cathedral were burned by Edward III, king of England. The harbor was improved in the late 18th century, and Aberdeen developed as a fishing port. Pop. (1991 prelim.) 201,099.

**ABERDEEN,** city, seat of Brown Co., NE South Dakota; inc. 1883. Situated in a rich grain-producing and livestock-raising area, the city is a trade and transportation center, with stockyards, meat-packing plants, and flour mills. Other manufactures include plastic goods and motor-vehicle parts. Northern State University (1902) and Presentation College (1952) are located here. The city was named by a railroad official for his birthplace, Aberdeen, Scotland. Pop. (1980) 25,956; (1990) 24,927.

**ABERDEEN, George Hamilton-Gordon, 4th Earl of** (1784–1860), British prime minister (1852–55), born in Edinburgh into a distinguished Scottish family. Having joined the foreign service, he represented Great Britain at the negotiations that resulted (1813) in the final European coalition against Napoleon and later served (1828–30) as foreign secretary under the duke of Wellington. Foreign secretary again (1841–46) under Sir Robert Peel, he settled two border disputes (1842, 1846) with the U.S. As prime minister, he succumbed to popular pressure by involving Great Britain in the Crimean War and then had to resign because of parliamentary criticism of the conduct of the war.

**ABERDEEN, UNIVERSITY OF,** institution of higher learning, in Aberdeen, Scotland. The university was incorporated in 1860, merging the College of Saint Mary, founded about 1495 and now called King's College, and Marischal College, established in 1593. Courses of instruction are offered in the arts, divinity, biological sciences, economic and social sciences, engineering and physical sciences, law, mathematics, and medicine. After a 3-year ordinary or a 4-year honors course of study, the university awards either the master of arts or the bachelor of science degree, approximately equivalent to the U.S. bachelor's degree. The university also awards graduate degrees of master (distinct from master of arts) and doctor. Aberdeen was the first institution in Great Britain to train students in medicine, a field in which it has achieved special fame.

**ABERDEENSHIRE,** former county, NE Scotland; Aberdeen was the county town. The county comprised a lowland area along the North Sea coast and, to the W and S, the Cairngorm and Grampian mountains. Numerous relics of prehistoric habitation survive here, as well as later Pictish and Roman remains. Aberdeenshire was a center of Royalist support in the English Revolution (17th cent.) and was prominent in the Jacobite uprising of 1715. Balmoral Castle within the county is the British royal residence in Scotland. In 1975 Aberdeenshire was made part of the newly created Grampian (q.v.) region.

**ABERHART, William** (1878–1943), Canadian statesman, premier of Alberta (1935–43). He was born near Seaforth, Ont., and educated in Kingston. In 1910 he went to Calgary, Alta., where he became a schoolteacher. During the depression he became acquainted with the monetary theories of Clifford H. Douglas (1879–1952), a British social economist. He then founded the Social Credit party, which in 1935 swept him into the premier's office, having won 56 out of 63 seats in the provincial legislature. Although unable to carry out the party's platform in practice, partly because of constitutional limitations, Aberhart remained in office until his death.

**ABERNATHY, Ralph David** (1926–90), American clergyman and civil rights leader, born in Linden, Ala. Abernathy, ordained a Baptist minister in 1948, received a B.S. degree in mathematics from Alabama State College in 1950 and an M.A. degree in sociology from Atlanta University in 1951. Later that year, he became pastor of the First Baptist Church, Montgomery, Ala. Together with the American clergyman and civil rights leader Martin Luther King, Jr., he founded the Montgomery Improvement Association in 1955 and the Southern Christian Leadership Conference (SCLC) in 1957, organizations devoted to achieving equality for blacks in the U.S. In 1961 he became pastor of the West Hunter Street Baptist Church, Atlanta, Ga. Abernathy was King's closest associate during the civil rights campaigns of the late 1950s and early '60s. When King was assassinated in April 1968, Abernathy succeeded him as president of SCLC. As such, he led a march in support of a strike by Memphis, Tenn., sanitation workers on April 8, 1969, and led the Poor People's Campaign march and encampment in Washington, D.C., in May 1969. He remained president of SCLC until 1977. His autobiography, *And the Walls Came Tumbling Down,* appeared in 1989.
**ABERRATION.** *See* OPTICS.

**ABERRATION OF LIGHT,** in astronomy, the angular discrepancy between the apparent position of a star and its true position, arising from the motion of an observer relative to the path of the beam of light observed. This motion is the resultant of such velocities as the speed of the diurnal rotation of the earth, its orbital speed in revolving around the sun, and the motion of the solar system through space. Although the resultant velocity of the observer is small (only about 0.2 percent of the velocity of light), it is enough to cause an apparent displacement of the rays of light from a celestial object, just as a drop of rain, falling vertically, leaves a diagonal trace on the window of a moving car. This displacement reaches a maximum of 20.47 sec of an arc, called the constant of aberration. The discovery of the aberration of light, by the British astronomer James Bradley (pub. in 1729), was one of the most important discoveries in physical science—initiating a series of investigations that led to the formulation of the theory of relativity (q.v.).

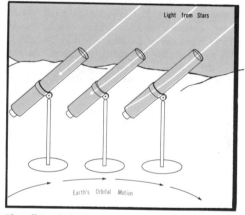

The effect of aberration of light on telescopic observation. A telescope receiving light from stars is moved by the earth's motion, causing a discrepancy between the actual and observed locations of the stars.

**ABERYSTWYTH,** town, Ceredigion District, Dyfed, central Wales, at the mouth of the Ystwyth and Rheidol rivers, on Cardigan Bay. A seaside resort and educational center, Aberystwyth is the seat of the University College of Wales (1872), the oldest college of the University of Wales (1893). Also here are the National Library of Wales (chartered 1907) and the remains of a 13th-century castle. Aberystwyth grew around a Norman castle founded in 1277. Pop. (1981 prelim.) 8666; (Ceredigion District, 1991 prelim.) 63,600.
**ABIATHAR,** in the Old Testament, the son of Ahimelech, a priest. He fled during a slaughter of priests in Nob under King Saul and became a

religious consultant to David, then an outlaw in Judea (see 1 Sam. 22:9–23). Later, as a priest, Abiathar supported King David during the rebellion of David's son Absalom (see 2 Sam. 15:29–37). Subsequently, Abiathar joined the unsuccessful rebellion of Adonijah, another son of David, against King Solomon. After the revolt was crushed, Solomon stripped Abiathar of priestly office and banished him from Jerusalem (see 1 Kings 1:5–7, 2:26–27).

**ABIDJAN,** city, SE Côte d'Ivoire, de facto capital, chief seaport, and largest city of the country. It is built on several converging peninsulas and islands, connected by bridges, in Ebrié Lagoon. Its modern port was opened in 1950, when the Vridi Canal was cut through a sandbar, linking the sheltered and relatively deep lagoon with the Gulf of Guinea and the Atlantic Ocean. Exports include coffee, cacao, timber, bananas, pineapples, and palm and fish products. Manufacturing, which has greatly expanded since the 1960s, includes vehicle and radio assembly and the production of textiles, metal products, clothing, foodstuffs, plastic, rubber, and petroleum products; tourism is of increasing importance. The city is the hub of the national road system and the terminus of the Abidjan-Niger Railway, which extends N into Burkina Faso.

Abidjan is an attractive, largely modern city, with parks and broad boulevards. Districts include Cocody, an elegant residential area to the E of the modern business district, and to the S, on Petit-Bassam Island, Treichville, with its large traditional market. Abidjan is the seat of the National University (1958) and several technical colleges and libraries; the national museum here contains collections of Ivorian art. Banco National Park, a forested area, lies N of the city. Abidjan was a small village in 1904, when it became the terminus of a railroad to the interior; it had no port facilities, however, and growth was slow. In 1934 the city succeeded Bingerville as the capital of the then French colony of Côte d'Ivoire, a position it retained after the colony gained independence in 1960. Although Yamoussoukro was named the administrative capital in 1983, Abidjan remains the center of the nation's cultural and commercial life. Pop. (1990 est.) 2,168,000.

**ABIGAIL,** in the Old Testament, wife of Nabal. After Nabal refused food supplies to David (the future king of Israel and Judah) while the latter was an outlaw in the Judean wilderness, Abigail intervened and persuaded David not to punish her husband. Her behavior so charmed David that soon after the death of Nabal, he married Abigail.

**ABILENE,** city, seat of Dickinson Co., E central Kansas, on the Smoky Hill R.; inc. 1869. Situated in a grain-farming and livestock-raising region, it is a trade and distribution center with some light industry. Among the points of interest here are the Eisenhower Center, which includes the boyhood home of President Dwight D. Eisenhower; Old Abilene Town, a re-creation of the area as it was in the 19th century; and the Greyhound Hall of Fame, which includes a museum of greyhound racing. Settled in the late 1850s, Abilene prospered in the late 1860s and early '70s as the N terminus of the Chisholm Trail, a major cattle-driving route. The city's name, taken from the Bible, means either "beautiful homeland" or "city of the plains." Pop. (1980) 6572; (1990) 6242.

**ABILENE,** city, seat of Taylor Co. and also in Jones Co., central Texas; inc. 1882. It is the commercial, financial, and industrial heart of a vast region of cattle ranches, grain farms, and oil wells. Manufactures include refined petroleum, aerospace structures, musical instruments, and processed food. Hardin-Simmons University (1891), Abilene Christian University (1906), and McMurry College (1923) are here. Dyess Air Force Base and the remains of Fort Phantom Hill, a

*Statue of President Dwight D. Eisenhower in his World War II uniform, with the famous Ike jacket, located in the Eisenhower Center, Abilene, Kansas.* **Photography House**

U.S. Army post of the late 19th century, are near-by. The city, founded with the coming of the railroad in 1881, is named for Abilene, Kans. Pop. (1980) 98,315; (1990) 106,654.

**ABIOGENESIS.** *See* SPONTANEOUS GENERATION.

**ABITIBI, LAKE,** shallow lake, E Canada, strad-dling the Ontario-Québec border. The remnant of an ancient glacial lake, it is 97 km (60 mi) long and has an area of 932 sq km (360 sq mi). Nearby coniferous forests are cut for pulpwood. From the lake, the Abitibi R. flows N to the Moose R. near James Bay.

**ABNAKI,** confederacy of North American Indian tribes, of the Algonquian-Ritwan language fami-ly, and of the Eastern Woodlands culture area. The most important Abnaki tribes were the Malecite, Norridgewock, Passamaquoddy, and Penobscot. The original habitat of these tribes included Maine and sections of New Brunswick and Québec. An early ally of the French, the confederacy was drawn into their struggle against the British. The confederacy was destroyed (1724–25), when the British severely defeated the Indians. Remnants of the Penobscot and Passamaquoddy tribes live on reservations in Maine. Most of the other sur-vivors live in Saint Francis, Québec, and are called Abnaki. *See* ALGONQUIAN; PASSAMAQUODDY; PENOBSCOT INDIANS.

**ABNER,** in the Old Testament, influential cousin of King Saul of Israel and captain of Saul's army (see 1 Sam. 14:50, 52) during the long struggle with the Philistines. After Saul's death Abner saved the crown for Saul's son Ish-bosheth. Later, resenting a charge made against him by Ish-bo-sheth, Abner went over to the side of David, king of Judah and Israel, who was Ish-bosheth's rival. Abner was murdered, however, by the Hebrew sol-dier Joab in revenge for Abner's earlier murder of Joab's brother Asahel (see 2 Sam. 2–3, 8).

**ABNORMAL PSYCHOLOGY.** *See* MENTAL DIS-ORDERS; PSYCHOANALYSIS; PSYCHOTHERAPY.

**ÅBO.** *See* TURKU.

**ABOLITIONISTS,** reformers of the 18th and 19th centuries dedicated to eliminating slavery, espe-cially in the English-speaking countries. Al-though the Quakers had long opposed slavery,

An antislavery convention in London in 1849 (from a 19th-cent. steel engraving). In the preceding year the first antislavery party in the U.S., the Liberty party, was founded.
The Granger Collection

John Brown's "fort" in the U.S. Arsenal at Harpers Ferry, Va., where his forces were surrounded by local militia and U.S. Marines in 1859.        Library of Congress

abolitionism as an organized force began in England in the 1780s, when William Wilberforce and the Clapham Sect—a group of wealthy evangelical Anglicans—began agitating against the African slave traffic. Their success (1807) stimulated further political assaults on slavery itself. With compensation to owners and apprenticeship arrangements, Parliament abolished West Indian slavery in 1833.

**Beginning of U.S. Abolitionism.** British example, Quaker traditions, evangelical revivalism, and northern emancipations (1776-1827) aroused interest in abolitionism in the U.S. The abolitionists differed from those of moderate antislavery feelings in that they called for an immediate end to slavery. The most extreme abolitionists denied the validity of any laws that recognized slavery as an institution; thus, they systematically violated the fugitive slave laws by organizing and operating the Underground Railroad (q.v.), which concealed and transported runaway slaves to Canada. The activities and propaganda of the abolitionists, although discredited in conservative northern quarters and violently opposed in the South, made slavery a national issue.

Most historians cite 1831 as the beginning of the U.S. abolitionist movement, when William Lloyd Garrison founded the *Liberator* in Boston. This newspaper soon became the leading organ of American abolitionism.. In 1833 the American Anti-Slavery Society (q.v.) was organized in Philadelphia under Garrison's leadership; this so-

ciety was the most militant of all the antislavery organizations. Viewed as fanatics by the general public, the abolitionists were relatively few in number—only about 160,000 in the period 1833-40. Most were educated church people of middle-class New England or Quaker heritage. Support among the working and upper classes was minimal.

**Split over Policy.** In 1839 the society split into two main groups, the radicals and the gradualists. The division was caused by disagreement concerning policy and tactics. The radical leaders, who besides Garrison included Wendell Phillips, Lucretia Mott, and John Brown, refused to join a party necessarily committed to gradual and legal emancipation of the slaves; these leaders retained control of the *Liberator* and the American Anti-Slavery Society. The gradualists, who included James Birney, Arthur Tappan (1786-1865) and his brother Lewis Tappan (1788-1873), and Theodore Weld (1803-95), believed that emancipation could be achieved legally by means of religious and political pressure.

In 1840 the Tappans founded the American and Foreign Anti-Slavery Society, which, along with numerous state organizations, carried on most of the U.S. antislavery agitation. One year earlier, a group led by Birney had founded the first antislavery political party, the Liberty party, in the U.S. Birney was the unsuccessful presidential candidate (1840 and 1844) of the party, the adherents of which later helped found the Free-Soil party (1848) and the Republican party (1854).

By the 1850s advocacy of violence against slave owners had replaced the earlier "moral suasion." This was especially true during the bitter contro-

*The radical abolitionist John Brown was hanged for attempting to free the slaves by force.*        Library of Congress

versy over extending slavery into Kansas. Only with the Union victory in the American Civil War could they claim a triumph. Blood and iron, not idealism, won the day. Most antislavery groups were dissolved after the adoption in 1870 of the 15th Amendment to the U.S. Constitution.

*See also* KANSAS-NEBRASKA ACT; MISSOURI COMPROMISE.

*For further information on this topic, see the Bibliography in volume 28, sections 209–10.*

**ABORIGINES,** earliest known inhabitants of a country. The term is generally applied to the original or native inhabitants of a country, as opposed to an intrusive conquering race from another area or colonists and their descendants. Most nations have instituted measures for the welfare of the aborigines within their territories. Such measures include those of the U.S. and Canada concerning Indians and Inuits and those of Australia concerning its aboriginal groups.

All aboriginal peoples have been affected by contact with contemporary civilization; in some cases, the introduction of disease, warfare, alcohol, and drugs has demoralized and decimated peoples. Others, such as the Ainu of northern Japan, have become almost wholly assimilated. The greatest degree of racial mixture has occurred among the native Polynesians of Hawaii. The Indian population of the U.S. has extensively intermarried with whites; those Indians living on reservations retain some traditional Indian folkways. In Central and South America and in the Caribbean region, many tribes have become ex-

*An aborigine from Elcho Island, northern Australia, displays a painting on bark. In addition to bark painting, traditional Australian aborigine art has included cave and rock painting.* HORIZON/Douglass Baqlin

tinct, in most cases after Spanish or Portuguese conquest. Among aborigines who have kept strong elements of their original identity are the Inuit, Maori, Dayak, and Australian aborigines. Tribes in such comparatively inaccessible areas as the Amazon River Basin of South America still live largely according to their traditional cultures.

**ABORTION,** termination of pregnancy before the fetus is capable of independent life. When the expulsion from the womb occurs after the fetus becomes viable (capable of independent life), usually at the end of six months of pregnancy, it is technically a premature birth.

**Types of Abortions.** Abortion may be spontaneous or induced. Expelled fetuses weighing less than 0.45 kg (16 oz) or of less than 20 weeks' gestation are usually considered abortions.

***Spontaneous.*** It is estimated that some 25 percent of all human pregnancies terminate spontaneously in abortion, with three out of four abortions occurring during the first three months of pregnancy. Some women apparently have a tendency to abort, and recurrent abortion decreases the probability of subsequent successful childbirth.

The causes of spontaneous abortions, or miscarriages, are not clearly established. Abnormal development of the embryo or placental tissue, or both, is found in about half the cases; these abnormalities may be due to inherent faults in the germ cells or may be secondary to faulty implantation of the developing ovum or to other characteristics of the maternal environment. Severe vitamin deficiencies have been shown to play a role in abortions in experimental animals. Hormone deficiencies also have been found in women who are subject to recurrent abortions. Spontaneous abortions may be caused also by such maternal abnormalities as acute infectious diseases, systemic diseases such as nephritis and diabetes, severe trauma, and excessive physical activity. Uterine malformations, including tumors, are responsible in some instances, and extreme anxiety and other psychic disturbances may contribute to the premature expulsion of the fetus. *See also* BIRTH DEFECTS.

The most common symptom of threatened abortion is vaginal bleeding, with or without intermittent pain. About one-fourth of all pregnant women bleed at some time during early pregnancy, however, and up to 75 percent of these women carry the fetus for the full term. Treatment for threatened abortion usually consists of bed rest. Almost continuous bed rest throughout pregnancy is required in some cases of repeated abortion; vitamin and hormone therapy also may be given. Surgical correction of uterine abnormalities may be indicated in certain of these cases.

Spontaneous abortion may result in expulsion of all or part of the contents of the uterus, or the embryo may die and be retained in the uterus for weeks or months in a so-called missed abortion. Most physicians advocate the surgical removal of any residual embryonic or placental tissue in order to avoid possible irritation or infection of the uterine lining.

**Induced.** Induced abortion is the deliberate termination of pregnancy by removal of the fetus from the womb. It is currently performed by any of four standard procedures, according to the period of gestation. Suction, or vacuum aspiration, is used in the first trimester (up to 12 weeks). In this procedure, which normally takes 5 to 10 minutes on an outpatient basis, the cervix (neck of the uterus) is opened gradually with a series of dilators and the uterine contents are withdrawn by means of a small flexible tube called a cannula, which is connected to a vacuum pump. To ensure that no fragments of tissue remain, a spoon-tipped metal instrument called a curette may then be used to scrape the uterine lining. Introduced in China in 1958, vacuum aspiration soon replaced the traditional early-abortion procedure, dilation and curettage (D&C), in which the curette is used to dislodge the fetus. Pregnancies in the earlier part of the second trimester may be terminated by a special suction curettage, sometimes combined with forceps, in a procedure called dilation and evacuation (D&E). After the 15th week of gestation, saline infusion is commonly used. In this technique, a small amount of amniotic fluid is withdrawn from the uterus by means of a fine tube or hypodermic needle through the abdominal wall and is slowly replaced with a strong (about 20 percent) salt solution. This induces uterine contractions in about 24 to 48 hours. The fetus is then usually quickly expelled and the patient leaves the hospital about a day later. Late abortions are accomplished by hysterotomy; this is a major surgical procedure, similar to a cesarean section (q.v.) but requiring a much smaller incision lower in the abdomen. When performed under proper clinical conditions, first-trimester abortions are relatively simple and safe. The risk of complications increases with length of gestation and includes infection, cervical injury, perforation of the uterine lining, and hemorrhage. Recent data, however, show that even late abortions place the mother at less risk than full term delivery.

An alternative to these procedures is use of RU-486, mifepristone, the so-called abortion pill. RU-486 was developed and approved for sale in France in 1988. In 1994 clinical trials began in the U.S. on women no more than 9 weeks pregnant. Use of the pill involves three steps. First a patient is given three mifepristone pills, which block the hormone progesterone needed to sustain pregnancy. Two days later two misoprostl pills are administered to cause contractions. It is in this stage, which can take from a few hours to a few days, that the patient aborts. Two weeks later a follow up visit is required. In 4 to 5 percent of patients the pill does not work and a surgical abortion is then performed.

**Regulation of Abortion.** The practice of abortion was widespread in ancient times as a method of birth control. Later it was restricted or forbidden by most world religions, but it was not considered an offense in secular law until the 19th century. During that century, first the English Parliament and then American state legislatures prohibited induced abortion to protect women from surgical procedures that were at the time unsafe, commonly stipulating a threat to the woman's life as the sole ("therapeutic") exception to the prohibition. Occasionally the exception was enlarged to include danger to the mother's health as well.

Legislative action in the 20th century has been aimed at permitting the termination of unwanted pregnancies for medical, social, or private reasons. Abortions at the woman's request were first allowed by the Soviet Union in 1920, followed by Japan and several East European nations after World War II. In the late 1960s liberalized abortion regulations became widespread. The impetus for the change was threefold: (1) infanticide and the high maternal death rate associated with illegal abortions, (2) a rapidly expanding world population, (3) the growing feminist movement. By 1980, countries where abortions were permitted only to save a woman's life contained about 20 percent of the world's population. Countries with moderately restrictive laws—abortions permitted to protect a woman's health, to end pregnancies resulting from rape or incest, to avoid genetic or congenital defects, or in response to social problems such as unmarried status or inadequate income—contained some 40 percent of the world's population. Abortions at the woman's request, usually with limits based on physical conditions such as duration of pregnancy, were allowed in countries with nearly 40 percent of the world's population.

**U.S. Legislation.** In the U.S., legislation followed the world trend. Fourteen states adopted the moderately restrictive type of abortion law between 1967 and 1972. Alaska, Hawaii, New York, and Washington legislated abortion on request with few restrictions. In 1973, the U.S. Supreme Court in the case of *Roe v. Wade* declared unconstitutional all but the least restrictive state statutes. Noting that induced early abortions had become safer than childbirth and holding that the word *person* in the U.S. Constitution "does not include the unborn," the Court defined, within each of the stages of pregnancy, the reciprocal limits of state power and individual freedom:

"(a) During the first trimester, the abortion decision and its effectuation must be left to the medical judgment of the pregnant woman's attending physician. (b) After the first trimester, the State, in promoting its interest in the health of the mother, may, if it chooses, regulate the abortion procedure in ways that are reasonably related to maternal health. (c) For the stage subsequent to viability, the State, in promoting its interest in the potentiality of human life may, if it chooses, regulate and even proscribe abortion, except where it is necessary, in appropriate medical judgment, for the preservation of the life or health of the mother."

***Resistance and controversy.*** Opponents of the 1973 Supreme Court ruling, arguing that a fetus is entitled as a "person" to constitutional protection, attacked the decision on a variety of fronts. State legislative bodies were lobbied for statutes narrowing the implications of the decision and circumscribing in several ways the mother's ability to obtain an abortion. A nationwide campaign was instituted to amend the Constitution to prohibit or severely restrict abortion. Right-to-life groups also engaged in grass-roots political activity designed to defeat abortion proponents and elect abortion opponents. Abortion became, rather than simply a legal and constitutional issue, a major political and social controversy. Many state legislatures passed laws imposing additional procedural restrictions on women who sought abortions; at first federal court decisions held these new statutes to be unconstitutional.

***Recent developments.*** The Reagan administration (1981–89) and the Bush administration (1989–93) supported the right-to-life position, as did many of their appointees to the federal judiciary. The U.S. Supreme Court, though sharply divided, generally declared unconstitutional those laws it found to place an undue burden on a woman's right to obtain an abortion. For example, in 1983 the Court reviewed three laws—from Akron, Ohio; Missouri; and Virginia—and struck down provisions requiring (1) a 24-hour waiting period; (2) that a doctor obtain a woman's "informed consent"; and (3) hospitalization for abortions after the first trimester of pregnancy. At the same time the Court upheld a Missouri provision that required a minor to obtain parental consent before an abortion but struck down an Akron or-

dinance with the same objective because a majority of the justices found the Akron law unduly restrictive. In a 1989 decision the Court let stand a Missouri requirement that before performing an abortion on any woman thought to be at least 20 weeks pregnant, a doctor must test whether the fetus could survive outside the womb. In a wide-ranging decision in 1992 on a Pennsylvania law, the Court reiterated its general support for a woman's right to an abortion but upheld most provisions of the statute, including requirements for "informed consent," a mandatory waiting period, and for the consent of at least one parent or a judge for anyone age 16 or under. In 1991 the Court had upheld a Reagan administration executive order banning abortion counseling at federally funded clinics. Fulfilling a campaign promise, President Bill Clinton reversed this ban in January 1993.

During the 1970s and '80s legislative action was often effective in cutting off public funds for abortions. In 1977 the Supreme Court ruled that neither the Social Security Act nor the Constitution prevented a state from restricting the use of Medicaid funds for "medically necessary" abortions. In a companion case the Court held that a city may refuse to allow elective abortions to be performed in a municipal hospital. Subsequently, a congressional limitation of Medicaid eligibility for elective abortions (the Hyde Amendment) was upheld. In 1994, despite protests from right-to-life groups, Congress passed a bill making it a federal crime for anyone to use force or "physical obstruction" to deny women their right to an abortion.                    C.T., C.C.M., & R.J.L.

*For further information on this topic, see the Bibliography in volume 28, sections 523–24.*

**ABRABANEL, Isaac** (1437–1508), Jewish statesman, philosopher, and theologian, born in Lisbon. He was a favorite of Alfonso V, king of Portugal, who made him his treasurer. Accused of conspiracy, he fled (1483) to Castile. He served (1484–92) as a minister under King Ferdinand V and Queen Isabella I. When the Jews were banished from Spain in 1492, he moved on to Naples and Venice (1503), where he was employed in diplomatic service. His theological writings include *Sources of Salvation* (1496) and *Salvation of His Anointed* (1497). The name is also spelled Abravanel.

**ABRABANEL, Judah León,** also called Leo Hebreus (c. 1460–c. 1523), Jewish physician and philosopher, son of Isaac Abrabanel, born in Lisbon. He followed his father to Spain in 1483, and when the Jews were expelled from there in 1492, he settled in Naples, where he was physician to the viceroy Hernández Gonzalo de Córdoba. Abrabanel is best known for his influential *Philosophy*

*Abraham, as painted by Lorenzo Monaco (c. 1375–1425).*
Bettmann Archive

*of Love* (1535; trans. 1937), which extols love as the motive force of the universe.

**ABRAHAM** *or* **ABRAM,** biblical patriarch, according to the Book of Genesis (see 11:27–25:10), progenitor of the Hebrews; regarded by Muslims, who call him Ibrahim, as an ancestor of the Arabs through Ishmael. Once considered a contemporary of Hammurabi, king of Babylonia, Abraham probably lived in the period between 2000 and 1500 BC. Because the biblical account of his life is based on traditions preserved by oral transmission rather than by historical records, no biography in the present sense can be written.

Originally called Abram, Abraham was the son of Terah, a descendant of Shem, and was born in the city of Ur of the Chaldees, where he married his half sister Sarai, or Sarah. They left Ur with his nephew Lot and Lot's family under a divine inspiration and went to Haran. Receiving a promise that God would make him a "great nation," Abram moved on to Canaan, where he lived as a nomad. Famine led him to Egypt, but he was driven out for misrepresenting Sarai as his sister. Again in Canaan, after quarrels between Abram and Lot and their herdsmen, they separated, Lot remaining near Sodom and Abram continuing his nomadic life. He later rescued Lot from the captivity of King Chedorlaomer of Elam and was blessed by the priest Melchizedek, king of Salem. Then God promised Abram a son by his wife Sarai, repeated his earlier promises, and confirmed these by a covenant.

When this covenant was later renewed, the rite of circumcision was established, Abram's name became Abraham, and Sarai's became Sarah. God subsequently repeated his promise of a male son by Sarah by means of visiting angels.

When God informed Abraham that he intended to destroy Sodom and Gomorrah because of the wickedness of their inhabitants, Abraham pleaded with him. Eventually it was agreed that God would spare the cities if he could find only ten righteous men. The ten men could not be found, and God destroyed both cities.

Ishmael, first son of Abraham, whose mother was Hagar, an Egyptian slave, was born when Abraham was 86 years old. Isaac, born to Abraham by Sarah in his 100th year, was the first of his legitimate descendants. God demanded that Abraham sacrifice Isaac as a test of faith, but because of Abraham's unquestioning compliance, God permitted him to spare Isaac and rewarded Abraham with a formal renewal of his promise. After Sarah died, Abraham married Keturah and had six sons by her. He died at the biblical age of 175 and was buried beside Sarah in the Cave of Machpelah, in what is now Hebron, West Bank.

Christians, Muslims, and Jews accept Abraham as an epitome of the man of unswerving faith, a view reflected in the New Testament.

**ABRAHAM, PLAINS OF.** *See* PLAINS OF ABRAHAM.

**ABRAHAM IBN DAUD** *or* **ABRAHAM BEN DAVID** (1110?–80?), historian and philosopher, born in Toledo, Spain. He was one of the first Jewish philosophers to introduce the Aristotelian system of knowledge to Judaism. His philosophical work, written in Arabic, *Al-akidah al-Rafiyah* and preserved in a Hebrew translation as *Emanah Ramah* (The Sublime Faith, 1168), influenced the philosopher Maimonides. Ibn Daud's historical work, *Sefer ha-Kabbalah* (Book of Tradition, 1161), includes a history of the Jews in Spain.

**ABRAHAMS, Peter** (1919– ), South African–born novelist and journalist. His first novel, *Mine Boy* (1946), describes the effects of the South African apartheid policy. Although Abrahams left for England in 1939 and in 1955 moved to Jamaica, Africa continued to dominate his work, including the short-story collection *Dark Testament* (1942), and *Wild Conquest* (1950), about the Boers' trek. His autobiography, *Tell Freedom: Memories of Africa* (1954), recreates his childhood in the Johannesburg slums. *A Wreath for Udomo* (1955), one of his most effective novels, tells of the murder of a native leader. His first work with a Caribbean setting, *This Island, Now* (1966; rev. 1971), views the future of the Third World pessimistically. *The View from Coyaba* (1985) is the story of four generations of a Jamaican family and the struggle for black autonomy.

**ABRAM.** *See* ABRAHAM.

**ABRASIVE,** substance employed in grinding or polishing an object by scraping or abrading its surface. Abrasives are usually very hard substances. Some are used in the form of fine powders; others break in such a way as to form sharp cutting edges and are used in larger pieces. Objects are ground to shape with a coarse abrasive, causing comparatively wide scratches on the surface of the object. Polishing is done with a fine abrasive, to produce narrow scratches. In each case the object must be softer than the abrasive. Rouge and similar agents are sometimes called abrasives, although they may be softer than the material that they are used to polish.

Most natural abrasives are minerals: corundum, diamond, emery, garnet, pumice, quartz, and sand; various types of diatomaceous earth have also been used. Among the older synthetic abrasives are rouge, crushed steel, and powdered glass. Since 1891 several synthetic abrasives (carbides, borides, nitrides) have been available. These synthetic abrasives are almost as hard as diamonds. In fact, carbon-coated synthetic abrasives can now be produced with a surface coating identical in hardness to that of synthetic diamonds. Among these are synthetic corundum, tungsten carbide, boron carbide, and silicon carbide, widely known as Carborundum.

**ABRUZZI,** region, S central Italy, on the Adriatic Sea, comprising four provinces named after their chief towns—L'Aquila, Chieti, Pescara, and Teramo. Topographically, the region includes two distinct areas. The W portion, almost contiguous with the province of L'Aquila, consists of three ranges of the Apennines, including their valleys and basins. Extending in a NW-SE direction, the highest range culminates at 2941 m (9650 ft) above sea level in Monte Corno, a peak of the Gran Sasso d'Italia section. In the E, sand and clay hills slope gradually downward to a broad coastal plain on the Adriatic Sea encompassing the provinces of Chieti, Pescara, and Teramo. The coastline lacks good natural harbors. The Pescara R., an important source of hydroelectric power, and the Sangro, Trigno, and Biferno rivers irrigate the lower valleys; all drain into the Adriatic Sea. Sheep and cattle grazing and the cultivation of potatoes and wheat in the highlands, of corn, olives, grapes, and citrus fruits in the coastal valleys, and of sugar beets in the drained basin of Lake Fucino are the primary economic activities of the region. Bauxite deposits are found in L'Aquila Province.

In the 4th century BC the inhabitants of the region were conquered by the Romans. From the 6th to the 11th century AD the area was under the control of the Lombards, and in the 12th and 13th centuries it was part of the Norman kingdom of Sicily. Governed as part of the kingdom of Naples from about 1240 to 1861, it was then incorporated into the unified kingdom of Italy. The region of Abruzzi e Molise became the two separate regions of Abruzzi and Molise in 1963. Area, 10,794 sq km (4168 sq mi); pop. (1991) 1,249,054.

**ABRUZZI, Luigi Amedeo, Duca d'** (1873–1933), Italian naval officer, mountaineer, and explorer,

*The death of Absalom, as represented in an American textile.*     Bettmann Archive

born in Madrid. He made the first ascent of Mount Saint Elias, Alaska, in 1897 and two years later led an expedition toward the North Pole. This expedition was the first to reach lat 86°34' N. He was the first to climb (1906) the peaks of the Ruwenzori in Africa and set a world record in ascending Mount Godwin Austen, or K2, in Kashmir, to a height of about 7500 m (about 24,600 ft). On Sept. 30, 1911, he commanded the squadron that attacked Préveza, Greece, in the first action of the Italian-Turkish War. Abruzzi commanded the Adriatic fleet of the Italian navy in World War I.

**ABSALOM,** in the Old Testament, third son of David, king of Israel and Judah. According to the Bible (see 2 Sam. 13–19), Absalom killed his brother Amnon for the rape of Tamar, their sister. Later he rebelled against David and after driving the king out of Jerusalem was defeated in battle in the forest of Ephraim. He was caught by his hair in an oak tree and killed by Joab, David's general. David lamented his son with the words: "O my son Absalom, my son, my son Absalom! Would I had died instead of you, O Absalom, my son, my son!" (2 Sam. 18:33).

**ABSALON** (c. 1128–1201), Danish soldier, statesman, and ecclesiastic, born near Ringsted, and educated in Paris. Having aided Waldemar I (1131–82) in gaining the Danish throne, he became bishop of Roskilde in 1158 and simultaneously acted as adviser to the king and his successor, Canute IV (1163–1202). A notable general, he led a long campaign against Wendish pirates in the Baltic, during which he fortified the village that later became Copenhagen; Absalon is often called the founder of the city. He captured and annexed the Wendish stronghold of Rügen in 1169 and finally rid Denmark of the Wendish nuisance with a naval victory over the duke of Pomerania in 1184.

Absalon was archbishop of Lund from 1177 to his death. A patron of culture and learning, he may have influenced his secretary, Saxo Grammaticus, to write his *Gesta Danorum* (c. 1200), a history of the Danes.

**ABSCESS,** collection of pus, a thick, yellowish fluid caused by bacterial, protozoan, or fungal invasion of body tissues. Abscesses can occur in the skin, the gums, in bone, and in body organs, such as the liver, lungs, and even the brain. The area of abscess becomes red and swollen; sensations of pain and localized heat are common. If the inflamed tissue encompassing the infected cavity thins out sufficiently, the abscess may rupture. Treatment may involve surgical incision or use of antibiotics or both.

**ABSENTEE BALLOT.** *See* ELECTION.

**ABSOLUTE,** term used to denote whatever is in no way dependent on or limited by anything else. Thus, in ethics an absolute value is one that is good in itself rather than useful for obtaining something else, and an absolute principle is one that permits of no exceptions. In political theory an absolute right is a right that society cannot take away from an individual.

In theology and metaphysics the term Absolute usually refers to God. According to the Dutch philosopher Baruch Spinoza, God is absolute; that is, unlimited, because by his very concept nothing can limit God. All other existing things exist through this absolute substance. The German philosopher Immanuel Kant defined the Absolute as an all-encompassing totality and argued that scientific knowledge of such a being is impossible. This position was adopted also by the British philosophers Herbert Spencer and Sir William Hamilton (1788–1856). The Absolute figures also as the central concept in the philosophies of the 19th-century German idealists. In particular, the German philosopher G. W. F. Hegel regarded the Absolute as a spiritual process that realizes itself through rationality alone, because only through the use of logic can reality be recognized. He maintained, as did the British idealist philosophers Bernard Bosanquet, Francis Herbert Bradley, and Thomas Hill Green, that all knowledge is indirectly and incompletely knowledge of the Absolute. The American idealist philosopher Josiah Royce identified the Absolute with a so-called cosmic community; his system of philosophy came to be known as absolute idealism. R.A.

**ABSOLUTE TEMPERATURE.** *See* HEAT.

**ABSOLUTE ZERO,** lowest temperature theoretically possible, characterized by complete absence of heat, at approximately −273.16° C (−459.69° F), or zero degree on the Kelvin scale (0 K). *See* HEAT; TEMPERATURE.

The concept of absolute zero temperature was first deduced from experiments with gases; when a fixed volume of gas is cooled, its pressure decreases with its temperature. Although this experiment cannot be conducted below the liquefaction point of the gas, a plot of the experimental values of pressure versus temperature can be extrapolated to zero pressure. The temperature at which the pressure would be zero is the absolute zero temperature. This experimental concept of a gas-thermometer temperature scale and of absolute zero was subsequently shown to be consistent with the theoretical definitions of absolute zero.

Absolute zero cannot be reached experimentally, although it can be closely approached. Special procedures are needed to reach very low, or cryogenic, temperatures (*see* CRYOGENICS). Liquid helium (q.v.), which has a normal boiling point of 4.2 K ($-268.9°$ C/$-452.0°$ F), can be produced by cryostats, extremely well-insulated vessels, based on a design by the American mechanical engineer Samuel Collins (1898–1984). If the helium is then evaporated at reduced pressures, temperatures as low as 0.7 K can be obtained. Lower temperatures require the adiabatic (no heat transfer) demagnetization of paramagnetic substances (substances of low magnetizability), such as chrome alum, while they are being surrounded with a liquid helium bath (*see* THERMODYNAMICS). The method, which was first developed in 1937 by the Canadian-American chemist William Giauque, utilizes a magnetic field that initially aligns the ionic magnets of the material. If the magnetic field is removed, the magnets again assume their random orientation, reducing the thermal energy of the material and thus its temperature. Temperatures as low as 0.002 K have been reached with the demagnetization of paramagnetic salts, and the demagnetization of atomic nuclei has yielded temperatures as low as 0.00001 K.

Temperature measurements at values close to absolute zero also present special problems. Gas thermometers can only be used up to the liquefaction point of helium. At lower temperatures, electric and magnetic measurements must be used to determine the effective temperature.

The concept of absolute zero temperature is also important in theoretical considerations. According to the third law of thermodynamics, the entropy, or state of disorder, of a pure crystal is zero at absolute zero temperature; this is of considerable importance in analyzing chemical reactions and in quantum physics.

*See also* CHEMICAL REACTION; QUANTUM THEORY; SUPERCONDUCTIVITY; SUPERFLUIDITY.     F.La.

**ABSOLUTION,** term in Christian theology, most often used to refer to sacramental absolution, the judicial act in the sacrament of penance, by which the priest, as the minister of God, grants to confessing penitents forgiveness of their sins. In the Roman Catholic and Orthodox churches, the practice is based on John 20:22–23. To be effective, absolution supposes a true contrition for sin and a firm purpose of amendment on the part of the penitent. Absolution is also a part of the Anglican ritual, but penance is not considered one of the sacraments instituted by Christ. Most Protestant denominations do not regard penance as a sacrament and therefore do not acknowledge the necessity for sacramental absolution. They recognize a broader interpretation of absolution,

that is, the remission of the sins of a repentant sinner. They believe this remission is achieved, not by the mediating judicial act of a minister or priest, but only through the direct acknowledgment of transgressions by the penitent to God and humble entreaty for his forgiveness. Although the term *absolution* is confined to Christian theology, the practice of penitently beseeching a deity's forgiveness for individual offenses is common to almost all religions.

In the Roman Catholic church, absolution can also mean release from ecclesiastical censure (penalty imposed on one who commits any of certain extremely serious sins specifically condemned as crimes in canon law) or the rite immediately following a funeral mass in which the mercy of God is implored for the soul of the dead.

**ABSOLUTISM,** political system in which total power is vested in a single individual or a group of rulers. Today the term is usually associated with the government of a dictator. It is considered the opposite of constitutional government such as that found in the U.S. Absolutism is distinguished from democracy by the unlimited power claimed for absolute rulers as contrasted with the constitutional limitations placed on heads of state in democratic governments.

The development of modern absolutism began with the emergence of European nation-states toward the end of the 15th century and flourished for more than 200 years. It is, perhaps, best exemplified by the reign (1643–1715) of King Louis XIV of France. His declaration *L'état, c'est moi* ("I am the state") sums up the concept neatly (*see* DIVINE RIGHT OF KINGS). A series of revolutions, beginning with the Glorious Revolution in England (1688), gradually forced the monarchs of Europe to yield their power to parliamentary governments.

Other forms of absolutism arose in the 20th century, most notably National Socialism in Germany and the Stalinist dictatorship in the USSR. Today absolute rulers are found in many countries, including some of the remaining Communist nations and various Latin American, Middle Eastern, and African countries.

**ABSORPTION,** in physics, the taking up of light, heat, or other radiant energy by molecules. The absorbed radiation is converted into heat; the radiation that is not absorbed is reflected and has changed characteristics. For example, sunlight striking an object will usually have some of its wavelengths absorbed and other wavelengths reflected. If the object looks white, it is because all or nearly all of the radiation is reflected. If the object appears to have any color other than white, however, it means that all the visible radiation has been absorbed except for those wavelengths that cause a color sensation when they strike the eye. Objects that absorb all the radiation striking them are known as black bodies.

Absorption in chemistry is the taking up of one substance by another. For example, a gas such as oxygen may be absorbed, or dissolved, in water.

Adsorption (q.v.), which is often confused with absorption, refers to the adhering of molecules of gases and liquids to the surfaces of porous solids. Adsorption is a surface phenomenon; absorption is an intermingling or interpenetration of two substances.

**ABSTRACT ART,** art that uses forms having no direct reference to external or perceived reality; it is usually synonymous with various types of 20th-century avant-garde art. The term *abstract* also refers to images that have been abstracted or derived from nature but which, in the process, have been considerably altered or have been simplified to their basic geometric or biomorphic forms. The term *nonobjective,* once used to describe certain kinds of abstract art, has been abandoned by most art critics and historians. *See* ABSTRACT EXPRESSIONISM; AMERICAN ART AND ARCHITECTURE; BAUHAUS; CANADIAN ART AND ARCHITECTURE; COLLAGE; CONSTRUCTIVISM; CUBISM; DADA; FUTURISM; MODERN ART AND ARCHITECTURE; PAINTING; PRINTS AND PRINTMAKING; SCULPTURE.

**ABSTRACT EXPRESSIONISM,** movement in painting that developed in the 1940s and was primarily concerned with expressing through line and color the artist's emotional experiences and reactions to the world rather than with representing the objective situations that occasioned them. The movement was part of the organic, emotional, expressionistic approach to art developed in Europe in the early 20th century in contrast to the geometrically structural, rationalist approach of the cubists. The roots of abstract expressionism are in the totally nonfigurative work of the Russian-born painter Wassily Kandinsky and that of the surrealists, who stressed the importance of the subconscious and spontaneity. The arrival in New York City during World War II of such avant-garde European painters as Max Ernst, Marcel Duchamp, Marc Chagall, and Yves Tanguy inspired a flowering of abstract expressionism among American painters in the late 1940s. They were also influenced by the subjective abstractions of the Armenian-born painter Arshile Gorky, who had immigrated to the U.S. in 1920, and by the German-born American painter and teacher Hans Hofmann, who stressed the dynamic interaction of colored planes.

The abstract expressionist movement centered in New York City, called the New York school, included at one extreme action painters, such as Jackson Pollock, whose unique approach to painting involved interlacing lines of dripped and poured paint that seemed to extend in unending arabesques. In the same wing were Willem de Kooning and Franz Kline, both of whom used broad impasto brush strokes to create rhythmic abstractions in virtually infinite space. At the other extreme of abstract expressionism were the quieter canvases of Mark Rothko, who created pulsating areas of saturated color. In between were the works of Bradley Walker Tomlin (1899–1953), Philip Guston (1913–80), William Baziotes (1912–63), Robert Motherwell, Adolph Gottlieb, and Clyfford Still.

Abstract expressionism also flourished in Europe, where it influenced such French painters as Nicolas de Stael (1914–55), Pierre Soulages (1919– ), and Jean Dubuffet. The European abstract expressionist schools *Tachism* (from Fr. *tache,* "spot"), which emphasized patches of color, and *art informel,* which rejected formal structure, had close affinities with New York action painting. Tachist painters include the Frenchmen Georges Mathieu (1921– ) and Camille Bryen (1907–77), the Spaniard Antoni Tàpies, the Italian Alberto Burri (1915–95), the German Wols (1913–51), and the Canadian Jean Paul Riopelle.

The movement's adherents in the 1980s and '90s have developed eloquent, sometimes disturbing, works. Among these painters are Elizabeth Murray (1940– ) and Katherine Porter (1941– ).

**ABSTRACT OF TITLE,** in law, a brief and orderly written statement concerning real property (land), which furnishes a history of the title to be transferred, showing not only the origin and nature of the interest of the seller but also all encumbrances and other interests, such as mortgages, easements, recorded judgments, and trusts that affect the title. In the U.S. public records provide the information for an abstract of title.

After entering into a contract of sale, a purchaser of land generally employs a lawyer or a title-abstract company to make a search of the title and compile a report. If the abstract shows any defects in the title, the purchaser may refuse to proceed with the sale or refuse to proceed until such defects are cured by the seller. A similar procedure is generally followed by a mortgagee before lending money on a mortgage.

**ABU AL-FARAJ.** *See* BAR HEBRAEUS.

**ABU AL-FIDA** (1273–1331), Arabian historian and geographer, born in Damascus (now in Syria). He took part in the sieges of Tripoli (1289) and Acre (1291), the last strongholds of the Crusaders. In 1310 Abu al-Fida was appointed governor of the

Abu Simbel. Two ancient temples of Ramses II were dismantled in 1964–66 and moved 64 m (210 ft) above their original sites to protect them from waters backed up behind the Aswan High Dam. Above: The four seated figures in the facade of the larger of the two temples, about 20 m (more than 65 ft) high, represent Ramses. Below: A portion of one of the statues of Ramses is moved.　　　Nenadovic–UNESCO; E. Streichen

city of Hamah, over which he ruled with almost absolute power. In 1312 he was made prince, and in 1320 he was given the title of sultan and the right to transmit the title to his descendants. Abu

al-Fida's most important work was *An Abridgment of the History of the Human Race,* a text that traces human history until 1329. This work is especially valuable as a source for the period of the Crusades. He also wrote *Geography,* which is valued primarily for its description of the Muslim world. His name is sometimes spelled Abulfida.

**ABU BAKR** (573–634), first caliph (632–34), father of Aisha, the wife of the prophet Muhammad. Born in Mecca, he became Muhammad's most trusted follower, accompanying him on the Hegira. After Muhammad died, Abu Bakr was made caliph, or successor to the Prophet, by an assembly of the faithful. As caliph, he prevented some tribes from reverting to heathenism and fought successfully against Persia and the Byzantine Empire. He was succeeded by Umar I (581?–644).

**ABU DHABI,** also Abu Zaby, city, N central United Arab Emirates, capital of the federation and of the emirate of Abu Dhabi, a port on the island of Abu Dhabi in the Persian Gulf. The city is also a financial, transportation, and communications center for a rich petroleum-producing region. It is the site of an international airport and an artificial deepwater port at Port Zayed. Products include steel pipe and cement. Urban development projects have been important in relieving a housing shortage, caused by rapid growth since the late 1960s. The main thoroughfare is the 7-km (4-mi) long Corniche, a landscaped, seafront boulevard. It is the site of a research institute and a large sports center. The settlement was founded in the 1760s and in 1795 became the seat of the rulers of the emirate of Abu Dhabi. The town had only local significance until the discovery of vast oil reserves in the area in the late 1950s. In 1971 it was made the federal capital of the newly formed United Arab Emirates. Pop. (1989 est.) 363,400.

**ABUJA,** city, central Nigeria, capital of the country, in the Federal Capital Territory. Abuja officially replaced Lagos as capital in December 1991, after 15 years of planning and construction. The city is located in a scenic valley of rolling grasslands in a relatively undeveloped, ethnically neutral area. Thus, planners hoped to create a national city where none of Nigeria's social and religious groups would be dominant. Government agencies began moving into the new capital in the early 1980s, as residential neighborhoods were being developed in outlying areas. Abuja has an international airport and is accessible to other cities in Nigeria by a network of highways. Projections called for a population of more than 1 million early in the 21st century.

**ABUKIR.** See ABU QIR.

**ABU QIR,** also Abukir, bay, N Egypt, between the Rosetta mouth of the Nile R. and the city of Alexandria. Abu Qir Bay was the scene of the defeat of the French fleet by British forces under the command of Adm. Horatio Nelson in the Battle of the Nile, on Aug. 1–2, 1798. The following year Napoleon defeated a Turkish army at the village of Abu Qir, which is on the shore of the bay, near Alexandria. The ancient Egyptian temple city of Canopus was located near Abu Qir.

**ABU SHEHR.** See BUSHIRE.

**ABU SIMBEL,** site of two temples, S Egypt, on the Nile River, south of Aswan. The temples were carved into a sandstone cliff about 1250 BC during the reign of Ramses II. The interior of the larger temple is more than 55 m (about 180 ft) in depth and consists of a series of halls and chambers leading to a central sanctuary. This temple was dedicated by Ramses II to the chief gods of Heliopolis, Memphis, and Thebes. It is oriented so that the rays of the rising sun illuminate the statues of the three gods and of Ramses II in the innermost sanctuary. The smaller temple was dedicated by Ramses to his queen, Nefertari, and to the goddess Hathor. The facade of the larger temple has four sitting statues of Ramses II, each about 20 m (more than 65 ft) in height. Smaller statues of Ramses II, Nefertari, and their children adorn the facade of Nefertari's temple. The larger temple has numerous inscriptions and reliefs, some of them of unusual historical interest. A series of reliefs depicts the battle between the Egyptians and the Hittites at Kadesh. Two of the large sitting statues of Ramses have inscriptions in Greek dating from the 6th century BC. They were written by Greek mercenary soldiers and are among the earliest dated Greek inscriptions.

The temples, the most important monuments of ancient Nubia, were unknown to the West until 1812, when they were discovered by the Swiss explorer Johann Ludwig Burckhardt (1784–1817). In 1964 an international project was begun to save the temples from inundation by Lake Nasser, the reservoir of the Aswan High Dam. The temples were cut apart and, in 1968, reassembled on a site 64 m (210 ft) above the river.

**ABYDOS,** city of ancient Phrygia in Asia Minor, on the Hellespont (now Dardanelles), opposite the ruined town of Sestos. King Xerxes I of Persia bridged the Hellespont with boats at Abydos in 480 BC in order to invade Greece. In Greek legend, Abydos is celebrated as the scene of the story of Hero and Leander.

**ABYDOS,** ancient city of Egypt, on the western bank of the Nile River, about 160 km (about 100 mi) downstream from the ancient city of Thebes. Most Egyptian kings of the 1st and 2d Dynasties (c. 3100–2755 BC) were buried here. Between the 1st Dynasty and the end of the 26th Dynasty (525 BC), one section of the town was the site of nine successive temples. The Great Temple of Abydos, constructed on another site during the reign (1291–1279 BC) of Seti I, is remarkably well preserved.

**ABYSSINIA.** See ETHIOPIA.

**ABYSSINIAN,** breed of short-hair cat, probably the result of selective breeding rather than of

*The Abyssinian cat is believed to be a descendant of the sacred cat of ancient Egypt. Always ruddy or reddish colored, it is extraordinarily lively, active, and affectionate.*
Alice Su

93

descent from an ancestor of definite Abyssinian origin. The animal does, however, resemble the sacred cat of ancient Egypt. Abyssinians were introduced into the U.S. in the 1930s. Several varieties exist; the Ruddy and the Red Abyssinian are recognized in both Great Britain and the U.S. Ideally, they should be free of any white markings, although most specimens have some white on the lower jaw and throat. Abyssinians are of medium size, lithe and muscular, with slightly rounded, wedge-shaped faces, gold or green eyes, large ears, and long tails thick at the base.

**AC.** *See* ELECTRIC MOTORS AND GENERATORS; ELECTRICITY.

*ACACIA,* important genus of trees or shrubs of the family Fabaceae (*see* LEGUME). Most of the 1200 species of the genus are native to tropical Africa or Australia. The normal type of leaf is bipinnate, but it is often modified, especially among the species that have had to adapt to the intense heat and drought of Australia. The Australian species have vertical phyllodes that are modified leaves. The genus is of great and varied economic importance, yielding edible seeds and valuable timber and gum.

**ACADEMIC ART AND ARCHITECTURE,** any painting, sculpture, or building created according to the tenets of an academy. Because European art academies were royal foundations of the 17th and 18th centuries, the art they sponsored was of necessity aristocratic and adhered to the ideals and principles of the ruling class. By the early 19th century, however, academic art and its instruction all too often fell into formularized sterility, although almost every artist of the past currently admired had some academic training. In particular the Parisian École des Beaux-Arts (School of Fine Arts), which trained both artists and architects, was held up to scorn by many 19th- and 20th-century artists, and the term *academic art* had, by 1930, become a pejorative for stilted, eclectic hack work. In the 1970s, however, as historians revised their judgment, much academic work returned to favor.

**ACADEMIC FREEDOM,** right of teachers and research workers, particularly in colleges and universities, to investigate their respective fields of knowledge and express their views without fear of restraint or dismissal from office. The right rests on the assumption that open and free inquiry within a teacher's or researcher's field of study is essential to the pursuit of knowledge and to the performance of his or her proper educational function. At present this right is observed generally in countries in which education is regarded as a means not only of inculcating established views but also of enlarging the existing body of knowledge. The concept of academic freedom implies also that tenure of office depends primarily on the competence of teachers in their fields and on their acceptance of certain standards of professional integrity rather than on extraneous considerations such as political or religious beliefs or affiliations.

**History.** The concept and practice of academic freedom, as recognized presently in Western civilization, date roughly from the 17th century. Although academic freedom existed in universities during the Middle Ages, it signified at that time certain juristic rights, for example, the right of autonomy and of civil or ecclesiastical protection enjoyed by the several guilds that constituted a *studium generale,* or *universitas* (*see* COLLEGES AND UNIVERSITIES). Before the 17th century, intellectual activities at universities were circumscribed largely by theological considerations, and opinions or conclusions that conflicted with religious doctrines were likely to be condemned as heretical. In the late 17th century the work of such men as the English philosophers John Locke and Thomas Hobbes helped pave the way for academic freedom in the modern sense. Their writings demonstrated the need for unlimited inquiry in the sciences and for a general approach to learning unimpeded by preconceptions of any kind. Neither Locke nor Hobbes, however, defended unlimited academic freedom. The German universities of Halle and Göttingen, founded in 1694 and 1737, respectively, were the first European universities to offer broad academic freedom, with few lapses, from their inception. The University of Berlin, founded in 1810, introduced the doctrine of *Lehr- und Lernfreiheit* ("freedom to teach and study"). In the 18th and 19th centuries, universities in Western Europe, Great Britain, and the U.S. enjoyed increasing academic freedom as acceptance of the experimental methods of the sciences became more widespread and as control of institutions by religious denominations became less rigorous. In Great Britain, however, religious tests for graduation, fellowships, and teaching positions were not abolished until late in the 19th century.

**Infringements.** During the first half of the 20th century academic freedom was recognized broadly in most Western countries. Infringements increased, however, as totalitarianism emerged in a number of countries. In Germany, for instance, educators were forced to follow the dictates of Nazism, including the teaching of racist theories in various fields. In the Soviet Union academic freedom was limited by the need to make instruction and research conform to Communist doctrines. From time to time the Politburo of the Central

Committee of the Soviet Communist party laid down decrees establishing the Marxist-Leninist viewpoint in various academic disciplines.

Infringements of academic freedom also occurred in the U.S. in the 20th century. A notable example was the Scopes trial, held in Dayton, Tenn., in 1925. A high school teacher was accused and convicted of violating a state law that forbade the teaching of the theory of evolution in the public schools (see FUNDAMENTALISM). This legislation was repealed in 1967.

After World War II fear was widespread that members of the Communist party had infiltrated the field of education, and some educators were accused of Communist party membership or of being under Communist party discipline. A number of teachers so accused were dismissed on the ground that their official instructions as party members required them to use their teaching positions for purposes of Communist indoctrination, and that they were consequently guilty of violating professional ethics. In the early 1950s, largely because of congressional investigations of communism in the U.S., many institutions of higher learning adopted regulations requiring loyalty oaths from members of their faculties. Some of these oaths, insofar as they were required only of teachers, were declared unconstitutional in some state courts. However, the right of the U.S. Congress to question teachers about their membership in the Communist party was upheld by the U.S. Supreme Court. All professional associations of teachers and administrators, including the National Education Association, the American Association of Colleges, and the American Association of University Professors, are opposed to special loyalty oaths and to all violations of academic freedom.

**Current Issues and Trends.** The 1960s and early '70s were marked by protest and violence on college campuses over U.S. involvement in the war in Vietnam. In some places professors were dismissed or arrested for protesting American participation in the war. This turmoil reached a tragic climax in 1970 with the killing of several students during campus demonstrations. In the long run, however, these disturbances led to a broad recognition of the legitimate concerns of students about the quality of higher education, and of the responsibility of universities, rather than the public or the government, to maintain essential academic order. By 1973, when U.S. troops were withdrawn from Vietnam, a general growth in higher education was under way.

Increasing enrollment and expansion of faculties, as well as a broader makeup of student and faculty populations, contributed to a vast enrichment of the academic curriculum, to increasing faculty control over the content of programs, and, overall, to the enhancement of the freedom to teach and to learn in colleges and universities.

Beginning in the early 1970s in the U.S. (and somewhat later in other countries such as Canada and Great Britain), however, institutions of higher education were faced with serious financial problems. Steps taken to deal with these difficulties also took a toll on academic freedom. For example, proliferation of irregular faculty appointments, intended to save money, created a virtual underclass of teachers lacking the employment security generally considered necessary for the exercise of academic freedom.

Threats to and violations of academic freedom continued in the 1980s. The U.S. government, in the name of national security, imposed severe restraints on the dissemination of research results. The influence of resurgent religious conservatism was felt in some areas in efforts to introduce religious teachings in elementary and secondary schools, and in limits on free expression at church-affiliated colleges and universities. In many other nations (among them, South Africa, the Soviet Union, Poland, and China) educators whose teachings were objectionable to the government were sometimes dismissed, harassed, or imprisoned. S.H. & W.W.B.

*For further information on this topic, see the Bibliography in volume 28, sections 156, 311.*

**ACADÉMIE FRANÇAISE.** *See* INSTITUT DE FRANCE.

**ACADEMY,** originally, in ancient Greece, a public garden outside Athens, dedicated to Athena and other deities and containing a grove and a gymnasium. In these gardens the Greek philosopher Plato met with and instructed his followers, and his informal school came to be known as the Academy. Subsequent schools of philosophy, modeled upon Plato's, were also called academies; the term was eventually used in ancient times to indicate any institution of higher education or the faculty of such an institution. The most notable academies of the ancient world were the Old Academy, founded (c. 387 BC) by Plato; the Middle Academy, founded by the Greek Platonic philosopher Arcesilaus (c. 316–c. 241 BC); and the New Academy, founded by the Greek skeptic philosopher Carneades.

**Learning Institutions.** Used to denote a school, the word *academy* has come to be applied to certain kinds of institutions of learning. The Ritterakademien, or schools for knights, appeared increasingly in Germany after the end of the Thirty Years' War in 1648. The term *academy* was adopted in England during the late 17th and the

18th centuries by Puritan religious sects as a name for secondary schools that they organized to provide for the general education of their children; these institutions were especially designed to train young men for the Puritan ministry, because such education could not be obtained in contemporary public schools. The word gradually lost its religious denotation, and by the 19th century it applied to a secondary school for boys corresponding roughly to the gymnasium in Germany. In colonial America, the term *academy* was introduced by Benjamin Franklin; his proposal resulted in the chartering (1753) of the Academy and Charitable School of the Province of Pennsylvania. In 1755 it was renamed the College and Academy and Charitable School of Philadelphia (now the University of Pennsylvania), with power to grant degrees. On the secondary-school level, the earliest academies, Phillips Andover and Phillips Exeter, founded in 1780 and 1781, respectively, introduced a modern curriculum. The academies were private, religion-oriented boarding schools. As they displaced the colonial Latin grammar schools, so were they largely superseded by the public high school after the American Civil War; those that survive, and other similar institutions, have largely become college-preparatory schools.

As a designation for a school, the word *academy* is also used in a looser sense to indicate institutions in which special accomplishments such as horseback riding, fencing, or dancing are taught. It may also be applied to schools that prepare students for a particular profession, such as the U.S. Military Academy, the U.S. Naval Academy, and the U.S. Air Force Academy.

**Scholarly and Professional Associations.** To describe a body of learned men (originally the faculty of a school of philosophy), the word *academy* has come to be applied to various associations of scholars, artists, literary men, and scientists, organized for the promotion of general or special intellectual or artistic interests and not necessarily connected with any distinct school. Thus, Charlemagne applied the name in 782 to a group of scholars organized at his court. During the Renaissance, academies achieved an intellectual prominence rivaling that of the universities and first displayed their typical modern form (*see* ED-UCATION, HISTORY OF). They characteristically consisted of a group of elected or appointed investigators, generally under royal or state patronage, who encouraged learning, literature, and art by research and publication. In the 15th century important academies were organized in Italy, notably at the courts of the Italian rulers Lorenzo and Cosimo de' Medici. In Italy, too, one of the

earliest academies devoted to science was organized in Naples in 1560; a later academy founded in the same city in 1603 included Galileo among its members. Scientific academies such as the Royal Society of London for Improving Natural Knowledge (q.v.), incorporated in London in 1662, have played roles of the highest importance in scientific progress by encouraging investigations and publicizing their results. Stimulated by royal patronage and more efficient methods of communication among scholars, the foundation of academies reached its height in Germany and northeastern Europe during the 18th century. In France, the most celebrated of all collections of academies was organized in 1795 as the Institut de France (q.v.). The institute now contains five distinct academies, all but one of which were founded as independent institutions in the 17th century; among the most notable of these are the French Academy and the academies of science and of fine art.

In the U.S., academies have not attained the complexity and prestige of their European models because American scholars have traditionally preferred to organize in learned societies open to all qualified applicants and independent of government support. Academies of the European type include the National Academy of Design and the National Academy of Sciences. The American Academy and Institute of Arts and Letters, a counterpart of the French Academy, is a subsidiary division of the National Institute of Arts and Letters, which, in turn, is modeled on the Institut de France.          S.H. & W.W.B.

*For further information on this topic, see the Bibliography in volume 28, sections 41, 309.*

**ACADEMY AWARDS.** *See* MOTION PICTURE ARTS AND SCIENCES, ACADEMY OF.

**ACADIA** (Fr. *Acadie*), original name of the parts of Canada now known as Nova Scotia, New Brunswick, and Prince Edward Island (qq.v.). The region was first colonized by the French in 1604, but the English claimed it by right of the explorations of the English navigator John Cabot in 1497–98. King James I of England granted Acadia to the Scottish poet and statesman Sir William Alexander in 1621, but control of it changed hands several times during the subsequent Anglo-French struggle for supremacy in North America. The British obtained permanent possession of mainland Acadia by the Peace of Utrecht (1713), which ended the War of the Spanish Succession. The Acadians, who attempted to remain neutral in the Anglo-French conflicts, suffered greatly.

In 1755, because of renewed war with France, the Seven Years' War, and doubts about the loyalty of the Acadians, the British colonial authorities removed the Acadians from their lands, dispossessed them of their property, and dispersed them among the other British colonies in America. The ordeal of the Acadian exiles was recounted in the poem *Evangeline* by the American poet Henry Wadsworth Longfellow.

**ACADIA NATIONAL PARK,** SE Maine, on the Atlantic coast, established as a national park in 1919. The park includes a rugged coastal region of great natural beauty with the highest land on the E seaboard of the U.S. It consists of most of Mount Desert Island, parts of Isle au Haut, and a number of other islets, as well as the tip of the Schoodic Peninsula, the only mainland section. The coast is characterized by wave-eroded granite cliffs. The inland portion of the park is forested with spruce and fir, and contains lakes and mountains carved by glacial action. A variety of land and marine life is found. The park has a nature center and a museum displaying Stone Age Indian relics. It was known as Lafayette National Park from 1919 to 1929. Area, 169.5 sq km (65.5 sq mi).

**ACANTHOCEPHALA.** *See* SPINY-HEADED WORM.

**ACANTHUS,** genus of ornamental plants of the family Acanthaceae, characterized by feathery leaves about 30 to 60 cm (about 12 to 24 in) long and by red, white, or purple flowers in spiny bracts. *Acanthus spinosus* and *A. mollis,* natives of southern Europe, are the species best known; the jagged leaves of the Mediterranean plant appear extensively in sculpture and decoration as stylized ornamental motifs. Acanthaceae are in the order Scrophulariales (*see* FIGWORT).

**ACAPULCO,** in full Acapulco de Juárez, town and seaport, S Mexico, in Guerrero State, on the Pacific Ocean. The city has scheduled air service and highway connections with the interior of Mexico. Its principal exports are agricultural: cotton, tropical fruits, sugarcane, coffee, tobacco, and sesame seed (the chief products of the surrounding region).

Endowed with a fine harbor, which is almost entirely landlocked, and located in a setting of great natural beauty, Acapulco is sometimes called the Riviera of Mexico. It has luxury hotels, gambling casinos, and excellent beaches and is popular for winter vacations and deep-sea fish-

*Acapulco, Mexico's oldest resort, is located on the Pacific coast in southern Mexico.*
© D. Donne Bryant

ing. The climate is warm and pleasant between December and April but becomes hot, humid, and rainy from May to November. The city was founded in 1550, and from 1565 to 1815 Acapulco was Mexico's principal port on the Pacific coast for Spanish trade with the Far East. Pop. (1990) 592,187.

**ACARNANIA,** region of ancient Greece, a mountainous, wooded section in the northwest (now part of Central Greece and Euboea Region). It was separated from Epirus on the north by the Ambracian Gulf, from Aetolia on the east by the Achelous River, and bounded on the south and west by the outer Corinthian Gulf and the Ionian Sea. Acarnania supported Athens in the Peloponnesian War (431–404 BC). In 390 BC it was conquered by Sparta. It was ruled successively by Sparta, Athens, and Thebes until 338 BC when it came under Macedonian control with the victory of Philip II of Macedon at Chaeronea. After nearly a century under Macedon, Acarnania was partitioned between the states of Aetolia and Epirus, but the Epirote section regained its independence in 230 BC. The Acarnanians sided with King Philip V of Macedonia in his unsuccessful wars against Rome; they were forced to send hostages to Rome in 167 BC. Rome, however, allowed Acarnania to retain its own government until about 22 BC, when the Roman emperor Augustus reorganized the Roman provinces. Some Acarnanians were then transported to the emperor's new city of Nicopolis in Epirus, while the rest remained in the province of Achaea.

**ACCELERATION,** rate at which the velocity, or speed, of a body changes per unit of time. Acceleration is called uniform acceleration if the rate of change remains the same over successive and equal intervals of time. (A decrease in velocity is sometimes called negative acceleration or deceleration.) Angular acceleration is the rate at which the velocity of a body changes when it is moving in a curved path. The force of gravity imparts to a body falling freely in a vacuum an acceleration that depends on the distance above sea level. The standard value of the acceleration of a freely falling body in a vacuum at sea level and 45° lat is 9.81 m/sec$^2$ (32.17 ft/sec$^2$).

**ACCELERATOR,** in chemistry, any substance that speeds up the rate of a reaction. For example, an accelerator speeds the action of: a developer in photography; the setting of concrete in construction; and the curing of epoxy and other resin-type plastics during manufacture. In engineering, an accelerator is a device (usually a pedal) used to control engine speed in a motor vehicle.

**ACCELERATOR, PARTICLE.** *See* PARTICLE ACCELERATORS.

**ACCENT** *or* **STRESS,** in language, special stress emphasis or relative force or loudness given to one syllable of a word, thereby making that syllable more prominent than the others. The strongest accent is called primary stress; the next most prominent is called secondary stress. In some languages tertiary and weaker stresses are also recognized. In many dictionaries the accents are indicated by such symbols as ' for primary or main stress and " for secondary stress. Almost every English word of two or more syllables has at least one stressed syllable. Frequently the secondary stress is placed on an early syllable of a word, as in *rec" om mend'* and *res" to ra' tion;* sometimes it falls on the last, as in *down' pour"* and *drum' head".* By changing the accent, many nouns may be made verbs, as *an ob' ject* but *to ob ject'.* Stress accent is more complex in the English language than in many other languages. The meters of English poetry are determined entirely by accent, rather than by the quantities of vowels. *See* VERSIFICATION. S.G.F.

**ACCESS, RIGHT OF,** legal incident of the ownership of property abutting on the sea or other navigable waters, or on a highway or other public lands. It is of the nature of a servitude or easement. Access to air as against a neighboring proprietor can be acquired only as an easement. The right of access to a highway over another's land is also of the nature of an easement that will be presumed to exist when such access is necessary for entrance and exit.

**ACCESSORY,** in criminal law, accomplice in the commission of an offense as distinguished from the chief offender. An accessory before the fact is one who deliberately encourages others to commit an offense, but who does not take a direct part in the offense. An accessory after the fact is one who, knowing that an offense has been committed, takes active steps to shelter the offender from justice or to enable the offender to escape. Accessories must be distinguished from principals in the second degree, that is, persons who, although not the actual perpetrators of the crime, were nevertheless present and aided and abetted in the commission of the offense. The tendency of modern legislation has been to convert accessories before the fact into principals, and an accessory before the fact is often subject to a punishment as severe as that imposed upon a principal. An accessory after the fact, on the other hand, is subject to less severe penalties.

**ACCIDENT,** unintended and unforeseen event, usually resulting in personal injury or property damage. In law, the term is usually limited to events not involving negligence, that is, the carelessness or misconduct of a party involved, or to a loss caused by lightning, floods, or other natural events (*see* ACT OF GOD). In popular usage, however, the term *accident* designates an unexpected event, especially if it causes injury or damage without reference to the negligence or fault of an individual. The basic causes of such accidents are, in general, unsafe conditions of machinery, equipment, or surroundings, and the unsafe actions of persons that are caused by ignorance or neglect of safety principles.

**Prevention of Accidents.** Organized efforts for the prevention of accidents began in the 19th century with the adoption of factory-inspection laws, first in Great Britain and then in the U.S. and other countries (*see* FACTORY SYSTEM). Fire insurance and accident insurance companies made efforts to enforce safety rules and to educate the public. Factory inspectors and inspectors from fire insurance and casualty insurance companies carried on a campaign against unsafe conditions and actions, and at the beginning of the 20th century a new branch of engineering developed, devoted to finding and eliminating such hazards (*see* INDUSTRIAL SAFETY).

Laws concerning workers' compensation (q.v.) were passed in Germany in 1884, Great Britain in 1897, and the U.S. in 1908. By placing on the employer the financial burden of caring for injured workers, such laws created an incentive for providing safe machinery and working conditions and for improved selection and training of employees. In the U.S., the National Safety Council was formed in 1913; this noncommercial organization has since been a leader in accident-prevention activities, especially in the publication of educational literature, the compilation of statistics, and the coordination of the work of schools, clubs, industrial organizations, and state and municipal agencies.

**Motor-Vehicle Accidents.** The single greatest cause of accidents in the U.S. is the automobile. In 1913 the American industrialist Henry Ford introduced assembly-line techniques in the manufacture of motor vehicles. The subsequent increase in the number of automobiles in use was huge and led to a great rise in the motor-vehicle accident rate. In 1991 in the U.S., automobile accidents were responsible for about 49.4 percent of all accidental deaths, as compared with accidents in the home (about 23.3 percent); accidents in public places, including railroads and airplanes (about 20.5 percent); and work-related accidents (about 11.3 percent). The second greatest cause of accidental deaths is falls, which account for some 13.9 percent of all fatalities. Accidental deaths reached a high of 110,000 in 1936, with a death rate of 85.9 per 100,000.

In 1991 the total was estimated at 88,000, with a death rate of 34.9 per 100,000; this was the lowest accidental death toll since 1924 (85,600).

*See also* HEALTH INSURANCE.

**ACCIDENT INSURANCE.** See HEALTH INSURANCE.

**ACCLIMATIZATION,** also physiological adaptation, process by which an organism becomes better adapted to exist in an environment different from the one to which it was indigenous. If the environmental difference is extreme, changes take place in the structure and physiology of the organism. Each organism, however, has certain limits of temperature and other conditions within which it can survive, and some alleged instances of acclimatizing have merely been instances of unsuspected hardiness in the organism.

Humans can acclimate to extreme conditions through changes in normal physiological processes. Persons who move from a temperate to a hot, dry climate undergo changes in heart rate and body temperature such that in time they perspire less, and their perspiration contains less salt. At an altitude of 7600 m (25,000 ft) most persons need to breathe high-pressure oxygen for survival, but through gradual acclimatization they may become able to breathe unaided. This is due to an increase in the number of red blood cells, which contain oxygen-carrying hemoglobin. The increase is mediated by the hormone erythropoietin, secreted by the kidneys. In addition, a change in chemical composition within the red blood cells promotes migration of hemoglobin into the body tissues, where oxygen is needed. The human organism also exhibits a response to the absence of natural light. As with most life forms, humans normally function in what is called a circadian rhythm corresponding to the length of the day. Humans who have lived underground under experimental conditions continue to show cyclical changes in physiology, demonstrating the existence of a natural biological clock (*see* BIOLOGICAL CLOCKS). The period dictated by this internal clock, however, is slightly longer than one day.

Acclimatization may also refer to psychological changes occasioned by a change in environments, as from a rural to an urban setting.

*See also* ADAPTATION.

**ACCOMPLICE,** in criminal law, any person who is in any way associated with another in the commission or attempted commission of a criminal offense. An accomplice is punishable either as principal or accessory. Under certain conditions, an accomplice is a competent witness either for or against his or her associates at every stage of the proceedings.

**ACCORDION,** free-reed musical instrument invented in Berlin in 1822. Wind is supplied to the reeds by a bellows, the access of air to each reed being controlled by a valve that the player opens by depressing a button or a pianolike key. The reeds and buttons or keys are mounted in two oblong frames, the bass reeds and buttons at the player's left-hand side of the bellows, the melody reeds and buttons or keys at the right-hand side. The reeds are small metal tabs set over a close-fitting frame; under air flow from their upper side, they vibrate through the frame, producing a tone of definite pitch.

The earliest accordions had ten melody buttons and two bass buttons. Each melody tone had one reed, and each melody button controlled two tones, the reeds for which were mounted in opposite directions so that one, say C, sounded on the draw of the bellows (that is, by suction) and the other, say D, on the push (that is, by pressure). One bass button controlled the tonic note (the keynote) and the other the three notes of the tonic chord on the push; they sounded the dominant note and chord on the draw. This "single-action" accordion was expanded by additional melody and bass buttons and continues to be popular in Austria and Switzerland.

The piano accordion, developed in France in the 1850s, substituted a pianolike keyboard for the melody buttons. It introduced a "double action," in which each key (or button) controls two reeds tuned to the same pitch (or, for chords, two threesomes of reeds). Thus, when the key for C is depressed, one reed sounds C on the push and the other sounds C on the draw. The piano accordion was greatly expanded by the addition of up to six rows of bass buttons, giving single bass notes, major and minor chords, and dominant- and diminished-seventh chords. In the 1930s the piano accordion was fitted with registers, that is, additional sets of reeds providing varied tone colors.

The concertina, invented in 1829 by Sir Charles Wheatstone, is a small, hexagonal, accordionlike instrument made in single-action and double-action versions.

**ACCOUNTING AND BOOKKEEPING,** the process of identifying, measuring, recording, and communicating economic information about an organization or other entity, in order to permit informed judgments by users of the information. Bookkeeping encompasses the record-keeping aspect of accounting and therefore provides much of the data to which accounting principles are applied in the preparation of financial statements and other financial information.

Personal record keeping often uses a simple single-entry system, in which amounts are recorded in column form. Such entries include the date of the transaction, its nature, and the amount of money involved. Record keeping of organizations, however, is based on a double-entry system, whereby each transaction is recorded on the basis of its dual impact on the organization's financial position or operating results or both. Information relating to the financial position of an enterprise is presented in a balance sheet, while disclosures about operating results are displayed in an income statement. Data relating to an organization's liquidity and changes in its financial structure are shown in a statement of changes in financial position. Such financial statements are prepared to provide information about past performance, which in turn becomes a basis for readers to try to project what might happen in the future.

**History.** Bookkeeping and record-keeping methods, created in response to the development of trade and commerce, are preserved from ancient and medieval sources. Double-entry bookkeeping began in the commercial city-states of medieval Italy and was well developed by the time of the earliest preserved double-entry books, from 1340 in Genoa.

The first published accounting work was written in 1494 by the Venetian monk Luca Pacioli (1450–1520). Although it disseminated rather than created knowledge about double-entry bookkeeping, Pacioli's work summarized principles that have remained essentially unchanged. Additional accounting works were published

*Print shows bookkeeping methods before modern mechanization. Bills were written by hand with quill pens, and all processes were handled individually.*
**Granger Collection**

during the 16th century in Italian, German, Dutch, French, and English, and these works included early formulations of the concepts of assets, liabilities, and income.

The Industrial Revolution created a need for accounting techniques that were adequate to handle mechanization, factory-manufacturing operations, and the mass production of goods and services. With the emergence in the mid-19th century of large, publicly held business corporations, owned by absentee stockholders and administered by professional managers, the role of accounting was further redefined.

Bookkeeping, which is a vital part of all accounting systems, was in the mid-20th century increasingly carried out by machines. The widespread use of computers broadened the scope of bookkeeping, and the term *data processing* now frequently encompasses bookkeeping.

## ACCOUNTING INFORMATION

Accounting information can be classified into two categories: financial accounting or public information and managerial accounting or private information. Financial accounting includes information disseminated to parties that are not part of the enterprise proper—stockholders, creditors, customers, suppliers, regulatory commissions, financial analysts, and trade associations—although the information is also of interest to the company's officers and managers. Such information relates to the financial position, liquidity (that is, ability to convert to cash), and profitability of an enterprise.

Managerial accounting deals with cost-profit-volume relationships, efficiency and productivity, planning and control, pricing decisions, capital budgeting, and similar matters. This information is not generally disseminated outside the company. Whereas the general-purpose financial statements of financial accounting are assumed to meet basic information needs of most external users, managerial accounting provides a wide variety of specialized reports for division managers, department heads, project directors, section supervisors, and other managers.

**Specialized Accounting.** Of the various specialized areas of accounting that exist, the three most important are auditing, income taxation, and nonbusiness organizations. Auditing is the examination, by an independent accountant, of the financial data, accounting records, business documents, and other pertinent documents of an organization in order to attest to the accuracy of its financial statements. Businesses and not-for-profit organizations in the U.S. engage certified public accountants (CPAs) to perform audit examinations. Large private and public enterprises

sometimes also maintain an internal audit staff to conduct auditlike examinations, including some that are more concerned with operating efficiency and managerial effectiveness than with the accuracy of the accounting data.

The second specialized area of accounting is income taxation. Preparing an income-tax form entails collecting information and presenting data in a coherent manner; therefore, both individuals and businesses frequently hire accountants to determine their taxes. Tax rules, however, are not identical with accounting theory and practices. Tax regulations are based on laws that are enacted by legislative bodies, interpreted by the courts, and enforced by designated administrative bodies. Much of the information required in figuring taxes, however, is also needed in accounting, and many techniques of computing are common to both areas.

A third area of specialization is accounting for nonbusiness organizations, such as universities, hospitals, churches, trade and professional associations, and government agencies. These organizations differ from business enterprises in that they receive resources on some nonreciprocating basis (that is, without paying for such resources), they do not have a profit orientation, and they have no defined ownership interests as such. As a result, these organizations call for differences in record keeping, in accounting measurements, and in the format of their financial statements.

**Financial Reporting.** Traditionally, the function of financial reporting was to provide proprietors with information about the companies that they owned and operated. Once the delegation of managerial responsibilities to hired personnel became a common practice, financial reporting began to focus on stewardship, that is, on the managers' accountability to the owners. Its purpose then was to document how effectively the owners' assets were managed, in terms of both capital preservation and profit generation.

After businesses were commonly organized as corporations, the appearance of large multinational corporations and the widespread employment of professional managers by absentee owners brought about a change in the focus of financial reporting. Although the stewardship orientation has not become obsolete, financial reporting in the mid-20th century is somewhat more geared toward the needs of investors. Because both individual and institutional investors view ownership of corporate stock as only one of various investment alternatives, they seek much more future-oriented information than was supplied under the traditional stewardship concept. As investors relied more on the potential of financial statements to predict the results of investment and disinvestment decisions, accounting became more sensitive to their needs. One important result was an expansion of the information supplied in financial statements.

The proliferation of footnotes to financial statements is a particularly visible example. Such footnotes disclose information that is not already included in the body of the financial statement. One footnote usually identifies the accounting methods adopted when acceptable alternative methods also exist, or when the unique nature of the company's business justifies an otherwise unconventional approach.

Footnotes also disclose information about lease commitments, contingent liabilities, pension plans, stock options, and foreign currency translation, as well as details about long-term debt (such as interest rates and maturity dates). A company having a widely distributed ownership usually includes among its footnotes the income it earned in each quarter, quarterly stock market prices of its outstanding shares of common stock, and information about the relative sales and profit contribution of its different industry segments.

## ACCOUNTING PRINCIPLES

Accounting as it exists today may be viewed as a system of assumptions, doctrines, tenets, and conventions, all encompassed by the phrase "generally accepted accounting principles." Many of these principles developed gradually, as did much of common law; only the accounting developments of recent decades are prescribed in statutory law. Following are several fundamental accounting concepts.

The *entity concept* states that the item or activity (entity) that is to receive an accounting must be clearly defined, and that the relationship assumed to exist between the entity and external parties must be clearly understood.

The *going-concern* assumption states that it is expected that the entity will continue to operate indefinitely.

The *historical-cost principle* requires that economic resources be recorded in terms of the amounts of money exchanged; when a transaction occurs, the exchange price is by its nature a measure of the value of the economic resources that are exchanged.

The *realization concept* states that accounting takes place only for those economic events to which the entity is a party. This principle therefore rules out recognizing a gain based on the appreciated market value of a still-owned asset.

The *matching principle* states that income is calculated by matching a period's revenues with the expenses incurred in order to bring about that revenue.

The *accrual principle* defines revenues and expenses as the inflow and outflow of all assets—as distinct from the flow only of cash assets—in the course of operating the enterprise.

The *consistency criterion* states that the accounting procedures used at a given time should conform with the procedures previously used for that activity. Such consistency allows data of different periods to be compared.

The *disclosure principle* requires that financial statements present the most useful amount of relevant information—namely, all information that is necessary in order not to be misleading.

The *substance-over-form* standard emphasizes the economic substance of events even though their legal form may suggest a different result. An example is the practice of consolidating the financial statements of one company with those of another in which it has more than a 50 percent ownership interest.

The *conservatism doctrine* states that when exposure to uncertainty and risk is significant, accounting measurement and disclosure should take a cautious and prudent stance until evidence shows sufficient lessening of the uncertainty and risk.

**The Balance Sheet.** Of the two traditional types of financial statements, the balance sheet relates to an entity's position, and the income statement relates to its activity. The balance sheet provides information about an organization's assets, liabilities, and owners' equity as of a particular date (such as the last day of the accounting or fiscal period). The format of the balance sheet reflects the basic accounting equation: Assets equal equities. Assets are economic resources that provide potential future service to the organization. Equities consist of the organization's liabilities together with the equity interest of its owners. (For example, a certain house is an asset worth $70,000; its unpaid mortgage is a liability of $45,000, and the equity of its owners is $25,000.)

Assets are categorized as current or long-lived. Current assets are usually those that management could reasonably be expected to convert into cash within one year; they include cash, receivables, merchandise inventory, and short-term investments in stocks and bonds. Long-lived assets encompass the physical plant—notably land, buildings, machinery, motor vehicles, computers, furniture, and fixtures. Long-lived assets also include real estate being held for speculation and intangibles such as patents and trademarks.

Liabilities are obligations that the organization must remit to other parties, such as creditors and employees. Current liabilities usually are amounts that are expected to be paid within one year, including salaries and wages, taxes, short-term loans, and money owed to suppliers of goods and services. Noncurrent liabilities are usually debts that will come due beyond one year—such as bonds, mortgages, and long-term loans. Whereas liabilities are the claims of outside parties on the assets of the organization, the owners' equity is the investment interest of the owners in the organization's assets. When an enterprise is operated as a sole proprietorship or as a partnership, the balance sheet may disclose the amount of each owner's equity. When the organization is a corporation, the balance sheet shows the equity of the owners—that is, the stockholders—as consisting of two elements: (1) the amount originally invested by the stockholders; and (2) the corporation's cumulative reinvested income, or retained earnings (that is, income not distributed to stockholders as dividends), in which the stockholders have equity.

**The Income Statement.** The traditional activity-oriented financial statement issued by business enterprises is the income statement. Prepared for a well-defined time interval, such as three months or one year, this statement summarizes the enterprise's revenues, expenses, gains, and losses. Revenues are transactions that represent the inflow of assets as a result of operations—that is, assets received from selling goods and rendering services. Expenses are transactions involving the outflow of assets in order to generate revenue, such as wages, rent, interest, and taxes.

A revenue transaction is recorded during the fiscal period in which it occurs. An expense appears in the income statement of the period in which revenues presumably resulted from the particular expense. To illustrate, wages paid by a merchandising or service company are recognized as an immediate expense because they are presumed to generate revenue during the same period in which they occurred. If, however, the wages are paid to process merchandise that will not be sold until a later fiscal period, they would not be considered an immediate expense. Instead, the cost of these wages will be treated as part of the cost of the resulting inventory asset; the effect of this cost on income is thus deferred until the asset is sold and revenue is realized.

In addition to disclosing revenues and expenses (the principal components of income), the income statement also lists gains and losses from other kinds of transactions, such as the sale of plant assets (for example, a factory building) or the early repayment of long-term debt. Extraordinary—that is, unusual and infrequent—developments are also specifically disclosed.

**Other Financial Statements.** The income statement excludes the amount of assets withdrawn by the owners; in a corporation such withdrawn assets are called dividends. A separate activity-oriented statement, the statement of retained earnings, discloses income and redistribution to owners.

A third important activity-oriented financial statement is the statement of cash flows. This statement provides information not otherwise available in either an income statement or a balance sheet; it presents the sources and the uses of the enterprise's funds by operating activities, investing activities, and financing activities. The statement identifies the cash generated or used by operations; the cash exchanged to buy and sell plant and equipment; the cash proceeds from stock issuances and long-term borrowings; and the cash used to pay dividends, to purchase the company's outstanding shares of its own stock, and to pay off debts.

**Bookkeeping and Accounting Cycle.** Modern accounting entails a seven-step accounting cycle. The first three steps fall under the bookkeeping function—that is, the systematic compiling and recording of financial transactions. Business documents provide the bookkeeping input; such documents include invoices, payroll time cards, bank checks, and receiving reports. Special journals (daily logs) are used to record recurring transactions; these include a sales journal, a purchases journal, a cash-receipts journal, and a cash-disbursements journal. Transactions that cannot be accommodated by a special journal are recorded in a general journal.

*Step one.* Recording a transaction in a journal marks the starting point for the double-entry bookkeeping system. In this system the financial structure of an organization is analyzed as consisting of many interrelated aspects, each of which is called an account (for example, the "wages payable" account). Every transaction is identified in two aspects or dimensions, referred to as its debit (or left side) and credit (or right side) aspects, and each of these two aspects has its own effect on the financial structure. Depending on their nature, certain accounts are increased with debits and decreased with credits; other accounts are increased with credits and decreased with debits. For example, the purchase of merchandise for cash increases the merchandise account (a debit) and decreases the cash account (a credit). If merchandise is purchased on the promise of future payment, a liability would be created, and the journal entry would record

A network of microcomputers, each able to enter and receive data from the company's mainframe, speeds modern bookkeeping.                                            Sperry Corporation

an increase in the merchandise account (a debit) and an increase in the liability account (a credit). Recognition of wages earned by employees entails recording an increase in the wage-expense account (a debit) and an increase in the liability account (a credit). The subsequent payment of the wages would be a decrease in the cash account (a credit) and a decrease in the liability account (a debit).

**Step two.** In the next step in the accounting cycle, the amounts that appear in the various journals are transferred to the organization's general ledger—a procedure called posting. (A ledger is a book having one page for each account in the organization's financial structure. The page for each account shows its debits on the left side and its credits on the right side, so that the balance—that is, the net credit or debit—of each account can be determined.)

In addition to the general ledger, a subsidiary ledger is used to provide information in greater detail about the accounts in the general ledger. For example, the general ledger contains one account showing the entire amount owed to the enterprise by all its customers; the subsidiary ledger breaks this amount down on a customer-by-customer basis, with a separate subsidiary account for each customer. Subsidiary accounts may also be kept for the wages paid to each employee, for each building or machine owned by the company, and for amounts owed to each of the enterprise's creditors.

**Step three.** Posting data to the ledgers is followed by listing the balances of all the accounts and calculating whether the sum of all the debit balances

agrees with the sum of all the credit balances (because every transaction has been listed once as a debit and once as a credit). This determination is called a trial balance. This procedure and those that follow it take place at the end of the fiscal period. Once the trial balance has been successfully prepared, the bookkeeping portion of the accounting cycle is concluded.

**Step four.** Once bookkeeping procedures have been completed, the accountant prepares certain adjustments to recognize events that, although they did not occur in conventional form, are in substance already completed transactions. The following are the most common circumstances that require adjustments: accrued revenue (for example, interest earned but not yet received); accrued expense (wage cost incurred but not yet paid); unearned revenue (earning subscription revenue that had been collected in advance); prepaid expense (expiration of a prepaid insurance premium); depreciation (recognizing the cost of a machine as expense spread over its useful economic life); inventory (recording the cost of goods sold on the basis of a period's purchases and the change between beginning and ending inventory balances); and receivables (recognizing bad-debt expenses on the basis of expected uncollected amounts).

**Steps five and six.** Once the adjustments are calculated, the accountant prepares an adjusted trial balance—one that combines the original trial balance with the effects of the adjustments (step five). With the balances in all the accounts thus updated, financial statements are then prepared (step six). The balances in the accounts are the data that make up the organization's financial statements.

**Step seven.** The final step is to close noncumulative accounts. This involves a series of bookkeeping debits and credits to transfer sums from income-statement accounts into owners' equity accounts. Such transfers reduce to zero the balances of noncumulative accounts; these accounts can then receive new debit and credit amounts related to the activity of the next business period.

REGULATIONS AND STANDARDS

Until 1973, accounting principles in the U.S. had traditionally been established by certified public accountants. Such persons are accountants licensed by their states on the basis of educational background, a rigorous certification examination, and, in some jurisdictions, relevant field experience. In 1973, the seven-member Financial Accounting Standards Board was created as an independent standard-setting organization. Regulations for auditors are promulgated by the American Institute of Certified Public Accountants. U.S. companies whose stocks or bonds are traded by the public must conform to rules set by the Securities and Exchange Commission (q.v.), a federal agency. Tax laws and regulations are administered at the federal level by the Internal Revenue Service (q.v.) and at the local level by state and municipal agencies. The U.S. has no standard-setting body for managerial accounting. From 1971 to 1980, however, the federal Cost Accounting Standards Board established accounting rules for contracts with parties that sell goods and services to the government. The nongovernmental Institute of Management Accounting, although not active in issuing technical standards, does administer a program qualifying candidates for a certificate in management accounting (CMA). The Institute of Internal Auditors has a program enabling an accountant to be designated a certified internal auditor (CIA).

Accounting has a well-defined body of knowledge and rather definitive procedures. Nevertheless, standard setters continue to refine existing techniques and develop new approaches. Such activity is needed in part because of innovative business practices, newly enacted laws, and socioeconomic changes. Better insights, new concepts, and enhanced perceptions have also influenced the development of accounting theory and practices. P.E.Me.

*For further information on this topic, see the Bibliography in volume 28, section 616.*

**ACCRA,** capital and largest city of Ghana, SE Ghana, on the Gulf of Guinea. Accra is an important commercial, manufacturing, and communications center. It is the site of an international airport and a focus of the country's railroad system, including a link to nearby Tema, which since 1962 has served as the city's deepwater port. Industries include vehicle and appliance assembly, petroleum refining, and the manufacture of foodstuffs, textiles, metal and wood products, plastics, and pharmaceuticals. A sprawling

*People in traditional African dress make for a colorful street scene in Accra, capital and largest city of Ghana.* Embassy of Ghana, Washington, D.C.

city, Accra presents a varied appearance, with buildings of modern, colonial, and traditional African architecture. Of note here are the 17th-century Christiansborg Castle, now the residence of the chief of state, and the National Museum (1957). Accra is the seat of the University of Ghana (1948) and several research and technical institutes.

The site of what is now Accra was occupied by villages of the Ga, the local people, when the Portuguese first visited here in the late 15th century. During the 17th century the Portuguese were forced to withdraw by the Dutch, who, along with the Danes and the English, founded rival trading posts, which became the settlements of Ussher Town, Christiansborg, and James Town, respectively. In the 19th century Great Britain purchased Dutch and Danish rights in the area, and in 1876 Christiansborg was made the capital of the Gold Coast Colony. The three separate towns grew and gradually coalesced to form the city of Accra. Much of the modern city's layout was planned in the 1920s, and since then growth has been rapid. Accra remained the capital city, when in 1957 the Gold Coast Colony became the independent state of Ghana. Pop. (1984) 964, 879.

**ACCULTURATION,** process by which continuous contact between two or more distinct societies causes cultural change. This can happen in one of two ways. The beliefs and customs of the groups may merge almost equally and result in a single culture. More often, however, one society completely absorbs the cultural patterns of another through a process of selection and modification. This change often occurs because of political or military domination. It may cause considerable psychological disturbance and social unrest.

The term *acculturation* was first used in anthropology in the late 19th century. After World War II it became an important field of study in applied anthropology.

**ACETALDEHYDE,** volatile, colorless, liquid, $CH_3CHO$, with a pungent, fruity odor. It is important as an intermediate in the manufacture of many chemicals, pharmaceuticals, and plastics (q.v.), including acetic acid (q.v.), butyl alcohol, chloral, and pyridine. It is miscible (mixable) in all proportions with water and most common organic solvents and is manufactured by the oxidation of ethyl alcohol or by the combination of water with acetylene. About half of the acetaldehyde produced in the U.S. is used in the manufacture of acetic acid. Acetaldehyde melts at $-123.5°$ C ($-190.3°$ F), boils at 20.8° C (69.4° F), and has a density of 0.778 g per ml at 20° C (68° F).

**ACETAMINOPHEN,** nonprescription drug used for the relief of minor pain, such as headaches and structural muscle aches, and for the reduction of fever. Like the other common analgesic (q.v.) drugs aspirin and ibuprofen, acetaminophen relieves pain by inhibiting the synthesis of prostaglandins (q.v.) in the body. It does not reduce inflammation as do those other two analgesics, but it also does not irritate the stomach lining, as aspirin tends to do for some users. A large overdose of acetaminophen may cause severe liver damage.

**ACETATE,** common name for a salt or ester of acetic acid (q.v.). The salts are formed by reacting acetic acid with a base, such as a metal hydroxide. The esters are formed by reacting the acid with an alcohol. The ester cellulose acetate, referred to commercially simply as acetate, is used in fabrics, fibers, and films (*see* CELLULOSE).

*See also* PLASTICS.

**ACETIC ACID,** common name of ethanoic acid, $CH_3COOH$, a colorless liquid with a sharp, irritating odor and sour taste. In aqueous solution, it functions as a weak acid. Pure acetic acid, because it freezes at slightly below ordinary room temperature, is called glacial acetic acid; mixtures of acetic acid with water solidify at much lower temperatures. Acetic acid is miscible (mixable) in all proportions with water and with many organic solvents.

Acetic acid can be prepared by the action of air on solutions of alcohol in the presence of bacteria (*Bacterium aceti*). Dilute solutions (4 to 8 percent) prepared in this way from wine, cider, or malt are called vinegar. Concentrated acetic acid is prepared industrially by the destructive distillation of wood. It is also produced synthetically by the oxidation of acetaldehyde (q.v.).

Acetic acid is used in the production of acetate rayon, plastics, photographic film, paint solvents, and pharmaceuticals such as aspirin. It boils at 118° C (245° F) and melts at 17° C (62° F).

**ACETIC ANHYDRIDE,** colorless, volatile, mobile (free-flowing) liquid, $(CH_3CO)_2O$, with an irritating odor. It is primarily employed as an intermediate in the manufacture of industrial chemicals, pharmaceuticals, perfumes, plastics (q.v.), synthetic fibers, explosives, weed killers, and other chemical products. It is manufactured by the dehydration of acetic acid or by the oxidation of acetaldehyde (q.v). About 75 percent of the acetic anhydride produced annually in the U.S. is used for the manufacture of cellulose acetate, and about 1.5 percent is used for the manufacture of aspirin (q.v.). Acetic anhydride melts at $-73°$ C ($-99.4°$ F), boils at 139.6° C (283.3° F), and has a density of 1.082 g per ml.

**ACETONE,** a colorless, flammable liquid, $CH_3COCH_3$, the simplest of the organic chemicals called ketones (q.v.). Completely soluble in water and organic solvents, acetone is itself an important solvent and is used both in the laboratory and in industry. Also called dimethyl ketone and 2-propanone, it has a mild, pleasant odor, boils at 56° C (133° F), and melts at –95° C (–139° F). Enormous quantities are used as solvents for cellulose acetate in the production of rayon and as a gelatinizing agent for explosives. Acetone is also used as an ingredient in lacquer solvent and to dissolve gums and resins. It is the solvent in rubber cement and in some cleaning fluids. Acetone can be prepared in the laboratory by oxidation of isopropyl alcohol or by heating of calcium acetate. Most acetone is obtained by synthesizing it from petroleum or by fermenting sugar with certain bacteria.

**ACETYLCHOLINE,** compound in the body of a vertebrate animal that functions as a neurotransmitter, conducting electrical impulses across synapses between nerve cells, and from nerve cells to muscle cells, causing the muscle cells to contract. The effect of acetylcholine is then neutralized by an enzyme, such as cholinesterase.

*See* BRAIN; NEUROPHYSIOLOGY.

**ACETYLENE,** colorless, odorless, flammable gas, $HC \equiv CH$, slightly lighter than air. As ordinarily prepared it has an unpleasant odor due to impurities. Acetylene, also known as ethyne, can be prepared from any of various organic compounds by heating them in the absence of air, but it is usually made commercially by the reaction of calcium carbide with water. Although acetylene can be liquefied at ordinary temperatures with high pressure, it is violently explosive as a liquid. Acetylene gas is usually stored in metal tanks, under pressure, dissolved in liquid acetone (q.v.). When acetylene is bubbled through a solution of ammonia and cuprous chloride, copper acetylide, a reddish precipitate, is formed. This is used as a test for acetylene. Copper acetylide is explosive when dry.

Acetylene burns in air with a hot and brilliant flame. It was formerly much used as an illuminant and is now mainly used in the oxyacetylene torch, in which acetylene is burned in oxygen, producing a very hot flame used for welding and cutting metal. Acetylene is also used in chemical synthesis, particularly in the manufacture of vinyl chloride for plastics, acetaldehyde, and the neoprene type of synthetic rubber. Acetylene has a melting point of –81.8° C (–115.2° F) and a boiling point of –88.5° C (–127.3° F).

**ACHAEAN LEAGUE,** confederation of 10 or 12 Greek towns established originally by the ancient Achaeans, a Greek-speaking people living on the northern coast of the Peloponnesus, the peninsula forming the southern part of Greece. The original league played little part in the wars of the 5th century BC but, toward the end of the 4th century BC, it was conquered by the Macedonians. By 280 BC, more than forty years after the death of Alexander the Great and the subsequent internal strife in Macedonia, the Achaean League was reestablished. The confederacy was further strengthened by the addition (251–229 BC) of Sicyon, Corinth, Megalopólis, and Argos.

The Achaean League was a federation. Each member state or town of the league was autonomous, but all members participated in a council that met twice a year to formulate common foreign policy and to enact legislation involving economic matters, such as coinage. The leading statesmen of the Achaean League included the generals Aratus of Sicyon (271–213 BC) and Philopoemen of Megalopólis (c. 253–182 BC).

About 235 BC Cleomenes III (260?–219 BC), king of Sparta, provoked a war with the league in an attempt to force the Achaeans into a Peloponnesian federation. After two serious defeats the Achaeans asked and received help from Macedonia. Cleomenes III was finally defeated at Sellasia in 222 BC. As the price of aid from the former enemy, Achaea again became subject to Macedonia. About 198 BC the Achaeans allied themselves with the Romans against the Macedonians. During the next 40 years the Romans completely subjugated the league, together with the rest of Greece; in 168 BC they took 1000 Achaeans to Rome as hostages, among them the Greek historian Polybius. In 146 BC Achaea became a Roman province that encompassed all of Greece south of Thessaly and Macedonia.

*See also* AETOLIAN LEAGUE.

**ACHAEANS,** people of Achaea, an ancient region in the northern Peloponnesus, Greece. The term was broadly used by Homer to designate all the inhabitants of ancient Greece. According to Greek mythology, the Achaeans were descendants of Achaeus, grandson of Hellen, the legendary ancestor of the Hellenes, or Greeks.

References to the western kingdom of Ahhiawa in Hittite documents of the 13th and 14th centuries BC have been thought by some scholars to refer to the city of Mycenae under Achaean domination. These documents characterize the Achaeans as a maritime people inhabiting western Asia Minor and the island of Lésvos in the Aegean Sea. In the Homeric period (c. 11th cent. BC) the Achaeans controlled southern Thessaly and most of the Peloponnesus, but from the 6th century to the 4th century BC they were restricted to a narrow strip on the north coast of the Peloponnesus. *See* ACHAEAN LEAGUE.

**ACHAEMENIDS,** ruling dynasty of Persia from about 550 BC to 330 BC. It was named for Achaemenes (Hakhamanish; fl. 681 BC), a minor ruler of Anshan (in southwestern Iran), but the real founder of the dynasty was his great-great-grandson, Cyrus the Great, creator of the Persian Empire. At the zenith of their power, under Darius I, called the Great, the Achaemenids ruled an empire extending from the Indus River in the east to Libya and Thrace in the west and from the Persian Gulf in the south to the Caucasus and the Jaxartes River (modern Syr Darya) in the north. They provided Persia with superb administration, a comprehensive code of laws, reliable currency, and efficient postal service. Although Zoroastrians themselves, they were tolerant of other religions, and under their rule art and architecture flourished. The dynasty ended with the death of Darius III.

**ACHATES,** in Roman mythology, the constant companion of the Trojan hero Aeneas.

**ACHEBE, Chinua** (1930– ), Nigerian novelist and poet, whose first novel, *Things Fall Apart* (1958), set the theme for his subsequent work: the impact of Western influences on traditional African society. Achebe's other works include *The Arrow of God* (1964), and *A Man of the People* (1966). Unsentimental, often ironic, they vividly convey tribal culture and the very speech of the Ibo people. Achebe's later works include a short-story collection, *Girls at War* (1972), and *Christmas in Biafra and Other Poems* (1973). Since 1971 he has been coeditor of *Okike,* one of Africa's most influential literary magazines.

**ACHERON,** in Greek mythology, river in Hades. It was also the name of a river in southern Epirus, Greece, which flowed underground for part of the 58-km (36-mi) course to the Ionian Sea.

**ACHESON, Dean Gooderham** (1893–1971), American statesman, born in Middletown, Conn., and educated at Yale University and Harvard Law School. From 1919 to 1921, he was private secretary to Louis D. Brandeis, associate justice of the U.S. Supreme Court. In 1933 he served as undersecretary of the treasury. He was assistant secretary of state (1941–45), under secretary (1945–47), and secretary of state (1949–53) under President Harry S. Truman. As secretary of state, Acheson continued the policies of his predecessor, George C. Marshall, most notably in the implementation of the European Recovery Program. He also represented the U.S. in the negotiations leading to the establishment of the North Atlantic Treaty Organization (NATO). In 1961 he was named head of an advisory group on U.S. policy toward NATO. Acheson received the U.S.

Presidential Medal of Freedom in 1964. Among his writings are *Power and Diplomacy* (1958) and *Present at the Creation: My Years in the State Department* (1969), for which he received the 1970 Pulitzer Prize in history.

**ACHILLES,** in Greek mythology, greatest of the Greek warriors in the Trojan War. He was the son of the sea nymph Thetis and Peleus, king of the Myrmidons of Thessaly. When he was a child his mother dipped him into the River Styx to make him immortal. The waters made him invulnerable except for the heel by which his mother held him. Achilles fought many battles during the 10-year siege of Troy. When the Mycenaean king Agamemnon seized the captive maiden Briseis from him, Achilles withdrew the Myrmidons from battle and sulked in his tent. The Trojans, emboldened by his absence, attacked the Greeks and drove them into headlong retreat. Then Patroclus, Achilles' friend and companion, begged Achilles to lend him his armor and let him lead the Myrmidons into battle. Achilles consented. When Patroclus was killed by the Trojan prince Hector, the grief-stricken Achilles returned to battle, slew Hector, and dragged his body in triumph behind his chariot. He later permitted Priam, king of Troy, to ransom Hector's body. Achilles fought his last battle with Memnon, king of the Ethiopians. After killing the king, Achilles led the Greeks to the walls of Troy. There he was mortally wounded in the heel by Paris. The quarrel between Achilles and Agamemnon, the subsequent battle, and the ransoming of Hector's body are recounted in the *Iliad.*

**ACHILLES TENDON,** in the legs of mammals, powerful, cordlike band of connective tissue that joins the fused muscles of the calf to the bone of the heel. Because bones are moved by muscles pulling on the connecting tendon, severance or rupture of the Achilles tendon results in immediate loss of the normal use of the leg and foot. The name of the tendon is derived from the legendary Greek warrior Achilles.

**ACHIN** (Indonesian *Atjeh* or *Aceh*), former sultanate, in the northwestern portion of the island of Sumatra. Originally a dependency of the neighboring state of Pedir, Achin became an independent sultanate during the first quarter of the 16th century; it was most powerful between 1607 and 1636. Imperialist rivalries among Portugal, Great Britain, and the Netherlands for control of Achin dominated its history during the remainder of the 17th century.

In 1819 the British government acquired exclusive trading privileges with the sultanate, but a subsequent Anglo-Dutch agreement (1824) made the sultanate virtually a protectorate of the

Netherlands. Achinese resistance to Dutch control culminated in a long and bitter conflict (1873–1908), which recurred at intervals until the establishment after World War II of the Republic of Indonesia. During this period the Dutch succeeded in subjugating only the coastal areas.

**ACHROMATISM,** in optics, property of a lens system of bending a beam of white light in such a way that all its component colors are brought to a focus at the same point, thus obtaining a sharp image. A single lens cannot achieve achromatic focus because different wavelengths of light are bent by differing amounts as they pass through the lens. For achromatic focus, at least two lenses that are made of glass with different refractive indexes must be combined. This principle was discovered in 1757 by John Dollond (1706–61), a British optician.

**ACIDOSIS.** See BLOOD: *Composition of Blood.*

**ACID RAIN,** form of air pollution (q.v.), currently a subject of great controversy because of widespread environmental damage for which it has been blamed. It forms when oxides of sulfur and nitrogen combine with atmospheric moisture to yield sulfuric and nitric acids, which may then be carried long distances from their source before they are deposited by rain. The pollution may also take the form of snow or fog or be precipitated in dry forms. In fact, although the term "acid rain" has been in use for more than a century—it is derived from atmospheric studies that were made in the region of Manchester, England—the more accurate scientific term would be "acid deposition." The dry form of such precipitation is just as damaging to the environment as the liquid form.

The problem of acid rain may be said to have originated with the Industrial Revolution, and it has been growing ever since. The severity of its effects has long been recognized in local settings, as exemplified by the spells of acid smog in heavily industrialized areas. The wide destructiveness of acid rain, however, has come to be realized only in recent decades. One large area that has been studied extensively is northern Europe, where acid rain has eroded structures, injured crops and forests, and threatened or depleted life in freshwater lakes. In 1983, for example, published reports indicated that 34 percent of the forested areas of West Germany had been damaged by acid rain. The northeastern U.S. and eastern Canada have also been affected by this form of pollution, as well as other areas of these countries and other regions of the world.

Industrial emissions have been blamed as the major cause of acid rain. Because the chemical reactions involved in the production of acid rain in the atmosphere are complex and as yet little understood, industries have challenged such assessments and stressed the need for further studies; and because of the cost of pollution reduction, governments have tended to support this attitude. U.S. government studies released in the early 1980s, however, strongly implicated industries as the main source of acid rain in the eastern U.S. and Canada. In 1988, as part of the UN-sponsored Long-Range Transboundary Air Pollution Agreement, the U.S., along with 24 other nations, ratified a protocol freezing the rate of nitrogen oxides emissions at 1987 levels. The 1990 amendments to the Clean Air Act of 1967 put in place regulations to reduce the release of sulfur dioxide from power plants to 10 million tons per year by Jan. 1, 2000. This amount is about one-half the emissions of 1990.

*For further information on this topic, see the Bibliography in volume 28, sections 566, 568.*

**ACIDS AND BASES,** two classes of chemical compounds that display generally opposite characteristics. Acids taste sour, turn litmus (a pink dye derived from lichens) red, and often react with some metals to produce hydrogen gas. Bases taste bitter, turn litmus blue, and feel slippery. When aqueous (water) solutions of an acid and a base are combined, a neutralization reaction occurs. This reaction is characteristically very rapid and generally produces water and a salt. For example, sulfuric acid and sodium hydroxide, NaOH, yield water and sodium sulfate:

$$H_2SO_4 + 2NaOH \rightleftarrows 2H_2O + Na_2SO_4$$

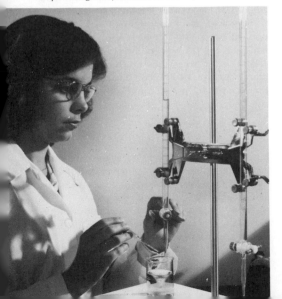

*Titration, a common laboratory procedure, is used to determine the concentration of an acid or a base in a sample being analyzed (the unknown).*  Union Carbide

# ACIDS AND BASES

**Early Theories.** Modern understanding of acids and bases began with the discovery in 1834 by the English physicist Michael Faraday that acids, bases, and salts are electrolytes. That is, when they are dissolved in water, they produce a solution that contains charged particles, or ions, and can conduct an electric current (*see* IONIZATION). In 1884 the Swedish chemist Svante Arrhenius (and later Wilhelm Ostwald, a German chemist) proposed that an acid be defined as a hydrogen-containing compound that, when dissolved in water, produces a concentration of hydrogen ions, or protons, greater than that of pure water. Similarly, Arrhenius proposed that a base be defined as a substance that, when dissolved in water, produces an excess of hydroxyl ions, $OH^-$. The neutralization reaction then becomes:

$$H^+ + OH^- \rightleftarrows H_2O$$

A number of criticisms of the Arrhenius-Ostwald theory have been made. First, acids are restricted to hydrogen-containing species and bases to hydroxyl-containing species. Second, the theory applies to aqueous solutions exclusively, whereas many acid-base reactions are known to take place in the absence of water.

**Brönsted-Lowry Theory.** A more satisfactory theory was proposed in 1923 by the Danish chemist Johannes Brönsted and independently by Thomas Lowry (1874–1936), a British chemist. Their theory states that an acid is a proton (hydrogen ion, $H^+$) donor and a base a proton acceptor. Although the acid must still contain hydrogen, the Brönsted-Lowry theory does not require an aqueous medium. For example, liquid ammonia, which acts as a base in aqueous solution, can act as an acid in the absence of water by transferring a proton to a base and forming the amide anion (negative ion) $NH_2^-$:

$$NH_3 + base \rightleftarrows NH_2^- + base = H^+$$

The Brönsted-Lowry definition of acids and bases also explains why a strong acid displaces a weak acid from its compounds (and likewise for strong and weak bases). Here acid-base reactions are viewed as a competition for protons. In terms of a general chemical equation, the reaction of Acid (1) with Base (2)

$$Acid\ (1) + Base\ (2) \rightleftarrows Acid\ (2) + Base\ (1)$$

results in the transfer of a proton from Acid (1) to Base (2). In losing the proton, Acid (1) becomes its conjugate base, Base (1). In gaining a proton, Base (2) becomes its conjugate acid, Acid (2). The equilibrium represented by the equation above may be displaced either to the left or to the right, and the actual reaction will take place in the direction that produces the weaker acid-base pair. For example, HCl is a strong acid in water because it readily transfers a proton to water to form a hydronium ion:

$$HCl + H_2O \rightleftarrows H_3O^+ + Cl^-$$

The equilibrium lies mostly to the right because the conjugate base of HCl, $Cl^-$, is a weak base, and $H_3O^+$, the conjugate acid of $H_2O$, is a weak acid.

In contrast, hydrogen fluoride, HF, is a weak acid in water because it does not readily transfer a proton to water:

$$HF + H_2O \rightleftarrows H_3O^+ + F^-$$

This equilibrium lies mostly to the left because $H_2O$ is a weaker base than $F^-$, and because HF is a weaker acid (in water) than $H_3O^+$. The Brönsted-Lowry theory also explains why water can be amphoteric, that is, why it can serve as either an acid or a base. Water serves as a base in the presence of an acid that is stronger than water (such as HCl), in other words, an acid that has a greater tendency to dissociate than does water:

$$HCl + H_2O \rightleftarrows H_3O^+ + Cl^-$$

Water can also serve as an acid in the presence of a base that is stronger than water (such as ammonia):

$$NH_3 + H_2O \rightleftarrows NH_4^+ + OH^-$$

**Measuring Acid or Base Strength.** The strength of an acid can be measured by the extent to which an acid transfers a proton to water to produce the hydronium ion, $H_3O^+$. Conversely, the strength of a base is indicated by the extent to which the base removes a proton from water. A convenient acid-base scale is calculated from the amount of $H_3O^+$ that is formed in water solutions of acids or of $OH^-$ formed in water solutions of bases. The former is known as the pH scale and the latter as the pOH scale (*see* pH). The value for pH is equal to the negative logarithm (q.v.) of the hydronium ion concentration—and for pOH, of the hydroxyl ion concentration—in an aqueous solution:

$$pH = -\log [H_3O^+]$$
$$pOH = -\log [OH^-]$$

Pure water has a pH of 7.0. When an acid is added, the hydronium ion concentration $[H_3O^+]$ becomes larger than that in pure water, and the pH becomes less than 7.0, depending on the strength of the acid. The pOH of pure water is also 7.0, and in the presence of a base, the pOH drops to values lower than 7.0.

The American chemist Gilbert N. Lewis has offered another theory of acids and bases that has the further advantage of not requiring the acid to contain hydrogen. This theory states that acids are electron-pair acceptors and bases are electron-pair donors. This theory also has the advantages that it works when solvents other than water are involved and it does not require the formation of a salt or of acid-base conjugate pairs. Thus, ammonia is viewed as a base because it can donate an electron pair to the acid boron trifluoride, for example

$$H_3N: + BF_3 \rightleftarrows H_3N{-}BF_3$$

to form an acid-base association pair.     P.L.G.

*For further information on this topic, see the Bibliography in volume 28, section 406.*

**ACKLINS ISLAND.**   *See* BAHAMAS.

**ACKNOWLEDGMENT,** in law in the U.S., the act of avowing before a proper officer or a court that one has executed a legal instrument, and of obtaining a certificate that admits the instrument as evidence in a legal proceeding without further proof of its genuineness. A commissioner of deeds or notary public is the regular officer before whom acknowledgments are made, although judges, clerks of court, mayors of cities, and in some states aldermen and justices of the peace are authorized to take acknowledgments. In all cases the acknowledgment must be signed by the person in whose presence it is made.

**ACLINIC LINE,** also magnetic equator, imaginary line on the surface of the earth approximately parallel to the geographical equator. A magnetic dipping needle shows no declination at this line. The line's location changes slightly each year.

**ACNE,** eruptive skin disease. It is primarily a disorder of the sebaceous follicles of the skin and appears most often on the face, neck, and back. The natural secretion, or sebum, of the follicles accumulates and mixes with dust and dirt. The follicles and surrounding tissue become inflamed and blackheads appear. If the follicle opening completely closes, the accumulated sebum is degraded by bacteria and forms a cyst.

Acne vulgaris, the most common form, is usually associated with adolescence but may also occur in adults. A severe form of the disorder is known as acne conglobata. Other forms of acne are also observed, such as the chloracne caused by chlorinated compounds. In acne rosacea, the capillaries in the cheeks, forehead, and nose are swollen with blood and the oil glands in the skin become infected.

Acne in adolescence results primarily from hormonal changes taking place in the body; the hormones stimulate sebum production. Outbreaks cannot be prevented by a controlled diet and are not a sign of uncleanliness. Good hygiene

should be observed, however, to prevent more serious infections. Severe acne may be treated by antibiotics, benzoyl peroxide, or vitamin A derivatives. Severe acne in adults may be a sign of an underlying endocrine disorder.

**ACOLYTE,** in some Christian churches, a layperson who assists the clergy during religious services by performing minor duties. Acolytes may be either adults (sometimes called servers) or young people (sometimes called altar boys or altar girls). In the Roman Catholic church, the term also applies to an official church ministry in which a man is officially installed to assist the deacon and priest. This ministry was considered one of the minor orders until 1972, when Pope Paul VI eliminated all minor orders.

**ACOMA,** American Indian pueblo (village), part of the Pueblo Indian Reservation, in Valencia Co., W central New Mexico. The small population of Keresan-speaking Indians who inhabit the pueblo live in long, terraced dwellings made of stone and adobe atop a steep sandstone mesa 109 m (357 ft) high. Founded about AD 1075, the pueblo is considered the oldest continuously occupied settlement in the U.S. and is a National Historic Landmark. Some cultivation and grazing are carried on in the plain below the mesa, but pottery is Acoma's major product. The pueblo was discovered by the Spanish in 1540 and was conquered by them about 1599. Not completely subdued, the residents took part in the Pueblo Rebellion of 1680. The community's name is derived from the Keresan word *Akome,* meaning "people of the white rock." San Esteban Rey Mission, built in the early 17th century, is here.

**ACONCAGUA,** mountain peak, W Argentina, highest of the Andes (q.v.) and of the western hemisphere, near the border with Chile. An extinct volcano, it is 6960 m (22,834 ft) high. The first ascent to the summit was made in 1897.

**ACONITE,** common name for perennial herbs of the genus *Aconitum* and for a preparation derived from them that was formerly used in medicine. The genus, with more than 100 species, belongs to the family Ranunculaceae (*see* BUTTERCUP) and is native to temperate regions of the northern hemisphere. Several species, including *A. napellus,* a well-known European species, are cultivated as garden plants in the U.S. The common aconites have fibrous or tuberous roots, mostly erect stems, and palmately divided or cleft leaves. The flowers in most aconite species are blue or purple, although some species have yellow or white flowers. The outer, showy parts of the bilaterally symmetrical flower are five in number, and the uppermost is shaped like a large, downward-opening hood. Because of this hood, which immediately distinguishes aconite from larkspur, aconites are commonly called monkshood. They are also known as wolfsbane.

Aconites contain highly active alkaloids, especially aconitine, and are poisonous to both humans and animals. *A. napellus* has long been considered one of the most dangerous plants of Europe. When eaten in small to moderate amounts, roots produce symptoms of restlessness, salivation, nausea, a weakened and irregular heartbeat, chest pain, prostration, and frequently death within hours.

**ACORN.** *See* OAK.

**ACORN WORM,** common name for simple, wormlike marine animals of the phylum Hemichordata. They are of special interest because of their close relationship to the phylum Chordata, which includes all vertebrates, including humans. This connection is evident in the adult anatomy. Some representative acorn worms have gill slits, traces of a supporting structure resembling a notochord, and a tubular nerve cord, which· are features characteristic of vertebrates (*see* VERTEBRATE). The larval stages of acorn worms, however, are very much like those of echinoderms such as starfish, indicating a remote common ancestry of echinoderms and vertebrates (*see* ECHINODERM).

The hemichordates are divided into 2 classes comprising about 50 species. The class Enteropneusta, the acorn worms, consists of animals that average 10 cm (4 in) long, but some are 1.5 m (5 ft). They construct burrows, commonly U-shaped, in sand of shallow seafloors, using an extendable, muscular proboscis attached to a thick collar that resembles an acorn—hence the name. They secrete a slime that collects food particles on the proboscis and collar, but some species filter sediments and sand through a complicated pharynx with many gill slits. The rare class Pterobranchia consists of small, usually colonial animals of the deep sea. They are not worm-shaped but stout, and they usually construct tubes. Food is captured by tentacles that project from the tube. The body is much simplified, and gill slits are reduced to one pair or none.                                          M.T.G.

**ACOSTA, José de** (1539?–1600), Spanish missionary and writer, born in Medina del Campo. He became a Jesuit in 1551, and 20 years later he became a missionary in Peru, serving as provincial of his order from 1576 to 1581. His catechism in the language of the Aymara and Quechua Indians was the first book printed (1583) in Peru. He became rector of the Jesuit college at Salamanca, Spain, in 1598. He is remembered chiefly for his monumental book about the natural history and aboriginal customs of Spanish America, *Natural and Moral History of the Indians* (1590; trans. 1604), which was translated into most of the major European languages within 15 years of publication.

**ACOSTA, Uriel** (c. 1585–1640), Portuguese Jewish rationalist. Born into a family of Marranos (Christianized Jews) in Oporto, he was named Gabriel da Costa and was educated as a Roman Catholic. When he was 21, however, he returned to Judaism and was received into the Jewish congregation at Amsterdam, adopting the name Uriel Acosta. After a period of controversy with his fellow religionists—he denied the immortality of the soul and the validity of revealed religion, advocating religion based on reason—he was charged with atheism and was excommunicated. He wrote his autobiography, *Exemplar Humanae Vitae* (Ideal of Human Life, 1687), shortly before committing suicide.

**ACOUSTICS** (Gr. *akouein*, "to hear"), term sometimes used for the science of sound in general, but more commonly for the special branch of that science, architectural acoustics, that deals with the construction of enclosed areas so as to enhance the hearing of speech or music. For the treatment of acoustics as a branch of the pure science of physics, *see* SOUND.

The acoustics of buildings was an undeveloped aspect of the study of sound until comparatively recent times. The Roman architect Marcus Pollio, who lived during the 1st century BC, made some pertinent observations on the subject and some astute guesses concerning reverberation and interference. The scientific aspects of this subject, however, were first thoroughly treated by the American physicist Joseph Henry in 1856 and more fully developed by the American physicist Wallace Sabine (1868–1919) in 1900.

**Problems of Design.** Acoustical design must take into consideration that in addition to physiological peculiarities of the ear, hearing is complicated by psychological peculiarities. For example, sounds that are unfamiliar seem unnatural. Sound produced in an ordinary room is somewhat modified by reverberations due to reflections from walls and furniture; for this reason, a broadcasting studio should have a normal degree of reverberation to ensure natural reproduction of sound. For best acoustic qualities, rooms are designed to produce sufficient reflections for naturalness, without introducing excessive reverberation at any frequency, without echoing certain frequencies unnaturally, and without producing undesirable interference effects or distortion.

The Central Target Simulation (CTS) anechoic chamber at the Naval Research Laboratory is used to test electronic equipment.　　　　Naval Research Laboratory–Dan Boyd

The time required for a sound to diminish to one-millionth of its original intensity is called reverberation time. An appreciable reverberation time improves acoustical effect, especially for music; a loud sound should still be barely audible for one to two seconds after the sound has stopped in an auditorium. In a private home a shorter but still discernible reverberation time is desirable.

**Materials.** For modifying the reverberations, the architect has two types of materials, sound-absorbent and sound-reflecting, to coat the surfaces of ceilings, walls, and floors. Soft materials such as cork and felt absorb most of the sound that strikes them, although they may reflect some of the low-frequency sounds. Hard materials such as stone and metals reflect most of the sound that strikes them. The acoustics of a large auditorium may be very different when it is full from when it is empty; empty seats reflect sound, whereas an audience absorbs sound.

In most cases, the acoustics of a room will be satisfactory if a proper balance between sound-absorbing and sound-reflecting materials is created. Troublesome echoes may frequently occur in a room that otherwise has a proper overall reverberation time if the ceiling or a wall is concave in shape and is highly reflecting; in such cases, sound may be focused at a particular point, making the acoustics bad at that point in the room. Similarly, a narrow corridor between parallel reflecting walls may trap sound by repeated reflection and cause troublesome echoes, even though the overall absorption is sufficient. Attention must also be given to the elimination of interference. Such interference arises from the difference in the distances traversed by the direct and the reflected sound and produces so-called dead spots, in which certain ranges of frequency

are canceled out. Reproduction of sound picked up by microphones also requires the elimination of echoes and interference.

**Insulation.** Another aspect of room acoustics is insulation from unwanted sound. This is obtained by sealing even the smallest openings that can leak sound, by using massive walls, and by building unconnected walls separated by dead spaces.

To evaluate the acoustical properties of rooms and materials, the acoustical scientist uses tools such as anechoic chambers and sound-level meters. The anechoic chamber is a room free from echoes and reverberations in which all sound is absorbed by glass-fiber wedges placed on the surfaces of the walls. A sound-level meter measures sound intensity, the rate of flow of sound energy, which is related to the loudness of a sound, and expresses the result in decibels (dB), a logarithmic unit. In a quiet residence the sound-level meter would read about 38 dB. An ordinary conversation would increase the sound level reading to about 70 dB. The sound intensity of an air-raid siren could reach about 150 dB; a jet-airplane noise, around 120 dB. When perceived sound intensity is doubled, its power level increases by 10 times, or 10 dB. Loudness levels, which depend upon the judgment of the listener, are measured in sones and phons.

*See also* SOUND RECORDING AND REPRODUCTION.

*For further information on this topic, see the Bibliography in volume 28, section 394.*

**ACQUIRED IMMUNE DEFICIENCY SYNDROME** (AIDS), disease that renders the body's immune system (q.v.) unable to resist invasion by several microorganisms that cause serious infections. It is usually characterized by severe weight loss and fatigue, and frequently by neurological complications due to damage of cells of the brain. There is also a high incidence of certain cancers, especially Kaposi's sarcoma, which shows up as purple lesions on the skin, and tumors known as B-cell lymphomas.

AIDS is transmitted by blood, through intimate sexual contact, from infected mothers to their babies in the uterus, and perhaps through infected mother's milk. Before a reliable test for screening blood was developed, a major route of transmission was through receiving transfusions of contaminated blood. A leading means of transmission and spread of the virus is through the use of blood-contaminated needles by intravenous drug abusers. Casual contact in general is not a risk factor for infection, and blood donors are definitely not at risk of catching the disease. The virus usually remains dormant for some time in infected T cells, and it may take up to 10 years for symptoms to develop.

Several strains of the AIDS virus have been isolated, and it appears to be continually changing in genetic makeup and, thus, its envelope, against which a person's immune system can make antibodies. This makes development of a vaccine that is able to raise protective antibodies to all virus strains an extremely difficult task. Nevertheless, dramatic progress has been made in AIDS research in a very short time in identifying the molecular makeup of the AIDS virus, its modes of transmission, and the mechanisms by which the virus produces the full-blown disease.

Much research centers on solving the problems of treating people who already have AIDS and those who have been infected with the virus but have not yet developed the syndrome. The first chemical that has shown to be partially effective in reducing clinical symptoms and controlling viral replication, zidovudine, formerly called azidothymidine (AZT), was developed in 1986–87. The fatality rate of those with AIDS indicates that few, if any, individuals with AIDS are likely to survive in the long run, until some adequate treatment is developed.

AIDS raises many legal, ethical, and civil rights issues. Among these are mandatory testing of all citizens or of particular populations (for example, marriage license applicants); discrimination in housing, employment, and medical treatment; and confidentiality versus notification of sex partners.

The first case of AIDS was identified in New York in 1979. The cause of the disease, a retrovirus (q.v.) now called human immunodeficiency virus (HIV; see HTLV), was identified in 1983–84 by scientists working at the National Cancer Institute in the U.S. and the Pasteur Institute in France. These workers also developed tests for AIDS, enabling researchers to follow the transmission of the virus and to study the origin and mechanism of the disease. Close relatives of the AIDS virus infect some African monkeys. This fact and the high incidence of infection of people in central Africa has led to the opinion that the AIDS virus originated there. In 1993 the World Health Organization announced that 611,589 cases of AIDS were reported worldwide by the end of 1992, and estimated the actual number of cases to be 13 million. R.C.G.

*For further information on this topic, see the Bibliography in volume 28, section 510.*

**ACQUITTAL,** in criminal law, judicial discharge of the accused. Acquittal automatically follows a determination by a judge or jury that the defendant is not guilty of the charge on which he or she was tried. After accused persons have been acquitted they may not lawfully be prosecuted a second time for the same act. Such a prosecution would place them in double jeopardy of losing their life, liberty, or property in violation of common law and of the U.S. and state constitutions. Protection against double jeopardy normally extends to any prosecution based on the same acts. Thus, if the accused has been acquitted on a charge of using a weapon to commit a murder, he or she may not be retried for having committed an assault on the alleged victim. If a trial is terminated because of procedural defect, however, the defendant is not protected by the rule against double jeopardy and may be prosecuted again on the same or a related charge.

**ACRE,** also Akko, city, W Israel, on the Bay of Haifa, near Haifa. An ancient seaport, it is one of the oldest continuously inhabited cities in the world. Founded before 1500 BC, it first appears in recorded history during the reign (1504–1450 BC) of the pharaoh Thutmose III. The town was captured by the Assyrians around 700 BC and practically depopulated under Ashurbanipal. In 332 BC it was incorporated into the empire of Alexander the Great. Ptolemy II, king of Egypt, seized the city in the 3d century BC and from that time until the Middle Ages it was known as Ptolemais. During the pre-Christian era, Acre was an important trading center and was successively a part of Syria and a colony of Rome.

After the permanent division of the Roman Empire in AD 395, Acre belonged to the Eastern (later Byzantine) Empire. The Arabs seized it in 638 and held it until its capture by King Baldwin I of Jerusalem in 1104. Saladin, sultan of Egypt and Syria, recaptured Acre in 1187, but the town was subsequently recovered by the Europeans during the Third Crusade. In 1291, after a long siege, Acre fell to the Saracens. The Ottoman Turks took possession of it in 1517. In 1918 it was captured by British troops and was included in the British mandate of Palestine. Acre was taken by the Israeli army in 1948 and incorporated into the state of Israel the following year. The town is now the center of the Israeli steel industry. Pop. (1992 est.) 41,600.

**ACROBATICS.** *See* GYMNASTICS.

**ACROMEGALY,** chronic disease marked by overgrowth of hands, feet, and lower part of the face, resulting from excessive production of somatotropin, the growth-stimulating hormone (*see* HORMONE). In many cases, oversecretion of the hormone can be traced to a tumor of the pituitary gland. Acromegaly is accompanied by progressive weakness and sometimes by diabetes mellitus; on occasion it occurs during lactation. The disease usually appears in adulthood and frequently affects more than one member of a family. Treatment generally consists of microsurgical removal

*The ruins of the Parthenon (center) and other buildings on the Acropolis bear witness to the glory of ancient Greece.*
© 1988 J. Messerschmidt–Bruce Coleman, Inc.

of hyperfunctioning tissue, pituitary irradiation, and drugs that suppress growth hormone. A similar disorder, gigantism, occurs in children, producing overgrowth of the long bones of the body. A deficiency in growth hormone production results in dwarfism, a condition marked by abnormally short bone development.

**ACROPOLIS** (Gr. *akros,* "highest"; *polis,* "city"), term originally applied to any fortified natural stronghold or citadel in ancient Greece. Primarily a place of refuge, the typical acropolis was built on a hill or eminence rising from the surrounding region. Because of this protection, the area adjacent to the base of the hill often became the site of a city. These acropolises include Acrocorinth at Corinth and the Cadmea at Thebes.

Lower defense walls were erected in certain cities, with the result that the acropolises, no longer useful as military bastions, were used as sites for temples and public buildings. The citadel of ancient Athens is traditionally referred to as the Acropolis. Built on a limestone hill about 150 m (about 500 ft) high, it dominates the city and houses the remains of some of the finest extant examples of classical architecture. Included are remains of the Parthenon, a Doric temple; the Propylaea, a monumental marble gateway on the west and the main entrance to the Acropolis; the Erechtheum, a temple famous for perfect detail; and the temple of Athena Nike. These were built in the Golden Age of Athens during the reign of Pericles. Later damaged and neglected, some were gradually restored after the Greek monarchy was established in 1833.

**ACROSTIC** (from Gr. *akros,* "pointed, first"; *stichos,* "a row"), group of phrases, words, or most often, verses, the first letters of which when taken consecutively form a word, name, phrase, or other predetermined entity. If a series of final or internal letters forms an additional such entity, it is termed a double acrostic. The acrostic was combined with the crossword puzzle to form the modern Double-Crostic.

**ACRYLIC,** chemical name for the organic group $H_2C{=}CHCO{-}$, which occurs in acrylic acid, $H_2C{=}CHCOOH$, and in the esters of this acid, called acrylates, such as methyl acrylate, $H_2C{=}CHCOOCH_3$. Acrylic resins, often called acrylics, are made by the polymerization of acrylates or other monomers containing the acrylic group. Acrylic compounds are thermoplastic (able to soften or fuse when heated and reharden upon cooling), impervious to water, and have low densities. These qualities make them suitable for the manufacture of a variety of objects and substances, including molded structural materials, adhesives, and textile fibers. Such fibers are used to weave durable, easily laundered fabrics that resist shrinkage. Acrylic paints—emulsions of pigments, water, and clear, nonyellowing acrylic resins—dry quickly without changing color and do not darken with time.

**ACRYLONITRILE,** colorless, volatile liquid, $CH_2{=}CHC{\equiv}N$, with a pungent odor. It is made by the reaction of hydrogen cyanide, HCN, with ethylene oxide, $(CH_2)_2O$, or acetylene, $C_2H_2$, and is used in the production of acrylic plastics (*see* PLASTICS). Most of the acrylonitrile produced in the U.S. is used for the manufacture of synthetic rubber (q.v.) and fibers (*see* FIBER). Acrylonitrile melts at $-83.5°$ C ($-118.3°$ F), boils at $77.5°$ C ($171.5°$ F), and has a density (q.v.) of 0.806 g per ml at $20°$ C ($68°$ F). In recent years acrylonitrile has been implicated as a carcinogen (q.v.).

**ACTA,** public acts or orders enacted by emperors and their predecessors in ancient Rome. The Romans also applied the term to certain public records. The Acta Diurna—called also Acta Po-

115

puli, Acta Urbana, or Acta Publica—were a daily record of the municipal, political, and social events in Rome, in some ways comparable to modern newspapers. These records were displayed in public places for a period of time and then preserved as historical material. Some historians believe that they were introduced by Julius Caesar in 59 BC, but others claim that they existed long before that date. The Acta Senatus, or Commentarii Senatus, were a record of the official transactions of the Roman Senate and included the opinions of the chief speakers and the final decision of the Senate. The Acta Senatus were regularly published after 59 BC along with Acta Diurna. The material for the various acta were gathered by reporters called *actuarii*.

**ACT OF GOD,** in law, any occurrence not caused by human intervention or negligence, such as lightning or floods. Because such events are beyond human control, ordinarily no person may be held legally responsible for the injuries and losses they may inflict. For example, a failure to deliver goods at the time contracted because unforeseeable floods have halted all transportation does not result in liability for legal damages. In this context, the exemption may not apply in the event of seasonal inundations such as monsoons. Most policies of insurance against property damage do not provide compensation for the consequence of acts of God. All standard fire insurance policies, however, do cover losses from fire caused by lightning; by the payment of an additional premium, so-called extended coverage is available to protect against damage from hazards such as the following: windstorms, hail, ice, snow, and falling trees.

**ACTH,** abbreviation for adrenocorticotropic hormone, hormone secreted by the anterior lobe of the pituitary gland. The specific function of ACTH is to stimulate the growth and secretions of the cortex of the adrenal gland. One of these secretions is cortisone, a hormone involved in carbohydrate and protein metabolism and in alleviation of the symptoms of allergies and arthritis. ACTH, also known as corticotropin, is a complex protein molecule containing 39 amino acids; its molecular weight is approximately 5000. The biological activity of the ACTH of various animal species is similar to that of humans, but the sequence of amino acids has been found to vary somewhat among species.

**ACTING.** *See* DRAMA AND DRAMATIC ARTS; THEATER PRODUCTION.

**ACTINIDE SERIES,** a series of 15 radioactive elements in the periodic table (*see* PERIODIC LAW) with atomic numbers 89 through 103. Only the first four in the series have been found in nature

in appreciable amounts; the remainder have been produced synthetically. Those elements with atomic numbers of 93 and above are called transuranium elements (q.v.). The elements constituting the actinide series are, in order of increasing atomic number, actinium, thorium, protactinium, uranium, neptunium, plutonium, americium, curium, berkelium, californium, einsteinium, fermium, mendelevium, nobelium, and lawrencium (qq.v.). Elements beyond the actinides are no longer being named in honor of scientists.

**ACTINIUM,** radioactive metallic element, symbol Ac, in the actinide series (q.v.) of the periodic table (*see* PERIODIC LAW); at.no. 89, at.wt. 227. Actinium melts at about 1050° C (about 1922° F), boils at about 3200° C (about 5792° F), and has a sp.gr. of about 10.

It was discovered (1899) by the French chemist André Louis Debierne (1874–1949). The element is found in all uranium ores to the extent of 2 parts to every 10 billion parts of uranium. Two naturally occurring isotopes of actinium are known. Actinium-227 is a member of the actinium series, called the actinium decay series, resulting from the radioactive decay of uranium-235 (*see* RADIOACTIVITY). It has a half-life of 21.8 years. The other isotope, actinium-228, is a member of the thorium series resulting from the decay of thorium-232. This isotope, known also as mesothorium-2, has a half-life of 6.13 hours. Isotopes ranging in mass number from 209 to 234 are known.

**ACTINIUM-K.** *See* FRANCIUM.

**ACTINOMYCOSIS,** infectious disease of horses, cattle, swine, and humans. Also called lumpy jaw or big jaw, it is caused by several species of bacteria of the genus *Actinomyces* (*see* FUNGUS INFECTIONS). In humans it is caused mainly by *A. israelii*, a component of the normal flora of the mouth and tonsillar crypts. The bacteria invade decayed teeth, diseased tonsils, and soft mouth tissues. The disease is characterized chiefly by abscessed, swollen, and lumpy tissues of the jaw. The lungs and intestinal tract may also become infected. It is treated by draining abscessed tissues and by using sulfonamides and antibiotics.

**ACTION PAINTING.** *See* ABSTRACT EXPRESSIONISM.

**ACTIUM, BATTLE OF,** decisive naval engagement fought off the promontory of Actium on Sept. 2, 31 BC, between the Roman fleet of Octavian (later first emperor of Rome as Augustus), under the command of Marcus Vipsanius Agrippa, and a combined Roman-Egyptian fleet commanded by Mark Antony and Cleopatra. The battle represented the culmination of the old rivalry between Antony and Octavian for control of the Roman world and had been preceded by a long period of skirmishing, which included large armies encamped on opposite shores of the Ambracian Gulf. Against the advice of his generals and allegedly at the behest of Cleopatra, who wanted an opportunity to withdraw to Egypt, Antony launched the initial phase of the engagement. His fleet of approximately 220 heavy craft equipped with missile-throwing devices attacked at close range. Octavian's fleet of some 260 light vessels had greater maneuverability. The outcome of the battle remained in doubt until Cleopatra, apparently alarmed by an enemy maneuver, ordered the Egyptian contingent, about 60 vessels, to withdraw. Antony himself followed her, but most of his remaining vessels were soon overtaken and annihilated. The deserted army later surrendered to Octavian.

**ACTIVATION ENERGY.** *See* CHEMICAL REACTION.

**ACTON, John Emerich Edward Dalberg, 1st Baron Acton** (1834–1902), British historian and liberal philosopher. A member of an English Roman Catholic émigré family, he was born in Naples and educated in England and Germany, where he was introduced to German historical methods by his teacher, the liberal Roman Catholic scholar Johann Joseph Ignaz von Döllinger. In 1859 Acton succeeded John Henry Newman as editor of the English Roman Catholic periodical *The Rambler,* but resigned in 1864, when the publication's liberal views were condemned by church authorities. He also came into conflict with church policy when he opposed defining the doctrine of papal infallibility at the time of the First Vatican Council in 1870.

In 1895, following many years of historical study, Acton was appointed Regius Professor of Modern History at the University of Cambridge. His scholarly legacy consists mainly of his university lectures, many of which were collected and published after his death, and The Cambridge Modern History (13 vol., 1902–12), which he planned and edited.

Through his writings and lectures, Lord Acton considerably influenced modern ideas about liberty. Upholding the sovereignty of the individual, he believed that concentration of power was harmful both in church and state, a belief expressed in his famous maxim "Power tends to corrupt; absolute power corrupts absolutely."

**ACTORS' EQUITY ASSOCIATION,** known popularly as Equity, American labor union of actors, singers, and dancers of the professional theater. It is affiliated with the Associated Actors and Artistes of America, a component of the American Federation of Labor and Congress of Industrial Organizations.

The objectives of Equity are twofold: (1) to protect the interests of its members through establishing standard conditions of employment in standard contracts for each kind of work carried out by performers and (2) to promote the welfare of the theater as a cultural and recreational institution. The essential condition for membership in Equity is a contract of employment with a theatrical producer. In the early 1990s the total membership was about 38,000. The organization maintains headquarters in New York City.

Originally, the jurisdiction of Equity included all actors in the U.S. entertainment field except those appearing in foreign-language productions and in vaudeville. As motion pictures and radio became important media of entertainment, the members in these fields formed their own unions, the Screen Actors Guild (1935) and the American Federation of Radio Artists (1937); in 1952 the latter became the American Federation of Television and Radio Artists.

**ACTORS STUDIO.** *See* STRASBERG, LEE.

**ACTS OF THE APOSTLES,** fifth book of the New Testament. The second part of a historical work, of which the Gospel According to Luke is the first volume, the Acts is the story of the development of the Christian church under the impulse of the Holy Spirit. The Holy Spirit is such a prominent figure in the Acts that the book is sometimes called the Gospel of the Spirit.

**Authorship.** Scholars agree that the Acts of the Apostles was written by the same person who wrote the Gospel of Luke. Because the book itself originally carried neither a title nor the name of the author, however, the identity of this person is far from clear. As early as the 2d century, the work was ascribed to St. Luke, the companion of St. Paul.

Recent research, however, has led to the opinion that the author merely had at his disposal a travel diary kept by someone who was an actual companion of St. Paul. Thus, the author may have been one of numerous early Christians known later solely from the anonymous pieces of literature they penned. For convenience of reference, scholars continue to refer to the author as Luke.

**Date of Composition.** Some of the text (Acts 16:10–17, 20:5–21:18, 27:1–28:16) refers to the author as one of the "we" who traveled with Paul, but Paul's execution is not mentioned, and no reference to his letters is made. Some scholars have reasoned therefore that the book was written before Paul's death (c. 61) and before the collection of his letters early in the 2d century. Because the Acts is designed to serve as a second volume, however, the book must be at least

117

slightly later than the Gospel of Luke, and the Gospel is almost certainly later than that of Mark. The result is to put Luke's two volumes sometime in the last two decades of the 1st century.

**Contents.** With a beginning that overlaps the ending of Luke's Gospel, the Acts tells the story of the birth of the church in Jerusalem (chap. 1–5); the martyrdom of Stephen and the conversion of Paul (chap. 6–9); the opening of Peter's eyes to God's intention of including Gentiles in the church (chap. 10–12); Paul's missionary travels (chap. 13–19); Paul's final journey to Jerusalem (chap. 20–21); his arrest, imprisonment, and hearings in Jerusalem and Caesarea (chap. 21–26); and finally his voyage to Italy and his confinement in a Roman prison in which he awaits trial before Caesar (chap. 27–28). Thus, the events described in the book are framed by the expansion of the church from its birth in Jerusalem, through the empire, all the way to Rome.

Covering a period of roughly 30 years, the story gives valuable insights into the Jewish Christian church in Palestine, led by Peter and James; but it finds its major focus in the remarkable growth of the mission to the Gentiles, pursued by Paul, who is thus the primary "hero" on the human level. Particularly notable are the numerous speeches made by the dominant characters. The one given by Paul on the Areopagus in Athens (chap. 17) may have been intended by Luke as a model for the preaching of the gospel to the Gentile world.                    J.L.Ma.

**ACTUARY,** person who applies the theories of probability and statistics and the principles of finance to problems of insurance, pensions, population studies, and related fields. Mortality tables and probability tables dealing with death, accidents, sickness, fires, and industrial losses, as well as natural disasters, are determined by an actuary. On the basis of these tables the rates for the various types of insurance are determined, and the various underwriting practices, such as the amount of money reserve that is required to settle expected claims, are established. The basic assumption in actuarial science is that the frequency with which events occurred in the past may be used to predict or measure the probability of their occurring in the future (see INSURANCE).

In addition to serving in the insurance field, actuaries are widely employed in various government agencies that deal with regulating the insurance agency industry and in connection with operating the social security, medicare, and pension programs. The relatively new field of operations research employs a large number of actuaries. The recent development of high-speed electronic computers and data processing machinery has created many new applications of actuarial science.

**ACT OF UNION,** name of several statutes enacted during the history of Great Britain that accomplished the joining of England with Wales (1536), England with Scotland (1707), Great Britain with Ireland (1800), and the provinces of Upper and Lower Canada (1840) in North America.

**Act of Union of 1536.** The Act of Union passed in 1536, during the reign of King Henry VIII, the second English monarch descended from the old Welsh house of Tudor, formally united England and Wales. By its terms, the Welsh Marches, estates held for centuries by semi-independent Marcher lords, became several new counties or were added to older counties. Counties and boroughs in Wales were given about 24 seats in the English Parliament. Firm administration led to greater peacefulness between the Welsh and the English.

**Act of Union of 1707.** The Act of Union passed in 1707 by the parliaments of England and Scotland created the kingdom of Great Britain. Although Scotland retained its judicial system and its Presbyterian church, its parliament was joined with that of England. Henceforth, Scotland sent 45 elected members to the British House of Commons and 16 of its peers to the House of Lords. Scots received the same trading rights as the English had in England and the overseas empire. Scotland also received money (called "the Equivalent") equal to the share it was assuming of England's national debt.

The crowns of the two countries had been united in 1603 when James Stuart (James VI of Scotland) succeeded Elizabeth I as James I of England, but the kingdoms otherwise remained separate except for nine years (1651–60) during the English Revolution. Impetus for union came from mounting disagreements between the two parliaments, most notably Scotland's refusal to approve the Act of Settlement (1701) passing the royal succession on to the German house of Hannover after the death of Queen Anne (the last Stuart sovereign), and from England's fear that Scotland might seek to restore an exiled Catholic Stuart to the throne.

**Act of Union of 1800.** The Act of Union passed in 1800 joined the kingdom of Great Britain and all of Ireland into the United Kingdom of Great Britain and Ireland. The merger followed a fierce but unsuccessful rebellion against British rule in Ireland. The Irish legislature was abolished, and the Irish were allowed 32 members in the British House of Lords and 100 members in the House of Commons. The act also provided for the continuation of the Anglican church as the established church in Ireland. The Roman Catholic Irish felt betrayed because they had not acquired the right to hold political office.

**Act of Union of 1840.** The Act of Union passed in 1840 by the British Parliament united the North American provinces of Upper and Lower Canada. Parliament had created the two provinces in 1791 due to the predominance of British colonists—many of them Loyalist refugees from the 13 American colonies—in Upper Canada and a Roman Catholic, French-speaking majority in Lower Canada. The 1840 act provided for a single government headed by a royally appointed governor and a legislative assembly equally apportioned between the former divisions. The union created the Province of Canada; the sections were known as Canada East and Canada West.    J.C.

**ACUPUNCTURE,** ancient Chinese medical procedure involving insertion and manipulation of needles at more than 360 points in the human body. Applied to relieve pain during surgery or in rheumatic conditions, and to treat many other illnesses, acupuncture is used today in most hospitals in China and by some private practitioners in Japan and elsewhere, including the U.S.

Acupressure, a variant in which the practitioner uses manipulation rather than penetration to alleviate pain or other symptoms, is in widespread use in Japan and has begun to find adherents in the U.S. Also known as shiatsu, acupressure is administered by pressing with the fingertips—and sometimes the elbows or knees—along a complex network of trigger points (see below) in the patient's body.

**History.** Acupuncture needles dating from 4000 years ago have been found in China. The first needles were stone; later, bronze, gold, or silver were used, and today needles are usually made of steel. Initially, needles were used only to prick boils and ulcers. Acupuncture was developed in response to the theory that there are special "meridian points" on the body connected to the internal organs and that "vital energy" flows along the meridian lines. According to this theory, diseases are caused by interrupted energy flow, and inserting and twirling needles restores normal flow.

**Treatment.** The primary use of acupuncture in China today is for surgical analgesia. Chinese surgeons estimate that 30 percent of surgical patients obtain adequate analgesia with acupuncture, which is now done by sending electrical current through the needles rather than by twirling them. American physicians who have observed surgery done under acupuncture have verified that it is effective in some patients, but put the figure closer to 10 percent. Brain surgery is especially amenable to this form of analgesia.

Chinese surgeons claim that acupuncture is superior to Western, drug-induced analgesia in that it does not disturb normal body physiology and therefore does not make the patient vulnerable to shock.

Chinese doctors also treat some forms of heart disease with acupuncture. As part of an attempt to put the practice on a more scientific basis, they studied the effects of acupuncture treatment on more than 600 people with chest pain caused by reduced blood flow to the heart. They claimed that almost all the patients greatly reduced their use of medicine and that most were able to resume work. Other physiological conditions treated with acupuncture are ulcer, hypertension (high blood pressure), appendicitis, and asthma.

How acupuncture works remains uncertain. Both Western and Eastern scientists have shown, by producing acupuncture analgesia in rabbits, that the effects are not simply a matter of suggestion. After the discovery in 1975 of enkephalins and endorphins (natural pain inhibitors in the body), some neurophysiologists suggested that the needles may trigger the release of one or more of these substances, which inhibit pain signals by blocking their pathway through the spinal cord. This view is supported by both American and Chinese studies showing that placing acupuncture needles in certain parts of the brain of dogs causes a rise in the level of endorphins in the spinal fluid. Scientists in the U.S. have also shown that acupuncture analgesia is at least partly reversible by naloxone, a drug that blocks the action of morphine and morphinelike chemicals such as endorphins. See also PAIN.

*For further information on this topic, see the Bibliography in volume 28, section 488.*

**ADAIR, James** (1709?–83?), American trader and writer, born in Ireland. He lived for almost 40 years among the Indians, primarily the Chickasaw, in the region now constituting the southeastern U.S. His book *The History of the American Indians* (1775), although it insists on the Jewish origin of the Indian race, is one of the best firsthand accounts of the habits and character of the Indian tribes of the region. The work contains an incomplete but valuable vocabulary of various Indian dialects.

**ADALBERT, Saint** (955?–97), Bohemian churchman, the son of a Bohemian noble. He became bishop of Prague in 983. Unpopular with the Bohemians because he attempted to convert them to Christianity, he withdrew to Rome, but returned to Prague at the request of Pope John XV (r. 985–96). He became a missionary in northern Germany and Poland and, during the course of his missionary activities, was murdered by a non-Christian priest. He is known as the Apostle of the Prussians; his feast day is April 23.

**ADAM,** family of 18th-century Scottish-born architects and furniture designers, who developed a refined, neoclassical style. The four Adam brothers were the sons of an Edinburgh architect. Working in London, they designed town and country houses and furnishings that reflected England's growing prosperity.

**Robert Adam** (1728–92) was the most important of the four. Initially trained by his father, he also studied the remains of ancient Roman architecture during his stay (1754–58) in Italy and other parts of the former Roman Empire, such as Diocletian's palace in Spalato (now Split, Croatia). Settling in London, he maintained a practice and served (1761–68) as royal architect. One of his most ambitious projects was the Adelphi (1768–72; demolished 1936), a section of riverfront London designed as a single architectural unit. It included docks and warehouses under arches supporting a terrace and streets of houses. Also notable was his remodeling of Osterley Park (1761–80) and Syon House (1762–69), two great houses near London, and his design for Kedleston Hall (c. 1765–70), Derbyshire. Especially important was his conviction that the interior of a building and its furnishings are the proper concern of the architect. Consequently, he designed furniture, textiles, and metalwork for his buildings. His *Ruins of the Palace of Diocletian at Spalato in Dalmatia* (1764) and *Works in Architecture of Robert and James Adam* (3 vol.—1773; 1779; posthumously 1822) established the Adam style—a simpler, more precise and delicate version of neoclassicism than the rich Palladian style previously in vogue. The Adam style was harmonious in design and proportion and gavea feeling of lightness and spaciousness. It used classical motifs, such as wreaths, swags, and urns. Adam furniture exhibits many similar qualities.

**James Adam** (1730–94) was draftsman for Robert and succeeded him as royal architect. John (1721?– 92) and William (c. 1738–1822) also assisted Robert.

**ADAM, Adolphe Charles** (1803–56), French composer, born in Paris. Although originally interested in a scientific career, he entered the Paris Conservatoire in 1817 and studied music composition under the French composer François Adrien Boieldieu (1775–1834). In 1829 Adam's one-act opera *Pierre et Catherine* was successfully produced; 52 more works followed, of which one of the most famous was the ballet *Giselle* (1841). His music is distinguished by its daintiness and finish. He became professor of musical composition at the Paris Conservatoire in 1849. His autobiography was published posthumously in 1860.

**ADAMAWA MASSIF,** plateau region, W central Africa, in central Cameroon, extending into SE Nigeria and W Central African Republic. An upland area of volcanic origin, it has an average elevation of about 1000 m (about 3300 ft). Savanna vegetation predominates. It is a sparsely populated region, cattle raising being the chief occupation. Its name is derived from the Fulani Muslim leader Modibbo Adama (d. 1848), who established an emirate incorporating much of the territory.

**ADAM DE LA HALLE,** also called Adam le Bossu (c. 1237–c. 1287), French trouvère, or poet-composer. Born in Arras, he was a member of the retinue of Charles of Anjou, later King Charles II of Naples. Adam's prose drama, *Le jeu de la feuillée* (The Play of the Greensward, c. 1262), a satirical fantasy, is commonly considered the earliest comedy in French. His musical play *Le jeu de Robin et Marion* (The Play of Robin and Marion, c. 1283), a pastoral comedy to his own music and text, is regarded as a precursor of comic opera. Adam also composed motets and polyphonic songs.

**ADAM AND EVE,** in the Bible, the first man and woman, progenitors of the human race. Adam (Heb. *ādām,* "man") was made of dust from the soil; Eve (Heb. *hawwa,* "the living one"?) was created from Adam's rib and given to him by God to be his wife. The story appears in two versions: Gen. 1:26–27 and Gen. 2:7–8, 18–24.

In prescientific times, it was commonly assumed that every species of life, the human included, had descended from a pair of aboriginal ancestors who had been created directly by God. In this respect the biblical story of Adam and Eve differs only in details from many other similar myths of the ancient Middle East and elsewhere. Similar motifs also appear in such ancient Mesopotamian sources as the Gilgamesh epic (q.v.), from about 2000 BC, for example.

In some other respects, however, the story of Adam and Eve is unique. The early chapters of the Book of Genesis underwent considerable editorial work, and what was at first a straightforward narrative of the beginning of the human species in general was converted into a more sophisticated accounting for the situation of men and women in relation to one another and to their environment. This is evident in the introduction of the theme of a separate creation of woman in Gen. 2:18–24, which, among other things, argues for the complementarity of the two sexes. It can also be seen in the use made of the story to assign to human culpability humankind's habitation of a less than perfect world,

*Adam and Eve in the Garden of Eden with the serpent (from an engraving by Albrecht Dürer).*

Parke-Bernet Galleries

Born in county Donegal, he entered the monastery on the island of Iona and in 697 was elected abbot. The Irish church then followed the Eastern method for dating Easter. Adamnan (also Adomnan or Eunan), a proponent of Roman observances, tried to adopt the Roman method in Iona. Disappointment at his failure to do so is thought to have caused his death. His works include *On the Holy Land,* an account containing valuable information about the Holy Land based on a pilgrimage made by a Frankish bishop. Adamnan is best known, however, for his *Life of Saint Columba,* a biography of the missionary who converted the ancient Picts and founded Iona. Along with accounts of miracles and many other stories, the biography contains nearly all extant information about the early Irish church. Adamnan's feast day is September 23.

**ADAMS, Abigail Smith** (1744–1818), wife of John Adams, second president of the U.S., and mother of John Quincy Adams, the sixth president. She was born in Weymouth, Mass., the daughter of the Reverend William Smith (1707–83), minister of the Congregational church there. Through her mother, Elizabeth Quincy (1721–75), she was descended from the 17th-century Puritan preacher Thomas Shepard (1605–49) of Cambridge. Although she had little formal education,

one in which the earth yields its fruits grudgingly (Gen. 3:17–19) and woman's social position is inferior to that of man (3:16). *See* ORIGINAL SIN.

These distinct directions given to the biblical story of human origins constitute its primary claim to consideration as a religious classic. In a precritical age, when the Bible was the only ancient literature known to the Western world, it was considered a historical document handing down authentic information about a relatively recent past in an unbroken tradition from generation to generation. It was taken for granted that the story was nothing less than sober history. This is the position still maintained by some Fundamentalists, who view the divine influence (inspiration) on the production of the biblical narratives as a guarantee that everything in them is literal fact. *See* FUNDAMENTALISM.

Most present-day biblical scholars, however, accept the story of Adam and Eve for what it appears to be: a Hebrew story of human origins having much in common with the myths of other ancient peoples and also a good deal that is distinctive. The religious values of the story are in no way diminished by this recognition but simply redefined.                                    B.V.

**ADAMNAN, Saint** (625?–704), Irish abbot and scholar, noted for his biography of St. Columba.

*Abigail Adams, wife of John Adams, second president of the U.S., and mother of John Quincy Adams, sixth president; portrait by Gilbert Stuart.*

National Gallery of Art–Gift of Mrs. Robert Homans

she was among the most influential women of her day, especially as a fashion leader and social arbiter. During and after the American Revolution she was separated for long periods of time from her husband, who was first a delegate to Congress and later a diplomat in Europe. Her letters to him present a vivid picture of the time. After 1800 she lived in Washington, D.C., and thereafter in Braintree, Mass. The *Familiar Letters of John Adams and His Wife, Abigail* (2 vol., 1876), published with a memoir by their grandson, Charles Francis Adams, and later collections of her letters show that she was perceptive, sagacious, warmhearted, and generous.

*For further information on this person, see the section Bibliographies in the Bibliography in volume 28.*

**ADAMS, Ansel Easton** (1902–84), American photographer of landscape in the American Southwest. Born in San Francisco and educated at Yale University, he was inspired by a 1916 trip to Yosemite, Calif., to film in black and white the majesty of the American wilderness. His camera caught raw mountains, harsh deserts, enormous clouds, and towering trees in sharp detail dramatized by light and shadow.

Adams held his first exhibition in San Francisco in 1939. He started the first college department in photography and published the Basic Photo-Books series on technique. Collections of his photographs include *Taos Pueblo* (1930), *Sierra Nevada* (1948), *This Is the American Earth* (1960), and *Yosemite and the Range of Light* (1979).

**ADAMS, Brooks** (1848–1927), American historian, youngest son of Charles Francis Adams, born in Quincy, Mass., and educated at Harvard University. Admitted to the bar in 1871, he practiced law for ten years before beginning his career as a writer. His first important work, *The Emancipation of Massachusetts* (1887), is a penetrating analysis of the religious and political forces that shaped the development of that colony. In *The Law of Civilization and Decay* (1895) he propounded an economic interpretation of history based on the factors governing the rise and fall of commerce. Adams applied the interpretation to his own times in *America's Economic Supremacy* (1901) and *The New Empire* (1902). His other writings include *The Theory of Social Revolutions* (1913), a brilliant, although pessimistic, study of the American democratic system.

**ADAMS, Charles Francis** (1807–86), American diplomat and editor, grandson of John Adams and son of John Quincy Adams, born in Boston, and educated at Harvard University. He was admitted to the bar in 1829. Adams served for five years in the Massachusetts legislature as a mem-

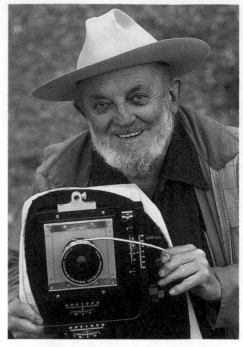

*Ansel Adams in 1979.*
© 1979 David Hume Kennerly–Liaison International

ber of the Whig party. In 1858 and again in 1860, he was elected to the U.S. House of Representatives from Massachusetts as a member of the Republican party. In 1861 he was appointed minister to Great Britain by Abraham Lincoln. His skillful handling of this position during the American Civil War (1861–65), when the British government rendered aid to the Confederacy, is an outstanding chapter in the history of American diplomacy. In the so-called Trent affair, the first major crisis in Anglo-American relations during the war, his calm and tact were instrumental in averting hostilities between the two nations. Although he failed to prevent the sailing of the *Alabama,* a raider built in Great Britain for the Confederacy, his efforts with the British government later resulted in the detention of other Confederate vessels. He resigned as minister to Great Britain in 1868. In 1871 he became a member of the *Alabama* claims tribunal. He edited the *Life and Works of John Adams* (10 vol., 1850–56), the *Memoirs of John Quincy Adams* (12 vol., 1874–77), and the *Familiar Letters of John Adams and His Wife, Abigail* (2 vol., 1876).

**ADAMS, Charles Francis** (1835–1915), American public official and historian, son of the elder Charles Francis Adams, born in Boston, and educated at Harvard University. After serving as an officer in the Union army during the American Civil War, he became railroad commissioner of

Massachusetts, and from 1884 to 1890 he was president of the Union Pacific Railroad. From 1893 to 1895 he was chairman of the Massachusetts Parks Commission. In 1895 he became president of the Massachusetts Historical Society and, in 1901, president of the American Historical Association. His works include *Railroads: Their Origin and Problems* (1878), *Richard Henry Dana: A Biography* (1891), *Three Episodes of Massachusetts History* (1892), and *Lee at Appomattox* (1902).

**ADAMS, Henry Brooks** (1838–1918), American historian, philosopher of history, and cultural critic, who wrote one of the most outstanding American autobiographies.

A son of the elder Charles Francis Adams, Adams was born in Boston, on Feb. 16, 1838, and educated at Harvard University. After his graduation (1858) from Harvard, Adams traveled for two years in Germany and Italy. From 1860 to 1868 he was private secretary to his father. He then decided to become a teacher and from 1869 to 1876 was assistant professor of history at Harvard, where he introduced the seminar system of instruction. During part of that period he also edited the periodical *North American Review.* After 1885 he devoted himself almost entirely to historical research and writing. Adams traveled extensively in Europe, spending considerable time in France. He died in Washington, D.C., on March 27, 1918.

Adams's most impressive achievement as a historian is his *History of the United States of America During the Administrations of Thomas Jefferson and James Madison* (9 vol., 1889–91), in which he contended that the decisions and policies of the period from 1801 to 1817 shaped the main course of subsequent American political development. Among his other writings are two biographies, *The Life of Albert Gallatin* (1879) and *John Randolph* (1882). He wrote two novels, *Democracy* (1880), a political satire, and *Esther* (1884), a story about New York City society.

His *Degradation of the Democratic Dogma* (1919) includes three essays on his philosophy of history. In this work Adams introduced his dynamic theory of history. Derived from the second law of thermodynamics, the theory maintains that mechanical energy is in a constant state of dissipation. Human history is similarly devoid of purpose and consists merely of a succession of energy phases. Another major contribution to the philosophy of history is found in the privately printed *Mont-Saint-Michel and Chartres* (1904), a sensitive and penetrating discussion of medieval culture. In his most widely read book, *The Education of Henry Adams* (1906; posthumous Pulit-

zer Prize, 1919), he discussed the fundamental character of the history of Western civilization. The book is an autobiography written in the third person with detached skepticism and delicate irony. Its main concern was to indict the educational system of his day for its failure to prepare an intelligent man for the chaos of modern life.

Adams's works reveal a profound concern with the destiny of the modern world. His prose style is forceful, as is his treatment of ideas. Although he thought of his privately published books as unsatisfactory, later critics place them among the important works of the 20th century.

**ADAMS, James Truslow** (1878–1949), American historian and editor, born in Brooklyn, N.Y., and educated at Brooklyn Polytechnic Institute and at Yale University. He worked as a stockbroker from 1900 to 1912. After serving as a captain in the U.S. Military Intelligence Division during World War I, he retired to write historical works. He won the 1922 Pulitzer Prize in history for *The Founding of New England* (1921). His *Epic of America* (1931) became a best-seller. He made a study of the famous Adams family of Massachusetts, to which he was not related; this study resulted in *The Adams Family* (1930) and *Henry Adams* (1933). He later became editor in chief of the *Dictionary of American History* (6 vol., 1940), the *Atlas of American History* (1943), and the *Album of American History* (1944–46). His other works include *The March of Democracy* (2 vol., 1932–33), *The Living Jefferson* (1936), and *Big Business in a Democracy* (1945).

**ADAMS, John** (1735–1826), second president (1797–1801) and first vice-president (1789–1797) of the U.S., and leader in the movement for independence. His presidency was marked by rivalry with fellow-Federalist Alexander Hamilton, controversy over government measures taken to curb political opposition, and a crisis in U.S. relations with France.

Adams was born on Oct. 30, 1735, in Braintree (now Quincy), Mass., a town in which Adamses had lived since 1638. His father had married into a wealthy Boston family, the Boylstons, and was thus able to send his son to Harvard College, from which young Adams graduated in 1755. He then selected law and soon found that in the courtroom his acquired erudition and intellectual precision overcame his natural timidity, and he became a powerful speaker and an adroit advocate. At the age of 29 Adams married Abigail Smith, a woman who was clearly his intellectual and psychological equal.

**The Coming of the Revolution.** The controversy that preceded the American Revolution catapulted Adams into a position of political leader-

*Portrait of John Adams, second president of the U.S., by John Trumbull.*                National Portrait Gallery

ship. His *Braintree Instructions* (1765) was a powerful denunciation of the Stamp Act, and his oddly titled *Dissertation on the Canon and Feudal Law* (1765) was a prescient analysis of the emotional and ideological demands facing the colonists. Chosen as a lawyer for several British soldiers charged with the death of five colonists in the Boston Massacre (1770), Adams successfully defended his clients by justifying their use of force out of fear for their lives. In his essays *Novanglus* (1774–75), he defended colonial resistance and argued that the British Empire was in reality a league of nearly autonomous entities; thus, he anticipated 19th-century self-government of British overseas possessions.

In the First and Second Continental Congresses, Adams emerged as a powerful exponent of the historic rights of the English and the natural rights of humankind. Along with his cousin Samuel Adams, he initiated (1775) the effort to secure the appointment of George Washington as commander of the new Continental army. Adams served on the committee to draft the Declaration of Independence, but when Thomas Jefferson later claimed that Adams had given him a free hand in composing it, Adams responded indignantly that the document was "a theatrical show" in which "Jefferson ran away with the stage effect ... and all the glory of it." Thus began a rivalry between the two men that continued for more than a decade.

More clearly perhaps than any other leading patriot of his day, Adams expressed the fear that he and his fellow revolutionaries might fail in summoning forth the virtue and objectivity required to avoid loss of nerve and internal factionalism. His *Thoughts on Government* (1776), in which he elaborated on these warnings, became a handbook on the writing of early state constitutions and particularly influenced the preparation of those documents in Virginia, North Carolina, and Massachusetts.

**Diplomatic Service and Vice-Presidency.** In 1778 Congress sent Adams and John Jay to join Benjamin Franklin as diplomatic representatives in Europe. Franklin remained the American envoy to France; Adams went to the Dutch Republic and had the responsibility for opening negotiations with Britain; Jay traveled to Spain. In 1782 and 1783, the three men together negotiated the Treaty of Paris, ending the 8-year war with Great Britain.

In 1785 Adams was appointed diplomatic envoy to Great Britain, a position he held until 1788. His duties in England caused him to miss the Constitutional Convention and the ratifying debates. He had played a crucial role earlier, however, in drafting the Massachusetts Constitution of 1780. While in London he wrote the three-volume *Defence of the Constitutions of Government of the United States of America*. This work rebutted a French critic of American politics and reiterated Adams's belief that only formal restraints on the exercise of power and on the impulses of the populace could militate against human evil and societal weaknesses.

Because he ran second to Washington in electoral-college balloting in both 1788 and 1792, Adams became the nation's first vice-president. In that capacity, he limited himself to presiding over the Senate.

**The Presidency.** In 1796 Adams was chosen to succeed Washington as president, winning over Thomas Jefferson and Thomas Pinckney. The threat of war with France, along with the resulting passionate debate over foreign policy and the limits of dissent, dominated the politics of his administration. The war scare was sparked by American indignation over French attempts to extort money from U.S. representatives in the so-called XYZ affair (q.v.). A conflict arose over the measures to be taken in preparation for possible hostilities. Adams favored strengthening the navy and building coastal fortifications, but an opposing group led by former secretary of the treasury Alexander Hamilton persuaded Congress to create a large standing army, with Hamilton himself as inspector general. Because the possibility of a French invasion of the U.S. was remote, the clear implication of this policy was the creation of an army the size and strength of which could intimidate opposition of the Republican voters.

*Alien and Sedition Acts.* The Hamilton Federalists added substance to those fears by pushing through Congress laws restricting the rights and privileges of aliens (presumed to be potential Republican voters or, worse yet, French radicals) and punishing as sedition the printing of false attacks on the dignity or integrity of high government officials. Adams found enough merit in these bills to sign them, and he acquiesced in 14 prosecutions under the Sedition Act. The Alien Acts, however, he refused to enforce.

One of Adams's most fateful decisions was to retain the cabinet he had inherited from Washington, several members of which were personally loyal to Hamilton. Together with Hamilton's supporters in Congress, they engineered the creation of the new army, which Hamilton in actuality controlled.

*Agreement with France.* Adams did, however, demonstrate the power of the presidency to confront challenges to executive leadership. In February 1799, he appointed new peace commissioners to go to France and reopen negotiations. Adams's timing and judgment were acute: The French foreign minister, Charles Maurice de Talleyrand-Périgord, had sent a diplomatic signal that he wanted peace with the U.S. When Secretary of State Timothy Pickering, a Hamilton follower, tried to sabotage the peace mission, Adams fired him; shortly thereafter the two nations came to terms.

The peace initiative enabled Adams to dismantle the new army, much to Hamilton's embarrassment. Adams's foreign policy, however, split the Federalist party on the eve of the 1800 election and contributed significantly to the election of Thomas Jefferson as well as to Republican victories in both houses of Congress.

**Retirement.** Adams lived for a quarter century after he left the presidency, during which time he wrote extensively. His guiding principles were embodied in a Whig philosophy to which he clung stubbornly. Ill-suited to adapt to the transition to 19th-century romantic culture, he was nevertheless a magnificent exponent of the pessimistic view of human society. He died in Quincy, Mass., on July 4, 1826.                                    R.M.C.

*For further information on this person, see the section Biographies in the Bibliography in volume 28.*

**ADAMS, John Quincy** (1767–1848), sixth president of the U.S. (1825–29), who combined brilliant statesmanship with skillful diplomacy. As secretary of state (1817–25) he ranks among the ablest holders of the office, and he played a major role in formulating American foreign policy. As an eight-term member of the House of Representatives (1831–48) he was a leading defender of freedom of speech and a spokesman for the antislavery cause.

**Early Career.** Adams was born in Braintree (now Quincy), Mass., on July 11, 1767, the eldest son of John and Abigail Adams. Remarkably precocious, at the age of 12 he accompanied his father to Europe. He served as French translator to Francis Dana (1743–1811), U.S. minister to Russia, in 1781–83 and as his father's secretary in 1783, during the peace negotiations that ended the American Revolution. He graduated from Harvard College and opened a law office in Boston.

Adams's "Publicola" essays, attacking the views Thomas Paine expressed in the *Rights of Man,* won him early political recognition. In 1793 President George Washington named him minister to Holland and then sent him to London to aid John Jay in negotiations with the British (*see* JAY'S TREATY). In London he met Louisa Catherine Johnson (1775–1852), whom he married in 1797; it was a happy union, marked by deep affection. That same year he became minister to Prussia, with which he concluded a pact incorporating the neutral rights provisions of Jay's Treaty.

In 1801 Adams was elected to the Masssachusetts Senate and two years later to the U.S. Senate. Although a Federalist, he followed an independent course. Adams supported the Louisiana Purchase. This and his endorsement of President Thomas Jefferson's policy of commercial warfare led to a break with his party and his resignation in 1808. The following year President

*John Quincy Adams, a portrait by Thomas Sully.*
National Gallery of Art, Washington, D.C.

James Madison appointed him minister to Russia, where he did much to encourage Czar Alexander's friendly feelings toward the U.S. As one of the delegates sent to Ghent to negotiate an end to the War of 1812, Adams found the British commissioners so intransigent that he had to approve a peace treaty (1814) that fell short of U.S. expectations. In 1815 he was appointed minister to Great Britain, where he did much to ease tensions resulting from the war.

**Secretary of State.** In 1817 President James Monroe chose Adams as his secretary of state, inaugurating a long and harmonious association, for the two men agreed on basic foreign policy aims. Both were expansionists, and both wanted the U.S. to follow a course distinct from that of the European powers. Monroe closely controlled foreign policy but relied heavily on the advice of Adams, who was an adroit negotiator. Adams's state papers are among the most brilliant ever penned by a secretary of state. With Monroe's support, he forced Spain to cede Florida and to make a favorable settlement of the Louisiana boundary in the Transcontinental Treaty drafted in 1819. His protracted negotiations with the French minister on outstanding issues between the two countries were less successful. The treaty concluded in 1822 only provided for a gradual reduction of France's discriminatory tariff, leaving other questions unsettled. His efforts to persuade Great Britain to open its West Indian trade to American ships were unsuccessful.

Adams did not share Monroe's apprehension that the European powers might intervene to suppress the South American revolutions and restore Spain's authority in its colonies. He was concerned, however, about Russian expansion on the west coast and thus welcomed Monroe's decision to formulate in his annual message of December 1823 a declaration (later known as the Monroe Doctrine) expressing American opposition to European intervention in the Americas. At Adams's suggestion, Monroe added a statement declaring that the U.S. regarded the western hemisphere as closed to further European colonization. As a result, Adams obtained a pledge from Russia to remain north of lat 54°40'. The British, however, refused to vacate the Columbia River area.

**President.** In 1824 Adams was involved in a bitter presidential contest in which none of the four candidates obtained a majority in the electoral college. Adams, with 84 votes (all from New England), ran behind Andrew Jackson (99) but ahead of William H. Crawford (41) and Henry Clay (37). Victory went to Adams in the House of Representatives, when Clay supported him. Adams's choice of Clay as secretary of state led to a charge (probably unfounded) of a "corrupt bargain"—in effect, that Clay had purchased the office with his votes.

Adams's presidency was marred by the incessant hostility of the combined Jackson and Crawford supporters in Congress, which prevented Adams from executing his envisaged nationalist program. His proposals for the creation of a department of the interior were rebuffed. Only after acrimonious debate did he obtain the appointment of delegates to a congress of the American nations in Panama (1826). Committed to the idea of a protective tariff, Adams in 1828 was maneuvered into signing the grossly unfair Tariff of Abominations, thereby alienating the South, as his enemies hoped he would. He steadfastly refused to use the federal patronage to strengthen his party support, allowing his postmaster general to appoint Jackson backers. In the election of 1828, pilloried as an aristocrat favoring special interests, Adams was overwhelmingly defeated by Jackson (178 to 83 electoral votes).

**Later Congressional Service.** Two years after the end of his presidency, Adams returned to politics, entering the House of Representatives. Now nominally a Whig, he still followed an independent course. For ten years he chaired the Committee on Manufacturers, which drafted tariff bills. He lauded Jackson's firm resistance to southern attempts to nullify the tariff of 1832, but condemned the compromise tariff of 1833 (not drafted by his committee) as being too great a concession to the nullificationists. After 1835 he was identified with the antislavery forces, although not with the abolitionists. Every year from 1836 to 1844 he led the fight to lift the gag rule that had ordered the tabling of all resolutions concerning slavery. He triumphed in 1844, when it was rescinded.

A vigorous speaker, Adams earned the sobriquet Old Man Eloquent. Throughout his lifetime he kept a voluminous diary, later edited by his son, Charles Francis Adams. On Feb. 21, 1848, he suffered a stroke on the floor of the House, and he died two days later without regaining consciousness.                                    H.A.

*For further information on this person, see the section Biographies in the Bibliography in volume 28.*

**ADAMS, Maude,** professional name of MAUDE KISKADDEN (1872–1953), American actor, born in Salt Lake City, Utah. She appeared in New York City in *The Midnight Bell* (1888), then spent three years with the Charles Frohman acting company. She played in *The Masked Ball* (1892) with John Drew, starred in *The Little Minister*

(1896) by Sir James Matthew Barrie, and played the duke of Reichstadt in *L'aiglon* (The Eaglet, 1900) by Edmond Rostand. From 1905 to 1907 she played the title role in Barrie's *Peter Pan*, probably her most popular performance. She retired at the height of her stage career after appearing in Rostand's *Chantecler* (1910–11). After 1937 she was instructor in drama at Stephens College, Columbia, Mo.

**ADAMS, Samuel** (1722–1803), American patriot, one of the leaders of resistance to British policy in Massachusetts before the American Revolution.

Adams was born in Boston on Sept. 27, 1722, and educated at Harvard College (now Harvard University). After leaving college in 1740, he was successively a law student, a clerk in a counting-house, and a merchant. His business failed, and he later became a partner with his father in a brewery. This enterprise also failed after his father died. Meanwhile, he had been an active participant in Boston political circles. In 1756 he was elected tax collector of Boston, a position he held for eight years. His outspoken opposition to strict enforcement of the Sugar and Molasses Act in 1764 brought him into prominence in colonial politics. In 1765, during the course of the controversy that was aroused by the Stamp Act, Adams drafted the instructions to the Boston representatives in the General Court, the legislative body of Massachusetts. He was elected to the lower house of the General Court in the same year. The radical majority in the lower house elected him clerk in 1766, and while serving in this position, which he held until 1774, he gradually assumed leadership of the movement in Massachusetts that advocated independence from Great Britain. As such he was a consistent and bitter opponent of Thomas Hutchinson, an aristocratic political leader, who served as the lieutenant governor (1758–71) and royal governor (1771–74) of the colony.

Adams decisively influenced every important aspect of the prerevolutionary struggle against British rule. In the realm of practical politics, he promoted the formation of the Boston chapter of the Sons of Liberty and sponsored the Committee of Correspondence of Boston. He led the fight against the Townshend Acts, headed the demonstrations that led to the Boston Massacre, directed the Boston Tea Party, and figured significantly in other outstanding events of the period. He rapidly acquired an intercolonial reputation both through these activities and as a literary agitator and revolutionary ideologist. Many of his writings, chiefly political pamphlets, were widely circulated and read. A proponent of the natu-

Portrait of Samuel Adams by John Singleton Copley.
Museum of Fine Arts, Boston

ral rights of man, he was in the vanguard of those Americans who challenged the authority of the British Parliament and championed rebellion. Stylistically, his writings are lucid, forceful, and epigrammatic. Adams's contributions to the *Gazette,* a Boston newspaper, constituted a voluminous phase of his agitational work. Frequently written under pseudonyms, his newspaper articles inveighed against reconciliation with Great Britain; they won many converts for the radical cause and generally deepened the mood for revolutionary action.

In June 1774, following the passage of the Boston Port Act, Adams climaxed his activities against that and similarly oppressive measures by securing the approval by the Massachusetts General Court of a resolution to send representatives to the First Continental Congress. Elected a delegate to the congress, he soon became the leader of the radical faction that demanded strong measures against Great Britain. Before adjourning, the Congress called for a boycott of British goods and recommended the use of force in resisting taxes that were imposed by the government in London.

Adams was a delegate to the Second Continental Congress, which convened at Philadelphia in May 1775, and he subsequently signed the Declaration of Independence. He remained a member of the Continental Congress until its dissolution (1781), but he was frequently at odds with his colleagues on matters of national policy. Because his strenuous opposition to a strong national government impeded mobilization of the nation for a speedy victory over Great Britain, his popularity and effectiveness as a leader gradually waned. In 1779, Adams was a member of the committee that drafted the Massachusetts State constitution, and he was instrumental also in securing the ratification by Massachusetts of the U.S. Constitution in 1788. He was lieutenant governor of Massachusetts from 1789 to 1793 and governor from 1794 to 1797. He died in Boston on Oct. 2, 1803.

**ADAMS, Samuel Hopkins** (1871–1958), American journalist and author, born in Dunkirk, N.Y., and educated at Hamilton College. From 1891 to 1900 he was a newspaper writer on the staff of the *New York Sun;* from 1903 to 1905 he was on the staff of *McClure's Magazine.* As a journalist he played an important role in the muckraking movement, an attempt to expose corruption in business and politics. His most notable disclosure was a series of magazine articles on the evils of the patent-medicine industry. His novel *Revelry* (1926) deals with corruption in the administration of President Warren G. Harding. He also wrote biographies, short stories, and several film scripts.

**ADAM'S PEAK** (Singhalese *Samanhela*), mountain, S Sri Lanka, E of Colombo. The 2243-m (7360-ft) summit contains a depression about 1.5 m (about 5 ft) long by about 76 cm (about 30 in) wide that is shaped like a human footprint. The origin of the footprint is explained in various ways depending on religious and cultural tradition. According to Muslim tradition, the summit was the scene of the penance of Adam (after his expulsion from Paradise), during which he stood on one foot for a thousand years. To Buddhists the footlike depression is the sacred footmark left by Buddha on his departure from Sri Lanka; the Hindus claim it is the footprint of the god Shiva.

**ADANA,** formerly SEYHAN, city, S Turkey, capital of Adana Province, on the Seyhan R., near the Mediterranean Sea. Adana is the marketing and distribution center for an agricultural region in which cotton, wheat, barley, grapes, citrus fruits, olives, and tobacco are produced. The chief industries in the city are textile manufacturing, tanning, and the processing of wool and various foods. Local points of interest include a great stone bridge, built in part during the reign (6th cent.) of the Byzantine emperor Justinian, and the ruins of a castle dating from 782.

Adana was probably founded in 63 BC by the Roman statesman Pompey the Great. For several centuries thereafter it was a way station on a Roman military road leading to the East. The city declined in importance after the fall of the Roman Empire (AD 476) but was rebuilt in the 8th century by Harun ar-Rashid, caliph of Baghdad. Adana was held by Egypt from 1832 to 1840, when it was restored to Turkish rule. Pop. (1990) 916,150.

**ADAPAZARI,** city, NW Turkey, capital of Sakarya Province, on the Sakarya R., near İzmit. A road junction and rail-spur terminus, Adapazari is a trade center in a farming area. Railroad and agricultural machinery are manufactured in the city, and iron, zinc, and copper are mined nearby. Pop. (1990) 171,225.

**ADAPTATION,** in biology, accommodation of a living organism to its environment. Two common forms of adaptation exist. Physiological adaptation involves the rapid acclimatization (q.v.) of an individual organism to a sudden change in environment; for example, a mammal sweats on a hot day to regulate its body temperature. Evolutionary adaptation, the focus of this article, occurs during the slow course of evolution and is inherited by successive generations.

**Mechanisms of Adaptation.** Evolutionary adaptations are the result of the competition among individuals of a particular species over many generations in response to an ever-changing environment, including other animals and plants. Certain traits are culled by natural selection (*see* EVOLUTION) favoring those individual organisms that produce the most offspring. This is such a broad concept that, theoretically, all the features of any animal or plant could be considered adaptive. For example, the leaves, trunk, and roots of a tree all arose by selection and help the individual tree in its competition for space, soil, and sunlight.

Biologists have demonstrated many cases of adaptive features in species; however, they find it difficult to be certain whether any particular structure of an organism arose by selection, and hence can be called adaptive, or whether it arose by chance and is selectively neutral. A classic example of an evolutionary development with evidence for adaptation is mimicry (q.v.). Biologists can show experimentally that some organisms escape predators by trying to be inconspicuous and blend into their environment and that other organisms imitate the coloration of species distasteful to predators. There are only a handful of tested cases. Many supposed cases of adaptation remain to be verified.

Some features of an organism may be retained because they are adaptive for special, limited functions, even though these features may be otherwise maladaptive. The large antlers of an elk or moose, for

Placentals

Marsupials

Wolf
(Canis)

Tasmanian wolf
(Thylacinus)

Ocelot
(Felis)

Native cat
(Dasyurus)

Flying squirrel
(Glaucomys)

Glider
(Petaurus)

Groundhog
(Marmota)

Wombat
(Vombatus)

Anteater
(Myrmecophaga)

Numbat or
Banded anteater
(Myrmecobius)

Mole
(Scapanus)

Mole
(Notoryctes)

Mouse
(Mus)

Mouse
(Phascogale)

*Australia's isolated marsupials evolved to fill environmental niches occupied by placentals on other continents.*
From *Evolution*, by T. Dobzhansky, F. J. Ayala, G. L. Stebbins, and J. W. Valentine. W. H. Freeman and Company. Copyright © 1977. After a chart in G. G. Simpson and W. S. Beck, *Life*, 2d ed., 1965, Harcourt Brace Jovanovich, Inc.

## HOMOLOGY (IN FORELIMB BONES)

ARM OF MAN    DOG FORELEG    BIRD WING    SEAL FLIPPER

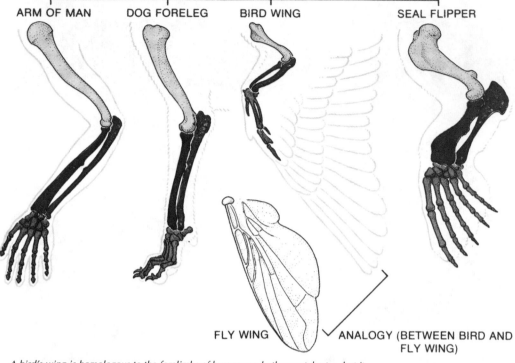

FLY WING    ANALOGY (BETWEEN BIRD AND FLY WING)

*A bird's wing is homologous to the forelimbs of humans and other vertebrates, but it is only analogous to an insect's wing. Bones of the five-digit mammalian "hand" are homologous to the human hand, the dog's paw, and the seal's flipper.*
Reprinted from E. O. Wilson et al., Life (1977), by permission of Sinauer Associates, Inc.

example, may be effective in sexual selection for mating but could well be maladaptive at all other times of the year. In addition, a species feature that now has one adaptive significance may have been produced as an adaptation to quite different circumstances. For example, lungs probably evolved in adaptation to life in water that sometimes ran low on oxygen. Fish with lungs were then adapted in a way that accidentally allowed their descendants to become terrestrial.

**Adaptive Radiation.** Because the environment exerts such control over the adaptations that arise by natural selection—including the coadaptations of different species evolving together, such as flowers and pollinators—the kind of organism that would fill a particular environmental niche ought to be predictable in general terms. An example of this process of adaptive radiation, or filling of environmental niches by the development of new species, is provided in Australia. When Australia became a separate continent some 60 million years ago, only monotremes and marsupials lived there, with no competition from the placental mammals that were emerging

on other continents. Although only two living monotremes are found in Australia today, the marsupials have filled most of the niches open to terrestrial mammals on that continent. Because Australian habitats resemble those in other parts of the world, marsupial equivalents can be found to the major placental herbivores, carnivores, and even rodents and moles.

This pattern can be observed on a restricted scale as well. In some sparsely populated islands, for example, one species of bird might enter the region, find little or no competition, and evolve rapidly into a number of species adapted to the available niches. A well-known instance of such adaptive radiation was discovered by Charles Darwin in the Galápagos Islands. He presumed, probably correctly, that one species of finch colonized the islands thousands of years ago and gave rise to the 14 species of finchlike birds that exist there now. Thus, one finch behaves like a warbler, another like a woodpecker, and so on. The greatest differences in their appearance lie in the shapes of the bills, adapted to the types of food each species eats.

**Analogy and Homology.** When different species are compared, some adaptive features can be described as analogous or homologous. For example, flight requires certain rigid aeronautical principles of design; yet birds, bats, and insects have all conquered the air. In this case the flight structures are said to be analogous—that is, they have different embryological origins but perform the same function. By contrast, structures that arise from the same structures in the embryo but are used in entirely different kinds of functions, such as the forelimb of a rat and the wing of a bat, are said to be homologous.                    J.T.B.

*For further information on this topic, see the Bibliography in volume 28, sections 138, 447.*

**ADDAMS, Jane** (1860–1935), American social reformer and Nobel laureate, born in Cedarville, Ill., and educated at Rockford Female Seminary and Women's Medical College and in Europe. In 1889, with Ellen Starr (1860–1940), Addams established Hull House in Chicago, one of the first settlement houses in the U.S. Addams played a prominent part in the formation of the National Progressive party in 1912 and of the Woman's Peace party, of which she became chairperson in 1915. She was elected (1915) president of the International Congress of Women at The Hague, Netherlands, and president of the Women's International League for Peace and Freedom, which was established by The Hague congress.

Jane Addams, *portrait by George de Forest Brush, c. 1920.*
National Portrait Gallery, Washington, D.C.–Art Resource

She was a delegate to similar congresses held in Zürich, Switzerland (1919), Vienna (1921), The Hague (1922), Washington, D.C. (1924), Dublin (1926), and Prague (1929). She won the Nobel Peace Prize in 1931, sharing the award with the American educator Nicholas Murray Butler. Her works include *Democracy and Social Ethics* (1902), *Newer Ideals of Peace* (1907), *Twenty Years at Hull House* (1910), and *The Second Twenty Years at Hull House* (1930).

*For further information on this person, see the section Biographies in the Bibliography in volume 28.*

**ADDAX,** genus of desert antelope with only one species, *Addax nasomaculatus,* of the family Bovidae in the order Artiodactyla. The addax inhabits the southwestern part of the Sahara in North Africa and is found in lesser numbers across the Red Sea into the Near East. A strictly herbivorous, cud-chewing mammal, it grazes in herds numbering up to 300. The addax is usually a little more than 91.4 cm (36 in) high at the shoulder and is yellowish white in color, with a brown mane and a black patch at the forehead. Both sexes have graceful, ringed horns, wound in an open spiral as long as 109 cm (43 in). Well adapted to the desert, the addax has large hooves for running over sand. By eating succulent leaves and wild watermelons it can survive without water for many days. The addax seeks shelter from the midday sun, sometimes in caves.

**ADDER,** common name for a snake of the viper family, the common adder or common European viper. Like all vipers, the common adder is poisonous, but it is less aggressive than most venomous snakes and its bite is rarely fatal to humans. This reptile is the only poisonous snake found in Great Britain. Its wide range throughout the Old World extends east to the Pacific Ocean and North to the Arctic Circle, the farthest north of any venomous snake.

The common adder seldom grows longer than 61 cm (24 in). Its color varies from gray, green, or brown to velvety black and, on all but the darkest skin, a regular series of zigzag black marks may be seen on the back. It eats mainly rodents.

Other vipers in the same genus with the common adder are also referred to as adders, including, on the one extreme, the Orsini viper of Europe, which lives largely on insects and appears to use its venom rarely, even when handled; and, on the other extreme, the daboia, or Russell's viper, of southeastern Asia, which has probably caused more human fatalities than any other species of viper.

In Africa, some larger snakes of the viper family, such as the puff adder, are also called adders.

Because of their appearance or behavior, other snakes completely unrelated to vipers are also known as adders. Australia's death adder is actually a member of the cobra family. In the U.S. several harmless snakes are called adders. For example, hognose snakes, called puff adders, spreading adders, or hissing adders, rarely even bite; these snakes puff up and hiss wildly when disturbed.

*See* DEATH ADDER; HOGNOSE SNAKE; VIPER.

| COMMON NAME | FAMILY | GENUS AND SPECIES |
|---|---|---|
| Common adder | Viperidae | *Vipera berus* |
| Orsini viper | Viperidae | *V. ursinii macrops* |
| Daboia | Viperidae | *V. russellii* |
| Puff adder | Viperidae | *Bitis arietans* |

**ADDER'S-TONGUE,** common name for plants of the fern genus *Ophioglossum* (*see* FERN) and also for *Erythronium americanum* of the lily family, Liliaceae. *E. americanum* (yellow adder's-tongue) is a beautiful spring wildflower found in the eastern U.S. Known also as the trout lily, it has mottled leaves, bears yellow, lilylike flowers, and reaches a height of 30 cm (12 in).

**ADDING MACHINE.** *See* COMPUTER.

**ADDIS ABABA,** city, central Ethiopia, the country's capital and largest city. It is situated at an elevation of about 2440 m (about 8000 ft) above sea level on a plateau that is crossed by numer-

ous streams and surrounded by hills. Addis Ababa is the country's commercial, manufacturing, and cultural center. It is the focus of a highway network, the site of an international airport, and the terminus of a railroad to the Gulf of Aden port of Djibouti. In the city are printing industries, and manufactures include footwear, clothing, asbestos and metal products, processed foods, cement, and plywood. Flourishing handicraft industries produce leather, metal, and textile goods, which are traded along with the regional agricultural produce, such as coffee, tobacco, and dairy items, in the vast open-air market known as the Mercato, on the W side of the city.

Addis Ababa is a sprawling city, well wooded, especially with eucalyptus trees, and crossed by broad avenues. Modern, multistoried buildings sit side by side with traditional one- and two-storied structures and open spaces. Its high elevation gives the city a mild, pleasant climate. The city is the seat of Addis Ababa University (1950), schools of music and art, and several research institutes. As headquarters of the Organization of African Unity and the UN Economic Commission for Africa, the city is the scene of many international conferences. Of note in the city are the octagon-shaped Saint George Coptic Christian Cathedral (1896), the modern Africa Hall with its dramatic stained-glass windows, and the Menelik II Palace, as well as several museums with col-

*Puff adder,* Bitis arietans, *venomous African snake that attains a length of 1.5 m (5 ft).*
© 1990 J. Carmichael, Jr.–The Image Bank

*Most roads in Ethiopia lead to the capital city, Addis Ababa, where modern multistory buildings stand side by side with traditional one-story houses.* **Bettmann Archive**

lections of art, ethnology, and archaeology.

The modern city was founded in 1887 at the site of a hot springs by Emperor Menelik II and given the name Addis Ababa, Amharic for "new flower." It became the national capital in 1889. The city's somewhat haphazard and unplanned growth was spurred by the completion in 1917 of the railroad to Djibouti. From 1936 to 1941 Addis Ababa was occupied by the Italians, who made it the capital of Italian East Africa and instituted extensive modernization projects. Between 1960 and 1970 the population of the city nearly doubled, and new light manufacturing industries were established. In 1963 the charter establishing the Organization of African Unity was signed here. Pop. (1984) 1,423,111.

**ADDISON,** village, Du Page Co., NE Illinois, a suburb W of Chicago; inc. 1884. It is largely residential with some varied manufacturing. The village is named for the British statesman and writer Joseph Addison. Pop. (1980) 28,836; (1990) 32,058.

**ADDISON, Joseph** (1672–1719), English essayist, poet, and statesman, whose work, particularly in the periodicals *The Tatler* and *The Spectator,* was one of the strongest influences in the formation of 18th-century English taste and opinion.

Addison was born on May 1, 1672, in Milston, Wiltshire, and educated at the University of Ox-

ford, where he was known for his skill in writing Latin verse. In 1699 he was granted a government pension, which he used for travel through Europe. In 1704, about a year after his return to England, Addison was commissioned by the government to write a poem celebrating the British victory at the Battle of Blenheim. His composition, "The Campaign," was such an aid to the Whig party that his position in both politics and letters was firmly established. In 1708, Addison entered Parliament as a Whig, and he retained his seat for the remainder of his life. In 1709 he became a contributor to *The Tatler,* a periodical founded by his friend the essayist Sir Richard Steele. Two years later, Steele founded another periodical, *The Spectator,* for which Addison subsequently wrote the finest of his many essays. Addison's literary reputation reached its highest point in 1713, when his tragedy *Cato* was produced in London. It was translated into several languages, and such influential critics as the French author Voltaire pronounced it the finest tragedy in the English language. In the opinion of most modern critics, this play, an artificial and undramatic work, was overestimated by Addison's contemporaries. Addison died on June 17, 1719, in London.

Addison's literary reputation has suffered a decline since his own time, when he was widely

*Joseph Addison*                    National Portrait Gallery, London

considered the most important of English authors. He is now remembered mainly as one of the founders of the modern familiar essay and as a prose stylist of polish, grace, and elegance. Addison's poetry is now generally read only as a typical product of his period, and his dramatic works are rarely produced.                    L.T.

**ADDISON'S DISEASE,** chronic disorder resulting from insufficiency of the adrenal glands. The disease was first described by the British physician Thomas Addison (1793–1860) in 1855. The insufficiency can occur after a severe infection, such as tuberculosis, after massive bleeding of the adrenals, or after surgery affecting the glands, such as removal of a tumor, but in most cases the origin of the disease is unknown. The resulting lack of hormone secretion causes such symptoms as weakness and fatigability, weight loss, low blood pressure, gastrointestinal distress, low blood sugar, depression and irritability, and increased skin pigmentation. Once fatal, the disease is now treated effectively with daily doses of cortisone or hydrocortisone and additional salt in the diet.

**ADDITION.** *See* ARITHMETIC.

**ADDRESS, FORMS OF,** conventional means of addressing persons of distinction. In most countries special forms of address are many and elaborate, but in the U.S. they are relatively few and simple. As sanctioned by usage, they include the following:

**Government.** In direct speech the president of the U.S. is addressed as *Mr. President;* in written communications he is addressed as *Dear Mr. President.* In diplomatic communications from other governments the president is styled *Excellency.* Similar forms are used for the vice-president. Members of the cabinet are addressed as *Mr./Madam Secretary* and are referred to as *The Honorable* John/Jane Doe. Ambassadors and governors of the states are styled *The Honorable* Jane/John Doe. The mayors of cities and assembly members are also called *The Honorable.*

The chief justice of the U.S. is addressed as *Chief Justice,* the other Supreme Court members as *Justice.* All justices in the U.S., whether federal, state, or local, are called *The Honorable* and addressed as *Judge.*

Members of the upper house of Congress, the Senate, are styled *The Honorable* Jane/John Doe and addressed as *Senator.* All other members of Congress and members of state legislatures are referred to as *The Honorable* John/Jane Doe.

**Physicians and Clergy.** The professional title *Doctor* sometimes precedes the name of a physician or a professor, but more usually follows it in the form of the appropriate initials, as in "Mary Jones, M.D." Physicians are addressed as *Doctor,* professors as either *Professor* or *Doctor.*

Clergy are referred to as *The Reverend* John/Jane Doe; never as *Reverend* or *The Reverend* Doe. They are addressed according to position in a given church, for example, *Pastor* or *Rector,* and as *Mr./Ms./Dr.* Jane/John Doe. Jewish clergy are called *Rabbi, Rabbi* Doe, or *Rabbi* John/Jane Doe.

Roman Catholic priests are styled *The Reverend;* if they are members of an order the initials of that order follow. They are addressed as *Father.* Women in religious orders are styled *Mother* or *Sister,* followed by the initials of the order; they are addressed as *Mother* or *Sister.*

**Army and Navy Officers.** Officers are styled by rank, as *General* Doe or *Captain* Doe, and addressed as *General* or *Captain;* naval officers below the rank of commander are addressed simply *Sir/Madam.*

**ADELAIDE,** city, S Australia, capital and chief city of South Australia State, on the Torrens R., near the Gulf of Saint Vincent (an arm of the Indian Ocean). Manufactures include motor-vehicle and electronic equipment, machinery, chemicals, textiles, and plastic goods. Shipping facilities are at nearby Port Adelaide. Adelaide is a modern city of broad streets, large squares, and extensive parks. Points of interest in Adelaide include the Adelaide Festival Centre complex (site of a biennial arts festival begun in 1960), Parliament House, Government House, the Natural History Museum, the National Gallery of South Australia, and the cathedrals of Saint Peter (Anglican) and Saint Francis Xavier (Roman Catholic). The University of Adelaide (1874) and the South Australian Institute of Technology (1889) are here.

Adelaide was founded in 1836 and named for Queen Adelaide, the consort of William IV, then the British king. It was designed and surveyed in 1837 by Col. William Light (1784–1838); in 1840 it was incorporated as a municipality. The community soon developed as the chief outlet for the agriculture of the lower Murray R. valley. It achieved city status in 1919. Pop. (1991, greater city) 1,023,597.

**ADÉLIE COAST** or **ADÉLIE LAND,** territory, Antarctica, lying between lat 66° and 67° S and between long 136° 20′ and 142° 20′ E, claimed by France. Jules Sébastien César Dumont d'Urville, commander of a French Antarctic expedition, discovered the region in 1840 and named it for his wife. Area, about 388,500 sq km (about 150,000 sq mi).

**ADEN** (anc. *Adana*), city, S Yemen, a major port on the Red Sea, economic capital of the Republic of Yemen. The city is located at the tip of the Arabian Peninsula on two small peninsulas of volcanic origin that rise to more than 300 m (1000 ft) in height. The E peninsula is known as Aden and the W peninsula as Little Aden. Its position near the entrance to the Red Sea has made the city one of the busiest fueling stations in the world, servicing most of the ships that pass through the Suez Canal. It is also a transshipment center for the region. A large oil refinery is located at Little Aden. The principal sources of employment are the refinery and the port complex. International air service is provided at the Aden Civil Airport, located at nearby Khormaksar.

An ancient trade center, the city of Aden was under Egyptian control from the 3d century BC until it became a Roman colony in 24 BC. It fell successively under Ethiopian and Persian control and became associated with Yemen about the 7th century AD. It fell to the Turks in 1538 and was incorporated into the sultanate of Lahej in 1728. After British forces seized Aden in 1839, it was administered as part of India. In 1937, it became a crown colony, encompassing the environs and the Kuria Muria and Perim Islands. Aden was declared a free port in 1850, and coastal areas were annexed to the port in 1881 and 1888. During World War II the colony of Aden was an important Allied air base.

In 1956 tension arose between Yemen (later the Yemen Arab Republic) and Great Britain over the Aden Protectorate territory. Trade union and nationalist elements in the colony generally sided with Yemen, and strikes and riots resulted from British efforts to deal with border clashes by force. These groups also opposed an announcement by the British government on Aug. 20, 1962, of a plan to merge the colony with the Federation of South Arabia, but the merger was effected in January 1963. In later years Aden was the focus of terrorist attacks by Arab nationalists trying to expel the British from South Arabia. When the federation won its independence on Nov. 30, 1967, Aden became the capital of the new state, known from 1970 to 1990 as the People's Democratic Republic of Yemen, which merged with the Yemen Arab Republic on May 22, 1990, to form the new Republic of Yemen. Pop. (1984 est.) 318,000.

**ADEN, GULF OF,** W arm of the Arabian Sea, between the S coast of the Arabian Peninsula and the N coast of the Horn of Africa (Somalia and Djibouti). It is about 885 km (about 550 mi) long and is linked to the Red Sea by a strait, the Bab al-Mandab. The gulf forms part of the commercial shipping route from the Indian Ocean to the Mediterranean Sea by the Suez Canal.

**ADENAUER, Konrad** (1876–1967), first chancellor (1949–63) of the Federal Republic of Germany.

Born in Cologne on Jan. 5, 1876, Adenauer was educated at the universities of Freiburg, Munich, and Bonn. From 1917 to 1933 he was lord mayor of Cologne and a member of the Prussian legislature. A member of the Catholic Center party, he opposed Nazism, and when Hitler came to power in 1933, Adenauer was barred from office

*Konrad Adenauer, leader of postwar Germany, at a reception in Bonn on the eve of his 90th birthday.* UPI

and forced into retirement. In 1944 he was sent to a concentration camp, but he was released when the Allies invaded Germany.

In 1945 he participated in the founding of the Christian Democratic Union (CDU) and became the new party's chairman in the British occupation zone. When the Federal Republic of Germany (West Germany) was established in 1949, Adenauer, favored by the occupying powers as an anti-Communist free of Nazi associations, became the new republic's first chancellor. For the next 14 years, Adenauer headed a coalition that was composed of the CDU, the Bavarian Christian Social Union, and the Free Democrats. From 1951 to 1955 he also served as foreign minister of the Federal Republic.

Adenauer's main goal was to establish West Germany as a bulwark of the Western alliance to contain Soviet expansion in Europe. To this end he promoted close relations with the U.S. and reconciliation with France, avoiding any move toward reunion with Communist East Germany. Under Adenauer's leadership, West Germany, a firm supporter of the North Atlantic Treaty Organization, achieved recognition as an independent nation (1955) and became one of the founding members of the European Economic Community, or Common Market (now European Union). In 1963 Adenauer and French president Charles de Gaulle concluded a long-desired treaty of cooperation between their two countries. Later that year he resigned from office at the age of 87. He died at Rhöndorf on April 19, 1967.

**ADENOIDS,** lymphoid tissue at the back of the throat, which usually shrinks and disappears by adolescence. Enlargement of this tissue, however, is fairly common in children and may interfere with breathing. Symptoms of enlarged adenoids include a nasal voice, persistent breathing through the mouth, snoring, and restless sleep.

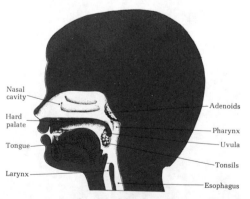

**Location of the Adenoids**

Nasal cavity
Hard palate
Tongue
Larynx
Adenoids
Pharynx
Uvula
Tonsils
Esophagus

Formerly these tissues were routinely removed in children, because it was thought that inflamed adenoids led to recurrent infections and colds. More recently, medical science has recognized this condition as usually benign, and the number of adenoidectomies has consequently declined. *See also* TONSIL.

**ADENOSINE TRIPHOSPHATE** (ATP), molecule found in all living organisms that is the main immediate source of usable energy for the activities of the cells. ATP is built up by the metabolism of foodstuffs in the cell, often in special compartments called mitochondria. Because the energy-

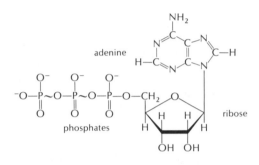

*Adenosine triphosphate (ATP)*

exchanging function of ATP and the catalytic (work-boosting) function of enzymes are intimately connected, ATP is characterized as a coenzyme. The adenosine part of the molecule is made up of adenine, a nitrogen-containing compound (also one of the principal components of the gene), and ribose, a five-carbon sugar. Three phosphate units (triphosphate), each made up of one phosphorus atom and four oxygen atoms, are attached to the ribose. The two bonds between the three phosphate groups are high-energy bonds, that is, they are relatively weak and yield their energy readily when split by enzymes. With the release of the end phosphate group, 7 kilocalories (7 calories, in common usage) of energy become available for work, and the ATP molecule becomes ADP (adenosine diphosphate). Most of the energy-consuming reactions in cells are powered by the conversion of ATP to ADP; they include the transmission of nerve signals, the movement of muscles, the synthesis of protein, and cell division. Usually, ADP quickly regains the third phosphate unit. In vertebrate muscle and brain cells, excess ATP can be transferred to creatine (q.v.) to provide a reserve energy store.

The release of two phosphate groups from ATP by the enzyme adenyl cyclase forms AMP (adenosine monophosphate), a nucleotide component of nucleic acids (q.v.), the material of DNA; this enzyme is important in many of the body's reactions. The American biochemist Earl Sutherland, Jr. (1915–74), won the 1971 Nobel Prize in physiology or medicine for work showing that one form of AMP called cyclic AMP, created by the action of the enzyme adenyl cyclase, is instrumental in regulating the activities of many hormones, including epinephrine and ACTH (qq.v.).

Plants produce ATP by direct utilization of the energy in sunlight. *See* PHOTOSYNTHESIS.

**ADHESION,** attraction between the surfaces of two bodies. The term is sometimes used to denote the tendency of two adjacent surfaces, which may be of different chemical compositions, to cling to each other, whereas cohesion is used to refer to the attraction between portions of a single body. For example, if a sheet of glass is lowered into water and withdrawn, some water will cling to the glass (adhesion) but the rest will be pulled back into the main body of water (cohesion).

The force of attraction is attributed to electromagnetic interactions produced by fluctuations in the distribution of electrons in the molecules of the facing surfaces. The distance between the molecules of the facing surfaces is a determining factor in the amount of force exerted. A surface that may appear smooth to the naked eye actually may be too rough to hold its molecules close enough to a facing surface to produce an electromagnetic bond. Gauge blocks, used for taking accurate measurements, have such smooth surfaces that their facing surfaces can be made to stick to each other by twisting them together.

In the human body, when tissues or organs that are normally separated unite or grow together, the process is called adhesion. It may occur after inflammation or during healing after a surgical operation.

**ADHESIVE,** a substance used to bond two or more surfaces together. Most adhesives form a bond by filling in the minute pits and fissures normally present even in very smooth surfaces. Adhesive bonds are economical, distribute the stress at the bonding point, resist moisture and corrosion, and eliminate the need for rivets and bolts. The effectiveness of an adhesive depends on a number of factors, including resistance to slippage and shrinkage, malleability, cohesive strength, and surface tension, which determines how far the adhesive penetrates the tiny depressions in the bonding surfaces. Adhesives vary with the purpose for which they are intended. Among such purposes is now included the increasing use of adhesives in surgery.

Natural adhesives have been replaced in many uses by synthetics; but animal glues, starches, gums, cellulose, bitumens, and natural rubber cements continue to be used in large volumes.

Organic adhesives derived from animal protein include glues made from collagen, a constituent of the connective tissues and bones of mammals and fish; blood albumen glue, used in the plywood industry; and glue made from casein, a protein constituent of milk, employed in wood bonding and in paint. Vegetable adhesives include starches and dextrins derived from corn, wheat, potatoes, and rice, used for bonding paper, wood, and textiles; gums such as gum arabic, agar, and algin, which when moistened provide adhesion in such products as stamps and gummed envelopes; cellulose adhesives, used to bond leather, cloth, and paper; rubber cements; and resins such as tree pitch and mastic.

Synthetic adhesives, used either alone or as modifiers of natural adhesives, perform better and have a greater range of application than the natural products. Most of them form polymers, huge molecules incorporating large numbers of simple molecules to form strong chains and nets that link surfaces in a firm bond. Thermosetting adhesives, which are transformed into tough, heat-resistant solids by the addition of a catalyst or the application of heat, are used in such structural functions as bonding metallic parts of aircraft and space vehicles. Thermoplastic resins, which can be softened by heating, are used for bonding wood, glass, rubber, metal, and paper products. Elastomeric adhesives, such as synthetic or natural rubber cements, are used for bonding flexible materials to rigid materials.

**ADIABATIC PROCESS,** in thermodynamics, any physical process in which quantities such as pressure and volume are varied without any essential transfer of heat energy to the surroundings (*see* HEAT; HEAT TRANSFER). A common example is the drop in temperature of an aerosol can when some of the can's contents are released. Energy was used up as the gases expanded too quickly for significant heat transfer to occur, hence the drop in temperature. A reverse effect of temperature rise is seen when a gas is compressed quickly. Various familiar systems, such as automobile engines, exhibit adiabatic phenomena.

**ADIGE,** river, N Italy. It rises in the Rhaetian Alps, flows E as far as Bolzano, and then courses in a generally S direction through Trento and Verona. Beyond Verona it flows toward the SE and E, finally emptying into the Adriatic Sea. The lower course is wide, but the swift current makes navigation difficult. In ancient times the lower course of the river, then known as the Athesis, lay somewhat to the N of the present course. The river is about 354 km (about 220 mi) long.

**ADIRONDACK MOUNTAINS** *or* **ADIRON-DACKS,** group of mountains, NE New York State, bounded by the Canadian border on the N, the Mohawk R. valley on the S, the Saint Lawrence R. and Black R. valleys on the W, and the Lake Champlain area on the E. The Adirondacks are composed mainly of metamorphic and igneous rock, among the oldest in the world (*see* PRECAMBRIAN ERA). Sometimes erroneously included in the Appalachian system, the Adirondacks are geologically related to the Canadian Shield (q.v.) and are generally considered a S extension of it. About half of the total acreage of the Adirondack Mt. range is part of the New York State Forest Preserve. More than 405,000 ha (2.4 million acres) of forest preserve land have been incorporated into Adirondack Park (created in 1892), where particular conservation and recreation efforts have been focused. The park, which has a total area of 209 million ha (516 million acres), 1.3 million ha (3.2 million acres) in private holdings, occupies the central portion of the mountain range and is magnificently scenic. In the park is Mt. Marcy (1629 m/5344 ft), the highest summit in the state, as well as 45 other peaks more than 1219 m (4000 ft) high, among them Algonquin Peak (1559 m/5114 ft) and Skylight, Haystack, and Whiteface peaks. The region has hundreds of lakes, notably Lakes Placid and George and Schroon, Cranberry, Upper and Lower Saranac, and Raquette lakes. The Hudson, Ausable, and Black rivers rise in the Adirondacks. The park is forested with spruce, pine, and hemlock and some deciduous trees. Wildlife is abundant.

There are no large cities or major industrial zones here. The area is a popular all-year sport and resort region. Because the climate is beneficial to sufferers from pulmonary ailments, several sanatoriums have been established here. Lumbering is carried on by private landholders, and some iron ore, talc, and zinc are mined.

*For further information on this topic, see the Bibliography in volume 28, sections 867, 1172.*

**ADJECTIVE.** *See* PARTS OF SPEECH.

**ADJUDICATION,** a way of resolving disputes or controversies, usually through action in a court of law. The issues settled by adjudication may be civil or criminal; they may arise between private parties or between private parties and public bodies. Issues are settled according to specific procedures involving submission of proofs and presentation of arguments for each side. The dispute is argued before an impartial judge and jury or judge, both of whom are empowered to decide in favor of one of the parties. Adjudication is also a function of legislative bodies, as in impeachment proceedings; administrative agen-

*A sylvan scene on the Ausable River in the Adirondacks, with Whiteface Peak in the background.*
J. Goerg–NY State Dept. of Environmental Conservation

cies, such as the Adjudication Division of the Federal Communications Commission; and labor arbitrators.

**ADJUTANT BIRD.** *See* MARABOU; STORK.

**ADLER, Alfred** (1870–1937), Austrian psychologist and psychiatrist, born in Vienna, and educated at the University of Vienna. He studied and was associated with Sigmund Freud, the founder of psychoanalysis (q.v.). In 1911 Adler left the orthodox psychoanalytic school to found a neo-Freudian school of psychoanalysis. After 1926 he was a visiting professor at Columbia University, and in 1935 he and his family moved to the U.S.

In his analysis of individual development, Adler stressed the sense of inferiority, rather than sexual drives, as the motivating force in human life. According to Adler, conscious or subconscious feelings of inferiority (to which he gave the name *inferiority complex*), combined with compensatory defense mechanisms, are the basic causes of psychopathological behavior. The function of the psychoanalyst, furthermore, is to discover and rationalize such feelings and break down the compensatory, neurotic will for power that they engender in the patient. Adler's works include *The Theory and Practice of Individual Psychology* (1918) and *The Pattern of Life* (1930).

**ADLER, Felix** (1851–1933), German-American educator and reformer, born in Alzey, Germany. In 1857 he went to the U.S., where his father had been called to the rabbinate of Temple Emanu-El in New York City. After graduating from Columbia College, he studied at the universities of Berlin and Heidelberg. On his return to the U.S. he was appointed professor of Hebrew and Oriental literature at Cornell University, a post he held for two years. In 1876 he organized the first Society for Ethical Culture (*see* ETHICAL CULTURE MOVEMENT). In 1880 he founded the Workingman's School, which in 1895 became the Ethical Culture School, and in 1928 he founded the Fieldston School. Both schools stress ethics and morality. Well known as a lecturer and writer, Adler also was editor of the *International Journal of Ethics*. In 1902 Columbia University created the chair of social and political ethics for him, which he held for the rest of his life. He wrote *Creed and Deed* (1877), *Life and Destiny* (1905), *The Religion of Duty* (1912), and *An Ethical Philosophy of Life* (1918).

**ADLER, Mortimer Jerome** (1902–  ), American scholar and author, born in New York City, and educated at Columbia University. He taught psychology at Columbia (1923–29) and philosophy of law at the University of Chicago (1930–52). In 1945 he became associate editor, with the American educator Robert Hutchins, of *Great Books of the Western World* (54 vol., 1945–52). He resigned from the University of Chicago in 1952 to head the newly established Institute for Philosophical Research at San Francisco. He wrote *How to Read a Book* (1940), *The Difference of Man and the Difference It Makes* (1967), and *Philosopher at Large: An Intellectual Autobiography* (1977). He was editor in chief of *The Annals of America* (20 vol., 1969) and director of planning for the 15th edition of *Encyclopaedia Britannica* (1974).

**ADMETUS.** See ALCESTIS.

**ADMINISTRATIVE LAW,** body of law applicable to the operations of agencies established by the legislature to carry out the functions of the executive branch of government. The Interstate Commerce Commission and the Federal Communications Commission are examples of such agencies in the U.S.

**Origins.** Although the term *administrative law* was not used until the 20th century, the concern with maintaining controls over the power of government goes back in English law as far as the Magna Charta. By the 19th century, courts in Europe had recognized a separate administrative law, which was known by the French term *droit administratif*. In the U.S. it was the New Deal of the 1930s, with its proliferation of government agencies, that led the courts to apply a distinctive body of law to the operation of these agencies.

**Administrative Law in the U.S.** Administrative bodies are created and given power by federal or state legislation. It is the function of administrative law to set forth the extent of this power, the limitations on it, and its applications to private individuals and groups. The law is basically concerned with whether proper standards are applied by administrative agencies in exercising their powers and in making and enforcing regulations. If an agency does not apply the proper standards, its failure may be redressed by application to the courts. Although a court may not substitute its own judgment for that of the agency in determining whether a given regulation is desirable, the court may declare the regulation a nullity if the agency, by promulgating such a regulation, has exceeded the authority conferred by the legislature. In determining that a regulation has been violated, substantial proof is required, but the agency is not bound by the laws of evidence that apply in court trials.

With the multiplication of federal administrative agencies in the U.S. during the 1930s, a means of making administrative regulations reasonably accessible to the public became necessary. The Federal Register Act (1935) provides that all federal regulations must be published in the *Federal Register;* a regulation that is not published in this manner is not binding upon persons who are unaware of its existence. Periodically, all federal regulations still in force must be codified and published in a compilation called the *Code of Federal Regulations.* The Administrative Procedures Act (1946) provides that before a federal agency promulgates a general regulation, interested parties must be afforded an opportunity to present their views. Another safeguard is that the investigation and prosecution of alleged violations may not be undertaken by the same persons who will render the judgment.

**ADMINISTRATOR.** See EXECUTOR.

**ADMIRAL** (Arab. *amir al*, "lord of the"), in common usage, a naval officer of the highest rank, also referred to as a flag officer. A system of gradations in the rank of admiral prevails in all major navies of the world. In the U.S. Navy the rank includes fleet admiral, admiral, vice admiral, and rear admiral, in descending order of seniority. In the British navy, except for the substitution of the title admiral of the fleet for that of fleet admiral, the grades are identical to those of the U.S. Navy.

Before the American Civil War, the highest rank in the U.S. Navy was that of commodore, a temporary rank assigned to the commander of a squadron. In 1862 the rank of rear admiral was created and bestowed on Capt. David G. Farragut. Congress also established the ranks of vice admiral and admiral for Farragut in 1864 and 1866, respectively. The rank of admiral of the navy was created for the American naval officer George Dewey in 1899; on his death the rank was abolished. Between 1899 and 1915 the ranks of admiral and vice admiral were also temporarily abolished. During World War II the rank of fleet admiral was created; it was first bestowed upon William Daniel Leahy (1875–1959) on Dec. 15, 1944. Within a year it was also bestowed upon Ernest Joseph King, Chester William Nimitz, and William Frederick Halsey. No fleet admirals have been named since World War II.

The rank of admiral is held by the chief and vice chief of naval operations, commanders in chief of the Atlantic and Pacific fleets, and others in highest ranking posts. Chiefs of other fleet commands, major shore commands, and the naval bureaus usually hold the rank of vice admiral or rear admiral. If the officers chosen to fill these posts do not hold appropriate rank, it is bestowed on them, temporarily. It can also be conferred by Congress as a mark of honor.

**ADMIRALTY,** in government, the department having control over naval matters. The Admiralty Board in Great Britain, established in the early 18th century, manages affairs similar to those of the Department of the Navy in the U.S.

**ADMIRALTY,** in law, special court exercising jurisdiction over all maritime issues. *See* MARITIME LAW.

**ADMIRALTY ISLANDS** *or* **ADMIRALTIES,** group of islands in the W Pacific Ocean, N of New Guinea, part of Papua New Guinea. The Admiralty Islands, which form part of the Bismarck Archipelago (q.v.), consist of about 18 islands. Manus Island (area, 1554 sq km/600 sq mi) and Rambutyo Island (area, about 207 sq km/about 80 sq mi) are the only large islands of the group. Coconut growing and pearl fishing are the leading industries. Lorengau, at the E extremity of Manus Island, is the chief town. The Admiralties were annexed by Germany in 1885. In 1920, following the defeat of Germany in World War I, the group was mandated to Australia. Japan occupied the islands in 1942, during World War II. Early in 1944 the Allies invaded the group. Japanese resistance ended on March 18, 1944. Administered by Australia after World War II, the islands became part of the newly independent nation of Papua New Guinea in 1975. Total area, 2072 sq km (800 sq mi); pop. (1990) 38,396.

**ADOBE,** Spanish-American name applied to a sun-dried brick and to the clay soil from which the brick is made. Adobe soils are found in many arid and semiarid regions worldwide, notably in Mexico and the southwestern U.S. Composed of a very fine mixture of clay, quartz, and other minerals, adobe has great plasticity when moist, but when dry is so coherent that tillage is almost impossible. The soils cover thousands of square miles in the western U.S. and under irrigation are very fertile, yielding undiminished yearly harvests

of grains, alfalfa, and other crops. Combined with straw, adobe soils are molded into bricks that are baked in the sun for 7 to 14 days. Because they lack cohesiveness when wet, adobe bricks can be used only in regions of limited rainfall. Dampness causes deterioration; hence, adobe structures often have eaves and stone foundations for protection against moisture. Such structures are most popularly associated with the Pueblo Indians, who built cliff dwellings and also ovens of adobe. Remains of their mud-brick communal villages still stand after centuries, and some Pueblos still use adobe as a building material.

**ADO-EKITI,** large town, SW Nigeria, in Ondo State. It is an important regional market center. Agricultural produce of the surrounding area includes yams, rice, corn, and livestock. Major manufactures are textiles, pottery, bricks, and footwear. Ado-Ekiti was founded by the Ekiti, a Yoruba people. It is also known as Ado. Pop. (1990 est.) 309,400.

**ADOLESCENCE,** stage of maturation between childhood and adulthood. The term denotes the period from the beginning of puberty (q.v.) to maturity; it usually starts at about age 14 in males and age 12 in females. The transition to adulthood varies among cultures, but it is generally defined as the time when individuals begin to function independently of their parents.

**Physical Development.** Dramatic changes in physical stature and features are associated with the onset of pubescence. The activity of the pituitary gland at this time results in the increased secretion of hormones, with widespread physiological effects. Growth hormone (q.v.) produces a rapid growth spurt, which brings the body close to its adult height and weight in about two years. The growth spurt occurs earlier among females than males, also indicating that females mature sexually earlier than males. Attainment of sexual maturity in girls is marked by the onset of menstruation (q.v.) and in boys by the production of semen. The main hormones governing these changes are androgen in males and estrogen in females, substances also associated with the appearance of secondary sex characteristics: facial, bodily, and pubic hair and a deepening voice among males; pubic and bodily hair, enlarged breasts, and broader hips among females. Physical changes seem to be related to psychological adjustment; studies suggest that earlier-maturing individuals are better adjusted than their later-maturing contemporaries.

*See also* GROWTH, HUMAN.

**Intellectual Development.** No dramatic changes take place in intellectual functions during adolescence. The ability to understand complex problems develops gradually. The French psychologist Jean Piaget determined that adolescence is the beginning of the stage of formal operational thought, which may be characterized as thinking that involves deductive logic. Piaget assumed that this stage occurs among all people regardless of educational or related experiences. Research evidence, however, shows that the ability of adolescents to solve complex problems is a function of accumulated learning and education.

**Sexual Development.** The physical changes that occur at pubescence are responsible for the appearance of the sex drive. The gratification of sex drives is still complicated by many social taboos, as well as by a lack of accurate knowledge about sexuality. Since the 1960s sexual activity has increased among adolescents in the U.S. Some recent studies suggest that almost 50 percent of adolescents under the age of 15 and almost 75 percent between the ages of 15 and 19 report having had sexual intercourse; yet, some adolescents are not interested in, or knowledgeable about, birth-control methods or ways in which to avoid contracting venereal disease. Consequently, births to young single mothers and the incidence of venereal disease are increasing.

**Emotional Development.** The American psychologist G. Stanley Hall asserted that adolescence is a period of emotional stress, resulting from the rapid and extensive physiological changes occurring at pubescence. Studies by the American anthropologist Margaret Mead, however, showed that emotional difficulties in the transition from childhood to adulthood varied from one culture to another. The German-born American psychologist Erik Erikson sees development as a psychosocial process going on through life.

The psychosocial task of adolescence is to develop from a dependent to an independent person, whose identity allows the person to relate to others in an adult fashion (intimacy). The occurrence of emotional problems varies among adolescents.

See also CHILD PSYCHOLOGY.    W.J.Me. & F.A.J.

For further information on this topic, see the Bibliography in volume 28, sections 151, 520.

**ADONAI.** See JEHOVAH.

**ADONIS,** in Greek mythology, beautiful youth beloved by the goddesses Aphrodite and Persephone. Born of the incestuous union of King Cinyras of Cyprus and his daughter, Adonis was placed in the custody of Persephone, queen of the underworld. When Adonis was slain by a wild boar while hunting, Aphrodite pleaded with the god Zeus to restore him to her. Zeus decreed that Adonis should spend the winter months with Persephone in Hades and the summer months with Aphrodite.

The story of his death and resurrection is symbolic of the natural cycle of death and rebirth.

**ADONIS,** genus of annual and perennial herbs of the family Ranunculaceae (see BUTTERCUP) containing about 20 species, grown for their showy flowers. They attain a height of about 30 cm (about 12 in) and have alternate, finely cut leaves; the flowers are usually red in the annual species and yellow in the perennial. Spring adonis, *Adonis vernalis,* is a perennial species bearing yellow flowers in May and June. Summer adonis, or pheasant's eye, *A. aestivalis,* is an annual with crimson flowers blooming from June to August. Autumn adonis, or flos adonis, *A. autumnalis,* is an annual; it bears small, dark-centered, red flowers from June through September.

**ADOPTION,** legal procedure recognized by statute in every state of the U.S. that permits, by means of a court action, a person who is not the lawful issue of the adopter to be admitted to all rights and privileges of a son or daughter. The practice and its legal sanction date from ancient Greece and Rome, when adoption served important estate-perpetuation purposes for citizens who otherwise would have had no heir. In modern societies the primary purpose of adoption is to enhance child welfare by allowing childless people, or couples with smaller families than they would like, to raise children who need parents. Adoption has long been an accepted procedure in the civil law, but it was not recognized by the common law courts of England. In the U.S. it has been necessary for individual states to pass specific legislation to permit adoption.

**Types of Adoptions.** Children may be adopted by stepparents or close relatives, or they may be adopted by nonrelatives, people who are strangers to the biological parents. Adoptions by relatives are not usually thought to pose serious risks to children or to the adoption process itself. Nonrelative adoptions, however, are regarded as involving potentially more serious problems.

Nonrelative adoptions are generally handled in one of two ways, through either licensed agencies or "independent placement." Both methods require judicial approval. In agency adoptions, applicants acquire the child from a public or private welfare agency following an investigation of their qualifications as prospective parents. In independent-placement adoptions, adoptive parents obtain a child directly from the natural parent, often using a doctor or lawyer as an intermediary, without any supervision or investigation by a social agency. During the last 35 years, some state legislatures and social agencies have become increasingly concerned about the risks of independent placement; thus, in a few states, welfare agencies have been given complete control of adoption.

The risks of independent placement are indeed formidable. Children may be purchased by adoptive parents who have more wealth than they have ability to give a child good and loving care. Professionals who arrange such adoptions, anxious to obtain children for clients, may attempt to coerce natural parents (often young and frightened unwed mothers with few economic resources). Many social-welfare experts believe that independent placement does not adequately protect the interests of the children because the adoptive parents may be less qualified for parenthood than are applicants investigated and approved by agencies.

Giving an adoption monopoly to agencies, however, also involves risks. Research suggests that agencies cater mainly to an upper-middle-class sample of prospective parents, whereas independent-placement adoption serves many couples from lower-income groups. Moreover, some evidence indicates that agencies also pressure unmarried parents into releasing their children for adoption. Allowing agencies the sole right to place children poses a serious threat that identically qualified applicants will be treated unequally, and that some prospective adoptive parents will be denied a child by arbitrary and unreviewable standards. For example, agencies often discriminate against qualified older couples, and sectarian agencies may reject those who do not adhere to strict religious practices.

In the last half of the 1970s, the number of babies available for adoption declined substantially; as a result, agency standards for adoptive parents became more stringent. As agency placements declined, the number of independent placements increased. The two methods of obtaining adopted children are likely to continue to create controversy until one or the other achieves more widespread public and professional support.

**Current Problems.** A notable decrease in the number of infants available for adoption (caused by increased abortions and by more mothers electing to keep their babies) has not led to an increase in the placement of children who are older, handicapped, or of mixed race, even though many such children are available for adoption. Most applicants continue to seek healthy babies of their own race. In addition, the complexity of the adoption process has led to a number of well-publicized legal conflicts between placing mothers who change their minds and adoptive parents who withhold the child despite a court order to the contrary. Many legal and mental health observers believe these controversies should be settled by looking solely to the "child's best interests," but the courts usually have preferred not to "reward" adoptive parents who seek to bond to a child while court orders returning the child to a natural parent have languished on appeal.

Single persons have sought—and, in some cases, gained—equal standing with couples to claim the limited number of children available for adoption. Interracial adoption has been vigorously supported by some agencies and adoptive parents and just as vigorously opposed by professional and political groups representing racial minority views. The U.S. Congress determined, in the Indian Child Welfare Act (1978), that Native American tribal rights to a child should be preferred to the claims of non-Indian adoptive parents even if the child was placed by a parent.

A different type of problem has resulted from the desire of some adopted persons to obtain information about their natural parents. Their attempts have been frustrated by agencies that will not allow even adults access to adoption records. The only one of these complex social problems close to resolution is the last. Many states have enacted statutes that authorize, under controlled conditions, the release of information about natural parents to adopted children.                    R.J.L.

*For further information on this topic, see the Bibliography in volume 28, section 295.*

**ADOPTIONISM** *or* **ADOPTIANISM.** *See* Monarchianism.

**ADOWA.** *See* Adwa.

**ADRENAL GLAND,** vital organ situated, in humans, on top of the upper end of each kidney. The two parts of the gland—the inner portion, or medulla, and the outer portion, or cortex—are like separate endocrine organs. They are composed of different types of tissue and perform different functions. The adrenal medulla, composed of chromaffin, secretes the hormone epi-

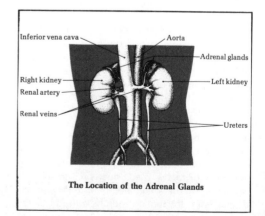

**The Location of the Adrenal Glands**

nephrine (q.v.), also called adrenaline, in response to stimulation of the sympathetic nervous system at times of stress. The medulla also secretes norepinephrine, a hormone that has a role in maintaining normal blood circulation. The hormones of the medulla are called catecholamines. Unlike the cortex, the medulla can be removed without endangering the life of an individual.

The cortex secretes about 30 steroid hormones, but only a few are secreted in significant amounts. Aldosterone, one of the most important hormones, regulates the salt and water balance in the body. Cortisone and hydrocortisone are also vital; they regulate fat, carbohydrate, and protein metabolism. Also secreted are adrenal sex steroids, which have a minor influence on the reproductive system. Modified glucocorticoids, now produced synthetically, are superior to naturally secreted steroids for treatment of Addison's disease and other disorders. See ACTH; HORMONE; HYDROCORTISONE.

**ADRENALINE.** See EPINEPHRINE.

**ADRIAN I** (d. 795), pope (772–95), who established the temporal power of the papacy.

A Roman aristocrat by birth, Adrian was elected pope by unanimous acclamation when he was only a deacon. After papal territory was attacked by the Lombard king Desiderius (r. 757–74), Adrian called Charles, king of the Franks (later Charlemagne), to his assistance. Charles defeated the Lombards and confirmed the pope in possession of many parts of Italy previously granted by Pepin, father of Charles. The borders of the Papal States remained much the same from that time until their disintegration in the 19th century. Adrian confirmed the decrees of the Second Council of Nicaea (787), ending the controversy over the veneration of images. A skilled administrator, he undertook the repair and construction of many buildings in Rome.

**ADRIAN IV** (1100?–59), pope (1154–59), the only Englishman to ascend to the papacy.

Born Nicholas Breakspear near St. Albans, Hertfordshire, he entered the monastery of Saint Rufus near Avignon, France. He was successively appointed abbot of the monastery (1137), cardinal bishop of Albano (c. 1150), and papal legate to Scandinavia (1152–54), where he reorganized the church hierarchy. When he returned to Rome, he was unanimously elected pope upon the death of Anastasius IV (b. 1073?; r. 1153–54).

Adrian almost immediately confronted Arnold of Brescia, the Italian monk and reformer who opposed the temporal power of the papacy. At Adrian's request, the German king Frederick I seized Arnold and then turned him over to the Roman Curia to be tried as a political rebel. After Arnold

was executed in 1155, Adrian crowned Frederick as Holy Roman emperor.

Adrian is said to have been called upon by Henry II of England to grant permission for the subjugation of Ireland. Because the popes claimed the "islands of the sea" by virtue of the Donation of Constantine, Adrian denied Henry absolute possession, but permitted him to occupy the island as a papal fief. The facts of the matter are uncertain, but the papal bull *Laudabiliter,* attributed to Adrian, may have been a forgery. The term Vicar of Christ began to be used to describe the pope during Adrian's pontificate.

**ADRIAN VI** (1459–1523), pope (1522–23), the only Dutchman and the last non-Italian elected to the papacy until the late 20th century. Born Adrian Florensz in Utrecht, he was a theologian and teacher, educated at the University of Louvain. He was appointed tutor to the future Charles V, Holy Roman emperor, and became (1516) administrator of Castile. Unanimously elected pope, even though he was not present at the conclave, he tried to initiate church reforms but was unsuccessful during the 20 months of his pontificate.

**ADRIANOPLE.** See EDIRNE.

**ADRIATIC SEA** (anc. *Adria* or *Mare Adriaticum*), arm of the Mediterranean Sea, S Europe, between the E coast of Italy and the W coast of the Balkan peninsula. At the S extremity is the Strait of Otranto, which connects it with the Ionian Sea. The Gulf of Venice, in the N, and the Gulf of Trieste, in the NE, are its main embayments. The W coast is comparatively low and has few inlets, and the N is marshy and edged with lagoons. On the E the Albanian coast is steep and rocky, and the coast of Croatia is fringed with islands. The area of the sea is about 155,000 sq km (about 60,000 sq mi). The rocky E coasts are dangerous for mariners in the winter because of the prevailing NE gales (bora). Trieste, Venice, Ancona, Bari, and Brindisi, Italy, are the chief ports. The fisheries of the Adriatic are highly productive.

**ADSORPTION,** the taking up by the surface of a solid or liquid (adsorbent) of the atoms, ions, or molecules of a gas or other liquid (adsorbate). Porous or finely divided solids can hold more adsorbate because of the relatively large surface area exposed. Similarly, the adsorbent surface of a quantity of liquid is increased if the liquid is divided into fine droplets. In some cases, the atoms of the adsorbate share electrons with atoms of the adsorbent surface, forming a thin layer of chemical compound. Adsorption is also an important part of catalysis and other chemical processes. Absorption (q.v.) occurs when the molecules of adsorbate penetrate the bulk of the solid or liquid adsorbent.

**ADULT EDUCATION,** all forms of schooling and learning programs in which adults participate. Unlike other types of education, adult education is defined by the student population rather than by the content or complexity of a learning program. It includes literacy training, community development, university credit programs, on-the-job training, and continuing professional education. Programs vary in organization from casual, incidental learning to formal college credit courses. Institutions offering education to adults include colleges, libraries, museums, social service and government agencies, businesses, and churches.

**Historical Background.** Early formal adult education activities focused on single needs such as reading and writing. Many early programs were started by churches to teach people to read the Bible. When the original purpose was satisfied, programs were often adjusted to meet more general educational needs of the population. Libraries, lecture series, and discussion societies began in various countries during the 18th century. As more people experienced the benefits of education, they began to participate increasingly in social, political, and occupational activities. By the 19th century, adult education was developing as a formal, organized movement in the Western world.

The largest early program in the U.S., the Lyceum, founded (1826) in Massachusetts by Josiah Holbrook (1788–1854), was a local association of men and women with some schooling who wanted to expand their own education while working to establish a public school system. The Lyceum movement encouraged the development of other adult education institutions such as libraries, evening schools, and endowed lecture series. By midcentury, employers and philanthropists began to endow institutions such as the Cooper Union for the Advancement of Science and Art (1859) in New York City and the Peabody Institute (1857) in Baltimore, Md., for adult education. Large audiences were attracted to the Chautauqua movement, which began (1874) in New York State as a summer training program for

*The summer encampment at Chautauqua Lake, near Chautauqua, in southwestern New York. Adherents of the Chautauqua movement cheer a speaker (from an 1880 newspaper engraving).*

The Granger Collection

Sunday school teachers and evolved into a traveling lecture series and summer school. Chautauqua was the prototype of institutions established to further popular education in the U.S. By 1876, universities started offering extension programs that brought education directly to the public.

Adult education was an early concern of the U.S. government. In 1862 Abraham Lincoln signed the Morrill Act, which led to the establishment of land-grant colleges offering training in agriculture and the mechanical arts. The need to develop and provide instruction in scientific farming techniques led to the establishment (1914) of the Federal Extension Service of the U.S. Department of Agriculture. The pattern of demonstration farming and extension advisers created by cooperative extension has been used to improve farming all over the world.

The rapid increase in immigration into the U.S. during the early 20th century resulted in the establishment of more English and citizenship classes and other Americanization programs for immigrants. During the Great Depression of the 1930s, the federal government established education projects as part of its work-relief programs. Public evening classes became the most popular means of adult education, allowing people to earn a living during the day and pursue vocational and intellectual interests in their spare time. Some institutions, such as the New School for Social Research in New York City, were devoted almost entirely to education for adults. After World War II, the adult education movement in the U.S. received a major impetus with the passage of the G.I. Bill of Rights, which enabled many veterans of World War II, and of later military service, to complete their education. The Higher Education Acts of 1966 and 1986 both reflected the growing importance of adult, part-time college students; they authorized a separate title devoted to continuing education and several financial-aid programs. Universities even began to offer graduate programs in this new field.

**Participation.** A person's desire to participate in an educational program often is the result of a changing personal, social, or vocational situation. Consequently, programs must be designed to satisfy the interests of participants. This individual orientation has resulted in the creation of a continually changing, dynamic field able to respond to the varied needs of society.

Programs for adults became the fastest-growing segment of education in the U.S. In 1991, part-time students accounted for approximately 45 percent of college enrollments in credit courses nationwide. Those over the age of 25 represented nearly the same percentage. Women, who have accounted for two-thirds of the increase in college enrollments since 1970, constituted some 54 percent of students in the early 1990s. During 1991 an estimated one-third of all Americans age 17 and over were enrolled in some type of adult education program. The general increase in adult participation is mainly the result of increased leisure time, the need to acquire job-related information and skills, and the feminist movement, which encourages women to begin or complete educational programs.

*Courtyard of the New School for Social Research in New York City, which was founded in 1919 for university-level adult education.*  © Debra P. Hershkowitz

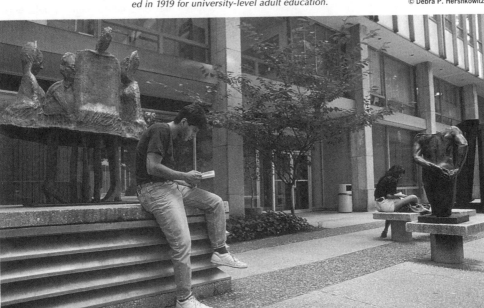

*English as a second language is one of the most popular adult education subjects in the U.S.*

Mark Sherman–Bruce Coleman, Inc.

Rapidly changing technical fields such as electronics require constant updating of information in order for workers to remain effective. Four out of five U.S. corporations with more than 500 employees now offer educational opportunities to workers, and many professional associations have educational programs for their members.

**Recent Developments.** In the last two decades, a rapid increase in continuing professional education programs has occurred, motivated by concern for improving the level of skills in fields as diverse as medicine, engineering, teaching, and accounting. Some states and professional associations have passed regulations requiring practitioners in licensed occupations such as medicine, accounting, and teaching to participate in a certain number of course-work hours each year. The need for continuing professional education is generally acknowledged, but there are disagreements as to whether such education should be mandatory. Controversy also exists over who should control such regulatory processes—government agencies, professional associations, or school faculties.

Another major development, perhaps the most important for future generations, is the increasing use of radio, network television, and cable television for adult education; broadcast media are being used worldwide to teach reading and writing, specialized seminars, and short courses, as well as to provide university-degree programs. With millions of personal computers and videocassette recorders in use in the U.S., teaching via these nonbroadcast technologies is also growing rapidly. Electronic media offer the means for reaching populations that are homebound or geographically isolated.

**International Movement.** Adult education has long been important in Europe, where formal programs began in the 18th century. For example, the Danish folk high school movement in the mid-19th century prevented the loss of Danish language and culture that a strong German influence threatened to absorb. In Great Britain, concern for the education of poor and working-class people resulted in the growth of adult education programs, such as the evening school and the Mechanic's Institute, to expand educational opportunities for all people. After the Russian Revolution the Soviet government virtually eliminated illiteracy through the establishment of various institutions and extension classes for adults.

In other areas of the world adult education movements are of a more recent origin. In 1960, Egypt established a "schools for the people" system designed to educate the adult population. The pattern used is similar to that developed in Great Britain a century ago. After many years in which the primary educational concern was with creating public school systems, in the 1970s countries in Africa, Asia, and Latin America began to increase opportunities for adult education. Innovative programs involving the mass media are being used in many countries. Tanzania, for example, has used mass-education techniques and the radio to organize national education programs in health, nutrition, and citizenship. In the 1980s, international educational exchange programs involving short-term nondegree study in specialized fields grew in popularity in the U.S. and many other countries.

A literate population is a necessity for any nation wishing to take advantage of modern technological growth. For instance, research has shown a direct relationship between literacy among women and improved health and child care in the family. The UN Educational, Scientific, and Cultural Organization (UNESCO) has long supported the concept that education must be considered an ongoing process. UNESCO has encouraged literacy programs, agricultural extension, and community instruction. The low cost and flexibility of such programs make adult education suitable for many areas of the world that do not yet have formal school programs.

See also CORRESPONDENCE EDUCATION; EDUCATION, TECHNICAL; EDUCATION, VOCATIONAL .

E.Co.; REV. BY H.J.S.

For further information on this topic, see the Bibliography in volume 28, section 324.

**ADULTERATION,** act of making any commodity impure by admixture of other or baser ingredients. This admixture may corrupt the nature of the original to the extent of destroying its identity, or it may merely lower the value or effectiveness of the finished product. Adulteration of foods and beverages has been performed with the same aim—increasing profits for the manufacturer or merchant—since early times, when laws in ancient Greece and Rome addressed the coloring and flavoring of wine. England has had laws against adulteration of beer, bread, and other commodities since the 13th century, culminating in the Adulteration of Food or Drink Act of 1872 with its stiff penalties—six months at hard labor for a second offense. The law was modernized with the 1955 Food and Drug Act.

In the U.S. numerous state and federal bills were introduced in the 1890s, finally resulting in the Pure Food and Drugs Act of 1906. This act was ineffective because of its light penalties, and in 1938 it was superseded by the Federal Food, Drug and Cosmetic Act, which outlaws foods and drugs dangerous to health that are sold in interstate commerce. The 1938 law has been amended to cover food colorings and additives and supplemented by similar state legislation aimed at foods and drugs that do not come within the scope of interstate commerce.

Adulteration not only functions to defraud consumers but it can also pose a health threat. In the case of illegal drugs sold on the street, adulteration is generally in the form of inert or harmless compounds, but deadly poisons, such as sodium cyanide, have sometimes been sold as heroin. Adulteration is not the only source of poor-quality or dangerous foods and drugs: The ingredients of junk foods need not be adulterated to ensure a virtual absence of nutritional value; potentially hazardous medicines will have more adverse effects if unadulterated. The consumer movement of recent times has focused not only on adulteration, but also on the nature of various unadulterated ingredients.

**ADUWA.** See ADWA.

**ADVENT** (Lat. adventus, "coming"), in the Christian ecclesiastical calendar, a season observed in preparation for Christmas. The earliest authentic record of Advent (AD 581) states that the season starts on the feast of St. Martin, November 11; this period is still observed in the Orthodox church. About 600, Pope Gregory I decreed that the season should start on the fourth Sunday before Christmas, but the longer period was observed in England for some years. The shorter period is now observed in the Roman Catholic, Lutheran, Anglican, and Episcopal churches, and the first Sunday of Advent is regarded as the commencement of the Christian ecclesiastical year. The season is also a preparation for the second coming of Christ at the end of the world.

**ADVENTISTS,** members of a number of related Protestant denominations that stress the doctrine of the imminent second coming (q.v.) of Christ. Adventism received its clearest definition and most earnest support under the leadership of an American Baptist preacher, William Miller. Miller and his followers, known initially as Millerites, proclaimed that the second coming would occur between March 21, 1843 and March 21, 1844. The failure of this prediction was called the First Disappointment, and many left the movement. Following this, a second date—Oct. 22, 1844—was set, and many Adventists disposed of their property in anticipation of the event. The movement was widely ridiculed after the day passed uneventfully. Thereafter many Adventists lost faith and returned to their former churches. Those remaining split into four main bodies, which still continue to flourish.

**Seventh-day Adventists.** By far the largest group is the Seventh-day Adventists, with more than 3.3 million members worldwide in 1980. The church originated between 1844 and 1855 under the leadership of three American Millerites, Joseph Bates (1792–1872) and James (1821–81) and Ellen White (1827–1915), but was not formally organized until 1863. Two tenets are prominent in the church's theology: belief in the visible, personal second coming of Christ at an early but indefinite date and the observance of Saturday as the Sabbath. Members accept the Bible as their sole religious authority, placing special trust in the literal interpretation of prophetic passages. They hold that grace alone is sufficient for salvation; they administer baptism by immersion and practice foot washing in connection with observance of the Lord's Supper.

Seventh-day Adventists expect the eventual destruction of the wicked and everlasting life for the just, including the living and the resurrected dead, at the second coming of Christ. In their social life, approved recreation replaces entertainments such as dancing and theatergoing. The denomination has a comprehensive program for youth. Holding that the body is the temple of the Holy Spirit, Seventh-day Adventists put great stress on health and avoid eating meat and using narcotics and stimulants. They maintain more than 360 hospitals and clinics around the world. The denomination also conducts missionary, educational, and philanthropic programs supported by a voluntary system of tithing (contributing a tenth of one's income) and by freewill offerings. Church activists are maintained in all parts of the world, and denominational publications are printed in 197 languages and dialects. The church conducts one of the largest school systems of any Protestant denomination.

**Other Adventist Churches.** The Advent Christian Church, first known as the Advent Christian Association and then the Advent Christian Conference, began in 1854 to withdraw gradually from the American Millenial Association, primarily because of a growing dispute over the question of immortality. First organized in 1860 in Salem, Mass., the Advent Christian Church preached a doctrine of "conditional immortality," according to which the dead remain in an unconscious state until the resurrection, which would take place at the second coming after the millennium. The church observes the sacraments of baptism by immersion and the Lord's Supper. Although organized into regional and central groups (the central group is the Advent Christian General Conference of America), each church governs itself independently. According to recent statistics, membership in the U.S. and Canada neared 30,000. The church supports missionary work in Mexico, Malaysia, Japan, India, and the Philippines; it founded Aurora College in Aurora, Ill., the Berkshire Christian College in Lenox, Mass., and two publishing houses. In 1964 the Life and Advent Union, founded in 1848, merged with the Advent Christian Church.

The Church of God (Abrahamic Faith) developed from several smaller groups of similar faith (some dating from 1800); some of them had organized in 1888 under the name Church of God in Christ Jesus. The churches, however, did not function as a unit until 1921, when a national conference was established and the name Church of God of the Abrahamic Faith was adopted. The corporate name is Church of God General Conference (Oregon, Ill.). Acceptance of the Bible as the supreme standard of the faith results in a literal interpretation of the biblical references to the kingdom of God; the premillennial coming of Christ, the belief that the return of Christ will precede the millennial kingdom of God predicted in Rev. 20:1–6, is central. The members maintain that the dead are merely asleep; at the time of the second coming the righteous will be resurrected on earth and the wicked will be finally destroyed. Acceptance of these doctrines, repentance, and purification through baptism by immersion are requirements for admission to the church. The individual churches are autonomous; recent figures indicate 9500 members. Missionary work is carried on in India, Mexico, and the Philippines.

The Primitive Advent Church is a recent offshoot of the Advent Christian Church; it has about 600 members, all in West Virginia, and its aim is to recover the principles and thought of early Adventism.

*For further information on this topic, see the Bibliography in volume 28, sections 93, 99.*

**ADVERB.** *See* PARTS OF SPEECH.

**ADVERTISING,** collective term for public announcements designed to promote the sale of specific products or services. Advertising is a form of mass selling, employed when the use of direct, person-to-person selling is impractical, impossible, or simply inefficient. It is to be distinguished from other activities intended to persuade the public, such as propaganda, publicity, and public relations. Advertising techniques range in complexity from the publishing of simple notices in the classified-advertising columns of newspapers to integrated marketing communications, involving the concerted use of advertising in newspapers, magazines, television, and radio, as well as direct response, sales promotion, and other communications vehicles in the course of a single campaign. From its unsophisticated beginnings in ancient times, advertising has burgeoned into a worldwide industry. In the U.S. alone in the early 1990s, about $138 billion was spent in a single year on advertising to influence the purchase of products and services.

American advertising leads the world not only in volume of business but in the complexity of its organization and of its procedures. For these reasons, this article deals primarily with advertising in the U.S. Modern advertising is an integral segment of urban industrial civilization, mirroring contemporary life in its best and worst aspects. Having proven its force in the movement of eco-

## NEWS! NEWS!!

AARON OLIVER, *Post-Rider*,

WISHES to inform the Public, that he has extended his Route ; and that he now rides thro' the towns of *Troy, Pittstown, Hoosick, Mapletown*, part of *Bennington* and *Shaftsbury, Petersburgh, Stephentown, Greenbush* and *Schodack*.

All commands in his line will be received with thanks, and executed with punctuality.

He returns his sincere thanks to his former customers ; and intends, by unabated diligence, to merit a continuance of their favours.

*O'er ruggid hills, aud vallies wide,*
*He never yet has fail'd to trudge it :*
*As steady as the flowing tide,*
*He bands about the* NORTHERN BUDGET.

*June 18,* 1799.

*Advertising in the early days of the U.S. took the form of handbills and personal messages transmitted by the town crier. Here a woodcut carries the announcement of a change in route served by a New England post rider.*
Bettmann Archive

nomic goods and services, advertising since the early 1960s has been directed in increasing quantity toward matters of social concern. The continuing cancer and antidrug abuse campaigns are only two examples of the use of the advertising industry as a means to promote public welfare.

Advertising falls into two main categories: consumer advertising, directed to the ultimate purchaser, and trade (or business-to-business) advertising, in which the appeal is made to business users through trade journals and other media.

Both consumer and trade advertising employ many specialized types of commercial persuasion. A relatively minor, but important, form of advertising is institutional (or image) advertising, designed solely to build prestige and public respect for particular business concerns as important U.S. institutions. Each year millions of dollars

are spent on institutional advertising, which usually mentions products or services only incidentally. Another minor, but increasingly popular, form of advertising is cooperative advertising, in which the manufacturer shares the expense of local television, radio, or newspaper advertising with the retailer who signs the advertisement. National advertisers occasionally share the same space in magazine advertising. For example, makers of pancake flour, of syrup, and of sausages sometimes jointly advertise this combination as an ideal cold-weather breakfast.

Advertising may be local, regional, national, or international in scope. The rates charged for the different levels of advertising vary sharply, particularly in newspapers; varying rates also are set by newspapers for amusement, political, legal, religious, and charitable advertisements.

*Advertisement for the American Cancer Society's Great American Smokeout, a campaign designed to get people to "take a day off from smoking."*

© Richard Hutchings–
Photo Researchers, Inc.

**Media.** Advertising messages are disseminated through numerous and varied channels or media. In descending order of dollar volume, the major media in the U.S. are newspapers, television, direct mail, radio, magazines, business publications, outdoor advertising, and farm publications. In addition, a significant amount of all U.S. advertising dollars is invested in miscellaneous media, such as window displays, free shopping-news publications, calendars, blimps, skywriting by airplanes, and even sandwich boards carried by people walking the streets.

In the U.S. a wide range of advertising media has been developed from sources whose potential importance formerly was ignored. Delivery trucks, once plainly painted, now often carry institutional or product messages, as do many shipping cartons. Some packages carry advertising for products other than those contained in them. Wrapping paper and shopping bags bearing advertisements are used widely by retail stores.

Newspapers have traditionally led all other media in the U.S. in terms of dollars invested in advertising; despite the popularity of radio and television, the daily papers have maintained a slight lead. Thus, in 1993 newspapers received about 23.2 percent of the advertising investment in the nation, totaling more than $32 billion from local and national advertisers. In second place was broadcast and cable television, with about 22 percent or approximately $30.5 billion. More than $27 billion was invested in direct mail. Radio received some $9.5 billion, and magazines got about $7.3 billion.

**Direct Advertising.** Direct advertising includes all forms of sales appeals mailed, delivered, or exhibited directly to the prospective buyer of an advertised product or service, without use of any indirect medium, such as newspapers or television. Direct advertising logically may be divided into three broad classifications, namely, direct-mail, mail-order, and unmailed advertising.

All forms of sales appeals (except mail-order appeals) that are sent through the mails are considered direct-mail advertising. The chief function of direct-mail advertising is to familiarize prospective buyers with a product's name, its maker, its merits, and its local distributors. A direct-mail appeal is designed to support the sales activities of retailers by encouraging the continued patronage of old and new customers.

When no personal selling is involved, other methods are needed to induce people to send in orders by mail. In addition to newspapers, magazines, radio, and television, special devices such as single-product folders or multiproduct catalogs are used in mail-order advertising. Mail-order promotions are designed to accomplish a complete selling job without salespeople.

Used for the same broad purposes as direct-mail advertising, unmailed direct advertising includes all forms of indoor advertising displays and all printed sales appeals distributed from door to door, handed to customers in stores, included in packages of merchandise, or conveyed in some other manner directly to the recipient.

With each medium competing keenly for its share of the business, advertising agencies continued to develop new techniques for displaying and selling wares and services. Among these techniques were vastly improved printing and reproduction methods in the graphic field, adapt-

This public-service message draws attention to the widespread problem of alcohol abuse in the U.S. today.

National Institute on Alcohol Abuse and Alcoholism

This television commercial for Alka Seltzer employed a humorous approach that was rapidly adopted by other advertisers and marked many campaigns of the 1970s.

Wells Rich Green, Inc.

ed to magazine advertisements and to direct-mail enclosures; the use of color in newspaper advertisements and in television; and outdoor signboards more attractively designed and efficiently lighted. Many subtly effective improvements are suggested by advertising research.

**Research.** During the 19th century it was possible only to approximate the effectiveness of various advertising techniques. Prospective advertisers were guided almost solely by estimates of magazine and newspaper readership. In the early days of broadcasting and outdoor advertising the industry lacked a reliable measure of the audience of these media. In 1914 the Audit Bureau of Circulations (ABC), an independent organization subscribed to principally by newspaper and magazine publishers, was established to meet the need for authentic circulation statistics and for a coordinated, standardized way of presenting them.

Eventually, greater scientific efforts to determine relevant facts about audience and readership developed as a result of competition among the media and the demand among advertisers for an accurate means of judging the relative effectiveness of the media. The media soon found ways of ascertaining not only how many people see or hear advertising messages, but what kinds of people and where they are located. Newspapers and magazines, either through their own research staffs or through specialized organizations employed for a fee, go to great lengths to analyze their circulations to show where their readers live, their income, education, recreational habits, age, and number of children and to provide other guides to determining their readers' susceptibility to certain classes of products.

Radio and television stations and networks similarly analyze their audiences for the guidance of advertisers. In this field, too, broadcast companies, advertising agencies, and advertisers subscribe to one or more audience-research organizations to determine how many viewers or listeners tune in regional and network shows at any given time. Special surveys of local broadcast programs can be arranged also. In a similar but less comprehensive manner, outdoor- and transportation-advertising companies have set up organizations to tally the numbers of persons exposed to their posters.

Because of the nature of advertising, depending as it does on psychological and other variables difficult to ascertain precisely, the whole field of audience research is complex and controversial. Researchers have found it necessary to consistently refine their techniques and make them increasingly reliable.

One by-product of this widespread interest in, and dependence on, advertising and marketing research is the Advertising Research Foundation, sponsored, directed, and subsidized by advertisers, agencies, and media. This organization, founded in 1936, not only initiates and commissions research projects of its own but also establishes criteria and standards of procedure that tend to enhance the authenticity, reliability, efficiency, and usefulness of all advertising and marketing research.

One major type of research project is the survey of test markets. Advertisers and agencies frequently conduct extensive and expensive surveys to determine the potential acceptance of products or services before they are advertised nationally at costs that may aggregate millions of dollars. In one common procedure the advertising-marketing division of a company dispatches a crew of surveyors to do a door-to-door canvass in various neighborhoods differing in average-income levels. Householders are shown various versions of the product intended for market. If the survey convinces the manufacturer that one of the versions exhibited will attract enough purchasers, a crew then pretests various sales appeals by showing provisional advertisements to consumers and asking them to indicate their preference. After the one or two best-liked advertisements or basic appeals are determined, the advertiser produces a limited quantity of the new product and introduces it in a test market. On the basis of this market test the advertiser-manufacturer can make a decision as to whether a national campaign should be launched.

The question of what motivates a consumer to buy challenges the imagination and ingenuity of the seller and presses research specialists forward into new fields of investigation. Motivational research, for example, attempts to probe the unconscious impulses that motivate buying decisions; advertising agencies then utilize these findings to influence the consumer and to attempt to break down sales resistance. Critical observers outside the advertising industry have assailed the motivational approach as unreliable and as unfair to the consumer, who should not, they feel, be subjected to such indirect sales attacks. Many researchers, however, regard motivational inquiry as only a means to delve deeper into the psychological springs of behavior than did earlier investigations. Through careful questioning and investigation it is often possible for an advertiser to trace a sale and learn what actually motivated the consumer to buy a product. Workers in motivational research try to explore these influences.

**Techniques of Persuasion.** While experts argue about new methods, they still rely mainly on basic appeals that have proved successful over the years. These appeals offer the hope of more money and better jobs, security against the hazards of old age and illness, popularity and personal prestige, praise from others, more comfort, increased enjoyment, social advancement, improved appearance, and better health. The modern advertiser stresses not the product but the benefits that may be enjoyed by purchasers. Thus, the advertiser purveys not cosmetics but the expectation of new beauty, allure, and hope. To attract the prospective buyer of automobiles, the manufacturer may stress not only the mechanical attributes of the car but also the excitement, comfort, and prestige it may bring the buyer.

The many techniques of persuasion are circumscribed only by the ingenuity of the creative mind, by the limits of the various channels of communications, by certain legal restrictions, and by standards self-imposed by the advertising industry. One fundamental technique, apparent in the earliest applications of advertising and still basic in the most modern procedures, is repetition. A typical national advertiser captures the attention of prospective customers by repeated appeals to buy. It is not unusual for a person to hear sales talks on radio and television, see advertisements for the same product in a local newspaper, receive additional reminders in various national magazines, and be confronted with a poster, counter card, or display on entering a store.

Another basic persuader is the trademark. Manufacturers have spent millions to establish their trademarks as symbols of reliability and value. A trademark is useless unless the manufacturer sets and maintains high standards of quality, but once consumers gain confidence in it, the owner can use it as a persuader, that is, as a device to reassure customers that all products bearing this symbol are reliable. The trademark is

Sports events provide an advertising opportunity for many consumer-goods companies. Diet Pepsi began its sponsorship of Dennis Connor and his racing yacht, Stars & Stripes, with the America's Cup races of 1987.  © Daniel Foster–Duomo

*The Fuji blimp has been flying around the United States since 1985, keeping the Fuji name before millions of people each year.* © 1988 David Madison–Duomo

especially useful when the manufacturer introduces a new item to an existing line of goods.

Price appeal probably motivates more decisions to buy than any other appeal, and the magic words *sale* and *bargain* are directed at consumers with great frequency. Closely allied to these plain and simple discount offers are the "something for nothing" lures, such as "buy one package and get a second one free," "send for free sample," and "trial offer at half price" and the big-money contest, for example, "finish this sentence and win $10,000 in cash, an automobile, or a trip to Bermuda for two." "No money down" is also a successful inducement.

Modern advertising employs an astonishing variety of persuaders. Among these are humorous and entertaining television and radio commercials, appeals to the sense of smell by the use of perfumed ink on paper, endorsements of products by celebrities, appeals to parents to give their children a better life and future, appeals to children to "ask mommy" to buy certain breakfast cereals, and the controversial use of "scare copy." Because fear is a principal human frailty, this last-mentioned motivation is applied to the advertising of thousands of products, sometimes boldly, sometimes subtly. Fear of poverty, sickness, and loss of social standing, and the specter of possible disasters, great and small, sometimes move previously unexcitable consumers to buy anything from insurance and fire extinguishers to cosmetics and vitamins.

**Structure of the Industry.** Big-budget advertising is a relatively new industry. Even in the late 1880s fewer than a dozen advertisers spent as much as $100,000 a year. The advertisers of that period had little need for agents. The publishers of magazines and newspapers, however, often found it difficult to sell space in their pages to advertisers, and they therefore began to commission brokers to go out and sell advertising space. These so-called space brokers were the first advertising agents. Present-day advertising agencies continue to act as space brokers in that they purchase space and time on behalf of the advertiser.

Their income derives from commissions based on an agreed-upon percentage (traditionally 15 percent) added to the amount they bill their clients to pay for media time and space. By the 1990s, these commissions had often been reduced to 12 or even 10 percent. Other methods of compensation, such as fees, retainers, and performance incentives, also are becoming popular and sometimes are used in addition to a reduced commission arrangement. Fees also are charged for such noncommissionable services as research, market analysis, and public relations.

Time and space buying, although highly specialized, is only one of the services rendered by the modern advertising agency. The agency spends most of its time planning, creating, and producing the advertising for its clients. A typical major agency maintains hundreds of executives and creative personnel. They include advertising and marketing specialists, designers, writers, artists, economists, psychologists, researchers, media analysts, product testers, librarians, accountants and bookkeepers, and mathematicians. An important group of people, making up the traffic department, follow and expedite the work from start to finish until the completed product is delivered at the end of the creative line.

The growth of radio and television as advertising media necessitated the creation of new departments devoted to the purchase of network- and local-station time, including spots on news reports, sports and entertainment shows, and other types of programs. The television-radio production staff of the agency supervises the purchase and production of commercials, most of which are produced by independent studios.

In simplest terms, the relationship between advertiser and agency may be described as follows. The advertiser tells the agency what product or service is to be sold and at what price. The agency, in consultation with the advertiser, then creates and produces the advertising and recommends the budget, the media to be used, and the scheduling of the various parts of the campaign.

The magnitude of such operations in the U.S. is

indicated by the volume of advertising placed by a leading firm in a recent year. The Procter & Gamble Co. in one year spent more than $2.1 billion to sell its soaps, detergents, dentifrices, toilet articles, food products, and other items worldwide through newspapers, consumer and other magazines, network radio and television, and outdoor advertising. A leading advertising agency, Young & Rubicam, Inc., recently handled accounts totaling about $7.2 billion in annual billings worldwide. That year the Interpublic Group of Companies, Inc., the parent of several advertising and public-relations agencies, reported combined billings of almost $14 billion. Although billings are the common measure of the size of an advertising agency, they do not represent the actual gross income of the agency, but rather the amount it spends placing advertising in the media on behalf of its clients.

Advertising also is becoming an increasingly important international business practice. In 1993 the top 55 U.S. advertising agencies derived more than $42.4 billion in billings from international operations. In addition, foreign agencies, most often from Great Britain, have acquired a number of U.S. advertising agencies.

**Economic and Social Effects.** With about 3 million business enterprises using one or more forms of advertising, almost every American citizen hears or sees advertising every day. In the U.S. the money invested in advertising equaled approximately $554 per capita in the early 1990s. The high per capita cost of U.S. advertising has led many critics to attack it as a wasteful, unnecessary, unreliable, and annoying institution. Such critics usually argue that the industry adds unnecessarily to the cost of goods and services it promotes. Proponents of advertising recognize some validity in these criticisms, but in rebuttal argue that by interesting consumers in making purchases, advertising enables manufacturers and others to sell their products and services in larger quantities; increased sales volume in turn enables companies to sell individual units at lower cost than would be possible if they were produced in small quantities. The personal computer business is a recent example of advertising leading to progressive lowering of per-unit costs to consumers.

In the opinion of most top business executives and of many economists, modern advertising plays an integral role in the development of markets for the low-cost goods made possible by the high productivity of American industry. At least one worldwide study of national investment in advertising, which showed a direct correlation with living standards, supported this thesis.

Advertising also supplies most of the operating funds of the principal communications media. According to an authoritative survey, the radio and broadcast television industry depends on advertising for all its revenue. Cable television carries both consumer-paid and advertising-supported programming. Metropolitan newspapers derive some 76 percent of their incomes from advertising, and national magazines, about 63 percent.

**Regulation.** Before the advertising industry became well organized, the sharp and unethical practices of some advertisers prompted the passing of many laws and legal restrictions by the federal, state, and municipal governments. At present, advertising is one of the most strictly regulated industries in the U.S. A number of federal bureaus exercise legal powers over advertising. An overlapping of authority exists among the bureaus, and in some instances one or more governmental bodies attempt to enforce conflicting regulations. The federal government has failed to develop a coordinated approach to the regulation of the industry. The federal agencies, however, wield considerable influence, mainly by threats of court action or of withdrawal of business licenses from firms accused of unethical practices. In 1969, for example, the Federal Communications Commission began pressing for a ban on the use of broadcast advertising by cigarette companies. On March 10, 1970, a bill was passed by the U.S. Senate prohibiting such cigarette advertising; the law became effective in January 1972. Recently, some municipalities have banned the display of posters advertising cigarettes in sports arenas where they may be transmitted by television cameras along with the game. In contrast, the distilled spirits industry voluntarily adopted a code in 1936 that prohibited broadcasting commercials on radio; the restriction on television advertising was added in 1946.

State laws and enforcement bureaus impose additional regulations on certain types of advertising, particularly those involving contests. These regulations may differ from state to state. Consequently, advertisers planning a national campaign through newspapers may have to prepare several different versions of an advertisement to comply with the varying laws. In some states the media are themselves regulated. For example, outdoor billboard advertising is banned in certain states.

Despite, or possibly because of, such widespread legal curbs, the advertising industry has resorted to self-regulation in a serious effort to stop abuses before they occur. These self-imposed codes of ethics and procedures aim principally to curtail not only bad taste but also misrepresentation and deception in copy and illustrations, as well as derogatory and unfair representations of competitors' products.

Several advertising trade associations are concerned with maintaining high standards. They feel it is good business practice to do so, inasmuch as advertising that weakens public confidence damages the impact and influence of all advertising.

Individual media and media groups often establish their own codes of ethics. Some newspapers and magazines refuse to publish advertising for tobacco and alcoholic beverages; most of them, in varying degree, investigate the reliability of advertisers before accepting their copy. Some publishers have strict rules about the presentation of advertising to prevent the publication of false or exaggerated claims and to preserve the aesthetic tone of their publications.

Radio and television stations generally try to investigate the company and its product before broadcasting advertising messages that might cause unfavorable reactions. The networks and the National Association of Broadcasters have established codes regulating the advertising of medical products and controlling contests, premiums, and other offers. All the networks maintain "clearance" or "acceptance" departments, which screen both commercial and noncommercial scripts, either deleting or challenging for substantiation any questionable material. Most magazine publishers have their own strict rules.

The American Advertising Federation has long campaigned, through its advertising clubs, for "truth in advertising." The Outdoor Advertising Association of America encourages its members to improve the design of their advertising posters and signs and to make sure they do not erect advertising billboards in locations where they will mar the landscape or otherwise offend the public.

The most active watchdogs in the field are the self-regulatory National Advertising Division of the Council of Better Business Bureaus, and its appellate body, the National Advertising Review Board. Another self-regulatory division of the council is the Children's Advertising Review Unit. These organizations review instances of false or misleading advertising and, when appropriate, bring pressure to bear on advertisers to change or cease to run offending advertising. The fact that this self-regulatory mechanism is subsidized by both advertisers and the media reflects the conviction of modern business management that "good advertising is good business."

**History.** The origins of advertising antedate the Christian era by many centuries. One of the first known methods of advertising was the outdoor display, usually a sign painted on the wall of a building. Archaeologists have uncovered many such signs, notably in the ruins of ancient Rome and Pompeii. An outdoor advertisement excavated in Rome offers property for rent, and one found painted on a wall in Pompeii calls the attention of travelers to a tavern in another town.

In medieval times word-of-mouth praise of products gave rise to an effective form of advertising, the use of town criers. They were citizens who read public notices aloud and were also employed by merchants to shout the praises of their wares. Later they became familiar figures on the streets of colonial America. The criers were forerunners of the modern announcer, who delivers radio and television commercials.

Although graphic forms of advertising appeared early in history, printed advertising made little headway until the invention of the movable-type printing press in Europe about 1440. The trademark, a two- or three-dimensional insignia symbolizing a company or industry, dates from about the 16th century, when trades people and guild members posted characteristic symbols outside their shops. Among the best-known trademarks from early modern times are the striped pole of the barber and three-ball sign of the pawnbroker.

In terms of both volume and technique, advertising made its greatest advances in the U.S. In the early stages of American advertising nationwide promotion was impractical because the nation itself was underdeveloped and lacked transcontinental transportation, distribution, and communications systems. Eventually, however, certain types of manufacturers conceived the idea of bypassing wholesalers and retailers and reaching the consumer through direct advertising, mainly by means of catalogs. The pioneers in this field were seed companies and book and pamphlet publishers. Mail-order houses selling general merchandise appeared on the scene in the 1870s. To the predominantly rural population of the day these catalogs offered all of the goods available to the city dweller, delivered right to the farmhouse door. Today's mail-order catalogs are much more sophisticated and specialized and many department stores conduct a profitable mail-order business in addition to their retail shops.

Patent-medicine companies loomed large in newspaper and magazine advertising starting in the late 1870s. They found a ready market because doctors and reliable pharmacists were scarce outside the populated areas, and the frontier settlers and farmers had to do much of their own doctoring. The patent-medicine bottlers made a gross profit of from 80 to 90 percent and could well afford to spend money publicizing their remedies.

Railroads and steamship lines were early users of advertising in the U.S., not only to praise the luxury and comfort of their modes of travel but also to publish their schedules and rates.

Late in the 19th century many American firms began to market packaged goods under brand names. This development initiated a new era in the history of advertising. Previously, everyday household products such as sugar, soap, rice, butter, milk, lard, beans, candy, candles, and pickles had been sold in neighborhood stores from bulk containers. Thus, consumers had seldom been aware of, or influenced by, brand names.

The soapmakers were early advertisers of packaged and branded products. The first "household name" soap brands, which date from about 1880, include Ivory, Pears', Sapolio, Colgate, Kirk's American Family, and Packer's. Soon afterward such brands as Royal Baking Powder, Quaker Oats, Baker's Chocolate, Hire's Root Beer, Regal Shoes, and Waterman's Pens were nationally advertised. Shortly after the turn of the century Americans began to be aware of such brand names as Bon Ami, Wrigley, and Coca-Cola.

After World War I advertising developed into a business so big that it became almost a trademark of America itself in the eyes of the world. The expanding U.S. industry inspired innovations and improved techniques that benefited other facets of business in the nation.

The invention of electricity led to the illuminated outdoor poster; photoengraving and other modern printing inventions helped both the editorial and advertising departments of printed journals. Advertising was used increasingly by public-relations specialists as an important means of communication. The advent of radio in the 1920s stimulated a new technique of selling by voice.

During World War II the American advertising industry founded the War Advertising Council, a nonprofit public-service organization that employed the resources of modern advertising to strengthen the American war effort. After the war the organization continued, as The Advertising Council, to function in the public interest. It has conducted nationwide drives to increase the sale of U.S. savings bonds, prevent forest fires and traffic accidents, encourage aid to higher education, and promote public health issues and crime prevention. Print and broadcast media contribute millions of dollars worth of advertising time and space to such projects every year. Many advertising agencies contribute their creative services to the Advertising Council campaigns. The Partnership for a Drug-Free America, founded in 1986, also conducts public-service campaigns with the voluntary participation of advertisers, agencies, and the media. The aim of their advertising is to eliminate the use of illegal drugs in America.

The most significant postwar development was television, a medium that forced the advertising industry to better its techniques of broadcast selling by the use of visual devices as well as by voice. By the 1980s the proliferation of videocassette recorders (VCRs) in U.S. homes caused concern among advertisers. The use of VCRs allows viewers to edit out commercials when recording or speed past them when viewing a taped show.

The advertising industry currently is looking into the possibilities offered by the "information superhighway," on which interactive advertising messages will be carried via television or computer screen and will enable consumers to place orders for products or services or to request further information about them. E.A.DeW.

*For further information on this topic, see the Bibliography in volume 28, sections 620–21.*

**ADVOCATE,** in a general sense, one who pleads for another in a court of law or other tribunal. In Great Britain, professional advocates are called barristers and plead or argue cases before the High Court of Justice; a barrister is distinguished from a solicitor, who conducts litigation in inferior courts (*see* COURTS). The *avocat* and *avoué* in France are analogous to the barrister and solicitor in England. In the U.S., most British colonies, and parts of Europe, the two branches are not separate (*see* ATTORNEY).

The term *advocate* was formerly used in Great Britain to denote a member of the College of Advocates at Doctors' Commons (abolished 1857). They had the exclusive right to plead in ecclesiastical and admiralty courts. In the U.S. Army, the judge advocate general is chief adviser to the army on military law (*see* MILITARY COURTS).

**ADWA** *or* **ADUWA** *or* **ADOWA,** town, N Ethiopia, in Tigre Province. The town lies in a fertile agrarian region, more than 1829 m (more than 6000 ft) above sea level, and is a trading center, with roads to Addis Ababa, Gondar, and Asmara. Cotton cloth, brassware, and iron products are manufactured here. On March 1, 1896, Adwa was the scene of a decisive Ethiopian victory over an invading Italian army. Italian forces bombed and later captured the town in the early stages of the Italo-Ethiopian War (1935–36). In 1941, during World War II, the Italian troops were expelled by British and Ethiopian forces. Pop. (est.) 16,400.

**Æ,** pseudonym of GEORGE WILLIAM RUSSELL (1867–1935), Irish writer and painter, born in Lurgan, Northern Ireland, and educated in Dublin. His poems and short stories and his essays on the question of Irish independence were a major contribution to the cultural movement known as the Celtic Renaissance (*see* IRISH LITERATURE). Æ's poetry, including *Collected Poems* (1913) and *The House of the Titans and Other Poems* (1934), reflects his preoccupation with theosophy and his belief in the world of nature as the chief connection between humans and God.

**AEACUS,** in Greek mythology, king of Aegina (now Aíyina). He was the son of the nymph Aegina, for whom his island kingdom was named, and the god Zeus. Hera, queen of the gods, angry with Zeus for his love of Aegina, sent a plague that destroyed most of the Aeginetans. Aeacus prayed to his father to change a group of industrious ants into human beings to people his deserted city. Zeus granted his wish, creating a race called the Myrmidons. Aeacus ruled over his people with such justice that after his death he became one of the three judges of the underworld. He was the father of Peleus and the grandfather of Achilles.

**AEDILES,** officers of the Roman Republic, corresponding approximately to directors of public works and exercising some police powers. The aediles supervised the maintenance (including fire fighting) and repair of the temples, public buildings, streets, sewers, and aqueducts of the city of Rome; supervised the public markets; regulated weights and measures; directed the public games; and maintained public order.

The office was founded in 494 BC with the establishment of two aedileships to be held by members of the plebs, or common people. They were elected annually by the plebs themselves. In 367 BC two additional aediles, known as curule aediles, were installed in office. Until the 2d century BC the curule aedileships rotated on a yearly basis between patricians and plebeians. Julius Caesar, himself a former curule aedile, installed two more plebeian aediles in 44 BC. Known as ceriales, they oversaw the grain supply.

Traditionally, the aedileship was the second magistracy, following the quaestorship in the career of Roman politicians. In the last years of the Republic the office was sought by ambitious politicians because it provided opportunity for building a public following. Under the Empire the office lost its importance, and by AD 235 it had disappeared.

**AËDON,** in Greek mythology, wife of Zethus, king of Thebes. She was insanely jealous of her sister-in-law Niobe, who had seven sons, while she had only one. Attempting to kill Niobe's eldest boy, Aëdon slew her own son by mistake. The god Zeus turned her into a nightingale whose melancholy song is a lament for the boy.

**AEGADIAN ISLES.** *See* EGADI ISLANDS.

**AEGEAN CIVILIZATION,** term used to denote the Bronze Age civilization that developed (C. 3000–1200 BC) in the basin of the Aegean Sea, mainly on Crete, the Cyclades Islands, and the mainland of Greece. It had two major cultures: the Minoan, which flourished in Crete and reached its height in the Middle Bronze period, notably at Knossos and Phaestos; and the Mycenaean, which developed in the Late Bronze period at Mycenae and other centers, including Tiryns and Pylos. *See* ACHAEANS; MINOAN CULTURE; MYCENAE.

Ancient Greek writers had related stories of an "age of heroes" before their time, but nothing definite was known about the Aegean civilization until the late 19th century, when archaeological excavations began at the sites of the legendary cities of Troy (q.v.), Mycenae, Knossos, and other centers of the Bronze Age.

**Greek Legends.** According to Greek mythology, there once was a time when great events had occurred and the gods had involved themselves in human affairs. The story of King Minos (q.v.) and the slaying of the Minotaur (q.v.) he kept in the labyrinth (q.v.) by the Greek hero Theseus may be the mythic rendering of the battle for hegemony in the Aegean in which Mycenae took over Knossos. Homer's epic the *Iliad* describes the Trojan War (q.v.), which is believed to have brought about the fall (traditionally in 1184 BC) of Troy at the hands of the Greeks, or Achaeans as the poet calls them. He also mentions well-known places believed to be the centers of the Mycenaean period, such as "golden Mycenae,"

*Pottery jug with typical Mycenaean design, in the Archaeological Museum, Iráklion, on Crete in Greece.*
Nimatallah–Art Resource

where King Agamemnon ruled; Pylos, where Nestor was king; and Phthia in Thessaly, home of the hero Achilles.

**Archaeological Discoveries.** A German amateur archaeologist, Heinrich Schliemann, was responsible for some of the most famous discoveries of the 19th century. In 1870 he began excavating a mound called Hissarlik, in Turkey, and found what is believed to be the ruins of Troy. In Greece he uncovered the sites of Mycenae in 1876–78 and Tiryns in 1884. Finds of fortress palaces, pottery, ornaments, and royal tombs containing gold and other artifacts demonstrated the existence of a well-developed civilization that had flourished about 1500–1200 BC. Schliemann's work has been continued by modern archaeologists, including the American Carl Blegen (1887–1971).

In 1900 the British archaeologist Sir Arthur Evans discovered at Knossos, Crete, a palace complex that he associated with King Minos and the labyrinth. He also found baked clay tablets with two types of writing from the middle of the 2d millennium BC, called Linear A and Linear B. Linear B tablets from about 1200 BC have been found at Pylos and other Mycenaean sites. The British cryptologist Michael Ventris (1922–56) and John Chadwick (1920– ), a classical scholar, proved that Linear B is an early form of Greek. Linear A, the language of Minoan Crete, has not yet been deciphered. The discovery of Linear B on Crete supported the theory that the mainland people, the Mycenaeans, gained ascendancy over the Minoans.

The existence of a Cycladic civilization that had connections with both the mainland and Crete is indicated by artifacts found in these islands. Since the 1930s Greek excavations of a Cycladic settlement on the island of Thera (Thira), also known as Santorin, have yielded frescoes and artifacts similar to the Minoan. Thera was destroyed by a great volcanic eruption about 1625 BC. The disaster may have been the basis for Plato's writings on the lost continent of Atlantis. More recent excavations on the islands encircling Delos traced back the Cycladic culture to the 4th millenium BC, when merchants, in search of obsidian (a volcanic glass), and fishermen established seasonal settlements there. Although no examples of writing have been identified, Cycladic culture possessed viable pottery, jewelry, and characteristic marble idols, generally of women and often life-size in scale, that were originally lavishly painted. Incorrectly termed "mother goddesses," these idols associate the deceased with the powers of the sea, which was central to Cycladic life.

*HISTORICAL RECORD*

Recent archaeological discoveries, such as the excavated village of Dimini in Thessaly, produced

*The citadel of Tiryns, Greece (13th century BC). These fortifications, along with those of Mycenae, Greece, and Knossos, Crete, are considered the most important monuments of the Aegean civilization.*

John Elk III–Bruce Coleman, Inc.

material evidence of a cultural progression from the Neolithic (New Stone Age) to the Bronze Age, which commenced about 3000 BC and of which three phases were recognized: Early, Middle, and Late.

**Early Bronze Age.** About 3000 BC new people apparently arrived in the Aegean, perhaps from Asia Minor. They used bronze for their weapons and tools, thus introducing the Bronze Age to the area. On the mainland their villages appear to have been small independent units, often protected by thick walls; over time, the buildings on Crete and in the Cyclades became more complex. Burials were communal throughout the Aegean, but burial practices varied. Pit graves and some graves of more elaborate construction were common on the mainland; stone-lined burial chambers (cists), in the Cyclades; and circular stone tombs, rectangular ossuaries (bone depositories), and caves, on Crete. All had places for cult

159

*Death mask of hammered gold found in a shaft grave at Mycenae by Heinrich Schliemann.*
**National Museum, Athens**

offerings, and the dead were often buried with beautiful objects.

**Middle Bronze Age.** About 2200–1800 BC another wave of newcomers arrived in the Cyclades and on the mainland. They caused considerable destruction, and for about two centuries civilization was disrupted, especially on the mainland. New pottery and the introduction of horses at this time indicate that the invaders were of the Indo-European language family, to which both Ancient and Modern Greek belong.

On Crete, impressive buildings, frescoes, vases, and early writing are evidence of a flourishing culture of the 2d millennium BC, which came to be known as Minoan. Great royal palaces built around large courtyards were the focal points of these communities. The most magnificent of the palaces was at Knossos. Destroyed presumably by an earthquake or a foreign invasion about 1700 BC, it was rebuilt on a grand scale. It seems likely that the Minoans maintained a marine empire, trading not only with the Cyclades and the mainland but also with Sicily, Egypt, and cities on the eastern shore of the Mediterranean.

Minoan religion featured a female snake deity, whose worship involved the symbolism of fertility and the lunar and solar cycles. The central cult figure may have been a goddess of a Middle Eastern type, together with her dying and resurrected consort, symbolic of the seasons.

**Late Bronze Age.** The destruction of the Cretan palaces about 1450 BC (that of Knossos took place shortly after 1400 BC) was followed by the decline of the Minoans and the rise of the Mycenaeans.

Some scholars have connected this change with the volcanic eruption on Thíra, but recent calculations place it some 200 years earlier. Mycenaean-style art and Linear B tablets found on Crete indicate the presence there of people from the peninsula. In any case, heavily fortified mainland cities became the new centers of Aegean civilization. Extant painted vases and weapons depict hunting and battle scenes that suggest the Mycenaeans were warlike. The styles are also more formal and geometric than those of earlier examples, anticipating the art of classical Greece.

A typical Mycenaean city had, at its center, the fortress palace of the king. The cities were fortified with massive structures of unevenly cut stones, known as Cyclopean walls. The Linear B tablets from this time include names of Greek gods, such as Zeus, and contain detailed records of royal possessions. The gold masks, weapons, and jewelry found by Schliemann at the royal burial sites suggest the great wealth and power gained by the Mycenaeans when they took over the Minoan trading empire. Troy, which is believed to have been situated on the mainland of Asia Minor (now Turkey) near the Hellespont, was in a good position to harass shipping and collect exorbitant tolls from the Mycenaeans. Archaeological evidence indicates that a city on this site was destroyed about 1200 BC, close to the date accepted by the ancient Greeks.

Shortly after 1200 BC the Aegean civilization collapsed, a fact that was attributed by some scholars to natural disasters, or, most likely, to the invasion of the Dorians (q.v.). A period generally described as the Dark Age followed (*see* ARCHAEOLOGY: *Greece*).　　　　J.Br.

## AEGEAN ART AND ARCHITECTURE

Aegean art is remarkable for its naturalistic pictorial style, originated in Minoan Crete; the movement and variety of Minoan art, even in its earlier abstract phases, suggest living things. From Crete, this style spread to the other Aegean islands and the Greek mainland, where it was modified by geometric tendencies. The rhythmic pulse that characterizes Aegean art suggests a deep reverence for the divinities of nature.

**Architecture.** The organic quality of Minoan style is seen most clearly in the palaces of Crete. The four major palaces known—at Knossos, Phaestos, Mallia, and Zakros—followed the same basic plan. Rooms, on several levels, were functionally organized around a large central court. These courts must have accommodated crowds of worshipers, who gathered in front of the cult rooms to the west. The palaces also had extensive basement storage areas, artists' workshops, dining halls, and sumptuous living quarters (including bathrooms) for the noble ruling families. The structures were light and flexible, rather than monumental, and entirely unfortified. The distinctive Minoan column, with its downward taper, suggests movement rather than stability. Another specifically Minoan feature was the polythyron, a wall made of doors, which allowed for flexibility in ventilating or closing off a room.

*Huge clay jars that once held grain and oil, found in the labyrinthine storerooms of the Palace of Knossos, Crete. Typically Minoan are the sinuous, wavelike bands of decoration in low relief.*　　　J. Baker–Shostal Associates

The private habitations of Minoan Crete ranged from simple peasant dwellings to rich mansions and villas, constructed with the same features and fine techniques as the palaces. A wide variety of buildings were constructed for burials. The most distinctive were the tholos tombs of southern Crete, circular buildings with corbelled stone vaulting, built large enough to accommodate family burials for many centuries.

On the Greek mainland, the palaces of the rulers were completely different from those of Crete. They incorporated the characteristic megaron, a dominant central hall. The megara of the best-known palaces—at Mycenae, Tiryns, and Pylos—were strikingly similar. Each was entered from a courtyard through a porch flanked by columns and had a large central hearth surrounded by four columns. The mainland sites tended to be fortified with huge walls of cyclopean masonry, constructed of massive, irregular blocks. Recent excavations at Mycenae indicate that, as in Crete, the palaces served as centers of worship as well as of government. For royal burials the Mycenaean Greeks first used shaft graves; later they adopted the Minoan tholos tomb and developed it into an impressive burial structure. The tombs were covered with earth tumuli, or artificial mounds, and were entered through long passageways. In the most developed tombs, such as the so-called Treasury of Atreus at Mycenae, the large, circular spaces were dramatically vaulted with thick canopies of stone.

**Painting and Sculpture.** Minoan painting is found in two forms, the vivid frescoes on the palace walls and the graceful designs that decorate Minoan pottery. Surviving Minoan sculpture, with a few exceptions, is largely restricted to statuettes and figurines in various materials and to intaglio–cut semiprecious stone seals.

*Frescoes.* In Crete the palaces and houses were often decorated with bright murals. The Minoans made a major contribution to the art of landscape painting. Only in the Aegean were landscapes depicted for their own sake, without human figures. Minoan artists represented the terrain with undulating contours and swirling striations of color to emphasize the life of the earth. The scenes were enlivened with animals, such as monkeys and birds, in sprightly movement amid swaying foliage. The Minoans had a special facility among ancient peoples for capturing motion. Figures were depicted in instantaneous moments of action and in a great variety of poses. Minoan figures are usually slender, which enhances their look of mobility. It is primarily in ritual scenes, such as the bull-leaping fresco from the palace at Knossos, that human figures are depicted. Occa-

*The throne room of the Palace of Knossos, Crete (2d millennium BC), is decorated with frescoes in the delicate naturalistic painting style characteristic of late Minoan civilization.*　　　　　　　J. Baker–Shostal Associates

sionally, frescoes were rendered in a special shorthand method of painting known as the miniature style, whereby crowds of people were depicted in a small area with a few light sketchy strokes.

Recently excavated on Thera, in the Cyclades, well-preserved frescoes from prosperous private homes show a close relationship to the art of Crete, although the nature scenes are rendered more abstractly. Many of the Thera frescoes feature children, who are portrayed at different ages and with their heads shaved, except for specific hairlocks. One especially important painting, from a site known as the West House, presents a narrative scene in an elaborate setting, the most extensive landscape known before the Hellenistic period. An entire Aegean world is depicted, with a fleet of lavishly ornamented ships sailing from town to town. Despite the remarkable achievement of the painting, the artist clearly had no notion of perspective.

The Minoan pictorial repertoire and fresco technique were later adopted on the Greek mainland, where religious scenes similar to those from Crete and Thera were depicted. Hunting and fighting scenes were also popular. Recent excavations at Tell-el-Daba in the western delta of Egypt have uncovered fragments of frescoes, the motifs of which include bull-jumping scenes and the like painted with Minoan, not Egyptian, colors. The relationships between Egyptian and Minoan painting must now be investigated anew.

**Sculpture.** Among the earliest examples of sculpture from the Aegean are those from the Cyclades in the form of schematic idols recalling the contours of violins. From these works evolved life-size, brightly painted marble figures, generally of women with their arms folded beneath their breasts, and an array of seated male figures generally playing harps or holding drinking cups.

Unique among the artifacts of the Aegean civilization are the bronze figurines associated exclusively with Minoan sites. These metal sculptures include male and female worshipers with their arms raised in adoration as well as an image of a crawling infant, a bull with its jumper, and a reclining goat. The Minoan artists excelled in the carving of ivory figurines to which secondary materials were added to enhance their effect. To the goddesses associated with animals can now be added an extraordinary image of a youthful god, the body of which is sculpted in ivory covered with gold leaf and the head of which is carved from a single piece of blue-gray serpentine. This image was first excavated at Palaikastro in 1987.

The Minoans excelled in the sculpting of stone vessels as well, many of which were enhanced with relief decoration. Stone sculpting on a large scale, however, is best represented by Mycenaeans, who embellished their architecture with reliefs. The facade of the so-called Treasury of Atreus at Mycenae is adorned with contrasting red and green marbles in the form of columns and a frieze of spirals. The stone stelae, or commemorative plaques, recovered above the royal shaft graves at Mycenae, contain both geometric and figural motifs. Within this context the monumental stone relief of the Lion Gate at Mycenae, in which the felines—whose heads were made of different material—heraldically flank a column, is not exceptional. The Mycenaeans excelled as well in the carving of circular ivory containers, statuettes, and decorative plaques.

**Pottery and Metalwork.** With the building of the great Cretan palaces came the development of pottery (q.v.) as a luxury art. Employing the same three-part firing technique later used by Attic potters, Cretan artists created splendid vases of numerous shapes and a seemingly endless variety of colorful decorations. Highly regarded in the ancient world, Minoan pottery was copied throughout the Aegean and even exported to Egypt and the Near East. In the later periods, the decoration included naturalistic motifs, such as floral forms and the well-known Marine style, with octopuses, shellfish, and seaweed painted in rich overall designs. Minoan pottery was imitated on the Greek mainland, where it gradually evolved in both shape and decoration into stricter, more disciplined forms. In the final phase, the Mycenaeans introduced pictorial elements, such as animals and human figures, as decoration.

The art of fine metalworking was also developed in Minoan Crete under palace patronage (*see* METALWORK). Although little remains, a few objects such as the granulated gold "bee pendant" from Mallia testify to Minoan expertise at working precious metals. The most impressive Mycenaean finds of metalwork were discovered in the shaft graves and tholos tombs of the mainland. They include gold masks and grave goods embossed with geometric designs. The burials also contained luxurious gold and silver vases and ornamented bronze weapons, many by Minoan artisans. Some of the vessels were decorated with elaborate figures and scenes hammered in repoussé relief. Other vessels, as well as daggers of bronze, were inlaid with designs of different colored metals, a technique sometimes referred to as "painting with metal." These intricate products of the metalworker were by no means minor arts; they were the most prized objects of the Aegean.                                E.N.D.

*For further information on this topic, see the Bibliography in volume 28,* sections 116, 647, 851–52, 891.

**AEGEAN ISLANDS,** numerous islands in the Aegean Sea between Greece and Asia Minor. The chief islands are Euboea (which is by far the largest and adjoins the mainland of Greece), Thásos, Samothráki, Lésvos, Límnos, Kos, Khíos, and Sámos. All the islands are included in either the Sporades or the Cyclades group. The islands, many of which are of volcanic origin, have a healthful climate and beautiful scenery. In ancient times they played an important part in Greek history, giving to the world many distinguished poets and philosophers. The islands came under the control of Rome in the 2d century BC and from the 5th to the 13th century AD were part of the Byzantine Empire. During the 15th and 16th centuries the islands were conquered by Turkey, and they remained under Turkish rule until 1829, when all but the Dodecanese became part of the independent kingdom of Greece. Italy took the Dodecanese in 1912, and Germany occupied them in 1943. In 1945 they were taken over by the British, and they formally became part of Greece in 1947.

**AEGEAN SEA** (Gr. *Aigaion Pelagos*), arm of the Mediterranean Sea, between Greece and Asia Minor. The name is variously explained in writings of antiquity as derived from Aegeus, king of Athens and father of Theseus, or from Aegea, a queen of the Amazons who drowned in the sea, or from an ancient Greek town named Aegae. The Aegean Sea is about 644 km (about 400 mi) long and about 290 km (about 180 mi) wide. It is connected with the Sea of Marmara to the NE by the Strait of the Dardanelles. The Aegean Sea is irregular in outline with numerous gulfs, and is studded with islands, including the Sporades, Cyclades, and Dodecanese. It was the center of one of the earliest known European civilizations. With the rise of the ancient Greek and Middle Eastern cultures, the lands surrounding the sea became the sites of widely differing civilizations, and the culture of the Aegean islands became identified with that of Greece.

**AEGEUS.**   *See* THESEUS.

**AEGINA.**   *See* AÍYINA.

**AEGIR,** in Germanic mythology, god of stormy seas. His wife, Ran, sank ships and drew mariners to the depths of the sea. The nine daughters of Aegir and Ran represented the different appearances of the ocean waves.

**AEGIS,** in Greek mythology, a garment of Zeus, the king of the gods, and of Athena, his daughter. A short cloak with golden tassels, generally worn over the shoulders, the aegis served as the symbol of Zeus's power; it not only protected him but terrified his enemies. Originally made for Zeus by Hephaestus, the god of artisans, it became the ordinary dress of Athena in later mythology. In art, Athena's aegis was frequently depicted as a breastplate or as a shield fringed with serpents. The garment was also occasionally used by other gods.

**AEGISTHUS,** in Greek mythology, the son of Thyestes and his daughter Pelopia. Desiring to avenge himself upon his brother Atreus and acting on the advice of the oracle at Delphi, Thyestes consummated an incestuous union with Pelopia. Shortly afterward, Atreus married Pelopia, not knowing she was his niece. When Aegisthus was born, Atreus accepted him as his own son. Aegisthus later learned his true identity and, urged by Thyestes, killed Atreus. While Agamemnon, king of Mycenae, was away fighting in the Trojan War, Aegisthus became the lover of Queen Clytemnestra. He helped Clytemnestra kill her husband upon his return from Troy. Together with the queen, Aegisthus then ruled Mycenae for seven years; he was murdered by Agamemnon's son Orestes.

**AEGIUM,** ancient town of Achaea, Greece, on the southern shore of the Gulf of Corinth. According to legend, it was the birthplace of Zeus, and a shrine to Zeus Homarios was nearby.

When the Achaean League was reestablished in 280 BC, Aegium became its chief city. The modern town is known as Aíyion.

**AEGYPTUS,** in Greek mythology, king of Arabia and Egypt, which he conquered and named for himself. He was the twin brother of Danaüs, who became king of Argos.

**AEHRENTHAL, Alois Lexa, Graf von** (1854–1912), Austro-Hungarian statesman, born in Bohemia, and educated at the universities of Bonn and Prague. In 1877 he entered the diplomatic service of Austria-Hungary and, after holding subordinate positions, was appointed minister to Romania in 1895. In 1899 he became ambassador to Russia and served until 1906, when he was appointed minister of foreign affairs. The high point of his tenure was the annexation of Bosnia and Hercegovina by Austria-Hungary in 1908, an act that had far-reaching effects. It is regarded as an important contributory cause of the Balkan Wars and as an indirect cause of World War I. Aehrenthal resigned in 1912.

**AELFRIC** (950?–1020?), English abbot and writer. His own works are the only source of information on his life. About 972, he entered the Benedictine school at Winchester and became a monk. In 987 he was summoned to rule over the abbey of Cernel in Dorset, where he taught and preached. Afterward, probably in 1006, he was made abbot of Eynsham. He is best known for his *Homilies,* written in Old English. Among his other works are *A Treatise on the Old and New Testaments;* the *Heptateuchus,* an abridged translation of the first seven books of the Old Testament; a Latin grammar and glossary, written in English for his students; and the *Colloquium,* designed to teach pupils to speak Latin correctly. On the basis of the last two, Aelfric is known as a grammarian. His writings include some of the best extant examples of Old English prose.

**AELURUS,** in Egyptian mythology, sacred cat worshiped as a deity and embalmed and buried after its death at Bubastis. According to the Greek historian Herodotus, Aelurus was identified with Artemis, Greek goddess of the hunt.

**AEMILIAN WAY** (Lat. *Via Aemilia*), ancient Roman road, about 282 km (about 175 mi) long, built by the consul Marcus Aemilius Lepidus (fl. 200–152 BC) in 187 BC. The road began where the Flaminian Way ended and ran from Ariminum (now Rimini) northwest to Placentia (now Piacenza). Later it was extended northwest across the Po River to Mediolanum (now Milan). The modern highway follows the same route and crosses some of the original bridges; the district between Rimini and Piacenza retains the name Emilia, derived from that of the ancient road.

**AENEAS,** in Roman mythology, the son of Anchises, a Trojan prince, and Venus, goddess of love. After the capture of Troy by the Greeks, Aeneas was able, with the help of his mother, to escape from the fallen city. Carrying his aged father and leading his little son by the hand, he made his way to the seacoast. In the confusion of flight, his wife was left behind.

A long, adventure-filled voyage took him to Thrace, Delos, Crete, and Sicily, where his father died. The goddess Juno, who hated Aeneas and wanted to keep him from founding Rome, which she knew was his destiny, tried to drown him in a violent storm. He and his crew were cast upon the African coast, where they were met by Dido, the beautiful queen of Carthage. Dido fell in love with Aeneas and begged him to remain. When he refused and set sail, she took her own life.

After years of wandering, Aeneas reached Italy and the mouth of the Tiber; there he was received by Latinus, king of Latium. He became betrothed to Lavinia, the king's daughter, but before they could marry, Juno caused Turnus, king of the Rutuli and a rejected suitor of Lavinia, to make war against Aeneas and Latinus. It was resolved by hand-to-hand combat, in which Turnus was defeated and slain by Aeneas. Aeneas then ruled

*Aeneas rescuing his father at the burning of Troy; detail from a painting by Federico Barocci (Galleria Borghese, Rome).* Scala–Art Resource

for several years in Latium and, marrying Lavinia, founded the Roman people.

The great Roman epic, the *Aeneid* by Vergil, tells the story of Aeneas' perilous wanderings in detail and ends with the death of Turnus.

**AENEID.** See VERGIL.

**AENESIDEMUS** (fl. 1st cent. BC), Greek skeptic philosopher, who attempted to demonstrate the relative character of all judgments and opinions. Born in Knossos, Crete, he taught at Alexandria. Ten well-known arguments (called *tropoi*) for skepticism (q.v.) are attributed to him. He held that judgment must be suspended in seeking knowledge and that nothing is certain either in itself or through anything else. This principle seemed evident to him, as objects appear differently to people according to the perspective taken, and proof of an assumption requires an infinite process of proof (that is, one assumption is based on another, and so on indefinitely).

**AEOLIAN HARP,** musical instrument in which several gut strings of equal length are stretched over a narrow, oblong box. When placed in a focused current of air (such as an almost-closed window), the Aeolian harp produces eerie chords, composed of the harmonics of a single fundamental tone, to which all the strings are tuned. The sounds range from pianissimo to forte and die away with the passing of the gust. The instrument was popular during the 19th century. Similar devices are mentioned in the Bible.

**AEOLIANS,** one of the three important ethnic divisions of the ancient Greeks, the other two being the Ionians and the Dorians. According to legend they were descendants of Aeolus, and their original home was in Thessaly. In the 11th century BC many migrated to the island of Lésvos (Lesbos) in the Aegean Sea; they also founded cities on the western coast of Asia Minor, between the Dardanelles and the Hermus River. This region became known as Aeolis or Aeolia. Aeolic, or Aeolian, their dialect, was one of the four linguistic divisions of the ancient Greek language, the other three being Ionic, Doric, and Arcado-Cyprian or Achaean. Aeolic was the language of the poets Alcaeus and Sappho; elements of the dialect are found in Homer's epics and Hesiod's writings. See GREECE.

**AEOLUS,** name of two figures in Greek mythology. The best known was keeper of the winds. He lived on the floating island Aeolia with his six sons and six daughters. The god Zeus had given him the power to still and arouse the winds. When the Greek hero Odysseus visited Aeolus, he was welcomed as an honored guest. As a parting gift, Aeolus gave him a favoring wind and a leather bag filled with all the winds. Odysseus's sailors, thinking the bag contained gold, opened it and were at once swept back to Aeolia. There Aeolus refused to help them again.

Another Aeolus was king of Thessaly. He was the son of Hellen, ancestor of the Hellenes, the ancient Greek peoples. Aeolus was himself the ancestor of the Aeolian Greeks.

**AEPYORNIS** (Gr., "tall bird"), genus of several fossil birds from Madagascar, especially the elephant bird. This bird may have survived until the first humans arrived on the island and thus gave rise to the legend of the roc, the gigantic mythical bird once believed to have inhabited India and later popularized in the *Arabian Nights*.

The adult elephant bird was about 2.4 to 2.7 m (about 8 to 9 ft) tall and massive, weighing perhaps as much as 450 kg (about 1000 lb), by far the heaviest of any known bird. Its eggs have been found fossilized in the mud of swamps.

**AERATION.** See WATER.

**AERIAL SURVEY,** photographing of the earth from an aircraft or an artificial satellite, for the purposes of military intelligence, mapping, geological or archaeological investigation, or meteorological observation. Long before the first balloon flight, the idea of viewing the earth from the air gave rise to imaginary bird's-eye representations. In the mid-19th century aerial survey became a reality; concurrent developments in flight and photography (q.v.) since then—often spurred by military requirements—have made possible ever more accurate observations.

**Military Applications.** Balloon observations for military intelligence were made during the American Civil War; by the end of the 19th century the armies of many nations had balloon observation units. The use of the camera and wireless radio from airplanes during World War I radically changed the collection and dissemination of intelligence. At first, cameras were held over the side of the plane; with the development of bigger planes, cameras could be positioned and focused vertically through apertures in the floor of the aircraft. By the war's end, cameras with rapid sequencing had been developed, providing photographs that overlapped and could be mounted to form a mosaic, and pairs of images of the same terrain that could be viewed stereoscopically (*see* STEREOSCOPE). Aerial reconnaissance had brought about the defensive use of ground camouflage; in turn, however, the development of infrared film lessened its effectiveness.

Postwar developments included electrically driven cameras and supersensitive film for night photography. During World War II strip cameras were developed; these expose a continuous strip of film making it possible to photograph at a rate geared to high-speed flight. Photo recon-

Aerial photo, taken by a radio-controlled balloon camera, shows complex detail of an excavated Minoan palace at Mallia, Crete. The building was restored sometime after 1700 BC, following a great earthquake; its present ground plan is about the size of a football field.
© 1992 J. Wilson Myers

naissance had a major impact on planning and evaluating air operations, locating rocket-launching sites, and mapping invasion targets.

Today the use of space satellites permits continuous observation of potential military operations around the world.

**Study of the Earth.** Air photography was first used for mapmaking in the early 1920s over Los Angeles and several French cities. Aerial survey is now the basis of cartography (see MAP), enabling geographers to map regions previously inaccessible and providing a broad range of physical and cultural data that would require much time to collect from ground observation.

The Landsats, a U.S. satellite series developed in the early 1970s, are multipurpose data-collecting vehicles. In addition to conventional cameras, the two that remain in orbit—Landsats 4 and 5, launched in 1983 and 1984—are equipped with sensors that can detect the different kinds of radiation emitted by natural and man-made features on the earth's surface. An array of devices such as these provides scientists and engineers with the information that, to list just a few useful applications, enables them to track earthquake faults, find oil and ore deposits, manage crops, and monitor the spread of drought. In recent years, civilian users of space-based imagery have turned increasingly to the French government instead of the U.S., the reason being that France's SPOT (Système Probatoire d'Observation de la Terre) satellite, launched in 1986, provides pictures with a resolution of 10 meters (about 33 ft), compared with the 30 meters (about 100 ft) available from Landsat. See REMOTE SENSING.

**Meteorological Surveys.** The first pictures showing weather data were taken from a V-2 rocket that was fired in 1946. By 1960 the Tiros (Television Infrared Observational Satellite) was sending such data to earth. Today's systems show cloud cover, track major storms and ice-flow movements, and even follow dust from volcanic ex-

plosions. See METEOROLOGY; SATELLITE, ARTIFICIAL.

**Archaeological Surveys.** In 1852, from a balloon, the American balloonist and inventor John Wise (1808–79) observed lines of prehistoric earthworks near Chillicothe, Ohio. In the 20th century archaeology has benefited from advances in aviation and space technology. Mapping planes and imaging satellites provide information not available from ground observations about the ways in which ancient peoples altered the broader landscape. Shooting at lower levels is necessary for surveying architectural details at individual excavations. These photographs, made from altitudes of 10 meters (about 33 feet) to 800 meters (about 2640 feet), are used by archaeologists to record successive levels of excavation, to help make sense of complex patterns, and to salvage eroding data for future study. To record at these lower levels, vertically mounted radio-controlled cameras are suspended from tethered balloons or blimps. D.J.B.

**AERODYNAMICS,** branch of fluid mechanics (q.v.) that deals with the motion of air and other gaseous fluids, and with the forces acting on bodies in motion relative to such fluids. The motion of an airplane through the air, the wind forces exerted on a structure, and the operation of a windmill are all examples of aerodynamic action (see AIRPLANE).

**Bernoulli's Principle.** One of the fundamental laws governing the motion of fluids is Bernoulli's principle (q.v.), which relates an increase in flow velocity to a decrease in pressure and vice versa. Bernoulli's principle is used in aerodynamics to explain the lift of an airplane wing in flight. A wing is so designed that air flows more rapidly over its upper surface than its lower one, leading to a decrease in pressure on the top surface as compared to the bottom. The resulting pressure difference provides the lift that sustains the aircraft in flight. The velocity of a wind that strikes the bluff surface of a building is close to zero near its wall. According to Bernoulli's principle,

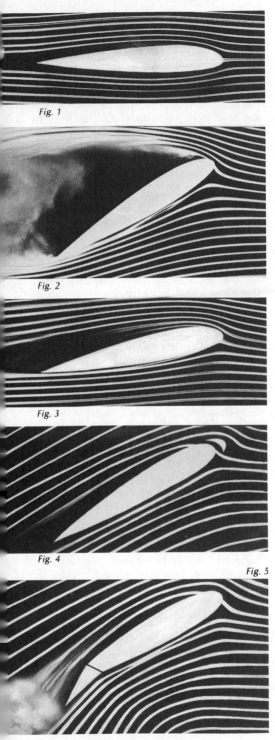

Fig. 1

Fig. 2

Fig. 3

Fig. 4

Fig. 5

Changes in airflow occurring under various conditions of flight provide greater or lesser lift with the different angles of attack.

this would lead to a rise in pressure relative to the pressure away from the building, resulting in wind forces that the structures must be designed to withstand.

Another important aspect of aerodynamics is the drag, or resistance, acting on solid bodies moving through air. The drag forces exerted by the air flowing over the airplane, for example, must be overcome by the thrust force developed by either the jet engine or the propellers (*see* PROPELLER). These drag forces can be significantly reduced by streamlining the body. For bodies that are not fully streamlined, the drag force increases approximately with the square of the speed as they move rapidly through the air. The power required, for example, to drive an automobile steadily at medium or high speeds is primarily absorbed in overcoming air resistance.

**Supersonics.** Supersonics, an important branch of aerodynamics, concerns phenomena that arise when the velocity of a solid body exceeds the speed of sound in the medium, usually air, in which it is traveling. The speed of sound in the atmosphere varies with humidity, temperature, and pressure (*see* SOUND). Because the speed of sound, being thus variable, is a critical factor in aerodynamic equations, it is represented by a so-called Mach number, named after the Austrian physicist and philosopher Ernst Mach, who pioneered the study of ballistics (q.v.). The Mach number is the speed of the projectile or aircraft with reference to the ambient atmosphere, divided by the speed of sound in the same medium and under the same conditions. Thus, at sea level, under standard conditions of humidity and temperature, a speed of about 1220 km/hr (about 760 mph) represents a Mach number of one, that is, M-1. The same speed in the stratosphere, because of differences in density, pressure, and temperature, would correspond to a Mach number of M-1.16. By designating speeds by Mach number, rather than by kilometers or miles per hour, a more accurate representation of the actual conditions encountered in flight can be obtained.

*Shock waves.* Studies of artillery (q.v.) projectiles in flight, by means of optical observations, disclose the nature of the atmospheric disturbances encountered in supersonic flight. A series of such photographs discloses the following characteristics of flight. At subsonic speeds, that is, below M-0.85, the only atmospheric disturbance is a turbulence in the wake of the projectile. In the transonic range, from M-0.85 to M-1.3, shock waves appear as speed increases; in the lower part of this speed range shock waves arise from any abrupt breaks in the smooth contour of the

167

projectile. As the speed passes M-1, shock waves arise from the nose and tail and are propagated from the projectile in the form of a cone, which has an apex angle inversely proportional to the speed of the projectile. Thus, at M-1, the nose wave is essentially a flat plane; at M-1.4 (1712 km/hr, or 1064 mph at sea level) the angle of the cone is about 90°; and at M-2.48 (about 3060 km/hr, or about 1900 mph), the shock wave preceding the projectile has a conical angle of slightly less than 50°. This line of research has already made possible the design of modern high-speed airplanes, in which the wings are swept back at angles as great as 60°, to avoid the shock wave from the nose of the plane.

**Maximum efficiency.** Other factors determined by research in the supersonic range of speeds of artillery projectiles include the shape of the projectiles and the rate of gas flow. The so-called tear-drop shape, which is the ideal streamlined shape for subsonic speeds, is extremely uneconomical in the supersonic range, because of the large frontal surface that must compress the atmosphere and give rise to energy-destroying shock waves of great amplitude.

If gaseous flow occurs through a constricted tube, for example the nozzle of a rocket (q.v.), at subsonic speeds, the speed of the flow increases and the pressure decreases in the throat of the constriction. The opposite phenomena take place at supersonic speeds, and speed of flow increases in a divergent tube. The exhaust gas of a rocket, therefore, increasing to sonic speed in the throat of a venturi tube or rocket nozzle, further increases its speed and consequent thrust in the diverging flare of the nozzle, thereby multiplying the efficiency of the rocket system. Another factor, long known to rocket designers, is the direct influence of ambient atmospheric pressures on the efficiency of the flight of planes in supersonic speed ranges. That is, the closer the surrounding medium is to a perfect vacuum (q.v.), the more efficient is the power plant of the plane. The range of the supersonic plane can also be increased by reducing the area, or cross section, displacing atmosphere. Increasing the weight by increasing the length, but at the same time making the plane more slender and equipping it with a needle nose, are necessary features of design for planes operating in the supersonic range in the atmosphere. In the years following World War II, the U.S. Air Force and the U.S. Navy established research institutions that included among their facilities wind tunnels capable of testing plane models and airplane parts in currents of air traveling at supersonic speeds. *See* WIND TUNNEL.

**Area rule.** A major development in aeronautics resulting from wind-tunnel research was the discovery by the American physicist Richard Travis Whitcomb (1921–  ) of the area rule, a new principle for the design of supersonic aircraft. According to this principle, the sharp rise in drag that occurs at transonic speeds results from the distribution of the total cross-sectional area at each point along the airplane. By pinching in the fuselage where the wings are attached, the reduction in the combined cross-sectional area of the fuselage and the wing produces a decrease in the drag characteristics of the aircraft. Whitcomb's so-called wasp-waist design made possible an increase of 25 percent in the supersonic-speed range without requiring any additional engine power.

The term *supersonics* was formerly used more broadly to include the branch of physics now known as ultrasonics (q.v.), which deals with high-frequency sound waves, usually in the range above 20,000 hertz (Hz).

*See also* JET PROPULSION.

*For further information on this topic, see the Bibliography in volume 28,* sections 393, 575.

**AERONAUTICS.** *See* AIRPLANE; AVIATION.

**AËROPE.** *See* ATREUS; THYESTES.

**AEROSOL,** suspension in a gas, usually air, of microscopic liquid or solid particles, such as smoke, dust, fog, or smog, that tend to remain dispersed rather than to settle. True aerosol particles range from $10^{-7}$ to $10^{-4}$ cm ($4 \times 10^{-8}$ to $4 \times 10^{-5}$ in) in diameter; however, turbulent media can keep in dispersion particles 100 times larger, as is often the case with fog and cloud droplets and dust particles. *See* COLLOID.

**AEROSOL DISPENSER,** container and valve designed to dispense a wide variety of substances in the form of fine sprays, foams, or liquid streams. The product to be dispensed, such as paint, cosmetics, or food, is sealed in the container with a propellant gas under pressure.

Certain propellants such as nitrous oxide or carbon dioxide remain gaseous when pressurized in these containers. Others, such as the chlorofluorocarbons, may liquefy (*see* FLUORINE). In a two-phase system the product mixes with the liquid propellant that expands into a gas when released and breaks the product into tiny droplets. A three-phase system consists of a layer of product between layers of nonmixing liquefied propellant at the bottom and gaseous propellant at the top. In both systems depressing the push button on the valve allows the product to be forced up a tube and through the valve. The liquefied gas in the bottom of the container vaporizes to keep the pressure constant.

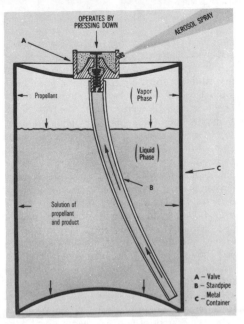

OPERATES BY
PRESSING DOWN

A

AEROSOL SPRAY

Propellant

Vapor
Phase

Liquid
Phase

C

B

Solution of
propellant
and product

A – Valve
B – Standpipe
C – Metal
      Container

*In this cross section of a typical aerosol container, designed for spraying an area or for surface coating, gas under pressure is used to spray atomized liquid.*
E. I. du Pont de Nemours & Compay

In the 1970s chlorofluorocarbons came under scrutiny as a possible threat to the atmospheric ozone layer. These propellants have been banned in the U.S. and in several other countries for all but essential uses (*see* ATMOSPHERE; OZONE LAYER).

**AEROSPACE INDUSTRY,** industry concerned with the design and construction of aircraft and spacecraft and the equipment on which they rely. In a technical sense, the aerospace industry is only about 30 years old. The term was not used until the late 1950s, when the first space flights were made. The industry's origins are much older, however, dating from the early 20th century, when the first airplanes flew. Many of the most important American aerospace companies, such as Boeing, Bell, Martin, and Douglas, are named after aircraft builders from the World War I period. Other important names, such as Lockheed, Northrop, Pratt and Whitney, Grumman, Vought, Sikorsky, and McDonnell, first appeared during the 1920s and 1930s.

Aerospace is a high-technology industry. Its products include not only space shuttles, satellites, rocket engines, helicopters, private propeller-driven and jet-powered airplanes, military aircraft (and the weapons they carry), and commercial airliners, but also electronic guidance, navigation, and safety systems, the turbo-fan jet engines that power large aircraft, and the special tools technicians need to service all these vehicles and systems.

Aerospace is an important component of the economies of most of the world's leading nations, including the U.S., Canada, Brazil, Taiwan, Israel, Japan, and the Western European nations. The U.S. is the leading aerospace nation. In 1991, 1,164,000 Americans worked for aerospace companies. Hundreds of thousands more work for government agencies connected to aerospace, such as the Air Force, the Navy, and the National Aeronautics and Space Administration. In 1991, the U.S. industry had sales worth $135 billion. Half of those sales were made to the federal government. Another 30 percent were made to buyers in other countries. Thus, aerospace is an important contributor to the U.S. balance of trade with foreign countries.

From the start, the technologies and industries of flight were international in scope. Most leading nations had an aircraft industry that was responsible for one technical advance or another, and the new knowledge quickly spread to other countries. The primary force behind the growth of the aircraft and aerospace industry has been war. The industry and its technologies developed most quickly when various countries were competing for air supremacy. For example, before World War II, the aircraft industries in such countries as the Soviet Union, the U.S., Great Britain, and Germany remained quite small, then grew at fantastic rates during the war. Technological breakthroughs were made that proved basic to aerospace. Jet and rocket engines and guided missiles were developed in Germany, but the Soviets and Americans made the most of these inventions during the cold war (q.v.) and international arms race. In 1947, Americans used jet engines to achieve supersonic speed, and in the 1950s they used jets to power large airliners. The Soviets made the first space flight in 1957, and both sides began an effort that lasted through the 1980s to outdo one another in this technology. Thousands of intercontinental ballistic missiles were built, and many satellites were sent into space to provide military intelligence, better communications, and weather information. In 1969, the U.S. used giant rockets to send astronauts to the moon.

The end of the cold war in the early 1990s promised to reduce military demand for aerospace products, but aerospace remains an important and dynamic industry worldwide.

*See also* AIRPLANE; DEFENSE SYSTEMS; GUIDED MISSILES; JET PROPULSION; ROCKET; SPACE EXPLORATION; WARFARE.                    J.A.V.M.

**AEROSPACE MEDICINE,** branch of preventive medicine that is concerned with the physiological and psychological stresses on the human body in flight. The study of effects within the earth's atmosphere is also called aviation medicine; beyond this atmosphere the study of effects is also called space medicine. Aerospace

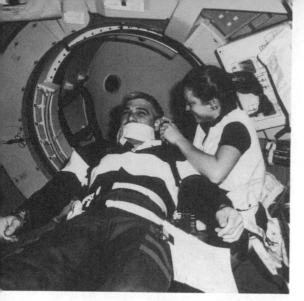

In one of the medical experiments aboard the space shuttle Columbia, on NASA's Spacelab Life Sciences Mission 1, astronaut Sidney M. Gutierrez gets his ears checked by fellow astronaut Tamara E. Jernigan. Gutierrez wears a medical restraint system.    **NASA**

medicine was recognized as a subspecialty by the American Medical Association in 1953.

## AVIATION MEDICINE

Specialists in aviation medicine study the reactions of humans to the stresses of air travel. They are concerned with the screening of candidates for flight training, the maintenance of maximum efficiency among aircrews, and with clinically oriented research into the effects of flight on the body. They also cooperate with aeronautical engineers in the development of safe aircraft.

**History.** Aviation medicine is rooted in the early 18th-century physiological studies of balloonists, some of whom were physicians. In 1784, a year

after the first balloon flight by the French physicist Jean Pilâtre de Rozier (1756–85), a Boston physician, John Jeffries (1744–1819), made the first study of upper-air composition from a balloon. The first comprehensive studies of health effects in air flight were made by the French physician Paul Bert (1833–86), who published his research on the effects of altered air pressure and composition on humans in 1878 under the title *La pression barometrique.* In 1894 the Viennese physiologist Herman Von Schrötter designed an oxygen mask with which the meteorologist Artur Berson (1859–1942) set an altitude record of 9150 m (30,000 ft). With the advent of the airplane, the first standards for military pilots were established in 1912. Significant work in this area was directed by the physician Theodore Lyster (1875–1933), an American pioneer in aviation medicine. Lyster set up the Aviation Medicine Research Board in 1917, which opened a research laboratory at Hazelhurst Field in Mineola, N.Y., in January 1918. The School of Flight Surgeons opened the following year, and in 1929 the Aero Medical Association was founded under the direction of Louis H. Bauer (1888–1964). In 1934 facilities were built at Wright Air Field in Dayton, Ohio, to study the effect of high-performance flight on humans. Technical advances included the first pressurized suit, designed and worn by the American aviator Wiley Post in 1934, and the first antigravity suit, designed by W. R. Franks (1901–  ) in Great Britain in 1942. In an effort to help design better restraint systems for military jet aircraft, the U.S. flight surgeon John Stapp (1910–  ) conducted a series of tests on a rocket-powered sled, culminating on Dec. 10, 1954, when Col. Stapp underwent deceleration from a velocity of 286 m (937 ft)/sec in 1.4 sec.

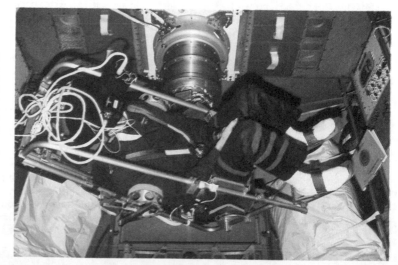

In orbit, astronaut David C. Hilmers sits in a moving chair and wears a helmet assembly as he participates in an experiment in the International Microgravity Laboratory aboard the space shuttle Discovery.
**NASA**

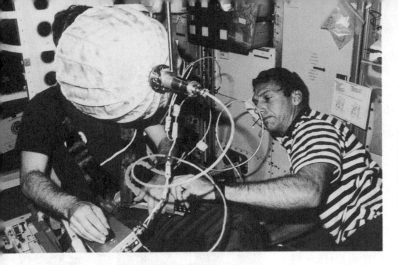

Aboard the space shuttle Discovery, astronaut David C. Hilmers assists Ulf Merbold, a specialist from the European Space Agency, in an experiment to study the effects of visual stimulation on someone in space. **NASA**

**Physiological Considerations.** Aviation medicine is concerned primarily with the effects on human beings of high speed and high altitude and involves the study of such factors as acceleration and deceleration, atmospheric pressure, and decompression. In civil aviation medicine, an additional concern is passenger airsickness.

*High speed.* In itself, high speed does not produce harmful symptoms. What can be dangerous are high acceleration or deceleration forces; these are expressed as multiples of gravity, or g's. In pulling out of a dive, for example, a pilot may be subjected to an inertial force as high as 9 g. If a force of 4 to 6 g is sustained for more than a few seconds, the resulting symptoms range from visual impairment to total blackout. Protection is provided by a specially designed outfit, called an anti-g suit, which supplies pressure to the abdomen and legs, thus counteracting the tendency for blood to accumulate in those areas. Proper support of the head is essential during extreme deceleration in order to avoid swelling of the sinuses and severe headaches. While facing backward in a seated position, properly supported human test subjects have been able to tolerate a deceleration force of 50 g without severe injury.

*Oxygen supply.* A critical consideration in aircraft travel is the continuing physiological requirement for oxygen. The only oxygen stored by the body is that in the bloodstream. Although muscles can function temporarily without oxygen, the buildup of toxic products soon limits activity. Brain and eye tissues are the most sensitive to oxygen deficiency.

The atmosphere, which contains 21 percent of oxygen by volume, is under a normal sea-level pressure of 760 torrs (14.7 lb/sq in). The barometric pressure (*see* BAROMETER) up to about 4575 m (about 15,000 ft) is sufficient to sustain human life. Above this altitude the air must be artificially put under pressure to meet the respiratory needs of human beings.

High-altitude military airplanes are provided with oxygen equipment, and military personnel are required to use it at all times when participating in flight above 3050 m (10,000 ft). Military craft that can fly above 10,675 m (35,000 ft) usually also have cockpits under pressure. Positive-pressure breathing equipment is also used in all other aircraft capable of flight above 10,675 m. Full or partial pressure suits with additional oxygen equipment are required in military aircraft capable of flight above 16,775 m (55,000 ft).

Commercial carriers provide oxygen systems and pressurized cabins in accordance with civil air regulations. An airliner flying at 6710 m (22,000 ft), for example, must maintain a "cabin altitude" of 1830 m (6000 ft).

*Altitude sickness.* This physiological condition results from a state of acute oxygen deficiency, known medically as hypoxidosis, at high altitudes. Ascending from the lower atmosphere, called the troposphere, the atmosphere is thin enough at 3900 m (13,000 ft) to produce symptoms of hypoxia, or oxygen hunger. At the lower limit of the stratosphere, about 10,675 m (about 35,000 ft), normal inhalation of pure oxygen no longer maintains an adequate saturation of oxygen in the blood.

Hypoxia produces a variety of reactions in the body. Mild intoxication and stimulation of the nervous system are followed by progressive loss of attention and judgment until unconsciousness occurs. Respiration and pulse rate increase, and the systemic oxygen is reduced. Prolonged lack of oxygen may cause damage to the brain.

*Aeroembolism.* Because of the reduction of barometric pressure at altitudes above 9150 m (30,000 ft), the body tissues can no longer retain atmospheric nitrogen in solution. As a result, liberated gas bubbles, as well as ruptured fat cells, may enter the circulatory system and form obstructions, or emboli, in the blood vessels. This condition, known medically as aeroembolism and popularly as the bends (q.v.), leads to confusion, paralysis, or neurocirculatory collapse. The most characteristic symptoms of the bends are pain in the large joints resulting from pressure of the gas on tendons and nerves, together with spasm of the blood vessels. Preflight inhalation of pure oxygen to eliminate nitrogen from the system has proved valuable as a preventive measure. Rapid decompression, resulting from accidental failure at high altitudes of the pressure within the cabin, causes major damage to the heart and other organs by the ram effect of gases formed in the body cavities.

**Airsickness.** This condition is produced by a disturbance of the labyrinthine mechanism of the inner ear (*see* EAR: *Equilibrium*), although psychogenic factors such as apprehension can also play a part. Motion sickness can be prevented by taking drugs containing scopolamine (q.v.) or some antihistamines (*see* ANTIHISTAMINE) before flight.

**Time change.** As transport planes became faster, pilots and passengers were able to travel across many time zones in less than a day. The resulting disturbance in the biological circadian ("about a day") rhythm (*see* BIOLOGICAL CLOCKS) can produce disorientation and reduce concentration and efficiency. This condition is popularly known as jet lag. While troublesome to passengers, the problem is more acute for pilots, who may have to fly another assignment in a short time. Concern has been expressed about the possible effect of this situation on air safety, although no air accident has been clearly identified as jet-lag-induced.

### SPACE MEDICINE

The U.S. National Aeronautics and Space Administration (NASA) is responsible for nonmilitary space flight for scientific purposes, which include medical studies. Specialists in space medicine—also known as bioastronautics—study the human factors involved in flight outside the atmosphere. Most of the potential dangers in space travel (such as acceleration and deceleration forces, the need for an artificial atmosphere, and noise and vibration) are similar to those encountered in atmospheric flight and can be compensated for in similar ways. Space medicine scientists, however, must consider two additional problems—weightlessness and the increased radiation outside the atmosphere.

**History.** The first information about human performance during space travel was gathered in

On June 17–24, 1985, the space shuttle Discovery made a busy experimental flight. Two guest astronauts, here, were payload specialists. Saudi Arabian prince Sultan Salman Abdel-Aziz al-Saud (left) eats, and Patrick Baudry of France conducts a phase of the French Postural Experiment on himself. NASA

Germany in the 1940s under the direction of Hubertus Strughold (1898–    ). In 1949 Strughold was made director of the department of space medicine at the School of Aviation Medicine at Randolph Air Force Base, Tex. (now the School of Aerospace Medicine at Brooks Air Force Base, Tex.). Both the U.S. and the USSR conducted rocket tests with animals beginning in 1948. In 1957 the USSR put a dog into earth orbit, and the U.S. used a monkey for tests in 1958. The tests suggested that few biological dangers existed in space flight. This was confirmed when human space flight began on April 12, 1961, with the launching of the Soviet cosmonaut Yury Gagarin into orbit.

The U.S. followed with the Mercury-Redstone suborbital flights and then the orbital Mercury and Gemini flights, the Apollo moon landings, the experimental orbital vehicle *Skylab,* and

Space Shuttle flights. Then, in the 1980s, when Soviet cosmonauts began setting records for time spent in the gravity-free or "microgravity" environment, the effects of long-term weightlessness began to be viewed as a serious medical problem.

**Physiological Findings.** Few serious biological effects were noted during the early years of space flight. Even the 21-day quarantine of astronauts returning from the Apollo moon mission was subsequently abandoned, because no infectious agents were identified. The body functions that were monitored (often with specially designed miniature instruments) included heart rate, pulse, body temperature, blood pressure, respiration, speech and mental alertness, and brain waves. Few changes occurred. Changes in the hormones and in the concentrations of salts in the blood did take place, but these were not detrimental. Eating in weightlessness was accomplished by packaging food in containers that could be squeezed directly into the mouth, and special systems were designed for collection of fluid and solid wastes. The lack of a natural time cycle in space was compensated for by keeping the astronauts' schedules synchronized with earth time.

Psychological changes were anticipated because of the close confinement of a few individuals in a small space with limited activity. Few psychological problems were noted, however, perhaps because the astronauts were chosen for emotional stability and high motivation and because they were assigned enough tasks to keep them almost constantly busy. Irradiation was also found to have little effect. Short orbital flights produced exposures about equal to one medical X ray—about the same as suborbital flight. The crew on the longer *Skylab* flight sustained many times this dose. Space flights are planned to avoid periods when solar flares are expected to occur, as these can emit dangerous levels of gamma radiation.

However, although it was assumed that gravity is necessary for normal growth, the magnitude of physiological changes induced by extended periods in a microgravity environment came as something of a surprise. Serious medical problems, including loss of bone matter and muscle strength, were observed to result from long-term weightlessness, as during the 237-day mission of three cosmonauts aboard a Salyut space station in 1984. Moreover, atrophy of certain muscles, particularly those of the heart, was seen to be especially dangerous because of its effect on the functioning of the entire cardiovascular system. The blood itself was found to be affected, with a

*An astronaut, on a movable platform, is lowered underwater in NASA's weightless environment training facility (WET-F). Mockups of space shuttle craft are completely submerged in a large pool to accommodate astronaut training.* NASA

measurable decrease in the number of oxygen-carrying cells.

On a seven-day *Challenger* Space Shuttle mission in 1985, these effects were studied in an experiment using 24 rats and 2 monkeys. Postflight examination revealed not only the expected loss of bone and muscle strength but a decrease in release of growth hormone as well.

These findings are taken into consideration now whenever plans are made for manned space flight. Astronauts' busy work schedules in space are designed to include regular exercise periods, thereby maintaining muscle tone. And plans for the operation of permanently manned space stations now include provisions for changing crews on a regular basis, so as not to subject astronauts to weightlessness for indefinite periods of time.

*For further information on this topic, see the Bibliography in volume 28, section 490.*

**AESCHINES** (389–314 BC), ancient Greek orator, born in Athens. Aeschines became one of the leading men of Athens through his eloquence and his legal knowledge. As a member of an embassy to Philip II, king of Macedonia, in 347 BC, he decided that Athenian resistance to the Macedonians would be futile. He thus became the leader of the peace party at Athens in opposition to the orator Demosthenes, the spokesman for those who believed that Philip should be resisted at any cost.

Aeschines' hatred of his rival, however, led to his downfall. In 337 BC he prosecuted the Athenian orator Ctesiphon (fl. 4th cent. BC) when the latter proposed that a golden crown be awarded to Demosthenes; the charge was actually an attack upon the whole foreign policy of Demosthenes. The trial took place in 330 BC. Aeschines lost the case and was fined heavily, whereupon he went into exile and, according to tradition, opened a school of oratory at Rhodes. His posthumous fame as an orator may be attributed to his three extant speeches: *Against Timarchus, On the Embassy,* and *Against Ctesiphon.*

**AESCHYLUS** (525–456 BC), Greek dramatist, the earliest of the great tragic poets of Athens. As the predecessor of Sophocles and Euripides, he is called the father of Greek tragedy. Aeschylus was born in Eleusis, near Athens.

He fought successfully against the Persians at Marathon in 490 BC, at Salamís in 480 BC, and possibly at Plataea in the following year. He made at least two trips, perhaps three, to Sicily. During his final visit he died at Gela, where a monument was later erected in his memory.

Aeschylus is said to have written about 90 plays. His tragedies, first performed about 500 BC, were presented as trilogies, usually bound by a common theme; each trilogy was followed by a satyr drama (low comedy involving a mythological hero, with a chorus of satyrs). The titles of 79 of his plays are known, but only 7 have survived. The earliest is *The Suppliants,* a drama with little action but many choral songs of great beauty; it is believed to be the first play of a trilogy about the marriage of the 50 daughters of Danaüs, which included the plays *The Egyptians* and *The Danaïds. The Persians,* presented in 472 BC, is a historical tragedy about the Battle of Salamís, the scene being laid in Persia at the court of the mother of King Xerxes I.

*The Seven Against Thebes,* produced in 467 BC, is based on a Theban legend, the conflict between the two sons of Oedipus, Eteocles and Polyneices, for the throne of Thebes. It is believed to be the third play of a trilogy, the first two being *Laius* and *Oedipus. Prometheus Bound,* a work of uncertain date, portrays the punishment of the defiant Prometheus by Zeus. It is probably the first play of a Promethean trilogy, the others being *Prometheus Unbound* and *Prometheus the Fire-Bringer.*

The remaining three plays, *Agamemnon, The Libation Bearers,* and *The Eumenides,* produced in 458 BC, form the trilogy known as the *Oresteia,* or story of Orestes. In *Agamemnon,* one of the greatest works of dramatic literature, King Agamemnon returns home from Troy and is treacherously murdered by his faithless wife Clytemnestra. In the second play, Orestes, the son of Agamemnon, returns to Argos and avenges his father's murder by slaying his mother and her paramour Aegisthus. This matricide is punished by the avenging goddesses, the Erinyes. In *The Eumenides,* the Erinyes pursue Orestes until he is cleansed of his blood guilt and set free by the ancient court of the Areopagus, through the intercession of Athena, goddess of wisdom.

By introducing a second actor into the play, he created dramatic dialogue; he also elaborated the staging of the drama, introducing costumes and scenery. His works are characterized by the profundity of theme and the grandeur of the poetry recited by the chorus. The *Oresteia,* probably his most mature work, offers an insight into his ideas of justice and mercy, and a belief in a divine will, with the aid of which humanity can achieve wisdom through suffering.                              G.E.D.

**AESCULAPIAN SNAKE,** common name for a harmless snake that symbolizes the Greek god of medicine, Asclepius. Two of these snakes are seen entwined on the caduceus, the physician's insignia.

Snakes were kept in the combination hospital-temples built by the ancient Greeks and, later, by the Romans in honor of the god. They are found not only in their original range of southern Europe, but also in the various places in Germany and Austria where Roman temples had been established; escaped snakes survived and flourished.

Smooth, glossy, and slender, the snake is uniformly brown with a streak of darker color behind the eyes. The snake's belly has ridged scales that catch easily on rough surfaces, making it especially adapted for climbing trees. The males engage in elaborate ritualistic combat dances.

| COMMON NAME | FAMILY | GENUS AND SPECIES |
|---|---|---|
| Aesculapian snake | Colubridae | *Elaphe longissima* |

**AESCULAPIUS.** See ASCLEPIUS.

**AESOP** (c. 620–560 BC), ancient Greek writer of fables, who is supposed to have been a freed slave from Phrygia. His name became attached to the beast fables, long transmitted through oral tradition. The beast fables are part of the common culture of the Indo-European peoples and constitute perhaps the most widely read collection of fables in world literature. Many of Aesop's fables were rewritten in verse by the Greek poet Babrius, probably in the 1st or 2d century AD, and in Latin verse by the Roman poet Phaedrus (c. 15 BC–c. AD 50) in the 1st century AD. The collection that now bears Aesop's name consists for the most part of later prose paraphrases of the fables of Babrius.

**AESTHETICS,** branch of philosophy concerned with the essence and perception of beauty and ugliness. Aesthetics also deals with the question of whether such qualities are objectively present in the things they appear to qualify or whether they exist only in the mind of the individual; hence, whether objects are perceived by a particular mode, the aesthetic mode, or whether instead the objects have, in themselves, special qualities—aesthetic qualities.

Criticism and the psychology of art, although independent disciplines, are related to aesthetics. The psychology of art is concerned with such elements of the arts as human responses to color, sound, line, form, and words and with the ways in which the emotions condition such responses.

Criticism confines itself to particular works of art, analyzing their structures, meanings, and problems, comparing them with other works, and evaluating them.

The term *aesthetics* was introduced in 1753 by the German philosopher Alexander Gottlieb Baumgarten, but the study of the nature of beauty had been pursued for centuries. In the past it was chiefly a subject for philosophers. Since the 19th century, artists also have contributed their views.

**Classical Theories.** The first aesthetic theory of any scope is that of Plato, who believed that reality consists of archetypes, or forms, beyond human sensation, which are the models for all things that exist in human experience. The objects of such experience are examples, or imitations, of those forms. The philosopher tries to reason from the object experienced to the reality it imitates; the artist copies the experienced object, or uses it as a model for the work. Thus, the artist's work is an imitation of an imitation.

Plato's thinking had a marked ascetic strain. In his *Republic* Plato went so far as to banish some types of artists from his ideal society because he thought their work encouraged immorality or portrayed base characters, and that certain musical compositions caused languidness or incited people to immoderate actions.

Aristotle also spoke of art as imitation, but not in the Platonic sense. One could imitate "things as they ought to be," he wrote, and "art partly completes what nature cannot bring to a finish." The artist separates the form from the matter of some objects of experience, such as the human body or a tree, and imposes that form on another matter, such as canvas or marble. Thus, imitation is not just copying an original model, nor is it de-

vising a symbol for the original; rather, it is a particular representation of an aspect of things, and each work is an imitation of the universal whole.

Aesthetics was as inseparable from morality and politics for Aristotle as for Plato. The former wrote about music in his *Politics,* maintaining that art affects human character, and hence the social order. Because Aristotle held that happiness is the aim of life, he believed that the major function of art is to provide human satisfaction. In the *Poetics,* his great work on the principles of drama, Aristotle argued that tragedy so stimulates the emotions of pity and fear, which he considered morbid and unhealthful, that by the end of the play the spectator is purged of them. This catharsis makes the audience psychologically healthier and thus more capable of happiness. Neoclassical drama since the 17th century has been greatly influenced by Aristotle's *Poetics.* The works of the French dramatists Jean Baptiste Racine, Pierre Corneille, and Molière, in particular, advocate its doctrine of the three unities: time, place, and action. This concept dominated literary theories up to the 19th century.

**Other Early Approaches.** The 3d–century philosopher Plotinus, born in Egypt and trained in philosophy at Alexandria, although a Neoplatonist, gave far more importance to art than did Plato. In Plotinus's view, art reveals the form of an object more clearly than ordinary experience does, and it raises the soul to contemplation of the universal. According to Plotinus, the highest moments of life are mystical, which is to say that the soul is united, in the world of forms, with the divine, which Plotinus spoke of as "the One." Aesthetic experience comes closest to mystical experience, for one loses oneself while contemplating the aesthetic object.

Art in the Middle Ages was primarily an expression of religion, with an aesthetic principle based largely on Neoplatonism. During the Renaissance in the 15th and 16th centuries, art became more secular, and its aesthetics were classical rather than religious. The great impetus to aesthetic thought in the modern world occurred in Germany during the 18th century. The German critic Gotthold Ephraim Lessing, in his *Laokoon* (1766), argued that art is self-limiting and reaches its apogee only when these limitations are recognized. The German critic and classical archaeologist Johann Joachim Winckelmann maintained that, in accordance with the ancient Greeks, the best art is impersonal, expressing ideal proportion and balance rather than its creator's individuality. The German philosopher Johann Gottlieb Fichte considered beauty a moral virtue.

The artist creates a world in which beauty, as much as truth, is an end, foreshadowing that absolute freedom which is the goal of the human will. For Fichte, art is individual, not social, but it fulfills a great human purpose.

**Modern Aesthetics.** The German philosopher Immanuel Kant was concerned with judgments of taste. Objects are judged beautiful, he proposed, when they satisfy a disinterested desire: one that does not involve personal interests or needs. It follows from this that beautiful objects have no specific purpose and that judgments of beauty are not expressions of mere personal preference but are universal. Although one cannot be certain that others will be satisfied by objects he or she judges to be beautiful, one can at least say that others ought to be satisfied. The basis for one's response to beauty exists in the structure of one's mind.

Art should give the same disinterested satisfaction as natural beauty. Paradoxically, art can accomplish one thing nature cannot. It can offer ugliness and beauty in one and the same object. A fine painting of an ugly face is nonetheless beautiful.

According to the 19th-century German philosopher G. W. F. Hegel, art, religion, and philosophy are the bases of the highest spiritual development. Beauty in nature is everything that the human spirit finds pleasing and congenial to the exercise of spiritual and intellectual freedom. Certain things in nature can be made more congenial and pleasing, and it is these natural objects that are reorganized by art to satisfy aesthetic demands.

The German philosopher Arthur Schopenhauer believed that the forms of the universe, like the eternal Platonic forms, exist beyond the worlds of experience, and that aesthetic satisfaction is achieved by contemplating them for their own sakes, as a means of escaping the painful world of daily experience.

Fichte, Kant, and Hegel are in a direct line of development. Schopenhauer attacked Hegel but was influenced by Kant's view of disinterested contemplation. The German philosopher Friedrich Nietzsche followed Schopenhauer at first, then disagreed with him. Nietzsche concurred that life is tragic, but thought that this should not preclude acceptance of the tragic with joyous affirmation, the full realization of which is art. Art confronts the terrors of the universe and is therefore only for the strong. Art can transform any experience into beauty, and by so doing transforms its horrors in such a way that they may be contemplated with enjoyment.

Although much modern aesthetics is rooted in German thought, German thinking was subject to other Western influences. Lessing, a founder of German romanticism, was affected by the aesthetic writings of the British statesman Edmund Burke.

**Aesthetics and Art.** Traditional aesthetics in the 18th and 19th centuries was dominated by the concept of art as imitation of nature. Novelists such as Jane Austen and Charles Dickens in England and dramatists such as Carlo Goldoni in Italy and Alexandre Dumas *fils* in France presented realistic accounts of middle-class life. Painters, whether neoclassical, such as J. A. D. Ingres, romantic, such as Eugène Délacroix, or realist, such as Gustave Courbet, rendered their subjects with careful attention to lifelike detail.

In traditional aesthetics it was also frequently assumed that art objects are useful as well as beautiful. Paintings might commemorate historical events or encourage morality. Music might inspire piety or patriotism. Drama, especially in the hands of Dumas and Henrik Ibsen, a Norwegian, might serve to criticize society and so lead to reform.

In the 19th century, however, avant-garde concepts of aesthetics began to challenge traditional views. The change was particularly evident in painting. French impressionists, such as Claude Monet, denounced academic painters for depicting what they thought they should see rather than what they actually saw—that is, surfaces of many colors and wavering forms caused by the distorting play of light and shadow as the sun moves.

In the late 19th century, postimpressionists such as Paul Cézanne, Paul Gauguin, and Vincent van Gogh were more concerned with the structure of a painting and with expressing their own psyche than with representing objects in the world of nature. In the early 20th century this structural interest was developed further by cubist painters such as Pablo Picasso, and the expressionist concern was reflected in the work of Henri Matisse and other Fauves and by the German expressionists such as E. L. Kirchner. The literary aspects of expressionism can be seen in the plays of August Strindberg, a Swede, and Frank Wedekind, a German.

Closely connected with these relatively nonrepresentational approaches to art was the principle of "art for art's sake," which was derived from Kant's view that art has its own reason for being. The phrase was first used by the French philosopher Victor Cousin in 1818. This doctrine, sometimes called aestheticism, was espoused in England by the critic Walter Pater, by the Pre-Raphaelite painters, and by the expatriate American painter J. A. M. Whistler. In France it was the credo of such symbolist poets as Charles Baudelaire. The "art for art's sake" principle underlies most of avant-garde Western art of the 20th century.

**Major Contemporary Influences.** Four philosophers of the late 19th and early 20th centuries have been the primary influences on present-day aesthetics. In France Henri Bergson defined science as the use of intelligence to create a system of symbols that supposedly describes reality but actually falsifies it. Art, however, is based on intuition, which is a direct apprehension of reality unmediated by thought. Thus art cuts through conventional symbols and beliefs about people, life, and society and confronts one with reality itself.

In Italy the philosopher and historian Benedetto Croce also exalted intuition, but he considered it the immediate awareness of an object that somehow gives that object form. It is the apprehension of things before one reflects about them. Works of art are the expression, in material form, of such intuitions; but beauty and ugliness are not qualities of the works of art but qualities of the spirit expressed intuitively in these works of art.

The American philosopher and poet George Santayana argued that when one takes pleasure in a thing the pleasure may be regarded as a quality of the thing itself, rather than as a subjective response to it. Just as one may characterize some human act as good in itself, instead of calling it good merely because one approves it, so one may say that some object is beautiful, not merely that one's aesthetic delight in its color and form leads one to call it beautiful.

John Dewey, the American educator and philosopher, viewed human experience as disconnected, fragmentary, full of beginnings without conclusions, or as experiences deliberately manipulated as means to ends. Those exceptional experiences that flow from their beginnings to consummations are aesthetic. Aesthetic experience is enjoyment for its own sake, is complete and self-contained, and is terminal, not merely instrumental to other purposes.

*Marxism and Freudianism.* Two powerful movements, Marxism in the fields of economics and politics and Freudianism in psychology, have rejected the art-for-art principle and reasserted art's practical uses. Marxism treats art as an expression of the underlying economic relations in society. Marxist proponents maintain that art is great only when it is "progressive," that is, when it supports the cause of the society under which it is created.

Sigmund Freud believed the value of art to lie in its therapeutic use: It is by this means that both the artist and the public can reveal hidden conflicts and discharge tensions. Fantasies and daydreams, as they enter into art, are thus transformed from an escape from life into ways of meeting it. In the surrealist movement in painting and poetry, the unconscious is used as a source of material. The stream-of-consciousness technique of fiction, notably in the novels of the Irish writer James Joyce, was derived not only from Freud's work but partly from *The Principles of Psychology* (1890) by the American philosopher and psychologist William James and partly from the French novel *We'll to the Woods No More* (1888; trans. 1938) by Édouard Dujardin (1861–1949).

*Existentialism.* More recently, the French philosopher and writer Jean Paul Sartre advocated a form of existentialism in which art is seen as an expression of the freedom of the individual to choose, and as such demonstrates the individual's responsibility for his or her choices. Despair, as reflected in art, is not an end but a beginning, because it eradicates the guilts and excuses from which people ordinarily suffer, thus opening the way for genuine freedom.

*Academic controversies.* Academic controversies of the 20th century have revolved about meaning in art. The British critic and semanticist I. A. Richards claimed that art is a language. He asserted that two types of language exist: the symbolic, which conveys ideas and information; and the emotive, which expresses, evokes, and excites feelings and attitudes. He regarded art as emotive language, giving order and coherence to experience and attitudes, but containing no symbolic meaning.

Richards's work was important also for its use of psychological techniques in studying aesthetic reactions. In *Practical Criticism* (1929) he described experiments revealing that even highly educated people are conditioned by their education, by handed-down opinion, and by other social and circumstantial elements in their aesthetic responses. Other writers have commented on the conditioning effects of tradition, fashion, and other social pressures, noting, for example, that in the early 18th century the plays of William Shakespeare were viewed as barbarous and Gothic art as vulgar.

Growing interest in aesthetics is revealed by the establishment of the periodicals *Journal of Aesthetics and Art Criticism,* founded in the U.S. in 1941; *Revue d'Esthétique,* founded in France in 1948; and the *British Journal of Aesthetics,* founded in 1960.                 A.C.D.

For further information on this topic, see the Bibliography in volume 28, sections 25–26, 28, 41, 642–43.

**AETA.** *See* PYGMY.

**AETNA.** *See* ETNA.

**AETOLIA,** district of ancient Greece on the northern coast of the Gulf of Corinth. It takes its name from a character in Greek mythology: Aetolus, son of King Endymion of Elis was said to have fled there after a manslaughter. The story probably reflects the southward migration of northern tribes in the 2d millennium BC. Aetolia is also prominent in Greek mythology as the site of the Calydonian boar hunt (*see* MELEAGER).

The Aetolians long retained their loose tribal organization, but in the 4th century BC they united in the Aetolian League. During the Middle Ages, Aetolia was part of the Byzantine Empire and later passed to the Ottoman Turks. It now forms part of the Greek department (nome) of Aetolia and Acarnina.

**AETOLIAN LEAGUE,** federation of cities in the ancient Greek district of Aetolia, formed sometime in the early 4th century BC. The league became prominent in the 3d century BC, when it opposed the Achaean League. Expanding with success, it soon dominated all of central Greece from the Ionian to the Aegean Sea and controlled areas of the Peloponnesus, Thessaly, Thrace, and Asia Minor as well. In 220 BC the league clashed with Philip V of Macedonia. Defeated, the Aetolians allied themselves with the Romans, who were also fighting Philip. Philip was defeated at Cynocephalae in 197 BC, but the Aetolians, failing to regain their possessions from their victorious ally, joined Antiochus III of Syria against Rome. When he was defeated by Rome in a series of battles (192–190 BC), they surrendered too. The league was formally dissolved in 167 BC.

**AFARS AND ISSAS, FRENCH TERRITORY OF THE.** *See* DJIBOUTI.

**AFFENPINSCHER** (Ger., "monkey terrier"), breed of toy dog. Its facial features mirror its namesake, the monkey, with pointed ears, bushy eyebrows, and a prominent chin tuft and mustache. The fur may be black, red, or gray. The coat is short and wiry except in the chest area and on the face, where it becomes shaggy. A sturdy dog, it stands about 25 cm (about 10 in) high at the shoulder and averages 3 to 3.6 kg (7 to 8 lb) in weight. It makes a friendly pet. The breed was recognized by the American Kennel Club in 1936.

**AFFIDAVIT,** in law, voluntary written statement sworn before an officer qualified to administer an oath. Both the person making the affidavit (that is, swearing to the truth of the facts contained in the document) and the witnessing offi-

*Afghan hound* © Pets by Paulette

cer (a judge, a commissioner of deeds, or a notary public) are usually required to sign the document. Affidavits are frequently used in preliminary legal proceedings, for example, in filing, or starting, a lawsuit. Persons who swear falsely in an affidavit may incur severe legal punishment. *See* DEPOSITION.

**AFGHAN HOUND,** breed of hound, long found in the hill country of northern Afghanistan. Its origin is unknown, although it was once believed that the Afghan existed in Egypt as far back as 4000 BC. Soldiers returning home after the Second Afghan War in the 1880s introduced the breed into England; it was brought to the U.S. in the 1920s. It has a narrow head, like the greyhound's; a long neck; straight, strong forelegs; and thick, silky hair. It weighs about 27 kg (about 60 lb) and stands about 69 cm (about 27 in) high. A hunter, the dog courses its game by sight. It is valuable in hilly country because of its ability to turn easily and leap powerfully. The breed was recognized by the American Kennel Club in 1926.

**AFGHANISTAN** (Pers. *Afghánistán*), officially Islamic State of Afghanistan, republic, SW Asia, bounded on the N by Turkmenistan, Uzbekistan, and Tajikistan; on the E by China and Pakistan; on the S by Pakistan; and on the W by Iran. It is roughly elliptical in shape and has a maximum length, from NE to SW, of about 1450 km (about 900 mi) and a width of about 725 km (about 450 mi). It has an area of about 647,500 sq km (about 250,000 sq mi), about the same as the state of Texas, with which it compares in latitude.

## LAND AND RESOURCES

Afghanistan is a predominantly mountainous country; about three-fourths of its surface consists of uplands. The main lowlands are a series of river valleys in the N and various desert regions in the S and SW. The principal mountain system of the country is the Hindu Kush, which, with its various offshoots, extends for about 800 km (about 500 mi) from the Pamirs, a range in the NE, to the borders of Iran in the W. The average altitude of the Hindu Kush is about 4270 m (about 14,000 ft); some peaks are about 7620 m (about 25,000 ft) high. Natural passes penetrate the mountains of Afghanistan at various points, facilitating travel within the nation as well as communication with neighboring countries. In the Hindu Kush the only pass lower than 3050 m (10,000 ft) is the Shibar (2987 m/9800 ft), which connects the Kabul region with the N part of the country. Probably the best known of the mountain passes is the historic Khyber Pass on the NE border, which traverses the Sulaiman Range and affords relatively easy access to Pakistan.

**Rivers.** The chief rivers of Afghanistan are the Amu Darya, known in ancient times as the Oxus, on the border of Tajikistan; the Kabul, which flows into the Indus R.; the Helmand, the longest river in the country, in the S; and the Harirud, in the W. All these rivers, except the Kabul, empty into lakes or swamps.

**Climate.** Climatic conditions in Afghanistan exhibit great daily and seasonal variations, largely because of the extremes in altitude that characterize the country. During the day, variations in temperature may range from freezing conditions at dawn to almost 38° C (100° F) at noon. Summer temperatures as high as 49° C (120° F) have been recorded in the N valleys. Midwinter temperatures as low as –9.4° C (15° F) are common at the 1980-m (6500-ft) level in the Hindu Kush. Kabul, situated at an altitude of about 1830 m (about 6000 ft), has cold winters and pleasant summers. Jalalabad (about 550 m/about 1800 ft high) is subtropical, and the climate of Kandahar (about 1070 m/about 3500 ft high) is mild. Afghanistan is a relatively dry country, the annual rainfall averaging about 305 mm (about 12 in). Most of the rainfall occurs between October and April. Sandstorms occur frequently in the deserts and arid plains.

**Natural Resources.** Despite the arid climate and mountainous terrain, the natural resources of Afghanistan are mainly agricultural. A variety of mineral deposits exists, but transportation difficulties and lack of native technical skills and equipment have hindered full exploitation of such resources. Much natural gas is located in the N, and the country also has major deposits of iron ore.

Arid climate and mountainous terrain are mainly responsible for the relative lack of soil development. The larger tracts of arable land in the fertile valleys are the only well-developed natural resource in Afghanistan.

**Plants.** The plant life of Afghanistan resembles that of Tibet and the Himalayan region in general, as well as that of the Middle Eastern plains and deserts. Forests of cedar, pine, and other conifers are found at elevations between about 1830 and 3660 m (about 6000 and 12,000 ft). As the result of overcutting, forests now occupy only about 3% of the land area. At lower altitudes are found such shrubs and trees as hazel, pistachio, ash, juniper, and tragacanth. Below the 914-m (3000-ft) level, vegetation, consisting largely of herbs and some shrubs, is quite sparse. Many varieties of wild flowers bloom in the spring, both in the mountains and on the grassy steppes. Forest products include resin, asafetida, and piñon (pine nuts), as well as timber and firewood. Among the various fruit trees are the apricot, peach, pear, apple, almond, and walnut. Date palms flourish in the extreme S, and pomegranates and citrus fruits grow in the vicinity of Kandahar and Jalalabad. Grapes and melons of excellent quality and unusual variety are common.

**Animals.** Indian, European, and Middle Eastern fauna inhabit Afghanistan. The dromedary and the Bactrian camel abound. Indigenous wild animals include mountain sheep, bear, ibex, gazelle, wolf, jackal, wildcat, hedgehog, and fox. The principal domesticated animals are sheep, cattle, and goats; others include donkeys, horses, mules, and the Afghan hound, a hunting dog. The Karakul sheep of Afghanistan are famous for their pelts. Waterfowl, pheasants, quail, and many varieties of smaller land and shore birds are also found.

## POPULATION

The population, predominantly rural, may be divided into four main ethnic groups. The Pathans, or true Afghans, make up about 52% of the total population and are divided into two subgroups, the Durani and Ghilzais. The Tajiks, of Iranian stock, make up about 20%, and most of the remainder consists of Uzbeks (9%) and Hazaras (9%).

**Population Characteristics.** A 1979 census placed the population at 15,551,358. The overall population density was 24 persons per sq km (62 per sq mi). The resident population of Afghanistan was estimated at 14,825,000 in 1989; another 5.6 mil-

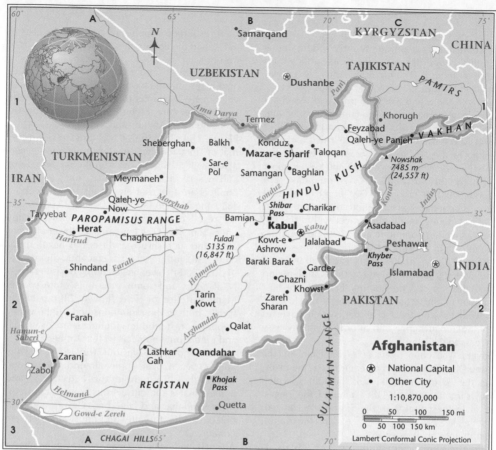

© GeoSystems Global Corp.

lion were refugees of the war of the '80s, living in Pakistan and Iran. More than half of these refugees returned to Afghanistan in the early 1990s. About 82% of the people live and work in rural areas, and approximately 2.5 million still lead a nomadic life.

**Political Divisions.** For administrative purposes, Afghanistan is divided into 31 provinces: Badakhshan, Badghis, Baghlan, Balkh, Bamian, Farah, Faryab, Ghazni, Ghor, Helmand, Herat, Jouzjan, Kabul, Kandahar, Kapisa, Konar, Kunduz, Laghman, Logar, Nangarhar, Nimruz, Nuristan, Paktika, Parwan, Patya, Samangan, Sar-e-Pol, Takhar, Uruzgan, Wardak, and Zabul.

**Principal Cities.** The capital of Afghanistan is Kabul (pop. 1988 est., 1,424,400), which, from its E location, commands vital routes through the mountain passes. Other major cities are the trading centers of Kandahar (225,500) and Herat (177,300), known for its many ancient mosques, palaces, and other architectural relics.

**Language.** Pashto, or Afghan, and Persian (Dari), divisions of the Iranian linguistic group, are the official languages of Afghanistan. Although Pashto has quite an extensive literature, Persian is used for cultural expression and business and government transactions. Of the many dialects spoken, the Turkish Uzbek, Turkoman, and Kirgiz are most prevalent in the border regions.

**Religion.** More than 99% of the people of Afghanistan are Muslims, mainly of the Sunni sect. Most of the remainder, notably the Hazara, belong to the Shiite sect. Small colonies of Hindus and Parsis are scattered in the towns. Mazar-e Sharif is the leading place of pilgrimage.

**Education.** Although elementary schooling is free and compulsory for children aged 7 through 15, only about 30% of the people aged 15 or more years are literate. In the late 1980s, elementary and secondary schools had an annual enrollment of more than 850,000. Institutions of higher education enrolled some 17,500 students. The University of Kabul (1932) is the main institute of higher education. The School of Commerce (1943), Kabul Polytechnic (1951), and the University of Islamic Studies (1988) are also in Kabul. The University of Nangarhar (1962) is in Jalalabad; Herat University was founded in 1987.

**Culture.** Afghanistan's rich cultural heritage is based on the traditions of its tribal society.

*Libraries and museums.* The few major libraries are located in Kabul. The Kabul Museum, largest in the country, is best known for its collection of early Buddhist relics.

*Literature.* The ancient art of storytelling continues to flourish largely as a result of widespread illiteracy. The Afghanistan Academy of Sciences fosters the study of languages, literature, and folklore, among other disciplines.

*Music and art.* Afghan cultural life is characterized by traditional arts and pastimes. Gold and silver jewelry, rugs in the Persian style, and various leather goods are still made at home. Music is rep-

resented chiefly by traditional folk songs, ballads, and dances. The *attan* is the national dance. It is performed in a large circle with the dancers clapping their hands and quickening the movements of their feet to the beat of the music.

**Recreation.** Popular sports include polo; *ghosai,* a team sport similar to wrestling; and *buzkashi,* a goal game that utilizes an animal carcass in place of a ball or puck.

ECONOMY

Afghanistan is one of the world's poorest countries, with annual income per capita estimated at $200. The economy is based on private ownership, modified by a limited form of socialism. A series of 5-year plans for the building of industry, agriculture, mining, transportation, and social services was begun in 1962. All mineral resources are state-owned. The economy was upset by the Soviet occupation and Afghan guerrilla resistance of the late 1970s and the '80s, and by factional fighting in the early '90s. Estimated annual government revenues in the early 1990s were $962 million; expenditures were $3.2 billion.

About 80% of the population is engaged in agriculture. The two most pressing labor problems are widespread unemployment and a lack of skilled workers and administrators.

**Agriculture.** Agriculture is the main source of income in Afghanistan; the country usually produces enough food for its own needs and a surplus for export. The leading crops are wheat, corn, rice, barley, garden vegetables, various fruits, and nuts. The major industrial crops are castor beans, madder, asafetida, tobacco, cotton, and sugar beets. Sheep raising is the major pastoral industry, which provides large quantities of meat, fats, and wool for domestic use and wool and hides for export; there were an estimated 13.5 million sheep in the early 1990s. The skin of the Karakul, a breed of broadtail sheep raised in the north, is highly valued. There are also large numbers of camels, horses, donkeys, cattle, goats, and poultry.

**Mining.** Since ancient times, deposits of gold, silver, copper, beryl, and lapis lazuli have been mined in small quantities in the mountainous areas. Salt has been mined in increasing quantities, and production now meets the needs of the country. Coal deposits have been exploited, and production stood at about 135,000 metric tons per year in the early 1990s. Large natural-gas deposits in N Afghanistan were developed with Soviet financing. Gas began flowing to the USSR in the mid-1970s. Other deposits, such as iron ore, sulfur, chrome, zinc, and uranium, are still largely unexploited.

**Manufacturing.** During the 1960s and '70s manufacturing greatly increased. With the opening in 1965 of a large West German-built wool mill,

At Jam, in Herat Province, Afghanistan, one of the world's tallest minarets (65 m/213 ft) stands on a bank of the Hari Rud. F. Jackson–Bruce Coleman, Inc.

woolen-textile production was more than doubled. Among the other factories, built primarily in Kabul, were plants manufacturing textiles, an important export product; government-operated cement plants; a fruit-processing plant; a coal-briquetting plant; and several cotton gins. Much of the country's industry was crippled by war during the 1980s and early '90s. The chief cottage industry (work done at home) is the weaving of rugs.

**Energy.** About two-thirds of Afghanistan's electricity is produced in hydroelectric facilities, and most of the rest is generated by thermal plants using coal or petroleum products. Major hydroelectric projects are situated on the Helmand and Kabul rivers. In the early 1990s Afghanistan annually produced about 1 billion kwh of electricity.

**Currency and Banking.** The unit of currency is the afghani, divided into 100 puls (1703 afghanis equal U.S.$1; 1994). The Central Bank of Afghanistan issues all notes, executes government loans, and lends money to cities and to other banks. Private banks were nationalized in 1975.

**Trade.** Most of the foreign trade of Afghanistan is controlled by the government or by government-controlled monopolies. In the early 1990s annual exports earned about $243 million, and yearly imports cost $737 million. The former Soviet republics, Pakistan, and Japan are the leading trade partners. Principal exports are fruits, nuts, rugs, Karakul skins, cotton, and natural gas.

Imports include textiles, building materials, petroleum, machinery, hardware, tea, and sugar.

**Transportation.** Travel within Afghanistan is severely limited by the rugged terrain. The country has no railroads, and its narrow, fast-flowing rivers are unnavigable and are used chiefly for transporting timber. Camels and other pack animals are extensively employed for conveying goods. The country has about 19,200 km (about 11,900 mi) of roads, mostly unpaved. Main highways link Kabul with the provincial capitals. Access to Pakistan is afforded by roads that traverse the Khyber Pass. Road maintenance is a constant problem in Afghanistan, mainly because of violent spring floods. Ariana Afghan Airlines is the nation's international and domestic air carrier.

**Communications.** The state-controlled telephone and telegraph lines serve all principal cities and smaller towns as well. Telegraphic communications exist among the major cities and between Kabul and Peshawar. In the mid-1980s about 32,000 telephones were in use.

Afghanistan had 13 daily newspapers in the early 1990s. The government broadcasting network serves about 1.5 million radios and 100,000 televisions.

### GOVERNMENT

Afghanistan was a monarchy until 1973, when the king was overthrown and a republic proclaimed. A constitution promulgated in February 1977 gave broad powers to the president, made the country a one-party state, and Islam the state religion. Legislative power was vested in a parliament (Shura), consisting of an upper house (House of the Elders) and a lower house (House of the People). This constitution was suspended in April 1978 following a coup d'état, and the Revolutionary Council became the chief governing body.

In 1987 the Soviet-backed Communist government issued a new constitution providing for a president to be indirectly elected to a 7-year term. The bicameral National Assembly (Meli Shura) consisted of the Senate and the House of Representatives. The People's Democratic party controlled the government, but 50 of the 234 seats in the House of Representatives were reserved for opposition parties.

Following the withdrawal of Soviet troops and the ouster of the Communist regime in April 1992, an interim council took power. An indirect election for president took place in December. An interim government, headed by a prime minister, was installed in June 1993.

**Judiciary.** Under the constitution, the highest tribunal in Afghanistan is the supreme court. Because of factional fighting, however, the national judicial system collapsed in the early 1990s, and justice was administered on an ad hoc basis by local leaders.

**Local Government.** Each province is administered by a governor appointed by the central government. The provinces are divided into districts and subdistricts.

**Health and Welfare.** Health conditions, already poor, have been aggravated by more than a decade of war. In the early 1990s, the infant mortality rate (168 per 1000 live births) was among the world's highest, and average life expectancy at birth was only 42 years for men and 43 years for women.

**Defense.** Until 1992, all male citizens between the ages of 15 and 40 were subject to conscription into the army of Afghanistan for a period of up to four years. In the early 1990s the army numbered 40,000; the air force, 5000; and paramilitary forces, more than 65,000. All military forces were reorganized after the ouster of the Communist regime In April 1992.

## HISTORY

Afghanistan first appeared in recorded history in the 6th century BC when it was included in the Persian empire of the Achaemenids. Along with the rest of the Persian Empire, the region was subjugated, about 330 BC, by Alexander the Great. After his death (323 BC) most of the region fell under the domination of Alexander's general, Seleucus I Nicator, and later under that of the Indian king Chandragupta. Later another Greek dynasty established itself in Bactria (northern Afghanistan) and founded a state that lasted from 256 BC until about 130 BC. The Greco-Bactrian state yielded in turn to Iranian nomads called the Sakas and then to the Kushans, who adopted Buddhism. In the 3d and 4th centuries AD, the Sassanid Persians invaded the country from the west. The Ephthalites, or White Huns, were largely in control of Afghanistan when the conquering Arabs swept the region in the middle of the 7th century.

**Early Muslim Dynasties.** Arab penetration affected Afghanistan probably more decisively than any previous foreign influence. Centuries passed, however, before Islam became the dominant religion. Arab political control was superseded meanwhile by Iranian and Turkish rule. Complete Turkish ascendancy in the area was established late in the 10th century and early in the 11th century by the Muslim sultan Mahmud of Ghazni (971–1030). Islamic culture subsequently achieved brilliant heights under the Afghan or Iranian Ghuri dynasty (1148–1215). The Ghurids gradually extended their rule into northern India but were overwhelmed by the hordes of the Mongol conqueror Genghis Khan, who came down

from the north about 1220. Most of the country remained under Mongol control until the close of the 14th century, when Tamerlane, a Turkoman Mongol conqueror, seized northern Afghanistan. Among Tamerlane's most prominent successors was Babur, founder of the Mughal dynasty of India, who conquered Kabul about 1504. Later in the 16th century Safavids from Iran and Uzbeks from the north made inroads in the region. The Iranians and the Mughal successors of Babur faced continuous Afghan revolts.

**The Foundation of the Afghan State.** During the 17th century, the native Afghans began to grow in power. The Ghilzai tribe conquered the Iranian capital of Isfahan in 1722. Subsequently, a vigorous Iranian counteroffensive was launched by Nadir Shah, who in 1738 reestablished Iranian authority over virtually all of Afghanistan. Nadir was assassinated in 1747, whereupon the Afghan chiefs selected one of his generals, a member of the Abdali tribe named Ahmad Shah, as their ruler. Ahmad Shah became known as Durri-i-Dauran ("Pearl of the Age"). The Abdali were thus designated thereafter as the Durani. Ahmad Shah enlarged his realm, acquiring eastern Iran, Baluchistan, Kashmir, and part of the Punjab. The emirate disintegrated under the succeeding rulers of his dynasty, falling in 1818. Anarchy prevailed during the ensuing period. In 1826 Dost Muhammad Khan (1793–1863), a member of a prominent Afghan family, took control of eastern Afghanistan, assuming the title of emir in 1835.

**Conflicts with Britain.** Meanwhile, Dost Muhammad had appealed to British colonial authorities in India for support of Afghan territorial claims in the Punjab. When the British rejected his appeal, he turned to Russia for help.

*First Afghan War.* Fearful that the Russian sphere of influence would be extended to the Indian frontiers, the British governor-general in India, George Eden, earl of Auckland (1784–1849), presented Dost Muhammad with an ultimatum that included demands for the expulsion of a Russian representative at Kabul. These demands were refused, and in March 1838 an Anglo-Indian army invaded Afghanistan, precipitating the First Afghan War (1838–42). Meeting little opposition, the army captured Qandahar in April 1839 and Ghazni in July. When Kabul fell in August Shah Shuja (1780?–1842), a grandson of Ahmad Shah, was installed on the Afghan throne in place of Dost Muhammad, who surrendered to the British.

On Nov. 2, 1841, Akbar Khan (fl. 1832–47), a son of Dost Muhammad, led a successful revolt against Shah Shuja's forces and the Anglo-Indian garrisons. An Anglo-Indian punitive expedition reinforced the garrisons for a brief period, but in

A gigantic Buddha, carved from a cliff of the Hindu Kush range. It is part of an ancient monastery excavated in Bamian, Afghanistan.    Peter Jackson–Bruce Coleman, Inc.

December 1842 the British finally left the country. Dost Muhammad was then released from custody and allowed to resume his throne.

Relations between Afghanistan and British-held India remained tense until 1855, when Dost Muhammad concluded a peace agreement with the Indian government.

**Second Afghan War.** Fratricidal strife among the emir's sons kept the country in turmoil for more than a decade after his death in 1863. Shere Ali Khan (1825–79), his third son and successor, aroused the enmity of the British by adopting a friendly policy toward Russia in 1878. Another British ultimatum was ignored, and in November 1878 Anglo-Indian forces again invaded Afghanistan. In the course of the ensuing conflict, known as the Second Afghan War (1878–79), the Afghans suffered a series of severe reversals. Kabul was occupied in October 1879; Yakub Khan (1849–1923), son of Shere Ali who had succeeded to the throne in the preceding March, was forced to abdicate; and, in 1880, Abd-ar-Rahman Kahn (1830?–1901), grandson of Dost Muhammad, was placed on the throne.

**Subsequent Anglo-Afghan relations.** The new ruler confirmed the cession, previously arranged

with the British by Yakub Khan, of the Khyber Pass and other Afghan territories. During his reign, which lasted until 1901, Abd-ar-Rahman Khan settled boundary disputes with India and Russia, created a standing army, and curbed the power of various tribal chieftains.

In 1907, during the reign of Habibullah Khan (1872–1919), the son and successor of Abd-ar-Rahman, the British and Russian governments concluded a convention pledging mutual respect for the territorial integrity of Afghanistan. Habibullah was assassinated in February 1919. His brother Nasrullah Khan, who held the throne for only six days, was deposed by the Afghan nobility in favor of Amanullah Khan (1892–1960), the son of Habibullah. Determined to completely remove his country from the British sphere of influence, Amanullah declared war on Great Britain in May 1919. The British, faced at the same time with the growing Indian liberation movement, negotiated a peace treaty with Afghanistan the following August. By the terms of the agreement, concluded at Rawalpindi, Great Britain recognized Afghanistan as a sovereign and independent nation. In 1926 Amanullah Khan changed his title from emir to king.

*Modernization.* The popularity and prestige that King Amanullah had won through his handling of the British were soon to be dissipated. Deeply impressed by the modernization programs of Iran and Turkey, he instituted a series of political, social, and religious reforms. Constitutional rule was inaugurated (1923), the titles of the nobility were abolished, education for women was decreed, and other sweeping measures aimed at the modernization of traditional institutions were enforced. The hostility provoked by the king's reform program led to a rebellion in 1929, and Amanullah quickly abdicated and went into exile. His brother, Inayatullah (1889?–1946), who succeeded him, was deposed, after a reign of three days, by Bacha Sakau, a rebel leader. In 1929, Amanullah's uncle, Nadir Shah (1880–1933), supported by several thousand tribesmen, defeated the rebels and executed Bacha Sakau. The crown was given to Nadir Shah.

The new ruler gradually restored order in the kingdom. In 1932 he initiated a program of economic reforms, but he was assassinated the following year. His son and successor, Zahir Shah (1914–    ), who was only 19 years old at the time of his accession, was dominated for the next 30 years by his uncles and cousins, particularly by his cousin and later brother-in-law, Prince Muhammad Daud Khan (1908–78). The government intensified the modernization program begun by Nadir Shah and established close commercial relations with Germany, Italy, and Japan. Zahir Shah proclaimed neutrality at the outbreak of World War II; in 1941, however, at the request of Great Britain and the Soviet Union, more than 200 German and Italian agents were expelled from the country. The U.S. established diplomatic relations with Afghanistan in 1942. In November 1946 Afghanistan became a member of the UN.

**The Pashtunistan Dispute.** The Afghan government closely scrutinized the events attendant upon the establishment in 1947 of India and Pakistan as independent states. Of particular concern to Afghanistan was the incorporation into Pakistan of the North-West Frontier Province Tribal Areas, a neighboring region largely populated by Pathans. Pakistan ignored Afghan demands for a plebiscite in the Tribal Areas on the question of self-determination. In retaliation, Afghanistan voted (1947) against the admission of Pakistan to the UN. Relations between Afghanistan and Pakistan continued to be strained during the next several years. Sporadic frontier clashes occurred between Pakistani forces and Pathan tribesmen, especially after 1949, when the latter, with the approval of the Afghan government, launched a movement to establish an independent state

to be called Pashtunistan or Pathanistan.

Afghanistan manifested displeasure over a U.S.-Pakistan military-aid pact concluded in 1954. The following year Soviet Premier Nikolay A. Bulganin, visiting Afghanistan, proclaimed support for a state of Pashtunistan. Subsequently the USSR and Afghanistan issued a joint statement advocating peaceful coexistence, universal disarmament, and UN membership for China. The Soviet government simultaneously extended technical-aid loans to Afghanistan.

Relations between Pakistan and Afghanistan improved briefly during the late 1950s. In 1961, however, the Pashtunistan dispute flared up, and relations were not fully restored until 1967.

**King Zahir's Personal Rule.** In 1963 King Zahir removed his cousin Muhammad Daud, who had been prime minister since 1953, and took full control of the reins of government. The following year he promulgated a new constitution, providing for a more liberal form of government. The first legislative elections under the new constitution were held in September 1965.

Afghanistan experienced major economic difficulties in the late 1960s. The situation was worsened by three years of drought, during which 80,000 persons were believed to have died of starvation. By 1973, the Soviet Union, the U.S., and China were all sending aid.

**The Republic and the Growth of Soviet Influence.** In 1968 King Zahir had made overtures to Daud, and a degree of harmony was believed to have been restored between them. In July 1973, however, Daud seized power, deposed the king, and proclaimed Afghanistan a republic. A new constitution was approved in early 1977, and Daud was elected to the powerful post of president. He appointed a civilian cabinet and maintained the country's policy of nonalignment. In April 1978 Daud was killed during a violent coup d'état. The new rulers, organized in a Revolutionary Council led first by Noor Muhammad Taraki (1917–79), and later by Hafizullah Amin (1929–79), suspended the constitution and initiated a program of "scientific socialism." This led to armed resistance by devout Muslims, especially among the mountain tribes. Unable to contain the rebellion, Taraki and Amin turned to the USSR for help. Despite Soviet military aid, resistance to the government continued in 1979. In December of that year Amin was overthrown and killed in a Soviet-backed coup, and Afghanistan was occupied by Soviet troops. The USSR then installed Babrak Karmal (1929–    ), a previous vice-president who had been purged and exiled in 1978, as president. Although Karmal diligently tried to placate the rebels, the insurgency persisted, and more than 3 million refugees fled to neighboring Pakistan. During the mid-1980s government forces and about 118,000 Soviet troops held major cities and roads but were unable to dislodge the rebels. In May 1986, probably at Soviet instigation, Karmal was replaced by Muhammad Najibullah (1947– ), formerly chief of state police. Between May 1988 and February 1989 the USSR withdrew all combat troops, as the civil war continued. Najibullah was deposed in April 1992, and rebels took over Kabul. The rival factions then agreed on an interim council to govern Afghanistan, with Burhanuddin Rabbani (1940– ) as provisional president. In December a special assembly voted to confirm President Rabbani for a 2-year term. An interim government, headed by a prime minister, was installed in June 1993, but factional fighting persisted.

*For further information on this topic, see the Bibliography in volume 28, sections 131, 1091.*

**AFONSO THE GREAT.** *See* ALBUQUERQUE, AFONSO DE.

**AFRICA,** second largest of the earth's seven continents, covering, with adjacent islands, about 30,300,000 sq km (about 11,699,000 sq mi), or about 20% of the world's total land area. In the mid-1990s about 12.5% of the world's population, some 700 million people, inhabited Africa.

Straddling the equator, Africa stretches about 8000 km (about 4970 mi) from its northernmost point, Cape Blanc (ar-Ras al-Abyad) in Tunisia, to its southernmost tip, Cape Agulhas in South Africa. The maximum width of the continent, measured from the tip of Cape Verde in Senegal, in the W, to Ras Hafun in Somalia, in the E, is about 7560 km (about 4700 mi). The highest point on the continent is the perpetually snowcapped Mt. Kilimanjaro (5895 m/19,340 ft) in Tanzania, and the lowest is Lake Assal (153 m/502 ft below sea level) in Djibouti. Africa has a regular coastline characterized by few indentations. Its total length is only about 30,490 km (about 18,950 mi); the length of its coastline in proportion to its area is less than that of any other continent.

The chief islands of Africa, which have a combined area of some 621,600 sq km (about 240,000 sq mi), include Madagascar, Zanzibar, Pemba,

## CHIEF POLITICAL DIVISIONS OF AFRICA

| Political Unit | Political Status | Political Unit | Political Status |
|---|---|---|---|
| Algeria | Republic | Mali | Republic |
| Angola | Republic | Mauritania | Republic |
| Benin (former Dahomey) | Republic | Mauritius | Republic within |
| Botswana | Republic within | | Commonwealth of |
| | Commonwealth of | | Nations |
| | Nations | Morocco | Constitutional monarchy |
| Burkina Faso (former Upper | Republic | Mozambique | Republic |
| Volta) | | Namibia | Republic |
| Burundi | Republic | Niger | Republic |
| Cameroon | Republic | Nigeria | Republic within |
| Canary Islands | 2 provinces of Spain | | Commonwealth of |
| Cape Verde | Republic | | Nations |
| Central African Republic | Republic | Réunion | Overseas department of |
| Chad | Republic | | France |
| Comoros | Republic | Rwanda | Republic |
| Congo, Republic of | Republic | St. Helena | British dependency |
| Côte d'Ivoire (Ivory Coast) | Republic | São Tomé and Príncipe | Republic |
| Djibouti (former French | Republic | Senegal | Republic |
| Territory of the Afars and | | Seychelles | Republic within |
| the Issas) | | | Commonwealth of |
| Egypt, Arab Republic of | Republic | | Nations |
| Equatorial Guinea | Republic | Sierra Leone | Republic within |
| Eritrea | Republic | | Commonwealth of |
| Ethiopia | Republic | | Nations |
| Gabon | Republic | Somalia | Republic |
| Gambia, The | Republic within | South Africa | Republic |
| | Commonwealth of | Sudan | Republic |
| | Nations | Swaziland | Independent monarchy |
| Ghana | Republic within | | within Commonwealth |
| | Commonwealth of | | of Nations |
| | Nations | Tanzania | Republic within |
| Guinea | Republic | | Commonweath of |
| Guinea-Bissau (former | Republic | | Nations |
| Portuguese Guinea) | | Togo | Republic |
| Kenya | Republic within | Tunisia | Republic |
| | Commonwealth of | Uganda | Republic within |
| | Nations | | Commonwealth of |
| Lesotho | Independent monarchy | | Nations |
| | within Commonwealth of | Western Sahara | Controlled by Morocco |
| | Nations | Zaire (former Democratic | Republic |
| Liberia | Republic | Republic of the Congo) | |
| Libya | Republic | Zambia | Republic within |
| Madagascar (former | Republic | | Commonwealth of |
| Malagasy Republic) | | | Nations |
| Malawi | Republic within | Zimbabwe | Republic within |
| | Commonwealth of | | Commonwealth of |
| | Nations | | Nations |

Cairo, the foremost African metropolis, seen from the island of az-Zamalik in the Nile, which flows through the city.

J. G. Ross–Photo Researchers, Inc.

Mauritius, Réunion, the Seychelles, and the Comoro Islands in the Indian Ocean; São Tomé, Príncipe, Annobón, and Bioko in the Gulf of Guinea; Saint Helena, Ascension, and the Bijagós Islands in the Atlantic; and the Cape Verde, Canary, and Madeira Islands in the North Atlantic.

## THE NATURAL ENVIRONMENT

Except for the N coast and the Atlas Mts. in the NW, the terrain of Africa consists of a vast, rolling plateau, marked by a number of large, saucer-shaped basins.

**Geological History.** A vast continental shield of Precambrian rocks, related in age and history to South America's Brazilian Highlands, extends south of the Atlas Mts. to the Cape of Good Hope. On the east, the shield encompasses two landmasses—the Arabian Peninsula and Madagascar—that were split off from Africa during the Tertiary Period (see PLATE TECTONICS). Among these ancient rocks some of the earliest traces of life on earth—fossil microorganisms 3.2 billion years old—have been found. Geologically, the Atlas Mts. of North Africa are part of Europe, having been raised by the same forces that created the Alpine mountain ranges of southern and central Europe.

The tectonic forces that split Africa and South America apart during the breakup of the supercontinent Gondwanaland, over 150 million years ago (see JURASSIC PERIOD), have continued into more recent times, creating East Africa's Rift Valley during the Tertiary Period and triggering eruptions there of the volcanic Mts. Kenya and Kilimanjaro.

**Physiographic Regions.** Africa may be divided into three major regions: the Northern Plateau, the Central and Southern Plateau, and the Eastern Highlands. In general, elevations increase across the continent from NW to SE, the average being about 580 m (about 1900 ft). Low-lying coastal strips, with the exception of the Mediterranean coast and the Guinea coast, are generally narrow and rise sharply to the plateau.

The outstanding feature of the Northern Plateau is the Sahara, the great desert that occupies more than one-quarter of Africa. At the fringes of the Northern Plateau are several mountainous regions. To the NW lie the Atlas Mts., a chain of rugged peaks linked by high plateaus, which extend from Morocco into Tunisia. Other prominent uplands are the Futa Jallon, on the SW, and the Adamawa Massif and the Cameroon mountain range, on the S. The Lake Chad Basin is situated in the approximate center of the Northern Plateau.

The Central and Southern Plateau is considerably higher than the Northern Plateau and includes W central and S Africa. It contains several major depressions, notably the Congo R. Basin and the Kalahari Desert. Other features S of this plateau, which averages more than 900 m (about 3000 ft) in elevation, are the Drakensberg Mts., running some 1125 km (about 700 mi) along the SE coast; and, in the extreme S, the Karoo, an arid plateau covering more than 259,000 sq km (more than 100,000 sq mi).

The Eastern Highlands, the highest portion of the continent, lie near the E coast, extending from the Red Sea S to the Zambezi R. The region has an average elevation of more than 1500 m (about 5000 ft), although in the Ethiopian Plateau it rises in stages to about 3000 m (about 10,000

With Africa's loftiest peak, Mt. Kilimanjaro, as background, elephants forage near the Kenya-Tanzania border.                    Herbert Lanks–Monkmeyer Press

ft). Ras Dashan (4620 m/15,157 ft) in N Ethiopia is the highest peak of the plateau. South of the Ethiopian Plateau are a number of towering volcanic peaks, including Mt. Kilimanjaro, Mt. Kenya, and Mt. Elgon. A distinctive topographical feature of the Eastern Highlands is the Rift Valley, a vast geologic fault system that traverses the region in a N to S direction. West of the Rift Valley is the Ruwenzori Range, which attains a maximum elevation of 5119 m (16,795 ft). The topography of the island of Madagascar features a rugged central highland extending in a generally N-S direction near the E coast.

Because most of the African continent has not been covered by the seas for millions of years, soils have developed locally, chiefly by weathering, and a few areas have benefited from soils transported by rivers or ocean currents. African soils, for the most part, have irregular drainage and no definite water tables. Most are relatively infertile as a result of mineral leaching from heavy rainfall and high temperatures. Desert soils (aridisols and entisols), which have little organic content, also cover large areas. The most fertile soils of the continent include the mollisols, also known as chernozems and black soils, of E Africa and the alfisols, or podzolic soils, of portions of W and S Africa.

**Drainage and Water Resources.** Six major drainage networks exist in Africa. With the exception of the Lake Chad Basin, all have outlets to the sea and all are cut by steep cataracts or rapids that impede navigation. The Nile R., with a length of 6650 km (4132 mi), drains NE Africa and is the longest river in the world. Formed from the Blue Nile, which

originates at Lake Tana in Ethiopia, and the White Nile, which originates at Lake Victoria, the Nile flows W and N before emptying into the Mediterranean Sea. The Congo R., some 4670 km (about 2900 mi) long, drains much of central Africa. It originates in Zambia and flows N, W, and S to empty into the Atlantic Ocean. The third longest African river, the Niger R. in W Africa, is about 4180 km (about 2600 mi) long; its upper portions are navigable only during rainy seasons. The Niger rises in the highlands of the Futa Jallon and flows N and E before turning S to empty into the Gulf of Guinea. The Zambezi R., about 3540 km (about 2200 mi) long, originates in Zambia in SE Africa and flows S and E to empty into the Indian Ocean. The Zambezi is cut by various rapids, the most spectacular of which is Victoria Falls. Draining S Africa is the Orange R., which, with its tributary, the Vaal R., has a length of about 2090 km (about 1300 mi). It rises in the Drakensberg Mts. and flows W to the Atlantic. Lake Chad, a shallow freshwater lake with an average depth of only about 1.2 m (about 4 ft), drains nearby rivers and constitutes the largest inland drainage area on the continent.

The deep rift valleys of the Eastern Highlands hold a great series of lakes. This equatorial lake system includes Lakes Turkana, Albert, Tanganyika, and Malawi (Nyasa). Lake Victoria, the largest lake in Africa and the third largest in the world, is, however, not part of this system; it occupies a shallow depression in the Eastern Highlands.

Achieving effective control of the water supply is a major problem in Africa. Vast areas suffer low rainfall; still larger areas receive only irregular

# Africa:
# Map Index

### Countries

### Cities and Towns

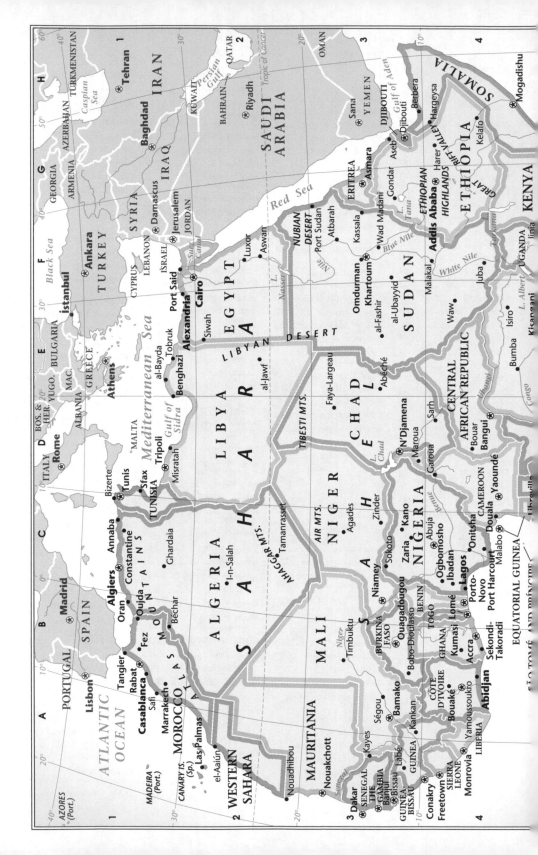

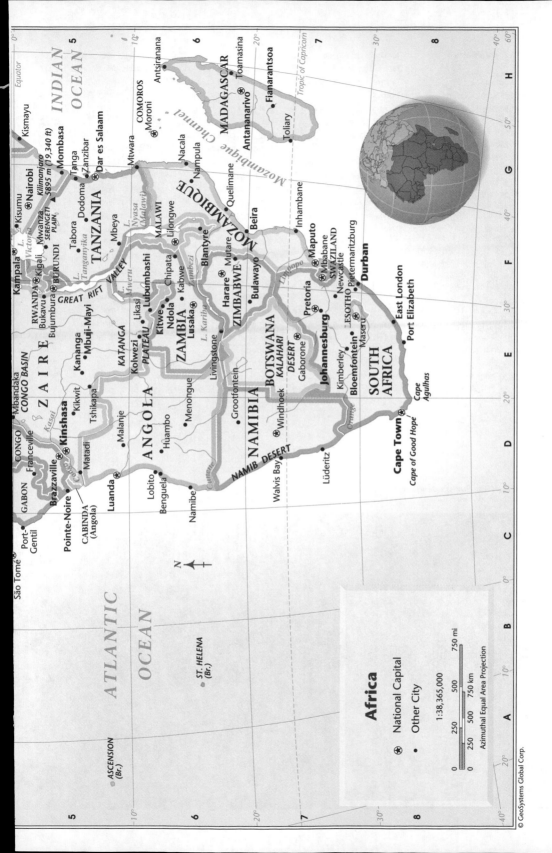

# Africa

⊛ National Capital

• Other City

1:38,365,000

```
0    250   500        750 mi
0  250  500  750 km
```

Azimuthal Equal Area Projection

© GeoSystems Global Corp.

# AFRICA

*This oasis in Tunisia, North Africa, offers a sharp contrast to the lush green growth in much of southern Africa.*          Marc & Evelyne Bernheim–Woodfin Camp & Associates

rainfall and must store water as insurance against delayed or deficient rains. Other areas have an overabundance of water. Great swamps exist, and large areas suffer from periodic flooding. In recent years, numerous dams and reservoirs have been constructed to channel water for irrigation and for hydroelectric power. The continent's numerous rivers and the abrupt descents of the waterways have led to estimates that Africa has approximately 40% of the total world hydroelectric potential.

**Climate.** The climate of Africa, more than that of any other continent, is generally uniform. This results from the position of the continent in the Tropical Zone, the impact of cool ocean currents, and the absence of mountain chains serving as climatic barriers.

Seven main African climatic zones can be distinguished. The central portion of the continent and the E coast of Madagascar have a tropical rain forest climate. Here the average annual temperature is about 26.7° C (about 80° F), and the average annual rainfall is about 1780 mm (about 70 in). The climate of the Guinea coast resembles the equatorial climate, except that rainfall is concentrated in one season; no months, however, are rainless.

To the N and S the rain forest climate is supplanted by a tropical savanna climate zone that encompasses about one-fifth of Africa. Here the climate is characterized by a wet season during the summer months and a dry season during the winter months. Total annual rainfall varies from about 510 mm (about 20 in) to more than 1520 mm (about 60 in). Away from the equator, to the N and S, the savanna climate zone grades into the drier steppe climate zone. Average annual rainfall varies between 250 and 510 mm (10 and 20 in) and is concentrated in one season.

Africa has a proportionately larger area in arid, or desert, climate zones than any continent except Australia. Each of these areas—the Sahara in the N, the Horn in the E, and the Kalahair and Namib deserts in the SW—has less than 250 mm (about 10 in) of rainfall annually. In the Sahara, daily and seasonal extremes of temperatures are great; the average July temperature is more than 32.2° C (90° F); during the cold season the nighttime temperature often drops below freezing.

Mediterranean climate zones are found in the extreme NW of Africa and in the extreme SW. These regions are characterized by mild, wet winters and warm, dry summers. In the highlands of E Africa, particularly in Kenya and Uganda, rainfall is well distributed throughout the year, and temperatures are equable. The climate on the high plateau of S Africa is temperate.

**Vegetation.** African vegetation can be classified according to rainfall and climate zones. The tropical rain forest zone, where the average an-

*Hippopotamuses near Murchison Falls in northwestern Uganda. Semiaquatic in nature, the animals are also called river horses.* William G. Levy–Photo Researches, Inc.

nual rain is more than 1270 mm (50 in), has a dense surface covering of shrubs, ferns, and mosses, above which tower evergreens, oil palms, and numerous species of tropical hardwood trees. A mountain forest zone, with average annual rainfall only slightly less than in the tropical rain forests, is found in the high mountains of Cameroon, Angola, E Africa, and parts of Ethiopia. Here a ground covering of shrubs gives way to oil palms, hardwood trees, and primitive conifers. A savanna woodland zone, with annual rainfall of 890 to 1400 mm (about 35 to 55 in), covers vast areas with a layer of grass and fire-resistant shrubs, above which are found deciduous and leguminous fire-resistant trees. A savanna grassland zone, with annual rainfall of about 510 to 890 mm (about 20 to 35 in), is covered by low grasses and shrubs and scattered, small deciduous trees. The thornbush zone, a steppe vegetation, with an annual rainfall of about 300 to 510 mm (about 12 to 20 in), has a thinner grass covering and a scattering of succulent or semisucculent trees. The subdesert scrub zone, with an annual rainfall of 130 to 300 mm (about 5 to 12 in), has a covering of grasses and scattered low shrubs. The zone of desert vegetation, found in areas with an annual rainfall of less than 130 mm (about 5 in), has sparse vegetation or none at all.

**Animal Life.** Africa has two distinct zones of animal life: the North and Northwestern zone, including the Sahara; and the Ethiopian zone, including all of sub-Saharan Africa. The North and Northwestern zone is characterized by animals similar to those found in Eurasia. Sheep, goats, horses, and camels are common to the region. Barbary sheep, African red deer, and two types of ibex are native to the N African coast. Desert foxes are found in the Sahara along with hares, gazelles, and the jerboa, a small leaping rodent. The Ethiopian zone is famous for its tremendous variety of distinctive animals and birds. Woodland and grassland areas are inhabited by numerous species of antelope and deer, zebra, giraffe, buffalo, the African elephant, rhinoceros, and the baboon and various monkeys. Carnivores, or meat-eating animals, include the lion, leopard, cheetah, hyena, jackal, and mongoose. The gorilla, the largest ape in the world, inhabits the rain forests of equatorial Africa. Monkeys, flying squirrels, bats, and lemurs also can be found in the rain forests.

Most bird life belongs to Old World groups.

*Most of the lions of the world dwell in the grasslands of sub-Saharan Africa. This male roams the Serengeti Plain of northern Tanzania, a land rich in wildlife.*
George Schaller–Bruce Coleman, Inc.

*Elephants in a water hole at Savuti, Botswana, in southern Africa, imbibe part of their daily requirement: 189 liters (50 gal).* C. Haagner–Bruce Coleman, Inc.

The guinea fowl is a leading game bird. Water birds, notably pelicans, goliath herons, flamingos, storks, and egrets, congregate in great numbers. The ibis is common in the Nile region, and the ostrich is found in E and S Africa. Reptiles are mainly of Old World origin and include lizards, crocodiles, and tortoises. A variety of venomous snakes, including the mamba, are encountered throughout the Ethiopian zone. Among the constricting snakes, pythons are found mainly in W Africa; boa constrictors are indigenous only to Madagascar. Freshwater fish abound, with more than 2000 species known. The continent has a variety of destructive insects, notably mosquitos, driver ants, termites, locusts, and tsetse flies. The last named transmit sleeping sickness to humans and animals (in animals, the disease is called nagana).

**Mineral Resources.** Africa is very rich in mineral resources, possessing most of the known minerals of the world, many of which are found in significant quantities, although the geographic distribution is uneven. Fossil fuels are abundant, including major deposits of coal, petroleum, and natural gas. Africa has some of the world's largest reserves of gold, diamonds, copper, bauxite, manganese, nickel, platinum, cobalt, radium, germanium, lithium, titanium, and phosphates. Other important mineral resources include iron ore, chromium, tin, zinc, lead, thorium, zirconium, vanadium, antimony, and beryllium. Also found in exploitable quantities are clays, mica, sulfur, salt, natron, graphite, limestone, and gypsum.

### THE PEOPLE

The Sahara serves as a vast barrier between the peoples of N Africa and those of sub-Saharan Africa. Although numerous classification systems have been applied to the people of the continent, the geographical division appears the most useful.

**Ethnography.** In the N portion of the continent, including the Sahara, Causasoid peoples—mainly Berbers and Arabs—predominate. They constitute about one-quarter of the continent's population. South of the Sahara, Negroid peoples, constituting some 70% of Africa's population, predominate. Pockets of Khoisan peoples, the San (Bushmen) and Khoikhoi (Hottentots), are located in S Africa. The Pygmies are concentrated

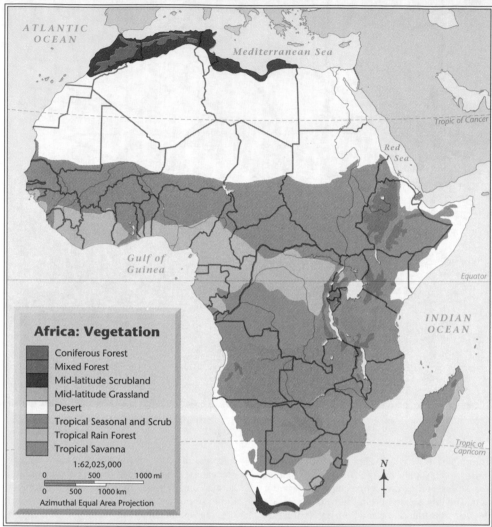

Africa: Vegetation

Coniferous Forest
Mixed Forest
Mid-latitude Scrubland
Mid-latitude Grassland
Desert
Tropical Seasonal and Scrub
Tropical Rain Forest
Tropical Savanna

1:62,025,000

0     500     1000 mi

0    500    1000 km

Azimuthal Equal Area Projection

© GeoSystems Global Corp.

in the Congo R. Basin and in Tanzania. Scattered through Africa, but primarily concentrated in S Africa, are some 5 million people of European descent. An Indian population, numbering some 1 million, is concentrated along the E African coast and in South Africa.

More than 3000 distinct ethnic groups have been classified in Africa. The extended family is the basic social unit of most of these peoples. In much of Africa the family is linked to a larger society through kin groups such as lineages and clans. Kin groups generally tend to exclude marriage among their members, and members marry outside the group. The village is frequently constituted of a single kin group united by either male or female descent.

**Demography.** Although Africa covers about one-fifth of the total world land surface, it has only

about 12.5% of its population. In the mid-1990s the total population of the continent was estimated at 700 million. Average density, some 23 people per sq km (60 per sq mi), is less than half the world average. This figure includes the large areas, such as the Sahara and Kalahari deserts, which are virtually uninhabitable. When the population living on arable land or pastureland is calculated, the average density almost triples. The most densely settled areas of the continent are those along the N and W coasts; in the Nile, Niger, Congo, and Senegal river basins; and in the E African plateau. Nigeria, with a population of more than 90 million, is the most populous nation of the continent.

The African birth rate is about 42 per 1000. (By contrast the birth rate in Europe is about 12 per 1000.) The availability of medical services since

World War II is responsible for a sharp decrease in the death rate, which averages about 13 per 1000. The continent's population increases annually by about 2.9%. These statistics vary greatly, however, from country to country and from region to region. The age distribution is weighted heavily toward the young. In most African countries, almost half the population is 15 years of age or younger.

The African population remains predominantly rural, with less than one-third of the population living in towns of more than 2000 inhabitants. Northern Africa is the most urbanized region, but major cities are located in every part of the continent. More than 20 African urban centers have populations of more than 1 million, including Cairo and Alexandria, Egypt; Algiers, Algeria; Casablanca, Morocco; Lagos, Nigeria; Addis Ababa, Ethiopia; Nairobi, Kenya; Abidjan, Côte d' Ivoire; Kinshasa, Zaire; and Johannesburg, Cape Town, Durban, and Pretoria, South Africa. The cities act as magnets, attracting large numbers of rural migrants who come either as permanent settlers or as short-term workers. Urban growth has been particularly rapid since the 1950s. A substantial international labor migration has also developed, particularly of Africans from central Africa to the mines and factories of Zambia, Zimbabwe, and South Africa, and of North Africans to France and, more recently, to the countries belonging to the European Union. Civil wars in a number of countries have led to massive refugee migrations, as have droughts and famines.

**Languages.** More than 1000 languages are spoken in Africa. Although more than 50 languages have 500,000 or more speakers each, the majority of

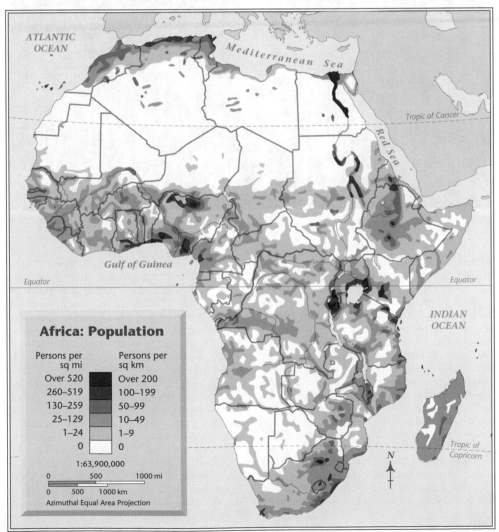

ATLANTIC OCEAN

Mediterranean Sea

Tropic of Cancer

Red Sea

Gulf of Guinea

Equator

Equator

INDIAN OCEAN

## Africa: Population

| Persons per sq mi | Persons per sq km |
|---|---|
| Over 520 | Over 200 |
| 260–519 | 100–199 |
| 130–259 | 50–99 |
| 25–129 | 10–49 |
| 1–24 | 1–9 |
| 0 | 0 |

1:63,900,000

0    500    1000 mi

0    500    1000 km

Azimuthal Equal Area Projection

Tropic of Capricorn

N

*Terraced farmland in western Uganda. Agriculture is the backbone of Uganda's economy—and that of the continent in general.* S.Trevor–D. B.–Bruce Coleman, Inc.

African languages are spoken by relatively few people. Apart from Arabic, the most widely spoken are Swahili and Hausa. The main linguistic families or groups are Niger-Kordofanian and Nilo-Saharan, the largest groups with more than 160 million speakers each; Hamito-Semitic, or Afro-Asiatic, which predominates in N and NE Africa; and Khoisan, spoken among the San and Khoikhoi of S Africa. Many Africans, particularly those of sub-Saharan Africa, are bilingual, speaking their own language as well as that brought by earlier European colonial administrations. *See* AFRICAN LANGUAGES.

**Religion.** Christianity, the most widespread religion, was introduced into N Africa in the 1st century and spread to the Sudan and Ethiopian regions in the 4th century. Christianity survived in Egypt through the Coptic church (q.v.), in Ethiopia and Syria (*see* EASTERN CHURCH) and in

Sudan but in the other areas, it was swept away by Islam. The religion was reintroduced and spread through tropical Africa with the 15th-century rise of European overseas expansion. Today Protestant and Catholic groups are about equally represented throughout the continent.

Islam, the second most widespread religion in Africa, was introduced throughout N Africa in the 7th century and in following centuries was spread along the E African coast and through the grasslands of W Africa. In the 20th century, Islam has penetrated into the rest of the continent. The earliest of the Muslim schools of law, the Maliki, prevails over most of Muslim Africa except in Egypt, the Horn, and the E African coast.

About 15% of African peoples practice indigenous, or local, religions. Although these are of great diversity, they tend to have a single god or creator figure and a number of subordinate spirits—nature spirits who inhabit trees, water, animals, and other natural phenomena—and ancestral spirits, such as founders of the family, lineage, or clan—who affect everyday life. *See* RELIGION: *Primitive Religions.*

Certain nativistic religious movements, arising primarily from Christianity, have fused orthodox Christian rites and beliefs with tribal religious elements. Led by individual prophets, these separatist groups have spread throughout Africa, although they appear most widespread and powerful in S and central Africa.

Small numbers of Jews are located in N and S Africa, and Hindu, Buddhist, and Taoist peoples are scattered through E and S Africa.

**Cultural Activity.** Much of Africa's cultural activity centers on the family and the ethnic group. Art, music, and oral literature serve to reinforce existing religious and social patterns. The Westernized minority, influenced by European culture and Christianity, first rejected African traditional culture, but, with the rise of African nationalism, a cultural revival occurred. The governments of most African nations foster national dance and music groups, museums, and to a lesser degree, artists and writers. *See* AFRICAN ART AND ARCHITECTURE; AFRICAN LITERATURE; AFRICAN MUSIC AND DANCE.

PATTERNS OF ECONOMIC DEVELOPMENT
Traditionally, the vast majority of Africans have been farmers and herders who raised crops and livestock for subsistence. Few markets existed, and trade usually took place between relatives and friends. Manufacturing and crafts were carried on as part-time activities. A few states developed long-distance trade systems, and in these places complex exchange facilities as well as industrial specialization, communication networks, and elaborate governmental structures maintained the flow of commerce.

With European colonization came overseas demand for certain agricultural and mineral products and internal labor migration; new and safe communication systems were constructed; European technology and crops were introduced; and a modern exchange economy evolved. Local industries and crafts—textiles and iron making, for example—were frequently undermined by cheaper or better European goods. Processing industries developed, as did ports and administrative centers. A variety of consumer industries sprang up to fill newly created local consumer needs. A feature of the African economy is the side-by-side existence of both subsistence and modern exchange economies. Future growth depends on the availability of investment funds, the world demand for local raw materials, the availability of energy sources, and the size of local markets.

**Agriculture.** Despite the expansion of commerce and industry, most Africans remain farmers and herders. In N and NW Africa, wheat, oats, corn, and barley are the important grain crops. Dates, olives, and citrus fruit are the main tree crops; a

*Completed in 1965, this dam on the Volta River near Akosombo, Ghana, is a major source of hydroelectric power.* Jacques Jongoux–Peter Arnold, Inc.

*A camel market is in progress outside Barmou, an adobe hut village of the Hausa tribe, in Niger.*                    **Marc & Evelyne Bernheim–Woodfin Camp & Associates**

variety of vegetables are grown. Goats and sheep are the most significant livestock raised. In the Sahara region, nomadic herders raise camels, and a few farmers, situated in oases, grow dates and grains. South of the Sahara, shifting agriculture—a method in which small areas were burned, cleared, and planted and then allowed to revert to bush—has given way in most areas to settled farming. Grain is the principal crop outside the rain forests; rice, yams, manioc, okra, plaintains, and bananas are raised for food. Cattle cannot be raised in tsetse fly-infested areas, which cover more than one-third of the continent. Outside tsetse fly areas and dense forests, however, cattle are raised in large numbers, but rarely for commercial purposes. Dairy farming is limited and is located primarily around urban centers in E and S Africa.

Although some 60% of all cultivated land is in subsistence agriculture, commercial or cash-crop farming is common in all parts of the continent. Foodstuffs are grown for local urban markets, but coffee, cotton, cacao, peanuts, palm oil, and tobacco are grown by Africans for export. For certain agricultural exports, such as cacao, peanuts, cloves, and sisal, Africa produces more than one-half of the world supply. European-owned plantations and farms, found mainly in E and S Africa, concentrate on citrus, tobacco, and other export foodstuffs.

**Forestry and Fishing.** Although about 22% of Africa is covered by forest, much of the timber has little value except as local fuel. Gabon is a major producer of okoume, a wood used in making plywood; Côte d'Ivoire and Ghana are exporters of hardwoods. Inland fishing is concentrated in the Great Rift Valley lakes and in the increasing numbers of fish farms. Ocean fishing is widespread for local consumption; it is commercially important off Morocco, Namibia, and South Africa.

**Mining.** Mineral extraction provides the bulk of African export earnings, and extractive industries are the most developed sectors in most African economies. Much of Africa's mineral income comes from South Africa, especially from gold and diamond mining. Other leading mineral-producing countries include Libya (petroleum), Nigeria (petroleum), Algeria (petroleum, natural gas), Botswana (diamonds), Zaire (copper, diamonds), and Zambia (copper, cobalt, lead, zinc). Petroleum is also found along the W African coast, in the Gabon Basin, the Congo, Zaire, and Angola. A significant share of the world's uranium is mined in Africa, chiefly in South Africa, Niger, Zaire, the

Central African Republic, and Gabon. The largest radium supply in the world is located in Zaire. Some 20% of the world copper reserve is concentrated in Zambia, Zaire, South Africa, and Zimbabwe. Zaire also possesses about 90% of the world's known cobalt, and Sierra Leone has the largest known titanium reserves. The continent produces a large share of the world's gold; South Africa, Zimbabwe, Zaire, and Ghana are the major producers. The mines of Zaire, Botswana, and South Africa together produce about 40% of the world supply of industrial diamonds. Iron ore is found in all parts of the continent. The majority of Africa's mineral wealth has been and is being developed by large, multinational concerns. Increasingly, in recent years, African governments have become substantial shareholders in the mining operations within their respective countries.

**Manufacturing.** Stemming from mineral and petroleum extraction are processing industries, such as refining and smelting, which are located in most mineral-rich countries with adequate energy. The bulk of Africa's manufacturing takes place in South Africa. Heavy industry, such as metal producing, machine making, and transport manufacturing, is concentrated in South Africa. Significant industrial centers have also developed in Zimbabwe, Egypt, and Algeria. Mineral-related industries are well developed in Zaire and Zambia; Kenya, Nigeria, and Côte d'Ivoire have developed primarily in textiles, light industry, and construction materials. Throughout much of the rest of the continent, manufacturing is limited to the making or assembling of consumer goods, such as shoes, bicycles, textiles, food, and beverages. Such industries are often confined by the relatively small size of the consumer market.

**Energy.** Nigeria, Libya, Algeria, and Angola are major world producers of petroleum. Africa's natural-gas exports are centered in Algeria. Coal is concentrated in Zimbabwe and South Africa; the bulk of their production is used internally. The rest of Africa must import fuels. Although Africa has some 40% of the world's hydropower potential, only a relatively small portion has been developed as a result of high construction costs, inaccessibility of sites, and their distance from markets. Since 1960, however, a number of major hydroelectric installations have been constructed; these include the Aswan High Dam on

*Dogon tribesmen in Mali perform a funeral dance. As the elaborate headdresses suggest, the tribe is known for skill in carving.* Wendy Watriss–Woodfin Camp & Associates

the Nile R., the Volta Dam on the Volta R., and the Kariba and Cabora Bassa dams on the Zambezi R.

**Transportation.** The economic development of virtually all African nations has been hindered by inadequate transportation systems. Most countries rely on road networks that are frequently composed largely of dirt roads, which become impassable during the rainy seasons. Road networks tend to link the interior of a country to the coast; few road systems link adjacent countries. Although most African nations support a national airline, rail and shipping systems are extremely limited outside S Africa.

**Trade.** The commercial sectors of most African states rely heavily on one or a few export commodities. The bulk of trade occurs with industrialized nations, which require raw materials and sell industrial and consumer goods. Trade between African states is limited by the competitive, rather than complementary, nature of their products and by trade barriers, such as tariffs and the diversity of currencies. Most former British colonies in Africa continue to have loose trade relations with Great Britain and keep monetary reserves in London. Former French colonies have even closer ties with France, and most are members of a French franc zone. In addition, most African states have economic ties with the European Union and benefit from some tariff barrier reductions. Few successful intra-African economic systems have emerged. The most durable and successful are the Economic Community of West African States and the Economic Community of Central African States. The Organization of African Unity (q.v.) also promotes intra-African trade and economic development. J.T.Sa.

### HISTORY

Some 5 million years ago a type of hominid, a close evolutionary ancestor of present-day humans, inhabited southern and eastern Africa. Between 1.5 and 2 million years ago this toolmaking hominid developed into the more advanced forms *Homo habilis* and *Homo erectus*. The earliest true human being in Africa, *Homo sapiens*, dates from more than 200,000 years ago. A hunter-gatherer capable of making crude stone tools, *Homo sapiens* banded together with others to form nomadic groups; eventually these nomadic Bushmanoid peoples spread throughout the African continent. Distinct races date from approximately 10,000 BC. Gradually a growing Negroid population, which had mastered animal domestication and agriculture, forced the Bushmanoid groups into the less hospitable areas. In the 1st century AD the Bantu, one group of this dominant people, began a migration that

lasted 2000 years, settling most of central and southern Africa. Negroid societies depended on subsistence agriculture or, in the savannas, pastoral pursuits. Political organization was normally local, although large kingdoms would later develop in western and central Africa.

The first great civilization in Africa began in the Nile Valley about 5000 BC. Dependent on agriculture, these settlements benefited from the Nile's flooding as a source of irrigation and new soils. The need to control the Nile floodwaters eventually resulted in a well-ordered, complex state with elaborate political and religious systems. The kingdom of Egypt flourished, influencing Mediterranean and African societies for thousands of years. Iron making was brought south from Egypt about 800 BC, and spread into tropical Africa. Ideas of royal kingship and state organization were also exported, particularly to adjacent areas such as Cush and Punt. The east Cushite state, Meroë, was supplanted in the 4th century AD by Aksum, which evolved into Ethiopia.

During the period from the late 3d century BC to the early 1st century AD, Rome had conquered Egypt, Carthage, and other North African areas; these became the granaries of the Roman Empire. The empire was divided into two parts in the 4th century. All lands west of modern Libya remained territories of the Western Empire, ruled by Rome, and lands to the east, including Egypt, became part of the Eastern or Byzantine Empire (q.v.), ruled from Constantinople. By this time the majority of the population had been converted to Christianity. In the 5th century the Vandals, a Germanic tribe, conquered much of North Africa. Vandal kings ruled there until the 6th century, when they were defeated by Byzantine forces, and the area was absorbed by the Eastern Empire.

*THE ERA OF EMPIRES AND CITY-STATES*
Islamic armies invaded Africa within a decade of Muhammad's death in 632 and quickly overcame Byzantine resistance in Egypt.

**North Africa.** From bases in Egypt, Arabs raided the Berber states to the west; in the 8th century they conquered Morocco. While the coastal Berbers began converting to Islam, many others retreated into the Atlas Mountains and beyond into the Sahara. Arab minorities established autocratic polities in Algeria and Morocco. The Christian states of Alwa and Makuria in the Sudan were conquered; only the Christian kingdom of Nobatia was strong enough to resist the invaders, forcing the conclusion of a treaty that maintained its independence for 600 years. Along the coast the Arab conquerors remained a small ruling minority for several centuries.

Trade across the Sahara became commonplace

In Ivory Coast, in West Africa, while members of his tribe look on in awe, a sorcerer dances with a poisonous black cobra in a ceremony to induce the forces of nature to provide abundant rain for his people's crops. By such public rites the elders pass on to the young traditional beliefs and attitudes that hold their culture together.

Hassoldt Davis–Raphto–Guillumette

by the 8th century. Caravan leaders and religious teachers spread political, religious, and societal values to the people along the trade routes. Even earlier, Muslim invaders from Yemen forced the peoples of coastal Aksum into the interior and established a series of city-states such as Adal and Harar. The Red Sea now belonged to the Muslim traders.

Several rival dynasties emerged on the North African coast. In the 8th century North African Muslims conquered most of the Iberian Peninsula, and they continued raids and expeditions of conquest against Christian Europe for centuries. By the time of the Crusades a few highly advanced Islamic states dominated the southern and eastern Mediterranean. In the 14th century Christian Sudan fell to the armies of Mameluke Egypt. The Ottoman Turks conquered Egypt in 1517 and within 50 years had established nominal control of the North African coast. The real power, however, remained in the hands of the Mamelukes (q.v.), who ruled Egypt until their defeat by Napoleon Bonaparte in 1798. The Ethiopians were overrun by the armies of the sultantate of Adal, but they defeated (1542) the Muslims with the aid of Portugal.

**West African Kingdoms.** In western Africa a number of black kingdoms emerged whose economic base lay in their control of trans-Saharan trade routes. Gold, kola nuts, and slaves were sent north in exchange for cloth, utensils, and salt.

*Ghana.* The earliest of these states, Ghana, came into being by the 5th century AD in what is now southeastern Mauritania. (Its capital, Kumbi Saleh, has been excavated in modern times.) By the 11th century, the armies of Ghana, equipped with iron weapons, made it master of the trade routes extending from present-day Morocco in the north to the coastal forests of western Africa in the south. Nomadic Berbers of the Sanhaja Confederation (in present-day central Mauritania) formed the main link between Ghana and the north. Once Arabs gained control of the northwestern coasts, they began to exploit these trade routes. By the early 11th century Muslim advisers were at the court of Ghana, and Muslim merchants lived in large foreign quarters from which they conducted lucrative large-scale trade. Late in the 11th century, Ghana was destroyed by the Almoravids, a militant Muslim movement founded among the Sanhaja Berbers. In the early 11th century they raised a jihad (holy war) and controlled the caravan routes of the Sahara. The movement then split; one group pushed north to conquer Morocco and Spain, while the other moved south to raze (about 1076) the capital of Ghana. During the next century the Soso people of the Futa Jallon, formerly vassals of Ghana, gained control of the area, but they in turn were conquered by the people of Mali about 1240.

*Mali and Songhai.* Centered on the upper reaches of the Senegal and Niger rivers, Mali evolved by the early 11th century from a group of Mande chieftaincies. In the mid-13th century, the state began a period of expansion under the vigorous ruler Sundiata (fl. 1203–60). Soon afterward the rulers of Mali appear to have converted to Islam. The high point of the Mali Empire was reached under Mansa (king) Musa, who conducted a pilgrimage to Mecca in 1324–25, opened diplomatic relations with Tunis and Egypt, and brought a number of Muslim scholars and artisans to the empire; from the time of Mansa Mūsa onward, Mali appeared on the maps of Europe. After 1400 the empire declined, and Songhai emerged as the leading state in the western Sudan. Although Songhai dates from before the 9th century, its greatest period of expansion occurred under Sunni Ali (r. 1464–92) and Askia Muhammad (r. 1493–1528). During the latter's rule Islam flourished at the court, and Timbuktu became a major center of Muslim learning, renowned for its university and its book trade. Attracted by its wealth, the armies of al-Mansur (1549–1603) of Morocco overran the Songhai capital of Gao in 1591. Following the collapse of Songhai, a number of small kingdoms—Macina, Gonja, Ségou, Kaarta—strove to dominate the western Sudan, but continual strife and economic decline were the only results.

*Hausa states and Kanem-Bornu.* To the east of Songhai, between the Niger River and Lake Chad, the Hausa city-states and the Kanem-Bornu Empire emerged. The Hausa states (Biram, Daura, Katsina, Zaria, Kano, Rano, and Gobir) originated before the 10th century, and after the fall of Songhai the trans-Saharan trade moved eastward, where it came under the control of Katsina and Kano. These became centers of flourishing commerce and urban life. Islam appears to have been introduced into the Hausa states in the 14th century from Kanem-Bornu.

The latter empire existed in the 8th century as a loosely knit state north and east of Lake Chad. It was first ruled by a nomadic people, the Zaghawa, but they were replaced by a new dynasty, the Saifawa, who ruled from about 800 to 1846. The new rulers were converted to Islam about the 11th century. In the late 14th century they moved into the Bornu region, and the older Kanem area fell to the Bulala people from the south. The best known Bornu ruler

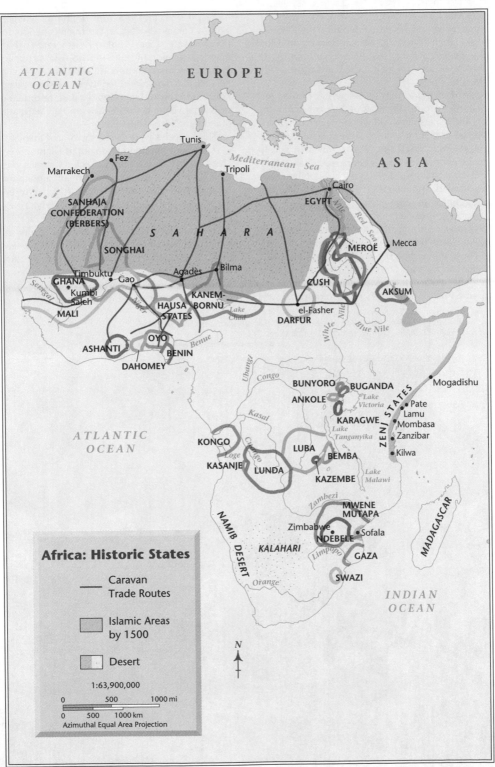

ATLANTIC
OCEAN

EUROPE

ASIA

Tunis

Fez

Marrakech

Mediterranean Sea

Tripoli

Cairo

SANHAJA
CONFEDERATION
(BERBERS)

EGYPT

Nile

Red Sea

S A H A R A

Mecca

SONGHAI

MEROË

Timbuktu

Agadès

Bilma

GHANA    Gao

CUSH

AKSUM

Kumbi
Saleh

Senegal

KANEM-
BORNU

Niger

HAUSA
STATES

Lake
Chad

el-Fasher

White Nile

Blue Nile

MALI

DARFUR

OYO

ASHANTI

Benue

BENIN

DAHOMEY

Ubangi

Congo

BUNYORO    BUGANDA

ATLANTIC
OCEAN

Kasai

ANKOLE

Lake
Victoria

Mogadishu

ZENI STATES

Pate
Lamu

KARAGWE

Mombasa

Lake
Tanganyika

Zanzibar

KONGO

LUBA

BEMBA

Congo

Loge

KASANJE    LUNDA

Kilwa

KAZEMBE

Lake
Malawi

MWENE
MUTAPA

Zambezi

NAMIB
DESERT

Zimbabwe

Sofala

MADAGASCAR

KALAHARI

NDEBELE

GAZA

Limpopo

SWAZI

Orange

INDIAN
OCEAN

## Africa: Historic States

— Caravan
    Trade Routes

▦ Islamic Areas
    by 1500

▨ Desert

1:63,900,000

0    500    1000 mi

0    500    1000 km

Azimuthal Equal Area Projection

N

was Mai Idris Alooma (r. about 1580–1617), who introduced firearms purchased from the Ottoman Turks. At its pinnacle, Kanem-Bornu controlled the eastern Saharan routes to Egypt, but by the middle of the 17th century it had begun a slow decline.

**Spread of Islam.** During the period of the great Sudanic empires, the lives of the masses of farmers and fishers remained virtually unchanged. Imported goods or luxuries were enjoyed only by the ruling classes; the farmers lived in subsistence economies, subject to periodic tax gathering and occasional slave raids. Islam was associated with the great urban centers and was the religion of some of the ruling classes and of the foreign residents. By the late 15th century, however, the nomadic Kunta Arabs began to preach, and during the mid-16th century the Qadiriyya brotherhood, to which they belonged, began to spread Islam throughout the western Sudan. At about the same time, the Fulani, a nomadic pastoral people, were moving slowly eastward from the Futa Toro region in Senegal, gaining converts for Islam. During this period, Islam became a personal religion rather than merely a religion of state. Indeed, Islam appears to have declined among the ruling classes, and non-Muslim dynasties ruled in old Muslim strongholds until the 18th century. Islamic reform and revival movements then began among the Fulani, Mandingo, Soso, and Tukolor.

Old dynasties were overthrown, and theocratic states were founded that spread Islam to new areas. In the Hausa states, Shehu Usuman dan Fodio, a Muslim teacher, led a revolt among the Fulani who between 1804 and 1810 overthrew the Hausa rulers and established new dynasties. An attempt to sweep into Bornu, however, was successfully resisted by the religious leader al-Kanemi (1774?–1835). The new Fulani Empire was initially divided between the shehu's brother Abdullahi (1756?–1828) and his son, Muhammad Bello (1781?–1837), but after 1817 Muhammad and his successors were the sole overlords.

At Meroë, in the Sudan, crumbling pyramids recall the vanished glories of the kings of the Cushite dynasty, who were buried inside them.

*Zebras are among the numerous animals indigenous to the continent. To ensure the preservation of their fauna, many African countries have established game reserves.*

Another theocratic state was formed in Macina in 1818 by Seku Ahmadu, a Fulani Muslim. During his rule an empire embracing the whole of the Niger River region from Jenne to Timbuktu was created. Upon his death in 1844 his son took power, but in 1862 Macina fell to another Muslim reformer, al-Hajj Umar, who created the vast Tukolor Empire in the Senegambia region before his death in 1864.

**East African Kingdoms.** The first records of East African history appear in the Periplus of the Erythræn Sea (AD 100?), which described the commercial life of the region and its ties to the world beyond Africa. Indonesian immigrants reached Madagascar during the 1st millennium AD bringing new foodstuffs, notably bananas, which soon spread throughout the continent. Bantu-speaking peoples settled in the immediate interior in clan-oriented polities, absorbing the Bushmanoid peoples, and Nilotic peoples occupied the so-called interlacustrine, or interlake, areas farther inland. Arab settlers colonized the coast and established trading towns. Ivory, gold, and slaves were the main exports. By the 13th century a number of significant city-states had been established. Among these Zenj states were Mogadishu, Malindi, Lamu, Mombasa, Kilwa, Pate, and Sofala. An urban Swahili culture developed through mutual assimilation of Bantu and Arabic speakers. The ruling classes were of a mixed Arab-African ancestry; the masses were Bantu, many of them slaves. These mercantile city-states were oriented toward the sea, and their political impact on inland peoples was virtually nonexistent until the 19th century.

The complex, advanced lake states first developed in the 14th century. Little is known of their early history. One theory is that more advanced Cushite peoples from the Ethiopian highlands came to dominate the indigenous Bantu. Other Cushites are believed to be ancestors of the Tutsi peoples of modern Tanzania, Rwanda, and Burundi. Located between Lakes Victoria and Edward, the early kingdoms ruled by the Bachwezi flourished before 1500, when they were supplanted by a wave of Luo peoples migrating from the Sudan. The new immigrants adopted local Bantu languages in Bunyoro country, but in Acholiland, Alurland, and in the Lango country (all in modern Uganda) they retained their own separate language. New states were founded later, among them Bunyoro, Ankole, Buganda, and Karagwe. Of these states, Bunyoro was the most powerful until the second half of the 18th century. Then Buganda began to expand, and its armies raided throughout wide areas. An elaborate centralized bureaucracy was founded, with a majority of the district and subdistrict chiefs appointed by the *kabaka* ("king").

Farther to the south, in Rwanda, a cattle-raising pastoral aristocracy founded by the Bachwezi (alternatively called Bututsi, or Bahima, in this area) ruled over settled Bantu peoples from the 16th century onward.

**Central African Kingdoms.** Even less known than the interlacustrine states are the ones formed in central Africa. In the Congo savanna, south of the tropical rain forests, Bantu-speaking peoples established agricultural communities by the beginning of the 9th century. In some places, long-distance trade to the east coast developed, with copper and ivory among the main exports. During the 14th century the Kongo Kingdom was established, dominating an area in present-day Angola between the Congo and Loge rivers and from the Cuango (Kwango) River to the Atlantic. An elaborate political system developed, with provincial governors and a king elected from among the descendants of the founding king Wene. In the area between the upper Kasai and Lake Tanganyika, small chiefdoms were organized, about 1500, into the Luba Empire. Its founding figure, Kongolo, subdued several small villages in one area and used this as a base for wider conquest. No adequate centralizing mechanisms were developed, however, so dynastic struggles and breakaway states were a continual problem. About 1600 one of the younger sons of the dynasty left the kingdom and founded the Lunda Empire. The Lunda state soon split, with members of the royal dynasty leaving to found such new states as the Bemba Kingdom, Kasanje, and Kazembe. The last became the largest and most powerful of the Luba-Lunda states; between 1750 and 1850 it dominated southern Katanga and parts of the Rhodesian plateau.

Bantu-speaking peoples moving east from the Congo region during the 1st millennium AD are thought to have assimilated local Stone Age peoples. Later Bantu immigrants, called the Karanga, were the ancestors of the present-day Shona people. The Karanga began constructing the Great Zimbabwe, an impressive stone compound housing the royal court. They also formed the Mwene Mutapa Empire, which derived its wealth from large-scale gold mining. At its height in the 15th century, its sphere of influence stretched from the Zambezi River to the Kalahari and to the Indian Ocean.

**Southern African Kingdoms.** Before the 19th century, Bantu-speaking peoples had pushed aside or assimilated their Bushmanoid predecessors in southern Africa and had established a number of sedentary states. In the early 19th century population pressures and land hunger resulted in a series of wars and large-scale migrations through south and central Africa. These began about 1816, when the Zulu ruler Shaka developed new military techniques and embarked on wars of conquest against neighboring peoples. The tribes defeated by the Zulu migrated from the southeast portion of South Africa; remodeling their own fighting techniques on those of the Zulu, they overwhelmed more distant peoples, who, in turn, were forced to seek new homes. The Ndwandwe, led by their chief Sobhuza (c. 1785–1836), moved north and established the Swazi Kingdom in the 1820s. The Ngoni also moved north, pushing through Mozambique and beyond Lake Malawi, where, about 1848, they split into five kingdoms, which raided extensively between Lake Victoria and the Zambezi. Another group, led by Soshangane (c. 1795–1859), migrated into southern Mozam-

*Tenerife is the largest of the Canary Islands. Pico de Teide, a peak on the island, is one of Africa's most compelling sights.*

Engraving from Théodore de Bry's Petits Voyages (1599), showing how 16th-century Europeans imagined the reception of Dutch traders by a black African king and his queen.
New York Public Library Picture Collection

bique, where they founded the Gaza state about 1830. The Kololo migrated north into Barotseland and began a struggle for domination with the local Lozi people. The Ndebele moved west (1824–34) and then north (1837) into what is now Zimbabwe, founding a kingdom there in Matabeleland.

*EARLY EUROPEAN IMPERIALISM*

The first sustained European interest in Africa developed through the efforts of Henry the Navigator, prince of Portugal. Numerous expeditions were sent out after 1434, each extending European knowledge of the African coastline southward, until, in 1497–98, Vasco da Gama rounded the Cape of Good Hope and reached India.

The Portuguese explorations were motivated by a variety of impulses: a desire for knowledge, a wish to bring Christianity to pagan peoples, the search for potential allies against Muslim threats, and the hope of finding new and lucrative trade routes and sources of wealth. Wherever the Portuguese, and the English, French, and Dutch who followed them, touched, they disrupted ongoing patterns of trade and political life and changed economic and religious systems.

**Trade Routes.** The Portuguese established a chain of trading settlements along the West African coast. El Mina, founded on the Gold Coast in 1482, was the most important; in fact, it was only on the Gold Coast and in the Kongo and Luanda areas that trade was really lucrative. African gold, ivory, foodstuffs, and slaves were exchanged for ironware, firearms, textiles, and foodstuffs. The Portuguese trade attracted rival European traders who, in the 16th century, created competing stations or attempted to capture the existing trade. In western Africa the new trade had profound effects. Earlier trade routes had been oriented northward across the Sahara, primarily to the Muslim world. Now the routes were reoriented to the coast, and as the states of the savanna declined in economic importance, states along the coast increased their wealth and power. Struggles soon developed among coastal peoples for control over trade routes and for access to the new firearms introduced from Europe.

*Slave trade.* With the rise of the slave trade to the Americas, wars over the control of African commerce became more intense. During the four centuries of the slave trade, untold millions of Africans fell victim to this traffic in human lives. Most were captured by other Africans and exchanged for various consumer goods. The first major kingdom to profit from the slave trade was Benin in modern west Nigeria, established in the 15th century. By the end of the 17th century, it had been supplanted by the kingdoms of Dahomey and Oyo. In the mid-18th century the Ashanti began their rise as a major West African power. Under Asantehene (king) Osei Kojo (r. 1764–77), Ashanti armies began to push south toward European trading stations located along the Gold Coast. Although they failed to clear the routes of middlemen, they secured steady supplies of firearms, which were used to expand northward and to contest their eastern frontiers with Dahomey. Farther east the Yoruba kingdom of Oyo declined in the late 18th century, bringing civil war and the intervention of Fulani forces from the north and an increase in the number of slaves available for trade. About 1835 the imperial capital, Old Oyo, was abandoned, but in the Battle of Oshogbo (c. 1840) the Fulani were driven back. The civil wars lasted until 1893, when Yoruba power was divided among several competitive states.

During the latter 18th century, sentiment in Britain turned against the slave trade. Following the Mansfield decision of 1772, which freed slaves in Great Britain, plans were made for a West African colony for former slaves. The first attempt (1787–90) at Saint George's Bay (in present-day Sierra Leone) failed; a second attempt was made by abolitionists, who, in 1792, founded Freetown in the same area. When the British outlawed the slave trade for British citizens in 1807, they saw Freetown as a desirable base for naval operations against such trade, and in 1808, Sierra Leone was made a crown colony. The example of Sierra Leone appealed to Americans interested in black colonization, and in early 1822 the American Colonization Society succeeded in establishing its colony, Liberia, at nearby Cape Mesurado.

**British expansion.** The British desire to suppress the slave trade found expression in attempts at redirecting African commerce toward other exports, such as palm oil, in heightened missionary activity, and in the imposition of British government jurisdiction over properties previously held by British merchants. Such developments frequently involved Great Britain inadvertently in struggles with African states and led to its assumption of sovereignty over certain African territory. On the Gold Coast the British government, in 1821, took control of a series of forts. Through misunderstandings the first of a series of Ashanti-British wars occurred from 1823

to 1826; these conflicts were to continue intermittently until the end of the century. Although the government gave up control of the forts in 1828, it again assumed jurisdiction in 1843. British authority over the Ashanti, however, was not firmly established until 1900. In the Niger delta of Nigeria, the British abolition of slavery brought about a shift in trade from slaves to palm oil, and in pursuit of this commodity Great Britain required a nearby port; in addition, the British were eager to eliminate the middlemen in such delta states as Calabar, Bonny, and Brass. In 1852, therefore, they forced the ruler of Lagos to accept British protection, and in 1861 Lagos was annexed as a crown colony.

**Central and East Africa.** In Central and East Africa the European impact was different. When the Portuguese arrived on the Congo-Angola coast in the 1480s, they quickly allied themselves with the rulers of the Kongo, who became converted to Christianity and attempted to create a westernized state. This aim was frustrated, however, by fraternal wars and by Portuguese introduction of the slave trade. The region was soon immersed in strife, and during the 16th century the kingdom collapsed. Farther south the Portuguese founded Luanda in 1575 as a base for their penetration of the Angolan hinterland, and it was here that about half of all the slaves sent to the Americas originated. When they reached the East African coast, the Portuguese attempted to cut off the area's trade with the Muslim world. In the process a number of the city-states were destroyed; others were occupied, and the entire area went into economic decline. After the Portuguese were finally expelled from Mombasa in 1698, the coast reverted to local rule, but during the 18th century the rulers of Oman established at least nominal control. In the early 19th century, Sultan Sayyid Said (1787?–1856), ruler of Oman, transferred his capital to Zanzibar, which then served as a base to strengthen his control of the coast and to penetrate inland for trade with the interlacustrine states. British efforts to control the East African slave trade led, in 1822, to a treaty prohibiting the sale of slaves to subjects of Christian countries. An active slave trade continued, however, for large numbers of Africans were seized for the clove plantations of Zanzibar and for Middle Eastern slave markets.

In Ethiopia the arrival of the Portuguese had helped stave off conquest by the Muslims. In 1542 a combined Portuguese-Ethiopian force crushed a Muslim army, and the Ethiopians regained much of their lost territory. After doctrinal disputes between Coptic churchmen and Portuguese Jesuits, however, the Portuguese

European depiction of a clash between British troops and Bantu warriors in the eastern frontier region of Cape Colony, South Africa, in 1851.

were expelled in 1632. Ethiopia went into a period of isolation, and by the 18th century, the monarchy was in collapse. From about 1769 to 1855, Ethiopia endured the "age of princes," during which the emperors were puppet rulers controlled by powerful provincial nobles. The era came to an end with the crowning (1855) of Emperor Theodore II (1818–68), a minor chief who rose to the throne by defeating his rivals. *See* ETHIOPIA: *History.*

**South Africa.** Although the Portuguese largely ignored southern Africa, their rivals, the Dutch, beginning in 1652, developed the area as a way station to the East Indies. For a short period colonists were encouraged to settle around Cape Town, and soon a new culture and people, the Boers, or Afrikaners, began to develop. Despite government resistance they began to move inland in search of better land and, after 1815, to escape control by the British government. As they trekked inland, they encountered the Zulu and other Bantu peoples expanding southward. The result was a series of wars for land. During the course of their migrations, the Boers were among the first whites to explore the African interior.

**Age of Exploration.** In the late 18th century, scientific interest and the search for new markets stimulated exploration. The British explorer James Bruce reached the source of the Blue Nile in 1770; his countryman Mungo Park explored (1796 and 1805) the Niger River; the German explorer Heinrich Barth traveled widely in the Muslim western Sudan; the Scottish missionary David Livingstone explored the Zambezi River and in 1855 named Victoria Falls; the British explorers John Hanning Speke and James Augustus Grant (1827–92), traveling downstream, and Sir Samuel White Baker, working upstream, solved the mystery of the source of the Nile in 1862. Following the explorers (and sometimes preceding them) were Christian missionaries and then European merchants.

**European Politics.** As European private interest in Africa grew, the involvement of their governments multiplied. The French began the conquest of Algeria and Senegal in the 1830s, but the systematic occupation of tropical Africa did not occur until the second half of the century. As European citizens and administrators penetrated inland, they encountered resistance from dominant peoples and welcome from subordinated peoples seeking allies or protectors. From about 1880 to 1905, most of Africa was partitioned among Belgium, France, Germany, Great Britain, Italy, and Portugal. In 1876 King Leopold II of the Belgians established the International Association of the Congo, a private company, for the exploration and colonization of the region. His principal agent for this task was Sir Henry M. Stanley. By 1884 the intense rivalry of the European powers for additional African territory, and the ill-defined boundaries of their various holdings, threatened their international relations. A conference was then called at Berlin, to which the nations of Europe, together with the U.S., sent delegates.

At the Berlin conference (1884-85) the powers defined their spheres of influence and laid down rules for future occupation on the coasts of Africa and for navigation of the Congo and Niger rivers. Among the important provisions of the General Act of Berlin was the rule that when a power acquired new territory in Africa or assumed a protectorate over any part of the continent, it must notify the other powers signatory to the conference. During the next 15 years, numerous treaties were negotiated between the European nations, implementing and modifying the provisions of the conference. Two such treaties were concluded in 1890 by Great Britain. The first, with Germany, demarcated the spheres of influence of the two powers in Africa. The second treaty, with France, recognized British interests in the region between Lake Chad and the Niger River and acknowledged French influence

A sale is transacted at an Algerian carpet market.
South African Tourist Corp.

in the Sahara. Other agreements, notably those between Great Britain and Italy in 1891, between France and Germany in 1894, and between Great Britain and France in 1899, further clarified the boundaries of the various European holdings in Africa.

**African Resistance.** No African states had been invited to the Berlin conference, and none was signatory to these agreements. Whenever possible, the decisions made in Europe were resisted when applied on African soil. The French faced (1870) a revolt in Algeria and resistance (1881-1905) to their efforts to control the Sahara. In the western Sudan the Mandinka ruler Samory Toure and Ahmadu, the son and successor of al-Hajj Umar of the Tukolor state, attempted to maintain their independence. Both were defeated by the French, however—Ahmadu in 1893 and Samory five years later. Dahomey was occupied by French forces in 1892, and the Wadai region was the last area to fall to the French, in 1900. British administrators encountered similar resistance from the Boers in South Africa during the periods 1880-81 and 1899-1902. British and Boer settlers conquered Matabeleland in 1893, and three years later both the Matabele (Ndebele) and their subordinates, the Shona, revolted. Revolts broke out in Ashantiland in 1893-94, 1895-96, and 1900 and in Sierra Leone in 1897. The British conquest of the Fulani Hausa states was resisted (1901-03). Sokoto revolted in 1906. The Germans faced (1904-08) the Herero insurrection in South-West Africa and the Maji Maji revolt (1905-07) in Tanganyika. Only the Ethiopians under Emperor Menelik II (r. 1889-1911) were successful in resisting European conquest, annihilating an Italian force at the Battle of Adwa (Aduwa) in 1896.

Liberian women shop for housewares in a public market in their capital, Monrovia.
United Nations

**Increasing Development.** Once the territories were conquered and pacified, the European administrations began to develop transportation systems so that raw materials could be shipped more easily to ports for export, and to institute tax systems that would force subsistence farmers either to raise cash crops or to engage in migrant labor. Both policies were well under way when World War I disrupted these efforts. During the course of the war, the German territories in West and South-West Africa were conquered and later were mandated by the League of Nations to the various Allied powers. Thousands of Africans either fought in the war or served as porters for the Allied armies. Resistance to the war was limited to the short-lived 1915 rebellion of John Chilembwe (c. 1860–1915), an African clergyman, in Nyasaland (now Malawi).

After World War I, efforts for the exploitation of the colonies were tempered, and greater attention was paid to providing education, health services, and development assistance and to safeguarding African land rights. Nevertheless, the white settler colonies, such as Algeria, Southern Rhodesia (now Zimbabwe), and Kenya, were given considerable internal self-government. Southern Rhodesia was made an internally self-governing crown colony in 1923 with virtually no provision for African voting. During the interwar years, various types of African-organized protest and nationalist movements began to emerge. On the whole, however, membership was limited to Western-educated African groups. Mass parties developed only in Egypt and Algeria, where large numbers of Africans had abandoned their traditional way of life and were developing new identities and allegiances. Ethiopia, which had earlier successfully resisted European colonization, fell to an Italian invasion in 1936 and did not regain its independence until World War II. With the coming of the war, Africans served in the Allied armies in even greater numbers than before, and the colonies generally supported the Allied cause. Fighting on the continent, which was limited to North and northeast Africa, ended in May 1943.

*THE NEW AFRICA*

Following the war, the European colonial powers were physically and psychologically weakened, and the balance of international power shifted to the U.S. and the USSR, both professed anticolonial nations. In North Africa, French rule was opposed from 1947 onward with sporadic terrorism and rioting. The Algerian revolution began in 1954 and continued until independence in 1962, six years after Morocco and Tunisia had received independence. In French sub-Saharan

Angora goats graze in Orange Free State, a province of the Republic of South Africa.　South African Tourist Corp.

Africa, an effort had been made to stave off nationalist movements by granting the inhabitants of the overseas territories full status as citizens and by allowing deputies and senators from each territory to sit in the French National Assembly. Nonetheless, the qualified franchise and communal representation given to each territory proved unacceptable. In the British areas the pace of change also quickened after the war. Mass parties, enrolling as wide a range of social, ethnic, and economic groups as possible, began to appear. In Sudan, disagreements between Egypt and Great Britain over the direction of Sudanese self-government led the British to accelerate the pace, and in 1954 Sudan achieved independence. During the 1950s, the examples of newly independent nations on other continents, the activities of the Mau Mau terrorist movement of Kenya, and the effectiveness of such popular African leaders as Kwame Nkrumah further quickened the pace. The independence of Ghana in 1957 and Guinea in 1958 set off a chain reaction of nationalist demands. In 1960 alone 17 sovereign African nations came into existence.

By the end of the 1970s almost all of Africa was independent. The Portuguese possessions—Angola, Cape Verde, Guinea-Bissau, and Mozambique—became independent in 1974–75 after years of violent struggle. France relinquished the Comoro Islands in 1975, and Djibouti gained independence in 1977. In 1976 Spain yielded Spanish Sahara, which then was divided between Mauritania and Morocco. Here, however, a bitter war for independence ensued. Mauritania gave up its part in 1979, but Morocco, taking over the entire territory, continued the fighting with the local Polisario front. Zimbabwe gained legal independence in 1980 (see ZIMBABWE: *History*). The last remaining large dependency on the continent, Namibia, attained independence in 1990.

213

The young African states face a variety of major problems. One of the most important is the creation of a nation-state. Most African countries retain the frontiers arbitrarily drawn by late 19th-century European diplomats and administrators. Ethnic groups may be divided by national boundaries, but loyalties to such groups are often stronger than loyalties to the state.

When the African states attained independence, the dominant nationalist movements and their leaders installed themselves in virtually permanent power. They called for national unity and urged that multiparty parliamentary systems be discarded in favor of the single-party state. When these governments proved unable or unwilling to fulfill popular expectations, the result often was military intervention. Leaving day-to-day administration to the permanent civil service, the new military leaders posed as efficient and honest public guardians, but they soon developed the same interest in power that had characterized their civilian predecessors. In many African states, the early 1990s brought renewed interest in multiparty parliamentary democracy.

Economic development also presented a major problem. Although a number of African states have considerable natural resources, few have the finances to develop their economies. Foreign private enterprise has often regarded investment in such underdeveloped areas as too risky, and this view has been justified in many instances. The major alternative sources of financing are national and multinational lending institutions.

Expectations in African nations for a better living standard have increased, and the prices of consumer and other manufactured goods have kept pace, but the prices of most African primary products have lagged behind. A worldwide recession in the early 1980s multiplied difficulties that were begun by the oil-price increases of the 1970s. Foreign-exchange problems and ballooning foreign debt aggravated public discontent. Famine and drought plagued the northern and central regions of Africa in the 1980s, and millions of refugees left their homes in search of food, increasing the problems of the countries to which they fled. Medical resources, already inadequate, were overwhelmed by epidemics of acquired immune deficiency syndrome (AIDS), cholera, and other diseases. Protracted local conflicts in Ethiopia, Somalia, Chad, the Saharan area, Rwanda, Liberia, southern Africa, and elsewhere have destabilized governments, halted economic progress, and cost the lives of hundreds of thousands of people.

Another major problem has been the inability to project a voice in international affairs. Most African states regard themselves as part of the Third World and the nonaligned nations, which they see as forces for moral leadership.

*A persistent drought brought wide-scale famine to Ethiopia in the mid-1980s, forcing many people off the land and into refugee camps like this one near Makale, in Tigre Province.*
© 1984 David Burnett–
Woodfin Camp & Associates

*A carved wood stool, its seat supported by a caryatid (female) figure, is typical of the work of the Luba tribe of central Congo.*

Marc & Evelyne Bernheim—Woodfin Camp & Associates

Because of their lack of military or financial power, however, the views of African nations rarely appear to be taken into account.

For additional information on historical figures, see biographies on most of those whose names are not followed by dates. J.T.Sa.

*For further information on this topic, see the Bibliography in volume 28, sections 118, 667, 725, 729, 856, 871, 873, 1009–41.*

**AFRICAN ART AND ARCHITECTURE,** in general, those works created by historical or contemporary African artists living south of the Sahara. The artists belong to a wide variety of African cultures, each of which is characterized by its own language, traditions, and artistic forms. Although the immense Sahara serves as a natural barrier within the continent, evidence has shown a considerable dissemination of influences through trade routes that traversed the continent from early times. Today, for example, many Islamic art and architectural forms of North African inspiration appear among cultures south of the Sahara. In addition, research has pointed to concurrent influences of sub-Saharan African arts and cultures on northern African areas closer to the

Mediterranean. Egypt, one of the most resplendent of African civilizations, can also be seen as having important ancient artistic and cultural parallels with sub-Saharan African civilizations (*see* EGYPTIAN ART AND ARCHITECTURE).

The arts of Africa illuminate the rich histories, philosophies, religions, and societies of the inhabitants of this vast continent. African artworks, in addition to their inherent significance to the peoples who produced them, also have inspired some of the most important artistic traditions emerging in Europe and America in the modern era (*see* MODERN ART AND ARCHITECTURE). Western artists of this century have admired both the African artists' emphasis on abstraction and their freedom from naturalism.

The history of art in Africa covers many centuries. Among the most ancient of these arts are the rock paintings and engravings from Tassili and Ennedi in the Sahara (6000 BC–1st cent. AD). Other examples of early arts include the terracotta sculptures modeled by Nok artists in northern Nigeria between 500 BC and AD 200, the decorative bronze works of Igbo Ukwu (9th–10th cent. AD), and the extraordinary bronze and terracotta sculptures from Ife (12th–15th cent. AD). The technical expertise and naturalistic qualities

*A carved wood mask embellished with cowrie shells, animals skins, and beads was made by the Dan-Ngere tribes of the Ivory Coast.*

Mark & Evelyne Bernheim—Woodfin Camp & Associates

A skin-covered mask with animal antlers attached is a type unique to the Ekoi tribe of eastern Nigeria.          Marc & Evelyne Bernheim—Woodfin Camp & Associates

of these latter arts led early viewers to assume erroneously that they must have been of classical Greek inspiration. Today rich African traditions continue, with artists working both within the traditional modes of expression and in nontraditional genres.

**The African Artistic Heritage.** African artists have developed diverse traditions of sculpture (figures and masks), architecture (principally domestic structures), furniture, pottery, textiles, and jewelry. In addition, body decoration (coiffure and cicatrization, or decorative scarring) and painting (on building, textile, and human surfaces) are also part of the African artistic heritage.

*Materials.* The most commonly employed materials include wood, fiber, metal (especially bronze, iron, and gold), ivory, clay, earth, and stone. The forms of representation within each medium vary from relative naturalism to general abstraction, with art styles conforming to the aesthetic tradition established within a particular cultural area. In African art, considerable concern is given both to the maintenance of traditional artistic forms within a culture and to the encouragement of creativity and innovation within the parameters of each artistic tradition.

*Artists.* African artists generally work as specialists, receiving their training from established artists living in the community or wider area. In some old kingships, such as that of Benin in Nigeria, active guild systems controlled the training of young artists. Among the nearby Yoruba, important schools of artists were developed at local family compound centers. Often the artistic profession was seen as hereditary, with talent being passed from generation to generation, and with

creativity and success often linked to a divine ancestral endowment. Among the Dogon and Bambara (or Bamana) of Mali, for this reason, sculptors were all selected from an ancient endogamous (intermarried by custom) group of blacksmiths. The place of work and the materials employed were also important to the artist during the creative process. Often these were controlled by religious proscriptions.

*Aesthetics.* Community criticism was an essential part of artistic traditions in many African cultures. Studies of the aesthetic canons followed by artists and critics in Africa indicate a deliberate concern for abstraction in the design process. Thus, for example, among the Yoruba of Nigeria, the criteria for sculptural beauty consist of a number of specifically nonrepresentational elements. These include visibility, even if this necessitates proportional distortion; straightness, which implies youth and good health; symmetry, to the exclusion of more natural poses or postures; ephebism, the depiction of each person at an idealized youthful age; smoothness, suggesting again youth and health without natural body imperfections; and hypermimesis, an emphasis on general resemblance rather than on exact representation.

In some African cultures correct aesthetic canons were intentionally distorted in order to portray characters whose behavior was antisocial. The Ibo and Ibibio of Nigeria, for example, carve masks with diseased, horrific, monstrous, or asymmetrical features to represent characters who were unruly, evil, or dangerous. In Ibo and Ibibio masquerade performances, such masks are often contrasted with other, more beautifully featured and aesthetically pleasing masks that are worn to portray persons who were orderly, good, or peaceful.

**Patronage.** Patronage, like aesthetics, plays an important role in the creation of African artworks. Kings and their courts are of particular significance in this regard because of their artistic requirements for the mounting of state pageants, the performance of religious ceremonies, and the manufacture of charismatic personal displays. In architecture, the palaces of kings such as those who lived in Nigeria (Yoruba, Benin), Ghana (Akan), Cameroon (Bamileke, Bamum), and Zaire (Kuba, Mangbetu) rank among the most elaborate and richly decorated structures in Africa. The expensive materials available to these rulers—ivory, bronze, gold, glass beads, and plush raffia velours—are amply displayed in the arts produced at these royal courts. Important types of art made for such regal patronage include staffs of office, thrones, state swords, crowns, royal memorial sculptures, drinking vessels, and serving containers.

Other important sources of art patronage in Africa included the various associations of men and women formed within many communities for social and political, as well as religious, control. The still-active Poro men's associations of the Dan and their neighbors in Liberia and Côte d'Ivoire are characteristic examples of this type of patronage association. Poro members commissioned many of the masks and figural sculptures found in this region.

Associations that united community members by age and occupation were also important African art patrons. Examples of artworks commissioned by such associations are found among the Bambara (Mali) and among the Ibo and Ejagham (Nigeria), among others. Often each age group or occupationally linked section of the association had its own distinctive representations or masquerade themes. Among the Ejagham, animal forms characterized the masks of hunting societies, and themes of human deformity were often found in conjunction with warfare masks; images of women were commonly employed for the headdresses of the women's clubs or ancestral associations.

Traditional religious and cult organizations were also important as sources of art patronage in Africa. Artworks were not only a central component of many traditional shrines and chapels but also played a critical role in the diverse religious pageants. Among the Yoruba of Nigeria, cults linked with the principal deities—Shango (thunder), Obatala (creativity), Oshun (water), Ifa (knowledge), Yemoja (sorcery), Eshu (exami-

nation), and Odudua (earth)—had a vast array of associated art forms, including figures, masks, pottery, textiles, and jewelry. Here, as elsewhere in Africa, the artworks used in conjunction with each particular cult were often identifiable through their iconography, materials, styles, and modes of manufacture.

**The Role of Art in African Society.** The multiple roles that art plays in African communities are as diverse as their forms of patronage. These include social, political, economic, historical, and therapeutic functions.

**Social role.** One of the most important functions of African art is distinctly social. In fulfilling this role, African art frequently depicts women as mothers, usually nursing or cradling their young. Men, on the other hand, are often presented both as elders—the traditional community leaders—and as successful warriors—appearing on horseback or with armaments. Social themes are prevalent in many African masquerade performances as well. In these masquerades, animal and human characters, in appropriate masks and garb, assume a variety of roles in demonstrating proper and improper forms of societal behavior. In performances of the Ijo and southern Ibo of Nigeria are found such diverse antisocial characters as the miser, the greedy person, the prosti-

*Highly stylized facial features characterize the elegant masks of the Fang tribe of Gabon in central Africa.*
Marc & Evelyne Bernheim–Woodfin Camp & Associates

A contemporary Nigerian artisan applies colors to decorative mud relief carvings on a building facade.

Lawrence Manning–Black Star

tute, the incompetent physician, and the unscrupulous lawyer. In the Egungun performances of the nearby Yoruba, the gossip, the glutton, and the strange-mannered foreigner have key parts as negative social models.

**Political role.** Political control is another major concern displayed through art in Africa. Among the Dan (Liberia), Kota (Gabon), Pende (Zaire), and others, special masks are worn by persons acting as community judges and policemen. The Kwele Gon maskers of Gabon are a particularly good example of this type of masked community official. Because of their anonymity and special powers, these Gon masked figures are able to break normal societal codes and proscriptions as a means of redistributing scarce food and animals at times of great community need. A different type of social control is achieved by certain African figures and architectural motifs. The reliquary figures of the Kota, Sogo, and Fang of Gabon, for example, are used as guardian images to protect the sacred ancestral relics of the community from theft or harm. The Dogon of Mali and the Senufo of Côte d'Ivoire carve elaborate doors that ritually protect the community food supplies and sacred objects in the same way.

**Economic role.** Art in Africa also fulfills an important economic role. The elegant wooden Chi Wara antelope headdresses of the Bambara of Mali are worn in planting and harvest ceremonies. Chi Wara, the mythical Bambara inventor of agriculture, is said to have buried himself in the earth as an act of self-sacrifice. The dance of the Chi Wara maskers on the agricultural fields (Chi

Wara's grave) serves both to honor this great being and to remind the young Bambara farmers of the arduous sacrifice that they in turn must make each year. Among the Senufo of Côte d'Ivoire, delicately carved figures are used in a similar way to encourage farmers in their difficult work. Here *daleu* staffs, with bird or female imagery, are secured in the ground at the end of cultivation rows. These staffs serve as goals, markers, and trophies for the field-planting competitions.

**Historical role.** An important historical role is also fulfilled in African art through its memorialization of important persons and events of the past. With this in mind, the Dogon of Mali have carved numerous images of their legendary ancestors, the Nommo, who descended from the sky at the beginning of time. Such Nommo figures (some of which have upraised hands pointing to the sky and their village of origin) find important places on granary doors, cave paintings, and sacred architectural supports.

In the powerful kingdom of Benin in Nigeria, elaborate relief plaques cast (lost-wax process) in bronze similarly carried images of important persons and events of the past, including the meetings of foreign dignitaries, battle scenes, court pageants, nobles in state dress, religious ceremonies, and musicians.

**Therapeutic role.** Traditional African therapies have also required special forms of art. Divination, the means by which problems and their potential resolutions could be determined, was particularly important in the production of African artworks. Yoruba (Nigeria) Ifa diviners, for example, used elaborately sculpted divination boards, bowls, and tappers as an essential part of their ritual equipment. Similarly, the Baule of Côte d'Ivoire used elaborately sculptured divination vessels for oracular purposes. Among the Kongo of Zaire, powerful wooden fetish figures (stuck through with iron nails) were employed therapeutically as a means of repelling personal danger and trauma.

**Regional Distinctions.** The widely differing cultures of sub-Saharan Africa are more readily comprehended if they are grouped by geographic regions, in view of the diversity in climate, topography, and social organization within this vast area. Although some of these cultures have vanished, fortunately much of their art remains; other cultures of this region have survived and continue to the present day to produce their traditional art.

*Arts of the western savanna.* Among the best known of the traditional western savanna arts are those of the Dogon, Bambara, Mossi, Bobo, and Tamberma living in the dry, grassy plains of Mali,

Burkina Faso, and Togo. The arts of the Dogon, one of the most isolated of these peoples, have been especially well researched. The Dogon have a rich and complex philosophical foundation on which their arts are based. The Dogon village plan, for example, is seen to have the form of a human, representing the Nommo, the first humans created by the Dogon sun and creator god. Important parts of the Dogon village physiognomy include its head (the smithy and men's house), chest (the houses of lineage leaders), hands (women's houses), genitals (a mortar and altar), and feet (shrines). Dogon masks, carved for the men's association, Awa, represent in their totality the Dogon image of the world with the animals and people that inhabit it. The antelope, the bird, the hare, Fulani women, and Samana men are some of the characters who appear in the funerary performances of this association. Other masks presented at such times depict more abstract philosophical concepts. One mask, the 9 m- (30 ft-) long serpentine "Great Mother" mask, recalls the origin of death. Another—the roughly cruciform Kanaga mask—

A bronze plaque (c. 1550–1680) depicting a king and his attendants was cast in the lost-wax method for the court of Benin of Nigeria's Bini tribe.

Metropolitan Museum of Art, Michael C. Rockefeller Memorial Collection of Primitive Art, Gift of Nelson A. Rockefeller.

re-creates, in its wearer's dance motions, the origin of the world.

Farther east, among the linguistically related Tamberma of Togo, house architecture has reached an apex of beauty and symbolic complexity. The two-story earthen "castles" of these people serve not only as their domiciles but also as their fortresses, cathedrals, theaters, and cosmological diagrams. The name that these people call themselves, Batammariba, or the "people who are the architects," bears out the importance of architecture among this group. Like the Dogon village, each Tamberma house is said to be distinctly human. Accordingly, its outer surfaces are scarified with the same patterns incised on women. Appropriate body parts are also found in the house, for example, the door "mouth," the window "eyes," the grinding stone "teeth," and so on.

**The western forests.** The great forested West Atlantic coast—often called the Guinea Coast—incorporates the diverse cultures and arts of Guinea, Sierra Leone, Liberia, and Côte d'Ivoire on the west and Ghana, Togo, Benin, and Nigeria on the east. In the western coastal forests, the dominant art patrons are associations of women and men such as Sandé and Poro, respectively. The women's Sandé society of the Mende (Sierra Leone) has a particularly important masquerade tradition. Sandé masks, which are polished a deep black to reflect the richness and beauty of the sea, are worn by female association leaders during the initiation ceremonies of young women in the community. The most beautiful of these masks reflect, in their form, the features that the Mende admire in themselves: a high, smooth forehead, an elaborate coiffure, and an elegant strong neck.

Poro, the parallel men's association, has elaborate masking traditions as well. Dan, Kran, and Guere Poro members from Liberia and nearby Côte d'Ivoire present in their association performances a diverse cast of players. These include, among others, the judge, the singer, and the runner. Elegance of form, shiny black facial surfaces, and complex woven coiffures are featured in these masks. When not being worn, the masks are secured in a special sacred *go* (*ge*) house under the guardianship of the *go*-master. The wife of this important man has her own special art form, a decorated spoon that she displays in feasts for the community.

From the eastern Atlantic coast region that encompasses the countries of Ghana, Togo, Benin, and Nigeria are found some of the most important aristocratic arts of Africa. Perhaps the most famous of the kingships is the Benin dynasty in Nigeria. The royal city of Benin (not be be confused with the recently named neighboring country of Benin) was at its height in the 17th and 18th centuries and was compared by travelers to the great contemporaneous cities of the Netherlands. The palace of the king, or *oba* as he was called, was especially impressive. At one time its walls were covered with beautifully cast bronze plaques that were said to shimmer like gold. The three main buildings at the palace were each surmounted by immense turrets supporting giant bronze birds and pythons. On the royal palace altars, bronze memorial heads and sculptures were displayed for private and state festivities.

**Central, South, and East Africa.** In the thick equatorial forests and drier savanna regions running from Gabon through the Congo, Zaire, and various countries to the east and south, still other artistic forms are emphasized. In the matrilinear cultures of southern Zaire, female figures are particularly important. The Pende chief's house, for example, often bears a full-scale image of a woman at the apex of the roof. This figure sometimes holds a child (the symbol of the family line and future heirs) as well as an ax (the symbol of power).

Among the remote Gato, Bongo, and Konso of

*A grave figure or reliquary of wood covered with brass was made by the central African Bakota tribe of Gabon.*
Sotheby Parke-Bernet–Editorial Photocolor Archives

Sudan and Ethiopia, memorial figures of wood were set up in prominent positions in the village to survey its entrance and the tombs of its important ancestors. In most other East African cultures monumental sculpture was rare. Instead, body decoration became an important focus of the arts. The Masai of Kenya and the Zulu of South Africa are particularly noted for their beaded jewelry. Circular forms such as one finds in the jewelry of the Masai are also emphasized in Bantu village planning in this area. The great elliptical stone building (c. 1200) of the ancient Monomotapa culture near Fort Victoria in Zimbabwe is conceptually part of this circular design and architectural tradition.

**Contemporary African Art.** Many of the so-called traditional arts of Africa are still being commissioned, carved, and used in active traditional contexts. As in all art periods, important innovations as well as significant retentions of established styles and modes of expression coexist. In recent years, with the changes in transportation and mass communications within the continent, a number of art forms have been disseminated widely among diverse African cultures. Today, for example, some Nigerian-style masks are being used in Ghanaian and other coastal centers on the eastern Guinea Coast.

In addition to distinctly African influences, a number of changes also have originated from the outside. For example, Islamic architecture and design motifs can be seen in many of the arts of the northern regions of Nigeria, Mali, Burkina Faso, and Niger. East Indian print motifs have similarly found their way into sculptures and masks of the Ibibio and Efik artists living along the southern coast of Nigeria. Christian themes have also been taken up by some contemporary artists in their designs for panels, doors, and baptismal fonts for Africa's Christian churches and cathedrals. In recent years artists have also found important sources of patronage for various art forms in the banks, commercial establishments, government offices, and courts of the new nations. Tourists have been responsible for still other art demands, particularly for decorative masks and ornamental African sculptures that are made of ebony or ivory.

The development of schools of art and architecture in sub-Saharan African cities has pushed artists to work in new mediums such as cement, oil and other paints, ink, stone, aluminum, and a variety of graphic modes. The images and designs they have created reflect a vibrant union of African and contemporary Western traditions. Artists such as Twins Seven Seven (1944?–   ) and Ashira Olatunde (1918–93) of Nigeria and

Nicholas Mukomberanwa (1940–   ) of Zimbabwe are among the most successful practitioners of these novel creative forms.                    S.P.B.

*See also* AFRICA; AFRICAN LITERATURE; AFRICAN MUSIC AND DANCE; MASK; as well as separate entries on individual kingdoms, nations, regions, and tribes.

*For further information on this topic, see the Bibliography in volume 28,* sections 642–43, 667.

**AFRICAN DAISY.** *See* ARCTOTIS.

**AFRICAN HUNTING DOG,** small, wild member of the dog family (q.v.), Canidae, in the carnivore (q.v.) order of mammals. The single species, *Lycaon pictus,* is found in Africa south and east of the Sahara and is also known as the African wild dog or Cape hunting dog. The black-skinned, long-legged body weighs up to 23 kg (up to 50 lb) and is covered with short, sparse fur in a wide range of black, yellow, and white patterns. The large ears are rounded, and each paw has only four toes. The animal lives and travels in packs numbering from a few to more than 50 individuals. They sometimes range widely in their search for food. The dogs exhibit complex social patterns; both parents care for the young, who learn much about hunting and game-trail patterns from the older dogs in the pack. A large pack of dogs can bring down large animals, such as lions and antelopes. After a gestation period of about 70 days, six to eight young are born to a litter.

**AFRICAN LANGUAGES,** languages indigenous to the African continent. More than 1000 different languages are spoken in Africa. Apart from Arabic, which is not confined to Africa, the most widely spoken African tongues are Swahili and Hausa, each with more than 10 million speakers. Several languages (often inaccurately termed dialects simply because they have few users) are spoken by only a few thousand people. On the average, an African language has about 200,000 speakers; only a few dozen languages have more than 1 million speakers. Although very few African languages have written literatures, the majority have long-standing traditions of oral literature.

**Language Groupings.** According to the most recent and widely accepted scholarly practice, the languages of Africa are grouped into four language families: Hamito-Semitic (or Afro-Asiatic), Nilo-Saharan, Khoisan, and Niger-Kordofanian. A language family is a group of related languages presumably derived from a common origin; a family is often further subdivided into branches composed of more closely related languages. At least some of the African linguistic families are believed to have a history of more than 5000 years. African languages that belong to different families are as little alike as English, Turkish, Chinese, and Navajo, although the disparate tongues may be spoken in the same locality. Even within a single family, African languages may be as different in sound and structure as English, Italian, Russian, and Hindi, all of which are members of the Indo-European language family. Within a given branch of one family, however, languages may frequently be as closely related to each other as German, Dutch, and Swedish.

Writing systems exist for only about half the languages of Africa, and in certain tongues the only written literature is a translation of some portion of the New Testament. Except for Arabic and certain languages of Ethiopia, the alphabets of most African languages are based on adaptations of the Roman alphabet and were introduced by missionaries. A few tribes, notably the Vai in Liberia and the Bamum in Cameroon, have developed their own syllabic writing systems.

The first European students of African languages were usually missionaries who, more than other groups, were interested in learning to speak with native populations and preparing literature for them. Much of the available information on African languages still comes from missionary sources. A major early work on African languages is the *Polyglotta Africana,* by the 19th-century missionary-teacher Sigismund W. Koelle (1823–1902); it contains a list of some 300 words and phrases in 156 different African languages. Koelle's information came from freed slaves living in the British West African protectorate of Sierra Leone. Twentieth-century scholars, such as the German linguists Carl Meinhof (1857–1944) and Diedrich Westermann (1875–1956), the South African linguist Clement Martyn Doke (1893–1980), and such British linguists as Ida Caroline Ward (1880–1949) and Malcolm Guthrie (1903–72), have made substantial contributions to the knowledge of African languages and the relationships of these languages to one another. The American linguist and anthropologist Joseph H. Greenberg (1915–    ) significantly revised earlier notions of the groupings of African languages, although some modifications and refinements of his 1963 classification can be expected from the increasing number of scholars in the field.

It is often suggested that the indigenous languages of Africa will eventually give way to internationally important European languages, or at least to a few of the major languages that are native to Africa. Despite an increasing number of African contacts with Europe and the U.S., however, most African languages are expected to continue in use over the next few centuries. As the continent develops, more and more speakers of minor languages will probably also learn at least one major African language and possibly a European language as well; but the use of the mother tongue in the family circle and in village and tribal affairs will without a doubt persist much longer than most people expect. The emergence of independent African states has been accompanied by a resurgence of interest and pride in the indigenous languages of Africa in many parts of the continent.

**The Hamito-Semitic Family.** The Hamito-Semitic languages (q.v.) constitute the most important group of languages spoken in North Africa. The Semitic branch of the family includes languages spoken in Asia as well as in Africa. The Arabic language (q.v.), the leading member of this branch, is the major language of North Africa and of the Republic of the Sudan. Amharic, which is spoken by more than 5 million people, is the official language of Ethiopia. The national book of Ethiopia, *Kebra nagast* (The Glory of the Kings), is written in ancient Ethiopic, or Ge<sup>c</sup>ez (q.v.), now no longer spoken. Ge<sup>c</sup>ez literature also includes several books of the Apocrypha not preserved in any other language. Other Semitic languages (q.v.) spoken in North Africa include Tigrinya and Tigré in Eritrea.

Languages of the Berber branch of the Hamito-Semitic family are spoken by a substantial portion of the population of Morocco, Algiers, and Tunisia; by scattered groups elsewhere in North Africa; and along the southern fringes of the Sahara Desert in western Africa. The Cushitic branch, confined to Ethiopia, Somalia, and the Red Sea coast, includes such major languages as Galla and Somali. The ancient Egyptian language (q.v.), which has no living descendant, was another branch of the Hamito-Semitic family (*see also* COPTIC LANGUAGE).

A number of languages spoken largely in northern Nigeria form another Hamito-Semitic grouping, known as the Chadic branch. By far the most important Chadic language is Hausa, one of the two most common languages of sub-Saharan Africa. Hausa is widely used in education and trade, even in regions far beyond its original borders. Several Hausa newspapers are published, and the body of Hausa literature is continually growing.

**The Nilo-Saharan Family.** The Nilo-Saharan languages are found in a broken chain from the great bend of the Niger River in West Africa to Ethiopia, throughout most of the upper Nile valley, and in parts of Uganda and Kenya. The westernmost member of this family is Songhai, spoken along much of the upper Niger River. The Saharan branch of this family includes the languages spoken in northeastern Nigeria, through the Republic of Chad to the east, and into the oasis settlements of Libya to the north. Although most of this area is sparsely populated, Kanuri, the major language of the Saharan branch, is spoken by about 1.5 million people.

Languages of the Chari-Nile branch are spoken in the northern part of Chad, in the Sudan, in much of Uganda and Kenya, and in the northeastern corner of the Congo. Along the Nile River near the southern border of Egypt and in scattered areas to the southwest are the Nubian languages, Chari-Nile languages spoken by about 1 million people. The Nubian alphabet was derived from that of the Coptic language. Nubian religious documents dating from the 8th to the 14th century form the only literature of a living African language that was written before the modern period. In the southern Sudan and in northern Uganda and Kenya a group of languages known as Nilotic belongs to this branch; important representatives are Dinka, Nuer, Shilluk, and Acholi (or Luo). Languages spoken farther to the southeast, including Masai in Kenya, have long been called Nilo-Hamitic; recent investigations, however, appear to prove that these tongues have no direct relationship to languages of the Hamito-Semitic family, but are most closely related to the Nilotic languages.

The very small Maban and Koman groups, and the single language Fur, also belong to the Nilo-Saharan family.

In many Nilo-Saharan languages, a system of noun suffixes indicates grammatical relationships; this system somewhat resembles the case system of Latin, but is quite unlike that of any other family of languages in Africa. In the northern Nilotic languages, similar grammatical relationships are expressed by an extremely complex system of internal vowel changes; many of the vowel sounds themselves are unusually difficult for the learner. Various verbal constructions are indicated by series of suffixes in some Nilo-Saharan languages (for example, Kanuri), or by both prefixes and suffixes in others (for example, the southern Nilotic languages). Many of these languages have a characteristic passive construction that is used much more freely than its counterpart in English. For example, "He bought cloth" is usually expressed as "Cloth was bought by him." This sentence can be shortened to "Cloth was bought." The action (buying) and the object (cloth) form the basic part of the sentence; the person who performed the action is comparatively unimportant.

**The Khoisan Family.** The Khoisan (or Click) languages comprise by all odds the smallest language family in Africa, with probably no more than 100,000 speakers altogether. Most of these languages are spoken by the Khoikhoi and San peoples of southern Africa; the largest of them is Nama, with about 25,000 speakers. Far to the northeast in Tanzania are two other representatives of this family: Sandawe, with about 23,000 speakers, and the much smaller Hadza. The Khoisan languages are best known for the unusual click consonants characteristic of most of them; in some Khoisan languages nearly every word begins with a click. The production of these sounds involves a sucking action of the tongue; by the positioning of the tongue and the way air is released into the mouth, distinctive kinds of clicks are produced. When these languages are written, the clicks are represented either by otherwise unused letters such as C, Q, X, or by special symbols such as /, !, //. Some of the Khoisan languages have a system of grammatical gender, which is found elsewhere in Africa only in the Hamito-Semitic family.

**The Niger-Kordofanian Family.** This family includes two subfamilies, Niger-Congo and Kordofanian. Of these, the Kordofanian languages number only about 30, all small; they are found in a small area of the Nuba hills in the southern Sudan, surrounded by languages of the Nilo-Saharan family and by Arabic. The Niger-Congo linguistic area, on the other hand, comprises almost all of the African continent below the Sahara Desert. Although migrations presumably separated certain branches of the Niger-Congo subfamily more than 5000 years ago, languages in each of the branches have similar words for many common objects and actions; the still more distantly related Kordofanian languages have a few such similar words and show some striking resemblances to the Niger-Congo languages in grammatical structure. In contrast to the small number of speakers in the Kordofanian subfamily, about three out of four African natives speak languages that belong to the Niger-Congo subfamily.

In this subfamily a relationship exists among most of the languages of southern and central Africa that has been recognized for more than a century. These languages have become widely known as Bantu (a word meaning "the people" in many languages of the group). Some of the more important Bantu languages are Zulu and Xhosa in South Africa; Makua in Mozambique; Nyanja in Malawi; Shona in Zimbabwe; Bemba in Zambia; Kimbundu and Umbundu in Angola; Swahili and Sukuma in Tanzania; Kikuyu in Kenya; Ganda in Uganda; Rwanda in Rwanda; Rundi in Burundi; Ngala and Kongo in the Congo and Zaire; and Fang and Bulu in Cameroon.

Some Bantu authors are now beginning to produce literature in their native languages.

The Bantu languages do not constitute a separate family, but should logically be grouped with certain languages of Nigeria, such as Tiv and Birom. All these languages together are classified as the Benue-Congo branch of the Niger-Congo subfamily. The Benue-Congo is by far the largest branch; the Bantu section alone numbers more speakers than all the rest of the Niger-Congo languages combined.

North of the Bantu language area, in the northern Congo and adjacent territory, is a second branch of the Niger-Congo subfamily, the Adamawa-Eastern branch. Its largest members are Zande and Ngbandi; a dialect of Ngbandi known as Sango is widely used as an intertribal language in the Central African Republic and is growing in importance.

From Nigeria west, five additional branches of the Niger-Congo subfamily, which have frequently been called West Sundanic languages, are found. A group of three or four closely related languages in the Niger delta, which together are known as Ijo, constitutes one of the five branches of the subfamily.

In a strip along the west coast from southeastern Nigeria to Liberia are found the languages of the Kwa branch. This branch includes such important languages as Efik, Igbo, and Yoruba in Nigeria; Ewe in Togo and Ghana; Fanti and Twi in Ghana; Anyi and Baule in Côte d'Ivoire; and Bassa and Kru in Liberia. Several of these languages are used in schools, and a small but growing body of published literature exists.

North of the Kwa language region, extending from western Nigeria into much of Côte d'Ivoire and Mali, are the languages of the Gur branch, including Moré in Burkina Faso, with about 2 million speakers.

Along the Atlantic coast, from Liberia to the desert north of Dakar, are several languages of the West Atlantic branch. These include Temne in Sierra Leone, Wolof in the vicinity of Dakar, and Fula (also known as Fulani, Fulfulde, or Peulh), by far the most widely spoken of the branch. The two large concentrations of Fulani-speaking people are located in Guinea and eastern Nigeria and Cameroon. Between these widely separated areas, Fulani-speaking people are spread out in numerous camps in which they raise cattle and sell meat, milk, and butter to neighboring tribes. Fulani is not, as has sometimes been thought, a Hamitic language.

Speakers of languages of the Mande branch inhabit most of the remaining portion of West Africa. One Mande language, known in various areas as Malinke, Maninka, Mandingo, Bambara, and Dyula, is spoken by some 3 million people from Senegal through much of Mali and northern Guinea and into northern Côte d'Ivoire. Other important Mande languages are Mende in Sierra Leone and Kpelle in Liberia. Small islands of Mande-language speakers are also scattered through areas farther east, as far as western Nigeria. The name Mandekan has recently been proposed as a name for the language as a whole and has gained substantial acceptance. The Mande languages are believed to be the oldest offshoots of the parent Niger-Congo language spoken more than 5000 years ago.

**Bantu Grammar.** The Bantu languages, now recognized as part of one branch of the Niger-Congo subfamily, have a system of noun classification that was formerly considered unique. In Swahili, a Bantu tongue, one group of nouns has a prefix *m* to indicate the singular and a prefix *wa* to indicate the plural; for example, *mtoto* ("a child"), *watoto* ("children"). Another group of nouns has a singular prefix *ki* and a plural prefix *vi;* for example, *kikapu* ("a basket"), *vikapu* ("baskets"). Words modifying a noun require corresponding prefixes; for example, *mtu mzuri* ("a good person"), *watu wazuri* ("good people"), *kikapu kizuri* ("a good basket"), *vikapu vizuri* ("good baskets"). Corresponding prefixes for some modifiers, and corresponding pronouns meaning "he," "she," "it," or "they," are not identical with the noun prefixes in all cases. Each set of prefixes and pronouns, whether singular or plural or neutral (such as the prefix *u* in *uhuru*, "freedom"), defines a class of nouns and its grammatical concords. A typical Bantu language may have from 12 to more than 20 noun classes.

Classification systems of the type described in the preceding paragraph are actually characteristic of languages belonging to all branches of the Niger-Congo subfamily except the Mande branch, and also of languages in the Kordofanian subfamily; this type of system was presumably present in the parent Niger-Kordofanian language thousands of years ago. Some languages of the Gur branch indicate the noun class by both prefix and suffix, and others by suffix only, but all have separate pronouns for each class, as do the Bantu languages. Many of the Kwa languages have noun prefixes, but no other characteristics of a class system. Some striking similarities are found throughout the Niger-Congo subfamily: for example, a class indicator such as *m* with words for oil, water, and other liquids.

Although grammatical structure among the Niger-Kordofanian languages varies considerably, in general these tongues emphasize the kind of action referred to (grammatical aspect), or the attitude toward the action (mode), rather than the time of the action (tense). Different constructions may indicate customary action ("He laughs all the time"), potential action ("He is likely to get sick"), experiential action ("He has met the chief"), hortative attitude ("He should go"), desiderative attitude ("If only he would come"), and so on. In many languages, the only construction referring primarily to time is one for the past tense. Such constructions, for which English often uses long phrases, are distinguished in Niger-Kordofanian languages by a single prefix, suffix, or particle, or even by a slight modification of a pronoun or verb form. On the other hand, passive constructions are rare or nonexistent in the non-Bantu languages of this family. Prepositions are also rare; ideas of motion ("to, from, up") are typically incorporated in verbs, while ideas of location ("under, beside, in") are typically incorporated in nouns.

**Tonality.** With few exceptions, the languages of the Nilo-Saharan, Niger-Kordofanian, and Khoisan families, as well as the Chadic languages and a few of the Cushitic languages in the Hamito-Semitic family, are tone languages—that is, distinctions in the pitch of a single syllable may differentiate completely different words or different grammatical functions of a word or of a prefix or suffix. For example, in a dialect of Jukun, a language of Nigeria, *kwī* with a high pitch means "knife," *kwī* with an intermediate pitch means "millstone," and *kwī* with a low pitch means "chicken." In the same dialect, *ku bi* with both syllables on an intermediate pitch means "He came," but *ku bi* with the first syllable on a high pitch means "Have him come." In scores of Niger-Congo languages, different pronouns may differ only in pitch. Distinctions in pitch or tone have generally been ignored in writing, although they are often crucial to understanding what the writer intended to say; tone is indicated by accent marks or other devices in only a relatively few modern grammars and dictionaries of African languages.

**Other Language Families.** Two other language families, Indo-European and Malayo-Polynesian, are represented to some degree in Africa. The former group includes Afrikaans and English, both native to many people in the Republic of South Africa and Zimbabwe. English is also indigenous to Liberia, having been introduced there by repatriated American blacks in the 19th century. Malagasy, the language of the island of Madagascar, is a member of the Malayo-Polynesian group.

Before 1959, academic involvement in African language studies was confined to a very few universities in England and Europe. Since then, a number of American universities, as well as the Foreign Service Institute of the U.S. Department of State, have begun teaching and research programs focused on African languages. With less emphasis on the implications of scientific linguistics for teaching and research, a number of other universities, colleges, and even high schools offer practical instruction in a single African language, usually Swahili.                    W.E.W.

*For further information on this topic, see the Bibliography in volume 28, sections 351, 856.*

**AFRICAN LITERATURE,** oral and written literature of the continent of Africa, not necessarily in the languages indigenous to Africa.

**Oral Literature.** Africa has a rich and varied oral literature, which has grown since the beginnings of African societies and continues to flourish today. The written literature of Africa has always shown a debt to the oral literature, which takes a variety of forms. Proverbs and riddles convey the accepted social codes of conduct, while myths and legends teach a belief in the supernatural as well as explain the origins and development of states, clans, and other important social organizations. Legends and myths are usually regarded as grounded in fact; in many instances, they have proved to be extremely accurate accounts of the history of a people. Folktales, on the other hand, are recognized as fiction. The most famous African folktales feature the tortoise, hare, and spider. Similar folktales are widespread on the continent and have been carried from Africa to the Caribbean, Latin America, and the U.S.

In the 20th century, largely through the efforts of anthropologists and historians, a good portion of the oral literature of certain areas, such as southern Africa, the regions formerly known as Ruanda and Buganda, and parts of the Congo region, have been recorded.

**Early Written Literature.** The earliest written African literature is North African. North African life and thought, however, have been more closely tied to that of Europe and the Middle East than to that of the rest of Africa. Therefore the early literature of Africa north of the Sahara, such as the works of the early Christian theologian St. Augustine and the 14th-century Islamic historian Ibn Khaldun, is more closely akin to Latin and Arabic literature.

Much of the early written literature of West Africa was influenced by Islamic writings, as transmitted by North Africans, in both form and content. The earliest known West African works were 16th-century writings by such Sudanese Islamic scholars as Abd al-Rahman al-Sadi (1596–

c. 1655), the author of *Tarikh as-Sudan* (History of the Sudan), and Mahmud Kati (1468?–1570?), who wrote *Tarikh al-Fettach.* These works set down the oral traditions of the western Sudanic empires of Ghana, Mali, and Songhai in the style of Arabic histories.

The earliest West African written poetry tended to be religious, and the best of it reflected a familiarity with pre-Islamic Arabic poetry as well as North African religious writing. Perhaps the most famous West African religious poet was Abdullah ibn Muhammed Fudi (1767–1828), emir of Gwandu and brother of the Muslim reformer Shedu Uthman (c. 1754–1817).

The written literature of East Africa has an equally long history and also shows the influence of Arabic models. An anonymous history of the city-state of Kilwa Kisiwani, written about 1520 in Arabic, is the earliest known example of East African written literature. Written Swahili versions of the histories of a number of city-states as well as "message" poems, usually written with a moral or religious point of view, soon began to appear. The earliest known original Swahili work, the epic poem *Utendi wa Tambuka* (Story of Tambuka), is dated 1728.

Swahili poetry was largely derived from Arabic poetry. Swahili writers of epic verse borrowed from the romantic traditions surrounding the Prophet Muhammad and then freely elaborated on them to meet the tastes of their listeners and readers. By the 19th century, Swahili poetry had gone beyond Arabic themes and taken up such indigenous Bantu forms as ritual songs.

The most famous Swahili poems date from the 19th and 20th centuries. The greatest religious poem, *Utendi wa Inkishafi* (Soul's Awakening), written by Sayyid Abdallah bin Nasir (c. 1720–1810), illustrates the vanity of earthly life through an account of the fall of the city-state of Pate. The oral tradition of Liyongo, a 13th-century contender for the throne of Shagga, is preserved in the epic poem *Utendi wa Liyongo Fumo* (Epic of Liyongo Fumo), written by Muhammad bin Abubakar in 1913.

Although the Sudanic areas of West Africa and the coastal areas of East Africa had a rich written literature predating contact with Europeans, the literature of the rest of sub-Saharan Africa remained oral until the establishment of European mission and government schools.

Among the first Africans to write in English was Olaudah Equiano (c. 1750–97), who was kidnapped as a child from the Benin region of Nigeria and shipped to the U.S. as a slave. As a free man in Great Britain, he wrote an autobiography (1789) under the pseudonym of Gustavus Vassa.

**Contemporary Literature.** Near the beginning of the 20th century, Africans began to publish creative writings in a number of African and European languages. There have been relatively fewer new African writers since the mid-1970s because of the increased involvement of intellectuals in political and academic concerns.

***South Africa.*** In South Africa a number of skilled poets and novelists appeared. Samuel E. K. Mqhayi (1875–1945) wrote extensively in Xhosa and showed its strength as a medium for written literature. Novelists such as Thomas Mofolo (1877–1948) and Solomon T. Plaatje (1877–1932), provoked by the indignities suffered by black South Africans at the hands of white Africans, sought to portray black Africans as complex, moral human beings. Mofolo's third novel, *Chaka the Zulu* (1925; trans. 1931), is a fictional treatment of Shaka, a 19th-century Zulu warlord. Written in Mofolo's native Sotho, the book is considered a classic in that language. Plaatje's novel *Mhudi,* a historical romance about Shaka's lieutenant Mzilikazi (c. 1790–1868), was published in 1930. Plaatje's style, which incorporates praise songs, is in the tradition of Bantu oral literature.

In the mid-20th century many black South African writers left their homes because of government policies. Among those emigrants were Peter Abrahams and Ezekiel Mphahlele (1919–  ). *Tell Freedom* (1954), an autobiography, is considered Abrahams's best work; in it he writes of the racial oppression he suffered as a child in Johannesburg. Mphahlele is a major critic of black African literature. In his work *The African Image* (1962), he discusses both black

*Thomas Mofolo, South Africa.*

Peter Abrahams, South Africa.    Granger Collection

Chinua Achebe, Nigeria    Nigerian Ministry of Information

and white African literature; he deplores its obsession with race relations and calls for a broader and deeper treatment of characters from other points of view. Other noted writers are A. C. Jordan (1906–68), writing in Xhosa, and the Zulu poet R. R. R. Dhlomo (1901–  ). Prose writers Alex La Guma (1925–85) and Bloke Modisane (1923–  ) and playwright and critic Lewis Nkosi (1936–  ) earned recognition after 1950. Dennis Brutus (1924–  ) is a prominent black South African poet. His most famous work, *Sirens Knuckles Boots,* depicts the effects of racial repression on everyday life.

White South Africans have a long tradition of creative writing, both in Afrikaans and in English. Writers in Afrikaans have included poets such as D. J. Opperman (1914–  ) and Breyten Breytenbach (1939–  ), who is considered one of the finest writers in the language; and several novelists concerned particularly with the effects of the apartheid policy, for example, J. M. Coetzee (1940–  ), author of *The Life and Times of Michael K.* (1984). Among writers in English is Olive Schreiner (1855–1920), whose novel *The Story of an African Farm* (1883) is regarded as a classic for its pioneering exploration of relations between the races and between the sexes. The effects of South African racial policy on private lives are reflected in the works of a number of internationally known 20th-century writers in English. These include the novelists Alan Paton and Doris Lessing, the short-story writer Nadine Gordimer (1923–  ), and South Africa's foremost playwright, Athol Fugard. Fugard's plays, such as *The Blood Knot* (1961),

*Boesman and Lena* (1969), and *Master Harold . . . & the Boys* (1982), openly defy government policies. Breytenbach, formerly a supporter of Afrikaner nationalism, wrote *The Confessions of an Albino Terrorist* (1985) in English; in exile in Paris, he renounced his native language. The book is an unflinching exploration of the effects of his seven years in South African prisons on charges of terrorism.

**West Africa.** Poetry has been the dominant literary form among Africans writing in French. Léopold Sédar Senghor, the poet-president of Senegal, led the *Négritude* movement, which was extremely influential in shaping the thinking of French-speaking intellectuals. *Négritude,* which reached its height in the 1930s and '40s, was a protest against the French policy of assimilation and a reassertion of the positive values of African culture. Birago Diop (1906–89) and David Diop (1927–60), both poets, were also associated with the movement.

Only a few West African novelists produced works in French. These writers have, however, been among the most talented on the continent. Camara Laye (1928–80) of Guinea was remarkable for the psychological insights of his novels. His autobiographical novel *The Dark Child* (1953; trans. 1954) is considered a masterpiece. Cameroon has produced two novelists, Mongo Beti (1932–  ) and Ferdinand Oyono (1929–  ), who have written extremely powerful and searching satire.

West Africans writing in English produced little of note until the 1940s. Since then, however, an impressive body of literature has been cre-

*Wole Soyinka, Nigeria.*                © J. Langevin–Sygma

ated. Nigeria in particular has many writers, of whom Amos Tutuola (1920– ) and Chinua Achebe are the most important. Tutuola became internationally known after publication of *The Palm-Wine Drinkard* (1952). Written as legend and myth, it has been compared by English critics with the 17th-century allegory *The Pilgrim's Progress* by the English writer John Bunyan. Achebe examined Western civilization's threat to traditional values in his early novel *Things Fall Apart* (1958). *A Man of the People* (1966) is a political satire on corruption in an unnamed African country. The Nigerian poet-dramatist Wole Soyinka, who was awarded the 1986 Nobel Prize in literature, writes in English but draws inspiration from Yoruba myths. An outspoken critic of Nigeria's military regime, he has produced a considerable body of poetry; plays such as *Death and the King's Horseman* (1975); and the novel *The Interpreters* (1965), a satirical analysis of modern Nigeria and its ancient traditions. Ijaw (Nigerian) myths and social situations have been used in a provocative way by the Nigerian poet and playwright John Pepper Clark (1935– ). The Nigerian poet Gabriel Okara (1921– ) wrote *The Voice,* one of the few African novels to concentrate exclusively on African characters and values. Sierra Leone's best-known novelist is William Conton (1925– ). His *African* (1960), about a young African who has been educated in England, accentuates cultural differences.

Ghana's Kofi Awoonor (1935– ) is considered one of Africa's most exciting poets. His works treat the conflicts of life and the ominous presence of death. Ayi Kwei Armah (1939– ), a Ghanaian novelist, depicted the end of the regime of Ghana's president Kwame Nkrumah in the novel *The Beautiful Ones Are Not Yet Born* (1968).

**East Africa.** Contemporary literature of East Africa includes important autobiographical works, such as those of Kenyans Josiah Kariuki (1929–75), who wrote *Mau Mau Detainee* (1963), and R. Mugo Gatheru (1925– ), who wrote *Child of Two Worlds* (1964). A younger Kenyan, James Ngugi (1938– ), is the author of several short stories and novels and one play. His works deal with the impact of Christianity on African life and are remarkable for their clarity and simplicity of writing. Jean Joseph Rabéarivelo (1901–37) of Madagascar wrote in French and is considered one of the greatest African poets. After modeling his earlier poems on French symbolist writings, Rabéarivelo turned to a brilliant use of the vernacular ballad form of Madagascar. Shaaban Robert (1909–62) of Tanganyika (now Tanzania) was East Africa's leading Swahili poet and essayist. His best-known work, *Kusadikika* (To Be Believed, 1951), examines political trends in Tanganyika. The work is an allegory patterned on *Gulliver's Travels,* an 18th-century work by the British writer Jonathan Swift. One of the most widely read works in East Africa, however, remains Shakespeare's *Julius Caesar* as translated into Swahili in 1966 by Tanzania's then president, Julius Nyerere.                J.T.Sa. & W.E.W.

*For further information on this topic, see the Bibliography in volume 28, section 856.*

**AFRICAN METHODIST EPISCOPAL CHURCH,** Protestant denomination organized in Philadelphia in 1816. On matters of doctrine and polity the denomination is in basic agreement with the Methodist church. A quadrennial General Conference is the chief policymaking body, and spiritual jurisdiction is exercised by a Council of Bishops. The church has 18 episcopal districts, including 4 in Africa. In addition to missionary activity within the U.S., the denomination maintains missions in Africa, South America, and the Virgin Islands. Its periodicals include the *A.M.E. Review* and the *Voice of Missions.*

The first congregation of what later became the African Methodist Episcopal Church was formed in 1787 by a group of black parishioners of Saint George's Church in Philadelphia. Led by the itinerant preacher and former slave Richard Allen, they withdrew from the church in protest against racial prejudice. The seceding group held religious services in a rented storeroom. Similar congregations of blacks were subsequently formed in the city, and in 1816 Allen, who had become a prominent Methodist preacher, took the lead in organizing the groups into a separate denomination, the African Methodist Episcopal Church. Elected the first bishop, he was ordained by the Anglo-American bishop Francis Asbury of the Methodist Episcopal Church. Immediately after the American Civil War, the denomination sent missionaries into the South. Largely through their labors, the membership increased in ten years from 70,000 to 390,000.

According to the latest available figures, the African Methodist Episcopal Church has more than 1,970,000 members and about 3050 separate congregations. It is the second largest Methodist denomination in the U.S.

**AFRICAN METHODIST EPISCOPAL ZION CHURCH,** Protestant denomination founded in New York City by a group of black congregations formerly belonging to the Methodist Episcopal Church. Its doctrine and polity are basically Methodist, and its chief policymaking body is the quadrennial General Conference. A bishop presides over each of the 12 episcopal areas.

In addition to missionary activity within the U.S., the church maintains missions in Africa, the West Indies, and South America. Publications include *Star of Zion,* the *Quarterly Review,* and *Missionary Seer.*

In 1796, a group of black parishioners of the John Street Methodist Episcopal Church in New York City, discontented over the smallness of their role in the management of church affairs, organized a separate congregation with the approval of the Anglo-American bishop Francis Asbury of the Methodist Episcopal Church. The group continued to meet in the John Street church until 1800, when they erected their own building, which they called Zion. In 1820 the group formally withdrew from the Methodist Episcopal Church, and in 1821, together with congregations from Connecticut, New Jersey, and Pennsylvania, held their annual conference at which James Varick (1750?–1828), leader of the original dissenters, was elected the first bishop. It was not until 1848, however, that the name African Methodist Episcopal Zion Church was adopted.

This movement spread rapidly throughout the northern states, but its major growth followed the end of the American Civil War; between 1866 and 1868 its membership increased fourfold the new recruits being largely southern blacks.

According to recent estimates the denomination has 1,125,000 members and 6020 separate congregations. The African Methodist Episcopal Zion Church is the third largest Methodist organization in the U.S.

**AFRICAN MUSIC AND DANCE,** indigenous African musical and dance expressions that are maintained by oral tradition and that are stylistically distinct from the music and dance of both the Arabic cultures of North Africa and the Western settler populations of southern Africa. African music and dance, therefore, are cultivated largely by societies in sub-Saharan Africa.

**Music.** In the precolonial period, trade, wars, migrations, and religion stimulated interaction among sub-Saharan societies, encouraging them to borrow musical resources from one another, including peoples exposed to Islamic and Arabic culture, who had integrated some Arabic instruments and techniques into their traditional music. Some usages became concentrated in particular culture areas, whereas others were widely distributed. Thus, the savanna belt of West Africa forms a music area distinct from the Guinea Coast because of its virtuosic instrumental styles and the presence of a class of professional praise singers, or griots, in that area. Similarly, the music of East Africa is distinguished from that of Central Africa by a number of instruments, and from that of southern Africa, which traditionally emphasizes certain kinds of choral organization and complex forms of musical bows.

Many features nevertheless unite the sub-Saharan musical traditions. Everywhere, music and dance are integrated into economic and political activities, life-cycle ceremonies, ancestral rites, and worship, as well as domestic life and recreation. On some occasions everyone may participate. In other instances, participation is restricted to particular social groups who perform their own kind of music, led by musician-specialists. Such specialists may also perform on their own, either individually or in small ensembles.

**Song.** All sub-Saharan traditions emphasize singing, because song is used as an avenue of communication. Because many African languages are "tone languages," in which pitch level determines meaning, the melodies and rhythms of songs generally follow the intonation contour and rhythms of the song texts. Melodies are usually organized within a scale of four, five, six, or seven tones. In group singing, some societies habitually sing in unison or in parallel octaves with sporadic fourths or fifths; others sing in two or three parts, using parallel thirds or fourths. Songs generally are in call-and-response form.

***Musical instruments.*** The musical instruments of sub-Saharan Africa include a wide variety of resonant solids (idiophones) such as rattles,

One of the masked dancers in the daylong Makishi ritual dance of Zambia, which celebrates a collective circumcision. Musicians in the background include hand clappers, drummers, and a xylophone player. Marc & Evelyne Bernheim–Woodfin Camp & Associates

bells, stamping tubes, the *mbira* (thumb piano), and the xylophone. Parchment-head drums (membranophones) are found in many forms, such as goblet drums; kettledrums; cylindrical, semicylindrical, and barrel-shaped drums; and hourglass drums with variable-tension heads. Among wind instruments (aerophones) are flutes made of bamboo, millet, reed, or the tips of animal horns and gourds; ocarinas; panpipes; horns (made from elephant tusks or animal horns) and trumpets (made of wood, sections of gourd, or metal tubes); single-reed pipes made from millet stalks; and double-reed pipes adopted from Arabic culture. Stringed instruments (chordophones) include musical bows, zithers, bowed and plucked lutes, harp-lutes, arched harps, and lyres. Body percussion is also exploited, the most common being handclapping and foot stamping.

In selecting any instrument for music making or communication, consideration is given to its melodic and rhythmic capacities, its evocative or dramatic power, or its symbolic references. The tuning systems, scales, and rhythms associated with instruments tend to be more complex than those of songs. Rhythm patterns in one line or several simultaneous lines may interlock, overlap, or form polyrhythmic structures. Such structures may utilize cross-rhythms or alternate double and triple rhythms in linear patterns.

**Dance.** African traditions also greatly emphasize dance, for movement is regarded as an important mode of communication. For this purpose the dance utilizes symbolic gestures, mime, props, masks, costumes, body painting, and other visual devices. The basic movements may be simple, emphasizing the upper body, torso, or feet; or they may be complex, involving coordination of different body parts and intricate actions such as fast rotation, ripples of the body, and contraction and release, as well as variations in dynamics, levels, and use of space. The dance may be open to all, or it may be an activity in which one, two, three, or four individuals (regardless of sex) take turns in the dancing ring. Team dances also occur. The formations may be linear, circular, serpentine, or columns of two or more rows.

**Modern Trends.** With urbanization and the impact of Western culture, traditional music and dance, although still practiced, have decreased. New idioms have emerged, however, that combine African and Western elements; they include West African highlife (showing certain Caribbean traits), Congolese popular music (reflecting Latin American influence), and in southern Africa, sabasaba and kwella (both akin to U.S. swing and jive music). Evidence suggests that the needs of the church and other transplanted institutions may stimulate a new art music. Traditional music and dance face serious threat of decline. Because of their political and cultural importance, however, their preservation is given special attention in many countries.                          J.H.K.N.

*For further information on this topic, see the Bibliography in volume 28, sections 725, 729.*

**AFRICAN UNITY, ORGANIZATION OF.** *See* ORGANIZATION OF AFRICAN UNITY.

**AFRICANUS, Sextus Julius** (160?–232?), early Christian historian and traveler, born in Libya. He is known for estimating the date of the creation in the *Chronographiæ,* a history of the world from the creation to AD 221. He set the creation 5499 years before the birth of Christ and dated Christ's birth three years earlier than the usual reckoning. His estimates were adopted by most of the Eastern churches. Only fragments of the *Chronographiæ* are extant.

*The drum unifies the African musical ensemble, providing basic rhythm, signaling changes of tempo, and developing rhythm patterns.*                          UPI

**AFRICAN VIOLET,** common name for flowering plants of the genus *Saintpaulia,* often grown as houseplants. Unrelated to violets, they are members of the family Gesneriaceae (*see* FIGWORT), which also contains gloxinia, but their petals are shaped like those of violets and are often violet in color. The genus contains about 20 species of small, hairy, herbaceous perennials with clusters of long-stalked, fleshy leaves at the base. The flowers are borne on loosely branched stalks that rise from between the leaves. All are native to the mountains of Tanzania and Kenya in East Africa, and most are cultivated. The common African violet is *S. ionantha;* numerous cultivars, including double-flowered forms and many color variations, have been developed from it.

**AFRIDI,** tribe of North-West Frontier Province, Pakistan, inhabiting the Afghan-Pakistan border region, a mountainous area that contains the Khyber Pass. The tribe is related linguistically and ethnologically to the Pathans, a people of Afghanistan and Pakistan.

**AFRIKAANS,** one of the two official languages of South Africa. Afrikaans, or Cape Dutch, is principally derived from the South Holland dialect of mid-17th-century Dutch settlers in South Africa. It gained loan-words from English, French, and German (through settlers) and from African languages and underwent grammatical simplification (for example, verb tense endings were dropped). Phonetic changes also occurred: *sch-* became *sk-* (Dutch *schoen;* Afrik. *skoen,* "shoes"), final *t* was lost after some consonants, and so forth. Until the mid-19th century Afrikaans was a spoken language only; Standard Dutch was used for writing. A movement then arose to make Afrikaans a literary language. It was gradually used in newspapers, schools, and churches, and in 1925 it officially replaced Standard Dutch.

**AFRIKANERS.** *See* BOERS; SOUTH AFRICA, REPUBLIC OF.

**AFRO-AMERICAN MUSIC,** music of the African natives sold into slavery in the Americas, and of their descendants. Early Afro-American music in the U.S. accommodated African musical practices with the vocabulary and structures of Euro-American music. Comprising work songs, calls, field and street cries, hollers, rhyme songs, and spirituals, this music provided the slaves with a means of effectively pacing their work, with a form of sung prayer and praise, with a means of surreptitious intragroup communication, and with psychic relief from the degradation of bondage. Many of the work songs used the African call-and-response form; a lead singer gave the line of melody and the others joined in for the refrain. This pattern, as well as a number of actual African tunes, was also carried over into the Afro-American spiritual (q.v.). Both the spiritual and the later blues (q.v.), a form of secular solo folk song, incorporated the African freedom to improvise variations in the melodic line. Also derived from African heritage was polyrhythmic drumming, simultaneously combining several different rhythmic patterns of different meters. The interplay of contrasting rhythms was eventually carried over into jazz (q.v.).

Although sacred music—the spiritual—was the most ubiquitous Afro-American music in the early 19th century, secular music also existed. Like the spirituals, the work songs, calls, and cries were performed a cappella; other secular songs were accompanied by instruments. The earliest slave instruments included drums and an African transplant, the banjo (q.v.); later, flute, violin, and guitar were also used. Guitar, violin, and banjo often constituted the string bands that provided music for the Afro- and Euro-American social dances of the 19th century—jigs, reels, the buck-and-wing, cotillions, and quadrilles. Makeshift instruments such as quills, gutbuckets (bass fiddles made from washtubs), and jugs were also used in string bands.

**Jazz and Its Predecessors.** Following the American Civil War, rhyme songs and ballads became plentiful, and the blues began to take on its modern forms. The music of the black minstrel shows, the string bands, the brass bands, and the honky-tonk pianos began to assert itself, and such genres as the cakewalk and ragtime gradually emerged. Having originated in the southern and midwestern U.S., ragtime reached its classic form in the 1890s in the St. Louis, Mo., school of ragtime pianists led by Scott Joplin. In the first decade of the 20th century, the musical practices of black Americans syncretized to form a new American music called jazz. It first flourished in New Orleans, La., then spread to cities all across the country. Among the most important jazz innovators in the first half of the 20th century were Louis Armstrong, Fletcher Henderson, Billie Holiday, Duke Ellington, and Dizzy Gillespie.

**Mid-20th Century.** In the 1940s, rhythm and blues emerged as a combined product of rural blues and black-oriented, big-band swing music, performed by small ensembles with a lead vocalist or instrumentalist and rhythm and backup sections. The pioneers and popularizers of it included T-Bone Walker (1910?–75), Little Walter (1930–68), Louis Jordan (1908–75), Fats Domino (1928– ), James Brown (1928– ), Ray Charles, and Ruth Brown (1928– ). Since the 1950s rhythm and blues has been the generic source of black music, as well as of American pop music.

Soul music was a further development of rhythm and blues. Essentially, it combines the rhythm-and-blues sound of the 1950s with techniques, effects, and performance practices borrowed from black gospel music (q.v.). It has two main substyles: the polished, sophisticated Detroit style, featuring such artists as Stevie Wonder (1950– ), The Supremes, and The Temptations; and the earthier, more gospel-oriented Memphis, Tenn., style, exemplified by Otis Redding (1941–67) and by Booker T. (Jones; 1944– ) and the MG's. Black gospel music had its beginnings in the black Holiness churches and in the published songs of the Philadelphia minister Charles A. Tindley (1851–1933). Using the resources of work songs, hollers, cries, spirituals, blues, and jazz, black gospel music was fully developed by both the hymnodist-composer Thomas A. Dorsey (1899–1992) and the singer Roberta Martin (1907–69). Famous performers of gospel music include Mahalia Jackson, James Cleveland (1931–91), and Andrae Crouch (1942– ) and the Disciples.

In the 1970s a new musical form called *rap*, or *rapping*, arose on the streets of New York City. The Sugar Hill Gang's "Rapper's Delight" (1979) was the first rap hit record. Using bits of funk and hard rock records, plus a miscellany of sounds, as background, rap performers chanted often-complicated rhyming couplets, generally about ghetto life. In the 1980s the music spread across the U.S. as young audiences responded to the rap performers' angry words about social injustice, racism, and drug abuse. Late in the decade and into the early 1990s controversy surrounded some artists accused of rapping racially and sexually inflammatory lyrics.

**Latin American Influence.** The relationship of Latin American music to black music in the U.S. is most evident in the offbeat accents that are common in both. Between 1900 and 1940, Latin American dances—the tango (Argentina), the merengue (Dominican Republic), and the rumba (Cuba)—were all introduced into the U.S. In the 1940s a fusion of Latin and jazz elements began; it was stimulated by the Afro-Cuban mambo and the Brazilian bossa nova. The late 1960s brought a mingling of Latin and soul music—notably by Mongo Santamaria (1927– ) and Willie Bobo (1934–83)—and the recognition of the Cuban-Puerto Rican salsa as an important genre. Reversing the direction of influence, Afro-American music of the U.S. also affected musical fusions in the Caribbean, Latin America, and Africa, giving rise to the Jamaican reggae and its predecessors, ska, rocksteady, and the African highlife.

**Concert and Recital Music.** Afro-Americans have also long contributed as composers and performers to North and South American concert and recital music in the European tradition (*see* BLACKS IN THE AMERICAS). S.A.F.

*See also* POPULAR MUSIC; ROCK MUSIC.

*For further information on this topic, see the Bibliography in volume 28,* sections 725, 729, 739, 742.

**AGADIR,** city, W Morocco, seaport on the Atlantic Ocean. It is situated within a mining region; cobalt, lead, manganese, and zinc are shipped by way of the excellent natural harbor of the city. The chief industries in Agadir are fishing, fish canning, and the manufacture of light metal products. An international airport is located near the city. Agadir was founded as a Portuguese settlement around 1500 and came under Moroccan rule about 1536. In 1911, at the height of the controversy caused by Franco-German rivalry in Morocco, Germany sent the warship *Panther* to Agadir. The incident, which nearly precipitated a general European war, led to the establishment of a French protectorate in Morocco in 1912. In 1960 Agadir was devastated by two earthquakes; about 12,000 persons died. Rebuilding of the city was begun shortly thereafter. Pop. (1990 est.) 779,000.

**AGA KHAN,** real name HASAN ALI SHAH (1800–81), believed to be a descendant of the Prophet Muhammad. Aga Khan was governor of the province of Kerman, Iran, until 1840, when he fled to India after an unsuccessful attempt to seize power in Iran. He helped the British government in India in its attempts to control frontier tribes. Aga Khan became leader of the Ismailis, a sect of Shiite Muslims, in India, Pakistan, Africa, and Syria.

**AGA KHAN II,** real name ALI SHAH (1831–85), son of Aga Khan, served as leader of the Ismaili sect for four years after the death of his father. His reign also emphasized close ties with the British government in India.

**AGA KHAN III,** real name AGA SULTAN SIR MAHOMED SHAH (1877–1957), son of Aga Khan II, born in Karachi, India (now in Pakistan), and educated in Europe. He became head of the Ismaili sect in 1885 after the death of his father, and during World War I he persuaded his followers and other Muslims to side with the Allies. In 1932 and from 1934 to 1937, he headed the Indian delegation to the Assembly of the League of Nations. He was a noted sportsman, and his extreme wealth enabled him to maintain the most valuable racing stables in the world before World War II. He also contributed generously to the Aligarh Muslim University in India. He wrote *India in Transition* (1918) and *Memoirs* (1954).

**AGA KHAN IV,** real name KARIM AL HUSSAINI SHAH (1936– ), grandson of Aga Khan III, born in Geneva, and educated in Switzerland and at Harvard University. Aga Khan III nominated his grandson to head the Ismaili sect, rather than a son, in the conviction that the Aga Khan should be "a young man brought up in the midst of the new age."

**AGAMEMNON,** in Greek mythology, king of Mycenae and commander of the Greek forces in the Trojan War. He was the son of Atreus and suffered the curse laid on his house. When the Greeks had assembled in Aulis for their voyage to Troy they were held back by adverse winds. To calm the winds, Agamemnon sacrificed his daughter Iphigenia to the goddess Artemis. His quarrel with Achilles over the captive princess Briseis and the consequences of that quarrel form much of the plot of Homer's *Iliad*. After a 10-year siege, Troy fell and Agamemnon returned in triumph to Mycenae. With him came the Trojan princess Cassandra, who had been awarded to him by the victorious Greek army.

Clytemnestra, Agamemnon's wife, greeted him with protestations of love, but while he was in his bath she threw a net over him. Her lover Aegisthus struck Agamemnon with a sword and while he was stunned from the blow, Clytemnestra beheaded him with an ax. His death was avenged seven years later by his son Orestes. The story of Agamemnon's death is told in the first play of the trilogy *Oresteia,* by the ancient Greek poet Aeschylus.

**AGANA,** town, U.S. unincorporated Territory of Guam, capital of the territory, on the W coast of Guam island, near Apra Harbor. The town was totally destroyed in World War II during the American reconquest of Guam from the Japanese in 1944. Reconstruction began in 1946 with appropriations from the U.S. government. Pop. (1980) 881; (1990) 1139.

**AGAR,** gel-forming colloidal material of widespread commercial use, found in the cell wall of several species of red algae (q.v.), especially Oriental members of the genus *Gelidium*. It is used as a solidifying agent in the preparation of candies, creams and lotions, and canned fish and meat; as a texturizer or emulsifier in ice cream and frozen desserts; as a clarifying agent in winemaking and brewing; and as a sizing material in fabrics. It is an excellent laboratory medium for growing bacteria, because it is not dissolved by salts or consumed by most microorganisms.

Agar is extracted from seaweed by boiling, and is cooled and dried and sold as flakes or cakes. Originally called agar-agar, a Malay word for a local seaweed, it was produced in the Far East but is now made in other Pacific coastal regions such as California and Australia.

**AGARIC.** *See* MUSHROOM.

**AGASSIZ, Alexander** (1835–1910), American zoologist, son of Louis Agassiz, born in Neuchâtel, Switzerland, and educated at Harvard University. He became curator of the Museum of Comparative Zoology at Harvard in 1873 and held the post until 1885, when poor health forced him to resign. As administrator of the Calumet and Hecla copper mines on Lake Superior (1865–69) and as a stockholder in the mines, Agassiz acquired a fortune. His gifts to the Harvard Museum of Comparative Zoology and to other institutions for biological research totaled over $1 million. In 1874–75 he explored Lake Titicaca, between Bolivia and Peru, and in 1875 established an aquarium at Newport, R.I. From 1877 to 1904 he made annual expeditions to study the marine life of the western Atlantic and the Pacific oceans. He was an authority on jellyfish, echinoderms, and corals.                                    N.E.M.

**AGASSIZ, LAKE,** immense glacial lake that formerly covered much of present-day NW Minnesota and N North Dakota and SW Ontario and S Manitoba. The lake existed in the Pleistocene epoch and was named in 1879 in honor of the naturalist Louis Agassiz. The historic existence of Lake Agassiz is indicated by deltas, created where former rivers flowed into the lake, and by well-marked shorelines that can be traced for long distances. Lake Agassiz discharged only relatively small amounts of water because its natural drainage toward the N was held back by the great Laurentide Ice Sheet. The outflow went through a channel 80 km (50 mi) long from the S end of the lake to the Minnesota R. and on to the Mississippi R. Because it retained so much water, the lake became very large; at its greatest extent it was about 1130 km (about 702 mi) long and covered about 284,900 sq km (about 110,000 sq mi). Lake Agassiz contracted drastically when the ice sheet melted sufficiently for an outlet to flow N via a channel (now the Nelson R.) to Hudson Bay. Lake of the Woods and Lakes Winnipeg, Winnipegosis, and Manitoba remain as remnants of Lake Agassiz. Most of the former bed of Lake Agassiz is now a fertile plain where much grain is produced.

**AGASSIZ, (Jean) Louis Rodolphe** (1807–73), Swiss-American naturalist, one of the best informed and most capable biologists of his day, with an ability to awaken the public's interest in natural science.

Born in Motiers, Agassiz was educated at the universities of Zürich, Heidelberg, Erlangen, and Munich. In 1826 he prepared a description of Brazilian fish from materials collected by the Bavarian naturalist Johann Baptist von Spix (1781–1826); the work attracted the notice of the French naturalist Georges Cuvier, with whom Agassiz later studied in Paris. From 1832 to 1846 Agassiz was professor of natural history at the University of Neuchâtel. During this time he prepared and published *Researches on Fossil Fishes* (1833–44, 5 vol., 311 plates) and *Studies on Glaciers* (1840). As a result of his observations in the Swiss Alps, he introduced the theory that at one time most of the earth was covered by glaciers—a glacial epoch. In 1846 Agassiz delivered a course of lectures at Lowell Institute, Boston, which resulted in his appointment in 1848 as professor of natural history in the Lawrence Scientific School of Harvard University. Although his later life was given to lecturing and exploration rather than to teaching, he held this position until his death.

In opposition to the Darwinian theory of evolution, Agassiz believed in a theory of epochs of creation. His explorations in the U.S. included the Lake Superior region (1848) and the Florida coral reefs (1850–51). From 1865 to 1866 he traveled in Brazil; the results of his research there were published under the title *A Journey in Brazil* (1868). In 1872 Agassiz made a journey to California, sailing around Cape Horn, and in the following year he established a summer school of zoology on Penikese Island, Buzzards Bay, Mass.
                                    N.E.M.

**AGATE,** mineral composed of layers of quartz sometimes of different colors. Agate usually occurs as rounded nodules or veins in traprock; the layers are often concentric. The composition of agate varies greatly, but silica is always predominant, usually with alumina and oxide of iron. Other types of quartz—chalcedony, carnelian, amethyst, jasper, opal, and flint—often occur as layers in agate. Among other forms of agate are star agate; clouded agate, with nebulous inclu-

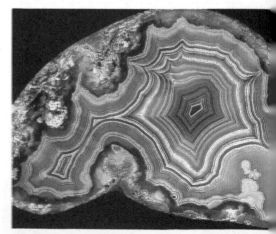

*Agate is a semiprecious stone that often occurs in bands of different colors. This specimen was found in Mexico.*
© A. Ruppenthal–Gemological Society of America

sions; and moss agate, with dark green mosslike inclusions. The mineral can be polished to a high gloss, and it is frequently used for ornamental purposes.

**AGATE FOSSIL BEDS NATIONAL MONUMENT.** *See* NATIONAL PARK SERVICE (table).

**AGATHA, Saint** (fl. 3d cent.), according to tradition, a noble Sicilian virgin of great beauty and wealth, who rejected the love of a Roman consul and as a result suffered cruel martyrdom. In art, she is frequently depicted with her severed breasts on a plate. Whether Agatha ever lived, and, if so, whether she died in the persecution of Christians conducted during the reign (249–51) of the Roman emperor Decius or that of Diocletian, 50 years later, is unknown. She is the patron saint of Malta and of Catania, Italy. Legend relates that several times the mere carrying of her veil (taken from her tomb in Catania) in procession averted eruptions of nearby Mount Etna, and that her intercession saved Malta from Turkish conquest in 1551. Saint Agatha's feast day is February 5.

**AGATHOCLES** (361–289 BC), tyrant of Syracuse, a Greek city in Sicily, born in Thermae Himerenses (now Termini Imerese), Sicily. After being exiled twice for attempting to overthrow the aristocratic government, he succeeded in his third attempt in 317 BC and became tyrant of all Sicily. Agathocles continued the previous Syracusan policy of constantly warring with the Carthaginians; he threatened the city of Carthage itself in 310 BC. As a ruler, he appears to have been popular and enlightened. Agathocles assumed the title of king in 304 BC. Later he formed an alliance with Ptolemy I of Egypt. He raided Italy and in 299 BC conquered the Greek island of Corcyra (now Kérkira) in the Adriatic Sea. In his will Agathocles provided for the restoration of the government to the people of Syracuse.

**AGAVE,** genus of plants of the family Agavaceae (*see* LILY), native to desert regions of the western hemisphere. The best-known species is *Agave americana,* the American aloe or century plant, which usually flowers only once, between the ages of 10 and 25 years. Shortly before it flowers, a long stalk grows rapidly upward to a height of about 12 m (about 40 ft). The flowers are large and greenish and cover short, horizontal branches that spring from the upper half of the stalk. Some plants die after flowering, but rhizomes of suckers often develop into new plants. The plant may also be grown from seeds, bulbs, or underground stems. The agave has large, thick, and fleshy leaves, which can store considerable quantities of water. They are spiked, particularly at the tips, are evergreen, and grow to a length

*Century plants,* Agave scabra, *found in northern Mexico.*
© M. P. L. Fogden–Bruce Coleman, Inc.

of about 2 m (about 6 ft) in a cluster around the base of the plant.

Many species of agave are of economic importance. *A. sisalana,* native to the West Indies but now also grown in Mexico and various tropical countries of the Old World, yields sisal or sisal hemp. Fibers up to 1.5 m (5 ft) long are obtained from the leaves of this plant. Other species of agave yield similar fibers that are called sisal or, more properly, false sisal. The roots of some species yield a pulp that produces a lather when wet and is used as soap. Such soap plants are called amoles. The sap of some agaves is fermented to obtain a drink called pulque, which can be distilled to make a colorless liquor, mescal. All agave is called maguey in Mexico. One species, *A. virginica,* the false aloe, is native to the southeastern U.S.

**AGAWAM,** town, Hampden Co., SW Massachusetts, on the Connecticut and Westfield rivers, near Springfield; settled 1635, inc. 1855. The town is a residential and trade center in a dairy-farming, poultry-raising, and truck-gardening area. Manufactures include machine tools and leather goods. The town's name is derived from an Indian word probably meaning either "crooked river" or "low meadowland." Pop. (1980) 26,271; (1990) 27,323.

**AGE OF CONSENT,** in law, the age when persons are considered to be fully bound by their words and deeds. The age of consent varies for different actions. For example, one has the right to consent to marriage at an earlier age than one may legally sign a contract. In most of the U.S. one acquires the legal capacity to conclude a contract at the age of 18. A boy at age 14 and a girl at age 12, however, are capable of matrimonial consent under common law, but again U.S. state statutes differ on the age of consent. The age at which a female is held capable of consenting to illicit sexual intercourse has generally been raised in the U.S. to as high as 18. Persons under the age of consent are said to be minors.

**AGEE, James** (1909–55), American writer, born in Knoxville, Tenn., and educated at Harvard University. A collection of his poetry, *Permit Me Voyage,* was published in 1934. His study of the life of sharecroppers, *Let Us Now Praise Famous Men,* appeared in 1941, illustrated by the American photographer Walker Evans. Agee's fiction was limited to the novelette *The Morning Watch* (1954) and the delicate and moving novel *A Death in the Family* (1957). For the latter novel Agee was posthumously awarded the 1958 Pulitzer Prize in fiction. The novel was successfully dramatized as a play (1960) and as a film (1963); both works appeared under the title *All the Way Home.* Agee also wrote several screenplays. His film criticism was published in *Agee on Film* (2 vol., 1958–60). *Letters of James Agee to Father Flye* (1962) suggests the complexity of his personality.

**AGEN** (anc. *Aginnum*), town, SW France, capital of Lot-et-Garonne Department, on the Garonne R. It is a farm-trade and manufacturing center; products include processed food (notably the dried plums called *pruneaux d'Agen*), clothing, and pharmaceuticals. Agen was the capital of the Nitriobriges, a Gallic tribe. Later it was made the capital of the county of Agenais. Agen became the seat of a bishopric in the 10th century; construction of the cathedral here was begun in the 12th century. Pop. (1990) 32,223.

**AGENCY FOR INTERNATIONAL DEVELOPMENT** (AID), agency of the federal government responsible for carrying out nonmilitary U.S. foreign assistance programs. It was created in 1961 to combine economic support and technical assistance operations, the loan activities of the Development Loan Fund, and the local currency-lending functions of the Export-Import Bank of the U.S.

Since 1979 AID has been part of the independent U.S. International Development Cooperation Agency. AID is headed by an administrator who is charged with the direction of the foreign economic assistance program. Based in Washington, D.C., AID has additional missions and offices located overseas.

Programs are directed to more than 75 developing countries. Much of the assistance involves contributing U.S. goods and services for specified activities, rather than granting money outright. AID provides loans to help develop specific social and economic projects, general importation programs to foster economic growth and technical assistance and training, and funds to assist nations during times of political emergency.

**AGERATUM,** genus of tropical American flowering annual herbs of the family Asteraceae (*see* COMPOSITE FLOWERS). The ageratum is known also as the flossflower. The genus comprises about 43 species, of which the best known is *Ageratum houstonianum,* a species native to Mexico. It is an attractive, low-growing plant with opposite, hairy leaves that are usually heart-shaped. Its flowers are generally blue and are borne in clusters of delicate, tassellike heads. It blooms throughout the summer and is often used for garden borders.

**AGE OF REASON, THE.** *See* PAINE, THOMAS.

**AGESILAUS II** (c. 444–360 BC), king of Sparta (c. 398–360 BC), son of King Archidamus II, and the successor of his half brother, King Agis II (r. about 426–398 BC). After Agesilaus became king, he took command of the forces in Asia Minor that were defending the Greek cities from the Persians. After winning several battles, he was recalled to defend Sparta against a hostile alliance of Athens, Thebes, Argos, and Corinth. Agesilaus was victorious against the alliance at the Battle of Coronea, in Boeotia, in 394 BC. He continued to lead his state in wars against other Greek states, especially Thebes. Despite the defeat of the Spartans at Leuctra in 371 BC, where Cleombrotus I (r. 380–371 BC), coruler of Sparta, was in command, Agesilaus continued to make war. He died on his way home from a mercenary expedition in Egypt against the Persians.

**AGGADA.** *See* HAGGADA.

**AGGRESSION,** form of animal behavior characterized by an assault or attack by one animal on another. Aggression can take two forms. One form of aggression is conflict between members of different species (interspecific aggression). It can include predatory aggression (food obtaining), defensive aggression, and aggression directed at competitors for resources such as food or water. Aggression of this sort typically does not involve emotions such as anger and can be regarded as a component of feeding and maintenance behavior.

A more significant kind of aggression involves attacks directed toward members of the same species (intraspecific aggression). Such fighting is observed in virtually all vertebrate species. Fish lock jaws and nip each other; birds attack one another, rats wrestle, kick, and occasionally bite; and steers, sheep, and goats butt their heads together. Animals fight in ways that are programmed by their genes—usually over some scarce resource. This kind of aggression exists because members of a given species have very similar needs and therefore find themselves in direct competition with one another for food, mates, and dwelling spaces. The form intraspecific aggression takes is determined in large part by the relative risks and potential benefits of the aggressive encounter. Some animals such as male sea elephants will fight to the death over possession of a breeding harem because defeat is equivalent to genetic suicide. Male American elk, on the other hand, engage in pushing contests with their antlers. When one becomes tired he retreats from the contest with the prospect that next year's mating season may bring better results. The antlers are not used to stab or wound and are shed at the end of the mating season. Most intraspecific aggression is of this sort and does not result in significant bodily harm.

**Limiting Aggression.** Because combat is dangerous and can lead to serious injury or death, evolutionary mechanisms tend to restrain the intensity of intraspecific aggressive behavior. One way aggression is minimized is through a genetically programmed tendency to establish territories. In this way conflicts are usually limited to occasional border skirmishes. The ritualization of aggressive behavior is another genetically programmed restraint on combat. Poisonous snakes wrestle without using their fangs; mountain sheep butt with well-armored heads without inflicting injury; some lizards make threat displays by expanding a skin fold in the throat; and apes shake branches, gesture, and shout fearsomely. The advantage of ritualization of combat is that even a sure winner has a great deal to lose if it becomes debilitated as a result of a fight. (The advantage to the probable loser in having the stronger animal not push its advantage is obvious.) An injured or exhausted victorious animal may not be able to defeat the next opponent and may become vulnerable to predation by other species. Therefore, most species have clear signals that indicate acceptance of defeat and terminate combat before injury occurs: A lizard will crouch; a cichlid fish will retract its fins; a stickleback will adopt a vertical posture; a dog will expose its unprotected belly; and a gull will offer the unguarded back of its neck to its opponent. Each of these maneuvers signals acceptance of defeat and immediately halts further aggression.

**Aggression in Humans.** Learned experience is an important determinant of aggressive behavior in humans. Elicitors of aggression such as personal insults, status threats, and the presence of weapons are all learned sources of aggressive behavior. Further, aggressive actions are often followed by rewards and are therefore likely to be repeated. Children learn that aggression can enable them to control resources such as toys and parental attention. Children also learn aggression by observing others behave aggressively. The violent behavior of some teenage gangs provides its younger members with aggressive role models. Children whose parents discipline with physical force tend to use more physical aggression when interacting with others, and parents who abuse their children were typically abused children themselves. The influence of the mass media, especially television, on promoting aggressive behavior is not yet well understood, but a growing body of research evidence indicates that watching violent entertainment is linked to subsequent aggression.

*See* ANIMAL BEHAVIOR; SOCIOBIOLOGY.

J.L.Go., C.G.G., & R.A.J.

**AGINCOURT, BATTLE OF,** military engagement during the Hundred Years' War, fought in France on Oct. 25, 1415, between an English army under King Henry V of England and a French one under Charles d'Albret (d. 1415), constable of France. Prior to the action, which took place in a narrow valley near the village of Agincourt (now Azincourt, in Pas-de-Calais Department), Henry, a claimant to the French throne, had invaded France and seized the port of Harfleur. At the time of the action, Henry's army, weakened by disease and hunger, was en route to Calais, from which Henry planned to embark for England. In the course of the march to Calais the English force, which numbered about 6000 men, for the most part lightly equipped archers, was intercepted by d'Albret, whose army of about 25,000 men consisted chiefly of armored cavalry and infantry contingents. The English king, fearful of annihilation, sought a truce with the French, but his terms were rejected. In the battle, which was preceded by heavy rains, the French troops were at a disadvantage because of their weighty armor, the narrowness of the battleground, the muddy terrain, and the faulty tactics of their superiors, notably in using massed formations against a mobile enemy. The French cavalry, which occupied frontal positions, quickly became mired in the mud, making easy targets for the English archers. After routing the enemy cavalry, the English troops, wielding hatchets, billhooks (a type of knife), and swords, launched successive assaults on the French infantry. Demoralized by the fate of their cavalry and severely hampered by the mud, the French foot soldiers were completely overwhelmed. D'Albret, several dukes and counts, and about 500 other members of the French nobility were killed; other French casualties totaled about 5000. English losses numbered fewer than 200 men. French feudal military strategy, traditionally based on the employment of heavily armored troops and cavalry, was completely discredited by Henry's victory. Although Henry returned to England after Agincourt, his triumph paved the way for English domination of most of France until the middle of the 15th century.                                                    S.R.Pa.

**AGING,** in biology, combination of changes in an organism that appear to occur inevitably and irreversibly with the passage of time, eventually resulting in death (see DEATH AND DYING). Such changes vary considerably in time and severity of occurrence among different species and from one individual organism to the next. Among humans they include a decrease in tissue flexibility, loss of some nerve cells, hardening of the blood vessels, and general decrease in body tone. Biologists concerned with aging may investigate such changes, or they may focus on bodily deficits and disabilities that accumulate with age but that appear to result more directly from disease, stress, or environmental trauma (see ALZHEIMER'S DISEASE). No scientific consensus exists as to the true nature of the aging process.

**Theories of Aging.** Although research into biological aging, therefore, is not guided by any single universally accepted theory, genetic, cellular, and physiological studies have yielded various hypotheses. One of the most prominent genetic concepts, the so-called error theory, assumes that the deficits of aging result from the accumulation of random genetic damage, or from small errors in the flow of genetic information (see GENETICS). Such damage or errors would reduce or prevent proper cell function.

In cellular research, the best-known theory of aging rests on the so-called Hayflick effect, named after the American microbiologist Leonard Hayflick (1928–   ). Hayflick found that certain human cells in a tissue culture are capable of only a limited number of cell divisions before they die. This finding may suggest that aging is programmed into cells, and it could account for

differences in the life span (q.v.) of different animal species, as well as differences in longevity between sexes within the same species. Among humans, for example, females typically outlive males by about eight years.

Physiological theories of aging focus on organ systems and their interrelationships. One area of much current investigation, for example, is the immune system (q.v.), which protects an organism from foreign cells. A characteristic of mammals is that the immune system gradually loses its capacity to fight off infections and other invaders as the organism ages. As a consequence, antibodies (see ANTIBODY) are produced that are unable to distinguish between "friendly," or "self," and "enemy," or "non-self," cells in the organism. Most experts now believe that aging is not the result of a single mechanism but represents many phenomena working in concert.

**Social and Behavioral Aspects.** The process of human aging must also be considered in the context of complex and changing societies. The ways in which people age are not entirely fixed by biology; they are also affected by individual environmental and social circumstances. Consequently, aging is increasingly being studied as a process that includes psychosocial and cultural components; in addition, the subject is being extended to include the entire course of life, rather than being restricted to the period of old age.

Knowledge gained through the work of social and behavioral scientists is helping to dispel some myths about the inevitability of the aging process. For example, one myth is that intelligence peaks in adolescence and then deteriorates; another is that sexual activity begins an irreversible decline in the middle years, whereas sexual activity is now known to continue even into the very late years of life.

Because the aging process is not unalterable, behavioral researchers are seeking ways in which it can be modified. For example, certain memory-aiding strategies have been found to help reverse the short-term memory loss experienced by some old people. Nursing-home arrangements to promote independent behavior have been found to bring patients to better levels of functioning, including some patients once thought to be hopelessly impaired. Relatively simple, research-tested changes in food flavorings have been found to solve nutritional problems that result from age-related declines in the senses of taste and smell. Also, artificial aids are being improved to meet the visual and hearing problems of later life.

**Ongoing Research.** Understanding the aging process more fully will require the combined efforts of psychosocial and biomedical scientists. Recent research methods being brought to bear on the subject include clinical trials in biomedical research and statistical analysis of data from long-term studies by social scientists. The following topics are of particular interest: nutritional requirements of the aged, age-related changes in reactions to drugs, and senile dementia (q.v.).

Some researchers are also asking longer-range questions about how social change—changes in smoking, exercise, and dietary habits; economic fluctuations; political shifts; medical advances; and new technologies—can affect the aging process. The importance of such research is evident in light of the number of persons over age 65 in U.S. society: more than 31 million (about 12 percent of the population) in 1990 and likely to rise to nearly 32 million (about 13 percent) by the year 2000. Research on aging is being conducted at many university centers around the world. In the U.S., the University of Southern California, Duke University, and the University of Michigan are among those prominent in the field. Nationally, the National Institutes of Health and especially the National Institute on Aging, founded in 1974, are sponsoring many research programs.

*See also* GERIATRICS; GERONTOLOGY.     M.W.R.

*For further information on this topic, see the Bibliography in volume 28,* sections 296, 450, 530.

**AGLAIA.** *See* GRACES.

**AGNES, Saint,** 4th-century Christian virgin and martyr, venerated in both the Eastern and Western churches. She was only 12 or 13 years old when she was executed; various accounts claim that she was beheaded, burned to death, or strangled. According to a 6th-century legend, Agnes was a beautiful Roman girl. After rejecting many suitors, she was denounced as a Christian and sent to a house of prostitution as her punishment. When a young man ventured to touch her, he lost his sight, but then regained it in answer to her prayers. Shortly thereafter she was executed and buried on the Via Nomentana in a catacomb eventually named for her. A church was built over her tomb about 350. In art she is often portrayed with a lamb, a symbol of innocence. On January 21, her traditional feast day, two lambs are blessed at her church in Rome. Their wool is then woven into palliums (bands of white wool), which the pope confers on archbishops as a token of their jurisdiction.

**AGNEW, Spiro Theodore** (1918–    ), 39th vice-president of the U.S. (1969–73). Born in Baltimore, Md., on Nov. 9, 1918, the son of a Greek-born father and an American mother, he served in the U.S. Army during World War II, then studied law at the University of Baltimore and became a practicing attorney.

In 1962 he was elected Baltimore County Executive as a Republican, and four years later he won the Maryland governorship. In 1968 and again in 1972 Agnew was elected vice-president on a ticket with Richard M. Nixon. As vice-president he became known for his flamboyantly phrased speeches denouncing liberals, radicals, and other critics of the Nixon administration.

In August 1973 it was revealed that Agnew was under investigation by the U.S. attorney's office in Baltimore on charges of bribery, extortion, tax fraud, and conspiracy. In October U.S. Attorney General Elliot Richardson (1920–    ) formally charged him with having accepted bribes totaling more than $100,000 while holding office as county executive, governor, and vice-president. Denying the bribery charges, Agnew pleaded no contest to a charge of tax evasion. On Oct. 10, 1973, he was fined $10,000 and sentenced to three years' probation. Just hours before, he had resigned, becoming the first U.S. vice-president to do so because of criminal charges. After leaving office he set up a business as a consultant in international trade. In his book *Go Quietly . . . or Else* (1980), Agnew charged that he had been pressured into resigning by threats on his life.

*For further information on this person, see the section Biographies in the Bibliography in volume 28.*

**AGNON, Shmuel Yosef** (1888–1970), Israeli writer and Nobel laureate. Originally surnamed Czaczkes, he was born in Galicia, then part of the Austro-Hungarian Empire. He published his first poetry, written in both Hebrew and Yiddish, at the age of 15. In 1910 he settled in Jerusalem. Except for two stays in Germany, between 1912 and 1932, Agnon lived in Israel until his death. In 1935 he was named the first recipient of the Bialik Prize, the most prestigious literary award in Israel. In 1966, Agnon and the German-Swedish poet Nelly Sachs shared the Nobel Prize in literature. Agnon was cited for his "profoundly characteristic narrative art with motifs from the life of the Jewish people."

Agnon's stories, written in classical Hebrew and very difficult to translate, are rich in Jewish folk legends and mysticism. They note the gradual decline of the Galician Jewish communities between the time of his youth and the beginning of World War I. Agnon's work that is set in Israel illustrates the differing outlooks of the religious and idealistic early Jewish settlers of Palestine and the predominantly secular present-day Israelis. Among his most admired works are his novels *The Bridal Canopy* (2 vol., 1919; trans.

1937) and *A Guest for the Night* (1938; trans. 1968).

**AGNOSTICISM,** doctrine that the existence of God and other spiritual beings is neither certain nor impossible. The term, derived from the Greek *agnostikos* ("not knowing"), was introduced into English in the 19th century by the British biologist Thomas Henry Huxley. The agnostic position is distinct from both theism (q.v.), which affirms the existence of such beings, and atheism (q.v.), which denies their existence.

Although usually regarded as a form of skepticism (q.v.), agnosticism is more limited in scope, for it denies the reliability only of metaphysical and theological beliefs rather than of all beliefs. The basis of modern agnosticism lies in the works of the British philosopher David Hume and the German philosopher Immanuel Kant, both of whom pointed out logical fallacies in the traditional arguments for the existence of God and of the soul. Another school of modern philosophy that, like agnosticism, rejects both atheism and theism, is empiricism (q.v.), also known as logical positivism, which maintains that metaphysical statements are meaningless.                    R.A.

**AGORA,** public square or marketplace of any ancient Greek city. It was originally the site of the popular assembly, but as time went by it was used increasingly for commercial purposes. Large and open and easily accessible, it was regarded as the center of political, commercial, religious, and social life in the city. The agora was surrounded by public buildings and temples, frequently with colonnades *(stoai)* on the side facing the square. The most famous agora is the Athenian, located northwest of the Acropolis.

**AGOUTI,** common name for rodents of the genera *Dasyprocta* and *Myoprocta,* (also called acouchi), of the family Dasyproctidae. The agouti is found in forested regions from southern Mexico south to Paraguay and in the West Indies. It is short eared, has practically no tail, and has a soft coat of golden-brown or reddish hair, sometimes speckled. *Dasyprocta* are rabbit-sized; *Myoprocta* are somewhat smaller. At first glance the agouti resembles the guinea pig, but it has slender, comparatively long legs and can run swiftly. The agouti lives in an underground den, from which it emerges usually at night. It feeds on green leaves, roots, and fallen fruit. Esteemed for its flesh and hated in farming areas because of its destructiveness, the agouti is hunted and killed in great numbers. The agouti reproduces rapidly, however; the female usually has two litters of two to four young each year. Born open-eyed and fully furred, the young agouti is ready to look after itself immediately.

*The Moti Masjid, or Pearl Mosque, an Indo-Saracenic building noted for its architectural beauty, is part of the Old Fort in Agra, India.*          Air-India Library

**AGRA,** city, N India, in Uttar Pradesh State, capital of Agra District, on the Jumna R. The city is a railroad junction and a commercial and industrial center for the surrounding agricultural area. Agra has an extensive trade in cotton, grain, tobacco, salt, and sugar. Factories are engaged in food processing and in the production of cotton textiles, carpets, iron and steel, and leather goods. Educational institutions include the University of Agra, a medical college, a teachers college for men, and a teachers college for women. Agra is celebrated as the site of the Taj Mahal and of several other outstanding examples of Indo-Saracenic architecture, including the Jahangri Mahal, a palace of white marble constructed for the Mughal emperor Akbar, and the Moti Masjid, or Pearl Mosque, built in the early 17th century.

Although Agra was the capital of some of the pre-Mughal dynasties of Indian rulers, the city did not attain prominence until after it was captured in 1526 by Babur, the first of the Muslim emperors. From that time until 1658, when the Mughal emperor Aurangzeb moved to Delhi, the city was the Mughal seat of government. The British captured Agra in 1803, and since 1835 it has been a provincial capital and administrative center. Pop. (1991, greater city) 955,694.

**AGRAPHA OF JESUS,** sayings attributed to Jesus that are not contained in the Gospels. These are preserved in the Acts of the Apostles (see 20:35) in the New Testament, the Apocryphal New Testament, the Apostolic Canons, Gnostic literature, the Talmud, and Muslim sources. In 1897 and 1903 valuable papyri containing such sayings were discovered at Oxyrhyncus, in what is now Egypt. A book of such sayings of Jesus was, in early traditions, attributed to St. Matthew, one of the 12 apostles.

**AGRICOLA, Georgius,** Latinized name of Georg Bauer (1494–1555), German scientist, generally regarded as the founder of the science of mineralogy. Agricola was born in Saxony and educated in medicine in Italy. He became the town physician in the mining center of Joachimsthal in 1527, but he made the study of mineralogy and geology his lifework. His greatest work, *De Re Metallica* (1556), which appeared after his death, served as a textbook and guide for mining engineers for almost two centuries. At the time of his death Agricola was burgomaster of the city of Chemnitz.

**AGRICOLA, Gnaeus Julius** (AD 40–93), Roman statesman and general, born in Forum Julii (now Fréjus in Var Department, France), and educated in philosophy in Massilia (now Marseille). He served with distinction in the Roman provinces of Britain, Asia, and Aquitania and held numerous civil offices at Rome, ending with the consulship in 77. The following year he was appointed governor of the Roman province of Britannia. During the seven years of his administration there he attempted to subdue the native peoples, winning victories over the Ordovices in Wales and over the Caledonians in Scotland. After he had defeated the Caledonians, his fleet circumnavigated Great Britain, proving it to be an island. His success, however, is said to have aroused the jealousy of Emperor Domitian, who recalled him to Rome. The suggestion, however, that Domitian was responsible for Agricola's death is unsubstantiated. Agricola was the father-in-law of the Roman historian Cornelius Tacitus, whose work *De Vita Iulii Agricolae* is a laudatory biography of the general.

**AGRICULTURAL ADJUSTMENT ACT.** *See* AGRICULTURE; NEW DEAL.

**AGRICULTURAL CHEMISTRY.** *See* AGRONOMY; CHEMURGY; HYDROPONICS; PEST CONTROL; WEED CONTROL.

**AGRICULTURAL EDUCATION,** formal or nonformal system designed to educate youths and adults about such subjects as animal and plant production, horticulture, natural resources and the environment, mechanics, and marketing and distribution. The high agricultural productivity in the U.S. stems in large measure from the educational delivery system available to the agricultural industry. This system includes agricultural colleges and experiment stations, the agricultural extension system, community colleges, vocational and technical schools, secondary school programs, and youth organizations.

The first agricultural schools were established during the 1850s in Michigan and Pennsylvania. Practical apprenticeship and self-training, how-

ever, were still the chief means by which farmers learned the techniques of farming. The first significant advance in agricultural education began in 1862, when President Abraham Lincoln signed the Morrill Act, which enabled the states to establish land-grant colleges. Under this measure each state received a grant of public lands to be used or sold to provide a college to teach the agricultural and mechanical arts. By the next year each state had established such a college.

To supplement the instruction given in agricultural colleges, in 1887 Congress passed the Hatch Act, establishing the system of the agricultural experiment station. By 1893, 49 such stations were in existence. Today more than 50 stations are in operation, one in each state, as well as in Puerto Rico, the Virgin Islands, and several U.S. territories. With fields, barns, greenhouses, and laboratories at their disposal, scientists at these stations study soils, crops, animals, diseases, pests, and social and environmental factors.

Complaints arose, however, that much of the new information was not reaching farmers. To meet this complaint, the Agricultural Extension Service, now called the Extension Service, was established in 1914. With money from state, county, and sometimes private sources, it became possible for each county to maintain a resident, college-trained expert, usually called the county agricultural agent or the county adviser. The Extension Service spread rapidly until nearly every rural county had an agricultural agent.

Even before the county-agent system appeared, it was recognized that farm children needed to be taught improved farming techniques. From this early recognition the nationwide 4-H clubs grew.

The Smith-Hughes Act of 1917 provided federal funds for vocational education, including instruction in farming. About 1928 the Future Farmers of America (FFA) was organized. Activities of this organization differ somewhat from those of the 4-H clubs, although the basic objectives are similar. The 4-H clubs are led by community volunteers, whereas FFA is integrated into the curriculum of the public schools (in grades 9–12). More than 5 million girls and boys participate each year in 4-H clubs and some 400,000 boys and girls belong to the FFA.

Along with the agricultural colleges, Extension Service programs, and youth organizations, the American farmer is also informed on farming techniques and management through the many farm journals, newspapers, newsletters, and more recently by means of direct satellite and computer network marketing systems. Some radio and television stations bring timely production and marketing news to members of the agricultural industry.                                         Ja.L.

**AGRICULTURAL EXPERIMENT STATION,** one of the agencies for agricultural research in each state of the U.S., the District of Columbia, Puerto Rico, the Virgin Islands, Guam, American Samoa, the Northern Marianas, and Micronesia. Provisions of the Hatch Act (1887) finance stations through state and federal funding. Each station focuses on the agricultural problems of its area, engaging in research and experiments to expand college courses and farm advisory services. Research projects are arranged through the Cooperative State Research Service of the U.S. Department of Agriculture (*see* AGRICULTURE, DEPARTMENT OF).

**AGRICULTURAL MACHINERY,** devices used to till soil and to plant, cultivate, and harvest crops. Since ancient times, when cultivation of plants was first undertaken, people have found the use of implements to be necessary. Primitive implements were pointed objects used for digging and keeping soil loosened, and sharp, knifelike objects were used for harvesting ripened crops. Modifications of these early implements led to the development of small hand tools still used in small-scale gardening, such as the spade, hoe, rake, trowel, and scythe, and larger implements, such as plows, larger rakes, and hoes, that are drawn by humans, animals, or simple machines. *See* AGRICULTURE.

Much of the arable land of the earth is still tilled under conditions that do not permit use of expensive modern machinery, such as that used extensively in the U.S., Canada, Great Britain, Western Europe, and Australia.

Modern large agricultural implements, adapted to large-scale farming methods, are usually powered by diesel- or gasoline-fueled internal-combustion engines. The most important implement of modern agriculture is the tractor (q.v.). It provides locomotion for many other implements and can furnish power, via its power shaft, for the operation of machines drawn behind the tractor in the field. The power shafts of tractors may also be harnessed to belts for operating such equipment as feed grinders, pumps, or electric-power generators. Small implements, such as portable irrigators, often are powered by individual motors.

**Implements for Growing Crops.** Many types of implements have been developed for the various types of activities involved in growing crops. These include breaking ground, planting, weeding, fertilizing, and combating pests.

Ground is broken by plows to prepare the seedbed. A plow consists of a bladelike plow-

*A rainbow finds the end of a movable irrigation system on a field in Driggs, Idaho, near Montana.*                    Tom Algire–FPG International

*Plowing under a field of wild flowers and preparing the soil for planting on a small farm in Pennsylvania.* © 1990 Michael Gadomski–Bruce Coleman, Inc.

*Harvesting pecans with a tree shaker, near Albany, Ga.* © 1990 Peter Davey–Bruce Coleman, Inc.

share that cuts under the soil and a curved mold-board, against which the soil is lifted, turned, and pulverized. Modern tractor plows are usually equipped with two or more plowshares, so that a wide area of ground may be broken at a single sweep. Harrows are used to smooth plowed land and sometimes to cover seeds and fertilizers with earth. The disk harrow, which has curved, sharp-edged steel disks, is used mainly to cut up crop residues before plowing and to bury weeds during seedbed preparation. Rollers with V-shaped wheels are used to break up clods of soil to improve the aeration of the soil and its capacity for taking in water.

Planting of some cereal crops is still accomplished by broadcasting seed, that is, scattering it over a wide area. Machines for broadcasting usually consist of a long seedbox mounted on wheels and equipped with an agitator to distribute the seed. Broadcast seeds are not always covered by a uniform or sufficient depth of soil, and so seeding is more often done with drills, which produce continuous furrows of uniform depth as seedbeds. The rate of sowing is adjustable in modern drills, but specialized implements called planters are necessary for sowing crops such as corn, which are planted in rows. Corn planters and other similar machines have a special feed wheel that picks up separate kernels or small quantities of grain and places them in the ground.

Fertilizer may be distributed during the winter or shortly before seeding time, but commercial fertilizers commonly are distributed, along with seeds, by drills and planters. Manure and other consolidated fertilizers are distributed most efficiently by a manure spreader, which is a wagon equipped with a bottom conveyor to carry the fertilizer back to a beater attachment, which disintegrates it and then scatters it on the ground.

After crops have begun to grow, a cultivator (q.v.) is used to destroy weeds and loosen and aerate the soil. A flame weeder, which produces a hot-air blast, can be used to destroy weeds in crops, such as cotton, which have stems of tough bark. Selective chemical herbicides applied in the form of a spray or as granules are used extensively for destruction of weeds (see WEED CONTROL). Insecticides also are applied to the soil and to crops in the form of granules, dust, or liquid sprays (see PEST CONTROL). A variety of mechanical spraying and dusting equipment is used to spread chemicals on crops and fields; the machinery may be self-powered or drawn and powered by a tractor. In areas where large crops of vegetables and grain are grown, airplanes are increasingly used to dust or spray pesticides. See also ENVIRONMENT.

**Implements for Harvesting Crops.** Machinery used for harvesting differs according to the crop being harvested. Most cereal crops are harvested by means of a combine, which is a machine equipped to remove the fruiting heads, beat off the grain kernels, and clean the grain as the combine moves through the fields. The cleaned grain is accumulated in an attached grain tank.

Corn for grain is harvested by means of a corn picker or a grain combine with a corn-picker attachment. As the corn picker moves along the rows, the ears are picked from the stalks and are husked. The ears may be transferred from the husking bed in the picker either to a sheller, which removes the kernels from the ear, mounted on the picker or to a wagon trailing behind the machine. When a combine is utilized, the whole cornstalk may be put through the machine to shell the ears, or the attachment may simply snap the ears from the stalks and feed them to the combine for shelling. Recently developed corn combines are capable of picking, husking, and shelling up to 13 metric tons (500 bu) of corn per hour.

Hay harvesting usually is a multiple operation because of the necessity of drying the hay after cutting it. Hay is first cut close to the ground with a mower. After drying in the sun, most hay is baled, although some is still put up as loose hay. In baling, the pickup baler lifts the hay to a conveyor that carries it to a baling chamber in which it is compressed into bales weighing up to 57 kg (125 lb) and automatically tied with heavy twine or wire. The field chopper is used to chop standing green hay and field-cured hay for silage. This machine can be equipped also to chop row crops, such as corn and sorghum. In harvesting grass silage, the

*Picking cotton, two rows at a time, by machine in the Mississippi delta. The enclosed cab shields the driver from the sun.* © Wendell Metzen–Bruce Coleman, Inc.

machine is provided with a cutter bar and a reel for direct cutting. Alfalfa and other legume hay is harvested in some areas with a hay cuber. This machine cuts the plants close to the ground and, after field curing, chops them into a fine mash and compresses the mash into cubes that are more easily shipped and stored than are bales. The cubes of hay must be of a size that cattle can eat readily.

Specialized machinery is used to harvest large root crops, such as potatoes and sugar beets. Mechanical cotton pickers and strippers are used in harvesting almost 95 percent of U.S.-grown cotton. Mechanical pickers are equipped with rotating spindles that twist the cotton fiber from the boll. Before picking, the leaves of the cotton plant are removed by means of a chemical defoliant spray. Light-boll, stormproof cotton is harvested by means of strippers that comb or brush the cotton from the plant and lift it into a trailed wagon. More efficient mechanical pickers continue to be developed. *See also* COTTON GIN.

Specialized machines are also used to harvest fruits and vegetables. For example, with a mechanical fruit picker, deciduous tree fruits, such as plums, cherries, and apricots, are literally shaken down. The machine, with arms attached to limbs of the tree, agitates the tree and causes the fruit to fall onto a raised catching frame that surrounds the tree. Nut crops may also be harvested in this manner. In addition, plant breeders use modern methods such as genetic engineering to develop varieties of fruits and vegetables that are tougher and hardier for easy harvesting by machines. For example, a variety of tomato has been bred for a tougher skin that reduces bruising.

In addition to the kinds of agricultural machinery being used on large modern farms, a wide range of automated devices has been made available to farmers through the revolution in electronics. Today farmers may even be linked by personal computers to information centers that can help them to solve problems they confront in the operation of their farms.

**Practical Significance.** Use of agricultural machinery substantially reduces the amount of human labor needed for raising crops. The average amount of labor required per hectare to produce and harvest corn, hay, and cereal crops has fallen to less than a fourth of what was required only a few decades ago. Mechanization, together with improved crop varieties, better techniques, and more efficient food processing, has enabled the small percentage of the U.S. population that remains living on farms to produce enough food to feed the nation.          REV. BY Wa.A.Wi.

*A combine picks corn from the stalk, husks it and removes kernels from the cob, and delivers the grain to a storage facility.*          © 1990 Alvis Upitis–The Image Bank

**AGRICULTURE,** art, science, and industry of managing the growth of plants and animals for human use. In a broad sense agriculture includes cultivation of the soil, growing and harvesting crops, breeding and raising of livestock, dairying, and forestry *(see* ANIMAL HUSBANDRY; CROP FARMING; DAIRY FARMING; FORESTRY; POULTRY FARMING; SOIL MANAGEMENT).

Regional and national agriculture are covered in more detail in individual continent and country articles. See also separate articles on the states of Australia and the U.S. and the provinces of Canada.

Modern agriculture depends heavily on engineering and technology and on the biological and physical sciences. Irrigation, drainage, conservation (qq.v.), and sanitation *(see* ENGINEERING: *Sanitary Engineering)*—each of which is important in successful farming—are some of the fields requiring the specialized knowledge of agricultural engineers.

Agricultural chemistry deals with other vital farm problems, such as uses of fertilizer (q.v.), insecticide, and fungicide *(see* FUNGICIDES; PEST CONTROL), soil makeup, analysis of agricultural products, and nutritional needs of farm animals.

Plant breeding (q.v.) and genetics (q.v.) contribute immeasurably to farm productivity. Genetics has also placed livestock breeding on a scientific basis. Hydroponics (q.v.), a method of soilless gardening in which plants are grown in chemical nutrient solutions, may solve additional agricultural problems.

The packing, processing, and marketing of agricultural products are closely related activities also influenced by science. Methods of quick-freezing and dehydration have increased the markets for farm products (see FOOD PROCESSING AND PRESERVATION; MEAT-PACKING INDUSTRY).

Mechanization, the outstanding characteristic of late 19th- and 20th-century agriculture, has eased much of the backbreaking toil of the farmer. More significantly, mechanization has enormously increased farm efficiency and productivity. See AGRICULTURAL MACHINERY.

Airplanes and helicopters are employed in agriculture for such purposes as seeding, transporting perishable products, and fighting forest fires, and in spraying operations involved in insect and disease control. Radio and television disseminate vital weather reports and other information that is of concern to farmers.

## WORLD AGRICULTURE

Over the 10,000 years since agriculture began to be developed, peoples everywhere have discovered the food value of wild plants and animals and domesticated and bred them. The most important are cereals such as wheat, rice, barley, corn, and rye; sugarcane and sugar beets; meat animals such as sheep, cattle, goats, and pigs or swine; poultry such as chickens, ducks, and turkeys; and such products as milk, cheese, eggs, nuts, and oils. Fruits, vegetables, and olives are also major foods for people; feed grains for animals include soybeans, field corn, and sorghum. Separate articles on individual plants and animals contain further information. See also GRASSES; HAY; LEGUME; SILAGE.

Agricultural income is also derived from non-food crops such as rubber, fiber plants, tobacco, and oilseeds used in synthetic chemical compounds, as well as raising animals for pelt.

The conditions that determine what will be raised in an area include climate, water supply, and terrain. See also CLIMATE; ECOLOGY; WATER SUPPLY AND WATERWORKS.

Nearly 50 percent of the world's labor force is employed in agriculture. The distribution in the late 1980s ranged from 64 percent of the economically active population in Africa to less than 4 percent in the U.S. and Canada. In Asia the figure was 61 percent; in South America, 24 percent; in Eastern Europe and the Soviet Union, 15 percent, and in Western Europe, 7 percent.

Farm size varies widely from region to region. In the late 1980s the average for Canadian farms was about 230 ha (about 570 acres) per farm; for U.S. farms, about 185 ha (about 460 acres). The average size of a single landholding in the Philippines, however, may be somewhat less than 3.6 ha (less than 9 acres), and in Indonesia, a little less than 1.2 ha (less than 3 acres).

Size also depends on the purpose of the farm. Commercial farming, or production for cash, is usually on large holdings. The latifundia of Latin America are large, privately owned estates worked by tenant labor. Single-crop plantations produce tea, rubber, and cocoa. Wheat farms are most efficient when they comprise some thousands of hectares and can be worked by teams of people and machines. Australian sheep stations and other livestock farms must be large to provide grazing for thousands of animals. The agricultural plots of Chinese communes and the cooperative farms held by Peruvian communities are other necessarily large agricultural units, as were the collective farms that were owned and operated by state employees in the former Soviet Union.

Individual subsistence farms or small-family mixed-farm operations are decreasing in number in developed countries but are still numerous in the developing countries of Africa and Asia. A "back-to-the-land" movement in the U.S. reversed the decline of small farms in New England and Alaska in the decade from 1970 to 1980.

Nomadic herders range over large areas in sub-Saharan Africa, Afghanistan, and Lapland; and herding is a major part of agriculture in such areas as Mongolia.

Much of the foreign exchange earned by a country may be derived from a single commodity; for example, Sri Lanka depends on tea, Denmark specializes in dairy products, Australia in wool, and New Zealand and Argentina in meat products. In the U.S., wheat, corn, and soybeans have become major foreign exchange commodities in recent decades.

The importance of an individual country as an exporter of agricultural products depends on many variables. Among them is the possibility that the country is too little developed industrially to produce manufactured goods in sufficient quantity or technical sophistication. Such agricultural exporters include Ghana, with cocoa, and Burma (Myanmar), with rice. On the other hand, an exceptionally well-developed country may produce surpluses that are not needed by its own population; such has been the case of the U.S., Canada, and some of the Western European countries.

Because nations depend on agriculture not only for food but for national income and raw materials for industry as well, trade in agriculture is a constant international concern. It is regulated by international agreements such as the General Agreement on Tariffs and Trade and by trading areas such as the European Union.

The Food and Agricultural Organization (FAO) of the UN directs much attention to agricultural trade and policies. According to the FAO, world agricultural production, stimulated by improving technology, reached a record high in the late 1980s. Further, agricultural output in developing nations increased 41 percent during the 1977–88 period, as compared to a rise of 9 percent in developed countries. On a per capita basis, however, food production rose by only 12 percent in developing nations, and less than 1 percent in developed countries. *See also* FOOD.

## HISTORY

The history of agriculture may be divided into four broad periods of unequal length, differing widely in date according to region: prehistoric; historic through the Roman period; feudal; and scientific.

**Prehistoric Agriculture.** Early agriculturists were, it is agreed, largely of Neolithic culture. Sites occupied by such people are located in southwestern Asia, in what are now Iran, Iraq, Israel, Jordan, Syria, and Turkey; in southeastern Asia, in what is now Thailand; in Africa, along the Nile River in Egypt; and in Europe, along the Danube River and in Macedonia, Thrace, and Thessaly. Early centers of agriculture have also been identified in the Huang He (Yellow River) area of China; the Indus River valley of India and Pakistan; and the Tehuacán Valley of Mexico, northwest of the Isthmus of Tehuantepec.

The dates of domesticated plants and animals vary with the regions, but most predate the 6th millennium BC, and the earliest may date from 10,000 BC. Scientists have carried out carbon-14 testing of animal and plant remains and have dated finds of domesticated sheep at 9000 BC in northern Iraq; cattle in the 6th millennium BC in northeastern Iran; goats at 8000 BC in central Iran; pigs at 8000 BC in Thailand and 7000 BC in Thessaly; onagers, or asses, at 7000 BC in Jarmo, Iraq; and horses at 4350 BC in Ukraine. The llama and alpaca were domesticated in the Andean regions of South America by the middle of the 3d millennium BC.

According to carbon dating, wheat and barley were domesticated in the Middle East in the 8th millennium BC; millet and rice in China and southeastern Asia by 5500 BC; and squash in Mexico about 8000 BC. Legumes found in Thessaly and Macedonia are dated as early as 6000 BC. Flax was grown and apparently woven into textiles early in the Neolithic period.

The farmer began, most probably, by noting which of the wild plants were edible or otherwise useful and learned to save the seed and to replant it in cleared land. Long cultivation of the

A figure of cast silver holds ears of corn and wears a costume of produce cultivated in early Latin America.
American Museum of Natural History

most prolific and hardiest plants yielded a stable strain. Herds of goats and sheep were assembled from captured young wild animals, and those with the most useful traits—such as small horns and high milk yield—were bred. The aurochs seems to have been the ancestor of European cattle, and an Asian wild ox of the zebu, the humped cattle of Asia. The cat, dog, and chicken were domesticated very early. The transition from hunting and food gathering to a dependence on food production was gradual, and in a few isolated parts of the world has not yet been accomplished. Crops and domestic meat supplies were augmented by fish and wildfowl as well as by the meat of wild animals.

The Neolithic farmers lived in simple dwellings—in caves and in small houses of sunbaked mud brick or of reed and wood. These homes were grouped into small villages or existed as single farmsteads surrounded by fields, sheltering animals and humans in adjacent or joined buildings. In the Neolithic period, the growth of cities such as Jericho (founded c. 9000 BC) was stimulated by the production of surplus crops.

Pastoralism may have been a later development. Evidence indicates that mixed farming, combining cultivation of crops and stock raising, was the most common Neolithic pattern. Nomadic herders, however, roamed the steppes of Europe and Asia, where the horse and camel were domesticated.

The earliest tools of the farmer were made of wood and stone. They included the stone adz; the sickle or reaping knife with sharpened stone blades, used to gather grain; the digging stick, used to plant seeds, and, with later adaptations, as a spade or hoe; and a rudimentary plow, a modified tree branch used to scratch the surface of the soil and prepare it for planting. The plow was later adapted for pulling by oxen.

The hilly areas of southwestern Asia and the forests of Europe had enough rain to sustain agriculture, but Egypt depended on the annual floods of the Nile to replenish soil moisture and fertility. The inhabitants of the so-called Fertile Crescent, around the Tigris and Euphrates rivers, also depended on annual floods to supply irrigation water. Drainage was necessary to prevent the carrying off of land from the hillsides through which the rivers ran. The farmers who lived in the area near the Huang He developed a system of irrigation and drainage to control the damage caused to their fields in the floodplain of the meandering river.

Although the Neolithic settlements were more permanent than the camps of hunting populations, villages had to be moved periodically in some areas, as the fields lost their fertility from continuous cropping. This was most necessary in northern Europe, where fields were produced by the slash-and-burn method of clearing. The settlements along the Nile, however, were more permanent, because the river deposited fertile silt annually.

*See also* ARCHAEOLOGY.

**Historical Agriculture Through the Roman Period.** With the close of the Neolithic period and the introduction of metals, the age of innovation in agriculture was largely over. The historical period—known through written and pictured materials, including the Bible, Near Eastern records and monuments, and Chinese, Greek, and Roman writings—was devoted to improvement. A few high points must serve to outline the development of worldwide agriculture in this era, roughly defined as 2500 BC to AD 500. For a similar period of development in Central and South America, somewhat later in date, *see* AMERICAN INDIANS.

Some plants became newly prominent. Grapes and wine were mentioned in Egyptian records about 2900 BC, and trade in olive oil and wine

was widespread in the Mediterranean area in the 1st millennium BC. Rye and oats were cultivated in northern Europe about 1000 BC.

Many vegetables and fruits, including onions, melons, and cucumbers, were grown by the 3d millennium BC in Ur. Dates and figs were an important source of sugar in the Near East, and apples, pomegranates, peaches, and mulberries were grown in the Mediterranean area. Cotton was grown and spun in India about 2000 BC, and linen and silk were used extensively in 2d-millennium China. Felt was made from the wool of sheep in Central Asia and the Russian steppes.

The horse, introduced to Egypt about 1600 BC, was already known in Mesopotamia and Asia Minor. The ox-drawn four-wheeled cart for farm work and two-wheeled chariots drawn by horses were familiar in northern India in the 2d millennium BC.

Improvements in tools and implements were particularly important. Metal tools were longer lasting and more efficient, and cultivation was greatly improved by such aids as the ox-drawn plow fitted with an iron-tipped point, noted in the 10th century BC in Palestine. In Mesopotamia in the 3d millennium BC a funnellike device was attached to the plow to aid in seeding, and other early forms of drills were used in China. Threshing was done with animal power in Palestine and Mesopotamia, although reaping, binding, and winnowing were still done by hand. Egypt retained hand seeding through this period, on individual farm plots and large estates alike.

Storage methods for oil and grain were improved. Granaries—jars, dry cisterns, silos, and bins of one sort or another containing stored grain—supported city populations. Indeed, without adequate food supplies and trade in food and nonfood items, the high civilizations of Mesopotamia, northern India, Egypt, and Rome would not have been possible.

Irrigation systems in China, Egypt, and the Near East were elaborated, putting more land into cultivation. The forced labor of peasants and the bureaucracy built up to plan and supervise the work of irrigation were probably basic in the development of the city-states of Sumer. Windmills and water mills, developed toward the end of the Roman period, increased control over the many uncertainties of weather. The introduction of fertilizer, mostly animal manures, and the rotation of fallow and crop land made agriculture more productive.

Mixed farming and stock raising were flourishing in the British Isles and on the continent of Europe as far north as Scandinavia at the beginning of the historical period, already displaying a

*Egyptian tomb painting from the tomb of Nahkt, 18th Dynasty, at Thebes, illustrates agricultural implements and practices of the period.* The Granger Collection

pattern that persisted throughout the next 3000 years. According to region, fishing and hunting supplemented the food grown by agriculturists.

Shortly after the time of Julius Caesar, the Roman historian Cornelius Tacitus described the "Germans" as a tribal society of free peasant warriors, who cultivated their own lands or left them to fight. About 500 years later, a characteristic European village had a cluster of houses in the middle, surrounded by rudely cultivated fields comprising individually owned farmlands; and meadows, woods, and wasteland were used by the entire community. Oxen and plow were passed from one field to another, and harvesting was a cooperative effort.

Rome appears to have started as a rural agricultural society of independent farmers. In the 1st millennium BC, after the city was established, however, agriculture started a capitalistic development that reached a peak in the Christian era. The large estates that supplied grain to the cities of the empire were owned by absentee landowners and were cultivated by slave labor under the supervision of hired overseers. As slaves, usually war captives, decreased in number, tenants replaced them. The late Roman villa of the Christian era approached the medieval manor in organization; slaves and dependent tenants were forced to work on a fixed schedule, and tenants paid a predetermined share to the estate owner. By the 4th century AD, serfdom (q.v.) was well established, and the former tenant was attached to the land.

**Feudal Agriculture.** The feudal period in Europe began soon after the fall of the Roman Empire, reaching its height about AD 1100. This period was also that of the development of the Byzantine Empire and of the power of the Saracens in the Middle East and southern Europe. Spain,

Italy, and southern France, in particular, were affected by events outside continental Europe.

In the Arab period in Egypt and Spain, irrigation was extended to previously sterile or unproductive land. In Egypt, grain production was sufficient to allow the country to sell wheat in the international market. In Spain, vineyards were planted on sloping land, and irrigation water was brought from the mountains to the plains. In some Islamic areas, oranges, lemons, peaches, and apricots were cultivated.

Rice, sugarcane, cotton, and such vegetables as spinach and artichokes, as well as the characteristic Spanish flavoring saffron, were produced. The silkworm was raised, and its food, the mulberry tree, was grown.

By the 12th century agriculture in the Middle East was static, and Mesopotamia, for example, fell back to subsistence level when its irrigation systems were destroyed by the Mongols. The Crusades increased European contact with Islamic lands and familiarized western Europe with citrus fruits and silk and cotton textiles.

The structure of agriculture was not uniform. In Scandinavia and eastern Germany, the small farms and villages of previous years remained. In mountainous areas and in the marshlands of Slavic Europe, the manorial system could not flourish. Stock raising and olive and grape culture were normally outside the system.

A manor required roughly 350 to 800 ha (about 900 to 2000 acres) of arable land and the same amount of other prescribed lands, such as wetlands, woodlots, and pasture. Typically, the manor was a self-contained community. On it was the large home of the holder of the fief—a military or church vassal of rank, sometimes given the title lord—or of his steward. A parish church was frequently included, and the manor might make up the entire parish. One or more villages might be located on the manor, and village peasants were the actual farmers. Under the direction of an overseer, they produced the crops, raised the meat and draft animals, and paid taxes in services, either forced labor on the lord's lands and other properties or forced military service.

A large manor had a mill for grinding grain, an oven for baking bread, fishponds, orchards, perhaps a winepress or oil press, and herb and vegetable gardens. Bees were kept to produce honey.

Woolen garments were produced from sheep raised on the manor. The wool was spun into yarn, woven into cloth, and then sewn into clothing. Linen textiles could also be produced from flax, which was grown for its oil and fiber.

The food served in a feudal castle or manor house varied—depending on the season and the lord's hunting prowess. Hunting for meat was, indeed, the major nonmilitary work of the lord and his military retainers. The castle residents could also eat domestic ducks, pheasants, pigeons, geese, hens, and partridges; fish, pork, beef, and mutton; and cabbages, turnips, carrots, onions, beans, and peas. Bread, cheese and butter, ale and wine, and apples and pears also appeared on the table. In the south, olives and olive oil might be used, often instead of butter.

Leather was produced from the manor's cattle. Horses and oxen were the beasts of burden; as heavier horses were bred and a new kind of har-

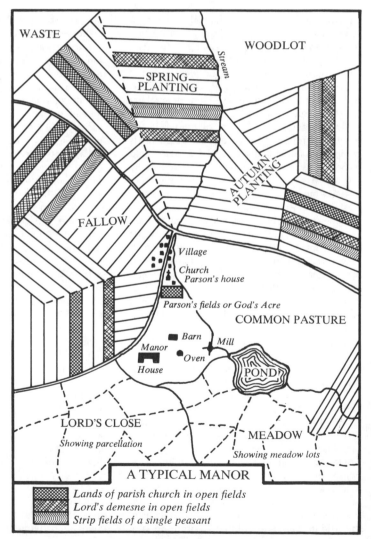

An English manor of the late feudal period typically employed a three-field system of cultivation, with each field divided into individual strips.

WASTE

WOODLOT

Stream

SPRING PLANTING

AUTUMN PLANTING

FALLOW

Village

Church
Parson's house

Parson's fields or God's Acre

COMMON PASTURE

Barn  Mill

Manor
House  Oven

POND

LORD'S CLOSE

Showing parcellation

MEADOW

Showing meadow lots

A TYPICAL MANOR

Lands of parish church in open fields
Lord's demesne in open fields
Strip fields of a single peasant

ness was developed, they became more important. A blacksmith, wheelwright, and carpenter made and maintained crude agricultural tools.

The cultivation regime was rigidly prescribed. The arable land was divided into three fields: one sown in the autumn in wheat or rye; a second sown in the spring in barley, rye, oats, beans, or peas; and the third left fallow. The fields were laid out in strips distributed over the three fields, and without hedges or fences to separate one strip from another. Each male peasant head of household was allotted about 30 strips. Helped by his family and a yoke of oxen, he worked under the direction of the lord's officials. When he worked on his own fields, if he had any, he followed village custom that was probably as rigid as the rule of an overseer.

About the 8th century a 4-year cycle of rotation of fallow appeared. The annual plowing routine on 400 ha would be 100 ha plowed in the autumn and 100 in the spring, and 200 ha of fallow plowed in June. These three periods of plowing, over the year, could produce two crops on 200 ha, depending on the weather. Typically, ten or more oxen were hitched to the tongue of the plow, often little more than a forked tree trunk. The oxen were no larger than modern heifers. At harvesttime, all the peasants, including women and children, were expected to work in the fields. After the harvest, the community's animals were let loose on the fields to forage.

Some manors used a strip system. Each strip, with an area of roughly 0.4 ha (about 1 acre), measured about 200 m (about 220 yd) in length and from 1.2 to 5 m (4 to 16.5 ft) in width. The lord's strips were similar to those of the peasants distributed throughout good and bad field areas. The parish priest might have lands separate from the community fields or strips that he worked himself or that were worked by the peasants.

In all systems, the lord's fields and needs came first, but about three days a week might be left for work on the family strips and garden plots. Wood and peat for fuel were gathered from the commonly held woodlots, and animals were pastured on village meadows. When surpluses of grain, hides, and wool were produced, they were sent to market.

About 1300 a tendency to enclose the common lands and to raise sheep for their wool alone first became apparent. The rise of the textile industry made sheep raising more profitable in England, Flanders, Champagne, Tuscany, Lombardy, and the region of Augsburg in Germany. At the same time, regions about the medieval towns began to specialize in garden produce and dairy products. Independent manorialism was also affected by the wars of 14th- and 15th-century Europe and by the widespread plague outbreaks of the 14th century. Villages were wiped out, and much arable land was abandoned. The remaining peasants were discontented and attempted to improve their conditions.

With the decline in the labor force, only the best land was kept in cultivation, and in southern Italy, for instance, irrigation helped to increase production on the more fertile soils. The emphasis on grain was replaced by diversification, and items requiring more care were produced, such as wine, oil, cheese, butter, and vegetables.

**Scientific Agriculture.** By the 16th century, population was increasing in Europe, and agricultural production was again expanding.

The nature of agriculture there and in other areas was to change considerably in succeeding centuries. Several reasons can be identified. Europe was cut off from Asia and the Middle East by an extension of Turkish power. New economic theories were being put into practice, directly affecting agriculture. Also, continued wars between England and France, within each of these countries, and in Germany consumed capital and human resources.

A new period of exploration and colonization was undertaken to circumvent Turkey's control of the spice trade, to provide homes for religious refugees, and to provide wealth for European nations convinced that only precious metals constituted wealth.

Colonial agriculture was carried out not only to feed the colonists but also to produce cash crops and to supply food for the home country. This meant cultivation of such crops as sugar, cotton, tobacco, and tea and production of animal products such as wool and hides. From the 15th to the 19th century the slave trade provided needed laborers, replacing natives killed by unaccustomed hard labor in unfavorable climates and substituting for imported Europeans on colonial plantations that required a larger labor force than the colony could provide. Slaves from Africa worked, for instance, in the Caribbean area on sugar plantations and in North America on indigo and cotton plantations. Indians were virtually enslaved in Mexico. Indentured slaves from Europe, and especially from the prisons of England, provided both skilled and unskilled labor to many colonies. Ultimately, however, both slavery and serfdom were substantially wiped out in the 19th century. See PEONAGE; PLANTATION; SLAVERY.

When encountered by the Spanish conquistadors, the more advanced Indians in the New World had intensive agricultural economies but no draft or riding animals and no wheeled vehicles. Squash, beans, peas, and corn had long since been domesticated. Land was owned by clans and other kinship groups or by ruling tribes that had formed sophisticated governments, but not by individuals or individual families. Several civilizations had risen and fallen in Central and South America by the 16th century. Those met by the Spanish were the Aztec, Inca, and Maya.

The scientific revolution resulting from the Renaissance and the Age of Enlightenment in Europe encouraged experimentation in agriculture as well as in other fields. Trial-and-error efforts in plant breeding produced improved crops, and a few new strains of cattle and sheep were developed. Notable was the Guernsey cow breed, still a heavy milk producer today. Enclosure was greatly speeded up in the 18th century, and individual landowners could determine the disposition of land and of pasture, previously subject to common use. Crop rotation, involving alternation of legumes with grain, was more readily practiced outside the village strip system inherited from the manorial period. In England, where scientific farming was most efficient, enclosure brought about a fundamental reorganization of landownership. From 1660 on, the large landowners had begun to add to their properties, frequently at the expense of small independent farmers. By Victorian times, the agricultural pattern was based on the relationship between the landowner, dependent on rents; the farmer, producer of crops; and the landless laborer, the "hired hand" of American farming lore. Drainage brought more land into cultivation, and, with the Industrial Revolution, farm machinery was introduced.

It is not possible to fix a clear decade or series of events as the start of the agricultural revolution through technology. Among the important advances were the purposeful selective breeding of livestock, begun in the early 1700s, and the spreading of limestone on farm soils in the late 1700s. Mechanical improvements of the traditional wooden plow began in the mid-1600s with small iron points fastened onto the wood with strips of leather. In 1797, Charles Newbold (1764–1835), a blacksmith in Burlington, N.J., introduced the cast-iron moldboard plow. John Deere, another American blacksmith, further improved the plow in the 1830s and manufactured it in steel. Other notable inventions included the seed drill of the English agriculturist Jethro Tull, developed in the early 1700s and progressively improved for more than a century; the reaper of Cyrus McCormick in 1831; and numerous new horse-drawn threshers, cultivators, grain and grass cutters, rakes, and corn shellers. By the late 1800s, steam power was frequently used to replace animal power in drawing plows and in operating threshing machinery.

The demand for food for urban workers and raw materials for industrial plants produced a realignment of world trade. Science and technology developed for industrial purposes were carried over into agriculture, eventually resulting in the agribusinesses of the mid-20th century.

In the 17th and 18th centuries the first systematic attempts were made to study and control pests. Before this time, handpicking and spraying were the usual methods of pest control. In the 19th century, poisons of various types were developed for use in sprays, and biological controls such as predatory insects were also used. Resistant plant varieties were cultivated; this was particularly successful with the European grapevine, in which the grape-bearing stems were grafted onto resistant American rootstocks to defeat the *Phylloxera* aphid. *See* PEST CONTROL.

Improvements in transportation affected agriculture. Roads, canals, and rail lines enabled farmers to obtain needed supplies and to market their produce over a wider area. Food could be protected in transport and shipped more economically than before as a result of rail, ship, and refrigeration developments of the late 19th and early 20th centuries. Efficient use of these developments led to increasing specialization and eventual changes in the location of agricultural suppliers. In the last quarter of the 19th century, for example, Australian and North American suppliers displaced European suppliers of grain in the European market. When grain production proved unprofitable for European farmers, or an area became more urbanized, specialization in dairying, cheesemaking, and other products was emphasized.

The impetus toward more food production in the era following World War II was a result of a new population explosion. A so-called green revolution, involving selective breeding of traditional crops for high yields, new hybrids, and intensive cultivation methods adapted to the climates and cultural conditions of densely populated countries such as India, temporarily stemmed the pressure for more food. A worldwide shortage of petroleum in the mid-1970s, however, reduced the supplies of nitrogen fertilizer helpful to the success of the new varieties. Simultaneously, erratic weather and natural disasters such as drought and floods reduced crop levels throughout the world. Famine seemed to be imminent in the Indian subcontinent and was common in many parts of Africa south of the Sahara. Economic conditions, particularly uncon-

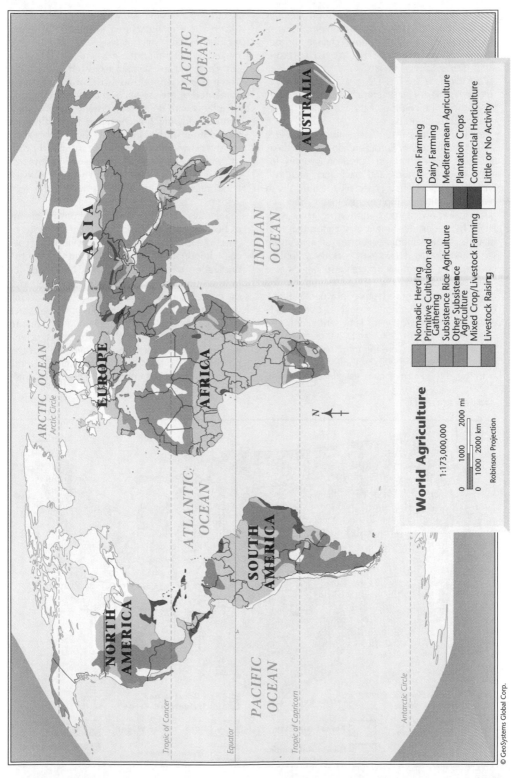

**World Agriculture**

1:173,000,000

Robinson Projection

0   1000   2000 km
0      1000   2000 mi

Nomadic Herding
Primitive Cultivation and Gathering
Subsistence Rice Agriculture
Other Subsistence Agriculture
Mixed Crop/Livestock Farming
Livestock Raising

Grain Farming
Dairy Farming
Mediterranean Agriculture
Plantation Crops
Commercial Horticulture
Little or No Activity

ARCTIC OCEAN
Arctic Circle

ASIA

EUROPE

AFRICA

AUSTRALIA

PACIFIC OCEAN

INDIAN OCEAN

ATLANTIC OCEAN

NORTH AMERICA

SOUTH AMERICA

PACIFIC OCEAN

Tropic of Cancer

Equator

Tropic of Capricorn

Antarctic Circle

trolled inflation, threatened the food supplier and the consumer alike. These problems became the determinants of agricultural change and development. *See* ENERGY SUPPLY, WORLD; ENVIRONMENT; FOOD SUPPLY, WORLD.

*AGRICULTURE IN THE U.S.*

In North America, agriculture had progressed further before the coming of the Europeans than is commonly supposed.

Until the 19th century, agriculture in the U.S. shared the history of European and colonial areas and was dependent on European sources for seed, stocks, livestock, and machinery, such as it was. That dependency, especially the difficulty in procuring suitable implements, made American farmers somewhat more innovative. They were aided by the establishment of societies that lobbied for governmental agencies of agriculture (*see* AGRICULTURE, DEPARTMENT OF); the voluntary cooperation of farmers through associations (*see* COOPERATIVES; NATIONAL GRANGE); and the increasing use of various types of power machinery on the farm. Government policies traditionally encouraged the growth of land settlement. The Homestead Act of 1862 and the resettlement plans of the 1930s were the important legislative acts of the 19th and 20th centuries.

In the 20th century steam, gasoline, diesel, and electric power came into wide use. Chemical fertilizers were manufactured in greatly increased quantities, and soil analysis was widely employed to determine the elements needed by a particular soil to maintain or restore its fertility. The loss of soil by erosion (q.v.) was extensively combated by the use of cover crops (quick-growing plants with dense root systems to bind soil), contour plowing (in which the furrow follows the contour of the land and is level, rather than up and down hills that provide channels for run-off water), and strip cropping (sowing strips of dense-rooted plants to serve as water-breaks or windbreaks in fields of plants with loose root systems). *See also* DUST BOWL.

Selective breeding produced improved strains of both farm animals and crop plants. Hybrids of desirable characteristics were developed; especially important for food production was the hybridization of corn in the 1930s. New uses for farm products, by-products, and wastes were discovered. Standards of quality, size, and packing were established for various fruits and vegetables to aid in wholesale marketing. Among the first to be standardized were apples, citrus fruits, celery, berries, and tomatoes. Improvements in storage, processing, and transportation also increased the marketability of farm products. The use of cold-

*Agriculture in the U.S.*

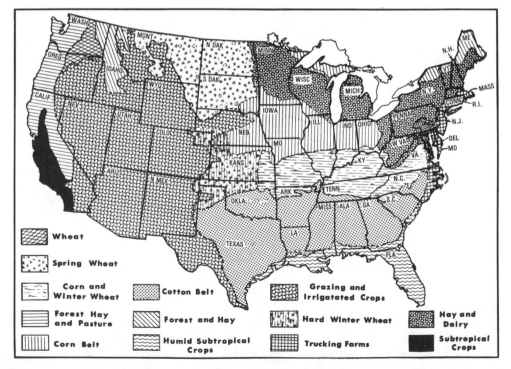

| | |
|---|---|
| ▨ **Wheat** | |
| ⁙ **Spring Wheat** | |
| ▤ **Corn and Winter Wheat** | ▦ **Cotton Belt** |
| ▦ **Forest Hay and Pasture** | ◎ **Forest and Hay** |
| ▥ **Corn Belt** | 〰 **Humid Subtropical Crops** |
| ▦ **Grazing and Irrigated Crops** | |
| ⷾ **Hard Winter Wheat** | ▩ **Hay and Dairy** |
| ▦ **Trucking Farms** | ■ **Subtropical Crops** |

## AGRICULTURAL INCOME IN THE UNITED STATES[1]

| Year | 1960 | 1970 | 1975 | 1980[2] | 1985 | 1989 |
|---|---|---|---|---|---|---|
| Income from livestock and livestock products | 18,989 | 29,563 | 43,059 | 68,000 | 69,800 | 83,700 |
| Income from crops | 15,259 | 20,976 | 45,150 | 71,700 | 74,200 | 75,400 |
| Government payments of subsidies and bonuses | 702 | 3,717 | 807 | 1,800 | 7,700 | 10,900 |
| Nonmoney income: value of housing and products used in farm homes | 3,303 | 3,770 | 6,689 | 12,200 | 11,800 | 19,200 |
| Gross income[3] | 38,894 | 58,575 | 100,338 | 149,300 | 166,200 | 189,200 |
| Cost of production | 27,376 | 44,424 | 75,863 | 133,100 | 134,000 | 142,600 |
| Net income[3] | 11,518 | 14,151 | 24,475 | 16,100 | 32,300 | 46,700 |

1. In millions of dollars. 2. Figures since 1980 rounded to nearest hundred million dollars. 3. Includes adjustments to income not otherwise shown.

storage warehouses and refrigerated railroad cars was supplemented by the introduction of refrigerated motor trucks, by rapid delivery by airplane, and by the quick-freeze process of preservation, in which farm produce is frozen and packaged the same day that it is picked. Freeze-drying and irradiation have also reached practical application for many perishable foods.

Scientific methods have begun to be applied to pest control, limiting the widespread use of insecticides and fungicides and applying more varied and targeted techniques. New understanding of significant biological control measures and the emphasis on integrated pest management have made possible more effective control of certain kinds of insects.

Chemicals for weed control have become important for a number of crops, in particular cotton and corn. The increasing use of chemicals for the control of insects, diseases, and weeds has brought about additional environmental problems and regulations that make strong demands on the skill of farm operators.

In the 1980s high technology farming, including hybrids for wheat, rice, and other grains, better methods of soil conservation and irrigation, and the growing use of fertilizers has led to the production of more food per capita, not only in the U.S., but in much of the rest of the world. U.S. farmers, however, still have the advantage of superior private and government research facilities to produce and perfect new technologies.

**Government Price-Support Policies.** One of the recurring problems of American agriculture in the 20th century has been the tendency of farm income to lag behind increases in the costs of production. The problem began in the 1920s, following a period of exceptional prosperity for U.S. farmers. The period 1910–14 was later taken as a standard for the level of farm prices in relation to the general price level and formed the basis for a concept called parity, aimed at maintaining farming as an essential part of the U.S. economy. After the outbreak of World War I the U.S. became the chief source of food for the warring nations of Europe, with U.S. farmers

bringing some 16 million additional ha (about 40 million acres) of land under cultivation and investing heavily in new land and equipment. These measures raised production levels until 1920, when the European demand for U.S. farm products suddenly declined, and prices began a continuing downward spiral.

Although attempts were under way to ease the economic difficulties of the farmer, farm income had not begun to recover when the Great Depression of the 1930s intensified them even more. By 1932 the level of farm prices was only about 65 percent of the 1910–14 average. Farmers continued to produce almost as much as before, and even increased their production in an attempt to maintain their income. That succeeded only in lowering farm prices further. By comparison, manufacturers could control their production, thereby maintaining price levels to a certain degree. Although prices for industrial goods declined, they did not drop as severely as farm prices, so that by 1932 farmers were receiving only 58 cents from the sale of their products for every dollar they had to pay for nonfarm items.

The federal government, which had done little in the 1920s to help farmers, initiated remedial programs during the administration of President Franklin D. Roosevelt. One approach was to reduce the supply of basic farm commodities. The Agricultural Adjustment Act of 1933 provided payments to farmers in return for agreements to curtail their acreage or their production of wheat, cotton, rice, tobacco, corn, hogs, and dairy products. The act was declared unconstitutional in 1936, but in 1938, after several changes in the membership of the U.S. Supreme Court, a second Agricultural Adjustment Act was passed under which production quotas were set as before. Payments were financed from taxes imposed on processors and were based on the parity concept.

The government also lent money to farmers to enable them to withhold crops from the market when prices were low and to store the produce so that it might be available in poor crop years.

A third method to limit production provided

payments for shifting acreage of soil-depleting crops such as corn, wheat, cotton, tobacco, and rice to soil-conserving plants such as grasses and legumes and for carrying out soil-building practices. In 1939, an all-risk crop insurance program was initiated for interested farmers to prevent economic distress in case of crop failure for hail, floods, and other natural disasters.

Until World War II the problem of low farm prices was not basically a result of overproduction. Rather, it was a consequence of the cycles of business and weather, and of problems of internal distribution, transportation, and credit. Following World War II, however, overproduction became a serious problem. Both during and immediately after the war, farm prices were generally high. Because production costs also were high, parity payments remained in force. Federal transactions in surplus commodities, principally the sale of such commodities at prices less than those paid to farmers, proved costly for the government. To reduce costs of the federal farm program, the administration of President Dwight D. Eisenhower proposed the substitution of flexible or variable price supports for the rigid 90 percent of parity that was in force. A bill authorizing a sliding scale of payments at 82.5 percent to 90 percent of parity on the basic commodities was enacted by the U.S. Congress in 1954.

The Agricultural Act of 1956, otherwise known as the soil-bank program, authorized federal payments to farmers if they reduced production of certain crops. A subsidy plan was formulated whereby farmers would be paid for converting part of their cropland to soil-conserving uses. In practice, the farmers shared the costs of planting trees or grasses and received annual payments compensating them for the economic loss incurred by the removal of some of their land from production.

The Department of Agriculture in the administrations of Presidents John Kennedy and Lyndon Johnson during the 1960s made control of overproduction a primary goal of farm policy. Farmers were offered what was in effect a rental payment for a part of their land that would be taken out of production during the following year. At the same time, measures were undertaken to expand the export market for agricultural products. During this period the ratio of a farmer's per capita income to that of a nonfarm person increased from about 50 percent to about 75 percent.

Direct subsidies for withholding agricultural land from production were phased out in 1973, as a result of a proposal by President Richard M. Nixon. In the same year, net farm income swelled to $33.3 billion.

Poor grain harvests throughout the world, particularly in the Soviet Union, prompted massive sales of U.S. government-owned grain reserves. World climatic conditions also helped keep demand for U.S. produce high through the mid-1970s. Toward the end of the decade, exports lessened, prices dropped, and farm income began to fall without a corresponding decrease in costs of production. U.S. net farm income in 1976 fell to $18.7 billion.

In 1978, a limited, voluntary output restriction was begun by President Jimmy Carter. Called the "farmer-held grain reserve program," the action took grains off the market for up to three years or until market prices reached stated levels. The program was intended also to provide an adequate reserve, lessen food-price gyrations and combat inflation, give livestock producers protection from extremes in feed costs, and contribute to greater continuity in foreign food aid.

On Jan. 4, 1980, President Carter declared a limited suspension of grain sales to the Soviet Union in response to that country's invasion of Afghanistan. Additional restrictions included a prohibition on sales of U.S. phosphate. Despite the grain embargo, the U.S. continued to honor a 5-year agreement already in effect that committed it to sell 8 million tons of grain to the Soviets yearly. The year 1980 was an election year, and despite efforts by President Carter's opposition to void the embargo, it continued. Administration officials argued that the Soviets had never been a major customer or even a reliable buyer. U.S. farmers maintained, however, that the action was at their expense and had made 1980 one of their worst years. In fact, U.S. farm exports in 1980 reached an all-time high of $40 billion, but the continued rise in costs of production and an extremely hot summer with accompanying droughts affected many farmers adversely. A new crop insurance program, passed by Congress in the fall of 1980, offered relief from such conditions rather than having to rely on disaster loans, which amounted to $30 million for feed alone in that year.

Whether the 1980 grain embargo had a strong effect on the USSR was a matter of conjecture. Beef production dropped 16 percent, pork was off 10 percent, and milk production fell 4 percent, but by the end of the year the Soviets had apparently obtained their needed grain from other sources. When President Ronald Reagan took office in 1981, he lifted the embargo and extended the agreement that allowed the USSR to purchase 8 million tons of grain yearly from the U.S. The two nations then signed a new 5-year agreement in 1983 that obliged the Soviet

Union to import a minimum of 9 million tons of U.S. grain every year.

**Farming Regions.** The U.S. has ten major farming areas. They vary by soil, slope of land, climate, and distance to market, and in storage and marketing facilities.

The states of the northeast and the Lake states are the country's principal milk-producing areas. Climate and soil there are suited to raising grains and forage for cattle and for pastures. Broiler farming is important to Maine, Delaware, and Maryland. Fruits and vegetables are also important to the region.

The Appalachian region is the major tobacco-producing area of the nation. Peanuts, cattle, and dairy production also are important.

Beef cattle and broilers are the major livestock products farther south in the states of the Southeast; fruit and vegetables and peanuts are also grown. Florida has vast citrus groves and winter vegetable production areas.

In the Delta states, principal cash crops are soybeans and cotton. Rice and sugarcane are grown in the more humid and wet areas. With improved pastures, livestock production has gained importance in recent years. It also is a major broiler-producing region.

The Corn Belt, extending from Ohio through Iowa, has rich soil, good climate, and sufficient rainfall for excellent farming. Corn, beef cattle, hogs, and dairy products are of primary importance. Other feed grains, soybeans, and wheat also are grown.

The northern and southern Plains, extending north and south from Canada to Mexico and from the Corn Belt into the Rocky Mountains, are restricted by low rainfall in the western portion and by cold winters and short growing seasons in the north. But about 60 percent of the nation's winter and spring wheat grows in the Plains states. Other small grains, grain sorghums, hay, forage crops, and pastures help make cattle important to the region. Cotton is produced in the southern part.

The Mountain states provide yet a different terrain. Vast areas are suited to cattle and sheep. Wheat is important in the north. Irrigation in the valleys provides water for hay, sugar beets, potatoes, fruits, and vegetables.

The Pacific region includes California, Oregon, and Washington plus Alaska and Hawaii. In the northern mainland, farmers raise wheat, fruit, and potatoes. Dairying, vegetables, and some grain are important to Alaska. Many of the more southerly farmers have large tracts on which they raise vegetables, fruit, and cotton, often under irrigation. Cattle are raised throughout the region.

Hawaii grows sugarcane and pineapple as its major crops.

**Agricultural Resources.** The total land area of the U.S. is about 917 million ha (about 2.27 billion acres), of which about 47 percent is used to produce crops and livestock. The rest is distributed among forestland (29 percent) and urban, transportation, and other uses (24 percent).

Approximately 161 million ha (about 399 million acres) make up cropland resources. Almost 83 percent of cropland is cultivated, including about 23 million ha (about 57 million acres) used for wheat, about 30 million ha (about 74 million acres) used for corn, and about 25 million ha (about 62 million acres) used for hay. More than 50 percent of croplands are prime farmland, the best land for producing food and fiber.

The nation has another nearly 400 million ha (almost 1 billion acres) of nonfederal rural land currently being used for pastures, range, forest, and other purposes. About 27.5 million ha (about 68 million acres) of this land are suitable for conversion to cropland if needed.

**Recent Changes.** The history of agriculture in the U.S. since the Great Depression has been one of consolidation and increasing efficiency. From a high of 6.8 million farms in 1935, the total number declined to 2.1 million in 1991 on a little less than the same area, about 397 million ha (about 982 million acres). Average farm size in 1935 was about 63 ha (about 155 acres); in 1991 it was about 189 ha (about 467 acres).

About 4.6 million people lived on farms in 1990, based on a new farm definition introduced in 1977 to distinguish between rural residents and people who earned $1000 or more from annual agricultural product sales. The farm population continues to constitute a declining share of the nation's total; about 1 person in every 54, or 1.8 percent, of the nation's 250 million people were farm residents in 1990.

Total value of land and buildings on U.S. farms in 1990 was $658 billion, substantially less than the value in 1980. Value of products sold was $170 billion per year. Overall net farm income was more than $46 billion in 1989, of which government subsidies accounted for 23 percent.

Not including real estate, major expenditures by farmers in 1989 were for feed ($22.7 billion); fuel, lubricants, and maintenance ($13.1 billion); hired labor ($11.9 billion); fertilizer ($7.6 billion); and seed ($3.7 billion).

Outstanding farm debt in 1989 was $146 billion, of which about 55 percent was owed on real estate. Interest payments on the mortgage debt were about $7.6 billion per year.

In 1980 a report based on projections by the U.S. government stated that in the next 20 years world food requirements would increase tremendously, with developed countries requiring most of the increase, and food prices would double. Less than five years later, however, the U.S. farmer was enveloped in a major crisis caused by exceptionally heavy farm debts, mounting farm subsidy costs, and rising surpluses. A number of farmers were forced into foreclosure.

The ailing Farm Credit System, a group of 37 farmer-owned banks under the Farm Credit Administration (q.v.) appealed to the government for a $5 to $6 billion fund that would keep the system solvent despite the weak national farm economy. After initial resistance, President Ronald Reagan signed legislation in December 1985 designed to create the Farm Credit System Capital Corp. to take over bad loans from the system's banks and to assume responsibility for foreclosing or restructuring distressed loans.

In December President Reagan also signed the Food Security Act of 1985, legislation designed to govern the nation's farm policies for the next five years, trim farm subsidies, and stimulate farm exports.

**Agricultural Exports.** The U.S. is the world's principal exporter of agricultural products. In 1989 the value of produce exported was about $39.7 billion, including roughly $1.5 billion in donations and loans to developing nations.

A substantial percentage of the wheat, soybeans, rice, cotton, tobacco, and corn for grain produced in the U.S. is exported. The principal foreign markets for the products are Asia, Western Europe, and Latin America. Japan heads the list of individual countries that import U.S. farm products.

*For further information on this topic, see the Bibliography in volume 28, sections 584–97.*

**AGRICULTURE, DEPARTMENT OF,** executive department of the U.S. government, begun about 1836 as a branch of the Office of the Commissioner of Patents, with the purpose of distributing plants and seeds to farmers. It was established as a department of agriculture by Congress in 1862 and raised to cabinet level in 1889. It is administered by a secretary appointed by the president with the approval of the Senate. The department carries out programs of research, education, conservation, forestry, marketing, credit, export expansion, food distribution, production adjustment, grading and inspection, and development of rural areas.

About the time the department was raised to cabinet level, the reserves of public lands available for homesteading were becoming depleted.

Instead of moving from worn-out land to free or less expensive fertile lands, farmers had to seek the aid of scientific techniques to increase production and income. Consequently, from about 1890 on, the responsibilities of the department grew rapidly. Existing units of the organization were merged and new units were created to carry on research and service activities and to administer regulatory laws.

The growth and expansion of the Department of Agriculture continued during the depression of the 1930s, when the problem of surplus farm products became extremely acute; the department was reorganized several times. During World War II, many bureaus were split off to establish the War Food Administration, but these bureaus were returned to the unified control of the department in a reorganization begun just after the war.

The following are among the major units of the department. The Agricultural Research Service, together with the Cooperative State Research Service, works with various state agencies to improve the effectiveness of research in such areas as human nutrition, soil and water conservation, processing and distribution of farm products, and climatic environmental conditions. With the continuing ability of farmers to produce more than the market demands, especially in grains, the Agricultural Stabilization and Conservation Service carries out programs aimed at keeping grain production balanced with needs. The Food and Nutrition Service administers food assistance programs, including food stamp, school breakfast and lunch, special milk, and summer food service programs.

The Agricultural Marketing Service assures safe, efficient movement of products from producer to consumer. The Animal and Plant Health Inspection Service safeguards the health and quality of animals and plants and protects the consumer by means of federal and state meat and poultry inspection. The Food Safety and Inspection Service provides for federal inspection of poultry, meat, and related products to be sure they are labeled honestly and informatively and that they are safe and wholesome. The Federal Grain Inspection Service sets standards and regulates the inspection and weighing of all types of grain.

The Economics Research Service publishes information that helps officials to develop and administer agricultural policies and programs. The National Agricultural Statistics Service prepares estimates of production, price, and supply figures on agricultural commodities, which appear in some 300 reports annually. The Foreign

Agricultural Service works to develop markets abroad and expand agricultural exports. Under its sponsorship, technicians work in developing nations to improve agriculture; officials of developing nations annually receive agricultural training in the U.S. The Soil Conservation Service helps to develop natural resources, control erosion and sedimentation, prevent floods, and plan community use of land. Technical service is given each year to landowners and land users in soil conservation districts and watershed projects.

Other units of the department include the Agricultural Cooperative Service, the Commodity Credit Corporation, the Extension Service, the Farmers Home Administration, the Federal Crop Insurance Corporation, the Forest Service, the Rural Development Administration, and the Rural Electrification Administration.

**AGRIGENTO** (Lat. *Agrigentum;* Gr. *Akragas*), city, Italy, S Sicily, capital of Agrigento Province, on the Mediterranean Sea. The city is a tourist and an agricultural center; manufactures include processed cement, sulfur, and furniture. The city has ruins of some 20 Doric temples (6th and 5th cent. BC) and an archaeological museum.

Agrigento was founded by Greeks from the city of Gela about 582 BC and became a trading and cultural center with a population of about 200,000. After 406 BC, when it was sacked by a force from Carthage, the city (then known as Akragas) declined in importance, although it remained large. In 262 BC it was incorporated into the Roman Empire and became known as Agrigentum. It was called Girgenti from the early Middle Ages until 1927, when the name was officially changed to Agrigento. Pop. (1990 est.) 56,400.

**AGRIPPA, Herod.** *See* HEROD AGRIPPA.

**AGRIPPA, Marcus Vipsanius** (63–12 BC), Roman general and statesman. In 36 BC he defeated Sextus Pompeius (d. 35 BC), son of the Roman general Pompey the Great, in the naval battles of Mylae (now Milazzo, Italy) and Naulochus. These victories helped Octavian, heir of Julius Caesar, become the sole ruler of the Roman Empire.

In 31 BC Agrippa commanded Octavian's fleet in the victory at Actium over the combined forces of the Roman general Mark Antony and Queen Cleopatra of Egypt. In 27 BC, when Octavian became the first Roman emperor, assuming the name Augustus, Agrippa is thought to have built the first Roman Pantheon in commemoration of the Battle of Actium.

Much of the success of the reign of Augustus was due to Agrippa. He was active in many campaigns and frequently served as provincial governor. He was one of the emperor's most trusted advisers and in 21 BC married Julia, the only child of Augustus. By Julia, Agrippa had three sons and two daughters, one of whom, Agrippina the Elder, married the Roman general Germanicus Caesar.

**AGRIPPINA THE ELDER** (c. 13 BC–AD 33), daughter of the Roman general and statesman Marcus Vipsanius Agrippa and Julia, daughter of the emperor Augustus. Agrippina was one of the most virtuous and heroic women of antiquity. She married the Roman general Germanicus Caesar and had nine children, the most famous of whom were Agrippina the Younger and Gaius Caesar, later the emperor Caligula. Agrippina accompanied Germanicus on many of his military expeditions. After the death of Germanicus in AD 19, Emperor Tiberius is said to have distrusted Agrippina, whose sons were possible successors to the throne. In AD 30, at the instigation of his minister Lucius Aelius Sejanus (d. 31), Tiberius banished her to the island of Pandateria (now Ventotene), near Naples, where she starved herself to death three years later.

**AGRIPPINA THE YOUNGER** (c. AD 15–59), daughter of the Roman general Germanicus Caesar and Agrippina the Elder, born in Oppidum Ubiorum, a Roman outpost on the Rhine River. The outpost was later named Colonia Agrippinensis (now Cologne, Germany) after her. She was thrice married. Her first husband was the father of her son Lucius, better known as Emperor Nero; she is said to have poisoned her second husband. In AD 49 she wed her uncle, Emperor Claudius I; he adopted Nero as his son and heir. In AD 54 Claudius was poisoned, almost certainly by Agrippina, who thus paved the way for Nero to become emperor. She attempted to rule through her son, but when she opposed his marriage to his second wife Poppaea Sabina (d. 65), Agrippina was killed on his orders.

**AGRONOMY,** agricultural science concerning methods of soil management and crop production. Agronomists study plant life and soils and the complex relationship existing between them. The scientists attempt to develop techniques that will increase the yield of field crops, improve their quality, and, at the same time, conserve the fertility of the soil. Agronomic research has resulted in important new strains of disease-resistant plants and in the development of such practices as the selective breeding of crops and the use of chemical fertilizers. *See* CROP FARMING; FERTILIZER; PEST CONTROL; PLANT BREEDING; SOIL MANAGEMENT.

**AGUA,** dormant volcano, S Guatemala, near the city of Guatemala. It is an imposing, cone-shaped mountain, with an elevation of 3766 m (12,356 ft). The original town of Guatemala, on a site near the modern city, was destroyed when the volcano erupted in 1541. In 1917 the modern city was severely damaged by an earthquake that originated near the base of Agua.

**AGUADILLA,** town, in Aguadilla Municipality, NW Puerto Rico, a port on Mona Passage (linking the Atlantic Ocean and the Caribbean Sea). It is a trade center with a major cargo airport. Machinery, apparel, leather products, and processed food are manufactured here. Aguadilla Regional College (1972) is in the city. Christopher Columbus is said to have visited the site of Aguadilla in 1493. The town was founded in 1775. Pop. (1980) 20,879; (1990) 18,347.

**AGUASCALIENTES,** city, central Mexico, capital of the state of Aguascalientes. The mild, pleasant climate of the area and the mineral springs near the city make Aguascalientes a favorite health resort. Local industries include the processing of many varieties of fruits and vegetables grown in the area, smelting works, railroad shops, tanneries, and cotton and other textile mills. The city is noted for the manufacture of serapes, as well as for its unique pottery. It has much fine colonial architecture and many plazas and parks. Points of interest include a network of immense catacombs, built by an unidentified pre-Columbian people. Founded in 1575 as a silver-mining town, it became an important commercial center in the 19th century, when a system of railroads was developed. Pop. (1990) 506,384.

**AGUINALDO, Emilio** (1869–1964), Filipino leader, born near Cavite, Luzon, and educated at the College of San Juan de Letran, Manila. Aguinaldo led a Filipino insurrection against Spanish rule in 1896, and two years later, during the Spanish-American War, he aided the American attack on the Philippine Islands. As head of the Filipino provisional government in 1899, he resisted American occupation; he continued to lead the struggle against the U.S. forces until March 1901, when he was captured. In April 1901 he took an oath of allegiance to the U.S. and retired to private life. He was taken into custody in 1945, during World War II, by invading American troops and held on suspicion of collaboration with the enemy during the Japanese occupation. He was subsequently exonerated.

**AGUIRRE, Lope de** (1508?–61), Spanish adventurer, born in Oñate. He took part in the civil wars among the Spanish conquerors in Peru after that country had been conquered by Francisco Pizarro in 1533. In 1559 Aguirre joined an expedition to search for the legendary El Dorado. The expedition sailed down the Amazon River and discovered its connection with the Orinoco River. During the voyage Aguirre renounced allegiance

to the king of Spain and sought to return to Peru to establish a kingdom there that would be independent of Spain. While he was marching through Venezuela, Spanish forces defeated his army and killed him at Barquisimeto.

**AGULHAS, CAPE.** *See* Cape Agulhas.

**AHAB,** king of Israel (869–850 BC), the son and successor of Omri (r. 876–869 BC). Ahab married Jezebel, a Tyrian princess, and through her influence the Phoenician worship of the god Baal was introduced into Israel. Ahab waged two successful wars against Ben-Hadad I (r. about 890-841 BC), king of Syria, but in a third campaign was killed by an arrow. His daughter Athaliah (d. 836 BC) married Jehoram (r. 849–842 BC), king of Judah. Ahab's entire family was later killed.

**AHAD HA-AM,** pseudonym of Asher Ginzberg (1856–1927), Russian writer, born near Kiev, Ukraine. In 1889 he founded the Zionist League at Odessa. He immigrated to England in 1906, living there until 1921, when he settled in Palestine. His writings, concerned with the problem of the Jewish peoples dispersed throughout the world, express his belief in the desirability of a Jewish homeland in Palestine based upon the common cultural and ethical heritage of the Jews. Ahad Ha-am's philosophy, adopted by numerous writers since his time and now called cultural Zionism, aimed at bringing about not a national state, similar to other national states, but a religious center in which the principles of the prophets could be reaffirmed. Among his other works, Ahad Ha-am wrote a collection of essays, *At the*

*Emilio Aguinaldo*

*Crossroads* (1895; trans. 1913), and a collection of letters, *Igeroth* (1923).

**AHAGGAR MOUNTAINS,** also Hoggar Mountains, plateau region, S Algeria, in the center of the Sahara. It is an arid, rocky, upland region that rises to a maximum elevation in Mt. Tahat (2918 m/9573 ft). On its SW edge is the oasis town and Saharan crossroads of Tamanrasset.

**AHASUERUS,** Hebrew form, as known from the Bible, of the Persian name Xerxes. The Ahasuerus of the Book of Esther is generally identified with King Xerxes I. Another Ahasuerus (see Dan. 9:1) is said to have been the father of Darius the Mede.

**AHAZ,** (r. 735–715 BC), son of Jotham (r. 742–735 BC), and 12th king of Judah. Judah was attacked early in his reign by King Pekah of Israel (737–732 BC) and King Rezin of Syria (r. about 742–732 BC), who attempted to force Ahaz into a coalition against Assyria. Additional incursions were made into Judaean territory by the Edomites, to whom Ahaz was forced to give up the important city of Elath (now al-Aqabah, Jordan). Ahaz asked help of the Assyrian king Tiglath-pileser III (r. 745–727 BC), who drove out the invaders but in return exacted tribute from Judah. Ahaz made various changes in the temple service and paid homage to the Assyrian gods. He was denounced for infidelity to Jehovah by the Hebrew prophet Isaiah, who opposed the alliance with Assyria. In 715 BC Ahaz was succeeded by his son Hezekiah.

**AHIDJO, Ahmadou** (1924–89), first president of Cameroon (1960–82). He was born in Garoua and educated at Yaoundé. Beginning his career as a radio administrator, he soon turned to politics and was elected to the Cameroonian territorial assembly in 1947. After an interim in the Assembly of the French Union, he was reelected to the territorial assembly and was its president from 1956 to 1957, when he was appointed minister of the interior and deputy prime minister; he was elevated to the post of prime minister the following year. When Cameroon became independent in 1960, Ahidjo was elected president. Reelected at 5-year intervals through 1980, he resigned the presidency in 1982 and leadership of the ruling National Cameroonian Union in 1983. While in exile in France, Ahidjo was accused of plotting to overthrow his successor.

**AHITHOPHEL,** in the Old Testament, friend and adviser to David, king of the Jews. According to the biblical story, he counseled Absalom, the son of David, to rebel against his father. After Absalom was killed in battle, Ahithophel committed suicide (see 2 Sam. 15:12, 16:20–17:23).

**AHMADABAD** *or* **AHMEDABAD,** city, W India, city in Gujarat State, on the Sabarmati R. Cotton, millet, and wheat are produced in the surrounding fertile agricultural region. An important industrial and commercial center, the city is especially noted for the manufacture of cotton textiles. Silk fabrics, soap, glass, carpets, tobacco products, matches, and high-quality brocades and metal and wood articles are also produced in the city. Architecturally, Ahmadabad is one of the most magnificent cities of India. Major buildings include the Jama Masjid, or Great Mosque, an Indo-Saracenic structure with 300 elaborately carved pillars; the temple of Hathi Singh, a Jainist shrine built in 1848; and the Mill Owners Association Building, designed by the French architect Le Corbusier. Across the river is Gandhi's Ashram and the Gandhi Memorial Museum. Ahmadabad was the capital of Gujarat State from 1960 to 1970, when the state capital was transferred to Gandhinagar. Pop. (1991, greater city) 3,297,655.

**AHMAD SHAH,** (1722? 73), first emir of Afghanistan (1747–73). Ahmad was the hereditary chief of the Abdali tribe of Afghans, whom he later renamed the Durani. He led a contingent of his tribesmen in the service of Nadir Shah, king of Persia, who won control of most of Afghanistan and part of India. When Nadir died, Ahmad founded an independent Afghan kingdom. He invaded the Indian Punjab six times between 1748 and 1752, and he seized and sacked Delhi. In 1761 he defeated an Indian army at Panipat, India. Although he was a powerful military leader, Ahmad never succeeded in permanently ruling India; he subsequently withdrew into Afghanistan.

**AHMADU,** sometimes called Seku (Chief) Ahmadu (c. 1775–1844), Fulani religious reformer and ruler of Macina, in present-day Mali. Inspired by Usuman dan Fodio, he set out to be a teacher, but soon rose up against the semipagan ruler of his homeland and overthrew him. A jihad (holy war) against the neighboring Tuareg and Songhai principalities ensued, and in 1826 he captured Timbuktu. Founding a capital at Hamdallahi (God Be Praised), Ahmadu ruled over his Islamic empire with fanatic zeal until his death.

Considered one of the three great jihad leaders of West Africa, Ahmadu was succeeded by his son and grandson, the latter being captured and killed by al-Hajj Umar in 1862.

**AHMED, Fakhruddin Ali** (1905–77), fifth president of India (1974–77) and the second Muslim to hold that office. Born in Delhi and educated in England, he joined the Congress party rather than the Muslim League upon returning to India and was first elected to the Assam state legislature in 1935; for most of the next 30 years Ahmed served in various state ministerial and legal positions.

In 1966 Prime Minister Indira Gandhi included him in her first cabinet, and she secured his election to the presidency in 1974. He, in return, remained a loyal ally who implemented her emergency rule of 1975–77. He died just before Gandhi's defeat in the March 1977 elections.

**AHMEDABAD.**  See AHMADABAD.

**AHMOSE I,** king of Egypt (r. 1570–1546 BC), founder of the 18th Dynasty, the first of the New Kingdom. A Theban prince, he completed (c. 1567 BC) the expulsion of the Hyksos begun by his brother Kamose (r. about 1576–1570 BC), recaptured northern Nubia, and reorganized Egypt as a unified country under his sole rule.

**AHMOSE II** (d. 526 BC), pharaoh of Egypt (570–526 BC). Born of humble parents, he became a general and was sent by the pharaoh Apries (r. 589–570 BC) to suppress a revolt of Egyptian troops. Ahmose joined forces with the rebels, who proclaimed him king. The combined forces defeated the hired troops of Apries and dethroned him. Two years later Ahmose repulsed an attack by the Babylonian king Nebuchadnezzar II. Ahmose added Cyprus to his kingdom, made alliances with Sámos and Lydia, and maintained friendly relations with Cyrene and the Greek states. He was succeeded by his son, Psamtik III (r. 526-525 BC), who, six months after he acceded to the throne, was defeated and dethroned by the Persians under Cambyses II. Egypt then became part of the Persian Empire.

**AHUACHAPÁN,** city, W El Salvador, capital of Ahuachapán Department, near the border with Guatemala. It is an important transportation and commercial center with a considerable trade in coffee, sugar, fruit, and grain. Hydroelectric power installations and thermal springs are nearby. The Pan-American Highway passes through the city. The area was the scene of civil warfare in the early 1980s. Pop. (1990) 83,885.

**AHVAZ,** also Ahwaz, city, SW Iran, capital of Khuzestan Province. It is an important railroad junction located at the head of navigation of the Karun R. Petroleum fields lie to the N, and several oil pipelines pass through the city. Manufactures include processed foods and textiles. It is the seat of a university and several technical institutes. Ahvaz is a city of ancient origins; by the 4th century AD it was an important city of the Persian Sassanian dynasty and was the seat of a bishop of the Nestorian Christian church. During the 12th and 13th centuries it was an Arab agricultural and commercial center but declined thereafter. The city revived in the early 20th century after oil was discovered in the vicinity. Ahvaz was the scene of heavy fighting during the war between Iran and Iraq in the early 1980s. Pop. (1991) 724,653.

**AHVENANMAA** (Swed. *Åland*), province, Finland, composed of the Åland islands, situated at the N end of the Baltic Sea, at the mouth of the Gulf of Bothnia, between Sweden and Finland. Of the approximately 6500 granite islands and rocky reefs, 80 are inhabited. Mariehamn, the administrative center and chief port, is located on Åland, the largest island, which is linked by daily ferry and steamship service to the Swedish and Finnish mainlands and by air service from Mariehamn Airport. Fishing, shipping, and tourism are the chief industries. Farming is confined to the cultivation of grains and vegetables and to cattle raising and dairy products. The population, entirely Swedish-speaking, is gradually immigrating to Sweden.

The Ahvenanmaa, inhabited since prehistoric times, were Christianized by Sweden in the 12th century; in 1809 they were ceded to Russia. The position of the islands made them strategically important during the Crimean War, after which they were demilitarized. At the end of World War I, Finland granted the islands autonomy to quiet a strong, pro-Swedish secessionist movement. Finnish sovereignty over the islands was confirmed by a 1921 decision of the League of Nations. Under pressure from the USSR in 1951, the Finnish parliament renounced the autonomy guaranteed by the earlier decision, but granted the islanders special rights, including their own flag. Area, about 1481 sq km (about 572 sq mi); pop. (1992 est.) 24,993.

**AIDS.**  See ACQUIRED IMMUNE DEFICIENCY SYNDROME.

**AIKEN, Conrad Potter** (1889–1973), American poet and novelist, born in Savannah, Ga., and educated at Harvard University. His first volume of verse, *Earth Triumphant and Other Tales in Verse* (1914), although derivative in style, reveals his talent for sensuous imagery and flowing rhythms. His *Selected Poems* won the 1930 Pulitzer Prize in poetry, and his *Collected Poems* won the 1954 National Book Award. Later volumes of his poetry include *Cats and Bats and Things with Wings* (1965), *Preludes* (1966), *Selected Poems* (1969), and *Thee* (1971).

Aiken wrote numerous novels and short stories, many of them based on psychoanalytic theory. One of his most notable stories is "Silent Snow, Secret Snow." *The Short Stories of Conrad Aiken* was published in 1950; his *Collected Novels* appeared in 1964; and *Collected Criticism* appeared in 1968. In recognition of his literary achievement, Aiken held the Chair of Poetry of the Library of Congress from 1950 to 1952 and was awarded the Gold Medal for Poetry by the National Institute of Arts and Letters in 1958.

**AILANTHUS,** common name for the family Simaroubaceae, a medium-size group of tropical and subtropical trees and shrubs, and for its representative genus *Ailanthus,* also called tree of heaven. Leaves of the ailanthus group are compound with many feathery leaflets and alternate on the leaf stems. The fruit is usually winged. The family comprises about 22 genera and 170 species and is a member of the order Sapindales (*see* SOAPBERRY), which also contains the mahogany and citrus trees. The ailanthus family is of limited importance as a source of timber; the trees are used for ornamentals and the bitter principles extracted from the bark are used in medicines. The tree of heaven, *A. altissima,* a native of northern China, was introduced into the U.S. in 1874. Its hardiness and rapid growth make it useful in urban settings, but it is difficult to eradicate once established and is considered a pest in some areas.

**AILEY, Alvin** (1931–89), American dancer and choreographer, best known for his works expressing the black heritage. Born in Rogers, Tex., he studied under the American dancers Lester Horton (1906–53), Martha Graham, Charles Weidman, and Hanya Holm, and the American actor Stella Adler (1902–92). In 1958 he formed his own company, which joined the New York City Center in 1972. In 1984 the Alvin Ailey American Dance Theater became the first predominantly black troupe to perform at the Metropolitan Opera House in New York. Ailey's works, incorporating techniques of modern dance, ballet, and tribal dance, include *Blues Suite* (1958), *Revelations* (1960), and *Mass* (1971; music by Leonard Bernstein). Ailey choreographed for several companies in addition to his own, including the Joffrey Ballet, the American Ballet Theatre, and the Paris Opera Ballet, for which he created *At the Edge of the Precipice* (1983), inspired by rock music. Active as a teacher of dance, Ailey devised a method of working with the visually handicapped. The American dancer Judith Jamison (1944–  ), an Ailey protégée, became artistic director of the Ailey company in 1990.

**AILLY, Pierre d'** (1350–1420), French philosopher and theologian, whose principal aim was to settle the Great Western Schism (1378–1417) that divided the Christian church (*see* SCHISM, GREAT). A native of Compiègne, he studied at the University of Paris, where he obtained a doctorate in theology in 1381. He quickly rose to prominence and by 1389 had become chancellor of the university. He became a bishop in 1395 and was made a cardinal in 1412.

D'Ailly participated in two assemblies that attempted to end the schism: the Council of Pisa (1409) and the Council of Constance (1414–18).

*Fruit of the tree of heaven, Ailanthus altissima.*
© Michael P. Gadomski–Photo Researchers, Inc.

He advocated a moderate form of the conciliar theory, holding that the supreme authority of the church lies with a general council (*see* COUNCIL) rather than with the pope. Many of his opinions were later adapted and developed by Martin Luther and the other religious reformers. D'Ailly also wrote on astrology, geography, and philosophy. His best-known work, *Imago Mundi* (Image of the World), in which he suggested that the Indies could be reached from the West, was known to Christopher Columbus.                J.W.O.

**AINU,** aboriginal people of Asia, chiefly occupying parts of the Japanese island of Hokkaido and the Russian-occupied islands of the Kurils and Sakhalin. The Ainu are thought to be descended from the ancient circumpolar people, who were gradually driven north on the Japanese archipelago by invaders now known as the Japanese. Many anthropologists believe that the ancestors of the Ainu belonged to the Caucasoid race; full-blooded Ainu are rare, primarily because so many have intermarried with Japanese. Typical members of this group possess various Caucasoid characteristics, including light complexions, heavy beards, and thick, wavy hair. They have short, sturdy bodies. A few isolated communities of upland Ainu are identical in some respects to those of prehistoric times. The Ainu language appears to be unrelated to any other. The reforms introduced into Japan after World War II caused rapid social and economic assimilation of most Ainu groups by the Japanese.

The Ainu social organization is based on patrilineal kin groups, each headed by a chief. Local groups usually consist of five to ten households. Spawning grounds of dog salmon are owned collectively; cooperative activities within local groups include housebuilding and a ceremony involving the dog salmon. Ainu pit houses, ground-stone celts, ground-bone projectile

Ainu couple and their household bear, in Hokkaido, Japan. The bear cult is a major part of the traditional Ainu religious practices.    ©1985 Joseph Nettis–Photo Researchers, Inc.

points, and grit-tempered, cord-marked pottery have been uncovered by archaeologists.

Ainu men hunt and fish; the women gather food and do some fishing. Ainu agriculture, essentially primitive until recently, was engaged in mainly by women, who practiced a method of crop rotation. The people have a basic diet of cherry salmon, dog salmon, deer, bear, and at least nine different plants. Tattooing of the face and arms is a common practice among the women, and both men and women frequently wear earrings. Adult males never shave. The traditional religion, based on faith in a supreme deity, is a form of nature worship that revolves around a belief in spirits associated with natural phenomena and forces. A bear cult is especially prominent; an annual religious festival is climaxed by the sacrifice of a bear approximately three years old, which has been reared from cubhood.

Some contemporary anthropologists contend that a pure Ainu culture no longer exists, having been absorbed by the Japanese culture.    E.I.K.

**AIR.**  See ATMOSPHERE.

**AIR COMPRESSOR,** also air pump, machine that decreases the volume and increases the pressure of a quantity of air by mechanical means. Air thus compressed possesses great potential energy, because when the external pressure is removed, the air expands rapidly. The controlled expansive force of compressed air is used in many ways and provides the motive force for air motors and tools, including pneumatic hammers, air drills,

sandblasting machines, and paint sprayers. See COMPRESSED AIR.

Air compressors are of two general types: reciprocating and rotating. In a reciprocating, or displacement, compressor (see Fig. 1), which is used to produce high pressures, the air is compressed by the action of a piston in a cylinder. When the piston moves to the right, air flows into the cylinder through the intake valve; when the piston moves to the left, the air is compressed and forced through an output-control valve into a reservoir or storage tank.

A rotating air compressor (see Fig. 2), used for low and medium pressures, usually consists of a bladed wheel or impeller that spins inside a closed circular housing. Air is drawn in at the center of the wheel and accelerated by the centrifugal force of the spinning blades. The energy of the moving air is then converted into pressure in

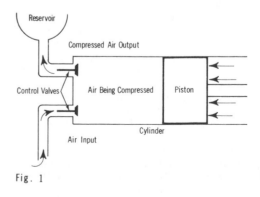

Fig. 1

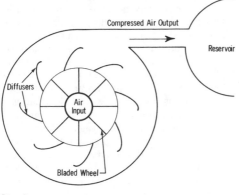

Compressed Air Output

Reservoir

Diffusers

Air Input

Bladed Wheel

Fig. 2

the diffuser, and the compressed air is forced out through a narrow passage to the storage tank.

As air is compressed it is also heated. Air molecules tend to collide more often with each other in a smaller space, and the energy produced by these collisions is evident as heat. This heat is undesirable in the compression process, so the air may be cooled on the way to the reservoir by circulating air or water. For high-pressure compressed air, several stages of compression may be employed, with the air being further compressed in each cylinder and cooled before each stage.

*See also* HEATING, VENTILATING, AND AIR CONDITIONING; HEAT TRANSFER; PUMP.

**AIR CONDITIONING.** *See* HEATING, VENTILATING, AND AIR CONDITIONING; REFRIGERATION.

**AIRCRAFT,** weight-carrying structure that can travel through the air, supported either by its own buoyancy or by the dynamic action of the air against its surfaces. *See* AIRPLANE; AIRSHIP; AUTOGIRO; AVIATION; BALLOON; GLIDER; HELICOPTER.

**AIRCRAFT CARRIER,** ship with a long, unobstructed flight deck that permits takeoffs and landings by high-performance airplanes; a carrier is in effect a mobile air base. Planes are stored below deck and brought up and down on elevators. They take off under their own power or may be launched by catapults. Mirror landing systems and arresting cables that catch a hook on the outside of incoming aircraft facilitate safe landings. Decks are angled so that pilots missing the arresting gear will be able to go around again without hitting other aircraft. Carriers, equipped with or capable of carrying missiles, are the heart of modern striking forces, accompanied by a variety of support vessels: destroyers and cruisers for protection and supply ships bearing fuel, ammunition, and food.

**History.** The earliest flight from a ship was made off an improvised platform on the U.S. cruiser *Birmingham* in 1910. The first true carrier designed to permit takeoffs and landings was the British merchant ship HMS *Argus,* completed in 1918. The first U.S. carrier, the *Langley,* a converted collier, joined the fleet in 1922, and in 1927 the *Lexington* and *Saratoga* were converted from battle cruisers.

After World War I, major carrier fleets were built by the U.S., Japan, and Britain; in the 1930s tactical exercises were held by the U.S. Navy to study and improve efficiency of its carrier operations. By World War II, however, Japan's carrier fleet was numerically and qualitatively superior to the American and British fleets in the Pacific. The use of six aircraft carriers by Japan to attack Pearl Harbor on Dec. 7, 1941, opened the war in the Pacific. No American carriers were present during the attack. The major carrier battle of Midway of June 3-6, 1942, cost the Japanese four carriers; America lost one, the *Yorktown.*

This victory gained the U.S. mastery of the skies and of the seas and turned the tide of the war. By 1944 the Japanese navy had been destroyed primarily by carrier-based aircraft assault, in addition to submarine action. In the European theater, England used carriers in support of operations in Norway and for convoy support in the Atlantic and Mediterranean. Carriers were also part of the British Eastern Fleet.

**Carrier Classes.** Since World War II, carriers have been designated by size and mission and grouped by class—that is, by similarity of construction and capabilities. All the present U.S. fleet is of the attack class, with capabilities for conversion to use as submarine warfare, utility, and assault helicopter aircraft carriers. They bear the classification symbols CV or CVN, the N denoting a carrier propelled by nuclear energy.

**Recent Developments.** In 1989 the U.S. was the world's principal user of carriers, with a fleet of 15 and 2 under construction. Two carriers were of the old Midway class, completed shortly after World War II, and eight were built in the 1950s and '60s. Five others were nuclear powered. One of these, the *Nimitz,* is 332 m (1092 ft) in length, displaces 96,000 tons, and is equipped with four steam catapults; it is capable of handling 90 aircraft with their associated maintenance facilities, fuel, ammunition, and parts. The ship accommodates a crew of 3300 plus an air wing of pilots and support crew, numbering about 3000. The *Nimitz* is capable of indefinite sea operation when supported by periodic reprovisioning. The angled flight deck permits simultaneous launching and landing of aircraft.

By the late 1980s the Soviet navy had four Kiev carriers, plus two nuclear carriers under construction. The Kiev carriers were 274 m (899 ft) long, displacing 38,000 tons. This class appeared to be designed for antisubmarine warfare and was equipped with helicopter and possible vertical-takeoff-and-landing (VTOL) aircraft. The two nuclear-powered carriers are 75,000-ton attack vessels. (In 1991 the Soviet navy became part of the armed forces of the Commonwealth of Independent States, but control of the Black Sea fleet was in dispute between Russia and Ukraine.)

The British fleet included three carriers, designed for antisubmarine warfare and command control missions. France had two carriers built in the 1950s, and a nuclear-powered 36,000-ton carrier under construction, all with antisubmarine warfare, helicopter, and command control functions. Two light carriers were maintained by the navies of India and Spain, and one each by Argentina and Brazil; most of these were acquired from larger powers.

*See also* AIRPLANE; AIR WARFARE. D.J.B.

**AIR-CUSHION VEHICLE,** also hovercraft, craft that operates above the surface of water or land while supported on a cushion of air 1.2 to 2.4 m (4 to 8 ft) thick. The air cushion is provided by a large fan that pushes air downward within a flexible skirt attached to the perimeter of the vehicle. The skirt makes the vehicle appear to be operating only a few inches above the surface. The vehicle is moved forward by propellers mounted above the vehicle or by control of the air exhaust through small openings around the skirt. Braking is controlled by reversing the pitch of the propeller or by changing the direction of airflow through the skirt vents. This phenomenon is also known in aerodynamics as ground effect.

The operating controls are essentially like those found in an airplane. A control wheel adjusts the pitch of the vehicle, and rudder pedals control yaw (side-to-side movement). The speed over water is limited by wave height and wind speed. Operation of the vehicle is much the same when moving from water to land or vice versa; the air cushion prevents the hull from striking the ground when the terrain changes.

Some air-cushion vehicles, such as the Bertin Hovertruck, have conventional wheel systems for travel over highways and solid ground, but for movement over marshland a built-in air-cushion system supports three-fourths of the weight of the truck. Most air-cushion vehicles, however, are designed for amphibious operation over water, marshy ground, and beaches.

An experimental air-cushion vehicle, designed to run on a track similar to a monorail, reached a speed of 346 km/hr (215 mph) on the 6.7-km (4.2-mi) concrete test track in Gometz-la-Ville, France. This so-called aerotrain rode on a cushion of air 0.25 cm (0.1 in) thick.

The vehicles have both commercial and military applications, and a number of 15- to 30-passenger craft have been placed in operation around the world. One of the largest air-cushion vehicles in use is the 150-metric-ton British SRN 4 hovercraft, *Mountbatten,* which began service in July 1968. Designed for ferry and passenger ser-

*The U.S. aircraft carrier* Constellation *on maneuvers in the Pacific Ocean.*
© 1990 FPG International

*Airedale terrier*                    Adolf Schmidecker

vice across the English Channel, the craft can carry 30 automobiles and 250 passengers.

**AIREDALE TERRIER,** breed of dog, that originated in Yorkshire, England. The Airedale weighs 18 to 23 kg (40 to 50 lb) and is the largest of the terrier class. It is wirehaired, with black crown, back, and sides and tan face, throat, and limbs. The forelegs are straight, and the general aspect is trim and powerful. Fast, sagacious, and noted for a keen sense of smell, the Airedale is also a natural swimmer and excellent hunter.

**AIRFOIL.** *See* AIRPLANE.

**AIR FORCE, DEPARTMENT OF THE,** one of the three major components of the U.S. Department of Defense, created by the National Security Act of 1947. It is headed by the secretary of the air force, a civilian who is appointed by the president with the consent of the Senate and functions under the secretary of defense. The secretary of the air force is responsible for and has authority to conduct all affairs of the air force establishment. The secretary is assisted by an under secretary and four assistant secretaries who are authorized to act, respectively, in the areas of financial management; manpower, reserve affairs, installations, and environment; acquisition; and space. This authority, subject to the secretary's direction, extends not only to actions within the air force establishment but also to actions and relationships involving Congress, governmental and nongovernmental organizations, and individuals. The secretary receives military advice from the Air Staff, headed by a chief of staff, who serves as the air force member of the Joint Chiefs of Staff. The chief of staff also advises the president, the National Security Council, and the secretary of defense.

**AIR FORCE, UNITED STATES.** *See* UNITED STATES AIR FORCE.

**AIR FORCE ACADEMY, UNITED STATES.** *See* UNITED STATES AIR FORCE ACADEMY.

**AIRLANGGA** (1001–49), king of East Java (1019–42), who restored native power after a long rule by the Sumatran kingdom of Sri Vijaya. After years of hiding from his enemies, he emerged in 1019 to be invested as king but could claim authority over only a fragment of the realm left to him. When Indian raids weakened Sri Vijaya about 1025, Airlangga moved in forcefully and by 1030 was recognized as the overlord of Java. His reign was marked by great economic resurgence and a flourishing of literary activity. Modern Indonesians regard him as a national hero.

**AIRLINE.** *See* AIR TRANSPORT INDUSTRY.

**AIRMAIL,** postal matter transported in aircraft over part of its trip, or the system for so transporting postal matter. The first airmail service consisted of a few irregular trips early in 1911 between two English cities near London. The first authorized U.S. airmail was flown between Garden City and Mineola, N.Y., in September 1911. Regular airmail service from London to Paris was begun in 1919 and air parcel post over the same route in 1922. The first regular airmail route in the U.S. was established between New York City and Washington, D.C., in 1918. Transcontinental service, between New York City and San Francisco, began in 1921; the scheduled flying time varied from 29 to 33 hours, but the planes flew only in the daytime. Day-and-night service over the same route began in 1924. Regular, scheduled, transoceanic airmail started in 1935, between the U.S. and the Philippines. Before 1935 the *Graf Zeppelin* had carried mail across the North Atlantic Ocean, and there had been airmail flights across the South Atlantic from Africa to Brazil, but regular airmail flights across the North Atlantic between Europe and the U.S. did not begin until 1939 when a route was established between New York City and Marseille, France.

In the meantime international airmail arrangements had been made. Some provisions were included in the agreements reached at the International Postal Convention held in Madrid in 1920. The International Air Mail Conference was held in 1927, at which it was agreed that a uniform cost would be established to enable each country's airmail service to carry airmail of countries with similar service. Lack of agreement concerning the right of the aircraft of one country to fly over the land of another has not affected the amicable workings of the airmail accords.

In 1935 there were about 46,349 km (about 28,800 mi) of regular airmail routes in the U.S. (excluding service within Alaska), over which approximately 4,963,898 metric-ton-km of mail were flown, at an average cost to the U.S. Post Office Department of $1.78 per metric-ton-km.

*Preparation for the first airmail trip from Boston to New York City on June 11, 1918. W. F. Murray (left), postmaster of Boston, hands a pouch of mail to pilot Torrey Webb (right). The map Webb used to guide him on his flight is attached to his left knee.*
U.S. Post Office

In 1945 there were more than 91,411 km (56,800 mi) of regular domestic routes (excluding Alaskan service), over which approximately 89,788,155 metric-ton-km were flown at an average cost of 39.2 cents per metric-ton-km. By 1968 more than 443,830,880 metric-ton-km of mail were flown.

In 1952 the Post Office Department experimented with shipping a limited amount of first-class mail by air between New York City and Chicago and between Chicago and Washington, D.C. This service was later expanded, according to the amount of unused cargo space available on regular airlines, and in 1975 the postal service merged domestic airmail with first-class mail. In 1977 the postal service established an overnight express mail service. By the mid-1980s all categories of domestic air-eligible mail transported exceeded 76 billion pieces, which equaled about 9 million metric tons.                                      L.A.B.

*For further information on this topic, see the Bibliography in volume 28, section 331.*

**AIRPLANE,** heavier-than-air craft that is propelled mechanically and supported by the dynamic action of the airstream on fixed-wing surfaces (*see* AERODYNAMICS). Other types of aircraft that are heavier than air include the glider, which is similarly equipped with fixed-wing surfaces but is not self-propelled, and rotary-wing aircraft, which are mechanically driven and supported by overhead rotors (*see* AUTOGIRO; HELICOPTER). Another type is the ornithopter, which is lifted and propelled by flapping wings. Toy-size ornithopters have been developed, but large-scale experiments have been unsuccessful. For the history of heavier-than-air craft, *see* AVIATION.

The term *airplane* generally denotes the landplane, or land-based airplane, but it applies also to several other categories of aircraft, including the carrier-based plane, the seaplane, and the amphibian. The principal variation in structure can be found in the landing apparatus. The carrier-based plane, a type of landplane designed for use on an aircraft carrier, is fitted with a tail hook that engages a cable stretched across the deck to arrest the plane after landing. The seaplane employs pontoons instead of the wheel gear of the landplane. In the variety of seaplane known as the flying boat, the fuselage is constructed as a hull, similar to that of a seagoing vessel, and serves to keep the plane buoyant. The amphibian is equipped with both wheel gear and hull or pontoons to permit operation with equal effectiveness on land and water.

Before World War II, flying boats were used for military transports and for intercontinental commercial service. These planes were limited to low flying speeds and to low landing speeds in water. With the advent of planes that fly and land much faster, large planes have been limited to land-based operation. The amphibian, even slower because of its double undercarriage, is less commonly employed than the landplane. For light sportplanes, amphibious floats have recently been made available. Generally resembling conventional pontoons, they have a recessed wheel located at the center of balance of the seaplane; the wheel-well is waterproof. The wheel tire does not extend far enough to add much drag to the float in the water, but it protrudes far enough to enable wheeled landings to be made on hard-surfaced runways or short-cut grass.

More successful types of heavier-than-air craft include the VTOL craft, the STOL craft, and the convertiplane. The VTOL (vertical takeoff and landing) craft is an airplane that can rise up vertically, fly horizontally, and then reverse the procedure for a landing. The term *VTOL* is limited to describing aircraft with performances similar to those of conventional airplanes but with additional vertical takeoff and landing ability. Several means are used to lift VTOL aircraft off the ground. The direct downward thrust of jet engines is used in several designs. Enormous power is needed to lift a craft in this manner, much more than is required to propel it horizontally. Rotating wings and ducted fans are also used for direct lift, but they tend to introduce drag into the horizontal flight. Convertiplanes, combining the rotating wings of helicopters with the fixed wings of airplanes, show promise for short-distance commercial VTOL operation. They compete directly with helicopters, however.

The STOL (short takeoff and landing) craft is an airplane that takes off and lands very steeply, thus requiring little runway. For a given payload, it is much more efficient in terms of fuel consumption and power requirements than a VTOL craft. It is also capable of higher speeds and longer-range flights than a helicopter. For lighter-than-air craft, *see* AIRSHIP; BALLOON.

## PRINCIPLES OF FLIGHT

An airplane flies because its surfaces, particularly its wings, are airfoils, which provide the lift necessary to overcome the force of gravity. An airfoil is shaped so that air moving above it travels faster than the air below it. This movement produces a difference in air pressure: low pressure above the airfoil exerts a pulling influence, and high pressure below the airfoil exerts a pushing influence. The resulting force, which is commonly called the lift, depends not only on the shape and area of the airfoil but also on its tilt and the air speed of the aircraft. The greater distance over

*The camber of an airfoil, which is the convexity of the curve from its leading edge to its trailing edge, is defined by the distance between the skeletal mean line and the chord line, as shown in the diagram.*

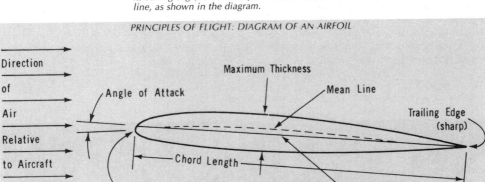

PRINCIPLES OF FLIGHT: DIAGRAM OF AN AIRFOIL

Direction of Air Relative to Aircraft

Angle of Attack

Maximum Thickness

Mean Line

Trailing Edge (sharp)

Chord Length

Leading Edge (Rounded)

Chord Line

*At left, airfoil in normal flight; at right, airfoil with flap depressed to produce high lift at low speeds.*

which the air must travel above the curved upper surface forces that air to move faster to keep pace with the air moving along the flat lower surface. According to Bernoulli's principle (q.v.), it is this difference in air velocity that produces the difference in air pressure.

**Lift.** Wing area influences lift; the more of the wing that is exposed to the air, the greater the lift. The up or down tilt of the wing, usually called its angle of attack, contributes to or detracts from lift. As a wing is tilted upward, that is, as its angle of attack is increased, its lift increases. The air passing over the top of an uptilted wing must travel a greater distance and thus produces a greater pressure differential between the upper and lower surfaces.

Aircraft speed has a great influence on lift. The faster the air moves over and under the surfaces of an airplane, the greater the pressure differential and, as a result, the greater the lift.

As an airplane flies on a level course, the lift contributed by the wing and other parts of the structure counterbalance the weight of the plane. Within certain limits, if the angle of attack is increased while the speed remains constant, the plane will rise. If the angle of attack is decreased, that is, the wing is tilted downward, the plane will lose lift and start to descend. An airplane will also climb from level flight if its speed is increased, and it will descend if its speed is decreased. Lift varies directly with speed.

During the course of a flight, a pilot frequently alters the speed and angle of attack of the aircraft. These two factors are often balanced against each other. For instance, if the pilot wishes to increase speed and yet maintain level flight, the angle of attack must be decreased to offset the extra lift that is provided by the increase in the speed of the aircraft.

In preparing to land, the pilot must ease the plane down and at the same time reduce its speed as much as possible. To compensate for the considerable loss of lift resulting from the decrease in speed, the pilot provides lift by altering the wing area, effective curvature, and angle of attack. This is done through the use of flaps, large wing extensions located at each trailing edge. Most flaps are normally tucked into the wing during straight and level flight. If extra lift is wanted, the pilot extends the flaps out and down.

**Drag.** Factors that contribute to lift in airplane flight also contribute to undesirable forces called drag. Drag is the force that tends to retard the motion of the airplane through the air. Most drag is a result of the resistance of the air to objects moving through it. This type of drag can be reduced by streamlining the aircraft. It is also reduced by placing slots in the wing so that the boundary layer or "wall of air" building up in front and around the wing can flow through it.

One form of drag, however, known as induced drag, is a result of the lift produced by the wing. In effect, induced drag is the penalty exacted for lift. Great differences in the pressure of the air flowing over and under a wing can cause whirlpools or eddies of air to billow up along the trailing edges of the wings. These whirlpools produce a braking or force toward the rear that must be overcome by the forward thrust of the engines.

As the angle of attack of an airplane is increased, the plane gains lift, but the lift is limited. As the angle of attack is increased, air turbulence spreads over the wing. Then at a certain critical point (an angle of about 14° in many airplanes), the wing loses lift and the plane stalls, nosing over into a dive.

*The McDonnell Douglas DC-10 is a wide-bodied commercial jet, first developed in the 1970s, that operates on high-density, long-distance passenger routes.*
McDonnell Douglas

The supersonic Concorde during takeoff. The delta-winged SST, developed jointly by France and Great Britain, made its first commercial flight in 1976, flying at more than twice the speed of sound. It is the fastest plane now in commercial service.

British Airways

Airplane designers try to design aircraft with high lift-to-drag ratios, that is, much more lift than drag. They are limited, however, by factors such as speed and the weight that the plane must carry. Faster planes usually have lower lift-to-drag ratios. A subsonic modern transport has a lift-to-drag ratio of about 15 and a light private plane may have a lift-to-drag ratio of about 25. Supersonic transports have a lift-to-drag ratio of about 6.

The supersonic age that aviation entered after World War II presented a number of new problems so revolutionary that aerodynamicists found themselves resorting to experimentation as dangerous and adventuresome as any faced by early pilots. Neither complex mathematical analyses nor improvement of such research tools as the wind tunnel (q.v.), in which models of airplanes are tested, could ensure completely satisfactory performance of an aircraft under the conditions encountered in supersonic flight.

**Sound barrier.** The first formidable problem confronted by aerodynamicists arose when planes attained the speed of sound (approximately 1223 km/hr, or about 760 mph, at sea level), known popularly as the sound barrier and scientifically as Mach 1. An airplane about to break the sound barrier is on the verge of catching up with the pressure waves created by its own forward thrust. The resulting distortion of the airflow at Mach 1 causes the formation of a shock wave, known as the compressibility shock, which greatly increases the drag of the plane. If the craft is not properly designed to cope with this abrupt change in the nature of the airflow, its control

will be severely if not disastrously impaired. *See* MACH NUMBER.

**Noise pollution.** A major problem caused by supersonic aircraft is noise. Engine noise of supersonic transports is louder and more high-pitched than that of subsonic jets, which are already a serious annoyance to airfield workers and residents of communities near airports. Medical concern, moreover, has been expressed about the effect of sonic booms, which are produced each time a supersonic plane exceeds the speed of sound. As an aircraft flies, the air rushing toward the plane should be deflected smoothly about the wing. In subsonic flight this does take place. At supersonic speeds, airflow can no longer adjust itself well ahead of the wing since disturbance signals "warning" the air cannot move faster than the speed of sound. As a result, the air has to adjust itself suddenly in the proximity of the leading edge of the wing by a sudden pressure rise or shock coupled with a redirection of the flow. The resulting shock front that travels with the aircraft extends over large vertical distances and reaches the ground with an impact which sounds like an explosion even if a plane flies at maximum altitudes. The shock wave may be so severe that it breaks windows on the ground far beneath the plane. Attempts were begun in the mid-1970s by designers, manufacturers, and various governmental agencies, including the Federal Aviation Administration (q.v.), to curb both engine noise and sonic booms.

**Heat barrier.** Among other serious problems associated with supersonic flight is the high temperature caused by the friction of the air against the outer surfaces of the airplane. This problem is known as the heat barrier. To withstand the extremely high temperatures and pressures generated at supersonic speed, the structural materials must be far more resistant to heat than the aluminum alloys used for subsonic aircraft. Titanium is an example of the type of heat-resistant, high-strength metal required in supersonic aircraft. The demands of the supersonic age for higher speeds, higher altitudes, and longer ranges have led not only to new aerodynamic designs, but also to research for new structural materials.

AIRPLANE STRUCTURE.

The present-day conventional airplane may be divided into four components: fuselage, wings, tail assembly, and landing gear, or undercarriage.

**Fuselage.** In the early days of aviation, the fuselage was merely an open structural mount to support the other components of the plane; the bottom of the airframe served as the landing gear. Subsequently, the need for greater strength and better performance resulted in the development of enclosed, boxlike, "strut-and-wire" fuselages that not only increased lift and decreased drag, but also provided protection for pilot and passenger, as well as space for cargo. This type of structure, known as truss, was gradually superseded by the monocoque (literally, single shell) fuselage. The loads imposed on such a structure are carried primarily by the skin, rather than by the internal framework, as in the trussed structure. In varying stages of advanced design, it is the most common fuselage in use.

**Wings.** Although the single-winged plane, known as the monoplane, made its appearance in the first decade of powered flight, early airplane construction favored the use of two wings (the bi-

plane), and occasionally even three or four. Multiple-wing planes have the advantage of superior lift, but the monoplane was subject to less drag. Once the cantilever (q.v.) principle of wing construction was developed, the dominance of the monoplane was assured, although it did not become the design of choice until the 1930s. Cantilever wings obtain their entire strength from structural elements inside the skin. In present-day aircraft, cantilever construction is employed in large aircraft, and external bracing is used only for small, light planes.

The structure of a typical wing consists of a spar-and-rib framework enclosed by a thin covering of metal sheet, of treated fabric, or, infrequently, of bonded plywood or of resin-impregnated glass fiber. The spar, or beam, extends from the fuselage to the wing tip. One or more spars may be used in the wing, but the single spar is the preferred design. The ribs, at right angles to the spar, give the wing its external shape. If the covering is of metal sheet, it contributes its own share of strength to the wing. This "stressed skin" type of wing is currently used in all large planes; fabric covering is employed for the wings of some small craft.

The size and shape of wings vary widely, depending on specific aerodynamic considerations. Wings of many supersonic planes have a high degree of sweepback (arrowhead tapering from the nose of the plane) and are as thin as possible, with a knifelike leading edge. Such streamlining helps to reduce the shock of compression when the plane approaches the speed of sound. The structural importance of the wing is dramatically demonstrated by the development of the so-called flying wing, a craft in which fuselage and

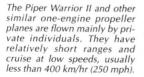

*The Piper Warrior II and other similar one-engine propeller planes are flown mainly by private individuals. They have relatively short ranges and cruise at low speeds, usually less than 400 km/hr (250 mph).*

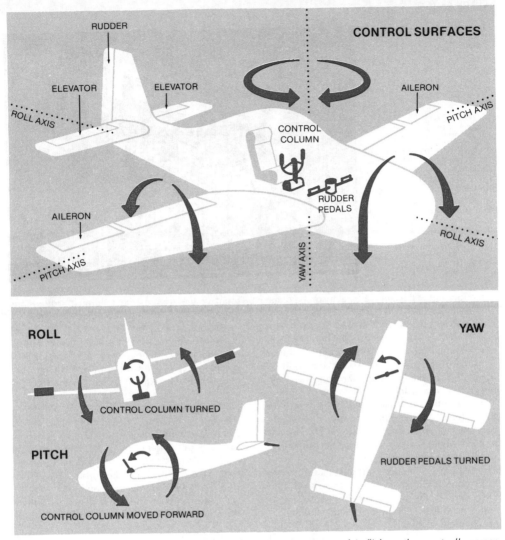

ROLL — CONTROL COLUMN TURNED

YAW — RUDDER PEDALS TURNED

PITCH — CONTROL COLUMN MOVED FORWARD

*The control surfaces of an aircraft orient a craft in flight on three mutually perpendicular axes. The ailerons control orientation on the roll axis; the elevators control pitch; and the rudder, yaw.*

tail are almost entirely eliminated. For speeds beyond the sound barrier, the nontapered wing is often the most efficient.

**Tail Assembly.** The conventional type of tail assembly consists of two basic surfaces, horizontal and vertical; each has movable sections contributing to control of the craft and fixed sections to provide stability. The leading section of the horizontal surface is known as the horizontal stabilizer, and the rear movable section, as the elevator. The stationary section of the vertical surface is called the fin, and the movable section is called the rudder. Two vertical surfaces are used in some aircraft; in that case, a double rudder is used. The **V**-shaped tail combines the rudder and

elevator functions in a single device. Tails vary in size according to the type of aircraft, but in supersonic flight the tail should be as small as possible. Its elimination would be the ideal design.

**Landing Gear.** Modern landing gear is one of the most intricate of all aeronautical mechanisms. Its components include the oleo strut, a hydraulic arm connecting the wheel with the wing or fuselage, which absorbs the shock of landing; the retracting mechanism, which raises and lowers the gear; the wheels; and the wheel brakes. A number of types of undercarriage are known, but two are most commonly employed: the conventional two-wheel gear and the tricycle gear. The former consists of two large wheels lo-

273

An F-4B Phantom II returns to the aircraft carrier USS America while participating in carrier tests in the Atlantic. F-4 aircraft are small, supersonic, tactical bombers that can be equipped with missiles or even nuclear weapons.          Wise-U.S. Navy

cated forward of the center of gravity of the plane with a small wheel at the tail. A tricycle gear consists of two large wheels behind the center of gravity and a third wheel, called the nosewheel, in front of the two main wheels. Landing is easier with the tricycle gear because braking and maneuvering are improved and the danger of nosing over is diminished. Other forms of landing gear include a caterpillar tread for handling heavy loads on poor landing fields, a swiveling gear for landing in crosswinds, and a combination ski-wheel gear for use on ice and snow.

*CONTROL COMPONENTS*

Components of modern aircraft necessary for flight control include devices manipulated from the cockpit by the stick or wheel, and instruments which provide the pilot with essential information. **Mechanical Controls.** The attitude of an airplane (its orientation relative to the horizon and to the direction of motion) is determined by three control devices, each of which provides for movement about a different axis. The three devices include the movable sections of the tail, the elevators and rudders; and the movable sections of the trailing (aft) edge of the wing, known as ailerons. The control surfaces are operated from the cockpit by means of a control stick or wheel column and rudder pedals. Stick control is used in smaller, lighter airplanes and in some military airplanes, and the wheel, with its greater leverage, is generally used in larger airplanes, as well as in some small ones.

Elevators provide for pitching movement around the lateral axis. A backward pull on the control stick or on the wheel column raises the elevators, thereby depressing the tail and lifting the nose of the plane for a climb. Forward move-

ment of the stick or the column produces the opposite effect, making the plane descend.

Ailerons, usually placed far out on the wing, control rolling movement around the longitudinal axis. Leftward movement of the stick or the wheel raises the left aileron and lowers the right, thereby banking the plane to the left. The reverse tilt occurs when the stick or wheel is moved to the right.

Rudders provide for turning movement around the vertical axis, changing the course of the plane to the left or the right. When the right rudder pedal is pressed, the rudder turns the plane to the right around the vertical axis. Pressing the left pedal produces a left turn.

To ensure easier and more dependable handling of all control surfaces, a number of secondary controls have been devised. Trim tabs are used on rudders, elevators, and ailerons as a means of adjusting the equilibrium, or trim, of the plane. Other controls include flaps (on trailing edges) and slots (on leading edges) to increase lift for takeoff or drag for landing, or to improve various other flight characteristics. Spoilers are surfaces that normally lie flush with the wing but can be raised to present a flat surface to the airstream and "spoil" the lift of the wing. Similar surfaces are called air brakes and extend at right angles to the fuselage or undersurface of the wing to slow the speed of the plane.

**Instruments.** Information required in flight is provided by various types of equipment, which may be divided into four general categories: power-plant instruments, flight instruments, landing instruments, and navigational aids (*see* NAVIGATION). Power-plant instruments indicate whether the engines are functioning properly and include the tachometer, which shows the revolutions per minute of each engine, various pressure gauges, temperature indicators, and the fuel gauges. The primary flight instruments provide indications of speed (the air-speed indicator), direction (the magnetic compass and the directional gyro), altitude (the altimeter), and attitude (the rate-of-climb and turn-and-bank indicators and the attitude gyro). Several of the flight instruments, including the automatic pilot, utilize the gyroscopic principle (see GYROSCOPE).

Landing instruments needed in poor visibility are of two types: the instrument-landing system (ILS), providing direct signals to the pilot to ensure a safe landing, and the ground-controlled approach (GCA), a system employing radar (q.v.) equipment on the ground to guide the pilot solely by radiotelephonic advice. The ILS is widely used in civil aviation; the GCA system, in military aviation. Both systems may also use the standard approach lighting system (ALS), which guides the airplane the last few hundred meters to the runway. See also AIRPORT; AIRWAY.

*PROPULSION*

Two basic means are used to provide the thrust for an airplane in flight: propeller and jet propulsion (qq.v.). In a propeller-driven airplane either a piston-driven internal-combustion engine (q.v.) or a turboprop engine is utilized to drive the propeller that thrusts the air backward by having airfoil-shaped blade sections cutting through the air in a screwlike fashion. In jet propulsion, the forward thrust is provided by the discharge of high-speed gases through a rear-facing nozzle.

An aircraft engine must satisfy a number of major design requirements, including high reliability, long life, low weight, low fuel consumption, and low frontal area. The most important factor is reliability. Long life is mainly an economic consideration, of special interest in commercial aviation. The relative importance of the other three requirements depends upon the type of plane that the engine is intended to propel. Low weight and low fuel consumption are naturally interdependent because the fuel itself is a weight factor. Low frontal area is desirable as a means of minimizing the drag caused by the engine.

**Internal-Combustion Engines.** The internal-combustion engine used in most propeller-driven aircraft is one of two types: the reciprocating engine and the compound engine. In the reciprocating engine, heat energy is utilized to move pistons operating within cylinders. Cylinder arrangement is generally in-line, horizontal-opposed, or radial, and either aircooling or liquid-cooling systems are used. Nearly all aircraft reciprocating engines are gasoline operated. In general, the advantages of the reciprocating engine are reliability and fuel economy.

The compound engine consists of a reciprocating engine and an exhaust-gas turbine (see GAS TURBINE) that drives a supercharger, an air compressor in the intake system of the engine. The supercharger compensates for the decreasing density of the atmosphere at higher altitudes. The chief advantage of the compound engine over the reciprocating engine is its high-power capacity at high altitudes. The compound engine served as the chief engine in U.S. military aircraft during World War II, before the advent of jet propulsion.

**Jet Engines.** Nonreciprocating aircraft engines, all of which operate on the principle of jet propulsion, include the turbojet, the turboprop, the ramjet, and the rocket engine. The turboprop, turbojet, and turbofan engines, which are modifications of the turbojet engine, are gas turbine engines, in which the air that enters the intake of the engine is first compressed in a compressor.

*The F-16 is a U.S. Air Force all-purpose supersonic fighter plane that carries a battery of assorted air-to-air missiles.*
**U.S. Air Force**

275

A U.S. Marine Harrier (AV-8A) lands aboard a U.S. naval ship after a training run. **U.S. Marines**

Fuel is then added to burn the oxygen in the air, increasing the gas temperature and volume. The high pressure gases are then partially expanded through a turbine which drives the compressor (and the propeller in a turboprop engine). The residual gas that is now at intermediate pressure is accelerated by expansion through a rear-facing nozzle, to produce a high leaving velocity and, with it, the desired thrust. Turbo-prop engines are efficient for medium-sized planes at speeds up to about 480 to 640 km/hr (about 300 to 400 mph). At higher speeds, turbojet or turbofan engines perform better. The performance of a propeller reaches such a low level of efficiency that jet engines are used only on aircraft that operate above 800 km/hr (about 500 mph).

The ramjet is an internal-combustion engine, in which the air compression needed for combustion is obtained from the speed of forward motion alone. As in the turbojet, its power output is delivered as the jet thrust of its expelled gases. Although the ramjet can be applied to piloted aircraft, its rate of fuel consumption is so prohibitively high that it is used only in guided-missile applications (see GUIDED MISSILES).

Like the ramjet, the rocket engine has its chief application in guided missiles. A solid-propellant rocket, rocket-assisted takeoff (RATO), is used for supplementary initial power in the takeoff of heavily loaded aircraft. See ROCKET.

*AIRPLANE TYPES AND USES*
Airplanes may be categorized according to function and field of operation into three main types: (1) commercial aircraft, including those for transportation of passengers and cargo by scheduled and nonscheduled airlines; (2) military aircraft; and (3) utility or general aircraft, which include all types of airplanes not included in the other two. The particular characteristics of each plane are de-

termined by the nature of the services to be performed. Increasing specialization in usage has resulted in wide variation in design requirements.
**Commercial Airplanes.** Although the airplane was adopted for passenger-transport service in Europe in 1919, it was not fully accepted as a common carrier in the U.S. until some years later; the carriage of mail by the U.S. Post Office Department, however, laid the foundation in the years from 1918 to 1927 for domestic airline service. The typical passenger aircraft evolved from two-engine propeller planes such as the DC-3, which carried 21 passengers and cruised at about 305 km/hr (about 190 mph), to the powerful four-engine planes of the 1950s, which could carry up to 100 passengers at speeds of over 480 km/hr (over 300 mph). During 1989, U.S. airlines carried about 452 million passengers on domestic and international routes.

Different types of passenger planes are used, depending on two factors: the volume of traffic and the distance between airports. The distance between airports is known as the stage length. The greatest number and variety of planes can operate profitably over stage lengths between 400 and 1600 km (between 250 and 1000 mi).

Commercial passenger jets were first used on long-distance runs; the British DeHavilland Comet began service in 1952, and the Boeing 707 in 1958. Also developed in the late 1950s were the DC-8 and the Convair 880 and 990. These planes cruised at about 885 km/hr (about 550 mph) and carried over 100 passengers.

Smaller jets such as the French Caravelle and the Boeing 727, both of which used a design with engines in the tail, were built for medium-distance runs of 800 to 2400 km (500 to 1500 mi). In the mid-1960s, even smaller two-engine jets were built to operate on short runs. These include the

Boeing 737, the DC-9, and the Fokker F-28.

The Boeing 747, which made its first flight in 1970, was the first of the wide-bodied planes that now serve on high-density medium- and long-distance runs. The 747 employs four turbofan engines and flies at over 885 km/hr (550 mph). It usually is fitted for 385 passengers, but can accommodate 500. The Boeing 757 and 767 represent a new generation of wide-bodied planes.

The DC-10 and the Lockheed 1011 Tristar are each capable of carrying more than 300 passengers. Both use a three-engines-aft design; they were built for Chicago-Los Angeles flights and comparable stage lengths. The DC-10 first flew in 1971, and the L-1011 in 1972.

The fastest passenger aircraft is the supersonic transport or SST. It is capable of flying back and forth across the North Atlantic in less time than it takes an ordinary jet to fly across one way. The Soviet TU-144, the first to be put in service, began making scheduled freight hauls within the USSR in 1975.

The British and French governments signed an agreement in 1962 to build the supersonic Concorde; the first test model flew in 1971. A certificate of airworthiness was granted in 1975, and the first commercial flights were made on Jan. 21, 1976. The French plane flew between Paris, Dakar in Senegal, and Rio de Janeiro, and the British plane flew from London to Bahrain.

From its inception the SST was criticized for being uneconomical and excessively noisy. Despite such objections, service to the U.S. began on May 24, 1976, with simultaneous flights from London and Paris to Dulles International Airport near Washington, D.C. The Port Authority of New York refused to allow the Concorde to land at Kennedy International Airport. Only after the British and French won a battle in the courts did the plane begin service to New York on Nov. 22, 1977. Except in the countries of the former USSR, SST flights over inhabited areas have to be at subsonic speeds.

Operating losses on the Concorde were in excess of $1 billion, and production of the plane ended in 1979. The French plane had extended service to Caracas, Venezuela, and to Dakar from Paris. The future of the SST was still not assured by the end of the 1980s.

The air-freight business has enjoyed an unprecedented boom since World War II. Leading commercial cargo planes include the Canadair CL-44 and the A-W Argosy, in addition to modified versions of the larger passenger jets.

**Military Airplanes.** Military planes of the U.S. may be divided into four categories: combat, cargo, training, and observation planes. In the category of combat planes are fighters and bombers for land, sea, and carrier operations.

The F-4 Phantom aircraft, used extensively by the U.S. Navy, U.S. Marines, and the U.S. Air Force, is a supersonic, missile-firing tactical fighter-bomber that can also deliver small nuclear weapons. It can be equipped with "smart" bombs that are guided to their targets by laser beams (see BOMB). The F-111 Aardvark is a jet fighter capable of flying at more than twice the speed of sound; a larger version of the plane is used as a bomber.

Aircraft recently developed include the F-15 Eagle, which excels at air-to-air defense tactics and has a maximum speed of over Mach 2.5 at over 11,000 m (over 36,000 ft); the F-16 Falcon, a highly maneuverable all-purpose fighter-bomber; the A-10 Thunderbolt, an attack plane designed for use in close support of ground troops; the F-117A Stealth, a $42 million, low-profile fighter-bomber developed to evade radar detection; and the E-3 airborne warning and control system (AWACS) surveillance aircraft developed to fly at high altitudes and detect threat aircraft. The principal carrier-based aircraft in use by the U.S. Navy are the F-14 Tomcat, a swing-wing jet with a maximum speed of Mach 2.34 at 12,000 m (about 40,000 ft); the F/A-18 Hornet, a fighter capable of launching air-to-air and air-to-surface missiles as well as bombs; and the A-6E

*The SR-71 strategic reconnaissance spy plane, known as the Black Bird, operates at high altitudes and has flown at more than 3200 km/hr (2000 mph).*  **Lockheed**

Intruder, a long-range attack bomber.

The B-52 Stratofortress, a subsonic plane developed in the 1950s, and the B-1B are the principal long-range heavy bombers used by the U.S. Air Force. As part of the Strategic Air Command (SAC), they can deliver nuclear weapons to any part of the globe. The main use of the B-52 in actual combat was in the Vietnam War, when it was employed in "carpet-bombing" missions against concentrations of enemy forces, and during Operation Desert Storm, the war in the Persian Gulf, when it dropped 750-lb free-fall bombs and 500-lb bombs with delayed fuses to penetrate reinforced shelters.

The Air Force C-5A cargo airplane, which made its first flight in 1968, is the largest and heaviest winged aircraft in the world. It can rush 120 metric tons of troops and equipment over a distance of 10,460 km (6500 mi) without refueling. In 1974 an intercontinental ballistic missile was successfully test-launched from the C-5A.

**General Aviation.** Planes used for private pleasure, for business, for agricultural or other special services, or for flight instruction may be termed utility, or general aviation craft. The most

widespread use of special-service airplanes is in agriculture. Agricultural applications include dusting and spraying with insecticides and herbicides, fertilizing, and seeding. Aerial inspection of pipe and power lines is an important industrial application. Other uses of special-service aircraft include mapping and surveying, forestry patrol, aerial photography, and game- and predatory-animal control. Airplanes were formerly used for policing and rescue operations, but the helicopter has proved more suitable for much of this type of work. L.A.B.; REV. BY H.L.Ta.

*For further information on this topic, see the Bibliography in volume 28, sections 283, 575–76.*

**AIR POLLUTION,** contamination of the atmosphere by gaseous, liquid, or solid wastes or by-products that can endanger human health and the health and welfare of plants and animals, or can attack materials, reduce visibility, or produce undesirable odors. While some air pollution is caused by natural sources, such as radon (q.v.) gas emitted from the earth, this article is concerned with air pollution caused by human activities. *See also* ENVIRONMENT.

Each year industrially developed countries

## MAJOR AIR POLLUTANTS

| Pollutant | Major Sources | Comments |
|---|---|---|
| Carbon Monoxide (CO) | Motor-vehicle exhaust; some industrial processes | Health standard: 10 mg/m$^3$ (9 ppm) over 8 hr; 40 mg/m$^3$ over 1 hr (35 ppm); no more than once per year (for both) |
| Sulfur dioxide (SO$_2$) | Heat and power generation facilities that use oil or coal containing sulfur; sulfuric acid plants | Health standard: 80 µg/m$^3$ (0.03 ppm) over a year; 365 µg/m$^3$ over 24 hr (0.14 ppm) no more than once per year |
| Suspended particulate matter ([PM$_{10}$] - particulate matter less than 10 µm in diameter) ([TSP], the measure formerly used - total suspended particulate matter of all sizes) | Motor-vehicle exhaust; industrial processes; refuse incineration; heat and power generation; reaction of pollutant gases in the atmosphere | Health standard: 50 µg/m$^3$ over a year; 150 µg/m$^3$ over 24 hr no more than once per year; composed of carbon, nitrates, sulfates, and many elements including lead, copper, iron, and zinc |
| Lead (Pb) | Motor-vehicle exhaust; lead smelters; battery plants | Health standard: 1.5 µg/m$^3$ over 3 months; most of lead contained in suspended particulate matter |
| Nitrogen oxides (NO, NO$_2$) | Motor-vehicle exhaust; heat and power generation; nitric acid; explosives; fertilizer plants | Health standard: 100 µg/m$^3$ (0.05 ppm) over a year for NO$_2$; react with hydrocarbons and sunlight to form photochemical oxidants |
| Photochemical oxidants (primarily ozone [O$_3$]; also peroxyacetyl nitrate [PAN] and aldehydes) | Formed in the atmosphere by reactions of nitrogen oxides, hydrocarbons, and sunlight | Health standard: 235 µg/m$^3$ (0.12 ppm) over 1 hr no more than one day per year |
| Nonmethane hydrocarbons ([NMHC], sometimes called nonmethane organic compounds [NMOC] or volatile organic compounds [VOC]; includes ethane, ethylene, propane, butanes, pentanes, acetylene, aldehydes, ketones, solvents) | Motor-vehicle emissions; solvent evaporation; industrial processes; solid waste disposal; fuel combustion; petroleum refineries; gasoline stations; dry cleaners; printing; many paints | React with nitrogen oxides and sunlight to form photochemical oxidants. Some VOC's, such as formaldehyde and benzene, are also hazardous to health. |
| Carbon dioxide (CO$_2$) | All combustion sources | Possibly injurious to health at concentrations greater than 5000 ppm over 2-8 hr; atmospheric levels have increased from a preindustrial level of about 280 ppm to over 350 ppm in the 1990s, and the rate of increase has speeded up. |
| Air toxics (for example, benzene, beryllium, asbestos, inorganic arsenic, mercury, vinyl chloride, formaldehyde) | Specific types of chemical processes; coke ovens; building demolition | Typically cause cancer, or are mutagenic, or are hazardous to unborn infants, or cause neurological disorders. Current levels of emission may result in 1000-3000 cancer deaths each year. |

Note: 1 cubic meter (1 m$^3$) is equal to 35.3 cu. ft; 1 milligram (1 mg) is equal to 0.00004 oz; 1 microgram (1 µg) is equal to 0.00000004 oz.

The city of Los Angeles, blanketed in yellowish smog, with the skyline barely visible in the distance. © 1990 Frank Whitney–The Image Bank

generate billions of tons of pollutants. The most prevalent and widely dispersed air pollutants are described in the accompanying table. The level is usually given in terms of atmospheric concentrations (micrograms of pollutants per cubic meter of air) or, for gases, in terms of parts per million, that is, number of pollutant molecules per million air molecules. Many come from directly identifiable sources; sulfur dioxide, for example, comes from electric power plants burning coal or oil. Others are formed through the action of sunlight on previously emitted reactive materials (called precursors). For example, ozone, a dangerous pollutant in smog (q.v.), is produced by the interaction of hydrocarbons and nitrogen oxides under the influence of sunlight. Currently more than 100 million Americans live in cities that do not meet public health standards for ozone. On the other hand, ozone in the upper atmosphere is a protection from the sun's ultraviolet rays. The discovery in the 1980s that air pollutants such as fluorocarbons were destroying the ozone layer (q.v.) has caused the phasing out of these materials.

**Meteorology and Health Effects.** Pollutant concentrations are reduced by atmospheric mixing, which depends on such weather conditions as temperature, wind speed, amount of sunlight, and the movement of high and low pressure systems and their interaction with the local topography, for example, mountains and valleys. Normally, temperature decreases with altitude. But when a colder layer of air settles under a warm layer, producing a temperature or thermal inversion, atmospheric mixing is retarded and pollutants may accumulate near the ground. Inversions can become sustained under a stationary weather system coupled with low wind speeds.

Periods of poor atmospheric mixing of only a few days, and sometimes only a few hours, can lead to high concentrations of hazardous materials in high-pollution areas and, under severe conditions, can result in illness and even death. An inversion in Donora, Pa., in 1948 caused respiratory illness in over 6000 persons and led to the death of 20. Severe pollution in London took 3500 to 4000 lives in 1952 and another 700 in 1962. Release of methyl isocyanate into the air during a temperature inversion caused the disaster at Bhopal, India, in December 1984, with at least 3300 deaths and more than 20,000 illnesses. The effects of long-term exposure to low concentrations are not well defined; however, those most at risk are the very young, the elderly, smokers, workers whose jobs expose them to toxic materials, and persons with heart or lung disease. Other adverse effects of air pollution are potential injury to livestock and crops.

Often, the first noticeable effects of pollution are aesthetic and may not necessarily be dangerous. These include visibility reduction due to tiny particles suspended in air, or bad odors, such as the rotten egg smell produced by hydrogen sulfide emitted from pulp and paper mills.

**Sources and Control.** The combustion of coal, oil, and gasoline accounts for much of air pollution. More than 80 percent of the sulfur dioxide, 50 percent of the nitrogen oxides, and 30 to 40 percent of the particulate matter emitted to the atmosphere in the U.S. are produced by fossil-fuel–fired electric power plants, industrial boilers, and residential furnaces. Ninety percent of the carbon monoxide and almost 50 percent of the nitrogen oxides and hydrocarbons come from burning gasoline and diesel fuels in cars and trucks. Other major pollution sources include iron and steel mills; coke ovens; zinc, lead, and copper smelters; municipal incinerators; petroleum refineries; cement plants; large solvent users; and nitric and sulfuric acid plants.

Potential pollutants may exist in the materials

Air pollution by automobile exhaust has spurred research into control devices. Above: Exhaust fumes are checked in a laboratory for hydrocarbons, carbon dioxide, carbon monoxide, and nitrogen oxide before and after the insertion of a catalytic convertor.

entering a chemical or combustion (q.v.) process (such as lead in gasoline), or they may be produced as a result of the process itself. Carbon monoxide, for example, is a typical product of internal-combustion engines. Methods for controlling air pollution include removing the hazardous material before it is used, removing the pollutant after it is formed, or altering the process so that the pollutant is not formed or occurs only at very low levels. Automobile pollutants can be controlled by burning the gasoline as completely as possible, by recirculating fumes from fuel tank, carburetor, and crankcase, and by changing the engine exhaust to harmless substances in catalytic converters (see INTERNAL-COMBUSTION ENGINE). Industrially emitted particulates may be trapped in cyclones, electrostatic precipitators, and filters. Pollutant gases can be collected in liquids or on solids, or incinerated into harmless substances.

**Large-Scale Effects.** The tall smokestacks used by industries and utilities do not remove pollutants but simply boost them higher into the atmosphere, thereby reducing their concentration at the site. These pollutants may then be transported over large distances and produce adverse effects in areas far from the site of the original emission. Sulfur dioxide and nitrogen oxide emissions from the central and eastern U.S. are causing acid rain (q.v.) in New York State, New England, and eastern Canada. The pH (q.v.) level, or relative acidity, of many freshwater lakes in that region has been altered so dramatically by this rain that entire fish populations have been destroyed. Similar effects have been observed in Europe. Sulfur dioxide emissions and the subsequent formation of sulfuric acid can also be responsible for the attack on limestone and marble at large distances from the source.

The worldwide increase in the burning of coal and oil since the late 1940s has led to ever increasing concentrations of carbon dioxide. The resulting "greenhouse effect" (q.v.), which allows solar energy to enter the atmosphere but reduces the reemission of infrared radiation from the earth, could lead to a warming trend that might affect the global climate and lead to a partial melting of the polar ice caps. Possibly an increase in cloud cover or absorption of excess carbon dioxide by the oceans would check the greenhouse effect before it reached the stage of polar melting. Nevertheless, research reports released in the U.S. in the 1980s indicate that the greenhouse effect is definitely under way and that the nations of the world should be taking immediate steps to deal with it.

**Government Action.** In the U.S., the Clean Air Act of 1967 as amended in 1970, 1977, and 1990 is the legal basis for air-pollution control throughout the U.S. The Environmental Protection Agency (EPA) has primary responsibility for carrying out the requirements of the act, which specifies that air-quality standards be established for hazardous substances. These standards are in the form of concentration levels that are believed to be low enough to protect public health. Source emission standards are also specified to limit the discharge of pollutants into the air so that air-quality standards will be achieved. The act was also designed to prevent significant deterioration of air quality in areas where the air is currently cleaner than the standards require. The amendments of 1990 identified ozone, carbon monoxide, particulate matter, acid rain, and air toxins as major air pollution problems. On the international scene, 49 countries agreed in March 1985 on a UN convention to protect the ozone layer. This "Montréal Protocol," which was renegotiated in 1990, calls for the phaseout of certain chlorocarbons and fluorocarbons by the year 2000 and provides aid to developing countries in making this transition.

See also OCCUPATIONAL AND ENVIRONMENTAL DISEASES; WATER POLLUTION.                    R.A.W.

For further information on this topic, see the Bibliography in volume 28, sections 566, 568.

**AIRPORT,** area of land or water adapted for the landing and takeoff of aircraft. Large airports provide terminal buildings for the arrival and departure of passengers, as well as maintenance and repair facilities for aircraft. Requirements for handling aircraft at large military airfields are similar to those of civil airports.

Airports evolved from grass and dirt strips. The growth in size and weight of German aircraft during World War I, and the concomitant requirements for longer takeoff runs, necessitated paved runways for heavy bombers. The first paved runways for a civil airport in the U.S. were built in 1928 at Newark, N.J. Before World War II, Newark also experimented with landing lights, illuminated wind vanes, and other innovations. In Europe, the first paved runways at civil airfields were built in the late 1930s, but Great Britain did not have paved runways until World War II. Airport development and construction of concrete runways in the U.S. benefited from federal relief programs in the depression of the 1930s. After 1941, global deployment of U.S. armed forces produced military airfields all over the world; many of these became the basis for later civil air networks. As air travel grew after the war, and a new generation of airliners demanded better facilities, thousands of new airports were built.

In 1990 the International Civil Aviation Organization reported 37,739 civilian airports in use throughout the world. The U.S. listed 17,327 airports at about the same time, 53 of which accounted for 73 percent of the 429,654,602 passengers enplaned in 1989. O'Hare in Chicago is the world's busiest airport; in 1989, it recorded more than 59 million passengers, about 790,000 takeoffs and landings, and 869,490 metric tons of cargo. London's Heathrow Airport, with the largest flow of international traffic in the world, had nearly 40 million passenger arrivals and departures. Typical of enormous traffic growth during the 1980s was the opening in 1990 of a

The second busiest airport in the U.S., Hartsfield International in Atlanta, Ga., is linked to downtown by a rail line that began operation in 1988 and runs through the main terminal buildings (center foreground). Aircraft arrive and depart from five parallel concourses to the rear of the terminal. Passengers travel within the airport on moving sidewalks or minitrains.                    City of Atlanta Aviation Department

third terminal at Florida's Orlando International Airport, where operations had swelled from 6 million passengers in 1981 to more than 17.2 million in 1989.

Throughout the 1980s, deregulation in the U.S. resulted in rate slashing and "frequent flyer" plans that brought unprecedented numbers of new travelers to the skies, creating congestion at major airports, as snarled ground transport systems proved ill-equipped to handle the strain of increased traffic. Meanwhile, rapidly growing international travel created similar problems at major airports in other parts of the world; Munich, for example, had to build an entirely new terminal, scheduled to begin operations in 1992, to replace an overcrowded facility whose traffic had grown from 1 million to 11.4 million passengers in less than three decades.

**Design and Construction.** With the growth of air travel, airports became symbols of international prestige after World War II, often designed by internationally renowned architects. An outstanding example was the award-winning 1962 design by the Finnish-American architect Eero Saarinen for the Trans World Airlines terminal at John F. Kennedy Airport in New York City. Typifying the enthusiasm for aviation prevailing at the time, the building suggests flight, with two winglike roof sections of concrete and glass over the waiting-room areas. A striking series of new airports in the Middle East integrated new structural concepts with traditional forms of domes and minarets.

Increasingly, development of wide-bodied jet transports, such as the Boeing 747, made it difficult for airports to allow adequate space on the ground for maneuvering such aircraft while permitting convenient movement of passengers transferring from one airline to another. This became particularly acute in the U.S. as airlines created more and more central-city hubs to collect passengers for long, nonstop flights and redistribute them to short-haul or commuter flights to smaller cities. One approach to the problem was that of the Dallas-Fort Worth Regional Airport: a central access route for cars serving as the spine for a series of semicircular terminals, flanked on either side by pairs of parallel runways. Charles de Gaulle Airport, near Paris, exemplified another solution for dealing with escalating international traffic: a larger main passenger terminal surrounded by satellite terminals with their own arrival and departure gates. Other major airports employed variations on such themes; passengers were transferred between or within terminals by buses, automated passenger trains, and moving walkways. At Dulles International Airport outside Washington, D.C., passengers boarded mobile lounges that ferried them across crowded taxiways to the airliners.

**Passenger Services.** Major airports provide a wide range of facilities for the convenience of millions of travelers. These range from such basic features as ticket-sales counters, baggage-claim areas, rest rooms, and restaurants to luxury hotels, conference centers, shopping malls, and play areas for children. Other amenities include newsstands, bars, barbershops, post offices, and bank branches. Taxi stands, rental-car agencies, and huge parking lots are necessary to accomodate ground connections. Many airports, particularly in Europe and Japan, also supply direct rail links to expedite such traffic. International terminals must also have customs areas and currency-exchange counters; most have duty-free shops as well. For international travelers, the problem of language barriers is met by using standardized symbols. At American airports, the threat of aerial hijacking and terrorist activities has led to elaborate security procedures and increasingly sophisticated baggage-inspection equipment to protect passenger safety.

**Airport Operation.** Because aircraft must land and take off into the wind, the location of terminals and the layout of runways depend largely on the pattern of prevailing winds. Other determinants include geographic features, such as surrounding hills and mountains, and the desirability of avoiding approach and departure routes over crowded residential areas. Such requirements have made it increasingly difficult to find locations for airports. Suppressing noise and reducing air pollution have been major concerns of both airport engineers and airplane designers but progress has not been rapid enough to quiet mounting protests by environmentalists and other concerned citizens. Airport designers must take into account the weight and wingspan of airplanes when laying out hangars, cargo-loading areas, parking ramps, taxiways, and runways; wide-bodied jets, requiring thick concrete runways 60 m (about 200 ft) or more in width and 4427 m (14,000 ft) or more in length, have added to such problems. Enormous maintenance hangars are also required; a 78.9 by 379-m (262 by 984-ft) building at Munich's new airport will accommodate six Boeing 747-400s under one roof. The same complex will include an even larger 100 by 499.9-m (328 by 1640-ft) air cargo terminal.

A standard feature of any airport is a control tower where air traffic controllers use computers, radar, and radio to keep track of air traffic and issue instructions for takeoffs, landings, and maintenance of safe distances between aircraft.

As traffic multiplied in the 1980s and numbers of controllers failed to grow apace, this became increasingly difficult. In 1989, approximately 1600 close calls were reported on airport runways in the U.S. alone; the collision of two jetliners at Detroit Metropolitan Airport the next year under foggy conditions intensified efforts by the Federal Aviation Administration to improve ground radar systems, runway and taxiway markings, and safety procedures. See AIR TRAFFIC CONTROL.

**Support vehicles.** Airport operations require a diverse array of support vehicles. Conventional cars, jeeps, and trucks—painted bright colors for high visibility—crisscross runways and taxiways. More specialized vehicles are also necessary; heavy-duty, four-wheel-drive "tugs" latch on to an airliner's forward landing gear in order to tow it in and out of parking ramp areas. Special catering and supply trucks, the cargo space of which can be raised and lowered by hydraulic hoists, are used to resupply airliners with food and with water for drinking and for lavatories. Other adjustable gantry equipment can be employed for inspection and maintenance. Trucks are still used to provide many types of aircraft with fuel brought from "fuel farms" located at safe distances from terminals, but at particularly large airports, where dozens of wide-bodied jetliners and other aircraft may await servicing, fuel must be delivered by insulated underground lines to ramp areas, where mobile units pump it directly into an airliner's tanks.

Other vehicles required for safe operation of an airport include emergency and fire-fighting equipment, such as fire-suppression vehicles equipped to discharge water, chemical foams, and powders at high velocity over considerable distances. Also available are medical units and ambulances. Busy airports experience frequent full alerts as traffic mounts.

**New Operations.** By 1990, with projections indicating that annual passenger volume might double to 900 million in the U.S. alone within 10 years and a similar increase looming in international traffic, major airports continued to be built throughout the world. In addition to Munich's new facility, examples included Airtropolis Terminal 2 at Changji Airport in Singapore, a technologically daring complex under construction in Japan's Osaka Bay, and a highly controversial new airport at Denver, Colorado.

See also AIRPLANE; AIR TRANSPORT INDUSTRY; AVIATION.                                       R.E.Bi.

*For further information on this topic, see the Bibliography in volume 28, sections 338–39.*

**AIR PUMP.** See AIR COMPRESSOR.

**AIRSHIP,** lighter-than-air craft equipped with a bag containing a gas to lift the ship, a means of propulsion, means for adjusting buoyancy, and one or more gondolas for the crew, passengers, and power units. The bag, usually containing helium or hydrogen, is elongated or streamlined to enable easy passage through the air. The means of propulsion usually comprises one or more engines and propellers. A means for releasing the ballast, usually sand or water, is used to increase buoyancy; and a means for releasing gas is used to reduce buoyancy. To steer the airship, the pilot uses one or more vertically hinged rudders; to control climb or descent, the pilot employs one or more horizontally hinged elevators.

Airships, or dirigibles, were developed from the free balloon (see BALLOON). Three classes of airships are recognized: the nonrigid, commonly called blimp, in which the form of the bag is maintained by pressure of the gas; the semirigid airship, in which, to maintain the form, gas pressure acts in conjunction with a longitudinal keel; and the rigid airship, or zeppelin, in which

The Goodyear blimp, a nonrigid dirigible, is one of a number of airships used for advertising and publicity and for aerial photography, especially of sports events.
**Goodyear Tire & Rubber Co.**

the form is determined by a rigid structure. Technically all three classes may be called dirigible (Lat. *dirigere,* "to direct, to steer") balloons.

The first successful airship was that of the French engineer and inventor Henri Giffard (1825–82), who constructed in 1852 a cigar-shaped, nonrigid gas bag 44 m (143 ft) long, driven by a screw propeller rotated by a 2.2-kw (3-hp) steam engine. He flew over Paris at a speed of about 10 km/hr (about 6 mph). Giffard's airship could be steered only in calm or nearly calm weather. The first airship to demonstrate its ability to return to its starting place in a light wind was the *La France,* developed in 1884 by the French inventors Charles Renard (1847–1905) and Arthur Krebs (1847–1935). It was driven by an electrically rotated propeller. The Brazilian aeronaut Alberto Santos-Dumont developed a series of 14 airships in France. In his *No. 6,* in 1901, he circled the Eiffel Tower.

The American inventor Thomas S. Baldwin (1854–1923) built a dirigible flown by Roy Knabenshue (1877–1960) in 1904. Walter Wellman (1858–1934) failed in an effort to cross the Atlantic Ocean in an airship in 1910. Although many successful flights were made before 1910, the best engine available for use in the early airship was too heavy in proportion to its power.

Count Ferdinand von Zeppelin, the German inventor, completed his first airship in 1900; this ship had a rigid frame and served as the prototype of many subsequent models. The first zeppelin airship consisted of a row of 17 gas cells individually covered in rubberized cloth; the whole was confined in a cylindrical framework covered with smooth-surfaced cotton cloth. It was about 128 m (about 420 ft) long and 12 m (38 ft) in diameter; the hydrogen-gas capacity totaled 1,129,842 liters (399,000 cu ft). The ship was steered by forward and aft rudders and was driven by two 11-kw (15-hp) Daimler internal-combustion engines, each rotating two propellers. Passengers, crew, and engine were carried in two aluminum gondolas suspended forward and aft. At its first trial, on July 2, 1900, the airship carried five persons; it attained an altitude of 396 m (1300 ft) and flew a distance of 6 km (3.75 mi) in 17 min.

The first commercial means of regular passenger air travel was supplied by the zeppelin airships *Deutschland* in 1910 and *Sachsen* in 1913. At the beginning of World War I, 10 zeppelins were in service in Germany, and others were built for the military services. By 1918 the total number of zeppelins constructed was 67, of which 16 survived the war. Those not captured were surrendered to the Allies by the terms of the Treaty of Versailles in 1919. At the outbreak of the war, France had a fleet of semirigid airships, developed by officers of the French army. The experience of the war, however, in disclosing the vulnerability of airships to airplane attack, caused the abandonment of the dirigible for offensive military purposes. Nonrigid airships became useful for aerial observation, coastal patrol, convoying, and locating enemy submarines and mines, because of their abilities to hover over a given location and to remain in the air for longer periods than the airplane.

Toward the end of World War I, the British began intensive development of rigid airships, stimulated by the prospect that nonflammable helium gas would soon be available in quantities sufficient to inflate large ships. The *R34,* with a length of 196 m (643 ft) and a gas capacity of 56,067,355 liters (1,980,000 cu ft), was commissioned in 1919. It made the first transatlantic flight of an airship, flying by way of Newfoundland, Canada, from East Fortune, Scotland, to Mineola, N.Y., and returning to Pulham, England. The total flying time for the round trip was 183 hr and 15 min and the aggregate distance traveled about 11,200 km (about 7000 mi). In 1921 the *R38,* some 25 percent larger than the *R34,* was completed; both were wrecked that same year.

The U.S. government purchased in 1921 a large semirigid airship named the *Roma.* It had a length of 125 m (410 ft), a gas capacity of 33,980,-215 liters (1,200,000 cu ft), and was powered by six 12-cylinder 298-kw (400-hp) motors. The ship

*The German airship* Hindenburg *crashes in flames at Lakehurst, N.J., on May 6, 1937.*　Associated Press

was lost in 1922; in 1923 the U.S. Navy commissioned the *Shenandoah,* originally known as the *ZR1,* the first zeppelin-type airship of entirely American construction and the first of the type filled with helium gas. It had a length of 206 m (677 ft) and a gas capacity of 59,890,129 liters (2,115,000 cu ft). In the two years following, it made several extended and successful flights, but in September 1925 it was completely wrecked in a windstorm, with the loss of 14 crew members. The 29 survivors undoubtedly owed their lives to the use of nonflammable helium for inflation. In 1924 the navy received delivery of the *ZR3,* later christened the *Los Angeles,* made by the zeppelin works in Germany as a partial payment of war reparations. This airship was 198 m (650 ft) long and had a gas capacity of 70,084,193 liters (2,475,000 cu ft). The control gondola also carried accommodations for 30 passengers, with sleeping facilities similar to those of a Pullman car. The *Los Angeles* made about 250 flights, including trips to Puerto Rico and Panama. It was decommissioned in 1932.

In 1926 the Italian airship *Norge,* a semirigid craft of about 18,405,949 liters (about 650,000 cu ft) capacity, flew from Spitsbergen, Norway, over the North Pole to Teller, Alaska, where the ship was dismantled. Another polar flight was tried two years later in a similar ship, the *Italia,* but, after passing over the Pole, it was wrecked on the return flight, with the loss of eight lives.

The German zeppelin plant in 1928 produced the *Graf Zeppelin,* which had a length of 235 m (772 ft) and a gas capacity of 105,055,490 liters (3,710,000 cu ft). It flew a total of more than 1,609,344 km (1 million mi) in nine years of service, crossing the Atlantic Ocean to North or South America 139 times and making a complete trip around the world with stops only at Tokyo, Los Angeles, and Lakehurst, N.J.

About the same time, the British resumed construction of rigid airships, launching the *R100* and the *R101* in 1929. With lengths of 215 m (707 ft) and 221 m (724 ft), respectively, these dirigibles had a gas capacity of 141,584,230 liters (5 million cu ft) each. The *R101* was powered by five 485-kw (650-hp) diesel engines and had dining, sleeping, and recreational accommodations for 100 persons built into the hull. In October 1930, on a flight to India, it crashed during a violent rainstorm into a hill near Beauvais, France, and was completely destroyed by fire; 46 of the passengers and crew lost their lives. The *R100,* which in the preceding August had made a round trip to Montréal, was scrapped after the destruction of the *R101,* and the British government abandoned construction of all dirigibles.

Meanwhile, in 1928, the U.S. Navy purchased two dirigibles, each with a length of 239 m (785 ft), a gas capacity of 184,059,490 liters (6,500,000 cu ft) of helium, and eight 418-kw (560-hp) engines. A novel feature of the design was provision for a hangar compartment in the ship capable of accommodating five scout airplanes, which could be released or taken aboard in flight. The first of these airships, the *Akron,* was completed in 1931 and was wrecked in a storm off the New Jersey coast in 1933; the wreckage was discovered by a marine research team in 1986. The second ship, the *Macon,* was completed in 1933 and wrecked in 1935. Since the *Macon,* the U.S. has built no rigid airships.

The famous German-built *Hindenburg* had a length of 245 m (804 ft) and a gas capacity of 190,006,030 liters (6,710,000 cu ft). After making ten transatlantic crossings in regular commercial service in 1936, it was destroyed by fire in 1937 when it was landing at Lakehurst, N.J.; 36 of its 92 passengers and crew were killed.

Since the destruction of the *Hindenburg,* airship activity has been confined to the nonrigid type of craft. In 1938 all military blimps in the U.S. were placed under navy jurisdiction, with the Naval Air Station at Lakehurst as center of operations. During World War II, blimps were employed for patrol, scouting, convoy, and antisubmarine work. A private commercial firm in the U.S. developed several small, nonrigid airships that have been used to provide aerial television views of sports events, to take people on rides, and for advertising purposes.

After World War II the U.S. Navy continued to develop the airship for such purposes as antisubmarine warfare, intermediate search missions, and early-warning missions. The largest of navy airships, the ZPG-2 type, was 99 m (324 ft) long and had a capacity of 24,777,240 liters (875,000 cu ft) of helium. An airship of this type stayed aloft without refueling for more than 200 hr. The navy discontinued the use of airships in 1961; however, during the later-1980s there was a renewal of military interest in airships, and both the U.S. Coast Guard and Navy began to study the feasibility of using airships for airborne early warning and electronic warfare as well as antisubmarine warfare. Some countries were also showing an equal interest in airships for civil aviation and advertising purposes.                    L.A.B.

*For further information on this topic, see the Bibliography in volume 28, sections 575–78.*
**AIRSICKNESS.** *See* MOTION SICKNESS.
**AIR TRAFFIC CONTROL,** management of aircraft proceeding along civil airways, including airport arrivals and departures. Different rules of opera-

tion apply to pilots proceeding under visual flight rules (VFR) and those under instrument flight rules (IFR).

The minimum instruments required under VFR include an airspeed indicator, altimeter, and magnetic direction indicator. Minimum flying conditions in radar-controlled airspace in transition areas specify a cloud ceiling about 215 m (700 ft) above ground level and 1.6 km (1 mi) visibility. Other VFR requirements for visibility and distance from clouds depend on altitude and operation in either controlled or uncontrolled airspace. VFR flight is permitted in all airspaces, but terminal control areas require positive (radar) air traffic control. Airport traffic areas typically encompass a radius of 8 km (5 mi) and can be extended laterally for controlling instrument-dependent departures and landings. Control zones around airports extend upward with no limit. Radio communications with the tower is required during landing and takeoff. Other regulations apply to high-speed, high-altitude operations in the continental control area above the U.S. and in the flight information regions on international routes. The remainder of this article will concern itself primarily with aircraft operating under IFR.

**Operation and Equipment.** At major airports, air traffic control begins with the ground controller in the airport tower, who guides airliners from the loading ramp, along the taxi strips, up to the runway threshold. The ground controller must consider other aircraft as well as the legions of vehicles, such as fuel pumpers, luggage and cargo vehicles, and maintenance vehicles needed for airport operation. The job continues

day and night, in all weather, so that at times of reduced visibility large airports rely on special radar to aid the ground controller. For takeoff, an air traffic controller located in the airport tower takes over, confirming an assigned runway clearance and providing information on wind and weather and other data needed for departure. Another departure controller may pass on additional data as the airliner is handed over to the air route traffic control (ARTC), the personnel of which remain in communication with the airliner from one ARTC center to the next, until the air traffic control tower at the plane's destination takes over. See AIRWAY.

The ARTC system of radar and computerized equipment represents a major advance in air traffic control, in that controllers are relieved of the accumulation and interpretation of immense amounts of routine material, thereby permitting them more time to assess data relevant to key decisions. In the control room, the controller wears earphones and a microphone for radio communication with aircraft and other controllers. The planes themselves are represented as a data block on a special radar screen in front of the controller (see RADAR). The data block includes a symbol for individual aircraft, along with each plane's identifying call sign, speed, and altitude. Some radar equipment can display additional information pertaining to a particular flight. All flights are kept at separate altitudes and at specific distances from one another. Flight plans are fed into computers and updated as the flight progresses. Air traffic controllers watch these displayed assignments carefully to prevent midair collisions. Collision-avoidance radar sys-

*Air traffic controllers, shown here at the Regional Air Traffic Control Center in Florida, are responsible for monitoring the flight paths of all aircraft over an area of 1000 sq km (400 sq mi). Radar screens and optical scanning devices line the walls of the control room.*
Art d'Arazian–Shostal Associates

tems for individual aircraft are under development. As aircraft converge on airports and begin descent for landing, aerial congestion can develop. In this case, new arrivals are directed to a holding area in the sky, about 50 km (about 30 mi) or so away from the field. Waiting planes in this area repeatedly circle a beacon, so that they create an aerial "stack," maintaining a vertical spacing of 305 m (about 1000 ft) between planes. Each time a suitable runway becomes available, a plane is taken from the bottom of the stack, permitting the others to spiral down one layer.

**Navigational Aids.** Navigation between airports increasingly relies on ground beacons and on electronic and computerized equipment within the airplane. The most widely used ground system is the very high frequency omnidirectional range beacon (VOR). VOR stations, which are not always located directly on an airport, operate on frequencies that are generally free of atmospheric noise and provide an accuracy lacking in previous equipment. Aboard the airplane, a visual display indicates the magnetic course the pilot must fly in order to travel directly to or away from the VOR station. Most VOR stations also have distance measuring equipment (DME), which tell the pilot distances to and from VORs. These VOR/DME stations provide excellent service for both private aircraft and scheduled airliners worldwide. For intercontinental routes, a radio and electronic system called Omega uses a network of eight global transmission sites that emit powerful long-range signals. A computer on board the aircraft receives the signals, analyzes their pattern, and calculates the position of the plane anywhere in the world. A different method, the inertial navigation system (INS), requires no ground stations or radio beams that might be subject to distortion or interruption. The INS uses a gyroscopically stabilized inertial platform, aligned to true north. Accelerometers associated with the system can determine the direction and speed of the aircraft, and a computerized display indicates this information, along with wind speed, drift, and other data. These systems, when combined with an autopilot, enable large jet transports literally to fly themselves on global routes. Many airlines also carry compact weather radar to detect storm conditions en route. Military equipment uses VOR, Omega, and other systems, including more sophisticated radar. *See also* NAVIGATION.

For instrument landings, pilots use an instrument landing system (ILS), similar to VOR signals. Cockpit instruments indicate deviations to either side of the localizer beam leading directly to the runway, and guidance information from the glide-slope beam indicates if the plane is too high or too low on the approach, which may start some 13 to 16 km (about 8 to 10 mi) from the airport. The ILS system, which is subject to "ground clutter" and occasional distortions, began to be replaced by a microwave landing system (MLS) in the early 1980s. The MLS equipment is more precise, permits multiple curving approaches (unlike the rigidly linear ILS-mediated approach) over a broader gateway area to accommodate more aircraft, and is cheaper to operate. Some existing ILS systems, however, can accommodate totally automatic landings, permitting operations in heavy fog. Elsewhere, special radar systems can be used by air traffic controllers to "talk down" aircraft in bad weather.

**Air Traffic Control Problems.** Despite the impressive sophistication of electronic aids and computerization, air traffic control continues to rely heavily on people, whether the airplanes are on the ground, approaching or departing the airport, or en route. Direct responsibility for people's lives rests with the men and women who control air traffic. Training standards are demanding, and the attrition rate for experienced controllers is high. The controllers also occupy an increasingly powerful position when they strike or initiate a work slowdown while bargaining on working conditions, pay scales, and other contract clauses. In the late 1970s, such actions created many problems for passengers and airline management alike, especially in Europe during busy air traffic seasons.

In August 1981, 11,800 members of the 15,000-member Professional Air Traffic Controllers Organization struck for a shorter work week, higher pay, and other benefits. The administration of President Ronald Reagan reacted by dismissing all 11,800 strikers and decertifying their union.

The growing number of private aircraft using major airport facilities creates additional problems in air traffic control planning. Some officials would prefer to ban all but scheduled airline traffic at major air terminals, citing the example of a midair collision in 1978 between an airliner and a private plane in California, as well as other near-misses. Even without the presence of private aircraft, increased airline traffic has intensified the concern for passenger safety. For this reason, collision-avoidance radar systems were developed during the 1980s.

*See also* AIRPLANE; AVIATION.     R.E.Bi.

**AIR TRANSPORT INDUSTRY,** area of commerce in which aircraft are employed to carry passengers, freight, and mail. Air transport companies operate scheduled airlines and nonscheduled services over local, regional, national, and inter-

*Wide-bodied cargo jets are the principal carriers of the air transport industry. Air transport is economical mainly for high-value items, such as the automobile shown here.*

David Vine–Shostal Associates

national routes. The aircraft operated by these companies range from small single-engine planes to large multiengine jet transports. *See* AIRPLANE; AVIATION.

**Origin and Development.** The first air passenger services began in 1910, when dirigibles began operating between several German cities. The first scheduled airplane service to carry passengers began in the U.S. in 1914. Several experimental airmail flights took place in India, Europe, and the U.S. before World War I, but sustained air transport services were not firmly established until after the war. In 1918 the U.S. Post Office Department began the nation's first scheduled air service, using planes and pilots furnished by the War Department. By the mid-1920s there were regular scheduled airmail flights from coast to coast. On night flights pilots were guided by a string of flashing beacons at ground stations along the flight path.

With the passage of the Air Mail (Kelly) Act in 1925, private lines began carrying mail under contract in single-engine, open-cockpit planes. Another federal law, the Air Commerce Act of 1926, established government agencies for development of airports, radio navigation, and

other services. Although several independent companies had begun passenger service early in the 1920s, none had succeeded. With subsidies from the Air Mail Act, however, new airlines like American, Delta, and United began to see their operations become profitable. These airlines soon were flying larger monoplanes with enclosed cabins, such as the Ford Trimotor, which carried up to 15 passengers.

In Europe many governments developed an extensive airline system. Although early airmail routes there compared unfavorably with American round-the-clock deliveries, European passenger operations became much more sophisticated. By 1929 Britain was operating a commercial air route to India, and within a few years other nations began combined mail, freight, and passenger service to distant countries and dependencies.

The era between 1919 and the outbreak of World War II in 1939 included significant advances in weather forecasting, navigation equipment, aerodynamics, and innovative management. Symbolizing these trends were airline specifications for modern equipment such as the DC-3 of the 1930s, a monoplane constructed of metal, carefully streamlined, with reliable and efficient radial engines, retractable landing gear, variable-pitch propellers, and many other refinements. Big flying boats began to link Europe and Asia with the U.S.

During World War II intercontinental air transport became firmly established. After the war the new long-range four-engine transports with fully pressurized cabins and advanced instrumentation were increasingly able to avoid storms and turbulent winds, enhancing passenger comfort and making operations more economical and consistent. These new planes and the jet airliners introduced in 1958 replaced railroad trains and ocean liners as the primary mode of long-distance travel. A new generation of wide-bodied, or "jumbo-jet," transports began operations in 1970, and the Anglo-French Concorde, a supersonic transport, entered passenger service in 1976.

Air transport operations are monitored and regulated by several national and international bodies. Within the U.S., the Air Commerce Act of 1926 charged the Commerce Department with encouraging civil aviation as well as with setting standards for both planes and pilots. In 1938, these duties were transferred to a new Civil Aeronautics Authority, which was then split in 1940 into two agencies, the Civil Aeronautics Board (CAB) and the Civil Aeronautics Administration (CAA). The CAB was entrusted with economic and safety rule-making as well as accident investigation; the CAA with airway development and enforcement of safety standards. In 1958, Congress gave the new Federal Aviation Agency (FAA) responsibility for rule-making and enforcement in the safety field and for maintaining a common civil-military system of air navigation and air traffic control. In 1967, the FAA was renamed the Federal Aviation Administration and placed within the newly created Department of Transportation. At the same time, accident investigation was transferred from the CAB to the new National Transportation Safety Board (NTSB). Legislation passed in 1978 phased out the CAB's remaining function, airline economic regulation, and in 1984 that agency ceased to exist. The International Civil Aviation Organization (ICAO) was created as a permanent body of the UN in 1947. Since then it has facilitated the establishment of worldwide standards for safety, reliability, and navigation. The ICAO also assists in resolving legal issues.

Modern airline operations include a significant effort in ancillary services, such as airframe and engine maintenance, personnel training (pilots, cabin attendants, ticket agents, ground crews), maintenance of computerized reservation and accounting equipment, food preparation, and the operation of hotels and resorts around the world. To meet federal standards for training and flight proficiency requirements, airlines rely heavily on computerized simulators, because exclusive training in complex jet transports is far too costly and time consuming.

**Air Cargo.** Along with airmail service, the shipping of commodities by air began in the 1920s. The private airline of American automobile manufacturer Henry Ford carried considerable amounts of bulky freight in the late 1920s, and one or two U.S. firms offered all-cargo schedules in the Great Lakes area about the same time. The air cargo business in the 1930s expanded as larger airliners came into service, but air cargo still lagged far behind passengers and mail as a source of revenue. Nonetheless, for certain categories of compact, lightweight, and high-value items, air transport proved highly useful. Typical air cargo in the pre–World War II era included jewelry, cut flowers, high-fashion clothing, movie reels, pharmaceuticals, and high-priority replacement and repair parts for machinery. Even some live animals were carried.

After World War II, when larger, more efficient planes became available, airlines increased their cargo operations, and several all-cargo companies were formed. Postwar freight was likely to include almost anything that would fit inside the fuselage of a plane. During the Berlin airlift (1948-49), military planes carried not only food but also tons of coal and construction equipment. With increasing frequency all kinds of livestock—from Thoroughbred horses to exotic zoo animals—traveled in pressurized cargo planes. Perishable produce, frozen foods, heavy machinery, automobile parts, and even complete autos were also characteristic of air cargo. Smaller shipments were usually packed in large containers, to make for easy handling and to cut down on pilferage. In the 1970s another kind of air cargo—the overnight delivery of letters, packages, and even larger cargo—took on increasing importance both within the U.S. and internationally. New carriers were now competing with national postal services.

Compared with truck, rail, and water transport, air cargo costs are still high in cost per mile, and air cargo still commands only a small share of total intercity tonnage moved by all forms of transport in the U.S. Nevertheless, many shippers still profit from air cargo by reducing inventories, warehouse requirements, and handling charges.

**General Aviation.** The general aviation sector of the air transport industry comprises such nonairline and nonmilitary activities as business flying, commercial flying, instructional flying, and recreational flying. Business flying involves individually owned planes, as well as larger corporate aircraft. Commercial activities run the gamut from chartered passenger and cargo flights to crop treatment, mapping, and advertising. Business and commercial activities account for well over half the total hours flown in general aviation. As many as one-third of all air passengers in intercity travel in the U.S. are carried in aircraft of the general aviation fleet.

From awkward beginnings in the early 1920s, general aviation has become an integral part of the air transport system in most nations. General aviation equipment includes helicopters, single-engine planes, twin-engine planes, and jets; the speeds of planes range from about 240 km/hr (about 150 mph) for single-engine planes to about 800 km/hr (about 500 mph) for executive jets.

The major development of business and commercial flying in the U.S. occurred after World War II, when the decentralization of American industry created a need for rapid business travel, especially to smaller urban areas where scheduled airline service was infrequent or nonexistent. Many of the single-engine and smaller twin-engine craft are being produced with supercharged or turboprop engines. The larger "cabin-class" twin-engine and jet craft introduced in the early 1960s are pressurized, permitting economical and efficient operations at high altitudes. Flown by full-time professional pilots, these planes seat up to 15 passengers and are equipped with such amenities as folding desks, snack and beverage compartments, and lavatories. Some airline jet transports have been converted into even more luxurious executive airplanes. Many small aircraft have weather radar, and the array of avionics (aeronautical electronics) on larger planes may rival the sophisticated equipment on commercial airliners.

Business aircraft consequently have remarkable flexibility in expediting the schedules of executives, permitting visits throughout a sales territory that would take far too long by car or that would be inconvenient because of airline schedules. Many large corporations operate their own regular air shuttle services between major plants and urban markets for their salespeople, engineers, and prospective customers. Using general aviation planes, some commercial operators contract to fly mail from smaller cities to major airline hub cities for redistribution. Other commercial operators make regular pickup and delivery of checks and securities for corresponding banks and Federal Reserve System institutions.

**Economic Trends.** As a result of the 1978 law deregulating the air transport industry, many airlines began to drop less profitable service to smaller cities, formerly required by law, and began intense competition in high-density passenger markets. New carriers, including the low-fare People Express, began flying. The major airlines adopted a hub-and-spoke system, in which each carrier funnels its routes into a handful of major regional airports. This scheme maximized the profitable use of an airline's fleet, but it also eliminated scores of direct flights between smaller cities. Fare wars that benefited passengers at first also created a profit squeeze for a number of carriers hard hit by rising costs. In the mid- and late 1980s there were several mergers, acquisitions, and bankruptcies. For example, in 1987 the undercapitalized People Express, which several years earlier had merged with Frontier, was absorbed by Continental Airlines. In that same year Continental also merged with New York Air. Then, in 1990, Continental filed for bankruptcy, although it continued to fly. TWA took the same course of action in 1992. Both restructured their finances and emerged from bankruptcy in 1993. In contrast, Eastern and Pan Am simply ceased operations in 1991; both had been major factors in the industry since the 1920s. Many small commuter lines, which generally had prospered for a time by taking over the low-traffic routes abandoned by the major companies, became subsidiaries of American, Delta, and other trunk lines that were able to remain in business.

During the 1980s the number of domestic passengers on U.S. airlines increased about 58%. In 1990 there were 423.7 million domestic passengers and 41.8 million international passengers; the latter figure was a 75% increase over 1980. The total amount of freight and express cargo flown by U.S. airlines almost doubled during the 1980s, from 5.7 billion to 10.6 billion (U.S.) ton-miles in 1990. Total airline profits were down, however; the industry lost a record $3.9 billion in 1990; employment also increased, however, from 355,000 in 1985 to 546,000 in 1990. Both employment and losses decreased in succeeding years, as the industry stabilized and attempted to recover from the turbulent 1980s.

Worldwide, 925 scheduled airlines operated 14,651 aircraft in 1990. In the U.S., the 22 scheduled airlines belonging to the Air Transport Association operated 4275 airplanes, including freight aircraft. The number of general aviation planes in the U.S. dipped to about 205,000, but production plummeted to an average of about 1100 units annually, well below the peak of 17,000 in the late 1970s. Many manufacturers had cut their production of single-engine aircraft in order to concentrate on the more profitable twin-engine turboprops and small jets for executive transportation.                                    R.E.Bi.

*For further information on this topic, see the Bibliography in volume 28, sections 334, 338–39.*

**AIR WARFARE,** military operations above the surface of the earth. Tactically, these operations include support of land and sea forces by aerial observation of the enemy; directing the fire of naval and ground weapons; and transporting troops, equipment, and supplies. Strategically, air warfare includes combat between fighter planes and bombardment of enemy factories, communications systems, and population centers.

**Balloon Observations.** The idea of warfare conducted from an aerial ship was proposed as early as 1670 by the Italian Jesuit Francesco de Lana Terzi (1631–87) in his book of inventions *Prodromo overo saggio di alcune invenzioni nuove.* A balloon was first used for military purposes in 1794, during the French revolution, when French army observers stationed in one directed ground fire against Austrian forces. Contemporary engravings illustrate another military application: a fanciful proposal to employ balloons as troop transports to invade England. During the American Civil War, in 1862–63 the Army of the Potomac used balloons to observe Confederate movements. A balloon sent to Cuba during the Spanish-American War was used to direct U.S. artillery fire at the Battle of San Juan.

**World War I.** The first U.S. military airplane, built by Wilbur and Orville Wright, was tested and accepted in 1909. As the threat of war in Europe grew before 1914, potential German use of zeppelins (*see* AIRSHIP) for military purposes led authorities to look seriously at military aviation; early in World War I, Paris and London were first bombed from zeppelins—which were subsequently withdrawn from use because of their extreme vulnerability.

The future of air warfare lay with propeller-driven aircraft, first used by the Italian army during the Italo-Turkish War of 1911–12 to observe movements of the Turkish forces. Great Britain founded the Royal Flying Corps in 1912. When hostilities broke out in 1914, the Allies and the Germans had about 200 aircraft each on the western front. The first planes were primarily scout and reconnaissance types, slow and vulnerable to antiaircraft fire. The French flying ace Roland Garros (1888–1918) was the first to shoot down a plane by firing a machine gun through his propeller (1915). The Dutch aircraft designer An-

*A German zeppelin spotlights the seaside town of Yarmouth, England, during World War I, in a composite photograph (1915).*                                    UPI

thony Fokker, working with the Germans, developed an interrupter gear to permit machine guns permanently mounted on a plane to fire through the propeller without damaging the blades; with this modification, and the development of speedier planes, the era of fighter aircraft was born.

Aerial combat produced the aces whose fame became legendary: Germany's Baron Manfred von Richthofen (the Red Baron); Georges Guynemer (1894–1917) and Charles Nungesser (1892–1927) of France; Albert Ball (1896–1917) of Great Britain; William Bishop (1894–1956) of Canada; Eddie Rickenbacker of the U.S.; and the American volunteers who flew (1915–17) with the French as the Lafayette Escadrille.

Earlier in the war, bombs were dropped by hand over the side of the cockpit; later, heavier aircraft were developed, and bombsights and standardized bomb fittings ensured greater effectiveness in striking military and civilian targets. By the war's end, 254 metric tons of bombs had been dropped in raids over England, causing 9000 casualties. Although not to be compared with World War II statistics, these raids were psychologically and strategically important, resulting in the diversion of aircraft from the front for air defense at home. The use of massed air power at the front reached its peak in 1918 in the battles of Château-Thierry, Saint Mihiel, and the Meuse-Argonne, with Allied forces led by the U.S. general Billy Mitchell.

The gutted hull of the Chuguko Press building stands alone on the main street of Hiroshima, Japan, on Aug. 6, 1945, in the devastation of the first atomic bomb used in warfare.                    UPI

**Between the Wars.** After the war, the chief European proponents of the development of air power were Hugh Trenchard (1873–1956), leader of the British Royal Flying Corps and first commander of the Royal Air Force (RAF) on its creation in April 1918, and Giulio Douhet (1869–1930), an Italian army officer who commanded his nation's first aviation unit from 1912 to 1915. Douhet's book *Command of the Air* (1921; trans. 1942) proposed the idea of strategic bombing of enemy centers. As the war ended, Trenchard and Mitchell were in fact planning extensive attacks on German war production sites and dropping soldiers behind the German lines. Mitchell's attempts to focus attention on the effectiveness of bombing by means of demonstrations conducted in 1921 and 1923 (several battleships were sunk in these tests) led to national prominence as a prophet of air power. His ideas bore fruit in World War II.

The development of high-speed offense bombers during the 1930s culminated in America's long-range Boeing B-17 Flying Fortress. Fighter aircraft did not receive the same attention in the U.S., because design modifications made bombers self-defending. The U.S. thus entered World War II with the P-39 and P-40 as its main fighter planes. Between 1935 and 1936

Great Britain and Germany developed the prototypes of the Hawker Hurricane, Supermarine Spitfire, and Messerschmitt Me 109 fighters; the Junkers Ju 87, better known as the Stuka dive bomber; and the Bristol Blenheim and Heinkel He 111 bombers. The war in Ethiopia in 1935 and Spanish civil war air battles, starting in 1938, served as testing grounds for aircraft design and tactics.

**World War II.** World War II began in 1939 with the invasion of Poland, the bombing of its major cities, and the immediate destruction of the Polish air force by the German *Luftwaffe*. In 1940 the defeat of Denmark, Norway, Holland, Belgium, and France was effected, in large part through air support. The Battle of Britain, in August–September 1940, concluded with the RAF Fighter Command having fought off the *Luftwaffe*. Strategic bombing efforts to destroy British factories and civilian morale had failed. The U.S. entry into the war began with the Japanese carrier-borne aircraft attacks on Pearl Harbor and the Philippines. Such attacks quickly destroyed most American land-based combat aircraft in the Pacific.

In the European theater, air defense systems in England were greatly aided by the development of radar (q.v.) to guide interception, as well as by the inability of German fighter planes to escort their bombers, because of low fuel capacity. The development of night-fighter systems by the Germans did not begin until after British night bombers began large-scale raids on Germany, such as the 1000-plane raid over Cologne in May 1942. At the same time, American bombers were carrying out early daylight attacks on specific industrial and military targets. This Combined Bomber Offensive included the costly Ploesti mission of Aug. 1, 1943 (planes launched from Africa to bomb Romanian oil fields) and the Regensburg-Schweinfurt mission of August 17 (the first large-scale American attack on Germany, launched from bases in England). American losses in these and other offensives were heavy until 1944, when long-range P-47 and P-51 escort fighters became available and made it possible for bombers to reach sites deep within Germany in relative safety. The Allies then gained air superiority by destroying German aircraft and aircraft-production facilities. On D-Day, June 6, 1944, Allied air superiority permitted only a few sorties by the *Luftwaffe* against land invasion forces.

German developments, however, indicated the future of air warfare. Their V-1, or "buzz bomb," a pilotless jet-propelled plane carrying 907 kg (2000 lb) of explosives, was directed against England in June 1944. The V-2, a true guided missile capable of carrying 748 kg (1650 lb) of explosives some 320 km (about 200 mi), was launched in September 1944. These attacks came too late to affect the final outcome of the war, as did the failure of the Germans to use the Me 262 as a jet fighter until 1945.

In the early days of World War II, the China-Burma-India theater was the site of the efforts of the American Volunteer Group, better known as the Flying Tigers. Following the Japanese conquest of Burma, supply flights from India to China over the "Hump" (the Himalayas) were as important as combat efforts. Bases in China later served in launching bombing operations against Japan.

In the Pacific, the Battle of Midway in June 1942 was a great victory for American carrier-based naval air power. The battles for the Gilbert, Marshall, and Mariana islands eventually provided bases for bomber attacks on Japan. The Japanese had not developed strong air defenses at home, and the use of the Boeing B-29 Superfortress, starting in 1944, caught them unprepared to detect bombers or to coordinate army and navy efforts. On March 9, 1945, a massive incendiary raid destroyed about one-fourth of all Tokyo's buildings, and on August 6, the B-29 *Enola Gay* dropped the first atomic bomb on Hiroshima.

The use of air power resulted in the defeat of Japan without an invasion and seemed to demonstrate that, in a future general war, ultimate defeat or victory would be settled by air battle. Some 20 years later, in 1967, this was demonstrated in the Six-Day War between the Arabs and Israel, which was decided in the first three hours when the Arab forces lost 452 aircraft.

*Paratroopers float earthward from C-119 planes in March 1951, as the U.S. moves to cut off retreating Communist units south of Munsan, Korea.*   **U.S. Army**

*The single-seat Lockheed F-117A Stealth Fighter has sophisticated electronic systems that can penetrate highly defended areas and attack targets with pinpoint accuracy. It was used extensively in the Persian Gulf War in early 1991.*     **Lockheed**

**Post-World War II.** By the 1950s surface-to-air, surface-to-surface, air-to-air, and air-to-surface missiles, as well as missiles fired from under water, were adopted by the major powers (*see* GUIDED MISSILES). The tactical use of piloted aircraft was, however, continued in the so-called limited wars fought after World War II.

The Korean War started with World War II propeller-driven aircraft, but soon became the occasion for the first aerial combats between jet fighters, notably the Russian-built MiG-15 and the U.S. F-80 and F-86. For political reasons U.S. Air Force and Navy strikes were limited to interdiction: the prevention of enemy movements and destruction of their communications and supply lines by gunfire and bombing. In 1954 the doctrine of "massive retaliation" suggested that in future conflicts the U.S. would not necessarily confine air strikes to the local area of hostilities, but might strike at the enemy's homeland.

In the mid-1960s the U.S. adopted the policy of "strategic persuasion," in which the application of military force is designed to dissuade an enemy from the prospect of overall gain by continued aggression.

**The Vietnam War.** Weaponry used in the war in Vietnam included supersonic jets; Russian-built MiG-17s and MiG-21s opposed F-105s and F-4s. American pilots faced the substantial new menace of surface-to-air (SAM) missiles used for air defense. Electronic technology, however, provided them with laser-guided and optically guided bombs, missile-detection and radar-jamming countermeasures, and air-to-air and air-to-ground rockets. The development of aerial refueling aided in extending the range of combat aircraft; on the other hand, the efforts of carrier-based aircraft were largely wasteful, compared with their successes in World War II. It was in Vietnam that helicopters, initially used for observation, trans-

port, and medical evacuation, became a significant combat weapon, and the World War II DC-3 cargo plane was converted into a gunship.

**Persian Gulf War.** In January 1991, the role of air power in modern warfare was dramatically demonstrated during the Persian Gulf War. Adhering to the military doctrine "Airland Battle," behind-the-lines attacks were made on enemy command and control centers, communication facilities, supply depots, and reinforcement forces, and air superiority was established before armored ground units moved in.

The initial attacks included Tomahawk cruise missiles launched from warships in the Gulf, F-117A Stealth fighter-bombers armed with laser-guided smart bombs, and F-4G Wild Weasel aircraft loaded with HARM anti-radar missiles. Timed to eliminate or reduce the effectiveness of Iraq's ground radar defenses, these attacks permitted the F-14, F-15, F-16, and F/A-18 fighter bombers to achieve air superiority and drop TV- and laser-guided bombs. The A-10 Thunderbolt, with its Gatling gun and heat-seeking or optically guided Maverick missiles, provided support for ground units and destroyed enemy armor. The AH-64 Apache and the AH-1 Cobra helicopters fired laser-guided Hellfire missiles, guided to tanks by ground observers or scout helicopters. Also essential to the allied victory were the E-3A Airborne Warning and Control System (AWACS), and an aging fleet of B-52Gs.

Over 2250 combat aircraft, including 1800 U.S. craft, participated against Iraq's approximately 500 Soviet-built MiG-29s and French-made Mirage F-1s. By the end of the fifth week, over 88,000 combat missions had been flown by allied forces, with over 88,000 tons of bombs dropped.     D.J.B.

*For further information on this topic, see the Bibliography in volume 28, sections 283, 286, 576.*

**AIRWAY,** originally defined as a straight line connecting navigational-radio transmitting sites, or the intersection of straight lines connecting two sites; the term *airway* now denotes any of the routes that airplanes follow in flying from one air terminal to another. By the 1980s the Federal Aviation Authority defined and maintained more than 560,000 km (350,000 mi) of airways in airspace over the continental U.S. The maximum ceiling is 22,500 m (75,000 ft); the minimum allowable height follows the contours of the ground and, at airports, touches the ground. Virtually all airspace over the continental U.S. that lies above 6400 m (18,000 ft) altitude is defined as Positive Control Area (PCA). All airways in the PCA are called jet routes, and all flights in this area are under positive radar control. Flights below the PCA are not, except for those operating under instrument flight rules.

**AISHA** or **AYESHAH** (c. 614–78), favorite wife of the Prophet Muhammad after the death of his first wife, Khadija (c. 555–619). In order to strengthen ties with Abu Bakr, his chief adviser, Muhammad married Aisha, Abu Bakr's daughter, when she was about nine years old. Even after subsequent marriages of the Prophet, she remained devoted to him; she is known among Muslims as Mother of the Believers. After the death of Muhammad in 632, Aisha, a childless widow of 18, helped her father become first caliph, or ruler, of the Muslims. She remained politically inactive during his caliphate (632–34), but she later opposed the succession of Ali as fourth caliph (656–61) and incited an unsuccessful revolt against him.

**AISNE** (anc. *Axona*), river, N France, a tributary of the Oise R. It rises in the Forest of Argonne, flows NW for the first two-fifths of its course, and then flows W to the Oise, which it joins above Compiègne. The Aisne is about 280 km (about 175 mi) long; more than 160 km (100 mi) are navigable, and canals connect it with the Meuse and Marne rivers.

**AIX** or **AIX-EN-PROVENCE,** city, SE France, in Bouches-du-Rhône Department, near Marseille. The city is a trade center for olives, almonds, and wine; industries produce textiles, leather, and processed food. The University of Aix-Marseille III (1409, reorganized 1970) is here.

Aix was founded about 123 BC by the Romans, who named its thermal springs Aquae Sextiae. In the 11th century it became a center of music and literature; later, many painters, including Paul Cézanne, worked in the picturesque city. Aix passed to France in the 1480s. Pop. (1990) 126,854.

**AIX-LA-CHAPELLE.** *See* AACHEN.

**AIX-LA-CHAPELLE, CONGRESS OF,** first of several meetings (1818) of Austria, Great Britain, Prussia, and Russia, the powers victorious over France in the Napoleonic Wars. At Aix-la-Chapelle (now Aachen, Germany), the four agreed to withdraw their occupation troops from France and to invite France to join them in an alliance to preserve order and combat revolutions in Europe. The most important result of the congress was the reconfirmation of the Holy Alliance between Russia, Austria, and Prussia.

**AIX-LA-CHAPELLE, TREATIES OF,** two pacts signed in the city of Aix-la-Chapelle (now Aachen, Germany). The first one (signed May 2, 1668) terminated the War of the Devolution (1667–68), the first war between France and Spain for the possession of the Spanish Netherlands. The treaty returned the district of Franche-Comté to Spain and gave to France 12 towns on the border of the Netherlands.

The second treaty of Aix-la-Chapelle (signed Oct. 18, 1748) ended the War of the Austrian Succession (1740–48), including the American campaigns of that war, which were known as King George's War. It restored Louisbourg (in Canada) to France, gave Madras (in India) to the British, accorded Silesia to Prussia, and confirmed the succession of Maria Theresa to the Austrian throne.

**AIX-LES-BAINS** (anc. *Aquae Gratianae*), town, E France, in Savoie Department, a fashionable resort and spa on Lake Bourget. The sulfur and alkaline springs in the town have been frequented since Roman times. Pop. (1990) 24,826.

**AÍYINA** or **AEGINA,** island, central Greece, in the province of Attikí, in the Saronic Gulf (an arm of the Aegean Sea), near Athens. The island is mountainous, triangular in shape, about 11 km (about 7 mi) long, and about 13 km (about 8 mi) wide. The principal city, Aíyina, is on the NW part of the island in a fertile plain in which grains, grapes, olives, figs, almonds, and peanuts are grown. Tourism and sponge fishing are the other major industries of the island.

Near the city are the ruins of an ancient temple of Apollo in which a group of several marble statues (now in the Munich Glyptothek) dating from the 5th century BC were discovered in 1811. The island, named for the mythological nymph Aegina whose son Aeacus was king of the island, was conquered by the Dorians about 1200 BC. It became a flourishing port, trading in corn, oil, wine, and slaves, but it declined in importance after being conquered by Athens in 459 BC. It was later conquered by the Romans and then by the Venetians. It remained in Turkish hands from the 16th to the 19th century. Aíyina served as the temporary capital of Greece in the late 1820s, during the Greek War of Independence. Area, 137 sq km (52.7 sq mi); pop. (1991) 11,243.

**AJACCIO,** city, France, capital of Corse-du-Sud Department, a seaport on the W coast of the island of Corsica, at the head of the Gulf of Ajaccio. The chief industries are anchovy fishing, diving for coral, shipbuilding, and the manufacture of macaroni and cigars. Considerable trade is carried on in wine, olive oil, hides, oranges, and timber. Napoleon was born in Ajaccio in 1769, and the house in which he lived is now a museum. The city was founded by Genoese colonists in 1492. Pop. (1990) 59,318.

**AJANTA CAVES,** group of about 30 caves carved out of the sides of a steep ravine, E central India, Maharashtra State (formerly Hyderabad), near the village of Ajanta. The caves, discovered in 1819, are famous for their frescoes and sculptures, which are works of Buddhist monks between 200 BC and AD 650. Most of the wall paintings represent themes of the Hindu fables known as the Jatakas. The feeling of the kinship of all living things, which plays so large a part in Buddhism, is apparent in all the paintings. Their astonishing liveliness, their rich and subtle colors, and the consummate skill of their execution make them the supreme monument of Buddhist painting.

**AJAX,** in Greek mythology, mighty warrior who fought in the Trojan War. He was the son of Telamon, king of Salamis, and led the Salaminian forces to Troy. A gigantic man, slow in speech but quick in battle, Ajax was called "bulwark of the Achaeans" by Homer. Angered because he was not awarded the armor of the dead Achilles, Ajax determined to kill the Greek leaders Agamemnon and Menelaus. The goddess Athena, to protect the two, struck him with madness. Ajax committed suicide by falling on his sword.

**AJAX THE LESSER,** in Greek mythology, chieftain from Locris in central Greece. He fought in the Trojan War. After the fall of Troy, he violated the temple of Athena by dragging the prophet Cassandra from the altar of the goddess. Athena appealed to the sea god Poseidon to avenge the sacrilege. When the Greeks sailed for home, Poseidon sent a great tempest. Ajax was shipwrecked, but managed to swim to shore. Clinging to a jagged rock, he boasted that he was a man whom the sea could not drown. Angered by his words, Poseidon split the rock with his trident, and Ajax was swept away by the waves.

**AJMER,** city, NW India, in Rajasthan State. In the city are many industrial and commercial establishments. Salt, textiles, and agricultural products are the principal articles of trade, and the chief industries include hand weaving, dyeing, cotton ginning, printing, oilseed processing, and the manufacture of leather products and soap. Among noteworthy landmarks are the ruins of an elaborately ornamented Jain temple, built in the 12th century and later converted to a mosque; the tomb of the Muslim religious leader Muin-ud-din Chishti (1142–1236); and Mayo Rajikumar College (1875). According to legend, Ajmer was founded in AD 145. Pop. (1991) 401,930.

**AKBAR** (1542–1605), third Mughal emperor of India (1556–1605), generally considered the true founder of the Mughal Empire. The son of Emperor Humayun, he was born in Umarkot, Sind (now in Pakistan), and succeeded to the throne at the age of 13. He first ruled under a regent, Bairam Khan (1504?–61), who recaptured for the young emperor much of the territory usurped at the death of his father. In 1560, however, Akbar took the government into his own hands. Realizing that Hindu acceptance and cooperation were essential to the successful rule of any Indian empire worthy of that name, he won the allegiance of the Rajputs, the most belligerent Hindus, by a shrewd blend of tolerance, generosity, and force; he himself married two Rajput princesses.

Having thus secured the Hindus, he further en-

*The Mediterranean sun casts a glow on the traditional buildings that line the harbor at Ajaccio, on the island of Corsica.*
© The Image Bank

larged his realm by conquest until it extended from Afghanistan to the Bay of Bengal and from the Himalayas to the Godavari River. Akbar's supreme achievement, however, was the establishment of an efficient administrative system that held the empire together and stimulated trade and economic development. Almost as notable was his promulgation of a new religion, the Din-i-Ilahi (Divine Faith), a blend of Islam, Brahmanism, Christianity, and Zoroastrianism. Although this attempt failed, Akbar surrounded himself with learned men of all faiths and, although illiterate himself, made his court a center of arts and letters.

**AKHENATON.** *See* IKHNATON.

**AKHMATOVA, Anna,** pseudonym of ANNA ANDREYEVNA GORENKO (1888–1966), Russian lyric poet. With Osip Mandelstam she was a leader of the early 20th-century acmeist movement, which, in opposition to the symbolists, called for use of poetic language that would convey exact meanings. Akhmatova's early romantic lyrics, *Vecher* (Evening, 1912) and *Chetki* (The Rosary, 1914), thus employ concrete images to render intimate details. Later works, such as *Anno domini MXMXXI* (1922), introduced patriotic themes but did not appease the Soviet critics, who branded the acmeists too personal. From then until 1940, the date of *Iva* (Willow), Akhmatova published no more verse. During the last decade of her life, however, she wrote several poems characterized by great beauty of visual imagery. Among these is her autobiographical *Poema bez geroya* (Poem Without a Hero, 1962).

**AKIBA BEN JOSEPH** (c. 50–c. 135), Jewish rabbi and martyr, resident in Palestine. During his youth, according to tradition, he was a shepherd. He began the study of law at age 40 and rose to a preeminent position as the father of rabbinic Judaism. He regarded the Jewish leader Simon Bar Kokhba, who headed the great Jewish revolt against Rome during the reign of Emperor Hadrian, as the promised Messiah and applied to him the title "son of the star." Imprisoned for transgressing Hadrian's edict forbidding the practice and teaching of the Jewish religion, he was later flayed to death in the ancient Palestinian city of Caesarea. Akiba is one of the ten martyrs named in the penitential prayers of the Jews.

Akiba laid the basis of the Mishnah by beginning the systematization of Jewish oral law. In addition he cultivated a method of scriptural explanation that is a characteristic feature of Talmudic literature. He taught that love for one's fellow humans is the central commandment, that people have free will, and that God's attitude toward the world is one of justice and mercy.

**AKIHITO,** full name AKIHITO TSUGONIMAYA (1933–  ), emperor of Japan (1989–  ), born in Tokyo, fourth child and first son of the emperor Hirohito. He attended Gakushuin University, Tokyo. In 1952 he was officially proclaimed heir to the throne. In 1953 he represented his nation at the coronation of Queen Elizabeth II of England. Akihito married a commoner, Shoda Michiko (1934–  ), in 1959, and their first son and heir, Crown Prince Naruhito, was born in 1960. Akihito succeeded to the throne on Jan. 7, 1989, designating his reign Heisei ("achieving peace").

**AKITA,** city, Japan, NW Honshu Island, capital of Akita Prefecture, a seaport on the Omono R. Oil refining, metalworking, and the manufacture of chemicals are the principal industries. Pop. (1993 est.) 301,800.

**AKITA,** breed of domestic dog, used both as a family guard dog and for hunting. A Japanese working dog, the akita dates to antiquity and still retains spiritual significance. Small statues of akitas are presented at the birth of a child or when a person is ill to express wishes for health and happiness. Ownership was formerly restricted to royalty and the ruling aristocracy, with special provisions for care and feeding and a special vocabulary to be used when addressing or referring to the dogs. From the 17th century they have been trained to hunt large game and retrieve waterfowl in the mountains of northern Japan. Akitas were first brought to the U.S. in 1937 by the American author Helen Keller; since World War II they have become increasingly popular.

The akita is large and powerful, with a massive head; full, broad muzzle; and broad, black nose.

*Akita*　　　　　　　©1988 D. H. Muska–Animal Images

The ears characteristically are erect, small in proportion to the head, and carried slightly forward over the eyes. The chest is wide and deep, the neck thick and muscular, and the skin pliant. The large, full tail is curled. The coat, of any color including white, is straight, harsh, and short. Males stand 66 to 71 cm (26 to 28 in) high; females, 61 to 66 cm (24 to 26 in).

**AKKA,** nomadic pygmy tribe dwelling in the Uele Basin of Zaire, and belonging to the Negrito branch of the Negroid race. The first European known to have encountered the Akka (also called Tiki-Tiki) was the German explorer Georg Schweinfurth (1836–1925), who visited their tribal domain in 1870. The Akka range in height from about 1.5 to 1.8 m (about 4 to 5 ft) and are brown skinned. They have protruding jaws, lips, and stomachs. The Akka hunt game with traps and poisoned arrows and collect ivory and honey, which they exchange with surrounding tribes for iron weapons and foodstuffs. Their houses are round and are made of leaves and branches. *See also* PYGMY; RACES, CLASSIFICATION OF.

**AKKAD.** *See* SUMER.

**AKKADIAN LANGUAGE AND LITERATURE,** extinct Semitic language, and the texts written in it, of the ancient region of Akkad (*see* SUMER). Two dialects of Akkadian eventually developed, Assyrian and Babylonian; for this reason it is also called Assyro-Babylonian. *See* ASSYRO-BABYLONIAN LANGUAGE; ASSYRO-BABYLONIAN LITERATURE.

**AKMOLA.** *See* TSELINOGRAD.

**AKOLA,** city, central India, in Maharashtra State, capital of Akola District. Cotton is grown extensively in the district, and the city is one of the chief centers of the cotton trade of Maharashtra. Pop. (1991, greater city) 327,946.

**AKRON,** city, seat of Summit Co., NE Ohio, at the highest point of the Ohio and Erie Canal and between the headwaters of the Cuyahoga and Tuscarawas rivers; inc. as a city 1865. Its name is derived from *akros,* Greek for "high place." A rail and road nexus, Akron is highly industrialized, with firms manufacturing aerospace, metal, plastic, chemical, and biomedical products. Polymer research and development is a growing industry. Known as the Rubber Capital of the World, it is an important center of rubber research and development, with several major tire and rubber companies headquartered here. The city is the site of the Goodyear Aerospace Airdock (1929), one of the world's largest structures without inner supports, where blimps were built. The University of Akron (1870) is located here, and in the region are several well-known golf courses and the Blossom Music Center, summer home of the Cleveland Symphony Orchestra. The

Inventor's Hall of Fame opened here in 1995.

The city was founded in 1825 in anticipation of the Ohio and Erie Canal, which was completed in 1832. The first rubber factory was built here in 1870; production declined in the 1970s. Pop. (1980) 237,177; (1990) 223,019.

**AKSAKOV, Sergey Timofeyevich** (1791–1859), Russian writer, born in Ufa. After completing his education he was a civil servant in Saint Petersburg and later in Moscow, where his home became a gathering place for members of the Slavophile movement, which proclaimed the superiority of Eastern European culture. In 1832 he befriended Russian writer Nikolay Gogol, who inspired him to embark on a literary career. Aksakov's popular works, *A Russian Gentleman* (1856; trans. 1917) and *Years of Childhood* (1858; trans. 1916), are based on his childhood experiences on the steppes of Russia. They gave impetus to the development of realism in Russian literature.

His two sons were also ardent Slavophiles. Konstantin Sergeyevich Aksakov (1817–60) was a literary critic who urged stronger ties with the Russian peasantry. Ivan Sergeyevich Aksakov (1832–86) was the editor of *Rus,* the official publication of the Slavophile party.

**AKSUM, KINGDOM OF,** ancient kingdom that flourished in what is now northern Ethiopia and Eritrea between the 1st and 6th centuries AD. It was founded probably by the gradual federation of earlier immigrants from southern Arabia and was centered at Aksum. It had well-established trade links with the Greco-Roman world, as well as with India, and was prominent in the commercial rivalry between the Roman and Persian empires. In the 3rd and 6th centuries AD, it also dominated Yemen on the Arabian Peninsula.

The kingdom was Christianized in the late 4th century by St. Frumentius (300?–80?), and the Bible was subsequently translated into Ge'ez, the language of Aksum. With the Muslim conquest of North Africa in the 8th century, however, contact with the rest of the Christian world was broken. Aksum later became the kingdom of Ethiopia. *See also* ETHIOPIA: *History.*

**AKUTAGAWA RYŪNOSUKE** (1892–1927), Japanese author, born in Tokyo, and educated at the University of Tokyo. His first published story, "Rashomon" (1915; trans. 1952), was combined with a later story, "In a Grove" (1921; trans. 1952), to form the basis for the beautiful Japanese film *Rashomon* (1950). Akutagawa's works reflect his interest in the life of feudal Japan.

**AKYAB.** *See* SITTWE.

**al-.** For most names beginning with al-, see the second part of the name; for example, for al-Hijaz, see Hijaz, al-.

*The semitropical Bellingrath Gardens in Mobile, Ala., begun in 1927, is famous for its live oaks, Spanish moss, azaleas, and lavish summer bedding displays.*

Gene Ahrens–Bruce Coleman, Inc.

**ALABAMA,** one of the East South Central states of the U.S., bounded on the N by Tennessee, on the E by Georgia, on the S by Florida and the Gulf of Mexico, and on the W by Mississippi. The Chattahoochee R. forms much of the E boundary.

Called the Heart of Dixie, Alabama entered the Union on Dec. 14, 1819, as the 22d state. In 1861 it became a founding member of the Confederate States of America during the American Civil War. Alabama's economy was long dominated by farming, but by the 1990s manufacturing, government, and services were the chief economic sectors. The name of the state is taken from the Alabama R., which was named for the Alabama, or Alibamon, Indians, who belonged to the Creek Confederacy.

### LAND AND RESOURCES

Alabama, with an area of 135,775 sq km (52,423 sq mi), is the 30th largest state in the U.S.; 1.7% of the land area is owned by the federal government. The state is roughly rectangular in shape, and its extreme dimensions are about 540 km (about 335 mi) from N to S and about 330 km (about 205 mi) from E to W. Elevations begin at sea level and extend up to 733 m (2405 ft), atop Cheaha Mt., in the E part of the state. The approximate mean elevation is 152 m (500 ft). Alabama's shoreline along the Gulf of Mexico is 85 km (53 mi) long.

**Physical Geography.** The S half of Alabama plus a narrow region in the NW are part of the East Gulf Coastal Plain. Roughly parallel, generally forested ridges (mostly less than 152 m/500 ft in elevation) stretch E-W across the plain. Soils are mainly clays and sandy clays, with the exception of the limestone-derived dark clays of the Black Belt, a fertile area in the center of the region. The delta formed by the Mobile and Tensaw rivers at the city of Mobile includes much swampland and marshland.

In N Alabama are the Interior Low Plateaus, a part of the Cumberland Plateau, the Valley and Ridge Region, and a section of the Piedmont Plateau. The Interior Low Plateaus, developed on flat-lying limestone and alluvium, are overlaid with relatively fertile sandy clay soils. The Cumberland Plateau region consists of flat to gently rolling land, developed principally on sandstone and sandy shale. The Valley and Ridge Region contains sandstone ridges and broad, moderately fertile valleys. It includes the Beaver Creek Mts. and part of Lookout Mt. The generally forested low hills and ridges of the Piedmont Plateau, developed on the oldest rocks in Alabama, are overlaid with clay and sandy clay soils. Situated in this region are Colvin Mt. and Talladega Mt.

**Rivers and Lakes.** With the exception of the Tennessee R. and its tributaries in N Alabama, all streams in the state flow generally S toward the Gulf of Mexico. Among the rivers are the Mobile, Alabama, Tombigbee, Chattahoochee, and Tensaw. The Alabama and Tombigbee rivers join to form the Mobile-Tensaw system. Principal tributaries of the Alabama R. include the Coosa,

299

Tallapoosa, and Cahaba rivers, and the Black Warrior R. is the chief affluent of the Tombigbee R.

All of Alabama's large lakes are constructed impoundments. These bodies of water include Lakes Guntersville, Wheeler, and Wilson, on the Tennessee R.; Weiss Lake, on the Coosa R.; and Walter F. George Reservoir, on the Chattahoochee R.

**Climate.** The temperate climate of N and central Alabama grades into a subtropical climate in the coastal area. The average annual temperature ranges from 15.6° C (60° F) in the N to about 21.1° C (about 70° F) near the Gulf of Mexico. The recorded temperature in the state has ranged from −32.7° C (−27° F), in 1966, to 44.4° C (112° F), in 1925. The average yearly rainfall for the state is about 1350 mm (about 53 in). The area near the Gulf receives approximately 1650 mm (approximately 65 in) of precipitation per year and is subject to occasional hurricanes in the summer months.

**Plants and Animals.** Forests cover about 65% of the total land area of Alabama; approximately 3% of the forest area is part of the National Forest system. Forests in N Alabama are mixtures of hardwoods and softwoods, whereas softwood pines are the dominant trees in S areas. A warm, humid climate, with a long growing season, has helped to produce more than 125 tree varieties and more than 150 species of shrubs in Alabama. Besides pines, notable trees include oak, hickory, cypress, and southern magnolia; among the shrubs are rhododendron, mountain laurel, azalea, and sumac.

Mammals in Alabama include white-tailed deer, red fox, squirrel, muskrat, nutria, beaver, and rabbit. Among the numerous birds are the yellowhammer (the state bird), bluebird, cardinal, blue jay, and mockingbird. Reptiles include snakes, alligators, turtles, and lizards. Fish abound here. Freshwater varieties include catfish, bream, bass, and crappie. Mullet, croakers, flounder, red snapper, and tarpon inhabit the Gulf of Mexico, as do oysters, shrimp, and crabs.

**Mineral Resources.** Among the major mineral deposits found in Alabama are coal, located mainly in the N half of the state, and petroleum and natural gas, situated principally in the East Gulf Coastal Plain. The state also has substantial deposits of limestone, iron ore, sand and gravel, bauxite, and clay.                          T.J.L.

## POPULATION

According to the 1990 census, Alabama had 4,040,587 inhabitants, an increase of 3.8% over 1980. The average population density in 1990 was 30 people per sq km (77 per sq mi). Whites made up 73.6% of the population and blacks 25.3%; additional groups included Asian or Pacific Islander, 0.5%, American Indian, Eskimo, or Aleut, 0.4%; and other races, 0.2%. About 24,600 persons were of Hispanic background. Baptists (51.4%), Methodists (10.4%), and Roman Catholics (4.5%) constituted the largest religious groups in the state; other Protestant groups made up most of the remainder. In 1990 about 60% of the people of Alabama lived in areas defined as urban, and the rest lived in rural areas. The state's largest cities were Birmingham; Mobile; Montgomery, the capital; and Huntsville.

## EDUCATION AND CULTURAL ACTIVITY

The number and variety of Alabama's educational and cultural institutions increased after 1950, as the state became more urban and developed sophisticated modern industries.

**Education.** The first school was established in Alabama in 1799, but the legislature did not provide for a statewide public educational system until 1854. In the late 1980s Alabama had approximately 1300 public elementary and secondary schools; the elementary schools had an enrollment of about 525,700 pupils per year, and the secondary schools about 197,600 students annually. In addition, some 57,600 students attended private schools. In the same period Alabama had 87 institutions of higher education, with a combined enrollment of about 208,600 students. Among the most notable of these schools were the University of Alabama, with campuses at University (near Tuscaloosa), Birmingham, and Huntsville; Auburn University, in Auburn; and Tuskegee University, near Tuskegee.

**Cultural Institutions.** Although many of Alabama's cultural activities are university related and thus distributed throughout the state, most of its cultural institutions are located in Birmingham, Mobile, and Montgomery. The most noteworthy art museums are the Birmingham Museum of Art, which contains part of the Samuel H. Kress Collection; the Fine Arts Museum of the South, in Mobile; and the Montgomery Museum of Fine Arts. The state's principal professional symphony orchestra is in Birmingham, as is the Birmingham Public and Jefferson County Free Library (1902), considered one of the outstanding libraries in the South. Also of interest are the George Washington Carver Museum, part of Tuskegee Institute National Historic Site; and the Women's Army Corps Museum, at Fort McClellan (near Anniston).

**Historical Sites.** Many of Alabama's historical sites commemorate battles of Indian wars and the American Civil War. Horseshoe Bend Na-

# Alabama: Map Index

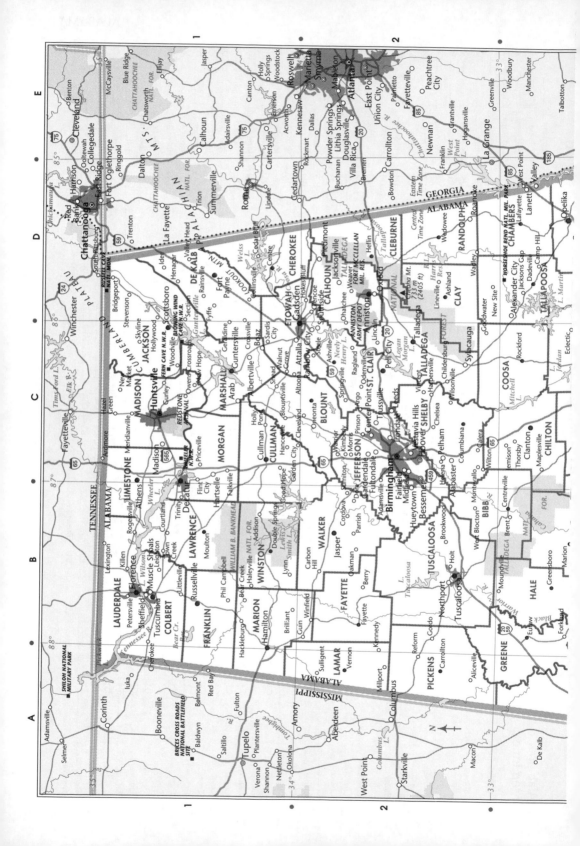

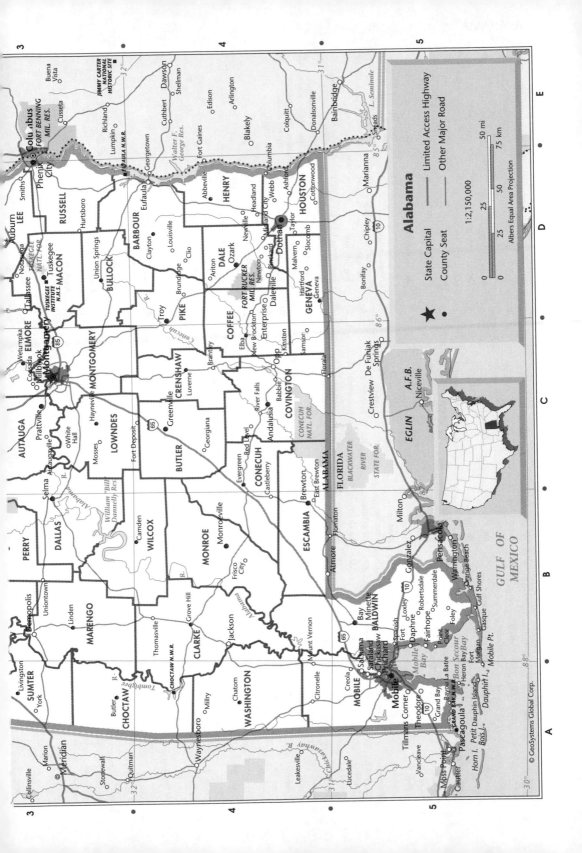

# Alabama

**State Capital** ★

**County Seat** •

**Limited Access Highway**

**Other Major Road**

1:2,150,000

Albers Equal Area Projection

0   25   50   75 km

0   25   50 mi

© GeoSystems Global Corp.

GULF OF MEXICO

The State Capitol at Montgomery, Ala., was the scene of the formation of the government of the Confederate States of America in 1861.    Björn Bölstad–Peter Arnold, Inc.

tional Military Park, near Alexander City, includes the site of Andrew Jackson's victory over the Creek Indians in 1814; and Fort Morgan and Fort Gaines in Mobile Bay are Civil War fortifications. The first White House of the Confederacy, in Montgomery, contains exhibits of personal furnishings of Jefferson Davis. The Civil Rights Memorial, in Montgomery, honors 40 persons who lost their lives in support of the civil rights movement between 1954 and 1968.

**Sports and Recreation.** Opportunities for outdoor recreation in Alabama are provided by numerous rivers and lakes, the Gulf of Mexico, and four national forests. Hiking, camping, fishing, hunting, golf, boating, and swimming are among the foremost recreational activities.

**Communications.** In the early 1990s Alabama was served by a comprehensive communications system, which included 160 AM radio stations, 117 FM radiobroadcasters, and 40 television stations. The first radio station in the state, WBRC in Birmingham, was licensed in 1925, and the first television station, WAFM-TV in Birmingham, was licensed in 1949. In 1955, Alabama began to run the nation's first state-owned educational television network. Alabama's first regularly issued newspaper, the *Mobile Centinel,* began publication in 1811. In the early 1990s the state had 27 daily newspapers with a total daily circulation of about 767,000 copies. Alabama's influential dailies included the *Birmingham News,* the *Huntsville Times,* and the *Montgomery Advertiser.*

## GOVERNMENT AND POLITICS

Alabama is governed under a constitution adopted in 1901, as amended. Five earlier constitutions had been instituted in 1819, 1861, 1865, 1868, and 1875. An amendment may be proposed by the legislature or by a constitutional convention. To become effective, it must be approved by a majority voting on the issue in an election.

**Executive.** The chief executive of Alabama is a governor, who is popularly elected to a 4-year term and may not serve more than two consecutive terms. The same requirements apply to the lieutenant governor, who succeeds the governor should the latter resign, die, or be removed from office. Additional members of Alabama's executive department include the secretary of state, attorney general, auditor, treasurer, and the commissioner of agriculture and industries.

**Legislature.** The bicameral legislature comprises a senate and house of representatives. The 35 members of the senate and 105 members of the house are popularly elected to 4-year terms.

**Judiciary.** Alabama's highest court, the supreme court, is made up of a chief justice who presides over the court and eight associate judges. The two intermediate appellate courts are the court of criminal appeals, with five judges, and the court of civic appeals, with three judges. The major trial courts are the circuit courts. The judges of all the courts are popularly elected to 6-year terms. District probate judges are also elected, but judges of municipal courts are appointed by the governing body of the municipality.

# ALABAMA

**DATE OF STATEHOOD:** December 14, 1819; 22d state

| | |
|---|---|
| **CAPITAL:** | Montgomery |
| **MOTTO:** | *Audemus jura nostra defendere* (We dare maintain our rights) |
| **NICKNAME:** | Heart of Dixie |
| **STATE SONG:** | "Alabama" (words by Julia S. Tutwiler; music by Edna G. Gussen) |
| **STATE TREE:** | Southern (longleaf) pine |
| **STATE FLOWER:** | Camellia |
| **STATE BIRD:** | Yellowhammer |
| **POPULATION (1990):** | 4,040,587; 22d among the states |
| **AREA:** | 135,775 sq km (52,423 sq mi); 30th largest state; includes 4332 sq km (1673 sq mi) of inland water |
| **COASTLINE:** | 85 km (53 mi) |
| **HIGHEST POINT:** | Cheaha Mt., 733 m (2405 ft) |
| **LOWEST POINT:** | Sea level, at the Gulf coast |
| **ELECTORAL VOTES:** | 9 |
| **U.S. CONGRESS:** | 2 senators; 7 representatives |

## POPULATION OF ALABAMA SINCE 1800

| Year of Census | Population | Classified As Urban |
|---|---|---|
| 1800 | 1,000 | 0% |
| 1830 | 310,000 | 1% |
| 1850 | 772,000 | 5% |
| 1880 | 1,263,000 | 5% |
| 1900 | 1,829,000 | 12% |
| 1920 | 2,348,000 | 16% |
| 1940 | 2,833,000 | 30% |
| 1960 | 3,267,000 | 55% |
| 1980 | 3,890,000 | 60% |
| 1990 | 4,040,587 | 60% |

## POPULATION OF TEN LARGEST CITIES

| | 1990 Census | 1980 Census |
|---|---|---|
| Birmingham | 265,968 | 284,413 |
| Mobile | 196,278 | 200,452 |
| Montgomery | 187,106 | 177,857 |
| Huntsville | 159,789 | 142,513 |
| Tuscaloosa | 77,759 | 75,211 |
| Dothan | 53,589 | 48,750 |
| Decatur | 48,761 | 42,002 |
| Gadsden | 42,523 | 47,565 |
| Hoover | 39,788 | 19,792 |
| Florence | 36,426 | 37,029 |

## CLIMATE

| | BIRMINGHAM | MOBILE |
|---|---|---|
| Average January temperature range | 1.1° to 12.2° C (34° to 54° F) | 5° to 16.1° C (41° to 61° F) |
| Average July temperature range | 21.1° to 32.2° C (70° to 90° F) | 22.8° to 32.8° C (73° to 91° F) |
| Average annual temperature | 16.7° C (62° F) | 19.4° C (67° F) |
| Average annual precipitation | 1346 mm (53 in) | 1702 mm (67 in) |
| Average annual snowfall | 30 mm (1.2 in) | 10 mm (0.4 in) |
| Mean number of days per year with appreciable precipitation | 118 | 124 |
| Average daily relative humidity | 72% | 71% |
| Mean number of clear days per year | 99 | 100 |

**NATURAL REGIONS OF ALABAMA**

INTERIOR LOW PLATEAUS
CUMBERLAND PLATEAU
VALLEY & RIDGE REGION
PIEDMONT PLATEAU
EAST-GULF COASTAL PLAIN
Black Warrior R.
Tombigbee R.
Alabama R.

# ECONOMY

State budget . . . . . . . . . . . . . . general revenue $7.6 billion
general expenditure $7.4 billion
accumulated debt $4.0 billion
State and local taxes, per capita . . . . . . . . . . . . . . . . $1328
Personal income, per capita . . . . . . . . . . . . . . . . . . . . $11,486
Population below poverty level . . . . . . . . . . . . . . . . . . 18.3%
Assets, insured commercial banks (221) . . . . $36.2 billion
Labor force (civilian nonfarm) . . . . . . . . . . . . . . . 1,588,000
    Employed in manufacturing              24%
    Employed in wholesale and retail trade    22%
    Employed in government                20%
    Employed in services                  19%

| | Quantity Produced | Value |
|---|---|---|
| **FARM PRODUCTS** . . . . . . . . . . . . . . . . . . . . . . . . . | | **$2.8 billion** |
| **Crops** . . . . . . . . . . . . . . . . . . . . . . . . . . . . . . . . . | | **$655 million** |
| Peanuts | 177,000 metric tons | $130 million |
| Cotton | 87,000 metric tons | $125 million |
| Hay | 1.0 million metric tons | $66 million |
| Soybeans | 203,000 metric tons | $44 million |
| Corn | 443,000 metric tons | $40 million |
| **Livestock and Livestock Products** | | **$2.1 billion** |
| Chickens | | |
|   (broilers) | 1.4 million metric tons | $1.2 billion |
| Cattle | 310,000 metric tons | $520 million |
| Eggs | 2.2 billion | $170 million |
| Hogs | 89,000 metric tons | $97 million |
| Milk | 237,000 metric tons | $84 million |
| **MINERALS** . . . . . . . . . . . . . . . . . . . . . . . . . . . . . | | **$2.5 billion** |
| Coal | 30.7 million metric tons | $1.1 billion |
| Natural gas | 3.6 billion cu m | $349 million |
| Petroleum | 19.8 million barrels | $342 million |
| Stone | 25.3 million metric tons | $167 million |
| Cement | 3.1 million metric tons | $144 million |
| **FISHING** . . . . . . . | **11,300 metric tons** | **$38 million** |
| | | Annual Payroll |
| **FORESTRY** . . . . . . . . . . . . . . . . . . . . . . . . . . . . . | | **$14 million** |
| **MANUFACTURING** . . . . . . . . . . . . . . . . . . . . . . . | | **$8.0 billion** |
| Apparel and textile mill products | | $1.3 billion |
| Transportation equipment | | $733 million |
| Primary metals | | $731 million |
| Paper and allied products | | $698 million |
| Industrial machinery and equipment | | $591 million |
| Fabricated metal products | | $548 million |
| Food and kindred products | | $536 million |
| Rubber and plastics products | | $506 million |
| Lumber and wood products | | $433 million |
| Electronic equipment | | $385 million |
| **OTHER** . . . . . . . . . . . . . . . . . . . . . . . . . . . . . . . . | | **$23.3 billion** |
| Government | | $7.4 billion |
| Services | | $5.2 billion |
| Retail trade | | $2.8 billion |
| Transportation, communications, | | |
|   and public utilities | | $2.1 billion |
| Wholesale trade | | $1.8 billion |
| Construction | | $1.8 billion |
| Finance, insurance, and real estate | | $1.6 billion |

# PRINCIPAL PRODUCTS OF ALABAMA

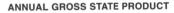

## ANNUAL GROSS STATE PRODUCT

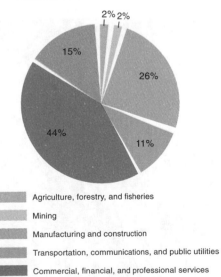

2% 2%
15%
26%
44%
11%

- Agriculture, forestry, and fisheries
- Mining
- Manufacturing and construction
- Transportation, communications, and public utilities
- Commercial, financial, and professional services
- Government

Sources: U.S. government publications

**Local Government.** In the early 1990s Alabama contained 67 counties, each of which was governed by a board of commissioners. Other important county officials include the county judge, probate judge, superintendent of education, and sheriff. Most of the state's towns and cities are governed under the mayor-council system.

**National Representation.** Alabama elects two senators and seven representatives to the U.S. Congress. The state has nine electoral votes in presidential elections.

**Politics.** In national, state, and local politics, Alabama has been a traditional stronghold of the Democratic party. The dominant political figure from the early 1960s through the mid-1980s was George Corley Wallace; first elected governor as a staunch segregationist, he later won with black support.

## ECONOMY

From the early 19th century, Alabama's economy was dominated by one crop—cotton. After 1915, however, boll weevils so damaged the state's cotton plants that farmers began to concentrate on raising livestock and crops other than cotton. Manufacturing began to be important to Alabama with the growth of the iron and steel industry during the early 20th century. Beginning in the 1930s low-cost power provided by the Tennessee Valley Authority (TVA), a federal agency, encouraged industrial development. Manufacturing, along with the government and service sectors, retained its importance in the early 1990s.

Federal facilities, notably the George C. Marshall Space Flight Center, in Huntsville, were major employers.

**Agriculture.** Farming accounts for about 2% of the annual gross state product in Alabama. The state has some 45,000 farms, which average 88 ha (218 acres) in size. Livestock products make up about 75% of Alabama's farm income. Broiler chickens and chicken eggs, produced mainly in the N part of the state, are the most important livestock products, and cattle and calves are next as sources of farm income.

Crops account for about 25% of Alabama's agricultural income. Peanuts, the leading crop, are grown in the SE part of the state. Cotton, hay, and greenhouse products are also important. Soybeans are grown mainly in the lowlands of SW Alabama and in the Tennessee R. valley.

**Forestry and Fishing.** The annual income from forestry and fishing in Alabama is relatively small. Yellow pine, the state's most common tree, is used for lumber and for making paper; some hardwood lumber also is produced.

In the late-1980s, about 11.3 million kg (about 24.9 million lb) of seafood was caught yearly in Mobile Bay and the Gulf of Mexico by Alabama commercial fishers. Most of the catch consisted of shrimp, the state's most valuable marine product. Catfish farming is a growing sector of the economy.

**Mining.** The mining industry accounts for about 2% of the annual gross state product of Alabama.

*The towers of the Sloss Furnaces in Birmingham, silhouetted against the sky. The making of iron and steel is one of the oldest and most important industries in Alabama.*
© 1988 Walter Bibikow—The Image Bank

Limestone quarrying, begun in the 19th century, is still an important part of Alabama's economy.

© 1990 Jim McNee–FPG International

Leading minerals are coal, natural gas, petroleum, and stone. Coal is mined primarily in N central Alabama, petroleum and natural gas are recovered in the SW, and limestone is quarried in the NE.

**Manufacturing.** Enterprises engaged in manufacturing have an annual payroll of $8 billion in Alabama and employ about 384,000 workers. Leading manufactures include apparel and textiles, transportation equipment, primary metals, and paper and paper products. Iron and steel production is centered around Birmingham, Anniston, and Bessemer. Aluminum plants are located in the tri-cities area of Florence, Sheffield, and Tuscumbia and in Mobile. Paper mills are situated in Mobile, Selma, Demopolis, Courtland, and Tuscaloosa. Birmingham, Mobile, Decatur, Sheffield, and Tuscaloosa have chemical plants. Other major manufactures of Alabama include industrial machinery, processed foods, and rubber and plastics products.

**Tourism.** Each year several million visitors produce more than $3.4 billion for the Alabama economy. Many persons visit the five areas in the state administered by the National Park Service; Horseshoe Bend National Military Park is

the most popular of these areas. The state maintains a system of 24 parks, including Cheaha State Park, near Anniston, which is the site of Cheaha Mt., the highest point in Alabama.

**Transportation.** Birmingham and Montgomery are important hubs within a network of about 146,000 km (about 90,700 mi) of federal, state, and local roads that serve all sections of Alabama. Some 1430 km (890 mi) of interstate highways link the major cities of the state. Alabama is served by about 6735 km (4185 mi) of railroad track. Birmingham is the major rail center.

Mobile is Alabama's only seaport. It handles more cargo than any other port on the Gulf of Mexico between Tampa, Fla., and New Orleans, La. The state includes a section of the Gulf Intracoastal Waterway and also has about 3200 km (about 1990 mi) of navigable inland waterways. The Black Warrior-Tombigbee-Mobile river system is the longest and most important such waterway in the state. The Tennessee R. links N Alabama with the Mississippi R. system.

Alabama has more than 150 airports. The Birmingham airport handles more than four-fifths of the state's air passenger traffic.

309

**Energy.** In the early 1990s, the electricity generating plants of Alabama had a total capacity of 20 million kw and produced about 76.2 billion kwh of electricity each year. Although Alabama ranked seventh among the states in hydroelectric capacity, about 70% of its electricity was coal-generated, and about 16% was produced by nuclear power plants. More than 40% of the state's electricity was generated by TVA facilities; these included the Browns Ferry nuclear plant, near Athens.                                   M.C.B.

## HISTORY

Earthen mounds and other archaeological evidence indicate that people have lived in Alabama for at least 9000 years. The major Indian groups at the time of European settlement were the Chickasaws and Cherokees in the north and the Creeks and Choctaws to the south.

The first known Europeans to explore Alabama were Spaniards and probably included Alonso Piñeda in 1519 and Pánfilo de Narváez in 1528. Hernando de Soto reached a site near the present-day city of Mobile on Oct. 18, 1540, after winning a costly victory over the Choctaw Indians in the Battle of Maubila. The French established the first permanent European settlements, at Fort Louis (1702), Port Dauphin (1702), and Mobile (1711). British claims to the area were recognized in the 1763 Treaty of Paris, but the Spanish regained Mobile and the Gulf coast by the 1783 Treaty of Paris. The U.S. took possession of the entire area after the War of 1812.

**Antebellum Alabama.** The Creek War (1813–14), in which the "Red Stick" Creeks tried to resist white encroachment, ended with Gen. Andrew Jackson's victory at the Battle of Horseshoe Bend in 1814. Alabama became a territory in 1817 and was accepted into the Union as the 22d state on Dec. 14, 1819.

The antebellum era in Alabama was characterized by the continued development of plantation agriculture in the central and southern parts of the state, the removal of the Indians to the West, and the rising controversy over the nature and legitimacy of slavery and its extension into new territories. The election of President Abraham Lincoln led to the special state convention that voted to secede from the Union in January 1861. Montgomery became the first capital of the Confederacy, and Jefferson Davis was inaugurated president there in February. Military operations in Alabama during the Civil War consisted of several Union raids into the state and the victory of Adm. David Farragut in the Battle of Mobile Bay in 1864.

**Alabama After the Civil War.** A new state constitution recognizing the abolition of slavery was adopted in December 1865. In March 1867, Alabama came under federal military control, and another constitution was adopted in November, affirming provisions of the 14th Amendment to the U.S. Constitution. Blacks responded to emancipation by attempting to exercise their new freedom and improve their condition, and a number of blacks were elected to public office during the Reconstruction era.

Conservative Democratic politics persisted throughout the last quarter of the 19th century, as did farm tenancy and poor agricultural conditions, despite the reform efforts of the People's party (Populists) in the 1890s. The growth of industry in northern Alabama was especially significant. Founded in 1871, Birmingham quickly became a center for iron and steel manufacture and one of the fastest growing cities in the South; it had 132,685 inhabitants in 1910 and 256,678 in 1930.

White supremacy was consolidated in the state constitution of 1901, which effectively prevented most blacks from voting. White political control resulted, among other things, in the casting of Alabama's electoral votes in 1948 for the states' rights candidate rather than for President Harry S. Truman, the regular Democratic party nominee, and in resistance to the black civil rights movement in the 1950s and '60s.

**Social and Economic Changes.** The Montgomery bus boycott by blacks in 1955 fueled the beginnings of civil rights protest. In May 1961, "Freedom Riders" of the Congress of Racial Equality were attacked by white mobs in Anniston, Birmingham, and Montgomery. In the spring of 1963, a series of demonstrations in Birmingham led by Martin Luther King, Jr., were met with mass arrests by city police, but resulted in a settlement containing most black demands. The Selma to Montgomery march of 1965, also led by King, furthered the passage of the federal Voting Rights Act.

Alabama's economic development in the 1960s and '70s, paced by the statewide growth of higher education, was greater than at any other time in the 20th century. The economy continued to grow in the 1980s, but Alabama lagged behind most other states in per capita income and educational attainment as the 1990s began.          B.A.Br.

*For further information on this topic, see the Bibliography in volume 28, sections 1183, 1189.*

**ALABAMA,** river, Alabama, one of the state's principal rivers. It is formed by the junction of the Coosa and Tallapoosa rivers near Montgomery, central Alabama. It is more than 500 km (more than 310 mi) long and is navigable for its entire length. The Alabama joins the Tombigbee R. to form the Mobile R., which flows into Mobile Bay of the Gulf of Mexico.

**ALABAMA, UNIVERSITY OF,** a system of three state-controlled institutions of higher learning, with campuses at University, near Tuscaloosa; Birmingham; and Huntsville. The university was established in 1820 and opened in Tuscaloosa in 1831. In 1943 a medical college was established in Birmingham, and in 1950 a branch campus in Huntsville. In 1969 the three campuses received autonomy, but a single board of trustees was retained.

The Tuscaloosa campus has colleges of arts and sciences, communications, education, commerce and business, nursing, and engineering; the division of continuing education; graduate school; graduate school of library service; the New College; and schools of human environmental science and social work. At Birmingham, the major divisions are the Medical Center, with schools of dentistry, health-related professions, medicine, nursing, optometry, and public health, and the university hospitals and clinics; and Academic Affairs, with schools of arts and humanities, business, education, engineering, natural sciences and mathematics, and social and behavioral sciences. The Huntsville campus has colleges of administrative science, engineering, health-related sciences, liberal arts, science, and graduate studies, and a division of continuing education. Degrees of bachelor, master, and doctor are granted.

*ALABAMA* CLAIMS series of claims for indemnity made by the U.S. upon Great Britain in the winter of 1862–63, during the American Civil War. The claims were for compensation for damages inflicted on U.S. property by the Confederate steamship *Alabama,* a vessel weighing more than 900 metric tons that was built at Birkenhead, England. Just before the British government issued an order calling for its detention in port, the ship put to sea, became a raider, and captured or destroyed 70 U.S. ships. When the *Alabama* reached Cherbourg, France, for refitting on June 11, 1864, the U.S. warship *Kearsarge* engaged it in battle outside the port and sank it.

The *Alabama* claims were not completely settled until 1885. The U.S. claims were based chiefly on the alleged failure of the British government to prevent the building of the *Alabama* and other Confederate ships and on the furnishing of supplies to the Confederate ships at British ports. A tribunal of arbitrators, appointed by representatives of the U.S., Great Britain, Italy, Switzerland, and Brazil, met in Geneva from 1871 to 1872 and decided that Great Britain should pay the U.S. damages of more than $16 million. Subsequently, two courts of commissioners ap-

pointed by the U.S. Congress sat (1874–76 and 1882–85) to determine the distribution to injured individuals and firms of the funds received through the *Alabama* claims. Congress also determined the distribution of other funds included within the award of the Geneva tribunal, based on depredations by the Confederate privateers *Florida* and *Shenandoah.*

**ALABAMA POLYTECHNIC INSTITUTE.** See AUBURN UNIVERSITY.

**ALABASTER,** name applied to two different minerals. One, Oriental alabaster, was extensively used by the ancient Egyptians. It is a variety of calcite, with a hardness (q.v.) of 3; it is usually white and translucent, but is often banded with dark or colored streaks. The other mineral, called true alabaster, is a variety of gypsum, usually snow-white in color with a uniform, fine grain. True alabaster is softer (hardness 1.5) than Oriental alabaster and is easily carved into intricate shapes. Deposits of fine gypsum alabaster are found in Italy and England.

**ALAI MOUNTAINS,** also Alay Mountains, range of lofty mountains, SW Kyrgyzstan, in Central Asia, an extension of the Tien Shan Mts. The average height of the Alai Mts. is about 4880 m (about 16,000 ft).

**ALAIN-FOURNIER,** pseudonym of HENRI ALBAN FOURNIER (1886–1914), French writer, born in La Chapelle-d'Angillon. He was the author of only one novel, *The Wanderer* (1913; trans. 1928), which, with its mystic overtones and spiritual quality, differed greatly from the realistic and naturalistic fiction of his contemporaries and exerted great influence on writers. His later promising career was cut short by World War I; he was reported missing after the fighting of Sept. 22, 1914, in France, and was presumed dead. Most of his writing was published after his death. *Miracles* (1924) is a collection of his early verse and prose, much of which had been published previously in various periodicals.

**ALAJUELA,** city, central Costa Rica, capital of Alajuela Province, on the slope of the 2704-m (8895-ft) Poás volcano, near San José. Sugar and coffee are grown in the surrounding area, and the city serves as an important marketplace for both of these commodities. Pop. (1991 est.) 158,276.

**ALAMANNI,** also Alemanni, confederacy of Germanic tribes inhabiting the region (called Alamannia) between the Main and Danube rivers in the 3d century. They invaded Gaul several times and, early in the 5th century, conquered the territory that is now Alsace and a large part of Switzerland. In 496 they were conquered by Clovis I, king of the Salian Franks, and the southern part of their territory was included in the duchy of Alamannia. The modern name for Germany in many Romance languages (Fr. Allemagne; Span. Alemania) is derived from the name of these tribes.

**ALAMEDA,** city, Alameda Co., W California, situated on islands in San Francisco Bay; inc. 1854. Although largely residential, it has some industry, including boatbuilding and aircraft repair, and is the site of the huge Alameda Naval Air Station and a major U.S. Coast Guard base. Originally located on a peninsula, Alameda became insular in 1902 with the completion of the Tidal Canal. The city is linked with Oakland by a tunnel and several bridges. Its name is Spanish for "poplar grove." Pop. (1980) 63,852; (1990) 76,459.

**ALAMO,** former Franciscan mission in San Antonio, Tex., erected about 1722, later used as a fort, and now preserved as a state monument. The Alamo was the site of the most heroic episode of the Texan war of independence against Mexico. On Feb. 23, 1836, a Mexican force of about 4000 men commanded by Antonio López de Santa Anna, general and later president of Mexico, reached the outskirts of San Antonio, which had been captured by Texan insurgents the previous December. The San Antonio garrison, only 155 men under the command of Col. William Barrett Travis, withdrew to the Alamo. Santa Anna deployed his troops around the structure and, when his artillery arrived, launched an intensive assault. The Texans, who were reinforced by 32 men on March 1, withstood the Mexicans until March 6, when the enemy succeeded in breaching the mission walls. Travis, his chief aides, including the American frontiersmen Davy Crockett and James Bowie, and the remainder of the garrison perished in the savage hand-to-hand struggle that followed. Of the 187 Texan defenders of the Alamo, only 6 survived the siege, and Gen. Santa Anna ordered them all killed. At the subsequent Battle of San Jacinto, in which Santa Anna was defeated, the battle cry of the Texans was "Remember the Alamo!"

**ALAMOGORDO,** city, seat of Otero Co., S New Mexico; founded 1898, with the coming of the railroad, inc. 1912. Situated at an altitude of 1326 m (4350 ft) in the foothills of the Sacramento Mts., it is a trade center for a ranching, vegetable-farming and fruit-growing area. Its economy revolves largely around Holloman Air Force Base and White Sands Missile Range, where the first atomic bomb was exploded in July 1945. The city is the seat of the Alamogordo branch (1958) of New Mexico State University, the New Mexico School for the Visually Handicapped (1903), and the International Space Hall of Fame; nearby are White Sands National Monument, Lincoln Na-

tional Forest, Oliver Lee State Park, and Mescalero Indian Reservation. The city's name, Spanish for "fat cottonwood," refers to cottonwood trees in the area. Pop. (1980) 24,024; (1990) 27,596.

**ALANBROOKE, Sir Alan Francis Brooke, 1st Viscount** (1883–1963), British field marshal, born in Bagnère-de-Bigorre, France, and educated at the Royal Military Academy, Woolwich, England. In World War II he organized the defensive operations that made possible the evacuation of British forces from Dunkirk in 1940. He thereafter commanded the home operations of the army. Alanbrooke was promoted to the rank of field marshal in 1944, and he was created a viscount in 1946.

**ÅLAND ISLANDS.** *See* AHVENANMAA.

**AL-ANON AND ALATEEN,** worldwide fellowships of people whose lives have been affected by others' addiction to alcohol. Membership in Al-Anon is open to families, friends, and employers of alcoholics; Alateen is a program designed for young people under the age of 21. The basic principle of both groups is that alcoholism is a family disease; those closely involved with alcoholics may suffer psychologically and spiritually and often physically. Both programs offer comfort, hope, and understanding to those who have lived in confusion and despair.

Al-Anon was started in New York City in 1952 by Lois W., wife of one of the founders of Alcoholics Anonymous (AA), and Anne B. Alateen groups were first organized in California in 1957. Although independent of AA, both programs use the AA 12 steps to recovery and conduct their meetings in a similar fashion. Support comes entirely through voluntary contributions from members.

By the late 1980s, about 25,000 Al-Anon and Alateen groups functioned in more than 70 countries. Al-Anon Family Group Headquarters, Inc., maintains its World Service Office in New York City.

*See also* ALCOHOLICS ANONYMOUS.

**ALANS,** Iranian-speaking nomadic tribe of the ancient world, one of the peoples known as Sarmatians. They first appeared in history north of the Caspian Sea; during the 2d, 3d, and 4th centuries, they migrated westward into the eastern provinces of the Roman Empire. They then divided into two groups. One group continued to migrate westward with the Germanic peoples, appearing in Gaul, Lusitania (Portugal), and finally North Africa, where they merged with the Vandals. The other group, wandering eastward, settled in the Caucasus Mountains, where they have survived into modern times as the Ossetians of the Republic of Georgia.

**ALAPPUZAH,** formerly ALLEPPEY, city, S India, in Kerala State, a seaport on the Indian Ocean. Trade is carried out with Kochi in the N and Trivandrum in the S and is facilitated by canals and lagoons along the coast. Major exports of Alappuzah include copra, pepper, and ginger. Pop. (1991) 264,887.

**ALARCÓN, Hernando de** (fl. 16th cent.), Spanish navigator and explorer in America. On May 9, 1540, Alarcón sailed to the head of the Gulf of California and completed the explorations begun by his countryman Francisco de Ulloa (d. 1540) in the preceding year. Subsequently he was the first European to ascend the Colorado River for a distance long enough to make important observations. On a second voyage he probably proceeded past the present site of Yuma, Ariz. A map drawn by one of Alarcón's pilots is the earliest accurately detailed representation of the gulf and the lower course of the river.

**ALARCÓN, Pedro Antonio de** (1833–91), Spanish writer and politician, born in Guadix. He served as a member of the Cortes, the national legislature. Alarcón was noted in his own time for his religious novels; *The Scandal* (1875; trans. 1945), a defense of the Jesuits, caused much discussion. He is now chiefly remembered, however, for his stories of rustic Spanish life, some of which are collected in *The Three-Cornered Hat* (1874; trans. 1891).

**ALARCÓN Y MENDOZA, Juan Ruiz de.** *See* RUIZ DE ALARCÓN Y MENDOZA, JUAN.

**ALARIC I,** (c. 370–c. 410) king of the Visigoths (395–410), born on an island in the delta of the Danube River. During his youth, the Visigoths migrated westward, under attack from the Huns at their rear. The Visigoths were used as auxiliary mercenary troops by the Roman emperor Theodosius I, and Alaric first appears in history in 394 as a leader of these troops. Upon the death of Theodosius in 395, the Visigoths renounced their allegiance to Rome and acknowledged Alaric as king. He led his troops into Greece; sacked Corinth, Argos, and Sparta; and spared Athens only in return for a heavy ransom. After being defeated by the Roman general Flavius Stilicho, Alaric retired with his plunder and secured from the new Eastern Roman emperor, Arcadius (c. 377–408), a commission as prefect of the Roman province of Illyricum. In 402 Alaric invaded Italy but was again defeated by Stilicho. Later Alaric was persuaded to join forces with the Western Roman emperor Honorius (384–423), who was planning war with the Eastern Empire.

When Arcadius died in 408, Rome abandoned its plan to move against the East, whereupon Alaric demanded 1814 kg (4000 lb) of gold as indemnity. On the insistence of Stilicho, the Roman government agreed to this demand, but soon afterward Honorius had Stilicho executed and abrogated the agreement. Alaric then invaded Italy, besieged Rome, and exacted a vast ransom. In 410 his troops captured and sacked Rome. A disastrous storm forced Alaric to abandon his next campaign, an invasion of Sicily and North Africa. He died shortly afterward and was succeeded by his brother, Ataulf (d. 415).

**ALARIC II** (d. 507), king of the Visigoths (484–507), succeeding his father, Euric (420?–84). He ruled all Gaul beyond the Loire and Rhône rivers and most of Spain. Like most Visigoths, Alaric adhered to Arianism; this gave the Frankish king Clovis I, an orthodox Christian, an excuse for making war on him. Alaric's forces were completely routed at Vouillé, near Poitiers (in present-day France), and he himself was overtaken and slain by Clovis. This defeat brought to an end the rule of the Visigoths in Gaul. Alaric is also known for the *Breviary of Alaric,* an abstract of Roman laws and decrees prepared at his direction for use in his domains. This document is a primary source of knowledge about the application of Roman law in nations formed from the disintegrated Roman Empire.

**ALA SHAN,** desert and mountain range, N central China. The mountains, with peaks as high as 3353 m (11,000 ft), are on the borders of Gansu Province and Ningsia Hui Autonomous Region, about 240 km (about 150 mi) NW of the city of Ning Xian. Northwest of the mountains, and shielded by them from moisture-carrying air currents, is the totally arid Ala Shan Desert, inhabited only by nomads.

**ALASKA,** one of the Pacific states, and the northern-most state of the U.S., occupying the NW extremity of North America; it is bounded on the N by the Arctic Ocean; on the E by the Yukon Territory and British Columbia; on the SE, S, and SW by the Pacific Ocean; and on the W by the Bering Sea, Bering Strait, and Arctic Ocean. The state includes two major island groups, the Aleutian Islands (q.v.), which extend in an arc W from the SW corner of the mainland, and the Alexander Archipelago (q.v.), adjacent to the SE coast of the mainland.

Sometimes called the Last Frontier, Alaska entered the Union on Jan. 3, 1959, as the 49th state. The wild grandeur of Alaska has fascinated people for several hundred years. Its economy, traditionally dominated by the exploitation of natural resources, entered a new phase in 1977, when production of petroleum began at the vast Prudhoe Bay oil field on the Arctic coast. The name of the state is derived from an Aleut word meaning "mainland."

*An active volcano in Katmai National Park, in southern Alaska.*  Shelly Grossman–Woodfin Camp & Associates

## LAND AND RESOURCES

Alaska, with a total area of 1,700,139 sq km (656,424 sq mi), is the largest state in the U.S.; about 81% of the land area is owned by the federal government. The state is roughly square in shape with two major projections: the Alaska Peninsula, with its geographical extension, the Aleutian Islands; and the Panhandle, which extends from the SE body of the state along the border of British Columbia. Its extreme dimensions are about 1770 km (about 1100 mi) from N to S and about 3220 km (about 2000 mi) from E to W. Alaska has the greatest relief range of any state; elevations begin at sea level and extend up to 6194 m (20,320 ft) in Mt. McKinley (Denali), the highest peak in North America. The approximate mean elevation is 579 m (1900 ft). Alaska has 8980 km (5580 mi) of shoreline on the Pacific Ocean and 1706 km (1060 mi) of shoreline on the Arctic Ocean.

**Physical Geography.** The entire S coastal area of Alaska belongs to the Pacific Mt. system. The group of ranges that form this area belong to a geologically unstable belt that surrounds the Pacific Ocean. Volcanic and earthquake activity is much in evidence in this region. The SE (or Panhandle) is a region of fjords and glaciers and consists of the rugged Boundary Range and the offshore Alexander Archipelago. Located here is the sheltered Inside Passage, a fine natural waterway and one of the most scenic in the world. At the NW corner of this region is the Saint Elias Range, with some of the highest peaks on the continent, largely covered with ice and snow and containing the spectacular Malaspina Glacier, the largest in the state.

The Pacific Mt. system also includes the Chugach Range, flanking the N periphery of the Gulf of Alaska and containing the massive Columbia Glacier. The Kenai Mts. constitute a SW continuation of the mountain system. Inland from the Chugach Range, the low relief of the Copper R. Basin is broken by the Wrangell Mts., which contain Mt. Wrangell (4269 m/14,006 ft), the highest active volcano in Alaska.

Inland from the Copper R. Basin is the extensive arc-shaped Alaska Range, which includes Mt. McKinley. The mountain system continues to the SW in a series of volcanoes, the Aleutian Range, which extends far W into the Pacific Ocean as an archipelago, the Aleutian Islands.

North of the Alaska Range is the complex Central Highland and Basin Region, sometimes called the Yukon Plateaus. In the W, elevations are low, and extensive areas flood with the spring thaw. A low range here, the elongated Kuskokwim Mts., separates the Yukon and Kuskokwim valleys. The E interior is occupied by the Yukon Highlands.

The Brooks Range has been little known until recently. It extends across the entire width of Alaska and consists of a complexly folded sedimentary mass with a series of longitudinal valleys, chiefly those of the Kobuk and Koyukuk rivers. Maximum elevations reach only about 3050 m (about 10,000 ft).

Alaska's Arctic Lowland, also known as the North Slope or Arctic Plain, slopes gradually downward from the base of the Brooks Range to the Arctic Ocean. In the S, where elevations exceed 610 m (2000 ft), drainage is good. In the N, however, are many hundreds of undrained ponds.

**Rivers and Lakes.** Alaska's major river, the Yukon, is one of the longest on the continent; it flows across the state from E to W, emptying in the Bering Sea. Its tributaries include the Porcupine, Koyukuk, and Tanana rivers. Among the state's shorter streams are the Colville and Kobuk rivers, which drain to the Arctic Ocean, and the Kuskokwim, Susitna, Matanuska, and Copper rivers, which drain to the Pacific Ocean. Thousands of small lakes and ponds are found in Alaska. The state's largest lakes (Iliamna, Becharof, and Ugashik) are located on the Alaska Peninsula.

**Climate.** Alaska can be divided into three major climate zones: a region of maritime influences (a marine west coast climate), a region of continental (or subarctic) climate, and a region of tundra (or arctic) climate.

The region of maritime climate comprises the Panhandle, the coast of the Gulf of Alaska, and the Aleutian Islands. This region is greatly affected by the relatively warm Alaska Current and by the proximity of the Gulf of Alaska, where storms form throughout the year, especially in winter. Gray skies, successive wet days, dampness, fogginess, and occasional gale winds are characteristic. Annual precipitation is heavy, amounting to more than 2540 mm (more than 100 in) in many places. The abundant snowfall provides the source for many glaciers. Summers are cool here, and winters, relatively mild.

Interior Alaska, the area N of the Alaska Range and S of the Brooks Range, is a region of continental climate, with mild, brief summers and harsh winters. This region is drier and has an average annual precipitation of about 610 mm (about 24 in). For half of the year the ground is covered with powdery snow that accumulates to depths of several feet. Invasions of warmer maritime air from the Gulf of Alaska may break the extreme winter cold for a week or so at a time. Average January temperature is −22.8° C (−9° F), with extremes of −51.1° C (−60° F) or colder. A record low temperature of −62.2° C (−80° F) was measured at Prospect Creek Camp, in NW Alaska, in 1971.

The area N of the Brooks Range is a region of tundra (arctic) climate and has weeks of continuous darkness in winter and of daylight in summer. Moderated by ocean influences, the winter is somewhat less harsh than in interior Alaska. While the snow cover is thin, strong winds at times create extremely cold windchill temperatures. The average annual precipitation is less than 203 mm (less than 8 in).

**Plants and Animals.** Slightly less than one-third of Alaska is forest covered, and the state contains the two largest national forests in the nation.

*The tundra, an autumn view. Behind loom mountains of the Alaska Range.*　　　Jon & Dee Bartlett–Bruce Coleman, Inc.

Lush coniferous forests, located in the Panhandle and on the coast of the Gulf of Alaska, are dominated by hemlock and spruce trees, with an understory of mosses and shrubs. Much of the interior is covered by taiga, or northern forest, consisting largely of spruce and birch; these forests are slow growing and of limited commercial value. Over much of W and N Alaska is the treeless tundra (q.v.), with a vegetation ranging from shrubs to mosses and sedges. Alaska's many flowers include fireweed, lupine, and the state flower, forget-me-not.

Alaska has a rich and diverse fauna. Surrounding waters are renowned for whale, fur seal, walrus, and sea otter, as well as salmon, halibut, crab, shrimp, and other marine life. Bears, including polar, brown, and black, are well represented. Great herds of caribou still migrate across the Brooks Range, followed by packs of wolves. Other mammals include moose, as well as such furbearers as beaver, wolverine, mink, otter, and muskrat. Several species of ptarmigan are widespread, and large numbers of ducks and geese spend summers on the Arctic slope. Mosquitoes swarm in vast numbers in summer; also present are flies and "no-see-ums," as the biting midges are known.

**Mineral Resources.** Petroleum and natural gas are by far Alaska's most important mineral resources. Considerable quantities of copper (from the Copper R. Basin) and gold (especially around Juneau, Fairbanks, and Nome) have been mined. Coal is found near the Alaska Railroad. Large deposits of molybdenum are known, near Ketchikan and in the W Brooks Range. Other mineral resources include sand, gravel, and clay. In the future, exploration is likely to reveal additional deposits of other minerals.                D.W.L.

## POPULATION

According to the 1990 census, Alaska had 550,043 inhabitants, an increase of 36.9% over 1980. The average population density in 1990 was less than 1 person per 3 sq km (less than 1 per sq mi), the lowest overall population density of any state. Whites made up 75.5% of the population and blacks 4.1%. Other major population groups included some 44,401 Inuit (Eskimo), amounting to 8.17% of the total population (see INUIT); 31,245 American Indians, or 5.7% of the total; and 10,052 Aleuts (see ALEUT), accounting for 1.8% of the total. Most of the Inuit population lived in the N and W parts of the state. The Tlingit, Haida, and Athabaska, the state's principal American Indian groups, lived in the S and SE. The Aleuts were concentrated in the Aleutian Islands and the Alaska Peninsula. Some 7976 persons of Filipino background and 2066 people of Japanese descent also lived in Alaska. In 1990, about 67% of all Alaskans lived in areas defined as urban, and the rest lived in rural areas. The largest cities in the state were Anchorage; Fairbanks; Juneau, the capital; Sitka; and Ketchikan.

*Juneau, seen from the harbor. Situated in the southeast, in the Alaskan Panhandle, the capital enjoys a temperate climate.*                Sullivan & Rogers–Bruce Coleman, Inc.

# Alaska: Map Index

## Cities and Towns

## Other Features

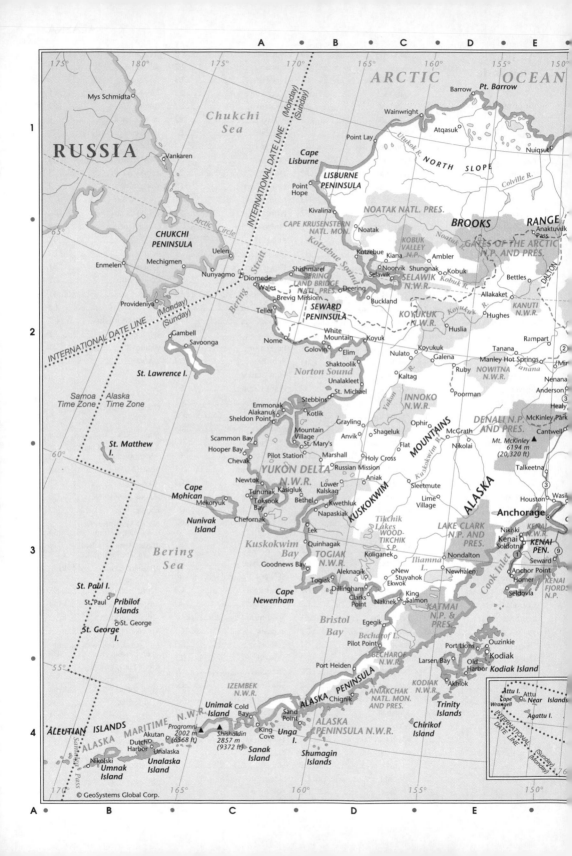

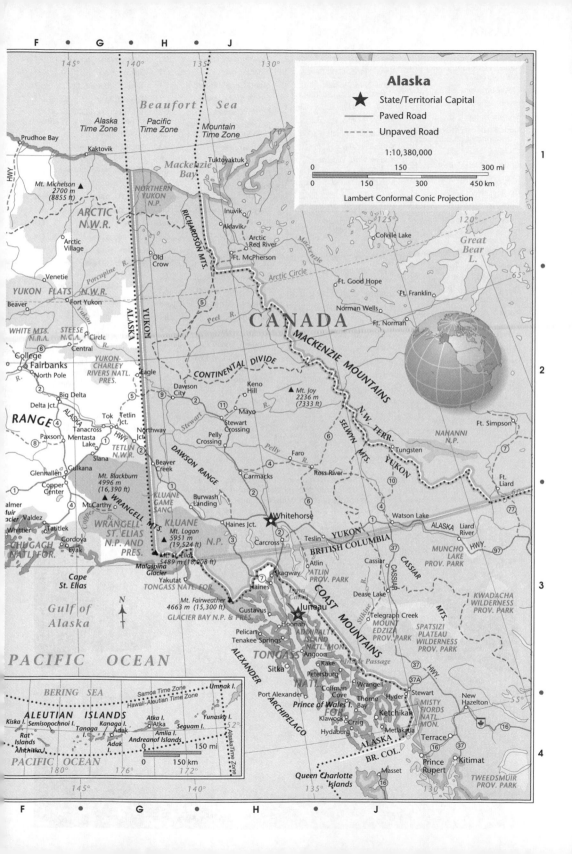

## Alaska

★ State/Territorial Capital
—— Paved Road
---- Unpaved Road

1:10,380,000

| 0 | 150 | 300 mi |
| 0 | 150 | 300 | 450 km |

Lambert Conformal Conic Projection

# ALASKA

*Much of the topography of Alaska has resulted from the region's extreme climatic conditions. In high latitudes where snow falls at a rate greater than it melts, glaciers form. The Portage Glacier (pictured here), on reaching water, spawned large masses of floating ice.*                    Bob & Ira Spring–FPG

*An Inuit (Eskimo) couple relax outside their igloo (house). The dome-shaped, snow-block igloo has never been built by the Alaskan Inuit.*

Alaska Tour & Marketing Serv., Inc.

## EDUCATION AND CULTURAL ACTIVITY

Many new educational and cultural facilities were opened in Alaska as a result of the influx of people and funds attendant to the start of large-scale petroleum production in the 1970s.

**Education.** The first mission school for native Alaskans was founded at Wrangell by Presbyterian missionaries in 1876. By 1884 the free public school system had been established in the territory. Today, general public schools are supported by the state and local governments. Schools for Native American children are operated by the U.S. Bureau of Indian Affairs.

In the late 1980s public education facilities included 207 elementary and secondary schools, and annual public school enrollment totaled about 81,700 elementary pupils and 27,600 secondary students. About 5000 children attended private schools. In the same period there were 8 institutions of higher education in Alaska, with a combined enrollment of about 28,600 students. These

institutions included the University of Alaska (1915), with its flagship campus at Fairbanks and branches in 11 communities, and Alaska Pacific University (1959), at Anchorage.

**Cultural Institutions.** The Anchorage Museum of History and Art contains outstanding collections on Alaskan history and native arts. The University of Alaska Museum, in Fairbanks, includes extensive exhibits on Alaskan archaeology and wildlife. The Alaska State Museum, in Juneau, and the Sheldon Jackson Museum, in Sitka, feature exhibits of Indian and Inuit artifacts. The state's largest public library is at Anchorage. The Alaska Center for the Performing Arts is located in Anchorage.

**Historical Sites.** The sites of 18th-century Russian settlements are found on Kodiak Island and at Sitka, and Sitka National Historical Park includes the site of a fort used by the Russians to gain control over the Tlingit Indians in the early 19th century. Klondike Gold Rush National Historical Park, at Skagway, commemorates the great gold rush of 1897–98.

**Sports and Recreation.** Alaska's leading resort area is Denali National Park and Preserve, where hiking, mountain climbing, and skiing are popular activities. Other outdoor sports in Alaska include fishing, hunting, swimming, ice skating, and dogsled racing. Popular indoor sports are basketball and bowling.

**Communications.** Alaska's communications facilities are concentrated in the state's few cities. Most small towns are connected with larger urban areas in both Alaska and the continental U.S. by radio and telephone service. In the early 1990s, Alaska had 40 AM radio stations, 43 FM radio-broadcasters, and 15 television stations. The state's first radio station, KFQD, began operation in Anchorage in 1924. In the early 1990s Alaska was served by seven daily newspapers, which had a combined daily circulation of about 136,300 copies. Among the leading dailies were the *Anchorage Daily News* and the *Fairbanks Daily News-Miner*. Alaska's first general newspaper, the *Sitka Times*, began publication in Sitka in 1868.

## GOVERNMENT AND POLITICS

Alaska is governed under a constitution adopted in 1956 (three years before it became a state), as amended. State constitutional amendments may be proposed by the legislature or by a constitutional convention. In order to become effective they must be approved by voters in a general election.

**Executive.** Alaska's chief executive is a governor, who is popularly elected to a 4-year term and may not serve more than two consecutive terms. The lieutenant governor, the only other state-wide-elected official, succeeds the chief execu-

321

# ALASKA

DATE OF STATEHOOD: January 3, 1959; 49th state

| | |
|---|---|
| **CAPITAL:** | Juneau |
| **MOTTO:** | North to the Future |
| **STATE SONG:** | "Alaska's Flag" (words by Marie Drake; music by Elinor Dusenbury) |
| **STATE TREE:** | Sitka spruce |
| **STATE FLOWER:** | Forget-me-not |
| **STATE BIRD:** | Willow ptarmigan |
| **POPULATION (1990):** | 550,043; 49th among the states |
| **AREA:** | 1,700,139 sq km (656,424 sq mi); the largest state; includes 222,871 sq km (86,051 sq mi) of inland water |
| **COASTLINE:** | 10,686 km (6640 mi) |
| **HIGHEST POINT:** | Mt. McKinley, 6194 m (20,320 ft) |
| **LOWEST POINT:** | Sea level, at the Pacific coast |
| **ELECTORAL VOTES:** | 3 |
| **U.S. CONGRESS:** | 2 senators; 1 representative |

## POPULATION OF ALASKA SINCE 1880

| Year of Census | Population | Classified As Urban |
|---|---|---|
| 1880 | 33,000 | 0% |
| 1900 | 64,000 | 25% |
| 1920 | 55,000 | 5% |
| 1930 | 59,000 | 14% |
| 1940 | 73,000 | 23% |
| 1950 | 129,000 | 26% |
| 1960 | 226,000 | 38% |
| 1980 | 400,000 | 65% |
| 1990 | 550,043 | 67% |

## POPULATION OF TEN LARGEST CITIES

| | 1990 Census | 1980 Census |
|---|---|---|
| Anchorage | 226,338 | 173,017 |
| Fairbanks | 30,843 | 22,645 |
| Juneau | 26,751 | 19,528 |
| Sitka | 8,588 | 7,803 |
| Ketchikan | 8,263 | 7,198 |
| Kodiak | 6,365 | 4,756 |
| Kenai | 6,327 | 4,324 |
| Bethel | 4,674 | 3,576 |
| Valdez | 4,068 | 3,079 |
| Wasilla | 4,028 | 1,559 |

## CLIMATE

| | FAIRBANKS | JUNEAU |
|---|---|---|
| Average January temperature range | −30° to −18.9° C (−22° to −2° F) | −7.8° to −1.7° C (18° to 29° F) |
| Average July temperature range | 10° to 22.2° C (50° to 72° F) | 8.9° to 17.8° C (48° to 64° F) |
| Average annual temperature | −3.3° C (26° F) | 4.4° C (40° F) |
| Average annual precipitation | 279 mm (11 in) | 1397 mm (55 in) |
| Average annual snowfall | 1072 mm (67 in) | 2794 mm (110 in) |
| Mean number of days per year with appreciable precipitation | 102 | 220 |
| Average daily relative humidity | 61% | 77% |
| Mean number of clear days per year | 68 | 44 |

ARCTIC LOWLAND

BROOKS RANGE

CENTRAL HIGHLAND & BASIN REGION

Yukon R.

PACIFIC MT. REGION

**NATURAL REGIONS OF ALASKA**

## PRINCIPAL PRODUCTS OF ALASKA

PETROLEUM

REINDEER

FURS

TIN
GOLD

GOLD

COAL

SILVER
GOLD

Fairbanks

POTATOES

GRAINS
DAIRY PRODUCTS
VEGETABLES

GOLD

Anchorage

FURS

PETROLEUM
NATURAL GAS

CRABS

FISH

FISH

FISH

FISH

FORESTRY
PRODUCTS

SEALS

# ECONOMY

State budget . . . . . . . . . . . . . . general revenue $4.8 billion
general expenditure $4.3 billion
accumulated debt $5.5 billion
State and local taxes, per capita . . . . . . . . . . . . . . . . . $4069
Personal income, per capita. . . . . . . . . . . . . . . . . . . . $17,610
Population below poverty level . . . . . . . . . . . . . . . . . . . . 9.0%
Assets, insured commercial banks (7). . . . . . . . $4.3 billion
Labor force (civilian nonfarm) . . . . . . . . . . . . . . . . . 227,000
  Employed in government                    30%
  Employed in services                      21%
  Employed in wholesale and retail trade    19%
  Employed in manufacturing                  7%

|  | Quantity Produced | Value |
|---|---|---|
| **FARM PRODUCTS** . . . . . . . . . . . . . . . . . . . . . . . | | **$27 million** |
| **Crops** . . . . . . . . . . . . . . . . . . . . . . . . . . . . . . . . . | | **$19 million** |
| **Livestock and Livestock Products** . . . . . . . . | | **$8 million** |
| Milk. . . . . . . . . . | 7200 metric tons | . . . . . . . . . . . . $3 million |

| | | |
|---|---|---|
| **MINERALS**. . . . . . . . . . . . . . . . . . . . . . . . . . . . . | | **$9.0 billion†** |
| Petroleum. . . . | 684 million barrels | . . . . . . . . . . $8.3 billion |
| Natural gas . . | 11.1 billion cu m | . . . . . . . . . . . $535 million |
| Gold . . . . . . . . | 5800 kg | . . . . . . . . . . . . . . . . . . . . $71 million |
| Coal . . . . . . . . | 1.4 million metric tons | . . . . . . . . . . . . . N/A |
| Sand, gravel . | 15.4 million metric tons | . . . . . $49 million |
| Stone . . . . . . . . | 2.6 million metric tons | . . . . . . $20 million |

†Excluding coal

| | | |
|---|---|---|
| **FISHING** . . . . . . . | 2.4 million metric tons | . . . . **$1.5 billion** |

Annual Payroll

**FORESTRY**. . . . . . . . . . . . . . . . . . . . . . . . . . . . . . . **$3 million**

**MANUFACTURING** . . . . . . . . . . . . . . . . . . . . . . . **$389 million**
  Food and kindred products . . . . . . . . . . . . . . $124 million
  Lumber and wood products . . . . . . . . . . . . . . $106 million
  Printing and publishing . . . . . . . . . . . . . . . . . . . $31 million
  Petroleum and coal products. . . . . . . . . . . . . . $16 million
  Stone, clay, and glass products . . . . . . . . . . . $13 million
  Fabricated metal products. . . . . . . . . . . . . . . . . . $9 million

**OTHER**. . . . . . . . . . . . . . . . . . . . . . . . . . . . . . . . . . . **$6.9 billion**
  Government. . . . . . . . . . . . . . . . . . . . . . . . . . . . . . $2.9 billion
  Services . . . . . . . . . . . . . . . . . . . . . . . . . . . . . . . . $1.2 billion
  Retail trade . . . . . . . . . . . . . . . . . . . . . . . . . . . . . $597 million
  Transportation, communications,
    and public utilities. . . . . . . . . . . . . . . . . . . . $544 million
  Construction . . . . . . . . . . . . . . . . . . . . . . . . . . . $541 million
  Wholesale trade. . . . . . . . . . . . . . . . . . . . . . . . . $247 million
  Finance, insurance, and real estate . . . . . $235 million

### ANNUAL GROSS STATE PRODUCT

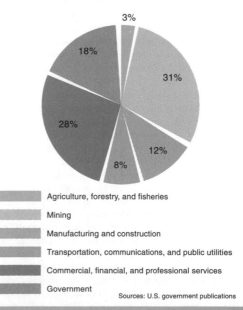

3%
18%
31%
12%
8%
28%

- Agriculture, forestry, and fisheries
- Mining
- Manufacturing and construction
- Transportation, communications, and public utilities
- Commercial, financial, and professional services
- Government

Sources: U.S. government publications

An aboveground length of the Trans-Alaska Pipeline. The pipeline wends its way to the southern port of Valdez, from which the oil it carries is shipped to the "South 48" (the conterminous states). Alyeska Pipeline

tive on the governor's death, removal from office, or incapacity to serve. The governor appoints cabinet officers, who are called commissioners.

**Legislature.** The Alaska legislature consists of a house of representatives of 40 members popularly elected to 2-year terms and a senate of 20 members popularly elected to 4-year terms. The senate elects a president from among its members, and the house chooses a speaker as its presiding officer. The legislature meets every January for a session of unlimited duration. A veto of legislation by the governor may be overridden by a two-thirds vote of the senate and house.

**Judiciary.** The highest judicial body in Alaska is the supreme court, made up of five justices, one of whom is chosen by the court to serve a nonrenewable 3-year term as chief justice. The governor appoints each justice, who must be confirmed in office by voters in the first general election held after the justice has served for three years on the court. Thereafter, the justice must be reconfirmed by voters every ten years. The chief trial courts in the state are the superior courts, which have a total of 30 justices.

**Local Government.** Alaska is not divided into counties; the chief units of local government in

the early 1990s were 12 boroughs, 3 unified home-rule municipalities (combining the functions of boroughs and cities), 149 other incorporated communities, and 132 unincorporated communities. Most of the boroughs and incorporated communities had elected mayors and councils.

**National Representation.** Alaska is represented in the U.S. Congress by two senators and one representative. The state casts three electoral votes in presidential elections.

**Politics.** Since statehood no single party has dominated politics in Alaska. Although Republicans outnumber Democrats among registered voters, nonpartisan registrants are in the majority. Control of the state governorship has been closely balanced between the two major parties; in the state legislature, Republicans tend to dominate the senate, while the Democrats usually control a majority of the house of representatives. In presidential elections, the state has generally gone Republican. The Libertarian party has a significant following, and Libertarians have won election to the state legislature.

### ECONOMY

Until the 1960s Alaska's economy developed slowly, despite the gold rushes of the Klondike (1897–98) and Nome (1898). Fishing and forestry have traditionally been important to the economy, but agriculture, at these high latitudes, employs few people. In the late 1970s, extraction of petroleum began along the Arctic shore, and substantial reserves of natural gas are also being developed. Although known mainly for the exploitation of natural resources, Alaska's economy is also heavily dependent on tertiary activities, largely government and service industries, which employ some three-quarters of the total labor force. The preponderance of military and government workers is a result of the state's strategic military location and the presence of vast areas of land under federal government jurisdiction.

**Agriculture.** Farming accounts for less than 1% of the annual gross state product in Alaska. The state has some 560 farms, averaging about 715 ha (about 1770 acres) in size. Crops account for about 70% of the annual farm income, and livestock and livestock products for about 30%. Greenhouse products, dairy products, potatoes, and cattle dominate agricultural output. Most agricultural activities are carried on in areas adjacent to or near the Pacific coast. The Matanuska Valley near Anchorage is the most important agricultural region, followed by the inland Tanana Valley and the Kenai Peninsula. Alaska is not self-sufficient in farm products.

**Forestry.** Forestry is important to Alaska's economy. In the early 1990s, the commercial timber-

*Alaska's richness in timber is suggested by this stand of evergreens along the Moose River, on the Kenai Peninsula in the south.* Dr. E. R. Degginger–Bruce Coleman, Inc.

land comprised about 9.2 million ha (about 22.8 million acres), or 6.2% of Alaska's land area. The principal species harvested in the state are western hemlock, Sitka spruce, cedar, and other softwoods that are used for lumber and for making paper.

**Fishing.** Alaska has excellent marine and freshwater fisheries. The value of the fish catch in the early 1990s exceeded $1 billion annually. Salmon accounts for a major share of the value of the annual catch, followed by shellfish (crabs, shrimp, scallops) and finfish other than salmon (halibut, herring, flounder).

**Mining.** The mining industry accounts for nearly one-third of the annual gross state product. Petroleum dominates the list of mineral products, accounting for at least 85% by value of the annual mineral output. Nearly all production now comes from Prudhoe Bay, with minor amounts taken from fields on the McArthur R., Middle Ground Shoal, Granite Point, the Swanson R., Trading Bay, and Beaver Creek. The Prudhoe field has an estimated 10 billion barrels of recoverable oil, and other fields on, or offshore, the Arctic coastline may contain even more reserves. Natural gas output is also substantial, most natural gas occurring with or near petroleum. Among the other minerals produced are sand and gravel, stone, coal, and gold.

**Manufacturing.** Manufacturing is a comparatively minor economic sector in Alaska, accounting for no more than 5% of the annual gross state product. Processing of fish and other food is the leading industry in the state, followed by production of lumber and wood products; printing and publishing are industries of lesser importance. These activities occur mainly along the Pacific coast, especially at Anchorage, but also inland at Fairbanks.

**Tourism.** Tourism is a growing industry in Alaska. Each year more than 600,000 people visit the state, a figure amounting to considerably more than that of the resident population. Income to Alaska from tourism exceeds $800 million each year. Large areas in the state are administered by the National Park Service; Denali and Glacier Bay national parks and preserves are two of the most popular areas. In addition the state maintains a system of 116 parks and recreation areas.

**Transportation.** Because of Alaska's enormous size and small population, water and air transportation are critically important. The state has numerous places that are officially recognized as ports, of which Anchorage is the most important; the great majority of these are located on the Pacific coast. The international airports serving Anchorage and Fairbanks are the busiest of the state's 477 airports. Alaska also has 105 seaplane bases and 20 heliports. The airplane not only links settled places but also allows isolated hamlets to maintain contact with one another and with more populated centers.

Anchorage and Fairbanks are important hubs in a network of about 21,710 km (about 13,490 mi) of federal, state, and local roads, of which 89% are rural and 11% urban. Principal highways connect Fairbanks with Anchorage, and Anchorage with the Kenai Peninsula. The Alaska Highway (q.v.), linked to this system, is a major overland route to Canada and the rest of the U.S. The publicly owned Alaska Railroad has about 845 km (about 525 mi) of operated track; it connects Fairbanks with Anchorage and extends S to Seward.

The Trans-Alaska Pipeline (opened 1977), 122 cm (48 in) in diameter, connects Prudhoe Bay to the Pacific port of Valdez, carrying crude petroleum. Lack of funding stalled a plan to build a natural-gas pipeline S from the same field.

**Energy.** Although Alaska has great hydroelectricity-generating potential, only a small amount of energy is consumed within the state, and this comes mostly from wood in rural areas and mostly from petroleum and natural gas in urban places. The electricity generating plants in Alaska have a total capacity of about 1.5 million kw and produce 4.5 billion kwh of electricity each year. More than three-quarters of all electricity comes from thermal plants consuming petroleum and natural gas.                                    R.S.Th.

### HISTORY

The original inhabitants of Alaska included four ethnological subdivisions. The Aleuts of the western Alaska Peninsula were expert mariners; their economy relied on sea otter, seal, sea lion, and fish, and they were skilled at basketry. The Inuit (Eskimo), inhabiting the coastal area from Bristol Bay to Point Demarcation on the Arctic, sailed in kayaks to hunt whale, seal, and walrus and to fish. On land they used dogs and sleds for hunting. The Inuit deftly carved ivory into tools, utensils, and ornaments. The Tlingit-Haida Indians of southeastern Alaska, skilled in totem-pole carving and basketry, were great traders and canoe builders who lived from the sea. Indian tribes of the interior belonged to the Athabascan family; they caught salmon and hunted land animals. The seminomadic Athabascans had few arts but made knives of stone and native copper.

**Russian Alaska.** The first Europeans to visit Alaska were part of a Russian expedition led by the Danish navigator Vitus Bering, who landed on the southern coast in 1741. Bering and much of the crew died on the return voyage; the remaining crew reached Russia in 1742, prompting ruthless *promshlenniki* ("fur traders") to swarm into the Aleutians. In 1784 Grigory Shelekhov (1747–95) colonized Kodiak Island; in 1786 Gerasim Pribilof (d. 1796) located the opulent Seal Islands. The Russian-American Co. was granted a monopoly over the fur trade in 1799.

Aleksandr Baranov (1746–1819), the first chief manager, founded Sitka as the colony's commer-

*Community house of the Tlingit Indians, near Ketchikan. The totem poles were designed specifically for the building, now little used.*     S. J. Krasemann–Peter Arnold, Inc.

cial center, along with 23 other posts. Despite penetrations by Spanish, British, French, and American explorers and traders, dating from the 1770s, Russian control over Alaska lasted until 1867. Although the Russians discovered gold, copper, and coal, they were mainly preoccupied with furs. A decline in fur profits and a threatened invasion by the British from Canada motivated Russia in the 1850s to consider selling Alaska to the U.S. The American Civil War delayed the purchase, astutely negotiated by Secretary of State William H. Seward, until 1867.

**Alaska Under the U.S.** Army troops garrisoned in Alaska from 1867 to 1877 constituted the first U.S. presence there. When the troops were withdrawn, the only U.S. officials present were customs collectors of the U.S. Treasury Department. After U.S. warships arrived in 1879, the commanding officers of those ships exercised de facto jurisdiction over Alaska until Congress established a civil and judicial district in 1884.

Salmon canning became a major industry by the 1880s; the Alaskan gold rush nearly doubled the population and attracted capital in the 1890s. In 1906 Alaska was given a delegate to Congress; in 1912 it gained territorial status. Its failure to achieve self-government hindered economic development, however, and the population declined between 1910 and 1930. New Deal measures of the 1930s improved housing, created public works, stimulated mining, and demonstrated greater agricultural potential for Alaska.

During World War II, the strategic importance of Alaska was belatedly recognized. In June 1942 the Japanese occupied the islands of Attu and Kiska in the Aleutians; it took U.S. forces 15 months to dislodge them. To circumvent a threat to Alaskan sealanes, the army built the Alaska Highway, connecting Alaska with British Columbia, in 1942.

The cold war with the USSR led to increased military construction in 1947 and the start of the radar stations of the DEW (Distant Early Warning) Line. The fishing industry, once the mainstay of the Alaskan economy, declined by the late 1940s. Between 1954 and 1959 the forest products industry, the first major year-round industry, expanded rapidly. The discovery of oil on the Kenai Peninsula in 1957 gave a new impetus to the economy.

**Statehood.** Alaska officially became the 49th state on Jan. 3, 1959. Tourism soon developed into a major industry, and a state ferry system was authorized in 1961. A devastating earthquake struck south-central Alaska in 1964.

The discovery of vast oil deposits on the Alaska North Slope in 1968 resulted in construction of the approximately 1300-km (approximately 800-mi) Trans-Alaska Pipeline from Prudhoe Bay to the ice-free port of Valdez, where the first oil arrived in July 1977. Oil revenues enabled the state to abolish its personal income tax and to distribute annual cash dividends to all state residents.

In 1980 Congress passed the Alaska Lands Bill, which excluded more than 42 million ha (more than 104 million acres) in the state from commercial development. Many Alaskans opposed what they felt were unjustifiable federal attempts to limit exploitation of the state's resources, but calls for secession were rejected. One of the worst environmental disasters in U.S. history occurred in March 1989, when an Exxon tanker ran aground in Prince William Sound, spilling more than 10 million gallons of oil.          B.F.G.

*For further information on this topic, see the Bibliography in volume 28, sections 1109, 1228–29.*

**ALASKA, UNIVERSITY OF,** statewide system of higher learning consisting of a flagship campus at Fairbanks and campuses in 11 other communities. Established by Congress in 1915 as a land-grant agricultural college, the University of Alaska Fairbanks today is a leader in research on the aurora borealis (northern lights) and other aspects of the northern environment. Associate's, bachelor's, master's, and doctoral degrees are awarded in arts and letters; behavorial sciences; business; earth sciences and mineral industry; economics and government; education; mathematics, physical sciences, and engineering; and natural sciences.

**ALASKA BOUNDARY DISPUTE,** early 20th-century controversy over the location of a portion of the boundary between Alaska and Canada. According to a vaguely worded 1825 treaty between Great Britain and Russia (the controlling colonial powers), the frontier north of lat 54°40` N was to follow a range of mountains 16.1 km (10 mi) inland from and parallel to the Pacific coast. In many places, no such mountains existed, but the ambiguous wording caused no problem until 1898, when the discovery of gold in the Klondike region east of Alaska gave Canada an interest in access to the Pacific coast adjacent to the goldfields. The Canadians argued that in many cases the mountains mentioned by the treaty were actually on offshore islands and that in those places the western border of Canada was the Pacific Ocean. The U.S., which had purchased Alaska from the Russians in 1867, maintained that the whole coastline was U.S. territory. In 1903 the U.S. and Britain referred the question to a commission of six members, three appointed by each power. The commission, which met in London, included three Americans, Secretary of War Elihu

Root and Senators Henry Cabot Lodge and George Turner (1850–1932); two Canadians, Sir Louis Jetté (1836–1920) and Allen B. Aylesworth (1854–1952); and England's chief justice, Lord Richard E. Webster Alverstone (1842–1915). Alverstone sided with the Americans, forming a majority in favor of the U.S.

**ALASKA HIGHWAY,** road, connecting Dawson Creek, B.C., with Fairbanks, Alaska. Formerly called the Alcan and the Alaskan International Highway, it is 2424 km (1506 mi) long and runs in a generally NW direction. Begun shortly after the U.S. entered World War II, it was to provide an overland military supply route and to link airfields in Canada and Alaska. From March to November 1942 the U.S. Army Corps of Engineers and contractors under the Public Roads Administration (now the Federal Highway Administration) constructed a pioneer trail. The following year an improved road, mostly on new alignment, was completed, in the main by private contractors. The Canadian section was turned over to Canada in 1946, and in 1948 the entire route was opened to civilian traffic. Today most of the 1946-km (1209-mi) section in Canada is surfaced with asphalt chip seal, while most of the Alaskan section has a hot-mix asphalt surface. The highway is open all year, with roadside services available along the entire route, although on a limited basis in winter.

**ALASKAN MALAMUTE,** hardy breed of working dog, originally bred by an Alaskan tribe known as Mahlemuts or Malemuit. The dog is the oldest known native Alaskan breed; akin to the wolf, it is often crossed with that animal. The Alaskan malamute is extensively used in the Arctic for hauling sledges. Some are also bred in the U.S., where they serve as pets and show dogs. The dog is large with a compact and powerful body and unusual powers of endurance. The male is 56 to 64 cm (22 to 25 in) high at the shoulder and weighs 29 to 39 kg (65 to 85 lb); the female is 51 to 58 cm (20 to 23 in) high and weighs 23 to 32 kg (50 to 70 lb). The animal has a thick, coarse outer coat and a woolly undercoat and is gray or black and white in color. It has a broad, moderately rounded skull; a large muzzle; dark, almond-shaped eyes; medium-sized ears, the upper halves of which are triangular; a deep chest; powerful legs; and a bushy tail carried high.

**ALASKA NORTH SLOPE,** region, N Alaska. It comprises a lowland area extending N from the Brooks Range to the Arctic Ocean. It is a treeless plain, the ground of which is permanently frozen except for a surface melting in the summer that results in swampy conditions. Large herds of car-

*Alaskan malamute. This purebred's formal name is Ch. Poker Flat's Snack Bar Annie CD.*
**Robin Haggard**

ibou are found in the region. In 1968 extensive petroleum deposits were discovered in the North Slope, notably at Prudhoe Bay; large-scale production began in 1977.

**ALASKA RANGE,** mountain range, S Alaska. It extends in a generally NE direction from the base of the Alaska Peninsula to the frontier of Yukon Territory. The Alaska Range averages about 80 km (50 mi) in width; it forms the parting between the Pacific drainage basin of Alaska, on the S, and the Bering Sea drainage basin, on the N and W; the highest peak is Mt. McKinley, or Denali, at 6194 m (20,320 ft), the tallest mountain in North America.

**ALAS Y UREÑA, Leopoldo** (1852–1901), Spanish writer, who used the pseudonym Clarín ("bugle"). As a noted reviewer of books, he is considered one of Spain's most influential literary critics of the late 1800s. His fiction, satirizing provincial and religious views, has been much praised. The novel La regenta (The Professor's Wife, 1884–85) is usually compared to the French novelist Gustave Flaubert's Madame Bovary.

**ALATAU,** name of several mountain ranges of the Tien Shan system, Central Asia, in Kyrgyzstan and Kazakhstan. The Alatau mountain ranges are located near Lake Ysyk Köl, and form part of the border with the Xinjiang Uygar Autonomous Region of China. The peaks of the Alatau ranges are from about 3050 to 5490 m (about 10,000 to 18,000 ft) above sea level.

**ALAY MOUNTAINS.** See ALAI MOUNTAINS.

**ALBA, Fernando Álvarez de Toledo, Duke of.** See ALVA, FERNANDO ÁLVAREZ DE TOLEDO, DUKE OF.

**ALBACETE,** city, E Spain, capital of Albacete Province, in Castile-La Mancha. It is on the main railroad line from Madrid to SE coastal points. The city is a market center for farm products; the major industry is the manufacture of matches. Pop. (1991) 128,718.

**ALBACORE.** See TUNA.

**ALBA IULIA** (Hung. Gyulafehérvár; Ger. Karlsburg), city, central Romania, in Alba Region, on the Mureş R. The city consists of an upper town, or citadel, built by Holy Roman Emperor Charles VI between 1716 and 1735; and a lower town, which contains a noted cathedral and the Batthyaneum, a museum founded in 1794. Constructed in the 11th century, the cathedral was rebuilt in the 15th century in the Gothic style. A library, an observatory, and a museum are in the Batthyaneum. Alba Iulia occupies the site of the Roman colony Apulum, and many Roman relics are in the museum. The tomb of the Hungarian patriot János Hunyadi is here. Pop. (1992) 71,254.

**ALBA LONGA,** city in ancient Latium; it was one of the oldest cities of Italy. According to

Roman legend, it was founded (c. 1152 BC) by Ascanius, son of the Trojan hero Aeneas. The city was long the head of the ancient confederacy known as the Latin League. It is said to have been destroyed in 665 BC by the Romans under Tullus Hostilius (r. 673–642 BC), the third king of Rome, and was never rebuilt. Alba Longa was located on a rocky ridge on the western shore of Lake Albano; an ancient necropolis containing tombs from about 1100 BC has been found here.

**ALBAN, Saint** (fl. about 287–304), first English martyr, probably born in the town of Verulamium (now Saint Albans, Hertfordshire) in the Roman province of Brittania. He served in the Roman army. During the persecution by the Roman emperor Diocletian, he was converted to Christianity and baptized by a fugitive priest whom he sheltered. When his house was searched by Roman soldiers, Alban, disguised as the priest, was arrested, tried, and beheaded. A shrine dedicated to him stands in Saint Albans Abbey, founded in 793 at the site of his martyrdom. His feast day is June 17 in the Church of England and June 22 in the Roman Catholic Church.

**ALBANIA** (Albanian Shqipëri, "Eagle's Country"), republic, SE Europe, located in the W part of the Balkan Peninsula; bounded on the NW and N by Yugoslavia (Montenegro and Serbia), on the E by the Republic of Macedonia, on the SE and S by Greece, and on the W by the Adriatic Sea. Albania, one of the smallest countries of Europe, has a maximum length from N to S of about 345 km (about 214 mi) and a maximum width of about 145 km (about 90 mi). The total area is 28,748 sq km (11,100 sq mi).

## LAND AND RESOURCES

Albania is predominantly mountainous with peaks averaging between 2100 and 2400 m (about 7000 to 8000 ft). Lowlands, which comprise less than one-quarter of the land area, are limited to a belt along the Adriatic coast N of Vlorë and to several river valleys extending inland from the coast. The rugged North Albanian Alps form the S end of the Dinaric Alps and include Albania's highest peak, Mt. Korab (2751 m/9026 ft). In the central and S parts of the country the mountains are interrupted by high plateaus and basins. The coastal lowlands possess rich soils, but in many places the land is marshy or poorly drained.

**Rivers and Lakes.** Most of Albania's rivers rise in the mountainous E and flow W to the Adriatic Sea. The largest of these—the Drin, Shkumbi, and Mat—have broad valleys. Albania's three large lakes straddle its borders: in the NW, Lake Scutari, and in the E, Lake Ohrid and Lake Prespa.

**Climate.** The Adriatic coastal region has a typical Mediterranean climate, with mild, wet winters and hot, dry summers. Inland, a more severe continental climate prevails, with marked seasonal temperature extremes. Average annual precipitation ranges from about 1000 mm (about 40 in) on the coast to nearly 2500 mm (about 100 in) in sections of the N mountains. Summer precipitation is scant in all parts of the country.

**Plants and Animals.** On the coastal region is found the typical Mediterranean chaparral vegetation of drought-resistant shrubs. Forests cover nearly 40% of the total land area. Thick forests are generally found only at higher elevations in the mountains; much of the other growth is scrub forests. Some common trees are oak, elm, pine, beech, and birch. Wildlife, found in the more inaccessible mountain regions, includes eagles, wolves, deer, and wild boar.

**Mineral Resources.** Albania is well endowed in mineral resources and is especially rich in high-quality chromium ores. Other minerals are petroleum, copper, nickel, coal (mostly low-quality lignite), iron ore, phosphates, and natural gas.

POPULATION

Albania is one of the most ethnically homogeneous countries in the world; about 98% of its people are Albanians, a group that is believed to be descended from the Illyrians, an Indo-European people who inhabited the area in ancient times. Minority groups include Greeks, Macedonians, Gypsies, Serbs, and Bulgarians.

The Albanians are divided into two main branches: the Ghegs and the Tosks. The border between the two groups is roughly formed by the Shkumbi R., the Ghegs occupying the area to the N and the Tosks occupying the area to the S. The groups are distinguished by minor differences in physical traits, dialects, and customs.

**Population Characteristics.** The population was estimated (1993) at 3,422,000. Albania has the highest rate of natural increase of any European nation (nearly 2% yearly in the early 1990s). Before World War II the population was mainly rural; since the 1950s rapid urbanization has occurred along with industrial development. About 36% was classified as urban in the early 1990s.

**Principal Cities.** The capital and chief city is Tiranë, with a population of 244,200 (1990 est.). Other major cities are the port and industrial center of Durrës (85,400), the agricultural marketing center of Elbasan (83,300), the ancient town of Shkodër (81,900), and the seaport of Vlorë (73,800).

**Language.** The Albanian language is usually classified in the Thraco-Illyrian subfamily of the Indo-European languages and has two main dialects: Gheg and Tosk. During the Communist period an official language, based on Tosk dialects, was adopted.

**Religion.** In 1967 the Albanian government abolished all religious institutions. Previously about 70% of the population was Muslim, 20% Greek Orthodox, and 10% Roman Catholic. Freedom of worship was officially restored in 1990.

*Durrës, Albania, seaport on the Adriatic, showing the main square and waterfront.*

## Albania: Map Index

### Cities and Towns

| | |
|---|---|
| Berat | A3 |
| Durrës | A2 |
| Elbasan | B2 |
| Ersekë | B3 |
| Fier | A3 |
| Gjirokastër | B3 |
| Kavajë | A2 |
| Korçë | B3 |
| Krujë | A2 |
| Kukës | B1 |
| Laç | A2 |
| Lushnjë | A3 |
| Peshkopi | B2 |
| Pogradec | B3 |
| Pukë | A1 |
| Sarandë | A4 |
| Shëngjin | A2 |
| Shkodër | A1 |
| Tiranë, *capital* | A2 |
| Vlorë | A3 |

### Other Features

| | |
|---|---|
| Adriatic, *sea* | A2 |
| Buene, *river* | A2 |
| Devoll, *river* | B3 |
| Drin, *river* | A1 |
| Erzen, *river* | A2 |
| Ionian, *sea* | A4 |
| Korab, *mt.* | B2 |
| Mat, *river* | B2 |
| North Albanian Alps, *range* | A1 |
| Ohrid, *lake* | B2 |
| Osum, *river* | B3 |
| Otranto, *strait* | A3 |
| Prespa, *lake* | C3 |
| Scutari, *lake* | A1 |
| Seman, *river* | A3 |
| Shkumbin, *river* | A2 |
| Vijosë, *river* | A3 |

© GeoSystems Global Corp.

## EDUCATION AND CULTURE

During most of the more than 400 years of Ottoman rule, the Albanian language and culture were suppressed. No Albanian-language school was permitted until the 1880s. While the Communist government held power, Albanian culture was influenced first by Soviet and then by Chinese models. Albania underwent a cultural revolution in the mid-1960s, and until the end of the 1980s most Western influences were suppressed.

**Education.** Primary education is free and compulsory for children between the ages of 7 and 15. In the early 1990s about 557,000 students were enrolled in primary schools; enrollment in secondary and technical schools totaled about 206,000 students. Institutions of higher education had a total combined enrollment of about 27,000 students. The University of Tiranë (formerly Enver Hoxha University), founded in 1957, has about 8750 students. The Communists combined education on the secondary and higher levels with work in factories or collective farms and military service. The literacy rate increased dramatically from 20% in 1939 to more than 90% in the late 1980s.

**Cultural Institutions.** Albania has more than 3600 libraries, the most important of which is the National Library (1922) in Tiranë with 1 million volumes. Also in Tiranë are the national companies of opera, theater, and ballet and the principal museums.

## GOVERNMENT

The constitution of 1946 proclaimed Albania a people's republic. A second constitution, enacted in 1976, was superseded in 1991 by an interim constitution that changed the name of the country to the Republic of Albania.

**Executive and Legislature.** Under the interim constitution of 1991, executive power rests with the president of the republic, who is commander in chief of the armed forces. The president, who is indirectly elected by the legislature, appoints the prime minister to head the Council of Ministers. The nation's first free multiparty legislative elections were held in 1991; voting for a reconstituted parliament of 140 seats (100 directly elected, and the remainder to be chosen by proportional representation) took place in March 1992.

**Judiciary.** The highest judicial body is the supreme court, the members of which are elected by the People's Assembly for terms of four years. Justice is dispensed by appellate and district courts. Judges of the lower courts are nominated by the Higher Judicial Council, which is headed by the president of the republic.

**Local Government.** Albania is divided into 27 districts. Local administration has been performed since 1991 by multiparty executive committees.

**Political Parties.** From the mid-1940s through the '80s the country's only political party was the Communist party, officially known as the Albanian Party of Labor (APL). Opposition parties were legalized in December 1990. In the March 1992 election, the Democratic party defeated the former Communists, running as the Albanian Socialist party.

**Health and Welfare.** The government provides retirement pensions, free medical care, workers' compensation, paid vacations, and other benefits for all workers and their families. Steps have been taken to correct the problem of insufficient medical personnel and facilities.

**Defense.** In the early 1990s Albania's army numbered about 60,000 persons; navy, about 2000; and air force, about 11,000.

## ECONOMY

Agriculture, mining, and manufacturing are the mainstays of the economy. Under the Communist government, industry was nationalized and foreign investment prohibited; agriculture was either collectivized or conducted on state farms. Since the fall of the Communist regime, land has been privatized, and foreign investment encouraged. Albania still remains one of the poorest European countries, with a gross national product estimated at $760 per capita as the 1990s began. Unable to produce enough grain to meet domestic needs in the early 1990s, Albania depended on food aid from Western Europe. As the country's unemployment rate rose to 40%, more than 300,000 Albanians found jobs abroad, mainly in Greece. The country's estimated annual budget included $1.1 billion in revenue and $1.4 billion in expenditure.

**Labor.** More than 1.4 million Albanians were economically active in the early 1990s; about 47% of the wage labor force engaged in agriculture, 30% in industry, and 23% in services. Under the Communist government, most workers belonged to the Central Council of Albanian Trade Unions, which was closely allied with the Communist party. Independent trade unions were established in 1991.

**Agriculture, Forestry, and Fishing.** About one-fifth of the country's land is arable. Major drainage and reclamation projects since the 1950s have added greatly to the total farmland. The major crops (with estimates of annual production in the early 1990s) include fruits and vegetables (248,000 metric tons), wheat (330,000 metric tons), corn (200,000 metric tons), sugar beets (140,000 metric tons), and potatoes (60,000 metric tons). Grapes, olives, cotton, and tobacco are also grown. Efforts have been made to improve the quality of a livestock population that includes some 500,000 cattle, 1 million sheep, and 170,000 pigs. Timberlands are an important natural resource and yield wood for fuel, lumber, and veneer. In the early 1990s the annual fish catch from the Mediterranean was 12,000 metric tons.

**Mining.** Mining is an important sector of the Albanian economy. In the early 1990s the annual output of crude petroleum was 7.8 million barrels. Albania is traditionally one of the world's largest producers of chromite ore, but annual output slumped to 612,000 metric tons in the early 1990s. Other major exploited minerals are copper, nickel, coal, iron ore, and phosphates.

**Manufacturing.** The Communist government emphasized the development of the formerly small manufacturing sector. Beginning in the late 1950s Albania established (first with Soviet and then with Chinese assistance) factories producing chemicals, cement, fertilizers, and machinery. Other plants included oil refineries, textile mills, and an iron and steel mill at Elbasan. Manufactured products also included asphalt, copper items, cigarettes, beer, and processed foods. Manufacturing declined drastically in the early 1990s, as many factories were dismantled.

**Energy.** With its numerous mountain streams, Albania has great potential for developing hydroelectricity. Annual electric-power production in the early 1990s was about 2.8 billion kwh, of which more than 90% was generated by hydroelectric plants.

**Currency and Banking.** The monetary unit of Albania is the lek (110 leks equal U.S.$1; 1994). The Albanian State Bank, which was organized in 1945, is the sole bank of currency issue. The National Commercial Bank of Albania, founded in 1993, functions as a central bank.

**Commerce and Trade.** The principal imports are heavy machinery, mineral fuels and lubricants, iron and steel items, and electronic and precision equipment. Exports include crude petroleum, asphalt, iron ore, chromium ore, copper, vegetables and fruit, tobacco, and wine. In the early 1990s annual exports earned about $45 million and imports cost about $120 million. Albania's main trading partners were Italy, the Republic of Macedonia, Germany, and other European countries.

**Transportation.** Albania had no railroads before 1948; Tiranë and Durrës are now linked by rail with other major industrial centers. In the early 1990s there were about 670 km (about 420 mi) of railroad and about 7450 km (about 4630 mi) of roads. The only navigable river is the Buenë R., in the NW. The major ports are Durrës, Vlorë, Sarandë, and Shëngjin. Albania's one airport (at Tiranë) has flights to cities in several neighboring countries.

**Communications.** During the Communist period all communications media in Albania were closely controlled by the government. In the late 1980s there were about 515,000 radios and 325,000 televisions. At that time the country had only two daily newspapers, and one of these, the daily *The Voice of the People,* was the official organ of the central committee of the Albanian Party of Labor. Several non-Communist dailies began publishing in the early 1990s.

## HISTORY

The Albanians are considered descendants of the Illyrians, an Indo-European people who settled the western part of the Balkan Peninsula at, or shortly after, the end of the Bronze Age (c. 1000 BC). The Illyrians established their own states during the 5th and the 3d centuries BC.

**Ancient Times.** The Adrians Kingdom, founded in the 3d century BC, was the most prominent of the ancient states. It extended from the Dalmatian coast to the coastal regions of present-day Albania and reached the peak of its power during King Agron's reign (250–231 BC). The Adrians Kingdom became a naval power, preying on Rome's shipping and endangering its trade in the Adriatic. In 168 BC Rome conquered the Illyrian Kingdom and thereafter ruled it for more than five centuries. In the beginning of the Roman occupation, Albania proper became an important center, connecting Rome with Byzantium by its Via Egnatia.

The Illyrians played an important role in the Roman Empire. Several of the emperors were of Illyrian origin, namely, Claudius II, Aurelian, Diocletian, and Probus (232?–282?) in the 3d century AD, Constantine the Great in the 4th century, and Justinian in the 6th century.

**Middle Ages.** With the division of the Roman Empire in AD 395, Albania became part of the Eastern Empire. During this period Albanian ports, such as Durrachium (Durrës), became important trade centers.

As the power of the empire declined, the Illyrian provinces were plagued by migrating tribes vying for control of the western parts of the Balkans. The Goths and Huns came in the 4th century, the Bulgars in the 5th century, and during the 6th and 7th centuries large numbers of Slavs began to penetrate Illyrian territories. Faced with the danger of assimiliation, the Albanians—who had been converted to Christianity—moved southward, settling mainly in the rugged mountain regions, where they were nominally under the rule of the East Roman, or Byzantine, Empire.

During the 11th and the 12th centuries Albania was overrun by the Normans, and in 1190, during a period of Byzantine weakness, the Albanian prince Progon established an independent state. This lasted until the middle of the 13th century, after which the country relapsed into disunity. In the 14th century it was conquered by the Serbs.

With the collapse of the Serbian Empire under Stephen Dushan (1308?–55) in 1355, Albania fell under the domination of local feudal lords. The Topias and the Dukagjinis ruled in the north, the Muzakas and the Shpatas in the south.

**Ottoman Rule.** The Ottoman Turks invaded Albania at the end of the 14th century. Under the leadership of George Kastrioti, called Scanderbeg, the Albanians waged a successful 25-year struggle against Turkish occupation. In 1448 and in 1466 Scanderbeg repulsed large Turkish expeditions, but after his death in 1468, Albania became part of the Ottoman Empire. Many Albanians immigrated to Italy, and the majority of the population converted to Islam. During the nearly five centuries of Turkish occupation, many Albanians rose to high positions in the empire.

The Turks never had total control over Albania. In the latter part of the 1700s, many native princes rose to prominence. From 1775 to 1796, the Bushatis ruled the Shkodër Duchy, extending their authority over northern and central Albania. From 1790 to 1822, Ali Pasha (1741–1822) ruled the duchy of Janina, which extended from Vlorë and Berat to Çamëria and Thessaly.

At the end of the 19th century nationalistic sentiments awakened. During the period of the Albanian League (1878–81), the Albanians waged a heroic struggle to preserve their territorial integrity against encroachments from their neighbors and to win autonomy from Turkey.

**Independence.** On Nov. 28, 1912, after a series of revolts against Turkey, Albanian patriots led by Ismail Qemal (1844–1919) proclaimed the country's independence. At the London Conference of December 1912, the Great Powers recognized Albania's independence. The 1913 frontier demarcation by a special commission appointed by the Great Powers, however, excluded from Albania more than half its territory, including Kosovë and Çamëria, and about 40 percent of its people.

Today several hundred thousand Albanians live in Greece, and about 2 million in Yugoslavia.

The Great Powers selected the German prince Wilhelm zu Wied (1876–1945) as Albania's ruler. Prince Wilhelm arrived in March 1914, but because of local opposition and the outbreak of World War I, he was forced to flee the country six months later. During the war, Albania became a battlefield for the Great Powers; with the coming of peace, it again faced the prospect of dismemberment by its neighbors. The Paris Peace Conference, however, rejected claims put forth by Greece, Serbia and Montenegro, and Italy, and Albania was saved from partition.

At the Congress of Lushnje, in January 1920, the Albanians established a provincial government and a council of regency; the following summer Italy recognized Albania's independence. During the next four years Albania was beset by a fierce struggle for power among competing political factions. By 1925 Ahmet Zogu (1895–1961) had achieved preeminence, and he ruled the country first as president, but from 1928 to 1939 as Zog I, king of the Albanians—a title that symbolically embraced the Albanian minorities in Greece and Yugoslavia. King Zog introduced broad cultural and economic reforms but entered into a political and military alliance with Fascist Italy. Heavy economic dependence on Italy in turn led to Italian interference in Albania's domestic and foreign affairs, and on April 7, 1939, Mussolini's troops occupied Albania. King Victor Emmanuel III of Italy was immediately proclaimed king of Albania.

**World War II.** Armed resistance to the invaders began soon after the invasion, but the few scattered Communist groups existing at the time did not participate in the resistance.

The Albanian Communist party was founded in November 1941, and Enver Hoxha, a young Western-educated schoolteacher, was elected its general secretary. The Communists launched their resistance movement against the invaders with the creation of the National Liberation Movement in September 1942 and the organization of the National Liberation Army in July 1943. The Allied command in Italy supplied material assistance.

In September 1943, preparing the ground for a seizure of power following the anticipated defeat of Germany, the Communists also launched a campaign against the nationalist organizations Balli Kombëtar (National Front) and Legaliteti (Legality Movement). After a bloody civil war, the nationalists were defeated, and by October 1944 the Communists were able to form a provisional government headed by Hoxha. A month later they seized control of the entire country.

*Ruins of a Roman amphitheater at Butrint, on the southwest coast of Albania.*            Malcolm J. Gilson—Black Star

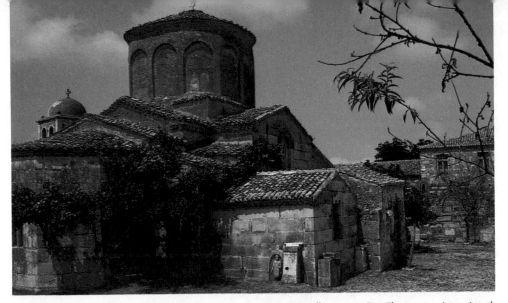

The Byzantine Church of St. Mary at Apollonia, near Fier. The area was intermittently under Byzantine rule from 535 to 1204.  Malcolm J. Gilson–Black Star

**The People's Republic.** On Jan. 11, 1946, a constituent assembly, elected the previous month, proclaimed the People's Republic of Albania. In March, a new constitution was promulgated and a new government formed, with Hoxha as prime minister. The Communist regime initiated a massive campaign of purges to eliminate real and potential opponents. Excessive wealth in private property was confiscated, all industrial plants and mines were nationalized, and a radical agrarian reform was instituted.

***Relations with neighbors.*** From 1944 to 1948, Albania's foreign policy was characterized by tense relations with Greece and the West and a close alliance with Yugoslavia. Plans, in fact, were under way for its absorption into Yugoslavia.

Following the Soviet-Yugoslav break in 1948, however, Albania aligned with the Soviet Union and subsequently received large-scale assistance from the USSR and other socialist countries. In 1949 it was admitted to the Council for Mutual Economic Assistance (COMECON), and in 1955 it became a member of the Warsaw Pact.

In 1954 Hoxha relinquished the premiership to his deputy, Mehmet Shehu (1913–81), but continued to dominate the country as head of the Albanian Communist party. Albania's relations with the Soviet bloc began to deteriorate in the mid- and late 1950s, when Hoxha refused to go along with Moscow's policies of de-Stalinization, peaceful coexistence with capitalist countries, and rapprochement with Yugoslavia.

***Alliance with China.*** Albania's views on the most important issues affecting the socialist camp were similar to those of China, and by late 1960 the government had clearly moved toward an alliance with Peking. In response, the Soviet Union and its East European allies cut off all assistance to Albania. Finally, in December 1961, the Soviet Union broke diplomatic relations with Albania.

China immediately sent in experts to fill the gap created by the withdrawal of Soviet advisers and provided low interest credits for Albania's five-year plans. This enabled the country to defy the Soviet Union and to proceed with its economic development.

The Soviet invasion of Czechoslovakia in 1968 caused Albania to reassess its foreign policy in general and its heavy reliance on China in particular. It normalized relations with Greece and Yugoslavia and expanded contacts with many Western and Third World nations.

***Going it alone.*** China's foreign policy reorientation in the early 1970s and the subsequent Sino-American rapprochement caused a cooling off in Albanian-Chinese relations. After several public Albanian condemnations of Chinese foreign policy, Peking cut off all aid to its former Balkan ally in July 1978. Following the break with China, Hoxha's regime adopted a strategy of independent economic development, maintaining that reliance on foreign assistance compromises a nation's political independence. The late 1970s and early '80s brought steady improvement in Albania's relations with Greece, West European nations, and the less developed countries; however, contacts with Yugoslavia were strained because of what the Albanian government alleged was mistreatment of ethnic Albanians in the southern Yugoslav province of Kosovo.

335

In December 1981 the government announced that Premier Shehu had committed suicide; he was later denounced as a foreign agent, and his supporters purged. Adil Çarçani (1922– ) became premier in January 1982, and Ramiz Alia (1925– ) replaced Haxhi Lleshi (1913– ) as president in November. After Hoxha's death in 1985, Alia became leader of the Communist party. With the wave of democratization sweeping Eastern Europe in the late 1980s, Albania eased restrictions on religion and foreign travel, legalized opposition political parties, and broadened contacts with the West; diplomatic relations with the U.S. were resumed in March 1991 after a 51-year break. The Communists won in Albania's first free multiparty parliamentary elections, and enacted a new interim charter creating the post of president of the republic, to which Alia was then elected by the People's Assembly. The Communist party, which in June changed its name to the Albanian Socialist party, was defeated in elections in March 1992. In April Alia resigned, and parliament elected Sali Berisha (1944– ), the first non-Communist president since World War II. Voters in November 1994 dealt a blow to Berisha by rejecting a new constitution he had supported.                    E.Bi.

*For further information on this topic, see the Bibliography in volume 28, sections 1002–4.*

**ALBANIAN LANGUAGE,** separate subfamily of the Indo-European languages (q.v.), sometimes classified as the only surviving branch of the Thraco-Illyrian subfamily. It is the official language of Albania, and is spoken in parts of Yugoslavia, and isolated pockets in southern Italy and Greece. Two major dialects have been developing differently for about 1000 years: Gheg, spoken in northern Albania, above the Shkumbi River; and Tosk, found to the south and in the Italian and Greek enclaves. The speakers generally can understand one another. A South Gheg dialect was the official language of Albania from 1909 until World War II; thereafter it was based on Tosk. Its grammar is most similar to that of Modern Greek and Romanian. The vocabulary includes many loanwords from Latin, Romanian, and Balkan languages. Written in Roman script, a limited amount of literature exists in Albanian, most of it produced after the 19th-century national revival.

**ALBANY,** city, seat of Dougherty Co., SW Georgia, on the Flint R.; inc. 1838. It is the shipping and industrial center of a farming area known for its pecans, peanuts, and livestock; large textile, meat-packing, and candy-manufacturing plants are here. Albany State College (1903), a junior college and a museum with Creek Indian artifacts are here, and a large U.S. Marine Corps supply base is nearby. The city hosts an annual pecan festival. Nearby is Radium Springs, a large natural spring. The city, named for Albany, N.Y., was an important cotton market until the early 20th century. Pop. (1980) 74,550; (1990) 78,122.

**ALBANY,** city, capital of New York State and seat of Albany Co., a port of entry on the Hudson R. at the E terminus of the New York State Barge Canal system, in the E part of the state, near Troy; inc. 1686. The city's economy is centered around state government activities, but it also is a transportation, banking, medical, and educational center; products include motor-vehicle equipment, sporting goods, felt, clothing, chemicals, and metal items. Albany serves as a gateway to resort areas in the Catskill, Adirondack, and Berkshire mountains. Among points of interest are the mansion (1762) in which the American Revolution general Philip Schuyler lived, now a state historic site; the Old Dutch Church (1799); and the State Capitol (1867–98). Government activities are concentrated at the Empire State Plaza. Institutions of higher education include the State University of New York at Albany (1844); Albany College of Pharmacy (1881); Albany Law School (1851); Albany Medical College (1839); and the College of Saint Rose (1920).

Visited in 1609 by the English navigator Henry Hudson during his exploration of the river that was later named for him, the city was settled in 1614 with the establishment of Fort Nassau, a Dutch trading post. In 1624 a group of Walloons built Fort Orange, which, in 1629, became the permanent settlement of Beverwyck. Following the surrender of Fort Orange to the British in 1664, the city's name was changed to honor the duke of York and Albany (later James II).

Albany's reputation as the Cradle of the Union was the result of the meeting here in 1754 of the Albany Congress, which adopted Benjamin Franklin's Plan of Union, a forerunner of the U.S. Constitution. Albany was heavily damaged by the British during the American Revolution. In 1797 it was chosen as the permanent state capital. Its commercial growth was spurred by the completion of the Champlain Canal (1822), Erie Canal (1825), and Mohawk and Hudson Railroad (1831), the first steam railway in the U.S. Albany's economy declined in the mid-1900s but was revived by the expansion of government facilities beginning in the 1960s. Pop. (1980) 101,727; (1990) 101,082.

*For further information on this topic, see the Bibliography in volume 28, sections 1172–3.*

**ALBANY,** city, seat of Linn Co. and also in Benton Co., W Oregon, at the junction of the Willamette and Calapooya rivers; settled 1846, inc. as a city 1864. Major industries include grass seed, food processing, and the production of zirconium, titanium, hafnium, and other metals; and wood and paper products. The city, site of a U.S. Bureau of Mines experimental station, is named for Albany, N.Y. Pop. (1980) 26,678; (1990) 29,462.

**ALBANY,** river, N Ontario, rising in Lake Saint Joseph. The river flows E for 982 km (610 mi) before emptying into James Bay, near Fort Albany. The Albany was once an important route for fur traders.

**ALBANY CONGRESS,** meeting in Albany, N.Y., in 1754, attended by representatives of New York, Pennsylvania, Maryland, the New England colonies, and the Iroquois Confederacy. Convened to strengthen ties with the Indians in preparation for war with France, it is best known for its espousal of a plan for colonial union devised by Benjamin Franklin. The Albany plan called for a common representative council elected by the colonial legislatures and a president-general appointed by the Crown. Although never implemented, the plan prefigured the later union of states.

**ALBANY REGENCY,** popular name for a group of Democratic party politicians whose activities were centered in Albany, N.Y., and who took a leading part in national and New York State politics between 1820 and 1850. The Regency was one of the earliest effective political machines in the U.S. Most of its members simultaneously held public offices and party positions, using both to bolster their own private fortunes and those of their party. Among its prominent members were Martin Van Buren, who rose from state office to the U.S. presidency, and William Marcy, who became governor of New York State and a cabinet member under Presidents James Knox Polk and Franklin Pierce. A split in the New York Democratic party after 1844 weakened the Regency, and eventually it was dissolved.

**ALBATEGNIUS** *or* **ALBATENIUS.** *See* AL-BAT-TANI.

**ALBATROSS,** common name applied to large seabirds of the family Diomedeidae in the order Procellariiformes, which includes the petrels and shearwaters. Albatross bills are characterized by a markedly hooked upper mandible with tubular nostrils protruding from the base. The feet are strongly webbed and lack a hind claw; the wings are long and narrow. Thirteen species of albatross can be found mainly throughout seas of the southern hemisphere, from the Antarctic region north to the Tropics.

Albatrosses are nomadic birds that spend months wandering great distances over the oceans. They sleep on the ocean surface, drink seawater, and feed on cuttlefish, other small marine animals, and refuse from ships. They return to land only to breed, at which time they perform a stylized courting ritual of elaborate bowing and posturing. Albatrosses nest on barren islands, close to shore; the nest usually is a depression in the ground containing a single egg. When hatched, the nestling is covered with brownish down, and it grows to adulthood relatively slowly. Their relative fearlessness around humans has led the albatrosses to be nicknamed "gooneys"; nesting sites near military airstrips on

*Hen and chick of the black-browed albatross,* Diomedea melanophrys, *which is native to the Falkland Islands.*                    Francisco Erize–Bruce Coleman, Inc.

islands have sometimes created problems because of the birds' interference with takeoffs and landings. At sea albatrosses often follow a ship for days, diving to recover refuse from the wake of the ship. They are seldom harmed because of a superstition held by sailors that killing the bird brings bad luck. The superstition forms the theme of "The Rime of the Ancient Mariner" by the English poet Samuel Taylor Coleridge.

Well-known species include the wandering albatross, *Diomedea exulans,* a huge bird with a 4-m (12-ft) wingspread. The plumage of adults is white with black wing tips; young birds are chocolate brown and become whiter yearly. The Laysan albatross, *D. immutabilis,* is a smaller, brown-winged species with a sooty-black spot near the eyes and a gray bill. Another smaller species is the black-footed albatross, *D. nigripes.*

**AL-BATTANI,** full name ABU-ABDULLAH MUHAMMAD IBN JABIR AL-BATTANI (c. 858–929), leading Arab astronomer and mathematician of his time, known also as Albatenius. His astronomical observations at ar-Raqqah, Syria, extended for a period of more than 40 years. He also made important contributions to pure mathematics. He introduced the use of sines in mathematical calculations, computed a table of cotangents, and formulated certain propositions in spherical trigonometry. His astronomical works, published as *De Motu Stellarum* (Concerning the Motion of the Stars, 1537), corrected errors of the Alexandrian astronomer Ptolemy in regard to the inclination of the ecliptic and the length of the year.

**ALBEE, Edward Franklin** (1928–    ), American playwright, born in Washington, D.C., and adopted as an infant by the American theater executive Reed A. Albee (1886–1961) of the Keith-Albee chain of vaudeville and motion picture theaters. Albee attended a number of preparatory schools and, for a short time, Trinity College in Hartford, Conn. He wrote his first one-act play, *The Zoo Story* (1959), in three weeks. Among his other plays are the one-act *The American Dream* (1961); *Who's Afraid of Virginia Woolf?* (1962); *The Ballad of the Sad Café* (1963), adapted from a novel by the American author Carson McCullers; *Tiny Alice* (1964); and *A Delicate Balance* (1966), for which he won the 1967 Pulitzer Prize in drama. For *Seascape* (1975), which had only a brief Broadway run, Albee won his second Pulitzer Prize. His later works include *The Lady from Dubuque* (1977) and *Three Tall Women* (1994), for which he received his third Pulitzer Prize in drama. His early plays are marked by themes that are typical of the theater of the absurd, in which characters are unable or unwilling to communicate meaningfully or to sympathize or empathize with one another. Albee's most successful plays focus on the subject of familial relationships.

**ALBEMARLE SOUND,** inlet of the Atlantic Ocean, NE North Carolina. Albemarle Sound extends inland for about 95 km (about 60 mi); the width varies from 6 to 24 km (from 4 to 15 mi). Depths seldom exceed 6 m (20 ft), and in many sections are less than 1.5 m (less than 5 ft). A narrow island at the mouth prevents the sound from being affected by the tides. The Roanoke and Chowan rivers flow into the upper extremity. The sound is connected by channels with Currituck and Pamlico sounds.

**ALBÉNIZ, Isaac Manuel Francisco** (1860–1909), one of the leading composers of Spanish music. Born in Camprodón, he was a child prodigy on the piano. At the age of 13 he ran away from home, working as an itinerant pianist in Latin America. He later studied at the Brussels Conservatory (1875–78), with the Hungarian pianist-composer Franz Liszt (1878), and in 1883 with the Spanish nationalist composer Felipe Pedrell (1841-1922). He settled in Paris in 1892, becoming associated with the French composer Vincent d'Indy. Albéniz is most noted for his piano works, imbued with the spirit of Spanish folk music; his masterpiece is the evocative suite *Iberia* (1906–9), virtuosic and musically complex. His most important nonpiano work is the opera *Pepita Jiménez* (1896).

**ALBERS, Josef** (1888–1976), American painter, graphic artist, and influential teacher, who investigated color relationships in his geometrical abstractions. Born in Bottrop, Germany, Albers attended art schools in Berlin, Essen, and Munich and then studied (1920–23) and taught design in the avant-garde Bauhaus (q.v.) for 10 years. He emphasized functionalism and suitability in modern design. After the Nazis closed the Bauhaus in 1933, Albers went to Black Mountain College, North Carolina, where he taught Bauhaus principles to his pupils, including the painter Robert Rauschenberg and the composer John Cage. When Yale University formed (1950) a department of design, Albers became its head, retiring from that position in 1958.

Albers emphasized rectilinear shapes of strong, flat color. The interplay of hues heightened the nonrepresentational, purely optical effect of the forms. In the famous experimental *Homage to the Square* series (started in the early 1950s), progressively smaller forms help illustrate his theories of how changes in placement, shape, and light produce changes in color. Albers's *Interaction of Color* (1963) is a basic text. His work influenced the op and minimal art of the 1960s.

**ALBERT I** (1875–1934), king of the Belgians (1909–34), nephew of King Leopold II. He was born in Brussels and educated privately and at the École Militaire. As count of Flanders he traveled widely, visiting the U.S. in 1898 and touring the Belgian Congo in 1900. His democratic manner made him the most popular member of the reigning house. After he acceded to the throne upon the death of Leopold II in 1909, Albert ordered many improvements in the administration of the Congo. He also called for strengthening of the Belgian military to meet the threat of war in Europe.

While on a visit to Berlin in 1913, Albert was informed of Germany's plans for war by Emperor William II. He immediately warned France and on July 31, 1914, sent a personal letter to the German emperor informing him that Belgium would remain neutral. Three days later German troops invaded. Albert assumed active command of his army but could only mount a delaying action. He and his army fought alongside British and French troops until the armistice was signed in 1918.

After the war Albert made a plea to the Allies for abolition of the Treaty of London, which made Belgium neutral ground and thus vulnerable to invasion. As a result, the abolition was incorporated into the Treaty of Versailles. Albert supported industrial expansion and the development of a strong merchant fleet as the best methods of national recovery. In 1934 he was killed by a fall while mountain climbing. He was succeeded by his eldest son, Leopold III.

**ALBERT II** (1934–    ), king of the Belgians, (1993–    ). The second son of King Leopold II and Queen Astrid (1905–35), he was born in Brussels and educated in Geneva and Brussels. During World War II he and his family were deported to Germany. He entered the Belgian military in 1953 and served with the navy. In 1959 he married the Italian princess Donna Paola Ruffodi Calabria (1937–    ). He has been a member of the nation's senate, president of the Belgian Red Cross, and a member of the International Olympic Committee. After the death of his brother, King Baudouin, Albert acceded to the throne on Aug. 9, 1993.

**ALBERT III** (1414–86), elector of Brandenburg (1470–86), born in Tangermünde, Germany. He was nicknamed Achilles and Ulysses, because his unusual physical strength and extraordinarily shrewd mind gave him in contemporary eyes a resemblance to these Greek heroes. In 1440, on the death of his father, Frederick I (b. 1372?), the territorial possessions of the Hohenzollerns were divided among Frederick's three sons. Albert received the principality of Ansbach, and John (1406–64), the principality of Bayreuth; Frederick (1413–71) became Elector Frederick II

of Brandenburg. His brothers' lands eventually came into Albert's possession; he inherited Bayreuth from John and received Brandenburg through the abdication of Frederick II in 1470. Albert strengthened the Hohenzollern hold on Brandenburg by warring against independent towns and princes and by providing against dispersal of the family lands after his death. His *Dispositio Achillea* (The Political Testament of Achilles), made public in 1473, provided that at his death Brandenburg should go intact to his oldest son, and the Hohenzollern lands in Franconia go intact to his two younger sons, and that in all succeeding generations both parts of the family holdings should descend only to oldest sons.

**ALBERT,** full name ALBERT FRANCIS CHARLES AUGUSTUS EMMANUEL OF SAXE-COBURG-GOTHA (1819–61), prince consort to Queen Victoria of England. He was born near Coburg, Germany, a younger son of Ernest I (1784–1844), duke of Saxe-Coburg-Gotha. In 1840 he married Victoria, who had been queen for three years, and he soon became her most trusted adviser. In this role he exerted enormous influence on policies and events, in international as well as national matters, becoming in truth the power behind the throne. He was an active and effective patron of the arts and sciences, organizing such enterprises as the epochal Great Exhibition of 1851 at the Crystal Palace, to stimulate the growth of British commerce, industry, and national pride. Although regarded by many Britons as a meddling foreigner, Albert succeeded in strengthening the monarchy and in encouraging social progress. Overburdened with work, he succumbed to typhoid fever at the age of 42.

**ALBERT I** (1248–1308), Holy Roman emperor (1298–1308) and duke of Austria (1282–1308). He received the duchy of Austria in 1282 from his father, Rudolf I of Habsburg, king of Germany and Holy Roman emperor. After Rudolf's death in 1291, the German imperial electors refused to recognize Albert's claim to the throne and named Adolf of Nassau (c. 1250-98) king of Germany. With the help of a coalition of German princes, Albert deposed and succeeded Adolf in 1298. Pope Boniface VIII recognized him as Holy Roman emperor in 1303, but he was never crowned. During his reign he adopted measures beneficial to serfs, Jews, and the mercantile class; obtained the crown of Bohemia for his son Rudolf (1282–1307); and in 1307 waged an unsuccessful war against Thuringia. He was murdered by a nephew, John of Swabia (1290–1313), whose inheritance he had withheld. He was succeeded by Henry of Luxemburg, Holy Roman emperor as Henry VII.

**ALBERT II** (1397–1439), Holy Roman emperor (1438–39) and duke of Austria (1404–39) as Albert

V. He inherited the duchy in 1404 and in 1437 succeeded his father-in-law, the Holy Roman emperor Sigismund, as king of Bohemia and Hungary. With him began the long Habsburg rule over the Holy Roman Empire. In 1438 he became king of Germany. Although recognized as Holy Roman emperor, he was never crowned. During Albert's brief reign, the Poles invaded Bohemia, and the Turks invaded Hungary.

**ALBERT** (1828–1902), king of Saxony (1873–1902), noted for his military ability. At the age of 21, he served as a captain in the army of the duchies of Schleswig and Holstein in their war against the Danes. In 1866, during the Seven Weeks' War between Austria and Prussia, Albert commanded a Saxon corps, which distinguished itself at the decisive Battle of Königgrätz by a firm stand against the Prussians. In the Franco-Prussian War of 1870–71, in which Saxony fought on the side of Prussia, Albert commanded the Saxon army that helped defeat the French at Gravelotte, France. He was then placed in command of the so-called Fourth Army, which fought at Sedan, France, and took part in the siege of Paris. After the armistice, Albert commanded the German army that occupied France, and upon the declaration of peace he became an inspector general and field marshal of the German army. During his reign, Albert encouraged industrialization and administrative reforms.

**ALBERT, LAKE,** also Albert Nyanza and Lake Mobutu Sese Seko, lake, E central Africa, in W Uganda and NE Zaire. Located in the Great Rift Valley, Lake Albert is elliptical in shape, about 160 km (about 100 mi) long and about 35 km (about 22 mi) at the widest part, with no depth exceeding 17 m (55 ft); the area is about 5350 sq km (about 2065 sq mi). The surface of the lake is about 610 m (about 2000 ft) above sea level and is estimated to have been about 915 m (about 3000 ft) above sea level in recent geological times. One of the sources of the Nile R., Lake Albert receives the waters of Lake Victoria to the SE by way of the Victoria Nile and of Lake Edward to the SW by way of the Semliki R. It is drained to the White Nile on the N by way of the Albert Nile. Lake Albert was sighted in 1864 by the British explorer Sir Samuel Baker, who named it in honor of Albert, prince consort of Great Britain. Since 1894 it has formed part of the boundary line between Uganda and Zaire.

**ALBERTA,** province, westernmost of the Prairie provinces of Canada, bounded on the N by the Northwest Territories, on the E by Saskatchewan, on the S by the state of Montana, and on the SW and W by British Columbia. Alberta is a wholly inland territory.

The province is called Sunny Alberta, because it has more hours of sunshine a year than any other province. Alberta entered the Dominion on Sept. 1, 1905, with Saskatchewan as the eighth and ninth provinces. With its extensive, fertile prairie lands, Alberta's economy was dominated by agriculture. Since the 1950s, however, mineral extraction has become a leading sector of the economy. Alberta is now Canada's largest producer of petroleum and natural gas. The province is named for Princess Louise Caroline Alberta (1848–1939), who was the wife of a Canadian governor-general and a daughter of Queen Victoria.

LAND AND RESOURCES

Alberta, with an area of 661,190 sq km (255,286 sq mi), is the fourth largest province in Canada; about 10% of the land area is owned by the federal government. The province is roughly in the shape of a rectangle lacking its SW corner; its extreme dimensions are about 1220 km (about 760 mi) from N to S and about 650 km (about 400 mi) from E to W. Alberta's highest point, Mt. Columbia (3747 m/12,294 ft), is in the Rocky Mts. along the SW border; the lowest, 170 m (557 ft), is in Wood Buffalo National Park in the NE.

**Physical Geography.** The Rocky Mts. and foothill region in the SW is Alberta's most striking relief feature. The NW–SE-trending fold mountains that make up this region have been heavily glaciated and provide some of Canada's most spectacular scenery. Numerous remnant glaciers dot the uplands. Soils here are thin or nonexistent.

The NE section of the province is occupied by the edge of the Canadian Shield (q.v.), a generally hilly but low-lying area. In the SE the Cypress Hills constitute a bedrock upland rising to about 610 m (about 2000 ft) above the surrounding plains. This is one of the few apparently unglaciated regions of the S prairies.

The remaining three-quarters of the province lies within the glaciated N Interior Plains of North America. This area has a certain uniformity throughout, imposed by the effects of continental glaciation on the natural landscape. Former glacial lake basins, till plains, end moraines, sandy outwash plains, and areas of rolling till provide a great deal of variety in the surface landforms. The Alberta Plain in the S is a gently rolling grasslands region, trees being confined to the river valleys; the soils of this region are notably fertile. The Alberta Plateau, to the N, is a forested region; it is bounded on the E by the Saskatchewan Plain, which contains great oil sand deposits.

**Rivers and Lakes.** Alberta's two longest rivers, the Peace and the Athabasca, flow from the Rockies N to the Arctic Ocean. Perhaps more important

The great Saskatchewan River system is represented in Alberta by the South and North Saskatchewan rivers. The valley of the latter is shown here, with Mt. Saskatchewan in the background.                    Keith Gunnar–Bruce Coleman, Inc.

in human terms are the various mountain streams that unite to form the North and South Saskatchewan rivers, for they flow E across the province's more heavily settled agricultural regions into Saskatchewan and eventually to Hudson Bay. In the extreme S, the Milk R. and its tributaries flow S into the Mississippi Basin. The province's largest lakes, Claire and Athabasca, are in the N, but numerous smaller lakes are also found in the region.

**Climate.** Alberta has a continental climate, with cold winters and mild summers. In the N and central regions the average annual temperature is 1.7° C (35° F); S of Calgary the average annual temperature is 4.4° C (40° F), except in the Rocky Mts., where it is about –1.1° C (about 30° F). Winter temperatures in the SW, modified by frequent chinooks (warm winds that descend the Rocky Mts.), are the mildest in the Prairie provinces. Summer temperatures, while generally cooler than in S Saskatchewan and S Manitoba, provide adequate heat for grain production. The maximum temperature recorded in Alberta is 43.3° C (109.9° F), in 1931 at Bassano Dam in the S; the minimum, –61.1° C (–78° F), in 1911 at Fort Vermillion. Because the Rocky Mts. prevent many of the moist air masses from reaching the province, the average annual rainfall is only about 430 mm (about 17 in). Winters are dry; much of the annual precipitation comes in the summer. Summertime thunderstorms are often severe, and south-central Alberta has a reputation as one of the worst hailstorm belts of North America.

**Plants and Animals.** Grasslands are found in the SE part of the province. Mixed grasses and a variety of flowering plants, such as vetch, anemone, and flowering cinquefoil, are found here. To the N and W the grasslands grade into a parkland, containing stands of aspens, which eventually give way to mixed and coniferous forests. The entire N half of Alberta is forest-covered; the principal tree species are spruce, pine, fir, aspen, larch, and poplar. Commercial forests cover about 39% of the total land area. In the mountains, coniferous forest gives way with increasing elevation to alpine vegetation. The provincial flower, the wild rose, is found in most areas.

Larger mammals found in the province include grizzly and black bear, moose, caribou, and elk, in the N and the mountainous regions. White-tailed and mule deer and coyote are numerous in the S and central areas. Mountain goat and bighorn sheep are found in the Rocky Mts. Migratory waterfowl, as well as the prairie chicken, partridge, and pheasant, are abundant in Alberta in the summer and fall. Mountain streams and the larger lakes support a large sports fishery and a small

341

commercial fishing industry. Among the most important species are trout, walleye, goldeye, whitefish, and northern pike.

**Mineral Resources.** Petroleum and natural gas, found in the sedimentary rocks that underlie nearly the whole province, are Alberta's greatest mineral resources. The oil-bearing sands in the vicinity of Fort McMurray constitute one of the world's great oil reserves. Coal is also abundant, not only in the foothills, where it is mined in several locations, but also on the plains. Other mineral resources include sulfur, sand, gravel, limestone, salt, and peat.                    A.H.P.

## POPULATION

According to the 1991 census, Alberta had 2,545,553 inhabitants, an increase of 7.6% over 1986. The average population density in 1991 was 4 people per sq km (10 per sq mi). The distribution of population, however, was very uneven; more than 60% of the province's inhabitants lived in the two largest metropolitan areas, and most of the N half of the province had a population density of less than 1 person for every 3 sq km (less than 1 per sq mi). English was the only mother tongue of about 85% of the population; French, for a little more than 5%. Approximately 15% of the population was foreign born, consisting largely of people from Great Britain and the U.S., but also from countries of N and E Europe. More than 68,000 American Indians lived in Alberta, mostly on reservations; the principal Indian groups included the Cree, Blackfoot, Blood, and Piegan. More than 40,000 Métis, or persons of mixed Indian and European ancestry, also resided in the province. The United Church of Canada and the Roman Catholic Church were the largest religious groups. About 80% of all Albertans lived in areas defined as urban and the rest in rural areas. The province's biggest cities are Calgary and Edmonton, the capital; the next largest cities—Lethbridge, Red Deer, and Medicine Hat—are much smaller.

## EDUCATION AND CULTURAL ACTIVITY

The number of educational and cultural institutions in Alberta has grown rapidly since the 1950s, when the provincial economy boomed with the exploitation of its vast mineral resources.

**Education.** The first schools in Alberta were established by missionaries in the mid-19th century. In 1884 the territorial government established a public school system and provided for school districts to be supported by local taxes. By the early 1990s Alberta had 1832 elementary and secondary schools, with a combined enrollment of about 534,400 students, and 23 institutions of higher education, with a total enrollment of 75,500 students. The University of Alberta (1906), in Edmonton, is the oldest and largest university in the province. Also prominent are the University of Calgary (1945), in Calgary; the University of Lethbridge (1967), in Lethbridge; and Athabasca University (1970), in Athabasca.

**Cultural Institutions.** Most of Alberta's noteworthy museums and other cultural facilities are in either Edmonton or Calgary. The Provincial Mu-

*Moraine Lake, in an exquisite setting, is a primary attraction of Banff National Park, along the British Columbia border.* Halle Flygare–Bruce Coleman, Inc.

# Alberta: Map Index

## Cities and Towns

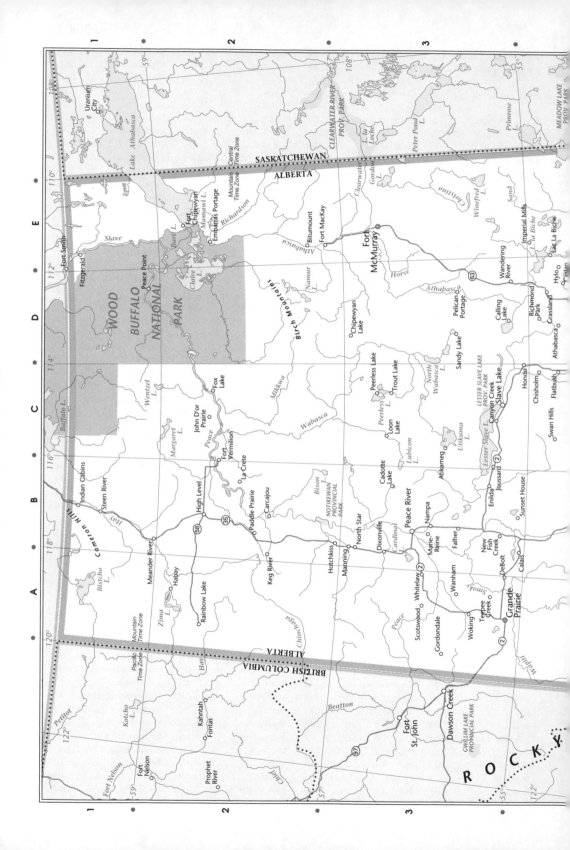

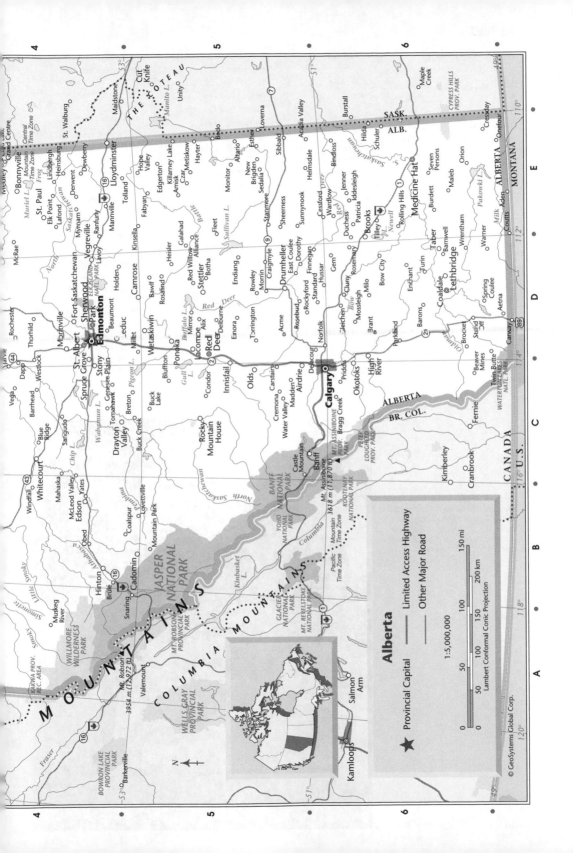

# ALBERTA

*Bighorn sheep were once numerous throughout Alberta. Today they are found only in remote areas, such as this glen in the shadow of Mt. Rundle, near Banff.*    **Canadian Consulate**

The Calgary business area skyline, showing Calgary Tower, an observatory column offering a spectacular view of the Rocky Mts. George Hunter–FPG International

seum and Archives; Edmonton Art Gallery, with a collection of Canadian art; the Space Sciences Centre; Muttart Conservatory, with extensive botanical displays; the University of Alberta Museum and Art Gallery; the Edmonton Symphony Orchestra; and the Edmonton Opera Company are all located in Edmonton. Calgary is the home of the Glenbow Museum, the Calgary Philharmonic Orchestra, and Theatre Calgary (both located in the Calgary Centre for Performing Arts), the Southern Alberta Opera, and Dinosaur Park. Three additional museums of note include the Luxton Museum, with exhibits exclusively on Indian themes; the Banff Park Museum, which displays stuffed animals and birds from the surrounding area; and the Whyte Museum of the Canadian Rockies, emphasizing local history and culture, all in Banff. Also of interest are the Nikka Yuko Japanese Garden, in Lethbridge; and the Royal Tyrrell Museum of Paleontology, featuring exhibits on the region's geological history, in Drumheller.

**Historical Sites.** For the most part, the historical points of interest in Alberta commemorate the province's early traders and settlers. Rocky Mountain House National Historic Site, in Rocky Mountain House, contains trading posts owned by the North West Co. and by its rival, the Hudson's Bay Co. Other sites of note are Heritage Park, in Calgary, an area of preserved historic buildings; Fort Edmonton Park, in Edmonton; Fort Whoop-up, a reproduction of the early fort, in Lethbridge; and Fort Macleod, a replica of Alberta's first North West Mounted Police post established in 1874, in Fort Macleod.

**Sports and Recreation** Alberta's national parks, provincial parks, and numerous rivers and lakes offer ideal conditions to sightseers and sports enthusiasts. Alberta has the largest area of national parks of any Canadian province. These include Banff National Park (Canada's first national park), Elk Island National Park, Jasper National Park, Waterton Lakes National Park, and Wood Buffalo National Park (qq.v.).

**Communications.** In the late 1980s Alberta had 37 AM and 14 FM commercial radiobroadcasting stations and 12 commercial television stations. The first radio station in the province, CFAC in Calgary, began operation in 1922. CHCT-TV in Calgary, Alberta's first commercial television station, went on the air in 1954. The *Edmonton Bulletin,* the first newspaper published in Alberta, went

# ALBERTA

**JOINED THE CANADIAN CONFEDERATION:** September 1, 1905,
with Saskatchewan, as the 8th and 9th provinces

| | |
|---|---|
| **CAPITAL:** | Edmonton |
| **MOTTO:** | *Fortis et liber* (Strong and free) |
| **NICKNAME:** | Sunny Alberta |
| **FLORAL EMBLEM:** | Wild rose |
| **POPULATION (1991):** | 2,545,553; 4th largest among the provinces and territories |
| **AREA:** | 661,190 sq km (255,286 sq mi); includes 16,800 sq km (6486 sq mi) of inland water; 4th largest province |
| **HIGHEST POINT:** | Mt. Columbia, 3747 m (12,294 ft) |
| **LOWEST POINT:** | 170 m (557 ft), in the northeast |
| **PRINCIPAL RIVERS:** | North Saskatchewan, South Saskatchewan, Athabasca, Peace, Red Deer |
| **PRINCIPAL LAKES:** | Athabasca, Claire, Lesser Slave |
| **CANADIAN PARLIAMENT:** | 6 members of the Senate; 26 members of the House of Commons |

## POPULATION OF ALBERTA SINCE 1901

| Year of Census | Population | Percentage of Total Can. Pop. |
|---|---|---|
| 1901 | 73,022 | 1.4% |
| 1911 | 374,295 | 5.2% |
| 1921 | 588,454 | 6.7% |
| 1931 | 731,605 | 7.0% |
| 1941 | 796,169 | 6.9% |
| 1971 | 1,627,874 | 7.5% |
| 1981 | 2,237,724 | 9.2% |
| 1986 | 2,365,825 | 9.3% |
| 1991 | 2,545,553 | 9.3% |

## POPULATION OF TEN LARGEST COMMUNITIES

| | 1991 Census | 1986 Census |
|---|---|---|
| Calgary | 710,677 | 636,843 |
| Edmonton | 616,741 | 573,982 |
| Lethbridge | 60,974 | 58,841 |
| Red Deer | 58,134 | 54,425 |
| Medicine Hat | 43,625 | 41,823 |
| Saint Albert | 42,146 | 36,710 |
| Fort McMurray | 34,706 | 34,949 |
| Grande Prairie | 28,271 | 26,471 |
| Leduc | 13,970 | 13,126 |
| Camrose | 13,420 | 12,968 |

## CLIMATE

| | CALGARY | EDMONTON |
|---|---|---|
| Average January temperature range | −15° to −3.3° C (5° to 26° F) | −18.3° to −8.3° F (−1° to 17° F) |
| Average July temperature range | 9.4° to 24.4° C (49° to 76° F) | 10.6° to 21.7° C (51° to 71° F) |
| Average annual temperature | 2.2° C (36° F) | 1.7° C (35° F) |
| Average annual precipitation | 437 mm (17 in) | 447 mm (18 in) |
| Average annual snowfall | 1539 mm (61 in) | 1321 mm (52 in) |
| Mean number of days per year with appreciable precipitation | 113 | 121 |
| Average dates of freezing temperatures (0° C/32° F or less): | | |
| Last in spring | May 28 | May 14 |
| First in autumn | Sept. 12 | Sept. 19 |

**NATURAL REGIONS OF ALBERTA**

ALBERTA — CANADIAN SHIELD
PLATEAU — SASKATCHEWAN PLAIN
Peace R.
Athabasca R.
Saskatchewan R.
N. Saskatchewan R.
ROCKY MOUNTAINS
ALBERTA PLAIN
Bow R.
CYPRESS HILLS

# PRINCIPAL PRODUCTS OF ALBERTA

## ECONOMY

Province budget................... revenue $14.0 billion
                              expenditure $14.7 billion
Provincial gross domestic product ......... $70.6 billion
Personal disposable income, per capita ........ $17,204
Labor force.................................... 1,358,000
 Employed in services     37%
 Employed in commerce    17%
 Employed in manufacturing and construction 14%
 Employed in agriculture    7%
 Employed in public administration  6%

| | Quantity Produced | Value |
|---|---|---|

**FARM PRODUCTS** ........................ **$3.7 billion**

**Crops**.................................... **$1.5 billion**
 Wheat ......... 7.8 million metric tons ... $627 million
 Canola ........ 1.6 million metric tons ... $309 million
 Barley ........ 5.9 million metric tons ... $191 million
 Vegetables.................................. $41 million
 Floriculture and nursery products.......... $40 million
 Potatoes....... 240,000 metric tons....... $38 million
**Livestock and Livestock Products**....... **$2.2 billion**
 Cattle, calves .. 1.2 million .............. $1.5 billion
 Hogs .......... 1.8 million............... $267 million
 Dairy products.. 581,000 kiloliters ........ $247 million
 Poultry........ 62,000 metric tons....... $100 million
 Eggs ......... 447 million ............... $42 million

**MINERALS**................................. **$16.1 billion**
 Petroleum ..... 72.2 million cu m......... $8.8 billion
 Natural gas .... 85.2 billion cu m ......... $4.3 billion
 Natural gas
  byproducts .. 23.7 million cu m....... $2.0 billion
 Coal.......... 32.4 million metric tons .. $541 million
 Sulfur,
  elemental ... 5.6 million metric tons ... $200 million

**FISHING** ........ **2200 metric tons** ........ **$2 million**

**FURS** ........... **125,000 pelts** ........... **$2 million**

**FORESTRY** ...... **12.3 million cu m** ...... **$184 million**

Value of Shipments

**MANUFACTURING**........................ **$19.3 billion**
 Food and beverage products ............. $4.7 billion
 Petroleum and coal products ............. $3.3 billion
 Chemical products ....................... $3.2 billion
 Fabricated metal products................ $1.1 billion
 Paper and allied products................ $912 million
 Primary metal products .................. $862 million
 Wood products........................... $841 million
 Machinery .............................. $831 million
 Printing and publishing ................. $761 million
 Nonmetallic mineral products ........... $707 million

Wages and Salaries

**SERVICE-PRODUCING INDUSTRIES**..... **$23.8 billion**
 Community, business, and
  personal services ..................... $10.6 billion
 Trade .................................. $4.9 billion
 Transportation, communications,
  and other utilities....................... $3.4 billion
 Public administration .................... $2.5 billion
 Finance, insurance, and real estate ....... $2.4 billion

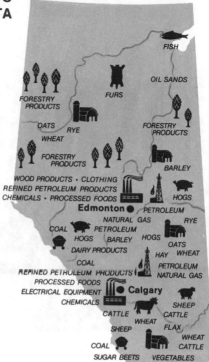

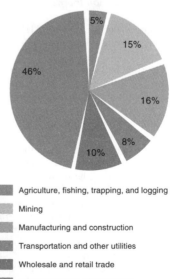

## ANNUAL GROSS DOMESTIC PRODUCT

5%
15%
46%
16%
8%
10%

&#9644; Agriculture, fishing, trapping, and logging

&#9644; Mining

&#9644; Manufacturing and construction

&#9644; Transportation and other utilities

&#9644; Wholesale and retail trade

&#9644; Government and other services

Sources: Canadian government publications
All figures are in Canadian dollars

*Giant excavator, Great Canadian Oil Sands Plant, in Alberta. Alberta is Canada's leading mineral producer, and the oil sands of the Athabasca River region make up one of the world's largest known petroleum deposits.* Photo Services, Government of Alberta

into print in 1880 in Edmonton. By the early 1990s Alberta had nine daily newspapers with a total circulation of about 510,000. Influential dailies included the *Edmonton Journal* and the *Calgary Herald.*

### GOVERNMENT AND POLITICS

The province of Alberta has a parliamentary form of government.

**Executive.** The chief executive of Alberta is the lieutenant governor, who is appointed by the Canadian governor-general in council to serve a 5-year term. The lieutenant governor, representing the British crown, holds a position that is largely honorary. The premier, the leader of the majority party, is the actual head of the provincial government and presides over the executive council. In the early 1990s Alberta's executive council had some 30 members, including the attorney general, provincial treasurer, minister of agriculture, minister of labour, and minister of education. Executive councilors are chosen by the premier from members of the majority party in the legislative assembly.

**Legislature.** The unicameral legislative assembly contains 83 seats, including those of the premier and the members of the executive council. Members of the legislature are popularly elected to a 5-year term; however, the lieutenant governor, on the advice of the premier, may call for an election before the term has been completed.

**Judiciary.** Alberta's highest courts are the court of appeal, with a chief justice and 13 other justices, and the Court of Queen's Bench, with 69 members. In addition, Alberta has provincial courts and family and juvenile courts.

**Local Government.** In the early 1990s Alberta had 30 counties, 16 cities, and 109 towns. Counties and cities were governed by a board of councilors elected to serve 3-year terms.

**National Representation.** Alberta is represented in the Canadian Parliament by 6 senators appointed by the Canadian governor-general in council and by 26 members in the House of Commons popularly elected to serve terms of up to five years.

**Politics.** Since Alberta entered the Dominion in 1905, four political parties have controlled the government: the Liberal party (1905–21), the United Farmers of Alberta (1921–35), the Social Credit party (1935–71), and the Progressive Conservative party (1971–  ).

### ECONOMY

Since the 1950s Alberta has been one of Canada's fastest-growing provinces in terms of income,

350

employment, and overall economic activity. The provincial economy was almost completely based on cattle raising and grain production until 1947, when the discovery of large oil deposits resulted in the establishment of energy-related and other industries. Between 1975 and 1983 total employment in the province rose 41%; growth lagged in the late 1980s, however, because of weak oil prices.

**Agriculture.** Farming accounts for about 4% of the gross domestic product in Alberta each year. The province has some 57,250 farms, which average 364 ha (898 acres) in size. Livestock and livestock products account for nearly 60% of agricultural income. Cattle and dairy farming are of greater importance in Alberta than in any other W Canadian province. About 36% of all cattle, 30% of all sheep, and 16% of all pigs on Canadian farms are located in the province. Crops account for approximately 41% of agricultural income. Wheat, canola, barley, vegetables, and potatoes are the most important crops. Wheat is the predominant crop in the dry-land area of SE Alberta. Irrigation projects, such as those on the Bow, Saint Mary, and Oldman rivers, furnish water for large areas of the province's farmland.

**Forestry and Fishing.** Annual income from forestry and fishing in Alberta is relatively small. Although 39% of the land area of the province is covered by commercial forest, Alberta supplies only 6% of the total Canadian output of lumber. Pulp and paper production is also small, accounting for only 2% of the total national output by value.

The annual commercial fishery production is about 2200 metric tons. Whitefish account for a dominant share of both the volume and the value of the annual catch. The province stocks more than 200 lakes, mainly with rainbow trout.

**Mining.** The mining industry accounts for about 15% of the annual gross domestic product in Alberta. The province is by far the most important Canadian mineral producer. Metallic mineral production is small, but about 83% of all natural gas, about 81% of the crude oil, and some 44% of the coal produced in Canada originate here. Since the opening of the Leduc field in 1947, numerous other oil and natural-gas deposits have been discovered, including the world's largest known reserve of oil-bearing sands—the Athabasca deposit, near Fort McMurray. The province's most important coal mines are in the foothills of the Rocky Mts.

**Manufacturing.** Enterprises engaged in manufacturing account for about 9% of the annual gross domestic product in the province. Although the manufacturing sector has grown steadily, in the early 1990s only about 5% of the total Canadian manufacturing employment was located in the province. Alberta's chief industries are those that produce processed food, refined petroleum and petrochemicals, fabricated metals, paper products, primary metals, wood products, and machinery. Since the 1960s Calgary has emerged as a financial center.

**Tourism.** Alberta ranks second only to British Columbia among the four W Canadian provinces in income derived from tourism. Each year between 3 and 4 million nonresident tourists generate more than Can. $1.8 billion for Alberta's economy. Located in the province are five national parks containing some of the world's most spectacular scenery; Banff and Jasper national parks lead all others in the country in terms of the number of visitors. In addition to federally operated parks, Alberta has 115 provincial parks; most are wilderness areas with camping facilities.

**Transportation.** In the late 1980s Alberta had about 171,200 km (about 106,380 mi) of highways and roads, of which about 35,165 km (about 21,850 mi) were paved. The highway network is densest in the N-S corridor between Edmonton and Calgary. The Alaska Highway (q.v.) passes through the Peace R. agricultural area, and the Mackenzie Highway provides the main land contact with the Northwest Territories. Alberta has about 4455 km (about 2770 mi) of operated mainline railroad track and is served by the two Canadian transcontinental railroads. Major airports are at Calgary and Edmonton.

**Energy.** Electricity-generating plants in Alberta have a total installed capacity of about 8 million kw and produce about 44.3 billion kwh annually. Some 90% of the electricity is generated in conventional steam-powered facilities, mainly from coal and gas. Mining and manufacturing account for about 38% of the total consumption; residences account for about 14%. M.A.M.

## HISTORY

The area that is now Alberta was first explored by French fur traders about 1750. Settlement began with the establishment of trading posts in the 1780s and '90s. From 1821 the region was controlled by the Hudson's Bay Co. In 1870 the new Dominion of Canada bought the company's lands and organized them as the Northwest Territories. Soon the Canadian government sent in the North West Mounted Police to keep order; they concluded treaties with the Indians.

In 1882 the Territories were subdivided into administrative districts. Canada's governor-general, the marquis of Lorne (later the 9th duke of Argyll), Sir John Douglas Sutherland Campbell (1845–1914), named the new district of Alberta after his wife, Princess Louise Caroline Alberta, daughter of Queen Victoria. Alberta was linked to the rest of Canada by the Canadian Pacific Railway in 1883. Settlement remained sparse until new Canadian prosperity after 1896 spurred immigration. Between 1901 and 1911 the population rose from 73,000 to 374,295. As the population grew, the federal government extended the boundaries of the district east and north and, on Sept. 1, 1905, made it a province.

Alberta was at first overwhelmingly agricultural. In the south, ranching predominated; farther north, the principal crop was wheat. Raising, marketing, and transporting agricultural products dominated both provincial and federal politics under a Liberal administration. Albertans, however, began to distrust the urban east and the established Liberal and Conservative parties. In 1921, Alberta elected a farmers' government drawn entirely from the United Farmers Party of Alberta. The Great Depression after 1929 hit the province hard. Wheat prices collapsed, and much of the population found itself on relief. In 1935, Alberta turned to the new Social Credit party, headed by the charismatic radio evangelist William Aberhart. His party, radical in monetary theory, turned out to be conservative in practice, largely because of constitutional limitations on its actions.

World War II was an economic turning point for Alberta. War industries were attracted to Edmonton and Calgary, near which oil had been found. In 1947 a new oil discovery at Leduc made the province a major oil and gas producer. The Social Credit party, which was led by Aberhart's successor, E. C. Manning (1908–   ), occupied itself with transporting oil and natural gas to markets located in the east. In 1958 a gas pipeline to eastern Canada was completed. As industries boomed, the farm population fell from 51 percent in 1931 to only 21 percent in 1961. Average income soared, particularly after world oil prices increased in 1973.

Premier Manning retired in 1968. Three years later the Progressive Conservatives, led by Peter Lougheed (1928–   ), for the first time were able to form Alberta's government. Lougheed's "Alberta-first" policies, stressing industrial development, sometimes led to confrontations with the federal government. Oil-based prosperity fostered a boom during the 1970s, but the recession of the early 1980s and the subsequent collapse of oil and grain prices hurt the province. Donald Getty (1933–   ), Lougheed's successor, easily won a majority in the 1986 election, but had more difficulty in winning in 1989. Largely because of increasing dissatisfaction among Albertans with the power of central Canada in national affairs, Getty was a major participant in the country's constitutional crisis, campaigning vigorously for Senate reform. Getty announced his impend-ing retirement as premier and party leader in September 1992, and Ralph Klein (1942–   ) was chosen in December to succeed him. Klein led his party to victory in the elections of June 1993.

R.Bw.; REV. BY P.R.

*For further information on this topic, see the Bibliography in volume 28, section 1113.*

**ALBERT OF BRANDENBURG** (1490–1545), archbishop of Magdeburg and archbishop and elector of Mainz. He was the younger son of John Cicero (1455–99), the elector of Brandenburg. In 1513 he became archbishop of Magdeburg. The following year he became archbishop and elector of Mainz, and in 1518 he was named a cardinal. In order to pay the expenses involved in obtaining high office, he was granted permission by the pope to sell indulgences. Among his agents in this enterprise was the German monk Johann Tetzel, against whom the 95 theses of Martin Luther were directed. In the ensuing struggle between Catholics and Protestants, Albert adhered to the Catholic church, but acted as peacemaker between the two factions at the Imperial Diet at Augsburg in 1530. Albert was the first German ruler to receive Jesuits in his dominions. Despite his loyalty to the church, he granted religious liberty to his Protestant subjects on condition that they pay his debts of about half a million florins.

**ALBERT EDWARD NYANZA.** See EDWARD, LAKE.

**ALBERTI, Leon Battista** (1404–72), Italian architect and writer, who was the first important art theorist of the Renaissance and among the first to design buildings in a pure classical style based on a study of ancient Roman architecture.

Alberti was born in Genoa on Feb. 14, 1404, the son of a Florentine noble. He received the best education available in the 15th century, first at the school of Barsizia at Padua and then at the University of Bologna. He was proficient in Greek, mathematics, and the natural sciences. As a poet, a philosopher, and one of the first organists of his day, Alberti greatly influenced his contemporaries. In 1432, he was appointed a papal secretary by Pope Eugene IV.

Alberti's architectural training began with the study of antique monuments during his first stay (1432–34) in Rome. Subsequently he joined the papal court in Florence, where he became intensely involved with the cultural life of the city. Among his friends and associates were the great architect Filippo Brunelleschi and the renowned sculptor Donatello. Probably at this time he became familiar with the mathematical laws of linear perspective, which Brunelleschi had studied. As explained in Alberti's treatise, Della Pittora (1436), they were of inestimable value to the

Cathari (from the Greek *katharos,* meaning "purified"), first appeared in northern France and the Low Countries toward the late 11th or early 12th century. Persecuted and expelled from the north, the Catharist preachers traveled south and found far greater success in the semi-independent province of Languedoc and the surrounding areas. There they became known as Albigenses.

The Albigenses believed that the whole of existence was a struggle between two gods: the god of light, goodness, and spirit, usually associated with Jesus Christ and the God of the New Testament; and the god of evil, darkness, and matter, identified both with Satan and the God of the Old Testament. Whether the two deities wielded equal power or whether the forces of evil were subordinate to the forces of good was a question subject to considerable debate; but, by definition, anything material, including wealth, food, and the human body itself, was evil and abhorrent. The soul had been imprisoned by Satan in the human body, and the only hope of human salvation was to live a good and spiritual life. By living a good life, a person could win freedom after death from material existence. Failure to achieve righteousness during one's lifetime would result in the soul's being born again as another human being or even as an animal. The Albigenses believed that Christ was God, but that during his time on earth he was a kind of angel with a phantom body taking the appearance of a man. They held that the traditional Christian church, with its corrupt clergy and its immense material wealth, was the agent of Satan and was to be avoided.

Adherents of the Albigensian doctrine were divided into the simple believers and the "perfects." The perfects vowed themselves to lives of extreme asceticism. Renouncing all possessions, they survived entirely from donations given by the other members. They were forbidden to take oaths, to have sexual relations, or to eat meat, eggs, or cheese. Only the perfects could communicate with God through prayer. The simple believers might hope to become perfects through a long initiation period followed by the rite called *consolamentum,* or baptism of the Holy Spirit through the laying on of hands. Some would receive this rite only when they were near death. They would then attempt to ensure their salvation by abstaining from all food and drink, in effect committing a form of suicide.

The Christian church initially attempted to reconvert the Albigenses through peaceful means. When every attempt failed, Pope Innocent III launched the armed Albigensian Crusade (c. 1209–29) that brutally repressed the Albigenses

and desolated much of southern France. Small groups of Albigenses survived in isolated areas and were pursued by the Inquisition as late as the 14th century.

*See also* BOGOMILS; CATHARI; DUALISM; MANICHAEISM; PAULICIANS.                                    T.N.T.

**ALBINO,** animal or plant without the normal pigmentation of its species. The pigment melanin, primary agent of normal human coloration, is absent in the tissues of human albinos because the enzyme tyrosinase, required for its formation, is lacking. As a result, albinos have pale skin, white or light yellow hair, and eyes that, although actually colorless, appear pink because the blood vessels of the retina are visible. Lacking the protection that pigment affords against strong light, albinos are photophobic (shunning light) and, in ordinary illumination, are inclined to squint. The absence of melanin in certain brain tissues is probably the cause of the nystagmus (oscillation of the eyeballs) characteristic of most albinos.

Albinos occur in all races of humans, most frequently among certain Indian tribes of the southwestern U.S., but nowhere in large numbers. Albinism is transmitted as a recessive hereditary characteristic. Several types of partial albinism exist, including dominant piebald albinism, dominant white forelock, and chromosomal, sex-linked ocular albinism.

Animal albinism, similar to that of humans in its cause, effects, and transmission, has been ob-

*Snowflake, an albino gorilla in the Barcelona, Spain, zoo. As in humans, albinism in animals is caused by a deficiency in normal pigmentation.*
© Marvin E. Newman–The Image Bank

painters of his own and succeeding generations. Alberti took an active part in the literary life of Florence and championed the literary use of Italian rather than the use of Latin. After spending nine years in Florence and other parts of Italy, Alberti returned to Rome in 1452. He was secretary to six popes. Under Pope Nicholas V, he was in charge of the projects for rebuilding Saint Peter's Basilica and the Vatican.

In the late 1440s, Alberti began to work as an architect. Although his buildings rank among the best architecture of the Renaissance, he was a theoretical rather than a practical architect. He furnished the plans of his buildings but never supervised their construction. The classical purity of Alberti's style, which prepared the way for Bramante and later architects, is evident in the facade of the Church of San Francesco at Rimini (1446–55), adapted from the arch of Augustus at Rimini. Alberti had a number of pupils and associates, who carried out his plans for the facade of Santa Maria Novella and the Palazzo Rucellai (1446-51), both in Florence, and other famous buildings. His *De Re Ædificatoria* (1485) was the first printed work on architecture of the Renaissance. He also wrote books on sculpture, the family, government, and literature. Alberti died in Rome on April 25, 1472.

**ALBERTI, Rafael** (1902–  ), Spanish poet, whose first training as an artist is reflected in *A la pintura* (On Painting, 1948), a brilliant attempt to describe one art in terms of another. His first volume of poetry, *Maniero en tierra* (A Sailor on Land, 1924), won a Spanish literary prize in 1925. His masterpiece, however, is considered to be *Sobre los ángeles* (Above the Angels, 1929), a surrealist allegory in which angels represent forces in the real world. After the Spanish civil war, Alberti immigrated to Argentina, returning to Spain in 1977.

**ALBERT NYANZA.** *See* ALBERT, LAKE.

**ALBERTUS MAGNUS, Saint** (c. 1200–80), called Albert the Great and known as *doctor universalis* for his wide interest in natural science. He was especially noted for his introduction of Greek and Arabic science and philosophy to the medieval world.

Born in Lauingen, Bavaria, to a noble military family, Albert was studying at Padua in 1223, when he was attracted to the Dominican Order of Preachers, then less than ten years old. He was ordained in Germany and taught there before going on to the University of Paris, where he became a master of theology in 1245 and subsequently held one of the Dominican chairs of theology. Among his early students was Thomas Aquinas. Albert was an influential teacher, church administrator, and preacher. He traveled through western Europe on behalf of his order and served as a provincial and, briefly, as bishop of Regensburg (1260-62) before returning to teaching and research.

Albert was a key figure in the assimilation of Aristotelian philosophy into medieval Scholasticism and in the revival of natural science that it inspired. Early in the 13th century, a body of philosophical and scientific writings previously unknown to Western philosophers and theologians became a disturbing force in Scholastic circles. These Latin writings, based on Arabic translations of the works of Aristotle, were accompanied by the writings of Arab commentators, notably Avicenna and Averroës. As such, they presented a point of view foreign to the church-trained Scholastics, whose knowledge of Aristotle was confined to his logic (q.v.), as taught and interpreted for centuries by the church, in the tradition of St. Augustine and the Neoplatonists. *See* SCHOLASTICISM.

Albert had, on his journeys, shown an intense interest in natural phenomena, and he seized on Aristotle's scientific writings. He examined them, commented on them, and occasionally contradicted them on the evidence of his own careful observations. He produced essentially new works and, according to the English philosopher Roger Bacon, held much the same authority in his time as did Aristotle himself.

As a theologian, Albert was outstanding among the medieval philosophers but not as innovative as his pupil Aquinas. In his *Summa Theologiae* (c. 1270), he attempted to reconcile Aristotelianism and Christian teachings. He maintained that human reason could not contradict revelation, but he defended the philosopher's right to investigate divine mysteries.

Albert died at Cologne on Nov. 15, 1280. He was beatified in 1622 and declared a saint by Pope Pius XI in 1931, at which time he was acclaimed an official Doctor of the Church. In 1941 Pope Pius XII made him the patron of all who study the natural sciences. His feast day is November 15.                                        D.J.F

**ALBIGENSES,** followers of the single most important heresy within the Christian church during the Middle Ages. They were named after the town of Albi, in southern France, a major center of the movement.

The Albigenses were believers in the Manichean dualistic system that flourished in the Mediterranean area for centuries. The dualists believed in the separate and independent existence of a god of good and a god of evil. Within western Europe, the adherents of dualism, ca

served in most species of domestic animals and in a wide variety of other mammals and birds. The white rabbits, white rats, and white mice common in biological laboratories are true albinos. Forms of albinism occur in cold-blooded animals, but their causes are different. Albinism in frogs and certain salamanders, for example, is apparently caused by hormonal deficiency, because it can be cured by an injection of pituitary hormone. In fish, complete or spotty melanism (atypical black color) or albinism can be induced by merely severing certain nerves. Most cases of so-called albinism in insects are probably color variations rather than the complete absence of pigmentation characteristic of albino mammals. Albinism in plants is always quickly fatal, because the plant cannot manufacture its food without the pigment chlorophyll.                              N.E.M.

**ALBINONI, Tomaso** (1671–1750), Italian composer and violinist, known today for his instrumental music. He was born and lived in Venice, where he produced most of his nearly 50 operas. His instrumental works, frequently played by modern chamber musicians, were admired by Johann Sebastian Bach. They include trio sonatas, concertos for one and for two oboes, and the 1710 concerto for solo violin.

**ALBOIN,** (d. 572), founder of the kingdom of Lombardy in Italy. He became chief of the Lombards in 565, when the tribe lived in the region between the Danube River and the head of the Adriatic Sea. Three years later, with the assistance of the Avars, Alboin defeated the Germanic people known as the Gepidae. After capturing and forcing the Gepidae princess, Rosamund, into marriage Alboin led the Lombards and some 20,000 Saxons across the Alps into northern Italy and established a kingdom in the valley of the Po River, with Pavia as its capital. Soon after, Rosamund had Alboin killed.

**ÅLBORG,** formerly AALBORG (anc. *Alburgum*), city, capital of Nordjylland Co., Denmark, a sea port on the NE portion of the Jutland Peninsula, on the S shore of the Limfjorden, near Århus. The chief products manufactured in Ålborg are cement, tobacco products, and liquor. Founded early in the 11th century, the city has been an episcopal see since 1554. Nearby is Rebild National Park, a memorial to Danish-American friendship dedicated in 1912. Pop. (1993) 157,270.

**ALBRIGHT, Ivan Le Lorraine** (1897–1983), American painter of the magic realist school, who depicted in precise detail the vitality of decaying, moribund objects. Born in Chicago, Albright studied architecture, made surgical drawings for the U.S. Army, and attended the Art Institute of Chicago. He worked ten years on *That Which I Should Have Done I Did Not Do* (1941, Art Institute of Chicago), a painstaking delineation of a decrepit door, weathered funeral wreath, and decayed hand. Albright's morbid subjects aroused much controversy.

**ALBRIGHT, William Foxwell** (1891–1971), American archaeologist and educator, noted for his work in the Middle East. Born of missionary parents in Chile, he studied at Upper Iowa University and earned his Ph.D. in archaeology and linguistics at Johns Hopkins University in 1916. He became director of the American School of Oriental Research in Jerusalem in 1921. In 1929 he was made professor of Semitic languages at Johns Hopkins, a post he held until he acquired emeritus status in 1958. Albright was one of the leading biblical archaeologists of his time, heading numerous expeditions in Palestine, southern Arabia, and adjacent regions. An expert in reconstructing past civilizations from their artifacts, he gained a wide reputation for his identification of "lost" biblical towns and his use of potsherds to date archaeological finds. His more than 800 publications include *From the Stone Age to Christianity* (1940) and *The Bible and the Ancient Near East* (1961).

**ALBUMIN,** one of a class of simple proteins, composed of carbon, hydrogen, oxygen, nitrogen, and a small percentage of sulfur. Albumin is coagulable by heat, mineral acids, alcohol, and ether and is soluble in water and in a weak salt solution. An important part of the diet, albumin is present in such animal tissues as egg white, milk, and muscle, and is found in blood plasma; it occurs also in plants, especially in seeds. Because albumin coagulates when heated to 71° C (160° F), it is useful for removing cloudy precipitates, thus clarifying solutions in sugar refining and other processes. Albumin forms insoluble compounds with many metallic salts, such as bichloride of mercury, copper sulfate, and silver nitrate, and is, therefore, used as an antidote to these poisons. A paste made of albumin mixed with slaked lime sets to a mass of stony hardness and is used as cement for broken earthenware.

**ALBUQUERQUE,** city, seat of Bernalillo Co., central New Mexico, on the Rio Grande; inc. as a city 1891. The largest city in New Mexico, it is a transportation, trade, and manufacturing center. Manufactures include electrical machinery, processed food, aerospace equipment, textiles, clothing, printed materials, and forest products. Albuquerque is also an electronic and nuclear research center; one of the largest employers is a nuclear and solar energy development company. Kirtland Air Force Base (site of the National Atomic Museum) is important to the economy, and many state and federal agencies have offices in the city. Albuquerque, which is served by an international airport, is the seat of the University of New Mexico (1889) and the College of Santa Fe at Albuquerque (1985) and is headquarters for Cibola National Forest. Situated at an altitude of about 1615 m (about 5300 ft), the city is a noted health resort and vacation spot. It has museums of art, natural history, and anthropology, and its Old Town retains a charming Spanish flavor. A hot-air balloon festival, the state fair, and many arts and crafts fairs are held here annually. Nearby are several Indian pueblos, notably at Coronado State Monument; Petroglyph State Park, with old Indian and Spanish carvings on lava; and the Sandia Mts., which have extensive winter-sports facilities.

Albuquerque, founded in 1706, is named for the duke of Alburquerque (d. 1733; the first *r* was later dropped), then viceroy of New Spain. It grew rapidly as a station on the Chihuahua Trail from Santa Fe to Mexico City and was an important U.S. military post from 1846 to 1870. Confederate troops briefly held Albuquerque in 1862, during the American Civil War. In 1880 a new town was laid out nearby to meet the railroad. It grew as a farming hub and health center, gradually enveloping Old Town, which it annexed in 1949. Pop. (1980) 331,767; (1990) 384,736.

**ALBUQUERQUE, Afonso de,** called Afonso the Great (1453–1515), Portuguese navigator, statesman, and founder of the Portuguese Empire in the Orient, born in Alhandra, near Lisbon. He spent his youth at the court of King Alfonso V of Portugal; he later took part in the expedition against the Turks that culminated in a Christian victory at Otranto, Italy, in 1481. In 1503 he made his first trip to the East, traveling with a Portuguese fleet around the Cape of Good Hope to India. Three years later King Emanuel of Portugal appointed him viceroy of all Portuguese possessions in Asia. His predecessor, Francisco de Almeida, at first refused to give up his office and imprisoned Albuquerque from 1508 to 1509. The new viceroy was eventually released to assume office when a fleet arrived from Portugal to free him. As viceroy, Albuquerque captured the Indian district of Goa in 1510. He went on to complete the conquests of Malabar, Sri Lanka, the Sunda Islands, the peninsula of Malacca, and the island of Hormuz at the entrance to the Persian Gulf. He maintained strict military discipline in the territories under his control but was respected and beloved by his subjects.

In spite of his valuable services, Albuquerque was the victim of intrigue at the Portuguese court. In 1515 King Emanuel, who had become suspi-

cious of him, appointed one of Albuquerque's enemies as his successor. Although he was offered assistance to help him resist Emanuel's arbitrary decree, Albuquerque would not violate his allegiance. A few days after receiving notice that he had been superseded, he died at sea off the Malabar coast near Goa. A biography containing his collected papers was written by his son Braz Albuquerque (1500–80) in 1557.

**ALCAEUS** (c. 620–580 BC), Greek poet, born on the island of Lésvos. Alcaeus became a leader against the Lesbian tyrant Pittacus (650?–570 BC); he was banished but after being pardoned, he returned to Lésvos. Of the ten books of his odes, only a few poems in fragmentary form still exist; these, all composed in the Aeolic dialect, are concerned with his grief over the state of Lésvos, his hatred of tyrants, and his own misfortunes; in some of the poems he praises love and wine. Alcaeus invented the Alcaic stanza, which Horace adapted to Latin lyric poetry.

**ALCALÁ DE HENARES,** town, central Spain, in Madrid Province, on the Henares R., near Madrid. An industrial center in which leather products and soap are produced, Alcalá is also a trading center for the surrounding agricultural area. The town was known to the Romans as Complutum. It was destroyed about 1000 and was rebuilt in 1083 by the Moors. The University of Alcalá, which became a leading educational center in Spain, was founded in 1508; it was moved to Madrid in 1836. A celebrated early Bible, the Complutensian Polyglot Bible, was printed in Alcalá in 1517. The town is the birthplace of the Spanish writer Miguel de Cervantes. Pop. (1991) 159,355.

**ALCAMENES** (fl. 420 BC), Greek sculptor, who was a pupil of the Athenian sculptor Phidias and subsequently became his artistic rival. Alcamenes was best known for the chryselephantine (gold and ivory) cult statues of Dionysus, Ares, and Hephaestus that he created for their Athenian shrines. These statues have been lost, but two surviving works in marble—*Procne and Itys* and *Athena of the Gardens*—in the Athens National Archaeological Museum, attest to his great skill.

**ALCAN HIGHWAY.** See ALASKA HIGHWAY.

**ALCATRAZ,** island, W California, in San Francisco Bay, near San Francisco. It rises 40 m (130 ft) above the surface of the bay and is about 535 m (about 1755 ft) long. The Spanish visited the island in 1769. From 1868 to 1933, when the army transferred it to the Department of Justice, it served as a military prison. The island then served as a federal prison for dangerous prisoners until 1963; in 1972 it became part of Golden Gate National Recreation Area.

**ALCESTIS,** in Greek mythology, daughter of Pelias, king of Iolcus in Thessaly. She married Admetus, king of Pharae and friend of the god Apollo. When it was time for Admetus to die, Apollo persuaded the Fates to let him live if he could persuade another to die in his place. Alcestis willingly took poison to spare Admetus's life. Later, Hercules rescued her from Hades.

**ALCHEMY,** ancient art practiced especially in the Middle Ages, devoted chiefly to discovering a substance that would transmute the more common metals into gold or silver and to finding a means of indefinitely prolonging human life. Although its purposes and techniques were dubious and often illusory, alchemy was in many ways the predecessor of modern science, especially the science of chemistry.

The birthplace of alchemy was ancient Egypt, where, in Alexandria, it began to flourish in the Hellenistic period; simultaneously, a school of alchemy was developing in China. The writings of some of the early Greek philosophers might be considered to contain the first chemical theories; and the theory advanced in the 5th century

BC by Empedocles—that all things are composed of air, earth, fire, and water—was influential in alchemy. The Roman emperor Caligula is said to have instituted experiments for producing gold from orpiment, a sulfide of arsenic, and the emperor Diocletian is said to have ordered all Egyptian works concerning the chemistry of gold and silver to be burned in order to stop such experiments. Zosimus the Theban (about AD 250–300) discovered that sulfuric acid is a solvent of metals, and he liberated oxygen from the red oxide of mercury.

The fundamental concept of alchemy stemmed from the Aristotelian doctrine that all things tend to reach perfection. Because other metals were thought to be less "perfect" than gold, it was reasonable to assume that nature formed gold out of other metals deep within the earth and that with sufficient skill and diligence an artisan could duplicate this process in the workshop. Efforts toward this goal were empirical and practical at first, but by the 4th century AD, astrology, magic, and ritual had begun to gain prominence.

*Two alchemists are portrayed in this woodcut from a 16th-century translation of* Summa Perfectionis, *an 8th-century work by Geber.*

A school of pharmacy flourished in Arabia during the caliphates of the Abbasids from 750 to 1258. The earliest known work of this school is the *Summa Perfectionis* (Summit of Perfection), attributed to the Arabian scientist and philosopher Geber; the work is consequently the oldest book on chemistry proper in the world and is a collection of all that was then known and believed. The Arabian alchemists worked with gold and mercury, arsenic and sulfur, and salts and acids, and they became familiar with a wide range of what are now called chemical reagents. They believed that metals are compound bodies, made up of mercury and sulfur in different proportions. Their scientific creed was the potentiality of transmutation, and their methods were mostly blind gropings; yet, in this way, they found many new substances and invented many useful processes.

From the Arabs, alchemy generally found its way through Spain into Europe. The earliest authentic works extant on European alchemy are those of the English monk Roger Bacon and the German philosopher Albertus Magnus; both believed in the possibility of transmuting inferior metals into gold. This idea excited the imagination, and later the avarice, of many persons during the Middle Ages. They believed gold to be the perfect metal and that baser metals were more imperfect than gold. Thus, they sought to fabricate or discover a substance, the so-called philosopher's stone, so much more perfect than gold that it could be used to bring the baser metals up to the perfection of gold.

Roger Bacon believed that gold dissolved in aqua regia was the elixir of life. Albertus Magnus had a great mastery of the practical chemistry of his time. The Italian Scholastic philosopher St. Thomas Aquinas, the Catalan churchman Raymond Lully, and the Benedictine monk Basil Valentine (fl. 15th cent.) also did much to further the progress of chemistry, although along alchemical lines, in discovering the uses of antimony, the manufacture of amalgams, and the isolation of spirits of wine, or ethyl alcohol.

Important compilations of recipes and techniques in this period include *The Pirotechnia* (1540; trans. 1943), by the Italian metallurgist Vannoccio Biringuccio; *Concerning Metals* (1556; trans. 1912), by the German mineralogist Georgius Agricola; and *Alchemia* (1597), by Andreas Libavius (c. 1540–1616), a German naturalist and chemist.

Most famous of all was the 16th-century Swiss alchemist Philippus Paracelsus. Paracelsus held that the elements of compound bodies were salt, sulfur, and mercury, representing, respectively, earth, air, and water; fire he regarded as imponderable, or nonmaterial. He believed, however, in the existence of one undiscovered element common to all, of which the four elements of the ancients were merely derivative forms. This prime element of creation Paracelsus termed *alkahest,* and he maintained that if it were found, it would prove to be the philosopher's stone, the universal medicine, and the irresistible solvent.

After Paracelsus, the alchemists of Europe became divided into two groups. One group was composed of those who earnestly devoted themselves to the scientific discovery of new compounds and reactions; these scientists were the legitimate ancestors of modern chemistry as ushered in by the work of the French chemist Antoine Lavoisier (*see* CHEMISTRY). The other group took up the visionary, metaphysical side of the older alchemy and developed it into a practice based on imposture, necromancy, and fraud, from which the prevailing notion of alchemy is derived.　　　　　　　　　　　　　　　S.Z.L.

*For further information on this topic, see the Bibliography in volume 28, section 407.*

**ALCIBIADES** (c. 450–404 BC), ill-fated Athenian statesman and general, whose opportunistic acts and divisive influence contributed to the defeat of Athens in the Peloponnesian War (431–404 BC). After the death of his father in 447 BC, Alcibiades was raised in the house of his uncle, the Greek statesman Pericles. Alcibiades was influenced by Socrates, who was his personal friend. Alcibiades gained great wealth through his marriage, but he squandered his money and led a dissipated life. By expensive public displays, especially at the Olympian Games of 420, he won the favor of the common people. His only political rival was the Athenian statesman Nicias (d. 413 BC), who had secured a treaty of peace for 50 years between the Athenians and the Spartans. In 415 Alcibiades made himself head of the army and induced the Athenians to undertake an expedition against Syracuse, for which he was elected one of the commanders. Before the departure of the expedition, all the statues of the god Hermes in Athens were mutilated in a single night; the blame for the sacrilege was laid—in all likelihood falsely—on Alcibiades, who was charged with impiety and recalled from the expedition. On his return he fled to Sparta, where he divulged the plans of the enterprise and helped the allied Spartans and Syracusans to defeat the Athenians. For this act of treason, a sentence of death was recorded against him at Athens, and his property was confiscated.

In 414 Alcibiades went with the Spartan expedition to the island of Khios, where he incited an

*An ancient bust of Alcibiades.*          Bettmann Archive

Ionian revolt against the Athenians. Difficulties with the Spartan leaders led to a plot to assassinate Alcibiades. On learning of the plot, Alcibiades fled to the Persian provincial governor Tissaphernes (fl. 413–395 BC) and attempted without success to win him over to the Athenians on the ground that it was in the interest of Persia to prevent Sparta from gaining complete ascendancy over Athens. Alcibiades then offered to bring Persian support to the Athenians if they would revoke the decree making him an exile. His offer was accepted, but he wished to render some service to Athens before returning. He therefore remained abroad and won important victories for the Athenians, including the capture of the cities of Cyzicus, Chalcedon, and Byzantium.

Alcibiades returned to Athens in 407 and was received with general enthusiasm. He was again sent to Asia with 100 ships, but the expedition was defeated at Notium in 406. As a result his enemies brought a new accusation against him, and he was relieved of his command. He thereupon again joined the Persians, taking refuge in Phrygia. At the request of the Athenian government, and with the approval of the Spartans, Alcibiades' residence was set on fire during the night, and, as he fled, he was killed by a volley of arrows.

**ALCINDOR, Lew.** *See* ABDUL-JABBAR, KAREEM.

**ALCMAEON,** in Greek mythology, son of Amphiaraus and Eriphyle. After Amphiaraus was killed in the expedition of the Seven Against Thebes, Alcmaeon led the Epigoni (the sons of the Seven) in a second expedition. To avenge his father's

death, on his return home he killed his mother, since she had coerced her husband to go on the expedition. He afterwards went mad and wandered from place to place, haunted by the avenging goddesses, the Erinyes, until he took refuge at Psophis in Arcadia. There, he married Arsinoe, the king's daughter. When the land was cursed with barrenness because of his presence, he fled to the mouth of the Achelous River and married Callirrhoe, daughter of the river god. The king and his sons pursued Alcmaeon and killed him.

**ALCMAN** (fl. about 625 BC), Greek poet, born in Sardis, in Lydia. Alcman was one of the earliest of the famous lyric poets of Greece and the first known to write choral lyrics in strophic form (*see* ODE). According to tradition, he was a slave who was freed and made a citizen of Sparta. He wrote, in the Doric dialect, *Parthenia* (songs for choruses of virgins), bridal hymns, and verses in praise of love and wine. Only fragments of his poems are extant.

**ALCMENE.** *See* AMPHITRYON; HERCULES

**ALCOHOL** (Arab. *al-kuhul*), term applied to members of a group of chemical compounds and, in popular usage, to the specific compound ethyl alcohol, or ethanol. The Arabic word denotes kohl, a fine powder of antimony used as an eye makeup. The word *alcohol* originally denoted any fine powder; the alchemists of medieval Europe later applied it to essences obtained by distillation, and this led to the current usage.

Alcohols are a class of organic compounds containing the hydroxyl group, OH, attached to a carbon atom. Alcohols have one, two, or three hydroxyl groups attached to their molecules and are thus classified as monohydric, dihydric, or trihydric, respectively. Methanol and ethanol are monohydric alcohols. Alcohols are further classified as primary, secondary, or tertiary, according to whether one, two, or three other carbon atoms are bound to the carbon atom to which the hydroxyl group is bound. Alcohols, although analogous to inorganic bases, are neither acid nor alkaline. They are characterized by many common reactions, the most important of which is the reaction with acids to form substances called esters (q.v.), which are analogous to inorganic salts.

Alcohols are normal by-products of assimilation and digestion and are found in the tissues and fluids of animals and plants.

**Wood Alcohol** Methyl alcohol, or methanol, $CH_3OH$, is the simplest of all the alcohols. It was formerly made by the destructive distillation of wood; however, almost all of the methanol produced today is synthetic, made from hydrogen and carbon monoxide. Methanol is used as a denaturant for grain alcohol (see below), as an anti-freeze, as a solvent for gums and lacquers, and in the synthesis of formaldehyde (q.v.) and other organic compounds. Methanol is also used as an automotive fuel, either by itself or mixed with gasoline to form gasohol (q.v.). When taken internally, by either drinking the liquid or inhaling the vapors, it is a violent poison (q.v.). Methanol melts at −97.8° C (−144.0° F), boils at 64.7° C (148.5° F), and has a sp.gr. of 0.7915 at 20° C (68° F).

**Grain Alcohol.** Ethyl alcohol, or ethanol, $C_2H_5OH$, is a limpid, colorless liquid, with a burning taste and characteristic, agreeable odor. Its low freezing point has made it useful as the fluid in thermometers for temperatures below −40° C (−40° F), the freezing point of mercury, and for other low-temperature purposes, such as for antifreeze in automobile radiators.

Ethanol is normally concentrated by distillation of dilute solutions, but the concentration cannot proceed beyond 97.2 percent by volume. Commercial ethanol contains 95 percent by volume of ethanol and 5 percent of water. Dehydrating agents remove the remaining water and produce absolute ethanol. Ethanol melts at −114.1° C (−173.4° F), boils at 78.5° C (173.3° F), and has a sp.gr. of 0.789 at 20° C (68° F).

Ethanol has been made since ancient times by the fermentation of sugars. All beverage ethanol and more than half of industrial ethanol is still made by this process. Starch from potatoes, corn, or other cereals can be the raw material (*see* FERMENTATION). The yeast enzyme, zymase, changes the simple sugars into ethanol and carbon dioxide. The fermentation reaction, represented by the simple equation

$$C_6H_{12}O_6 \rightarrow 2C_2H_5OH + 2CO_2$$

is actually very complex because impure cultures of yeast produce varying amounts of other substances, including fusel oil, glycerin, and various organic acids. The fermented liquid, containing from 7 to 12 percent ethanol, is concentrated to 95 percent by a series of distillations. In the production of beverages such as whiskey (q.v.) and brandy, some of the impurities, which supply the flavor, are of great value. Much ethanol not intended for drinking is now made synthetically, either from acetaldehyde (q.v.) made from acetylene, or from ethylene made from petroleum. A small amount is made from wood pulp.

Ethanol can be oxidized to form first acetaldehyde and then acetic acid (q.v.). It can be dehydrated to form ether (q.v.). Butadiene (q.v.), used in making synthetic rubber, may be made from ethanol, as are chloroform (q.v.) and many other organic chemicals. Ethanol, like methanol,

is used as an automotive fuel by itself and can be mixed with gasoline to form gasohol. Ethanol is miscible (mixable) in all proportions with water and with most organic solvents. It is useful as a solvent for many substances and in making perfumes, lacquer, celluloid, and explosives. Alcoholic solutions of nonvolatile substances are called tinctures; if the solute is volatile, the solution is called a spirit.

Most industrial ethanol is denatured to prevent its use as a beverage. Completely denatured ethanol contains small amounts, 1 or 2 percent each, of several different unpleasant or poisonous substances. The removal of all these substances would involve a series of treatments more expensive than the federal excise tax on alcoholic beverages. These denaturants render ethanol unfit for many industrial uses. In such industries especially denatured ethanol is used under close federal supervision.

**Higher Alcohols.** Higher alcohols, those of greater molecular weight than ethyl alcohol, have many uses. Isopropyl alcohol is used extensively as a rubbing alcohol, butyl alcohol is a base for perfumes and fixatives, and others are important flavoring agents and perfumes. Polyhydric alcohols, those containing more than one OH group, are also important, as, for example, the trihydric alcohol known as glycerol (q.v.).

**ALCOHOLICS ANONYMOUS** (AA), worldwide fellowship of men and women who meet together to attain and maintain sobriety. It originated in 1935 when Bill W., a New York stockbroker, and Dr. Bob S., a surgeon, met in Akron, Ohio, and started to help each other stay sober. From that modest beginning, AA has grown to an estimated 90,000 groups in 132 countries, with a total membership of more than 2 million.

Men and women of all ages and walks of life are welcome to join in the common cause to help each other toward sobriety. The only requirement for membership is a desire to stop drinking. No dues or fees are required; contributions are entirely voluntary. The AA program is one of total abstinence, in which members are encouraged to stay away from one drink, one day at a time. Their sobriety is maintained through sharing their experience, strength, and hope at group meetings, and following the suggested Twelve Steps to recovery. Even isolated alcoholics in remote regions, without access to AA groups, can seek help from the "Loners" program through the General Service Office in New York City. Intergroup offices in most urban areas provide information on times and places of nearby meetings.

A board of trustees, of whom 7 are nonalcoholics and 14 are AA members, administers the organization's activities in the U.S. and Canada. Regional delegates vote on matters of general significance at annual conferences; an international convention is held every five years. *Alcoholics Anonymous* (1939; 3d ed., 1976), by Bill W., and others, explains the philosophy of AA and contains the Twelve Steps recovery program.

See also AL-ANON AND ALATEEN.

ALCOHOLICS ANONYMOUS

**ALCOHOLISM,** chronic and usually progressive illness involving the excessive inappropriate ingestion of ethyl alcohol (*see* ALCOHOL), whether in the form of familiar alcoholic beverages or as a constituent of other substances. Alcoholism is thought to arise from a combination of a wide range of physiological, psychological, social, and genetic factors. It is characterized by an emotional and often physical dependence on alcohol, and it frequently leads to brain damage or early death.

Some 10 percent of the adult drinkers in the U.S. are considered alcoholics or at least they experience drinking problems to some degree. More males than females are affected, but drinking among the young and among women is increasing. Consumption of alcohol is apparently on the rise in the U.S., countries of the former Soviet Union, and many European nations. This is paralleled by growing evidence of increasing numbers of alcohol-related problems in other nations, including the Third World.

**Development.** Alcoholism, as opposed to merely excessive or irresponsible drinking, has been variously thought of as a symptom of psychological or social stress or as a learned, maladaptive coping behavior. More recently, and probably more accurately, it has come to be viewed as a complex disease entity in its own right. Alcoholism usually develops over a period of years. Early and subtle symptoms include placing excessive importance on the availability of alcohol. Ensuring this availability strongly influences the person's choice of associates or activities. Alcohol comes to be used more as a mood-changing drug than as a foodstuff or beverage served as a part of social custom or religious ritual.

Initially, the alcoholic may demonstrate a high tolerance to alcohol, consuming more and showing less adverse effects than others. Subsequently, however, the person begins to drink against his or her own best interests, as alcohol comes to assume more importance than personal relationships, work, reputation, or even physical health. The person commonly loses control over drinking and is increasingly unable

to predict how much alcohol will be consumed on a given occasion or, if the person is currently abstaining, when the drinking will resume again. Physical addiction to the drug may take place, sometimes eventually leading to drinking around the clock to avoid withdrawal symptoms.

**Effects.** Alcohol has direct toxic as well as sedative effects on the body, and failure to take care of nutritional and other physical needs during prolonged periods of excessive drinking may further complicate matters. Advanced cases often require hospitalization. The effects on major organ systems are cumulative and include a wide range of digestive-system disorders such as ulcers, inflammation of the pancreas, and cirrhosis of the liver. The central and peripheral nervous systems can be permanently damaged. Blackouts, hallucinations, and extreme tremor may occur. The latter symptoms are involved in the most serious alcohol withdrawal syndrome, delirium tremens (q.v.), which can prove fatal if not treated or treated improperly. This is in contrast to withdrawal from narcotic drugs such as heroin, which, although distressful, rarely results in death. Recent evidence has shown that heavy— and even moderate—drinking during pregnancy can cause serious damage to the unborn child: physical or mental retardation or both; a rare but severe expression of this damage is known as fetal alcohol syndrome.

**Treatment.** Treatment of the illness increasingly recognizes alcoholism itself as the primary problem needing attention, rather than regarding it as always secondary to another, underlying problem. Specialized residential treatment facilities and separate units within general or psychiatric hospitals are rapidly increasing in number. As the public becomes more aware of the nature of alcoholism, the social stigma attached to it decreases, alcoholics and their families tend to conceal it less, and diagnosis is not delayed as long. Earlier and better treatment has led to encouragingly high recovery rates.

In addition to managing physical complications and withdrawal states, treatment involves individual counseling and group therapy techniques aimed at complete and comfortable abstinence from alcohol and other mood-changing drugs of addiction. Such abstinence, according to the best current evidence, is the desired goal, despite some highly controversial suggestions that a safe return to social drinking is possible. Addiction to other drugs, particularly to other tranquilizers and sedatives, poses a major hazard to alcoholics. Antabuse, a drug that produces a violent intolerance for alcohol as long as the substance remains in the body, is sometimes used after withdrawal. Alcoholics Anonymous (q.v.), a support group commonly used for those undergoing other treatment, in many cases helps alcoholics to recover without recourse to formal treatment.

Despite these encouraging signs, estimates of the annual number of deaths related to excessive drinking exceed 97,000 in the U.S. alone. Economic costs related to alcoholism are at least $100 billion a year. Additional data are needed on various societal costs of alcoholism as well as on the costs of various modes of treatment compared with their actual results.

*See also* DRUG DEPENDENCE.                         L.B.

*For further information on this topic, see the Bibliography in volume 28, section 501.*

**ALCOTT, (Amos) Bronson** (1799–1888), American educator and philosopher, born in Wolcott, Conn. He developed a method of teaching young children by means of conversation and in 1834 established a school at Boston in which this system was employed. The school was criticized by the press and regarded by the general public as a revolutionary innovation. In 1839 Alcott closed the school and later moved to Concord, Mass. Thereafter he became widely known as a lecturer. He was a prominent abolitionist and a leader of the philosophic doctrine of transcendentalism. His writings include *Observations on the Principles and Methods of Infant Instruction* (1830), *Concord Days* (1872), *Table Talk* (1877), and *Sonnets and Canzonets* (1882).

**ALCOTT, Louisa May** (1832–88), American writer, the daughter of Bronson Alcott, born in Germantown, Pa. She was raised in Boston and was tutored by the American writers Ralph Waldo Emerson and Henry David Thoreau. While serving as a nurse during the American Civil War, she wrote letters to her family that were later published as *Hospital Sketches* (1863). Her most famous works—*Little Women* (1868–69), an autobiographical novel of her childhood, and its sequels, *Little Men* (1871) and *Jo's Boys* (1886)—are considered classics. Like her other books for children, they are characterized by their intimate depiction of family life and loyalties. In order to support her own often poverty-stricken family, Alcott also wrote a number of thrillers. These well-crafted, suspenseful yarns were published pseudonymously in various magazines.

**ALCUIN** or **ALBINUS** (735–804), English scholar and ecclesiastic, born in Yorkshire, and educated at the cathedral school of York. He became the head of the school in 778. During a mission to Rome in 780, he became acquainted with Charlemagne. At the request of Charlemagne, Alcuin directed an educational program among the

Franks from 781 to 790, thereby exercising lasting influence upon the intellectual life of the Western world. In 794 at the council held at Frankfurt he led the successful fight against adoptionism, a heretical belief then dividing the Catholic church. After a brief visit to his native country, he returned to France, where he was made abbot of St. Martin of Tours in 796. He wrote many letters, works on rhetoric, and poems. His letters are among the most valuable sources of information about the social life and humanistic learning of 8th-century France. The impetus given to humanistic studies by Alcuin and his successors led not only to a revival of learning but also to the development of the Carolingian, or Caroline, minuscle, a script that influenced the handwriting of the Renaissance in Italy and, indirectly, the Roman letters of the early Italian typesetters, from which modern type is derived.

**ALDEHYDES,** class of organic compounds that are important in the manufacture of plastics, dyes, food additives, and other chemical compounds. Aldehydes have the general formula

$$R-C=O$$
$$|$$
$$H$$

where R is either a hydrogen atom, as in the case of formaldehyde, or an aliphatic or an aromatic hydrocarbon group.

**ALDEN, John** (1599?–1687), one of the Pilgrims, born in Southampton, England. He went to America on the *Mayflower* in 1620 and was a signer of the Mayflower Compact. He was one of the founders of Plymouth, the first permanent English settlement in New England. In 1623 Alden married Priscilla Mullens (1602?–85?), another Pilgrim. In 1627 or shortly afterward, together with the Plymouth colonist Myles Standish, he founded Duxbury, where he lived until his death. Alden was active in the affairs of Plymouth Colony, serving alternately as assistant to the governor and as deputy from Duxbury. He lived longer than any of the other signers of the Mayflower Compact.

Alden's fame rests chiefly on the romantic tale written by the American poet Henry Wadsworth Longfellow, "The Courtship of Myles Standish" (1858). In the poem, Alden, deeply in love with Priscilla Mullens, proposes to her on behalf of his shy friend Standish, whereupon she inquires, "Why don't you speak for yourself, John?"

**ALDER,** common name for plants of the genus *Alnus*, of the family Betulaceae (*see* BIRCH), order Fagales. They are trees or shrubs, natives of cold and temperate climates. Because the wood resists decay underwater, it is used for bridge pilings. Dye was formerly obtained from the bark of many species. The black alder, *A. glutinosa,* is a native of Europe. It usually grows to about 15 m (about 50 ft). Among the varieties used for ornamental planting are the golden alder, with bright golden-yellow leaves, and the cut-leaved alder, with narrow, deeply incised leaves. The gray alder, *A. incana,* has acute leaves, downy underneath, and grows to a height of about 24 m (about 80 ft).

**ALDER, Kurt** (1902–58), German chemist and Nobel laureate, born in Königshütte (now Chorzów, Poland), and educated at the University of Kiel. Under the guidance of the German chemist Otto Diels (1876–1954), his chief instructor at Kiel, Alder specialized in diene synthesis (later known also as the Diels-Alder reaction), which is essentially the analysis and formation of complex organic compounds. As early as 1928 he and Diels coauthored a paper on this process. Alder was professor of chemistry at the universities of Kiel and Cologne. In 1950 he and Diels were jointly awarded the Nobel Prize in chemistry for their work in diene synthesis.

**ALDERNEY,** most northerly of the Channel Islands (q.v.).

**ALDRICH, Thomas Bailey** (1836–1907), American writer and editor, born in Portsmouth, N.H. He served (1866–74) as editor of *Every Saturday* and later (1881–90) as editor of the *Atlantic Monthly.* His most famous work, *Story of a Bad Boy* (1870), was based on his boyhood experiences in Portsmouth. His collection of short stories, *Marjory*

*Daw and Other People* (1873), is written in a graceful style. Among his other works are the novels *Prudence Palfrey* (1874), *Queen of Sheba* (1877), and *Stillwater Tragedy* (1880).

**ALDRIN, Edwin Eugene, Jr.** (1930– ), American astronaut, known as Buzz, born in Glen Ridge, N.J. He received a B.S. degree (1951) from the U.S. Military Academy. Aldrin served as a combat jet pilot during the Korean War. After receiving an Sc.D. degree (1963) from the Massachusetts Institute of Technology, he became an air force representative at the Manned Spacecraft Center, Houston, Tex., and entered the astronaut training program the following year. During his first space flight in November 1966 as copilot of the earth orbital rendezvous mission *Gemini 12,* Aldrin achieved a record 5.5 hour space walk. In July 1969, Col. Aldrin, as part of the *Apollo 11* lunar mission, became the second man to set foot on the moon. His companions on the mission were Michael Collins and Neil Armstrong.

**ALE,** fermented cereal beverage brewed from an infusion of grain, primarily malted barley, and flavored with hops. About 1524, before the introduction of hops from the Netherlands into England and Germany, the term *ale* was used for any fermented malt beverage. After 1524 the term was applied to all hop-flavored brews, but has since gradually come to indicate only those produced by the top-fermentation process. Ale has a stronger hop flavor and higher alcoholic content than beer. *See also* BREWING.

**ALEICHEM, Shalom.** *See* SHALOM ALEICHEM.

*Alders, Alnus glutinosa, alongside the River Wye in Monmouth, England. A young alder leaf, freshly opened, is shown at right.* 1. © 1973 J. Markham–Bruce Coleman, Inc.
2. © D. Hardley–Bruce Coleman, Inc.

**ALEIJADINHO,** real name Antonio Francisco Lisboa (1738–1814), outstanding Brazilian rococo architect and sculptor. Aleijadinho ("Little Cripple") suffered from a progressively disabling ailment, probably leprosy, that forced him to have his carving implements strapped to his forearms. His masterpieces, the 12 prophets, in soapstone, and 6 polychromed wood scenes of Christ's Passion that he carved (1800–5) for the Church of Bom Jesus de Matozinhos at Congonhas do Campo, are powerfully and superbly executed, with no evidence of his physical handicaps.

**ALEIXANDRE Y MERLO, Vicente** (1898–1984), Spanish poet and Nobel laureate. The lyrical poems in his first book, *Ambito* (Environment, 1928), show an interest in nature, but, as an antifascist in the 1940s, his surrealistic, pessimistic free verse became more concerned with human life, especially with love and death. He widely influenced Spain's poets after the 1930s. Major collections of his works include *Poesías completas* (1960) and *Antología total* (1975). In 1977 he was awarded the Nobel Prize in literature.

**ALEKHINE, Alexander** (1892–1946), Russian chess grand master and world champion, born in Moscow, and educated at the universities of Petrograd (now Saint Petersburg) and Paris. After the Russian Revolution of 1917 he immigrated to France and became a French citizen. He won the rank of chess master at the age of 16 and the rank of grand master at 21. Alekhine won the chess world championship in 1927 from the Cuban chess player José Rául Capablanca and lost it to the Dutch chess player Max Euwe in 1935. Alekhine regained it from Euwe in 1937 and maintained it until his death.

**ALEMÁN, Mateo** (1547–1610?), Spanish novelist, born in Seville, and educated at the University of Seville. He is best known as the author of the novel *The Rogue* (1599; Pt. II, 1604; trans. 1623), which revived the Spanish picaresque novel, or story of a rogue (Span. *pícaro*) and his adventures. Alemán is the first picaresque author whose identity is definitely known. Among Spanish novels of this type *The Rogue* is ranked second only to *Lazarillo de Tormes,* a novel written by an unknown author before 1555. *The Rogue* went through more than 15 editions in five years and has been widely translated.

**ALEMANNI.** *See* Alamanni.

**ALEMÁN VALDÉS, Miguel** (1902–83), president of Mexico (1946–52), born in Sayula, and educated at the National University in Mexico City. In 1930 he was elected deputy from the state of Veracruz, becoming senator in 1935 and governor in 1936. He was minister of the interior from 1940 to 1945, when he resigned to run for president as the candidate of the National Revolutionary party. Elected president of Mexico in 1946, he embarked upon a vigorous program of industrialization, for which he negotiated a large loan from the Export-Import Bank of the U.S. in 1947. Alemán also made long-range plans for the government-controlled oil industry, presided over the expansion of the rail system, and improved Mexico City's water supply. His administration, however, was accused of pervasive corruption, and financial problems surfaced soon after his tenure ended. In his later years, Alemán was involved in promoting tourism and helped to bring the Olympic Games to Mexico City in 1968.

**ALEMBERT, Jean le Rond d'** (1717–83), French mathematician, philosopher, and Encyclopedist. Born in Paris, he was the illegitimate son of the French writer Claudine Guérin de Tencin (1681?–1749) and was left as an infant on the steps of the Chapel of Saint Jean le Rond, from which he received his name. He was educated at the Collège Mazarin, where he excelled in mathematics, physics, and astronomy. At the age of 22 he wrote his first published work, *Mémoire sur le calcul intégral* (Report on Integral Calculus, 1739). His most important scientific work, *Traité de dynamique* (Treatise on Dynamics, 1743), which marks an epoch in the science of mechanics, is based on the theory known as d'Alembert's principle, discovered by him at the age of 26 and expressed in the proposition: The resultant of the forces impressed upon a system is equivalent to the effective force of the entire system. His *Réflexions sur la cause générale des vents* (Reflections on the General Cause of Winds, 1746) contains the first conception of the calculus of partial differential equations. In 1749 he proposed the first analytical solution of the precession of the equinoxes. In 1751 he became associated with the French Encyclopedist Denis Diderot in editing the great French *Encyclopédie.* Although he withdrew from the editorship in 1758 because of government interference with the publication, d'Alembert continued to contribute articles on science and philosophy.

**ALENÇON,** town, N France, capital of Orne Department, on the Sarthe R., in Normandy. Manufactures include motor-vehicle parts, textiles, and printed materials. In addition, the production of *point d'Alençon,* a fine lace, begun in 1665, is still carried on. Crystals of smoky quartz, known as Alençon diamonds, are found nearby. The town, capital of the old county and duchy of Alençon, was generally a royal possession from the 13th century and formally passed to the Crown in the mid-16th century; it was the seat of the court of Margaret of Navarre. Alençon was damaged in World War II. Pop. (1990) 31,139.

**ALEPPO.** *See* HALAB.

**ALESSANDRIA,** city, NW Italy, capital of Alessandria Province, in Piedmont Region, on the Tanaro R. It is a commercial and industrial center; manufactures include hats and furniture. Alessandria was founded in 1168 by the people of Cremona, Milan, and Placentia (now Piacenza) as a bulwark against Frederick I, Holy Roman emperor, who was attempting to subjugate N Italy. It was named in honor of Pope Alexander III, chief opponent of the emperor, and was brought into the Lombard league. Massimiliano Sforza (1493–1530), duke of Milan, plundered Alessandria in 1522. In 1707 it was taken by the Austrian general Eugene, prince of Savoy, during the War of the Spanish Succession. Following the defeat of Austria by France at the Battle of Marengo in 1800, during the Napoleonic Wars, the French held the city for 14 years. It was the principal stronghold of the Piedmontese during the insurrection of Lombardy and Venetia in 1848–49. Pop. (1991) 93,866.

**ALESSANDRI PALMA, Arturo** (1868–1950), Chilean statesman, born in Linares, and educated at the University of Chile. In 1897 he was elected to the Chamber of Deputies of the National Congress and served for six consecutive terms. After holding a number of cabinet posts, he began to campaign for the presidency in 1918 as a spokesman for labor and the middle class. He was elected in 1920; in 1921 he introduced a broad program of social and political reform, including the separation of church and state and the direct election of the president and vice-president by popular vote. He resigned in 1924, after a military junta seized power. He was recalled, however, by another junta of young army officers that seized power in 1925, but remained in office only a short time before resigning. During this period he drafted and had ratified by popular vote the constitution under which Chile was long governed. He was president again from 1932 to 1938. During this term he created a central bank to stabilize the Chilean currency and introduced reforms of the tax system and monetary and banking laws. He was elected senator in 1946. His son, Jorge Alessandri Rodríguez (1896–1986), was president from 1958 to 1964.

**ALETSCH,** glacier, S Switzerland, largest glacier of Europe, in the Alps. It is about 20 km (about 12.5 mi) long and sweeps around the S side of the Jungfrau in the Swiss Alps. At the E extremity lies a glacier lake, Märjelensee (2350 m/7711 ft above sea level). To the NW rises Aletschhorn (4195 m/13,763 ft), which was first climbed in 1859.

**ALEUT,** native people of the Aleutian Islands, generally classified as a North American Indian group, of the Eskimo-Aleut language family and of the Arctic culture area. Most Aleuts are of average height and stocky build and have dark skin and coarse black hair.

The Aleuts originally moved to the islands from Alaska. They led a primitive existence, dependent on the sea for food, clothing, fuel, and materials for shelter such as driftwood and whalebone. When the islands came under Russian domination in the 1740s, the native population numbered about 25,000. The Aleuts, who were skillful hunters of sea mammals, were exploited by the fur traders. Harsh treatment by the Russians and smallpox and influenza epidemics took their toll on the native population. Today, most are members of the Russian Orthodox church. They live in wood frame houses, engage in fishing, hunting, and raising sheep, and eat processed foods. In 1990, 23,797 people claimed Aleut ancestry.

*See also* AMERICAN INDIANS.

*For further information on this topic, see the Bibliography in volume 28, section 1109.*

**ALEUTIAN ISLANDS,** chain of about 150 small islands, SW Alaska, separating the N Pacific Ocean from the Bering Sea. The archipelago extends about 1930 km (about 1200 mi) W from the Alaska Peninsula toward Kamchatka Peninsula in Russia. The four main subgroups of the Aleutian Islands from E to W are the Fox Islands, Andreanof Islands, Rat Islands, and Near Islands.

Geologically, the archipelago is a continuation of the Aleutian Range, which is on the Alaskan mainland, and contains a number of volcanic peaks. Shishaldin (2857 m/9372 ft), on Unimak Island, is the highest volcano. Few trees, all of stunted growth, are found, but grasses grow in abundance. Although a few good harbors are found in the archipelago, navigation is dangerous because of perpetual fog and numerous reefs. The native people, known as Aleuts, belong to the Eskimo-Aleut language family and are generally classified ethnologically as North American Indians. Fishing, hunting, and sheep raising are the principal pursuits of the inhabitants. The chief trade center is Unalaska, on the island of Unalaska. The Aleutians were visited in 1741 by the Russian navigator Alexey Ilich Chirikov (1703–48) and Vitus Bering, a Danish navigator in the service of Russia. During World War II, in June 1942, Japanese forces occupied Attu and Kiska islands in the Aleutians, but were forced to surrender them to U.S. forces the following year.

**ALEWIFE,** common name for a food fish, *Alosa pseudoharengus,* of the family Clupeidae (*see* HERRING). It resembles the shad in shape and color but is only about 25 to 30 cm (about 10 to 12 in) long. Early in the summer alewives appear in great numbers on the east coast of North America and enter the rivers to spawn. Many are harvested for pet food or fertilizer. Alewives are also called spring herring; the French-Canadian name for the fish is gaspereau.

**ALEXANDER III** (c. 1105–81), pope (1159–81), who vigorously championed papal authority.

Born Rolando Bandinelli in Siena, Italy, he studied law under the Italian scholar Gratian, later called the father of canon law. Bandinelli taught at Bologna, and his writings in law and in theology earned him the reputation of a scholar. Named a cardinal in 1150, he became papal chancellor in 1153. That same year he was sent as a legate to negotiate the Treaty of Constance with Holy Roman Emperor Frederick I.

Following the death of Pope Adrian IV in 1159, Bandinelli was elected pope as Alexander III, over the opposition of Frederick I. Much of his pontificate was involved in the complex politics of the time, as he and European rulers strove to reduce one another to subservience. He forced Henry II of England to do public penance for the murder of Thomas à Becket, archbishop of Canterbury. After a long struggle with three successive antipopes who were supported by Frederick I, Alexander, aided by the Lombard League, forced Frederick to recognize his elevation to the papacy.

Forced by Frederick I into exile in 1162, Alexander III spent much of his pontificate in France. One of the great medieval popes, he presided over the Third Lateran Council (1179) and fostered the Scholastic revival of his time.

**ALEXANDER VI** (c. 1431–1503), pope (1492–1503), noted for his worldliness and corruption.

Born Rodrigo de Borja (Ital. *Borgia*) in Játiva, near Valencia, Spain, he was adopted into the family of his maternal uncle, Alfonso Borgia (later Pope Callistus III). Even as a teenager, Rodrigo was given ecclesiastical grants and revenues. After studying law at Bologna, he became successively a cardinal, a bishop, and an able administrator in the papal court. As a member of the powerful Borgia family, he acquired wealth and lived a life of worldly pleasure. He had four children by a Roman noblewoman, Vanozza Catanei (fl.1470–80); the most famous were Cesare and Lucrezia Borgia. During the conclave of 1492, after the death of Innocent VIII (1432–92), Rodrigo was elected pope. Even though he used bribery to secure the necessary two-thirds of the votes, his election was generally welcomed.

The course of his pontificate was determined by economic and political considerations. He established the machinery for a reform of papal finances; recovered the territories of the Papal States, which had been ruled by local tyrants; and tried to unite Christendom against the Turks. Other notable acts included his issuance (1493) of the Bull of Demarcation (*See* DEMARCATION, LINE OF), which divided the New World between Spain and Portugal, and his sending of the first missionaries to America. In 1498 he ordered the execution of the Florentine church reformer Girolamo Savonarola. The course of Alexander's pontificate was also determined by family considerations; he greatly increased the fortunes of his children through ecclesiastical and political appointments and marriages. Some modern studies have tended to minimize the spiritual laxity of his pontificate, but the positive aspects of his reign remain overshadowed by corruption and ambition. He died Aug. 18, 1503.

**ALEXANDER I** (1777–1825), emperor of Russia (1801–25), son of Emperor Paul I (1754–1801). He abolished many barbarous and cruel punishments then practiced and in 1802 introduced a more orderly administration of government by the creation of eight ministries. He improved the condition of the serfs and promoted education, doubling the number of Russian universities by establishing those at Saint Petersburg, Kharkov, and Kazan. Alexander was for a time the ally of Prussia against Napoleon of France. In 1807, however, after the battles of Eylau and Friedland, Alexander allied himself with the French. He broke the alliance in 1812, and later that year Napoleon invaded Russia, only to lose his army in a disastrous retreat from Moscow. Alexander was prominent thereafter in the European coalition that led to Napoleon's fall. In 1815 Alexander instituted the Holy Alliance of Austria, Russia, and Prussia. The purpose of the alliance, as it was conceived, was to achieve the realization of high Christian ideals among the nations of Europe, but it soon ceased to have any real importance. The last years of Alexander's life and reign were reactionary and despotic. He was succeeded by his brother Nicholas I.

**ALEXANDER II** (1818–81), emperor of Russia (1855–81), son of Emperor Nicholas I and nephew of Alexander I. He ascended the throne during the Crimean War and in 1856 signed the Treaty of Paris, which brought the hostilities to an end. After establishing committees to study the need for reform, Alexander II abolished serfdom throughout Russia in 1861. He also abolished corporal punishment, established local self-government, initiated judicial reform, revised the educational system, and developed a system of universal military service. Under his rule the administration of the police was greatly improved, and military operations in Central Asia and in a war with Turkey (1877–78) were highly successful. The Russian possessions in North America, now constituting the state of Alaska, were sold to the U.S. in 1867. Alexander was assassinated by a bomb thrown into his carriage by a member of a revolutionary group, the Narodnaya Volya (People's Will).

**ALEXANDER III** (1845–94), emperor of Russia (1881–94), son of Alexander II. In reaction to the assassination of his father, he restored much of the absolutism of the reign of Nicholas I and sternly repressed all revolutionary agitation. Alexander tried to impose the Russian language on all of his subjects, persecuted the Jews, and restricted education. His foreign policy was marked by a close union with France in opposition to the Triple Alliance. He was succeeded by his son, Nicholas II.

**ALEXANDER I** (c. 1078–1124), king of Scotland (1107–24). He was called Alexander the Fierce for his stern suppression of an insurrection in northern Scotland. He worked for the independence of the Scottish church and founded a number of bishoprics as well as the abbeys of Scone in Perth Co. and Inchcolm, on an island in the Firth of Forth.

**ALEXANDER II** (1198–1249), king of Scotland (1214–49), the son of William the Lion. He supported the English barons in their rebellion against King John, helping them to secure the Magna Charta (1215), but in 1217 he recognized John's successor, Henry III, as his overlord, and in 1221 he married Henry's sister, Joan. After Joan's death in 1238, he took a second wife, Mary of Coucy, who bore him a son in 1241. By the Peace of York (1237), Alexander and Henry established the permanent boundary between England and Scotland. At home, Alexander imposed his rule over outlying parts of Scotland and strengthened the power of the monarchy.

**ALEXANDER III** (1241–86), king of Scotland (1249–86), son of Alexander II and his second wife, Mary of Coucy. In 1251 Alexander married Margaret, the daughter of King Henry III of England, and the English repeatedly attempted to interfere in Scottish affairs during his minority. He successfully resisted an invasion by King Håkon IV of Norway at the battle of Largs (1263), and in 1266 he forced Håkon's successor, Magnus VI, to surrender the Isle of Man and the Hebrides Islands to Scotland. Alexander was succeeded by his granddaughter Margaret, the Maid of Norway (1282?–90).

**ALEXANDER I** (1888–1934), king of Yugoslavia (1921–34), second son of Peter I of Serbia. He became crown prince of Serbia in 1909, upon the renunciation of the succession by his brother George. Alexander served in the Serbian army in the Balkan War (1912) and in World War I. In 1918 he became prince regent of the newly established kingdom of the Serbs, Croats, and Slovenes, and three years later he became king. Disorders in the kingdom, arising chiefly from the Croatian autonomy movement, caused him to dismiss the parliament in 1929, to abolish the constitution, and to set up a royal dictatorship. To emphasize the unity that he hoped to enforce, he changed the name of the kingdom to Yugoslavia. On Oct. 9, 1934, while on an official visit to France, he was assassinated in Marseille, together with Louis Barthou (1862–1934), French foreign minister, by a Croatian nationalist. He was succeeded by his son, Peter II.

**ALEXANDER, Grover Cleveland** (1887–1950), American baseball player, born in Saint Paul, Nebr. He played in the National League from 1911 to 1929 for the Philadelphia, Chicago, and Saint Louis teams. Considered one of the finest pitchers in the history of the game, he was elected to the Baseball Hall of Fame in 1938.

**ALEXANDER, Harold Rupert Leofric George, 1st Earl Alexander of Tunis** (1891–1969), British field marshal, born in county Tyrone (now in Northern Ireland), and educated at the Royal Military College, Sandhurst. Following distinguished service as an officer during World War I, he held various positions in the British army, including command of a brigade in India. In 1938 he was appointed major general. In 1939, after the outbreak of World War II, Alexander commanded the 1st Division in France. Later, as commander of the I Corps, he directed the evacuation of the British army from Dunkirk. Appointed commander in chief of British forces in the Middle East in August 1942, he organized the drive on Tunis the following October to December. In February 1943 he became deputy commander in chief, under Gen. Dwight D. Eisenhower, of all Allied ground forces in North Africa; later that year he directed the invasions of Sicily and Italy. He succeeded Eisenhower as supreme allied-commander in the Mediterranean Theater of Operations in 1944 and advanced to the rank of field marshal in November. Alexander was governor-general of Canada from 1946 to 1952 and British defense minister from 1952 to 1954. He was granted the title of viscount (1946) and of earl (1952). He wrote *The Alexander Memoirs, 1940–1945* (1962).

**ALEXANDER, Samuel** (1859–1938), British philosopher, born in Sydney, Australia, and educated in Melbourne and at the University of Oxford.

He gave up a fellowship at Oxford to study psychology in Germany (1890–91) because he wanted to relate philosophy to the new discoveries in experimental psychology. He was one of the few philosophers of the 20th century to develop a comprehensive metaphysical system. The basic tenets of this system are expressed in his major work, *Space, Time, and Deity* (1920). Space-time is the cosmic system from which different categories of existence evolve in an infinite series. The primary categories are matter, life, and mind. Alexander found the cosmic order tending toward an end, which he termed Deity. Mind, one of the primary categories, is endowed with the unique property of consciousness, through which it may achieve Deity. Within the context of this system, Alexander dealt with traditional philosophical problems, such as the relation of mind and body, moral values, and the nature of knowledge. In his later years, he became interested in aesthetics, with which *Beauty and Other Forms of Value* (1933) is concerned. Alexander was awarded the British Order of Merit in 1930.

**ALEXANDER, Sir William, Earl of Stirling** (1567?–1640), Scottish poet and courtier, born probably in Menstrie, and educated probably at the universities of Glasgow and Leiden. He was tutor to the oldest son of James VI of Scotland (later James I of England). Alexander became secretary of state for Scotland in 1626. His principal works include the collection of sonnets *Aurora* and the tragedies *Darius* (1603), *Croesus* (1604), *The Alexandrean* (1605), and *Julius Caesar* (1607). The tragedies contain several distinguished soliloquies. Alexander's other works include the epic *Doomesday, or the Great Day of the Lord's Judgment* (1614).

**ALEXANDER, William,** known as Lord Stirling (1726–83), American soldier, born in New York City. He served in the French and Indian War, first as commissary and then as aide-de-camp to the American colonial governor of Massachusetts William Shirley. In 1756 he went to England to defend Shirley against the charge of neglect of duty and to urge a claim of his own before the House of Lords to the earldom of Stirling. This claim was rejected, and in 1761 he returned to America. Alexander soon became surveyor-general and a member of the Provincial Council, and in November 1775 he enlisted as a colonel in a New Jersey regiment. In 1776 he was promoted to the rank of brigadier general. In this position he took part in the American revolutionary battles of Long Island, Brandywine, Germantown, and Monmouth. Later Alexander was a founder and the first governor of King's College (now Columbia University).

**ALEXANDER ARCHIPELAGO,** group of about 1100 islands, SE Alaska, in the Pacific Ocean. The islands and the mainland coast form the Alaskan Panhandle. The principal islands include Admiralty, Baranof, Chichagof, Etolin, Kuiu, Kupreanof, Prince of Wales (the largest in the archipelago), and Revillagigedo. The largest city in the archipelago is Sitka, on Baranof Island, which is named for the Russian fur trader Aleksandr Andreyevich Baranov (1746–1819), who took possession of the island in 1799 for Russia. The second largest city, Ketchikan, is on Revillagigedo. The islands, which are a submerged mountain system, form the sheltered channels that are part of the maritime tourist route between Seattle, Wash., and Alaska. Industries include canning, fishing, fur trapping, lumbering, and uranium mining.

**ALEXANDER THE GREAT** (356–323 BC), king of Macedonia, conqueror of the Persian Empire, and one of the greatest military geniuses of all times.

Alexander, born in Pella, the ancient capital of Macedonia, was the son of Philip II, king of Macedonia, and of Olympias (c. 375–316 BC), a princess of Epirus. Aristotle was Alexander's tutor; he gave Alexander a thorough training in rhetoric and literature and stimulated his interest in science, medicine, and philosophy. In the summer of 336 BC Philip was assassinated, and Alexander ascended to the Macedonian throne. He found himself surrounded by enemies at home and threatened by rebellion abroad. Alexander disposed quickly of all conspirators and domestic enemies by ordering their executions. Then he descended on Thessaly, where partisans of independence had gained ascendancy, and restored Macedonian rule. Before the end of the summer of 336 BC he had reestablished his position in Greece and was elected by a congress of states at Corinth. In 335 BC as general of the Greeks in a campaign against the Persians, originally planned by his father, he carried out a successful campaign against the defecting Thracians, penetrating to the Ister (modern Danube) River. On his return he crushed in a single week the threatening Illyrians and then hastened to Thebes, which had revolted. He took the city by storm and razed it, sparing only the temples of the gods and the house of the Greek lyric poet Pindar, and selling the surviving inhabitants, about 8000 in number, into slavery. Alexander's promptness in crushing the revolt of Thebes brought the other Greek states into instant and abject submission.

Alexander commenced his war against the Persian Empire during the spring of 334 BC. He began his conquest by crossing the Hellespont (modern Dardanelles) with an army of 35,000 Macedonian and Greek troops; his chief officers, all Macedonians, included Antigonus, Ptolemy, and Seleucus. At the river Granicus, near the ancient city of Troy, he attacked an army of Persians and Greek mercenaries totaling 40,000 men. His forces defeated the enemy and, according to tradition, lost only 110 men; after this battle all the states of Asia Minor submitted to him. In passing through Phrygia he is said to have cut with his sword the Gordian knot (q.v.). Continuing to advance southward, Alexander encountered the main Persian army, commanded by King Darius III, at Issus, in northeastern Syria. The size of Darius's army is unknown; the ancient tradition that it contained 500,000 men is now considered a fantastic exaggeration. The Battle of Issus, in 333, ended in a great victory for Alexander. Cut off from his base, Darius fled northward, abandoning his mother, wife, and children to Alexander, who treated them with the respect due to royalty. Tyre, a strongly fortified seaport, offered obstinate resistance, but Alexander took it by storm in 332 after laying siege to it for seven months. Alexander captured Gaza next and then passed on into Egypt, where he was greeted by the people as a deliverer. As a result of these successes Alexander secured control of the entire eastern Mediterranean coastline. Later in 332 he founded, at the mouth of the Nile River, the city of Alexandria, which later became the literary, scientific, and commercial center of the Greek world. Cyrene, the capital of the ancient North

African kingdom of Cyrenaica, submitted to Alexander soon afterward, thus extending his dominion to Carthaginian territory.

In the spring of 331 Alexander made a pilgrimage to the great temple and oracle of Amon-Ra, Egyptian god of the sun, whom the Greeks identified with Zeus. The earlier Egyptian pharaohs were believed to be sons of Amon-Ra; and Alexander, the new ruler of Egypt, wanted the god to acknowledge him as his son. The pilgrimage apparently was successful, and it may have confirmed in him a belief in his own divine origin. Turning northward again, he reorganized his forces at Tyre and started for Babylon with an army of 40,000 infantry and 7000 cavalry. Crossing the Euphrates and the Tigris rivers, he met Darius at the head of an army of unknown size, which, according to the exaggerated accounts of antiquity, was said to number a million men; this army he completely defeated in the Battle of Gaugamela, on Oct. 1, 331. Darius then fled as he had done at Issus and was later slain by two of his own generals. Babylon surrendered after Gaugamela, and the city of Susa with its enormous treasures was soon conquered. Then, in midwinter, Alexander forced his way to Persepolis, the Persian capital. After plundering the royal treasuries and taking other rich booty, he burned the city during a drunken binge and thus completed the destruction of the ancient Persian Empire. Alexander's domain now extended along and beyond the

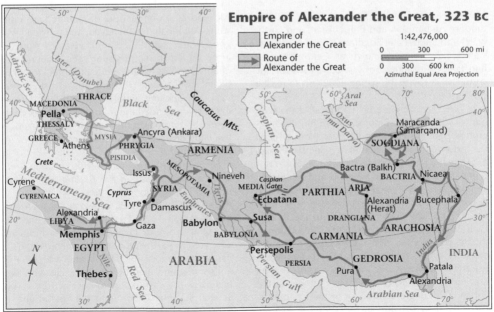

## Empire of Alexander the Great, 323 BC

■ Empire of Alexander the Great

→ Route of Alexander the Great

1:42,476,000

0       300       600 mi

0    300   600 km

Azimuthal Equal Area Projection

© GeoSystems Global Corp.

*A mosaic depicting Alexander the Great in battle.*
Scala–Art Resource

his empire, in his own words, "to the strongest"; this ambiguous testament resulted in dire conflicts for half a century.

Alexander was one of the greatest generals of all time, noted for his brilliance as a tactician and troop leader and for the rapidity with which he could traverse great expanses of territory. He was usually brave and generous, but could be cruel and ruthless when politics demanded. The theory has been advanced that he was actually an alcoholic having, for example, killed his friend Clitus (d. 328 BC) in a drunken fury. He later regretted this act deeply. As a statesman and ruler he had grandiose plans; according to many modern historians he cherished a scheme for uniting the East and the West in a world empire, a new and enlightened "world brotherhood of all men." He trained thousands of Persian youths in Macedonian tactics and enrolled them in his army. He himself adopted Persian manners and married Eastern wives, namely, Roxana (d. about 311 BC), daughter of Oxyartes of Sogdiana, and Barsine (or Stateira; d. about 323 BC), the elder daughter of Darius; and he encouraged and bribed his officers to take Persian wives. Shortly before he died, Alexander ordered the Greek cities to worship him as a god. Although he probably gave the order for political reasons, he was, in his own view and that of his contemporaries, of divine birth. The order was largely nullified by his death shortly after he issued it.

To bind his conquests together, Alexander founded a number of cities, most of them named Alexandria, along his line of march; these cities were well located, well paved, and provided with good water supplies. Greek veterans from his army settled in them; young men, traders, merchants, and scholars were attracted to them; Greek culture was introduced; and the Greek language became widely known. Thus, Alexander vastly extended the influence of Greek civilization and prepared the way for the kingdoms of the Hellenistic period and the conquests of the Roman Empire.

*For further information on this person, see the section Biographies in the Bibliography in volume 28, and sections 878, 1052.*

**ALEXANDER OF HALES,** known as Doctor Irrefragabilis (1185?–1245), English theologian and philosopher, born in Hales, Gloucestershire, and educated in Paris. About 1237 he entered the Order of the Franciscans. He became a lecturer on philosophy and theology in Paris. His work was included in a vast exposition of doctrine known as the *Summa Theologica* (Compendium, or Summary, of Theology), compiled after his death and credited to him. Alexander of Hales intro-

southern shores of the Caspian Sea, including modern Afghanistan and Baluchistan, and northward into Bactria and Sogdiana, the modern Russian Turkestan, also known as Central Asia. It had taken Alexander only three years, from the spring of 330 BC to the spring of 327 BC, to master this vast area.

In order to complete his conquest of the remnants of the Persian Empire, which had once included part of western India, Alexander crossed the Indus River in 326 BC and invaded the Punjab as far as the river Hyphasis (modern Beas); at this point the Macedonians rebelled and refused to go farther. He then constructed a fleet and passed down the Indus, reaching its mouth in September 325 BC. The fleet then sailed to the Persian Gulf. With his army, he returned overland across the desert to Media. Shortages of food and water caused severe losses and hardship among his troops. Alexander spent about a year organizing his dominions and completing a survey of the Persian Gulf in preparation for further conquests. He arrived in Babylon in the spring of 323 BC. In June he contracted a fever and died. He left

duced Aristotelian principles into Christian theological discussion.

**ALEXANDER NEVSKY** (1220?–63), Russian national hero and saint. The son of Yaroslav Vsevolodovich (1191?–1246), grand prince of the medieval Russian state of Vladimir, Alexander was elected prince of the state of Novgorod in 1236. In 1240 he won a victory over the Swedes on the Neva River near present Saint Petersburg, thus acquiring his surname, Nevsky ("of the Neva"). The following year, he led the army of Novgorod against the Teutonic Knights, driving them from Russian soil and defeating them in a battle at Lake Peipus, Estonia, in April 1242. Later generations viewed this victory as having saved Russia from Western domination. When the Mongols invaded Russia from the east, Alexander collaborated with them, acting as mediator between his people and the Mongol Golden Horde. In 1246 the Mongols made him grand prince of Kiev, and in 1251 they installed him as prince of Vladimir, replacing his brother Andrei (d. 1264). As ruler of Vladimir, Kiev, and Novgorod, he did much to unify the principalities of northern Russia. Alexander is recognized as a saint by the Russian Orthodox church; his feast day is September 12.

**ALEXANDRIA,** city and major seaport, N Egypt, in the Nile R. delta, on a ridge that separates Lake Mareotis from the Mediterranean Sea. The city was founded in 332 BC by Alexander the Great, king of Macedonia, who planned it as one of the finest ports of the ancient world. A mole (breakwater made of large stones or masonry) nearly 1.6 km (1 mi) in length called the Heptastadium ("seven furlongs") was built to the island of Pharos, enclosing a spacious harbor. A famous lighthouse, considered one of the Seven Wonders of the Ancient World, was also built on Pharos. Another smaller harbor was open to the W. A canal joined Lake Mareotis to the Canopic branch of the Nile.

The ancient city was about 6.4 km (about 4 mi) long, and regularly built, with streets crossing at right angles and colonnades adorning the principal streets. The most magnificent quarter of the city, called the Brucheium, was situated on the E harbor. Farther W was the Serapeion, or temple of the Egyptian deity Serapis; the Soma, or mau-

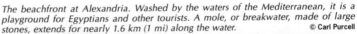

*The beachfront at Alexandria. Washed by the waters of the Mediterranean, it is a playground for Egyptians and other tourists. A mole, or breakwater, made of large stones, extends for nearly 1.6 km (1 mi) along the water.*     © Carl Purcell

soleum of Alexander and the Ptolemies; the Poseidonium, or temple of Poseidon, god of the sea; the museum; the great theater; and the emporium, or exchange. The NE quarter was occupied by the Jews. In Alexandria the Jews came into contact with Greek learning, which profoundly influenced the later religious thought of the world; here the Greek translation of the Old Testament, called the Septuagint, was made before AD 100. Later philosophers attempted to fuse the doctrines of Christianity with the ideals of Greek philosophy.

Soon after the city was founded, the population, consisting chiefly of Greeks, Jews, and Egyptians, numbered 300,000 free citizens, exclusive of slaves and strangers. Alexandria was made the capital of Egypt; numerous palaces were built by the Ptolemies; the Alexandrian Library and Museum were founded; and influential schools of philosophy, rhetoric, and other branches of ancient learning were established.

Under the Ptolemies, the city became the literary and scientific center of the ancient world. After the defeat of Cleopatra, queen of Egypt, at Actium in 31 BC and her suicide the following year, the city came under the rule of Octavian, later the Roman emperor Augustus, and was governed by a prefect appointed by him. Its position made it the center of commerce between East and West, and fleets of grain ships sailed from Alexandria to Italy year after year. Gradually, however, the city lost its prosperity. A Jewish revolt in AD 116 resulted in the annihilation of the Jewish population and the destruction of a large portion of the city. In 215 the Roman emperor Caracalla ordered a massacre of the male inhabitants of the entire city for reasons that remain obscure but may have involved a punishment for some form of seditious conduct. The founding of Constantinople further eclipsed the Egyptian metropolis. The Muslims, under the general Amr ibn-al-As (c. 594–663), besieged, captured, and almost destroyed the city in 638 and again about 646. Under Muslim rule the city declined, particularly after the rise of Cairo after about 968 and the opening of the sea route to India in the 15th century. Alexandria was captured and held from 1798 to 1801 by Napoleon.

The modern city is situated mainly on a peninsula about the mole, reaching to and including the island of Pharos, and on the portion of the mainland immediately S of the E harbor. The part of the modern city on the peninsula is a characteristically Egyptian town; the European quarter is on the mainland. Alexandria has had, since ancient times, two harbors, of which the W one is the chief commercial center and the site of the

customs house and many warehouses for cotton, grain, sugar, and wool. More than 80 percent of the imports and exports of the country pass through the city. Pop. (1991 est.) 3,295,000.

**ALEXANDRIA,** city, seat of Rapides Parish, central Louisiana, on the Red R., opposite Pineville; inc. 1882. It is the transportation and processing center of a region in which timber, livestock, and soybeans are produced. Manufactures include toiletries, industrial valves, and forest products. Louisiana State University at Alexandria (1960) is here, and Louisiana College (1906) is in Pineville. Named for the daughter of the merchant and landowner who subdivided land here in 1805, Alexandria was almost completely destroyed by Union troops in 1864, during the American Civil War. The city was rebuilt and by about 1900 had become a prosperous timber-processing and trade center. Pop. (1980) 51,565; (1990) 49,188.

**ALEXANDRIA,** independent city, N Virginia, on the Potomac R., a suburb of Washington, D.C.; inc. 1749, reincorporated as an independent city 1852. It is a commercial and transportation center, with large railroad freight yards and a port accommodating oceangoing vessels. Manufactures include railroad equipment, printed materials, and processed food. Among the city's historic structures are Christ Church (1773), where George Washington worshiped; Gadsby's Tavern, frequented by Washington and other patriots; many colonial and Georgian houses; and the boyhood home of the Confederate general Robert E. Lee. Washington's home, Mount Vernon, is nearby. Alexandria is named for John Alexander (1603?–77), who purchased land here in 1669. In 1749 Washington helped plat the city, which became a thriving colonial trade center and tobacco port. It was part of the District of Columbia from 1801 to 1847. It was occupied by Union troops from 1801 until the end of the American Civil War. Pop. (1980) 103,217; (1990) 111,183.

**ALEXANDRIA, LIBRARY OF,** famous ancient library of Alexandria, Egypt. Founded by Ptolemy I Soter, king of Egypt, it was expanded by his son Ptolemy II Philadelphus into the greatest collection of books in the ancient world early in the 3d century BC. The scholars in charge included the ablest Alexandrian men of letters of the period. Zenodotus of Ephesus (325?–260? BC), whose specialty was the classification of poetry, was the first to hold the position of librarian. The poet Callimachus made the first general catalog of the books and apparently was also librarian. The two most noted librarians were Aristophanes of Byzantium (257?–180? BC) and Aristarchus of Samothrace (220?–150? BC), both great editors and grammarians. In the time of Ptolemy II, according to one historian, the main library in the Alexandrian Museum contained nearly 500,000 volumes, or rolls, and an annex in the Temple of Serapis contained some 43,000 volumes. Most of the writings of antiquity were preserved in these collections from which copies were made and disseminated to libraries throughout the civilized world.

It is largely through such copies that ancient works have survived to modern times, for the Alexandrian library was partially or wholly destroyed on several occasions. In 47 BC, during the civil war between Julius Caesar and the followers of Pompey the Great, Caesar was beseiged in Alexandria; a fire that destroyed the Egyptian fleet spread through some stores of books, about 40,000 of which were ruined. A few years later the Roman emperor Mark Antony presented to Cleopatra, queen of Egypt, books from the library of the city of Pergamum, in Asia Minor. According to legend, the library at Alexandria was burned three times: in AD 272 (by order of the Roman emperor Lucius Domitius Aurelian), in 391 (under the Roman emperor Theodosius I), and in 640 (by Muslims under the caliph Umar I, 581?–644).

**ALEXANDRINE,** in verse, a line of 12 syllables (or 13 if the last syllable is unstressed), consisting of 6 iambic feet. Some scholars think the name is derived from a 12th-century collection of romances concerning Alexander the Great. The alexandrine became popular in the 16th century, through the work of Pierre de Ronsard, and soon became accepted as the standard line for epic narrative, tragedy, and high comedy. It remained characteristic of French heroic verse until the middle of the 19th century. The alexandrine also occurs in English poetry, probably the most famous example being the line in Alexander Pope's *Essay on Criticism:*

A needless alexandrine ends the song
that like a wounded snake, drags its
    slow length along.

**ALEXIS I** (1629–76), second Russian czar (1645–76) of the house of Romanov, and father of Peter the Great. He succeeded his father Michael (1596–1645). As a result of two campaigns by Alexis against the Poles (1654–56 and 1660–67), Russia gained Smolensk, Kiev, and the lands east of the Dnepr River. The war with Sweden (1656–58) was not as successful; Alexis was forced to withdraw from the lands he had taken. The reign of Czar Alexis was also marked by internal revolt, a schism in the Russian Orthodox church, and the formulation of a legal code that extended the serfdom of the Russian peasants.

**ALEXIUS I COMNENUS** (1048–1118), Byzantine emperor (1081–1118). Coming to the throne at a time when the Byzantine Empire was threatened by foreign enemies on every side, Alexius began his reign by combining with the Venetians to resist Norman invaders led by Robert Guiscard in Greece. In 1091 he defeated the Pechenegs, a Turkic tribe raiding the empire from the north; in the same year he stabilized the situation in the east by concluding a treaty with the Seljuk Turks. In 1095 Alexius appealed to Pope Urban II for help in recovering Anatolia from the Seljuks, thus helping to inspire the First Crusade. He exacted an oath of allegiance from the Crusade's leaders (among them, Bohemond, the son of his old enemy Robert Guiscard) when they arrived in Constantinople the following year. With their help, he regained control of western Anatolia, but he failed to prevent them from establishing independent states in Syria and Palestine. A dispute with Bohemond over the lordship of Antioch ended when the Norman acknowledged Alexius as his overlord in 1108. Alexius's biography, the *Alexiad,* was written by his daughter, Anna Comnena. It is considered a valuable source of historical information.

**ALFALFA,** common name for a fodder plant, *Medicago sativa,* known also as lucerne, of the family Fabaceae (*see* LEGUME). It is believed to have originated in southwestern Asia. Historical accounts indicate that it was first cultivated in Persia. From there it was taken to Greece in the 5th century BC and to Spain in the 8th century AD. Spaniards introduced alfalfa to North and South America. Its extension over the irrigated sections of the western U.S. began in 1854, when it was taken to San Francisco from Chile. With the development of improved varieties and the use of better fertilizing and soil-management practices, its culture has spread throughout the U.S.

One of the most nutritious crops grown for fodder, alfalfa is rich in proteins, minerals, and vitamins. Because its root extends as much as 9 m (30 ft) into the soil, alfalfa can reach stores of plant food and, in sections of limited rainfall, can withstand extremes of drought. The plant is remarkably adaptable to various climatic conditions, but it must have certain soil conditions and proper sowing. The effect of alfalfa on irrigated land is to increase the value per hectare of subsequent crops. Alfalfa is used as a soil-conditioning crop and as pasturage, and in the form of silage and hay it is fed to dairy cows, beef cattle, sheep, hogs, horses, and poultry. It is also an excellent honey crop for bees and is used to increase the vitamin content of prepared foods. Its sprouted seeds are often used in salads.

*Alfalfa,* Medicago sativa, *also known as lucerne.*
Hans Reinhard–Bruce Coleman, Inc.

The principal alfalfa-producing states include California, Washington, Idaho, Kansas, and Oregon. Alfalfa production in the U.S. averages about 70 million metric tons harvested annually for hay and about 60,000 for seed.

**ALFIERI, Vittorio, Conte** (1749–1803), Italian dramatist and poet, who was one of the leading literary and patriotic figures of modern Italian history.

Alfieri was born in Asti, Piedmont, on Jan. 16, 1749, and educated at a military academy in Turin. He inherited a fortune and at the age of 17 set out on travels throughout Europe. In 1772 he returned to Turin, and in 1775 he wrote a tragic drama, *Cleopatra,* which was enthusiastically received. He then devoted himself to writing tragic dramas and patriotic poems. Alfieri moved to Florence in 1776 to study the purer Italian spoken in the province of Tuscany. While living in Florence he fell in love with Louise de Stolberg (1753–1824), the countess of Albany, who became his mistress. She encouraged his writing and became a stabilizing influence in his life.

During the next 13 years he produced 19 tragic dramas; *Saul* (1783), the most notable, is based on the biblical account of the destruction of Saul because of his jealousy of David. His other tragic dramas of this period include *Agamemnon* (1783), *Philip the Second* (1781), *Antigone* (1786), and *Sophonisba* (1788). In his most im-

portant prose writings of these years, *On Tyranny* (1789) and *The Prince and Literature* (1801), he argued that honest literature could be created only in a free society. In five odes, published from 1776 to 1783, he celebrated American independence. He died in Florence on Oct. 8, 1803.

The whole body of Alfieri's writings, inspired by his own love of freedom, awakened the national pride of Italians and helped promote the Italian independence movement known as the Risorgimento.

**ALFÖLD,** also Great Alföld (Hung. *Nagy Alföld*) and Great Hungarian Plain, fertile agricultural lowland, E Europe; covering most of the region E of Danube in central and SE Hungary, it extends into N Yugoslavia, where it is known as the Pannonian Plains, and into W Romania, as the Tisza Plain. The plain is drained by the Tisza and Danube rivers. It has a semiarid climate and was a stock-raising and grassland region before being irrigated and brought under cereal cultivation in the late 19th century. The Little Alföld (Hung. *Kis Alföld*), in NW Hungary, also extends into S Slovakia.

**ALFONSO II** (1152–96), king of Aragón, the son of Ramón Berenguer IV (1115–62), count of Barcelona. Alfonso became count of Barcelona in 1162 and king of Aragón in 1164, and in 1167 he inherited the county of Provence. A poet and musician, Alfonso is remembered for his patronage of Provençal literature.

**ALFONSO I** (1073?–1134), king of Aragón and Navarre (1104–34). He married Urraca (1081–1126), daughter of King Alfonso I of Castile, thus joining the two principal Christian kingdoms in Spain. He won many victories over the Moors and played an important part in the Christian reconquest of the Iberian Peninsula. The Moors defeated him at Braga in 1133, and he died the following year of wounds received there.

**ALFONSO V,** called The Magnanimous (1385–1458), king of Aragón and Sicily (1416–58), and as Alfonso I, king of Naples (1443–58). He was the son of King Ferdinand I of Aragón. He earned his nickname when, upon his ascension to the throne, he destroyed a list containing the names of nobles who had been hostile to him. He is renowned chiefly for having brought southern Italy under the dominion of Aragón. In 1420 Alfonso attacked Corsica, but hastened to Naples at the request of its queen, Joanna II (1371–1435), who, in return for his aid against Louis III of Anjou (1403?–34), named Alfonso her heir. In 1423 the queen transferred her favor from Alfonso to his rival, Louis. On her death in 1435 Alfonso claimed the kingdom, but Duke René of Anjou (1409–80), successor of Louis, opposed him. The pope and Genoa sided with René. The

Genoese fleet defeated the fleet of Aragón, and Alfonso was captured. He was sent to Francesco Sforza, duke of Milan, who set him at liberty and formed an alliance with him. After several battles Alfonso defeated René and entered Naples in triumph, transferring his court there and becoming the founder of Spanish power in Italy.

**ALFONSO I,** called The Brave (1030–1109), king of Castile (1072–1109), and as Alfonso VI, king of León (1065–1109). His father, King Ferdinand I of Castile and León, died in 1065 and left his kingdom, divided into three parts, to his three sons. Alfonso received only León, but he succeeded to nearly all his father's dominions as a result of a war with his brothers, and he also added Toledo and New Castile to his holdings. In 1086 the Abbadids of Seville, with Almoravid help, defeated him at Zalaca and stopped the gradual reconquest of Spain by the Christian rulers. Alfonso regained some of his power, but in 1108, a year before his death, the Almoravids defeated him again and killed his only son.

**ALFONSO VIII** (1155–1214), king of Castile (1158–1214); he succeeded to the throne on the death of his father, Sancho III (c. 1134–58). Troubled by interference from Navarre in his youth, he later allied Castile with Aragón, forming a connection that was eventually to become the basis for the unification of Spain. He also established Castilian dominance over León. In 1170 he married Eleanor (d. 1214), daughter of King Henry II of England. From the 1170s, he resisted encroachments by the Almohads, Muslim invaders from northern Africa. Defeated by the Muslim caliph Yakub al-Mansur (c. 1160–99) at Alarcos in 1195, Alfonso and his allies won a major victory over the Muslim commander al-Nasir (1158–1225) at Navas de Tolosa in 1212.

**ALFONSO IX** (1166?–1230), king of León (1188–1230). In 1197 he married Berengaria (1171–1246), daughter of his first cousin King Alfonso VIII of Castile and granddaughter of King Henry II of England. Pope Innocent III annulled the marriage in 1214 because of the family relationship of Alfonso and Berengaria. Alfonso founded the University of Salamanca and captured Cáceres, Badajoz, and Mérida from the Muslim Almohads.

**ALFONSO X,** called The Wise (1226?–84), king of León and Castile (1252–82), son of Ferdinand III, whom he succeeded. His reign was turbulent, marked by fighting with the Moors, a series of civil wars, and an extended but unsuccessful attempt on his part to gain the crown of the Holy Roman Empire. He was deposed in 1282, after an insurrection led by his son Sancho IV (1258–96), and died a fugitive at Seville. Alfonso promulgated the law code known as Las Siete Partidas (The Seven

Parts). Himself a poet and author, he greatly stimulated the intellectual life of his time. A famous set of planetary tables, still known as the Alphonsine Tables, was prepared under his direction in 1252.

**ALFONSO XI** (1310?–1350), king of León and Castile (1312–50). A strong defender of the royal prerogative, he courted the lower classes with his economic policies while curtailing the authority of the nobles. On Oct. 30, 1340, he and Alfonso IV of Portugal crushed the resurgent Moors in Spain in the Battle of the Salado River.

**ALFONSO I,** in Portuguese, Alfonso Henriques (1109?–85), first king of Portugal (1139–85), and son of Henry of Burgundy (1069?–1112), count of Portugal. As an infant, he inherited his father's title, and in 1128 he defeated his mother, Teresa (1070?–1130), the erstwhile regent, in battle. He began a long struggle for independence from León soon thereafter; he won this war in 1139. On July 25 of that year he also won a decisive victory over the Moors at Qurique and proclaimed himself king of Portugal. His subsequent victories over the Moors included the capture of Santarém in 1147, and, with the help of Crusaders en route to the Holy Land, the capture of Lisbon in October of that year.

**ALFONSO II,** called The Fat (1185–1223), king of Portugal (1211–23), the son of Sancho I (1154–1211), whom he succeeded. In 1217 he defeated the Moors at the village of Alcácer do Sal. He was excommunicated later by Pope Honorius III (fl. 1188–1227) for misuse of church moneys. His son Sancho II (1208–48) succeeded him.

**ALFONSO III** (1210–79), king of Portugal (1248–79), the son of Alfonso II. He seized the throne after a two-year civil war with his brother Sancho II, who had ruled since 1223. In 1250–51 Alfonso conquered the Moorish kingdom of Algarve for Portugal.

**ALFONSO IV,** called The Brave (1290–1357), king of Portugal (1325–57), the son of Diniz, whom he succeeded, and grandson of Alfonso III. He ordered the murder of Inés de Castro, the wife of his son Dom Pedro (1320–67). She was a member of the Castilian royal family, and Alfonso IV feared the marriage would hurt Portugal politically.

**ALFONSO V,** called The African (1432–81), king of Portugal (1438–81), son of King Edward (1391–1438), born in Cintra (now Sintra). He succeeded to the throne in 1438, but his powers were delegated to a regency. In 1448 he dissolved the regency and assumed control of the government. In 1449 he quelled an insurrection led by his uncle Pedro (1392?–1449), who had seized the regency from the queen mother. Between

1458 and 1471 he fought a series of successful wars against the Moors in northwestern Africa. He attacked the kingdom of Castile in 1476, but was defeated. Portuguese exploration of the west coast of Africa, a project begun by Henry the Navigator, prince of Portugal, continued during the reign of Alfonso V.

**ALFONSO VI** (1643–83), king of Portugal (1656–67), son of King John IV, founder of the house of Braganza, whom he succeeded. In 1662 he expelled the queen regent from his court. Paralyzed from the age of three and unsound in mind, he was deposed in 1667 and exiled to the Azores by his brother Pedro (1648–1706), who acted as regent until Alfonso's death and then became Pedro II, king of Portugal.

**ALFONSO XII** (1857–85), king of Spain (1870–85), born in Madrid. His mother, Queen Isabella II, took him with her from Spain when she was deposed in the Revolution of 1868. He was educated in Paris, Vienna, and Sandhurst, England. Isabella formally abdicated in favor of her son in 1870, but he did not return to Spain to take up his royal duties until 1875, when the monarchist general Arsenio Martínez de Campos (1831–1900) summoned him to the throne. In 1876 Alfonso suppressed the last of the Carlists—that is, those who supported the claim of the descendants of Don Carlos (1788–1855) to the Spanish throne. In the same year he ordered the Cortes, the representative assembly, to draft a new constitution that introduced a two-party system on the English model into Spanish politics. Throughout his reign Alfonso was greatly influenced by his prime minister, Antonio Cánovas del Castillo (1828–97). His untimely death was followed by the long, troubled regency of his second wife, Maria Christina of Austria (1858–1929).

**ALFONSO XIII** (1886–1941), king of Spain (1886–1931), posthumous son of King Alfonso XII. Until he attained his majority in 1902, his mother, Queen Maria Christina (1858–1929), acted as regent. The principal event of this period was the Spanish-American War, in which Spain lost the Philippines and all its possessions in the New World. Alfonso's reign was marked by revolutionary, antidynastic uprisings, notably in Madrid and Barcelona from 1909 to 1911. He pursued a neutral policy during World War I, but was blamed for Spanish defeats in Morocco in 1921. From 1923 to 1930, he associated himself with the unpopular dictatorship of Miguel Primo de Rivera. Following a period marked by strikes and riots, Alfonso was forced to flee Spain in 1931; he spent the rest of his life in exile.

**ALFRED,** called The Great (849–99), king of the West Saxons (871–99), and one of the outstanding figures of English history. Born in Wantage in southern England, Alfred was the youngest of five sons of King Ethelwulf (790?–858). On the death of his brother Ethelred (r. 866–71) Alfred became king, coming to the throne during a Danish invasion. Although he succeeded in making peace with the Danes, they resumed their marauding expeditions five years later, and by early 878 they were successful almost everywhere. About Easter of 878, however, Alfred established himself at Athelney and began assembling an army. In the middle of that year he defeated the Danes and captured their stronghold, probably at present-day Edington. During the following 14 years Alfred was able to devote himself to the internal affairs of his kingdom. By 886 he had captured the city of London, and soon afterward he was recognized as the king of all England.

In 893 the Danes invaded England again, and the following four years were marked by warfare; eventually, the Danes were forced to withdraw from Alfred's domain. The only ruler to resist Danish invasions successfully, Alfred made his kingdom the rallying point for all Saxons, thus laying the foundation for the unification of England.

Alfred was a patron of learning and did much for the education of his people. He began a court school and invited British and foreign scholars, notably the Welsh monk Asser (fl. 885–909)

*Alfonso XII*

Bettmann Archive

and the Irish-born philosopher and theologian John Scotus Erigena, to come there. Alfred translated such works as *The Consolation of Philosophy* by the Roman statesman and philosopher Boethius, *The History of the World* by the Spanish priest Paulus Orosius (c. 385–420), and *Pastoral Care* by Pope Gregory I. Alfred's laws, the first promulgated in more than a century, were the first that made no distinction between the English and the Welsh peoples.

**ALGAE,** common name for various phyla of single-celled or simple multicellular organisms that are capable of photosynthesis but have little or no differentiation into tissue systems. A few algae in some phyla are closely related to photosynthetic forms, but derive their energy by other means. The best-known forms occur as seaweeds and pond scum. Algae are the most ancient form of life capable of photosynthesis; blue-green algae identical to forms living today have been found in fossil deposits at least 3.4 billion years old in the Fig Tree Formation of South Africa.

In the classification system followed in this encyclopedia, the blue-green algae are placed in the primitive kingdom Monera, the members of which have no defined nucleus or membrane-enclosed cell structures. A recently discovered green alga, a unicellular organism called *Prochloron,* also lacks nuclei. *Prochloron* is therefore not placed with the true green algae but in a new phylum, Prochlorophyta, within the kingdom Monera. One phylum, the Chrysophyta, or golden algae, is placed in the kingdom Protista, the members of which have bounded nuclei and specialized cellular structures. The remaining algal phyla—Chlorophyta, or green algae; Rhodophyta, or red algae; Phaeophyta, or brown algae; and Charophyta, or stoneworts—are intermediate between the protists and the plant kingdom (Plantae). The colors of these algae often correspond to their common names and are attributable to specific pigments that are important in algal classification. The green algae and the more complex stoneworts have two forms of the photosynthetic pigment chlorophyll: chlorophyll a and chlorophyll b. Because the only other organisms in which these chlorophylls occur are such green land plants as mosses, ferns, and flowering plants, it is believed that green algae represent the ancestors of green land plants.

Most algae are aquatic, but some can survive on dry land by means of spores; others can grow on moist soil. More species are found in salt water (where the algae probably evolved) than in fresh water, but fresh waters are often rich in algae. Some algae grow as epiphytes; that is, attached to, but not nutritionally dependent on, land plants. The widely distributed alga *Protococcus* grows as an epiphyte: It is found as a green mat on tree bark and rocks. Some green algae, including *Protococcus,* live in symbiotic association with a fungus as a composite organism called lichen (q.v.).

Algae are widely distributed and can live in extreme environments. For example, a few blue-green algae grow in the hot springs in Yellow-

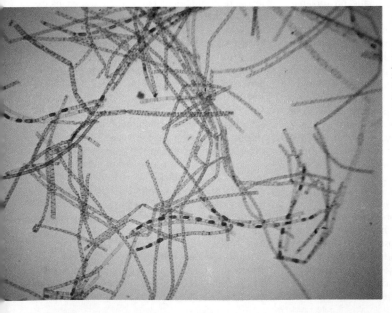

*Magnified filaments of blue-green algae of the genus* Spirogyra. *Blue-green algae represent a form of life more primitive than either plants or animals.*

E. R. Degginger—Bruce Coleman, Inc.

A magnified section of a colony of green algae. Green algae are most commonly found as a scum on both freshwater and saltwater ponds.
A. Grotell–Peter Arnold, Inc.

stone National Park, in water close to the boiling point, whereas a pink-orange algae related to the blue-green thrives under a thick ice cover in cold Antarctic lakes. Red algae were discovered in 1984 on a Bahamas seamount at a depth of 268 m (879 ft), far deeper than it had been thought light-dependent plant life could exist.

In size, algae vary from tiny unicellular forms visible only under a microscope to such giant forms as the kelp *Pelagophycus,* which can grow 60 m (200 ft) in a year. Microscopic algae that float in the ocean are part of the phytoplankton—the main food source, either directly or indirectly, for most marine animals. *See* PLANKTON.

Algae also are a food for humans; principal sources include the brown kelps—known in Japan as kombu—and certain red algae (*Porphyra*) and green algae (*Ulva,* the sea lettuce). Commercially important products include alginates, which are gelatinous extracts of the cell walls of brown algae. Alginates give ice cream a creamy texture and prevent ice-crystal formation; they also prevent the settling out of pigment particles in paints. Some red algae *Gelidium* are a source of agar, used in making soups and other foods and as a solidifier of media used in laboratories for growing microorganisms.

**Blue-Green Algae.** The Cyanophyta are found in both salt and fresh waters. They can grow at temperatures higher than those tolerated by any other organism and can endure extreme dryness and high light intensity. The pigment phycocyanin is responsible for the deep green or blue-green color of many species. Blue-green algae

occur as single cells, colonies, or filaments, and they reproduce by cell division. *See* BLUE-GREEN ALGAE.

**Green Algae.** The Chlorophyta is the largest of algal phyla. Green algae are most abundant in fresh water (often visible as pond scums), but also inhabit salt water and terrestrial environments. They may exist as single cells, colonies, filaments, or plates of cells. Most species form motile reproductive cells (zoospores) that develop directly into new plants. Various types of sexual reproduction occur, and many species exhibit alternation of generations (q.v.). *See* GREEN ALGAE.

**Brown Algae.** Most species of the phylum Phaeophyta are marine. They grow as seaweed (q.v.), mainly in the shallow waters of the sea in temperate regions. These are the largest of the algae and the most highly differentiated in structure. The color of brown algae is due to pigments called xanthophylls, which mask the color of the chlorophylls. Common forms are the kelps (*see* KELP), the sea palm, and the sea-otter's cabbage. Most large species are attached to the ocean bottom by a long, thick stalk. Gulfweeds of the genus *Sargassum* are found as masses of free-floating algae on the Sargasso Sea. The Phaeophyta are a source of fertilizer, vitamins, iodine, and food. *See* BROWN ALGAE.

**Red Algae.** Most Rhodophyta are marine and grow in the deeper waters of subtropical seas. The vegetative body of these organisms is small and delicate. Their color is imparted by the pigment phycoerythrin, which obscures the color of the chlorophylls. Some species secrete lime, which they take from seawater, forming limestone deposits that play an important role in the formation of coral reefs. The so-called Irish moss (*Chondrus crispus*), long used for food, is a red alga that grows off the coasts of Great Britain, Ireland, and North America. *See* RED ALGAE.

*See also* GOLDEN ALGAE; STONEWORT.

*For further information on this topic, see the Bibliography in volume 28, section 457.*

**ALGARDI, Alessandro** (1595–1654), Italian baroque sculptor and architect, born in Bologna. He studied painting, but later turned to sculpture. He executed such marble groups as *St. Philip Neri and the Angel* for Santa Maria del Popolo in Rome and *Beheading of St. Paul* for San Paolo in Bologna. He succeeded Bernini as papal court sculptor in 1644; he designed the Villa Doria-Pamphili and a large bronze statue of Pope Innocent X (1574–1655), now in the Palazzo dei Conservatori, both in Rome. In 1650 he completed the tomb of Pope Leo XI (1535–1605) and a huge bas-relief for the altar of Pope Leo I in Saint Peter's Basilica, Rome, representing Leo's confrontation with the warrior Attila the Hun.

**ALGEBRA,** branch of mathematics in which letters are used to represent basic arithmetic relations. As in arithmetic (q.v.), the basic operations of algebra are addition, subtraction, multiplication, division, and the extraction of roots. Arithmetic, however, cannot generalize such mathematical relations as the Pythagorean theorem,

which states that the sum of the squares of the sides of any right triangle is also a square. Arithmetic can produce specific instances of these relations (for example, 3, 4, and 5, where $3^2 + 4^2 = 5^2$). But algebra can make a purely general statement that fulfills the conditions of the theorem: $a^2 + b^2 = c^2$. Any number multiplied by itself is termed squared and is indicated by a superscript number 2. For example, 3 x 3 is notated $3^2$; similarly, $a$ x $a$ is equivalent to $a^2$ *(see* EXPONENT; POWER; ROOT).

Classical algebra, which is concerned with solving equations, uses symbols instead of specific numbers and employs arithmetic operations to establish procedures for manipulating symbols *(see* EQUATION; EQUATIONS, THEORY OF*)*. Modern algebra has evolved from classical algebra by increasing its attention to the structures within mathematics (q.v.). Mathematicians consider modern algebra a set of objects with rules for connecting or relating them. As such, in its most general form algebra may fairly be described as the language of mathematics.

**History.** The history of algebra began in ancient Egypt and Babylon, where people learned to solve linear ($ax = b$) and quadratic ($ax^2 + bx = c$) equations, as well as indeterminate equations such as $x^2 + y^2 = z^2$, whereby several unknowns are involved. The ancient Babylonians solved arbitrary quadratic equations by essentially the same procedures taught today. They also could solve indeterminate equations.

*Brown algae of the genus Fucus are a form of seaweed with long vegetative strands and round, yellowish air bladders that increase the algae's buoyancy.*
Robert P. Carr–Bruce Coleman, Inc.

# ALGEBRA

The Alexandrian mathematicians Hero and Diophantus continued the traditions of Egypt and Babylon, but Diophantus' book *Arithmetica* is on a much higher level and gives many surprising solutions to difficult indeterminate equations. This ancient knowledge of solutions of equations in turn found a home early in the Islamic world, where it was known as the "science of restoration and balancing." (The Arabic word for restoration, *al-jabru*, is the root of the word algebra, and algebra as a science is an Arabic contribution.) In the 9th century, al-Khwarizmi wrote one of the first Arabic algebras, a systematic exposé of the basic theory of equations, with both examples and proofs. By the end of the 9th century the Egyptian Abu Kamil (850–930) stated and proved the basic laws and identities of algebra and solved such complicated problems as finding $x$, $y$, and $z$ such that $x + y + z = 10$, $x^2 + y^2 = z^2$, and $xz = y^2$.

Ancient civilizations wrote out algebraic expressions, using only occasional abbreviations, but by medieval times Islamic mathematicians were able to talk about arbitrarily high powers of the unknown $x$, and work out the basic algebra of polynomials (without yet using modern symbolism). This included the ability to multiply, divide, and find square roots of polynomials as well as a knowledge of the binomial (q.v) theorem. The Persian Omar Khayyam showed how to express roots of cubic equations by line segments obtained by intersecting conic sections, but he could not find a formula for the roots. A Latin translation of al-Khwarizmi's *Algebra* appeared in the 12th century, and in the early 13th century appeared the writings of the great Italian mathematician Leonardo Fibonacci (1170–1230), among whose achievements was a close approximation to the solution of the cubic equation $x^3 + 2x^2 + cx = d$. Because Fibonacci had travelled in Islamic lands, he probably used an Arabic method of successive approximations.

Early in the 16th century, the Italian mathematicians Scipione del Ferro (1465–1526), Niccolò Tartaglia (1500–57), and Gerolamo Cardano (1501–76) solved the general cubic equation in terms of the constants appearing in the equation. Cardano's pupil, Ludovico Ferrari (1522–65), soon found an exact solution to equations of the fourth degree, and as a result, mathematicians for the next several centuries tried to find a formula for the roots of equations of degree five, or higher. Early in the 19th century, however, the Norwegian Niels Abel and the French Évariste Galois proved that no such formula exists.

An important development in algebra in the 16th century was the introduction of symbols for the unknown and for algebraic powers and operations. Thus Book III of the French philosopher and mathematician René Descartes' *La géometrie* (1637) looks much like a modern algebra text. Descartes is most significant in mathematics, however, for his discovery of analytic geometry, which reduces the solution of geometric problems to the solution of algebraic ones. His geometry text also contained the essentials of a course on the theory of equations, including his so-called rule of signs for counting the number of what Descartes called the "true" (positive) and "false" (negative) roots of an equation. Work continued through the 18th century on the theory of equations, but not until 1799 was the proof published, by the German mathematician Carl Friedrich Gauss, that every polynomial equation has at least one root.

By the time of Gauss, algebra had entered its modern phase. Attention shifted from solving polynomial equations to the structure of systems of elements that arose as abstractions of systems, such as the complex numbers, that mathematicians had met in their study of polynomial equations. Two examples of such systems are groups (*see* GROUP) and quaternions, which share some of the properties of number systems (q.v.) but also depart from them in important ways. Groups began as systems of permutations and combinations (q.v.) of roots of polynomials, but they became one of the chief unifying concepts of 19th-century mathematics. Important contributions to their study were made by the French mathematicians Galois and Augustin Cauchy, the British mathematician Arthur Cayley, and the Norwegian mathematicians Niels Abel and Sophus Lie (1842–99). Quaternions were the discovery of the British mathematician William Rowan Hamilton, who extended the arithmetic of complex numbers (See COMPLEX NUMBER) to quaternions (quadruples of real numbers).

Immediately after Hamilton's discovery, the German mathematician Hermann Grassmann (1809–77) began investigating vectors (*see* VECTOR). Despite its abstract character, American physicist J. W. Gibbs recognized in vector algebra a system of great utility for physicists, just as Hamilton had recognized the usefulness of quaternions. The widespread influence of this abstract approach led to the publication in 1854 of George Boole's *The Laws of Thought*, an algebraic treatment of basic logic. Since that time, modern algebra—also called abstract algebra—has continued to develop. Important new results have been discovered, and the subject has found applications in all branches of mathematics and in many of the sciences, as well.    J.Le.B.

**Symbols and Special Terms.** The symbols of algebra include numbers, letters, and signs that indicate various arithmetic operations. Numbers are, of course, constants, but letters may represent either constants or variables. Letters used to represent constants are taken from the beginning of the alphabet; those used to represent variables are taken from the end of the alphabet.

*Signs of aggregation and operation.* The grouping of algebraic symbols and the sequence of arithmetic operations rely on grouping symbols to ensure that the language of algebra is clearly read. Grouping symbols include parentheses ( ), brackets [ ], braces { }, and horizontal bars (also called vinculums) that are used most often for division and roots, as in the following:

$$\frac{ax + b}{c - dy} \qquad \sqrt{b^2 - 4ac}$$

The basic operational signs of algebra are familiar from arithmetic: addition ($+$), subtraction ($-$), multiplication ($\times$), and division ($\div$). Often, in the case of multiplication, the $\times$ is omitted or replaced by a dot, as in $a \cdot b$. A group of consecutive symbols, such as $abc$, indicates the product of $a$, $b$, and $c$. Division is commonly indicated by bars as in the preceding example. A virgule, or slash (/), is also used to separate the numerator from the denominator of a fraction, but care must be taken to group the terms appropriately. For example, $ax + b/c - dy$ indicates that $ax$ and $dy$ are separate terms, as is $b/c$, whereas $(ax + b)/(c - dy)$ correctly represents the fraction

$$\frac{ax + b}{c - dy}$$

*Order of operations.* Multiplications are performed first, then divisions, followed by additions, and then subtractions. Grouping symbols indicate the order in which operations are to be performed: Carry out all operations within a group first, beginning with the innermost group. For example

$$\{2\,[3 + (6\cdot 5 + 2)]\} = \{2\,[3 + (30 + 2)]\} =$$
$$\{2\,[3 + (32)]\} = \{2\,[35]\} = 70$$

*Special definitions.* Any statement involving the equality relation ($=$) is called an equation. An equation is called an identity if the equality is true for all values of its variables; otherwise an equation is said to be conditional, if it is true for some values and false for others. A term is any algebraic expression consisting only of products of constants and variables; $2x$, $-a$, $\frac{1}{4}s^4x$, and $x^2(2zy)^3$ are all examples of terms. The numerical part of a term is called its coefficient. The coefficients of each term above are, respectively, 2, $-1$, $\frac{1}{4}$, and

8 (the last term may be rewritten $8x^2(zy)^3$).

An expression containing one term is called a monomial; two terms, a binomial; and three terms, a trinomial. A polynomial is any finite sum (or difference) of terms. For example, a general polynomial of degree $n$ might be expressed as

$$a_1x^n + a_2x^{n-1} + a_3x^{n-2} + \ldots + a_nx$$

Degree in this context refers to the largest exponent of the variables in a polynomial. For example, if the largest exponent of a variable is 3, as in $ax^3 + bx^2 + cx$, the polynomial is said to be of degree 3. Similarly, the expression $x^n + x^{n-1} + x^{n-2}$ is of degree $n$.

A linear equation in one variable is a polynomial equation of degree one, that is, of the form $ax + b = 0$. These are called linear equations because they represent the equation of straight lines in analytic geometry.

A quadratic equation in one variable is a polynomial equation of degree two, that is, of the form $ax^2 + bx + c = 0$.

A prime number is any integer (whole number) that can be evenly divided only by itself and by the number 1. Thus, 2, 3, 5, 7, 11, and 13 are all prime numbers, being divisible by no integers other than themselves and 1.

Powers of a number are formed by successively multiplying the number by itself. The term $a$ raised to the third power, for example, can be expressed as $a \cdot a \cdot a$, or as $a^3$.

The prime factors of any number are those factors to which it can be reduced such that the number is expressed only as the product of primes and their powers. For example, the prime factors of 15 are 3 and 5. Similarly, the prime factors of 60 are $2^2$, 3, and 5. *See* FACTOR.

A root is one of the equal factors of a given number. For example, given the number 4, 2 is the square root of 4, because $2^2 = 4$.

**Operations with Polynomials.** In operating with polynomials, the assumption is made that the usual laws of the arithmetic of numbers hold. In arithmetic, the numbers dealt with are the natural numbers, or positive integers (*see* NUMBER; NUMBER THEORY), the negative integers, and all quotients, producing the set of rational numbers. Arithmetic alone cannot go beyond this, but algebra and geometry can include both irrational numbers, such as the square root of 2, and complex numbers. The set of all rational and irrational numbers taken together constitutes the set of what are called real numbers.

*Laws of Addition.* A-1. The sum of any two real numbers $a$ and $b$ is again a real number, denoted $a + b$. The real numbers are closed under the operations of addition, subtraction, multiplication, division, and the extraction of roots.

A-2. No matter how terms are grouped in carrying out additions, the sum will always be the same: $(a + b) + c = a + (b + c)$. This is called the associative law of addition.

A-3. Given any real number $a$, there is a real number zero (0) called the additive identity, such that $a + 0 = 0 + a = a$.

A-4. Given any real number $a$ there is a number $(-a)$, called the additive inverse of $a$, such that $(a) + (-a) = 0$.

A-5. No matter in what order addition is carried out, the sum will always be the same: $a + b = b + a$. This is called the commutative law of addition.

Any set of numbers obeying laws A-1 through A-4 is said to form a group. If the set also obeys A-5 it is said to be a commutative Abelian group.

**Laws of Multiplication.** Laws similar to those for addition also apply to multiplication. Special attention should be given to the multiplicative identity and inverse, M-3 and M-4.

M-1. The product of any two real numbers $a$ and $b$ is again a real number, denoted $a \cdot b$ or, more simply, $ab$.

M-2. No matter how terms are grouped in carrying out multiplications, the product will always be the same: $(ab)c = a (bc)$. This is called the associative law of multiplication.

M-3. Given any real number $a$, there is a number one (1) called the multiplicative identity, such that $a(1) = 1(a) = a$.

M-4. Given any real number $a$, there is a number $(a^{-1})$, or $(1/a)$, called the multiplicative inverse, such that $a(a^{-1}) = (a^{-1})a = 1$.

M-5. No matter in what order multiplication is carried out, the product will always be the same: $ab = ba$. This is called the commutative law of multiplication.

Any set of elements obeying these five laws is said to be a commutative, or Abelian, group under multiplication. The set of all real numbers, excluding zero (because division by zero is inadmissible), forms such a commutative group under multiplication.

**Distributive Laws.** Another important property of the set of real numbers links addition and multiplication in two distributive laws as follows:

D-1. $a(b + c) = ab + ac$

D-2. $(b + c)a = ba + ca$

Any set of elements with an equality relation and for which two operations (such as addition and multiplication) are defined, and which obeys all the laws for addition A-1 through A-5, the laws for multiplication M-1 through M-5, and the distributive laws D-1 and D-2, constitutes a field.

**Multiplication of Polynomials.** The following is a simple example of the product of a binomial and a monomial:

$$(ax + b)(cx^2) = acx^3 + bcx^2$$

This same principle, multiplying each term of the one polynomial by each term of the other, is directly extended to polynomials of any number of terms. For example, the product of a binomial and a trinomial is carried out as follows:

$$(ax^3 + bx^2 - cx)(dx + e) = adx^4 + aex^3 + bdx^3 + bex^2 - cdx^2 - cex$$

After such operations have been performed, all similar terms should be combined whenever possible to simplify the entire expression:

$$= adx^4 + (ae + bd)x^3 + (be - cd)x^2 - cex$$

**Factoring Polynomials.** Given a complicated algebraic expression, it is often useful to factor it into the product of several simpler terms. For example, $2x^3 + 8x^2y$ can be factored as $2x^2(x + 4y)$. Determining the factors of a given polynomial may be a simple matter of inspection or may require trial and error. Not all polynomials, however, can be factored, and these are called prime polynomials.

Some common factorizations are given in the following examples.

Trinomials of the form:
$$x^2 + 2xy + y^2 = (x + y)(x + y) = (x + y)^2$$
$$x^2 - 2xy + y^2 = (x - y)(x - y) = (x - y)^2$$
$$25x^2 + 20xy + 4y^2 = (5x + 2y)^2$$

The difference of two squares:
$$x^2 - y^2 = (x + y)(x - y)$$
$$25x^2 - 16y^2 = (5x + 4y)(5x - 4y)$$

Trinomials of the form:
$$x^2 + (a + b)x + ab = (x + a)(x + b)$$
$$x^2 + 7x + 10 = (x + 5)(x + 2)$$

Sums and differences of cubes:
$$x^3 \pm y^3 = (x \pm y)(x^2 \mp xy + y^2)$$
$$x^3 + 8y^3 = (x + 2y)(x^2 - 2xy + 4y^2)$$

Grouping may often be useful in factoring; terms that are similar are grouped wherever possible, as in the following example:

$$2x^2z + x^2y - 6xz - 3xy = x^2(2z + y) - 3x(2z + y)$$
$$= (x^2 - 3x)(2z + y)$$
$$= x(x - 3)(2z + y)$$

**Highest Common Factors.** Given a polynomial, it is frequently important to isolate the greatest common factor from each term of the polynomial. For example, in the expression $9x^3 + 18x^2$, the number 9 is a factor of both terms, as is $x^2$. After factoring, $9x^2(x + 2)$ is obtained, and $9x^2$ is the greatest common factor for all terms of the original polynomial (in this case a binomial). Similarly, for the trinomial $6a^2x^3 + 9abx + 15cx^2$, the number 3 is the largest numerical factor common to 6, 9, and 15, and $x$ is the largest variable factor common to all three terms. Thus, the greatest common factor of the trinomial is $3x$.

**Least Common Multiples.** Finding least common multiples is useful in combining algebraic fractions. The procedure is analogous to that used to combine ordinary fractions in arithmetic. To combine two or more fractions, the denominators must be the same; the most direct way to produce common denominators is simply to multiply all the denominators together. For example

$$\frac{a}{b} + \frac{c}{d} = \frac{a}{b} \cdot \frac{d}{d} + \frac{c}{d} \cdot \frac{b}{b} = \frac{ad + bc}{bd}$$

But $bd$ may not be the *least* common denominator. For example

$$\frac{2}{3} + \frac{1}{6} = \frac{2 \cdot 6}{3 \cdot 6} + \frac{1 \cdot 3}{6 \cdot 3} = \frac{12 + 3}{18} = \frac{15}{18}$$

But 18 is only one possible common denominator; the least common denominator is 6, and

$$\frac{2}{3} \cdot \frac{2}{2} + \frac{1}{6} = \frac{4}{6} + \frac{1}{6} = \frac{5}{6}$$

In algebra, the problem of finding least common multiples of denominators is similar. Given several algebraic expressions, the least common multiple is the expression of lowest degree and least coefficient that can be divided evenly by each of the expressions. Thus, to find a common multiple of the terms $2x^2y$, $30x^2y^2$, and $9ay^3$, all three expressions could simply be multiplied together, and it would be trivial that $(2x^2y)(30x^2y^2)(9ay^3)$ is evenly divisible by each of the three terms; however, this would not be the *least* common multiple. To determine which is the least, each of the terms is reduced to its prime factors. For the numerical coefficients 2, 30, and 9, the prime factors are $2$, $2 \cdot 3 \cdot 5$, and $3 \cdot 3$, respectively; the least common multiple for the numerical coefficients must therefore be $2 \cdot 3 \cdot 3 \cdot 5$, or 90. Similarly, because the constant $a$ appears only once, it too must be a factor. Of the variables, $x^2$ and $y^3$ are required, so that the least common multiple of the three terms is $90ax^2y^3$. Each term will evenly divide this expression.

**Solution of Equations.** Given an equation, algebra proceeds to supply solutions based on the general idea of the identity $a = a$. As long as the same arithmetic or algebraic procedure is applied si-

multaneously to both sides of the equation, the equality remains unaffected. The basic strategy is to isolate the unknown term on one side of the equation and the solution on the other. For example, to solve the linear equation in one unknown

$$5x + 6 = 3x + 12$$

the variable terms are isolated on one side and the constant terms on the other. The term $3x$ can be removed from the right side by subtracting; $3x$ must then be subtracted from the left side as well:

$$\begin{array}{rcr} 5x + 6 = & 3x + 12 \\ -3x & -3x \\ \hline 2x + 6 = & 12 \end{array}$$

The number 6 is then subtracted from both sides:

$$\begin{array}{rcr} 2x + 6 = & 12 \\ -6 & -6 \\ \hline 2x \quad = & 6 \end{array}$$

To isolate $x$ on the left side, both sides of the equation are divided by 2:

$$\frac{2x}{2} = \frac{6}{2}$$

and the solution then follows directly: $x = 3$. This can easily be verified by substituting the solution value $x = 3$ back into the original equation:

$$5x + 6 = 3x + 12$$
$$5(3) + 6 = 3(3) + 12$$
$$15 + 6 = 9 + 12$$
$$21 = 21$$

*Solution of quadratic equations.* Given any quadratic equation of the general form

$$ax^2 + bx + c = 0$$

a number of approaches are possible depending on the specific nature of the equation in question. If the equation can be factored, then the solution is straightforward. For instance

$$x^2 - 3x = 10$$

First the equation is put into the standard form

$$x^2 - 3x - 10 = 0$$

which can be factored as follows:

$$(x - 5)(x + 2) = 0$$

This condition can be met, however, only when the individual factors are zero, that is, when $x = 5$ and $x = -2$. That these are the solutions to the equation may again be verified by substitution.

**Method of completing the square.** If, on inspection, no obvious means of factoring the equation directly can be found, an alternative may exist. For example, in the equation

$$4x^2 + 12x = 7$$

the expression $4x^2 + 12x$ could be factored as a perfect square if it were $4x^2 + 12x + 9$, which equals $(2x + 3)^2$. This can easily be achieved by adding 9 to the left side of the equation. The same amount must then, of course, be added to the right side as well:

$$4x^2 + 12x + 9 = 7 + 9$$
$$(2x + 3)^2 = 16$$

This can be reduced to

$$(2x + 3) = \sqrt{16}$$

or

$$2x + 3 = +4$$

and

$$2x + 3 = -4$$

(because $\sqrt{16}$ has two values). The first equation leads to the solution $x = \frac{1}{2}$ (because $2x + 3 = 4$, $2x = 1$ [subtracting 3 from both sides], and $x = \frac{1}{2}$ [dividing both sides by 2]). The second equation leads to the solution $x = -7/2$, or $x = -3\frac{1}{2}$. Both solutions can be verified, as before, by substituting the values in question back into the original equation.

**The quadratic formula.** In factoring or completing the square, any quadratic equation can always be solved by application of the quadratic formula. This formula provides a method for determining the solutions of the equation if it is in the form

$$ax^2 + bx + c = 0$$

In all cases the two solutions of $x$ are given by the formula:

$$x = \frac{-b \pm \sqrt{b^2 - 4ac}}{2a}$$

For example, to find the roots of

$$x^2 - 4x = -3$$

the equation is first put into the standard form

$$x^2 - 4x + 3 = 0$$

As a result, $a = 1$, $b = -4$, and $c = 3$. These terms are then substituted into the quadratic formula

$$x = \frac{-(-4) \pm \sqrt{(-4)^2 - 4(1)(3)}}{2(1)}$$

$$= \frac{4 \pm \sqrt{16 - 12}}{2}$$

$$= \frac{4 \pm \sqrt{4}}{2} = \frac{4 \pm 2}{2} = 3 \text{ and } 1$$

**Solution of two simultaneous equations.** Algebra frequently has to solve not just a single equation but several at the same time. The problem is to find the set of all solutions that satisfies both equations. These are called simultaneous equations, and specific algebraic techniques may be used to solve them. For example, given the two linear equations in two unknowns

$$3x + 4y = 10 \qquad (1)$$
$$2x + y = 5 \qquad (2)$$

a simple solution exists: The variable $y$ in equation (2) is isolated ($y = 5 - 2x$), and then this value of $y$ is substituted into equation (1):

$$3x + 4(5 - 2x) = 10$$

This reduces the problem to one involving the single linear unknown $x$, and it follows that

$$3x + 20 - 8x = 10$$

or

$$-5x = -10$$

so that

$$x = 2$$

When this value is substituted into either equation (1) or (2), it follows that

$$y = 1$$

A faster method of solving simultaneous equations is obtained by observing that if both sides of equation (2) are multiplied by 4, then

$$3x + 4y = 10 \qquad (1)$$
$$8x + 4y = 20 \qquad (2)$$

If equation (1) is subtracted from equation (2), then $5x = 10$, or $x = 2$. This procedure leads to another development in mathematics, matrices, which help to produce solutions for any set of linear equations in any number of unknowns (*see* MATRIX THEORY AND LINEAR ALGEBRA). *See also* MATHEMATICAL SYMBOLS. J.W.D.; REV. BY J.Le.B.

*For further information on this topic, see the Bibliography in volume 28, section 369.*

**ALGECIRAS,** city and seaport, S Spain, in Cádiz Province, on Algeciras Bay, near Gibraltar. The city is a popular resort area because of the mild winters and nearby beaches and mineral springs. It serves as a port city for the surrounding agricultural region, in which cereals, tobacco, and livestock are produced. The major industries of the city are fishing and the processing of cork. The present city was founded on the ruins of a Moorish city in 1704 by Spanish refugees from Gibraltar, when the promontory was captured by a combined British and Dutch force. The ruins of a Moorish aqueduct are nearby. Algeciras was the site of a famous naval battle in 1801, in which the British fleet defeated the combined French and Spanish forces, and of the Algeciras Conference held (1906) to settle the dispute of the European powers over Morocco. Pop. (1991) 101,063.

**ALGER, Horatio** (1834–99), American writer of juvenile fiction, born in Revere, Mass., and educated at Harvard College and Harvard Divinity School. Ordained (1864) a Unitarian minister in 1866, he became chaplain of a lodging house for newsboys in New York City.

In Alger's first volume of fiction, *Ragged Dick* (1867), and in similar works, he portrayed underprivileged youths who win fame and wealth by practicing such virtues as honesty, diligence, and perseverance. *Luck and Pluck* and *Tattered Tom* appeared in 1869 and 1871, respectively. Alger wrote more than 100 such works. Although of little literary significance, his novels influenced American youth by emphasizing merit, rather than mere social status, as the chief determinant of success.

**ALGERIA** (Arab. *al-Jazairiyah*), officially Democratic and Popular Republic of Algeria, republic of W North Africa; bounded on the N by the Mediterranean Sea; on the E by Tunisia and Libya; on the S by Niger, Mali, and Mauritania; and on the W by Morocco. Its total area is 2,381,741 sq km (919,595 sq mi).

### LAND AND RESOURCES

Algeria has four main physical regions, which extend E to W across the country in parallel zones. In the N, along the Mediterranean coast and extending inland for 80 to 190 km (50 to 118 mi), is the Tell. The region consists of a narrow and discontinuous coastal plain backed by the mountainous area of the Tell Atlas (see ATLAS MOUNTAINS). The numerous valleys of this region contain most of Algeria's arable land. The country's principal river, the 725-km (450-mi) long Chelif, rises in the Tell Atlas and flows to the Mediterranean Sea; no permanent streams are found S of the Tell. The next region, lying to the S and SW, is the Hauts Plateaux, a highland region of level terrain. Several basins here collect water during rainy periods, forming large, shallow lakes; as these lakes dry they become salt flats, called chotts, or shotts. South of the Hauts Plateaux region lie the mountains and massifs of the Saharan Atlas. The fourth region, comprising more than 90% of the country's total area, is the great expanse of the Algerian Sahara. Much of the terrain is covered by gravel, although the Grand Erg Oriental and the Grand Erg Occidental are vast regions of sand dunes. In the S, rising above the desert, are the Ahaggar Mts., which culminate in Mt. Tahat (2918 m/9573 ft), the highest peak in Algeria.

*Illustrated title page of one of the* Luck and Pluck *series telling how poor boys achieved wealth and fame through virtue and hard work.* **Bettmann Archive**

**Climate.** The Tell region in the N has a typical Mediterranean climate, with warm, dry summers and mild, rainy winters. This is the most humid area of Algeria, with an annual precipitation ranging from 400 to 1000 mm (16 to 39 in). The mean summer and winter temperatures are 25° C (77° F) and 11.1° C (52° F), respectively. During the summer an exceedingly hot, dry wind, the sirocco (known locally as the Chehili), blows N from the Sahara. To the S the climate becomes increasingly dry. Annual precipitation in the High Plateau and Saharan Atlas ranges from about 200 to 400 mm (about 8 to 16 in). The Sahara is a region of daily temperature extremes, wind, and great aridity; annual rainfall is less than 130 mm (5 in) in all places.

**Natural Resources.** Most of the natural wealth of Algeria lies in its sizable mineral deposits, notably crude petroleum, natural gas, phosphates, and iron ore. Other minerals include coal, lead, and zinc. The arable land comprises only about 3% of the total area and is located mainly in the valleys and plains of the coastal region.

**Soils.** Rich soils are rare in Algeria. The most fertile lands, in the Tell region nearest the coast, are relatively poor in humus and suffer from overcultivation. The plains have considerable alluvial deposits, but the uplands have poorer soils and can support only grasses suitable for grazing.

The west gate of the Roman ruins at Timgad, in northeastern Algeria.
© 1987 F. Jackson–Bruce Coleman, Inc.

**Plants and Animals.** The N sections of Algeria have suffered from centuries of deforestation and overgrazing. Remnants of forests exist in a few areas of the higher Tell and Saharan Atlas. Trees include pines, Atlas cedar, and various oaks, including cork oak. Lower slopes are bare or covered with a scrub vegetation of juniper and other shrubs. Much of the High Plateau is barren, but tracts of steppe vegetation containing esparto grass and brushwood are present. Saharan flora is widely scattered and consists of drought-resistant grasses, acacia, and jujube trees.

The relatively sparse vegetation of the country is able to support only a limited wildlife population. Scavengers, such as jackals, hyenas, and vultures, are found in most regions. Antelopes, hare, gazelles, and reptiles are also present in smaller numbers.

### POPULATION

The population consists almost entirely of Arabs, Berbers, and persons of mixed Arab-Berber stock. Until 1962 about 1 million European settlers, mainly French, and an indigenous population of 150,000 Jews lived in Algeria; 90% of this group, however, emigrated after Algeria became independent in 1962. About 52% of the population is classified as urban.

**Population Characteristics.** The resident population of Algeria (1994 est.) was 27.9 million. The overall population density was about 12 people per sq km (about 30 per sq mi). More than half the population is concentrated in the coastal Tell region. Another 2.5 million Algerians live in France.

**Political Divisions.** Algeria is divided into 48 departments (*wilaya*). These are subdivided into nearly 700 local communes.

Algiers is the capital, chief seaport, and largest city (pop., 1987 census, 1,507,241). Other important cities include Oran (628,558), a trading center, and Constantine (440,842), the center for a livestock- and wheat-producing region.

**Language and Religion.** Arabic is the official language and is spoken by more than 80% of the population; most of the remainder speak a Berber dialect. French is still widely read and spoken by many educated Algerians. Islam is the official religion and is professed by the vast majority of the population.

### EDUCATION AND CULTURE

French tradition formerly dominated the cultural life of Algeria. Even before independence, however, there was a growing movement among Algerian artists and intellectuals to revive national interest in Arab-Berber origins, a movement that, since 1962, has gained official support.

**Education.** Primary education is free and compulsory for all children between the ages of 6 and 15, and more than 85% of school-age children receive primary education. The Algerian educational system, long patterned after the French, was changed by a program of Arabization shortly after independence. The government introduced new teaching methods and began training Algerian teachers and bringing in foreign, Arabic-speaking teachers. In 1976 all private schools were abolished and a compulsory period of nine years of education was introduced.

In the early 1990s some 4.3 million pupils attended primary schools and about 2.2 million were enrolled in secondary schools. The government also maintains vocational and teacher-training schools.

Algeria's ten universities include two universities of science and technology; the total enrollment at all institutions of higher education exceeds 258,000. The University of Algiers (1879) has faculties of law, medicine, science, and liberal arts.

Nine of the universities and most of the 20 or so university centers, institutes, and specialized colleges have been founded since independence.

**Cultural Institutions.** Foremost among Algerian libraries is the National Library (1835) in Algiers, which has about 1 million volumes, including important works on African subjects. Collections are maintained by the University of Algiers, which has more than 700,000 volumes, and by the Municipal Library in Constantine, which contains about 25,000 volumes.

The Prehistory and Ethnographic Museum ("Le Bardo"; 1930), the National Museum of Antiquities (1897), and the National Museum of Fine Arts of Algiers (1930) are located in Algiers. The Museum of Cirta (1853) in Constantine contains art and archaeological collections.

**Literature.** Although much Algerian writing was suppressed by the French during the 1950s, the war for independence stimulated a considerable resurgence of interest in the Arabic-language national literature. Noted 20th-century Algerian

*Oran is Algeria's second largest city and a main Mediterranean port. The city is the principal center of exporting, food processing, and manufacturing in Western Algeria.*
John Elk III–Bruce Coleman, Inc.

# ALGERIA

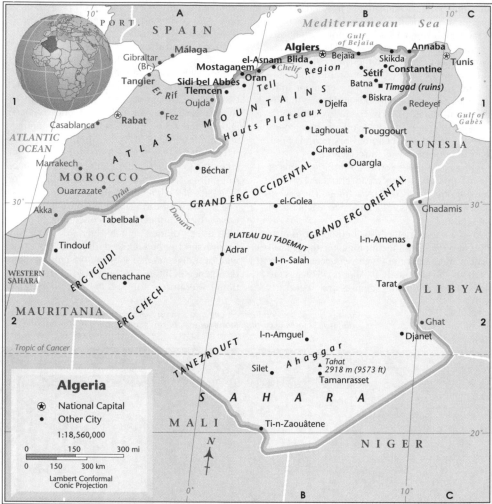

© GeoSystems Global Corp.

writers (who wrote in French) are Kateb Yacine (1929–89), Mohammad Dib (1920–  ), and Malek Haddad (1927–  ). The French novelist Albert Camus was born and educated in Algeria.

## ECONOMY

Algeria is one of the wealthiest nations of Africa, with an annual gross national product of $1840 per capita in 1992. Agriculture plays a declining but still important role in the Algerian economy, while mineral production accounts for the largest part of the gross domestic product. Since the late 1960s the government has instituted major industrialization programs. The annual national budget in the early 1990s included $14.4 billion in revenue and $14.6 billion in expenditure.

**Labor.** The General Union of Algerian Workers, founded in 1956, consists of 800,000 members divided by trade into ten sectors. In 1973 a National Union of Algerian Peasants was formed, consisting of about 700,000 farmer members. The labor force consists of about 6.2 million, of whom some 36% engage in industry and commerce, 16% in agriculture, and 23% in government.

**Agriculture.** Although farming employs more than 15% of the work force, it accounts for only about 7% of the gross domestic product. Productivity is low and foodstuffs must be imported. The principal crops are wheat, barley, potatoes, citrus fruits, grapes, olives, tobacco, vegetables, and dates. Of the livestock raised, sheep numbered about 18,600,000 in the early 1990s, goats 2,500,000, and cattle 1,420,000.

**Forestry and Fishing.** Forests, which contain much brushwood, cover less than 2% of Algeria's land area. Substantial reforestation projects were undertaken in the 1970s. Lumber is used principally for heating and industrial needs. Bark is cut for tanning and cork for commercial purposes. Charcoal, made from charred wood, is also used for fuel.

Fishing is an important industry; in the early 1990s the country's total annual catch was about 91,100 metric tons. The bulk of the yield included sardines, anchovies, sprats, tuna, and shellfish.

**Mining, Manufacturing, and Energy.** The chief mineral products are crude petroleum and natural gas from the Sahara. Oil production in the early 1990s was about 290 million barrels a year; natural gas production totaled 43.3 billion cu m (1.53 trillion cu ft) annually.

Other major mineral products are iron ore and pyrites, coal, zinc, lead, and mercury. More than 500 million tons of phosphates are thought to exist in hilly regions in the north. Virtually all mining and industrial activity is state controlled. Much of the industry is centered around the cities of Algiers and Oran. Major products are carpets and textiles, chemicals, refined petroleum, plastics, construction materials, olive oil, wine, and processed tobacco. Other industries produce iron and steel, paper, and electrical items.

In the early 1990s electric power production in Algeria exceeded 17.3 billion kwh. More than 98% of the power was produced in conventional thermal plants using fossil fuels.

**Currency and Banking.** The chief monetary unit of Algeria is the dinar (36.19 dinars equal U.S.$1; 1994). All government banking and monetary functions are carried out by the Bank of Algeria. Since 1966 all domestic banks have been nationalized.

**Commerce and Trade.** The principal Algerian exports are natural gas, petroleum, iron ore, vegetables, tobacco, phosphates, fruit, cork, and hides. Major imports are machinery, textiles, sugar, cereals, iron and steel, coal, and gasoline. The European Union is Algeria's main trading partner, taking more than two-thirds of its exports, including much of its oil. Other major partners are the U.S. and Japan. In the early 1990s, annual exports totaled about $12.3 billion and imports about $6.9 billion. Algeria's trade volume and balance depend heavily on petroleum prices.

**Transportation.** The rail and road systems mainly serve the N third of the country. Five railroad lines run to the N edge of the Sahara, and roads link the Sahara oil fields to the coast. In the early 1990s Algeria had about 4290 km (about 2670 mi) of railroad track and about 90,000 km (about 55,920 mi) of roads, of which 70% was paved. Algeria's segment of a trans-Saharan highway, extending from the Mediterranean coast past Tamanrasset to the Niger border, was completed in 1985. Air Algérie, the national airline, provides domestic and international air service.

**Communications.** All news media, including the country's 11 daily newspapers, are government controlled, as are book publishing and the radio and television networks. In the early 1990s the country had an estimated 2 million televisions and 3.5 million radios.

## GOVERNMENT

Under the constitution adopted in February 1989, Algeria is a socialist republic.

**Executive and Legislature.** The constitution of 1989 provides for a president elected to a 5-year term by universal adult suffrage. A unicameral National People's Assembly of 295 members was elected in 1987. The National Liberation Front has dominated Algerian politics since independence. Elections were annulled and the Assembly was suspended in January 1992 to prevent the Islamic Salvation Front, a Muslim fundamentalist party,

*Farming the traditional way in the Kabylian Mountains, Algeria.*
©1987 Henneghien–Bruce Coleman, Inc.

from gaining a legislative majority. Since then, Algeria has been ruled by the High Security Council (HSC), supported by the military. A five-member council, the High Committee of State, exercised executive powers until January 1994, when it was dissolved by the HSC and replaced by a single appointed president.

**Judiciary.** The highest court in Algeria is the supreme court, which sits in Algiers. A total of 183 lower courts and 31 appellate courts are organized on a regional basis. The judicial system also includes military courts and special antiterrorist tribunals.

**Local Government.** Each department (*wilaya*) is headed by a governor appointed by the federal government. Municipal councils enact local laws and elect all administrative officers.

**Health and Welfare.** The government sponsors social welfare programs providing allowances for the aged, needy, and disabled; benefits for non-agrarian workers; agrarian reform; public works; and accelerated public-housing programs.

Since 1974, medical care has been provided free to all Algerian citizens. Health services have improved significantly in recent decades; the infant mortality rate declined from 139 per 1000 live births in 1970 to 55 in 1992. In the early 1990s average life expectancy at birth was 68 years for women and 66 years for men, among the highest in Africa.

**Defense.** Military service in Algeria is compulsory for a period of 18 months. The nucleus of the 105,000-troop army was provided by the liberation forces after Algerian independence was secured. A 10,000-member air force is equipped with Soviet- and French-built jet planes and helicopters. Naval forces numbered 6700 in the early 1990s.

### HISTORY

**Ancient Times.** The earliest inhabitants of what is now Algeria were Berbers, tribal peoples of unknown origin. Cave paintings in the Ahaggar region depict a people who raised cattle and hunted game in the area between 8000 and 2000 BC. Much later, about 1100 BC, the Phoenicians, a seafaring people from the eastern Mediterranean, founded a North African state at Carthage in what is now Tunisia. During the Punic Wars (3d–2d cent. BC) between Carthage and Rome, Massinissa (238?–148 BC), a Berber chief allied with Rome, established the first Algerian kingdom, Numidia. His grandson, Jugurtha, was subjugated by Rome in 106 BC.

Numidia prospered under Roman rule. Large estates produced so much grain and olive oil that the region became known as the granary of Rome. A system of military roads and garrisoned towns protected the inhabitants from nomadic tribes. In time, these towns grew into miniature Roman cities.

The decline of Rome brought many changes. Roman legions were withdrawn to defend other frontiers, and in the 3d century AD regional independence was briefly expressed in the Donatist movement, a North African Christian sect persecuted by the Roman authorities. The Vandals, a Germanic tribe, invaded the region in the 5th century and stayed on there to establish their own kingdom. Barely a century later these warriors were themselves overthrown by an army of the Byzantine emperor Justinian, whose dream was to restore the glory of the Roman Empire.

**Medieval Islamic Dynasties.** Justinian's dream was short-lived. In the 7th century the Arabs invaded North Africa, bringing with them a new religion, Islam. In Algeria they were resisted by a woman leader—Kahina (fl. 670–98), the high priestess of a tribe supposedly converted to Judaism—but eventually the Berbers submitted to Islam and Arab authority; Algeria became a province of the Umayyad caliphate. The Arabs, however, remained largely an urban elite.

An internal conflict over the succession to the caliphal throne enabled the Berbers to form their own Islamic government in the 8th century. Many of them joined the branch of Islam known as Shia, and they established several tribal kingdoms. One of the most prominent kingdoms was that of the Rustamids at Tahert in central Algeria. Tahert prospered in the 8th and 9th centuries. Between the 11th and 13th centuries two successive Berber dynasties, the Almoravids and the Almohads, brought northwest Africa and southern Spain under a single central authority. Tlemcen, the capital under the Almohads, became a city of fine mosques and schools of Islamic learning, as well as a handicrafts center. Algerian seaports like Bejaïa, Annaba, and the growing town of Algiers carried on a brisk trade with various European cities, supplying the famed Barbary horses, wax, fine leather, and fabrics to European markets.

**Ottoman Turkish Rule.** The collapse of the Almohads in 1269 set off fierce trade competition among Mediterranean seaports, both Christian and

*The central market in Ghardaia, Algeria.*       © 1979 John Elk III–Bruce Coleman, Inc.

*A modern road cut through the rocky, once impassable, gorges of Chabet el Akra, near the town of Kerrata.*

Trans World Airlines

Muslim. To gain advantage, city governments began to hire corsairs—pirates who seized merchant ships and held crews and cargo for ransom. Algiers became a primary center of corsair activities.

In the 16th century the Christian Spaniards occupied various North African ports. Algiers was blockaded and forced to pay tribute. Other ports were captured outright. The desperate Muslims called for help from the Ottoman sultan, then the caliph of all Islam. Two corsair brothers, the Barbarossas ("Redbeards"), persuaded the sultan to send them with a fleet to North Africa. They drove the Spaniards out of a majority of their new possessions, and in 1518 the younger Barbarossa, Khayr ad-Din (1483?–1546), was appointed beylerbey, the sultan's representative in Algeria.

Because of its distance from the Turkish capital at Constantinople, Algiers was governed as an autonomous province. Externally, the effectiveness of its corsair fleet made Algiers a power in its

own right; Algerian pirates dominated the Mediterranean. European states paid tribute regularly to ensure protection for their ships, and prisoner ransoms brought a rich income to the province. Internal security was maintained by Ottoman janissary garrisons.

In the late 18th century improved firepower and ship construction enabled the Europeans to challenge corsair domination. By then, the days of Ottoman Algiers were numbered. International agreements to outlaw piracy made collective action against the corsair capital possible. In 1815 the U.S. sent a naval squadron against Algiers. The following year an Anglo-Dutch fleet nearly destroyed its defenses, and in 1830 the city was captured by a French army.

**French Colonization.** France annexed Algeria in 1834, and the new regime aroused fierce resistance from tribes accustomed to indirect Turkish rule. Their leader, Abd al-Qadir (1803-83), an Islamic holy man who claimed descent from Muhammad, employed hit-and-run tactics that were extremely effective; he was not completely subdued until 1847, and he remains a hero to modern Algerian nationalists.

With Abd al-Qadir out of the way, France began to colonize Algeria in earnest, and European settlers poured into the country. To encourage settlement, the French confiscated or purchased lands at low prices from Muslim owners. Algeria became an overseas department of France, controlled for all practical purposes by the European minority, the colons (colonists). The colons formed a privileged elite. With the help of large infusions of capital, they developed a modern economy, with industries, banks, schools, shops, and services similar to those at home. Algerian agriculture was geared to the French economy; large estates produced wines and citrus fruit for export to France, just as North Africa had once served Rome. Some Europeans made vast fortunes, but the majority were small farmers, tradespeople, shopkeepers, and factory workers. All, however, shared a passionate belief in Algérie Française—a French Algeria.

The Muslim population, although benefiting from social services and economic development, remained a disadvantaged majority, subject to many restrictions. By French law they could not hold public meetings, carry firearms, or leave their homes or villages without permission. Legally, they were French subjects, but to become French *citizens,* with full rights, they had to renounce their faith. Few did so.

The Muslim population grew steadily; by 1930, it numbered 5 million. A small minority, educated in French schools, adopted French culture, although they were not accepted as equals by the colons. From this group came the initial impetus for Algerian nationalism.

### Rise of Algerian Nationalism.
Algerian nationalism developed after World War I among groups of Muslims who at first wanted only equality with the Europeans. Ferhat Abbas and Ahmed Messali Hadj (1898–1974), a Communist, were among the most prominent Algerian leaders in the 1920s and '30s. In 1936 the French government devised a plan providing full equality for Muslim war veterans and professionals, but it was scuttled by colon deputies in the French National Assembly. Frustrated by the colons' stubborn resistance to reform, Abbas joined forces with Messali during World War II to organize a militant anti-French party, the Friends of the Manifesto and Liberty. After the war the Algerian Organic Statute (1947) set up Algeria's first parliamentary assembly, with an equal number of European and Muslim delegates, but this satisfied neither natives nor colons and proved ineffective. The more militant nationalists were by then beginning to favor armed revolt. In the early 1950s many went into hiding or exile.

### War of Independence.
In March 1954 Ahmed Ben Bella, an ex-sergeant in the French army, joined eight other Algerian exiles in Egypt to form a revolutionary committee that later became known as the National Liberation Front (Front de Libération Nationale, FLN). A few months later (November 1), the FLN launched its bid for Algerian independence by coordinated attacks on public buildings, military and police posts, and communications installations.

A steady rise in guerrilla action over the next two years forced the French to bring in reinforcements; eventually, 400,000 French troops were stationed in Algeria. FLN strategy combined Abd al-Qadir's guerrilla tactics with deliberate use of terrorism. The guerrilla tactics effectively immobilized superior French forces, while indiscriminate murders and kidnappings of Europeans and Muslims who did not actively support the FLN created a climate of fear throughout the country. This in turn brought counterterrorism, as colons and French army units raided Muslim villages and slaughtered the civilian population.

In 1956 the war spread to the cities. In Algiers, even cafés, schools, and shops became targets, as the nationalists sought to weaken colon morale and draw international attention to their cause. The Algiers uprising was ruthlessly put down. Elsewhere, the French gradually gained the upper hand by using new tactics. Collective punishment was meted out to whole villages suspected of aiding guerrillas. Other groups were deported to guarded refugee camps. Electrified fences along the Tunisian and Moroccan borders cut off the main FLN army from units inside Algeria.

Despite their military superiority, the French were unable to find a political solution satisfactory to both the colons and the FLN. International criticism of France increased, and its allies in the North Atlantic Treaty Organization worried about the commitment of French forces to an unpopular war.

In May 1958 the colons and French army officers joined hands in Algiers to overthrow the French government, charging it with vacillation. A Committee of Public Safety demanded the return to office of Gen. Charles de Gaulle, the wartime leader of the Free French, as the only one who could settle the war and preserve French Algeria. De Gaulle, however, was a realist. Once in power, he recognized that the war was unwinnable. In 1959 he announced his intention of allowing Algerians to choose between independence and continued association with France.

The plan struck the colons like a thunderbolt. They staged a failed revolt against de Gaulle early in 1960, and in 1961 a group of army generals again tried to overthrow him. Both times the bulk of the army remained loyal to the government. Associated with the generals' plot was a group of military and colon extremists, called the Secret Army Organization, which at the same time carried on a brutal campaign of counterterrorism against both the FLN and French authorities.

In March 1962 a cease-fire was finally arranged between government and FLN representatives at Evian, France. In the long-awaited referendum, held the following July, Algeria voted overwhelmingly for independence. The colons began a mass evacuation; before the end of the year most of them had left the country.

**Independence.** The Evian agreements gave immediate independence to Algeria, with aid from France to help the country recover from eight years of devastation. The French also returned the Sahara, with its vast French-developed oil and gas deposits. On its side, the FLN guaranteed protection and full civil rights for the remains of the European population; after a 3-year period they would choose between Algerian and French citizenship.

The material and human costs of the war were staggering. French casualties were about 100,000, Algerian more than 1 million, and another 1.8 million were refugees. An additional 150,000 pro-French Muslims became victims of the FLN as it settled old accounts after the cease-fire.

The departure of the Europeans deprived Algeria of nearly all its skilled labor force. To make matters worse, factional rivalries within the FLN,

papered over during the war, now became visible. At a meeting in Tripoli, Libya, FLN leaders approved a charter that specified Algeria as a socialist state, with the Front as the only legal political organization. Authority would be exercised by a central FLN political bureau. The economy would be state controlled, with former colon lands managed by committees of their workers.

The leaders agreed on little else, and open warfare soon broke out between factions. Col. Houari Boumedienne, chief of staff of the Army of National Liberation, threw his support to Ahmed Ben Bella, who in September 1962 was elected the first president of independent Algeria.

Ben Bella served as president for three years and made a start toward putting the country back on its feet. The first constitution was approved by voters in 1963, providing a presidential form of government. The only check on the president's power would be censure by two-thirds of the National Assembly. With such unrestricted authority, Ben Bella became totally absorbed in his personal power and prestige, more and more preoccupied with international leadership, and at the same time more autocratic at home. By mid-1965 Boumedienne, then minister of defense, felt Ben Bella had gone too far; he had him arrested in a bloodless coup and assumed supreme power.

**The Boumedienne Regime.** Under Boumedienne Algeria finally began to capitalize on its vast resources. The army rather than the FLN became a dominant force. Boumedienne formed a 26-member Council of the Revolution as supreme authority; its members were army commanders and his close associates. Factionalism and personal rule were strictly prohibited. Although Bou-

*Algerian President Chadli Benjedid and President Zail Singh of India at a meeting of the nonaligned nations in New Delhi in the 1980s.*         A. Nogues–Sygma

medienne remained first among equals—he was simultaneously president, prime minister, and minister of defense—the principle of collegial leadership was maintained.

In addition to economic growth, Boumedienne brought to the country a viable political system. The constitution of 1976 defined Algeria as a socialist state under FLN leadership. Boumedienne was legally elected president. When he died in 1978, Col. Chadli Benjedid succeeded him. Benjedid continued Boumedienne's policies but relaxed some of his strict controls; he released and pardoned (1980) former president Ben Bella. Benjedid was reelected in 1984.

In 1988, prompted by clashes between mostly youthful protesters and government troops, Benjedid loosened the FLN's monopoly on political power. Reelected in December to a third 5-year term, he secured passage of a new constitution in February 1989. In the 1990 provincial and municipal elections, the fundamentalist Islamic Salvation Front defeated the FLN by an overwhelming margin. In January 1992, after a first round of balloting made it likely that the fundamentalists would win control of parliament, a group of military and civilian officials, constituting themselves as the High Security Council (HSC), forced Benjedid to resign. They canceled the election, suspended parliament, and established a new executive committee headed by Mohammed Boudiaf (1919–92). When Boudiaf was assassinated, Ali Kafi (1928–    ) was named to replace him. The HSC dissolved the executive committee in January 1994 and named the defense minister, Liamine Zeroual (1941–    ), as head of state. By late 1994 at least 10,000 people had been killed in the escalating conflict between the Algerian government and Islamic militants.                                          W.S.

For additional information on historical figures, see biographies of those whose names are not followed by dates.

*For further information on this topic, see the Bibliography in volume 28, sections 1009–11, 1021.*

**ALGIERS** (Arab. *al-Jazair*), city, N Algeria, capital and largest city of the country and of Algiers Department, on the Bay of Algiers. It is the main Mediterranean port of NW Africa.

The city's strategic position and fine harbor combine to make Algiers a major shipping center and a principal Mediterranean refueling station. It has a major international airport and is the hub of a network of railways and roads.

**The Urban Landscape.** The city is divided into two sections. The lower part is the modern city, built by the French, with wide boulevards, theaters, cathedrals, museums, an opera house, and many educational institutions, including the University of Algiers and several Muslim schools. The upper part is the old city, with narrow, twisting streets dominated by the Casbah, a 16th-century fortress built by the Turks, which lends its name to the entire quarter. With the post–World War II population increase, and the crowding in the old quarter, suburbs have burgeoned.

**History.** By 1200 BC the Phoenicians had colonized the site and set up a coastal trading post. Following the Punic Wars, Algiers, then called Icosium, became (146 BC) part of the Roman Empire and remained Roman until the middle of the 5th century, when it was overrun by the Vandals. Next, it was ruled by the Byzantines, who, in turn, were ousted in 650 by Arabs. The present city was founded about 950 by Berbers. During the next five centuries control of the city was gained and lost by various European, Arabian, and Berber warlords. In 1510 Spain captured and fortified the islet in front of the harbor, known as the Peñón. In 1518 Algiers proclaimed itself part of the Ottoman Empire, and the Spanish were driven out. While ruled by the Ottomans, it became the capital of the infamous Barbary Coast. For 300 years Barbary pirates preyed upon European, and later U.S., shipping. In 1815 the American naval captain Stephen Decatur led an expedition against Algiers, forcing its governor to sign a peace treaty promising to end attacks on U.S. ships. The piracy continued, however, and in 1816 the combined Dutch and British navies almost completely destroyed the Algerian fleet. Algiers remained a pirate port until 1830, when France, retaliating against attacks on its vessels, captured the city and, in time, the entire country. They retained control until 1962, when Algeria won independence. During World War II, Algiers served (1942–44) as the headquarters of Allied forces in North Africa and of the Free French government of Gen. Charles de Gaulle. Pop. (1987) 1,507,241.

**ALGOA BAY,** large inlet of the Indian Ocean, S South Africa. The bay is of commercial importance. On the W side is Port Elizabeth, one of the main seaports of South Africa. In the early 16th century Portuguese navigators stopped here on the way to Goa, in India. In 1820 it was the landing place of early British immigrants to South Africa.

**ALGOL,** variable star, also called β (Beta) Persei, the second brightest star in the northern constellation Perseus. It is about 115 light-years from the earth; its light varies over a period of 68 hr 48 min 56 sec. For about 59 hr the light is almost constant; during the next 5 hr it decreases to 30 percent of its original strength; it then increases again in another 5 hr. Algol is composed of two stars of unusual brightness about 10 million km (about 6 million mi) apart. These two stars revolve around each other, and periodically the eclipse is not total because the plane of revolution of the stars is inclined to the line of sight by about 8°. The stars are each about 2.5 million km (1.5 million mi) in diameter. About 300 other variable stars of this type are now known. These are called Algol-type variables, or eclipsing binaries. Their periods vary from 6 hr to 29 years.

**ALGONQUIAN,** most populous and widely distributed of the North American Indian linguistic stocks, originally comprising several hundred tribes that spoke nearly 50 related languages. The Algonquian people occupied most of the Canadian region south of Hudson Bay between the Rocky Mountains and the Atlantic Ocean and, excluding certain territory held by Siouan and Iroquoian tribes, that section of what is now the U.S. extending northward from North Carolina and Tennessee. Algonquian tribes inhabited various isolated areas to the south and west, including parts of what are now South Carolina, Iowa, Wyoming, and Montana. The best-known Algonquian tribes include the Algonquin, from which the stock takes its name, Amalecite, Blackfoot, Cheyenne, Conoy, Cree, Delaware, Fox, Gros Ventre, Kickapoo, Massachuset, Miami, Micmac, Mohegan, Mohican, Montagnais, Musi, Narragansett, Naskapi, Nipmuc, Ojibwa, Ottawa, Pequot, Potawatomi, Sac, Shawnee, Tête de Boule, and Wampanoag. Some of the principal Algonquian confederacies were the Abnaki, Pennacook, and Illinois. *See* AMERICAN INDIAN LANGUAGES. For additional information, see separate articles on many of the tribes mentioned.

**ALGONQUIN,** North American Indian tribe of the Algonquian linguistic stock, dwelling originally in the vicinity of the Gatineau River, in what is now Québec Province. French explorers and colonizers in Canada, whom the Algonquins (or Algonkins) befriended, applied their name to various neighboring tribes. As a result of their alliance with the French, the Algonquins became involved in mortal struggle with the Iroquois. The warfare ended in complete victory for the latter, and by the middle of the 17th century the remnants of the Algonquin tribe had been dispersed westward. About 2000 Indians of Algonquin ancestry live in present-day Canada, mainly in Ontario and Québec. *See* AMERICAN INDIAN LANGUAGES; AMERICAN INDIANS.

*For further information on this topic, see the Bibliography in volume 28, sections 364, 1105–8.*

**ALGORITHM,** in mathematics, method of solving a problem by repetitive application of a sequence of well-defined steps. A basic example is the process of long division in arithmetic (q.v.). The term

*algorithm* is now applied to many kinds of problem solving that employ a mechanical sequence of steps, as in setting up a computer program. The sequence may be displayed in the form of a flowchart in order to make it easier to follow.

As with algorithms used in arithmetic, algorithms for computers can range from simple to highly complex. In all cases, however, the task that the algorithm is to accomplish must be definable. That is, the definition may involve mathematical or logic terms or a compilation of data or written instructions, but the task itself must be one that can be stated in some way. In terms of ordinary computer usage, this means that algorithms must be programmable, even if the tasks themselves turn out to have no solution.

In computational devices with a built-in microcomputer logic, this logic is a form of algorithm. As computers increase in complexity, more and more software-program algorithms are taking the form of what is called hard software. That is, they are increasingly becoming part of the basic circuitry of computers or are easily attached adjuncts, as well as standing alone in special devices such as office payroll machines. Many different applications algorithms are now available, and highly advanced systems such as artificial intelligence (q.v.) algorithms may become common in the future.

**ALHAMBRA,** city, Los Angeles Co., S California, a suburb of Los Angeles; inc. 1903. A gateway to the San Gabriel Valley, it is chiefly residential. The San Gabriel Mission (1771) is nearby. The city is named for the Alhambra, a Moorish fortress and palace in Spain. Pop. (1980) 64,615; (1990) 82,106.

**ALHAMBRA,** 13th- to 14th-century fortress palace of the Moorish kings of Granada, Spain. *See* ISLAMIC ART AND ARCHITECTURE.

**ALI,** in Arabic, Ali ibn Abi Talib (600?–61), fourth caliph of Islam and son-in-law of the Prophet Muhammad. He was born in Mecca, the son of Abu Talib (c. 540–619), Muhammad's uncle. Ali was one of the first converts to Islam and one of the most faithful followers of the Prophet. He married Muhammad's daughter Fatima, who bore him two sons, Hasan (624?–79?) and Husayn (626?–80). In 632, when Muhammad died, Ali claimed the right of succession. He was preceded in the caliphate, however, by Abu Bakr, Umar I (581?–644), and Uthman ibn Affan (575?–656), and did not become caliph until 656.

In the first year of Ali's reign he was forced to deal with a rebellion led by Aisha, whom Muhammad had married after the death of Fatima's mother and who bitterly opposed Ali's claim of succession. Although the rebellion was sup-

*The manner of their attire and painting themselues when they goe to their generall huntings or at theire Solemne feasts.*

*Among the first Indians encountered by the Europeans were southeastern members of the Algonquian stock. Drawings of them reached Europe as early as the 1560s, after the French and Spanish settlements in Florida were established. This water-color painting, by John White, Great Lord of Virginia, is dated 1585 by the Smithsonian Institution. The artist shows the Indian chief painted as he would be for "generall huntings" or "Solemne feasts."*

Granger Collection

pressed in 657, disputes over Ali's right to the caliphate were not resolved. Muawiyah I, a member of Uthman's family, refused to recognize Ali as caliph and claimed the caliphate himself. This dispute continued until 661, when Ali was murdered at Kufah by a member of the Kharijite sect; Muawiyah I was then acknowledged caliph.

Dissension betwen Ali's adherents and his opponents continued to shake the Muslim world. This conflict led to the first and most important schism in Islam, between the Shiites (adherents of Ali) and the Sunnites (orthodox Muslims). Ali is the ancestor of the Fatimid line of caliphs, who traced their descent from Ali and Fatima.

**ALI,** called Sunni Ali (d. 1492), ruler of Songhai (1464–92), who transformed his small inherited kingdom, centered at Gao (in modern Mali), into the most powerful empire of West Africa; his entire reign was occupied with conquests and punitive expeditions. A superb strategist who made skillful use of both cavalry and river flotillas, he drove the Tuaregs out of Timbuktu in 1468, crippled the resistance of the powerful Mossi and Dogon tribes, and, after a seven-year siege captured Djenné in 1471. At the time of his death, his realm extended some 3218 km (some 2000 mi) along the Niger River.

Although professing Islam, Sunni Ali ruled essentially as an African magician-king and ruthlessly persecuted Muslim scholars, whom he saw as a threat to the African nature of his empire. Administratively, he divided his territory into provinces under trusted governors and organized the traditional African cults in the service of the state. His fleet patrolled the Niger, keeping the peace, and held restive tribes in check. He died mysteriously while returning from a campaign.

**ALI, Muhammad** (1942– ), American boxer, originally named Cassius Marcellus Clay, Jr., born in Louisville, Ky. After winning the light heavyweight title at the 1960 Olympic Games, he turned professional, and in 1964 he made good his claim of being "The Greatest"; after only 20 professional fights he upset Sonny Liston (1934–70) and became world heavyweight champion. In the same year, after joining the Black Muslims (q.v.), he assumed the name Muhammad Ali. In 1967 he refused induction into the U.S. Army on the grounds that he was a Muslim minister and therefore a conscientious objector. He was soon convicted of draft evasion, and the ruling bodies of boxing declared his title vacant. Ali returned to the ring in 1970 and won two fights, but he lost a championship bout to Joe Frazier (1943– ) in March 1971. Later that year the U.S. Supreme Court overturned his conviction.

Ali made a comeback in 1974, regaining the heavyweight title by knocking out the champion, George Foreman (1949– ), in Kinshasa, Zaire. He lost the title to Leon Spinks (1953– ) in February 1978, then regained it in September of the same year. Ali thus became the first heavyweight boxer in history to win the championship three times. He retired in 1979, having lost only three bouts in his career; in 1980 he returned to challenge World Boxing Council heavyweight champion Larry Holmes (1949– ) but was defeated.

**ALI BEY** (1728–73), Mameluke ruler of Egypt, born in Abkhasia (now Abkhaz autonomous region, Georgia), in the Caucasus. In his youth he was carried off to Egypt as a slave. By 1766 he had become one of the Mameluke beys, or governors. Gaining followers in the next five years, he slaughtered the other beys, proclaimed Egypt independent of Turkey, and took the title of sultan. He conquered Syria and part of Arabia, but one of his sons-in-law, Muhammad Bey, called Abu al-Dhahab (1743?–75), turned against him and defeated him in battle near Cairo in 1773.

**ALICANTE** (anc. *Lucentum*), city, SE Spain, in Valencia, capital of Alicante Province, a seaport on the Mediterranean Sea. It is in a fertile agricultural region, especially noted for wines. Other products include olives, almonds, oranges, dates, rice, and barley. Mining of rock salt and calcium phosphate and fishing and manufacturing are leading industries. The city is the export outlet of the province; its manufactures include textiles, acids, and other products. Pop. (1986) 265,543.

**ALICE,** city, seat of Jim Wells Co., S Texas; inc. 1910. It is a highway and rail junction and a center of oil and natural-gas production in an area of large ranches, cotton farms, and major petroleum fields. The enormous King Ranch is nearby; the city is named for Alice Kleberg, the wife of one of the ranch's owners. Pop. (1980) 20,961; (1990) 19,788.

**ALICE SPRINGS,** town, central Australia, in the Northern Territory. Formerly called Stuart, it is a transportation and commercial center for the surrounding livestock and mining region. Tourism is also important. Alice Springs is in the virtual center of the country and one of the few population centers in Australia's vast, arid interior region known as the Outback or the Centre. The town was founded in 1871. Pop. (1991) 25,585.

**ALIEN,** in law, a person residing in one country while being a citizen of another. If aliens do not become citizens by naturalization, they do not possess such political rights as voting and holding public office. Most countries distinguish between temporary aliens and those who wish to reside permanently. In the U.S. long-term aliens are subject to military conscription and taxation, and they may acquire, convey, and transmit title to real and personal property. In accordance with the Alien Registration Act of 1940, aliens over 14 years of age must register each year. Aliens who are criminals, paupers, or diseased may be excluded from a country or denied entrance. *See* IMMIGRATION; NATIONALITY; NATURALIZATION.

**ALIENATION,** estrangement from other people, society, or oneself. The term is widely used in sometimes contradictory ways. Psychiatrists consider alienation a blocking or dissociation of a person's feelings, causing the individual to become less effective. The focus here is on the person's problems in adjusting to society. Some philosophers, on the other hand, believe that alienation is inevitably produced by a shallow and depersonalized society. In popular concern, alienation reached its peak with the "generation gap" of the 1960s and has been employed to account for activities running the gamut from aggressive violence to total inactivity.

The roots of the concept are old. Saint Augustine wrote that due to its sinful nature, humanity was alienated from God; he believed that a reconciliation could be achieved through belief in Christ. Karl Marx gave an economic interpretation to alienation. People were alienated from fellow human beings because of economic competition and class hostility; the cause was capitalism, and the cure was socialism. To Sigmund Freud, alienation was self-estrangement caused by the split between the conscious and unconscious parts of the mind. Sociology provided another viewpoint: Émile Durkheim's anomie, or rootlessness, stemmed from loss of societal and religious tradition. Subsequent sociologists further expanded Durkheim's theme of alienation. The existentialists Søren Kierkegaard, Martin Heidegger, and Jean Paul Sartre saw some measure of self-estrangement and powerlessness over one's destiny as an inevitable part of the human condition.

**ALIEN AND SEDITION ACTS,** in American political history, four laws passed in 1798. The Naturalization Act, raising from 5 to 14 the number of years of U.S. residence required for naturalization, was repealed in 1802. The Alien Act, empowering the president to arrest and deport any alien considered dangerous, expired in 1800. The Alien Enemies Act, which expired in 1801, provided for the arrest and deportation of subjects of foreign powers at war with the U.S. The Sedition Act made it a criminal offense to print or publish false, malicious, or scandalous statements directed against the U.S. government, the president, or Congress; to foster opposition to the lawful acts of Congress; or to aid a foreign power in plotting against the U.S. Although the Sedition Act enacted some reforms in the existing law of seditious libel—evidence of the truth of the alleged libel could be pleaded in justification—its penalties were severe: imprisonment for up to five years and fines up to $5000.

The Alien and Sedition Acts were enacted by a Congress dominated by the Federalist party (q.v.) and signed by President John Adams during the war crisis with France that followed publication of the XYZ letters (see XYZ AFFAIR). These documents had revealed that French officials had demanded bribes from American diplomats in Paris as a condition for negotiations to preserve the peace between the two nations.

The Naturalization and Alien Acts were aimed largely at Irish immigrants and French refugees who had participated in political activities critical of the Adams administration. The Sedition Act was an attempt to curb newspaper editors who supported the Republican party and who, in many cases, were also immigrants and refugees. The duration of the law (until March 3, 1801) indicated that its purpose was to obstruct Republican party activities during the presidential election of 1800. Before it expired, about 25 people were arrested and about 10 were convicted, some of whom were later pardoned.

The most prominent opponents of the Alien and Sedition Acts were the Republican party leaders, Thomas Jefferson and James Madison. They drafted, respectively, the Kentucky and Virginia Resolutions (q.v.) of 1798 as part of their campaigns to protest Federalist violations of civil liberties and the freedom of the press clause of the 1st Amendment to the U.S. Constitution. The resolutions also became important in American political history after 1830 as precedents to justify the doctrine of nullification (the principle that the states could nullify federal laws). The Alien and Sedition Acts were widely unpopular and played a major role both in the downfall of the Federalist party and the election of Jefferson to the presidency in 1800.

**ALIGARH,** city, N India, in Uttar Pradesh State, capital of Aligarh District, near Agra. It is a railroad junction and the commercial center of an agricultural region where wheat, corn, millet, barley, cotton, and sugarcane are produced. The principal industries in the city include flour milling, the processing of raw cotton, and the manufacture of butter and glass. Among points of interest are the old city of Koil; the ruins of Fort Aligarh, dating from the 16th century and captured from the Marathas by the British in 1803; and Aligarh Muslim University, founded in 1875 as the Muhammadan Anglo-Oriental College. The university is one of the foremost institutions in Asia for the study of Western culture. Pop. (1991, greater city) 479,978.

**ALIMENTARY CANAL,** in anatomy, the principal part of the digestive system. It begins at the mouth and extends to the anus, having, in humans, an average length of about 9 m (about 30 ft). Passing through the head, neck, and body, it includes the mouth, pharynx, esophagus, stomach, small intestines, cecum, and large intestines. *See* DIGESTIVE SYSTEM.

**ALIMONY,** amount of money ordered by a court to be paid by one spouse to the other—usually by the husband to the wife—for some period, limited or indefinite, after a divorce (q.v.). The traditional legal standard governing the amount of alimony was that which would allow the wife to live in the style to which she had become accustomed during the marriage.

The requirement that a husband support his wife after dissolution of their marriage was a long-standing tradition in the U.S. The financial support rules adopted by the American states were originally created by ecclesiastical courts in England for a society that recognized only judicially approved separation (q.v.), but not divorce. Under these circumstances, permanent support for the dependent spouse made sense—especially in a traditional society in which the husband earned the income and owned all family wealth and the wife was responsible for maintaining the home and rearing the children.

Today most states recognize that marriage is essentially an economic partnership of the spouses. Divorce doctrines, therefore, often rely on civil-law community-property jurisdiction; they authorize the court to award to each spouse, in some equitable fashion, property acquired during the marriage regardless of formal ownership.

In the last part of the 20th century, the increasing divorce rate, the greater participation of women in the labor market, and feminist ideology all contributed to the need for reform of the alimony-award system. Most divorce reform statutes of the 1970s included a variety of modifications of alimony awards, which take account of changes in American culture and in marriage as an institution. The term *alimony* has often been changed to *maintenance* in an effort to minimize both the connotation the older term conveyed of female dependence and the resentment many husbands had of continuing support obligations. In most statutes alimony became payable to either spouse, based strictly on the economic needs of the dependent spouse. The reform statutes preferred a short-term support award, called rehabilitative alimony, for younger spouses to finance continued or renewed education to enable them to join the work force and become self-supporting. The new maintenance statutes, however, spawned controversy. In a few instances, judges have denied alimony or awarded quite limited rehabilitative alimony, even to older women whose marriages were of the traditional type and who were not equipped for gainful employment. Another subject of contention during the 1980s was whether, in the absence of marriage, one cohabiting partner could compel the other to pay "palimony" when their relationship dissolved.

R.J.L.

**ALIPHATIC COMPOUNDS,** large class of organic molecules consisting essentially of straight or branched chains of carbon atoms. Aliphatic compounds include the alkanes, alkenes, and alkynes and their derivatives. The other major class of organic molecules, aromatic compounds, forms closed ring structures.

**AL ITTIHAD.** *See* MADINAT ASH-SHAB.

**ALKAHEST.** *See* ALCHEMY.

**ALKALIES** (Arab. *al-qili*, "ashes of the saltwort plant"), originally the hydroxides and carbonates of potassium and sodium, leached from plant ashes. The term now applies to the corresponding compounds of ammonium, $NH_4$, and the other alkali metals, and to the hydroxides of calcium, strontium, and barium. All of these substances produce hydroxide ions, $OH^-$, when dissolved in water. The carbonates and ammonium hydroxide give only moderate concentrations of hydroxide ions and are termed mild alkalies. The hydroxides of sodium and potassium, however,

produce hydroxide ions in high enough concentration to destroy flesh; for this reason they are called caustic alkalies. Solutions of alkalies turn red litmus blue, react with and neutralize acids, feel slippery, and are electrical conductors.

Caustic soda, or sodium hydroxide, NaOH, is an important commercial product, used in making soap, rayon, and cellophane; in processing paper pulp; in petroleum refining; and in the manufacture of many other chemical products. Caustic soda is manufactured principally by electrolysis of a common salt solution, with chlorine and hydrogen as important by-products.

Sodium carbonate, $Na_2CO_3$, one of the mild alkalies, is made chiefly from common salt brines by the Solvay ammonia-soda process. It is used in the manufacture of glass and as a cleaning agent and water softener.

**ALKALI METALS,** series of six chemical elements in group 1 (or Ia) of the periodic table (*see* PERIODIC LAW). They are soft compared to other metals, have low melting points, and are so reactive that they are never found in nature uncombined with other elements. They are powerful reducing agents, that is, they give up an electron easily, and react violently with water to form hydrogen gas and hydroxides, or strong bases. The alkali metals are, in order of increasing atomic number, lithium, sodium, potassium, rubidium, cesium, and francium (qq.v.). Francium exists only in a radioactive form.

**ALKALINE EARTH METALS,** series of six chemical elements in group 2 (or IIa) of the periodic table (*see* PERIODIC LAW). They are strong reducing agents, that is, they give up electrons easily. They are less reactive than the alkali metals, but reactive enough not to be found free in nature. Although rather brittle, the alkaline earth metals are malleable and extrudable. They conduct electricity well, and when heated, burn readily in air. The alkaline earth metals are, in order of increasing atomic number, beryllium, magnesium, calcium, strontium, barium, and radium (qq.v.). Their oxides are called alkaline earths.

**ALKALOIDS,** group of mildly alkaline compounds, mostly of plant origin and of moderate molecular complexity. Even in very small amounts, they produce strong physiological effects on the body. All contain nitrogen atoms that are structurally related to those of ammonia.

Nearly 3000 alkaloids have been recorded; the first to be prepared synthetically (1886) was one of the simplest, called coniine, or 2-propyl piperidine, $C_5H_{10}NC_3H_7$. It is highly poisonous; less than 0.2 g (0.007 oz) is fatal. Coniine, obtained from seeds of the hemlock (*see* HEMLOCK, POISON), was the poison used in the execution of Socrates.

Some 30 of the known alkaloids are used in medicine. For example, atropine, obtained from belladonna, causes dilation of the pupils; morphine is a painkiller; quinine is a specific remedy for malaria; nicotine is a potent insecticide; and reserpine is a valuable tranquilizer.

**ALKALOSIS.** *See* BLOOD.

**ALKMAAR,** town, W Netherlands, in North Holland Province, on the North Holland Canal, near Amsterdam. It is a trading center for cattle, corn, and dairy products; cheese is a major export, and sailcloth is manufactured here. In 1573 the town successfully withstood a Spanish siege. In October 1799, during the Napoleonic Wars, the commander in chief of the Anglo-Russian army in the Netherlands signed the French terms of capitulation in Alkmaar. Pop. (1993 est.) 91,500.

**ALKYD,** term for the macromolecular ester formed by the reaction of a polyhydric alcohol, the molecules of which contain two or more —OH groups, with a polybasic acid, the molecules of which contain two or more —COOH groups. The alkyds, or alkyd resins, are widely used for protective coatings.

**ALLAH,** Muslim name for the Supreme Being. The term is a contraction of the Arabic *al-Ilah,* "the God." Both the idea and the word existed in pre-Islamic Arabian tradition, in which some evidence of a primitive monotheism can also be found. Although they recognized other, lesser gods, the pre-Islamic Arabs recognized Allah as the supreme God.

The Koran, the holy book of Islam, asserts that Allah is the creator and the one who rewards and punishes; that he is unique and can only be one; that he is eternal, omniscient, omnipotent, and all-merciful. The core of the religion is submission to the will of Allah; people must abandon themselves entirely to God's sovereignty.

Although as creator Allah is utterly transcendent and not to be compared to any of his creatures, he is nevertheless a personal god, a fair judge, merciful and benevolent. Each chapter of the Koran begins with "Allah, the Merciful, the Compassionate," and before fulfilling religious obligations the Muslim recites, "In the name of Allah, the Merciful, the Compassionate."

Islam does not admit of any mediator between Allah and humans; a person approaches Allah directly in personal prayer and in reciting the Koran, which is considered literally the speech of Allah. The prophets, who conveyed the word of Allah, are not considered in any way divine.

**ALLAHABAD,** city, N India, in Uttar Pradesh State, capital of the Allahabad District, at the confluence of the Yamuna and Ganges rivers. An important railroad junction, Allahabad is a trading center for agricultural products, notably rice, pulse, wheat, tobacco, cotton, and sugarcane. Known originally as Prag, it is one of the oldest and holiest cities in India, visited annually by thousands of Hindu pilgrims. The Mughal emperor Akbar gave the city the present name in 1575. Points of interest include a stone pillar dating from the reign of the Indian king Asoka, a fort and the ruins of a palace, both built by Akbar, and the Jama Masjid (Great Mosque). The city is the site of the University of Allahabad, an institute for teachers, and several technical schools. Allahabad was formerly the capital of the United Provinces of Agra and Oudh, now Uttar Pradesh State. The ashes of the assassinated Indian leader Mahatma Gandhi were consigned to the sacred Ganges at Allahabad in 1948. Pop. (1991, greater city) 858,213.

**ALL-AMERICAN CANAL,** irrigation canal, SE California, near the Mexican border. It stretches from the Colorado R. near Yuma, Ariz., where it is fed by reservoirs formed by the Laguna and Imperial dams, W across the Colorado Desert to Calexico, Calif. Built between 1934 and 1940, it is 129 km (80 mi) long and about 61 m (about 200 ft) wide. Its water is used to irrigate the fertile but arid Imperial Valley. The Coachella Canal (completed 1948) branches from the All-American Canal, extending 198 km (123 mi) NW to irrigate the Coachella Valley.

**ALLEGHENY,** river, Pennsylvania and New York. It rises in N Pennsylvania, nearly 610 m (nearly 2000 ft) above sea level, flows into SW New York state then flows through W Pennsylvania and merges with the Monongahela R. at Pittsburgh, Pa., to form the Ohio R. Although the Allegheny flows through a hilly region, the river is navigable by small boats for nearly 322 km (nearly 200 mi) above Pittsburgh. Unusually heavy flooding has necessitated the building of several reservoirs. The Allegheny is about 523 km (about 325 mi) long and drains an area of about 28,490 sq km (about 11,000 sq mi).

**ALLEGHENY MOUNTAINS** *or* **ALLEGHENIES,** complex of ranges and uplands of the Appalachian system. The name is usually applied to the ranges W of the Blue Ridge in Pennsylvania, Maryland, Virginia, and West Virgina. Varying from 610 m (2000 ft) to more than 1372 m (more than 4500 ft) in height, the range is composed of stratified rocks of the Silurian, Devonian, and Carboniferous ages and is rich in timber and minerals.

**ALLEGORY,** fictional literary narrative or artistic expression that conveys a symbolic meaning that is parallel to but distinct from, and more important than, the literal meaning. Allegory is also defined as an extended metaphor. The symbolic meaning is usually expressed through personifi-

*Ethan Allen confronts the British commander of Fort Ticonderoga and demands that he surrender; colored engraving, 19th century.* **The Granger Collection**

cations and other symbols. Related forms are the fable and the parable, which are didactic, comparatively short and simple allegories.

The art of allegory reached its height during the Middle Ages (in the work of Dante and the English poet Geoffrey Chaucer) and the Renaissance. It remained a popular literary form until the end of the 17th century. Two early examples are *Le Roman de la Rose* by the French poets Guillaume de Lorris and Jean de Meun (c. 1240–1305) and *The Vision of Piers the Plowman,* attributed to the late 14th-century poet William Langland. The former is an allegory of human love, the latter an allegorical protest against the clergy. In Edmund Spenser's *Faerie Queene,* social commentary on conditions in 16th-century England is concealed beneath a surface of chivalric romance. One of the greatest of all allegories is John Bunyan's *Pilgrim's Progress,* a 17th-century prose narrative symbolically concerning the search for spiritual salvation.

Although modern authors generally favor less abstract, more personal symbolism, allegories are still written, an extremely popular example of which is *Animal Farm* by George Orwell.

In art, an allegorical painting or sculpture is one that has a symbolic meaning underlying the surface image.

*See also* BIBLICAL SCHOLARSHIP.

**ALLELE.** *See* GENETICS.

**ALLEMANDE** (Fr., "German"), 16th- and 17th-century courtly dance for a line of couples, and a stylized version of its music. The dance, in moderate $\frac{2}{4}$ or $\frac{4}{4}$ time, originated in Germany and had the gliding steps and balances of its ancestor, the French *basse danse.* It was developed into an independent form by 17th-century English harpsichord composers and became the usual first movement of the baroque suite. The name *allemande* was also used for some 18th-century country dances.

**ALLEN, Ethan** (1738–89), patriot of the American Revolution, leader of the Green Mountain Boys, and champion of statehood for Vermont.

Allen was born on Jan. 21, 1738, in Litchfield, Conn. In 1769 he moved to the region known as the New Hampshire Grants, comprising present-day Vermont. After settling in Bennington, he became prominently involved in the struggle between New York and New Hampshire for control of the region. Following rejection by the New York authorities of an appeal that the region be established as a separate province, Allen organized a volunteer militia, called the Green Mountain Boys, to resist and evict proponents of the New York cause. He was thereupon declared an outlaw by the royal governor of New York. At the outbreak of the American Revolution, Allen and his force offered their services against the British. On orders from the Connecticut legislature, he, the Connecticut soldier Benedict Arnold, and a contingent of the Green Mountain Boys captured Fort Ticonderoga early in the morning of May 10, 1775. Allen demanded surrender from the British commander "in the name of the Great Jehovah and the Continental Congress." Subsequently, as a member of the army of Gen. Philip John Schuyler, he rendered valuable service in the American military expedition against Canada. He was taken prisoner near Montréal in September 1775 and held in confinement until exchanged in 1778. Following his release by the British, he returned to his home and was commissioned a lieutenant colonel in the Continental army and major general of militia.

In 1778 Allen appeared before the Continental Congress in behalf of a claim by Vermont for recognition as an independent state. With his brother Ira Allen and other Vermonters he devoted most of his time thereafter to the territorial dispute. He negotiated with the governor of Canada between 1780 and 1783, ostensibly to establish Vermont as a British province. On the basis of this activity he was charged with treason but, because the negotiations were demonstrably intended to force action on the Vermont case by the Continental Congress, the charge was never substantiated. He wrote *Narrative of Colonel Ethan Allen's Captivity* (1779). Allen died in Burlington, Vt., on Feb. 12, 1789.

**ALLEN, Florence Ellinwood** (1884–1966), American jurist, born in Salt Lake City, Utah, and educated at Salt Lake College, Western Reserve University, the University of Chicago, and New York University. After a brief career as a music editor and lecturer, she began to practice law in Cleveland in 1914. Elected judge of the Supreme Court of Ohio, she served from 1922 to 1934, the first woman in America to hold such office. She gained national recognition during this time by her decision upholding the city-manager plan of government (*see* MUNICIPAL GOVERNMENT). President Franklin D. Roosevelt appointed her judge of the U.S. Court of Appeals for the Sixth Circuit in 1934. She retired in 1959. Allen wrote *This Constitution of Ours* (1940) and *The Treaty as an Instrument of Legislation* (1952).

**ALLEN, Fred,** professional name of JOHN FLORENCE SULLIVAN (1894–1956), American comedian, who made successful transitions from vaudeville and stage to radio, television, and film. He was born in Cambridge, Mass., and educated at Boston University. His Broadway shows include *The Passing Show of 1922* and *The Greenwich Village Follies*. He was producer, writer, and star of the *Fred Allen Show* on radio (1939–49) and starred on television in *Judge for Yourself* (1953–54). His humor combined sharp commentary, erudition, and faultless timing. Among his films (1932–54) are *Thanks a Million, Love Thy Neighbor, We're Not Married, O'Henry's Full House,* and *Sally, Irene, and Mary.* He wrote an autobiography, *Treadmill to Oblivion* (1954).

**ALLEN, Ira** (1751–1814), soldier in the American Revolution, born in Cornwall, Conn. In 1772 he moved to Vermont and joined the Green Mountain Boys in support of his brother Ethan. He was active (1780–91) in obtaining statehood for Vermont and largely responsible for the founding (1791) of the University of Vermont. He wrote *The Natural and Political History of Vermont* (1798).

**ALLEN, Richard** (1760–1831), American clergyman, born in Philadelphia. The son of a slave, Allen was freed after his master was converted to Methodism. He was ordained a minister in 1784 at the first conference of the Methodist church in the U.S. During the next two years he was an itinerant preacher. While preaching at Saint George's Church in Philadelphia in 1786, an incident of racial prejudice occurred, which is believed to have started him working for the establishment of an independent Methodist church for black members. This separate church was formed in 1799. In 1816 the African Methodist Episcopal Church (q.v.) was formed, uniting congregations of blacks in New York, New Jersey, Delaware, and Maryland. Allen was elected its first bishop, a post he held until his death.

**ALLEN, Woody** (1935– ), professional name of ALLEN STEWART KONIGSBERG, American actor, director, and writer, born in Brooklyn, N.Y. Allen began his career as a writer for television before writing and acting in his first film, *What's New, Pussycat?* (1965). His subsequent films, which he also directed, include *Annie Hall* (1977; Academy Award for best picture) and *Hannah and Her Sisters* (1986; Academy Award for best screenplay).

**ALLENBY, Edmund Henry Hynman, 1st Viscount Allenby** (1861–1936), British field marshal, born in Felixstowe, England, and educated at Haileybury College and at the Royal Military Academy, Sandhurst. Between 1884 and 1902 he was stationed with the Inniskilling Dragoons in Bechuanaland (now Botswana) and Zululand (in present-day South Africa) and served in the Boer War. He had held various cavalry commands before becoming inspector of cavalry in 1910. During World War I he headed the British cavalry in France. He was given command of the Fifth Army Corps in 1915. Subsequently, as head of the Third Army, he figured prominently in the Second Battle of Ypres and in the capture of Vimy Ridge. As a result, he was promoted to the rank of general and made a knight commander of the Bath.

Assigned in 1917 as commander in chief of the Egyptian Expeditionary Force, he led an offensive against the Turkish armies in the Middle East, capturing Jerusalem on Dec. 10, 1917, winning decisively at Megiddo in September 1918, and taking Damascus on Oct. 1, 1918. The campaign forced the Turks to capitulate; he was promoted to the rank of field marshal and made a viscount. From 1919 to 1925 he was British high commissioner in Egypt. He became lord rector of the University of Edinburgh in April 1936.

**ALLENDE GOSSENS, Salvador** (1908–73), president of Chile (1970–73), born in Santiago, and educated as a physician at the University of Chile. He joined the Socialist party when it was founded in 1933, was elected to Congress in 1937, and served as minister of health from 1939 to 1942. In 1945 Allende was elected to the Senate, where he remained active for 25 years. During that period he was three times the presidential candidate of his party. Running his fourth race in 1970, supported by a leftist coalition, he won a narrow plurality. As president, Allende set out to revamp Chilean society, nationalizing industries and enterprises, but met with resistance from the right and dissatisfaction from the radical left. As inflation soared, powerful U.S. interests exploited the situation to stir up the middle class. Chaos resulted, and in a military coup on Sept. 11, 1973, Allende lost his life.

**ALLEN PARK,** city, Wayne Co., SE Michigan, a suburb of Detroit; inc. 1957. The mainly residential community was founded in the 1860s and named for Lewis Allen (1814–94), an early settler here. Pop. (1980) 34,196; (1990) 31,092.

**ALLENTOWN,** city, seat of Lehigh Co., E Pennsylvania, on the Lehigh R., in the Pennsylvania Dutch region, near Bethlehem; inc. as a city 1867. It is a manufacturing and distribution hub; products include chemicals, communications and transportation equipment, electrical goods, and fabricated metals. Cedar Crest College (1867), Muhlenberg College (1869), and United Wesleyan College (1921) are here. Colonial buildings include the Zion Reformed Church where the Liberty Bell was hidden during the British occupation of Philadelphia in 1777–78. The community, established in 1762 as Northamptontowne, was renamed in 1838 for its founder, the jurist William Allen (1704–80). Pop. (1980) 103,758; (1990) 105,090.

**ALLEPPEY.** See ALAPPUZAH.

**ALLERGY,** a condition of hypersensitivity in certain persons or animals to substances harmless to most individuals. Some people have characterized allergy as immunity "gone wrong." In the immune reaction, contact with a disease-producing microorganism or a toxin prompts an individual to build up antibodies (proteins related to globulin serum) against the offending organism or toxin so that he or she will be protected against further exposure. Normally, people are able to produce such protective antibodies, but in some the capacity to differentiate potentially harmful substances from harmless ones is absent. These persons produce antibodies against one or many inoffensive substances and thus are said to be allergic. When an antibody reacts with an antigen (a substance that stimulates the formation of antibodies) an allergic reaction results. The symptoms of that reaction will depend on where it takes place. If it occurs in the nose, it may cause sneezing and running of the nose, giving rise to hay fever. In the air passages it may cause contraction, leading to wheezing, coughing, and difficulty in breathing, as in asthma. In the skin, it may produce itching spots, hives, or welts (urticaria). If the reaction takes place in the circulating

blood, a severe reaction known as serum sickness may ensue. The allergen, the substance producing the reaction, is usually a protein or protein-carbohydrate complex. It may be inhaled, as dust or pollen; it may be eaten, as eggs or shellfish; it may be injected, as penicillin; or it may act by mere contact, as wool.

The variety of substances to which a person may be allergic is almost infinite; diagnosis involves discovering the particular substance or substances to which the patient is hypersensitive. A history of the development of the allergic reaction may give a clue, particularly when it is seasonal, when it is associated with exposure to a specific substance, or when it occurs only in a particular place. Often it is possible to remain unaffected merely by avoiding the allergen to which the victim reacts allergically, but common allergens such as dust or pollen cannot easily be avoided. See IMMUNE SYSTEM.

An allergic individual may develop new hypersensitivities, or old hypersensitivities may die out, at any time during a person's life. Sometimes psychic factors, stemming from emotional conflicts, play an important role in allergy. See STRESS-RELATED DISORDERS.

The mechanism of allergic reactions is not fully understood. Most likely the antigen becomes localized in a particular tissue, such as the cells lining the nasal passages or the bronchial tubes. The antibody reacts with the antigen at these sites, causing the release of certain chemical substances, including histamine, which mediates, or brings about, the reaction. Sometimes testing the skin with a wide variety of common allergens can pinpoint the specific allergen or allergens that are causing the difficulties.

The simplest and best treatment is, when possible, to avoid contact with the allergen. A person allergic to feathers, particular pollens, foods, or medicines, for example, should avoid them. Where this is not feasible, because the allergen is unknown, because it affects more than one part of the body, or because too many allergens are present, drugs such as antihistamines or, in more serious cases, adrenal cortical steroids may be used to decrease the reaction. In other cases desensitization (the process of making the patient able to tolerate the antigen without having a reaction) may be accomplished by giving injections of antigen, first in minute doses and then in gradually increasing doses as tolerance builds up. Skin testing is always needed when desensitization treatment is being considered. Symptomatic treatment, such as the administration of drugs to relax spasms in the walls of the bronchi in asthmatics, decongestants for hay fever sufferers, or local ointments to relieve itching for hives may also be useful. *See also* ASTHMA, BRONCHIAL; HIVES. L.J.V.

*For further information on this topic, see the Bibliography in volume 28, section 512.*

**ALL FOOLS' DAY,** the first day of April, commonly referred to as April Fools' Day.

**ALLIANCE,** city, Stark and Mahoning counties, NE Ohio, at the headwaters of the Mahoning R.; inc. as a village in 1854, with the consolidation of Freedom, Liberty, and Williamsport; inc. as a city 1889. Alliance is an industrial center in a productive farming and mining region. The city's many manufactures include machinery and steel products. Mount Union College (1846) is here. The name of the community was chosen (1854) in anticipation of the union of two railroads here. Pop. (1980) 24,315; (1990) 23,376.

**ALLIANCE,** in international politics, an association of two or more nations united by a formal treaty for some agreed-upon purpose. Most alliances are defensive in form, involving a pledge of mutual military assistance against an actual or potential common enemy. Alliances have existed throughout history, from ancient China and India to the modern nations, often as responses to acts of aggression. The threat of Soviet expansion after World War II caused the U.S. to change its traditional policy of nonalignment. It now maintains a system of alliances with non-Communist countries around the world, for example, the North Atlantic Treaty Organization. An alliance may sometimes be made to achieve economic goals, for example, the Alliance for Progress.

*See also* CONFEDERATION; HOLY ALLIANCE; TREATY; TRIPLE ALLIANCE; TRIPLE ENTENTE.

**ALLIANCE FOR PROGRESS,** program for technical and financial cooperation and development among the American nations of the Organization of American States (OAS). The alliance was established by the Charter of Punta del Este, signed in August 1961 at the suggestion of U.S. President John F. Kennedy. The U.S. agreed to provide assistance for the development goals to be carried out within the framework of the OAS to benefit developing countries of Latin America.

The economic objectives of the alliance included raising national incomes and distributing them more equitably, accelerating industrialization and agricultural productivity, and stabilizing prices and increasing exports. Social objectives included improving education and reducing illiteracy, improving health and nutrition, and increasing trained medical personnel.

After ten years in operation the program had mixed results. Per capita economic growth of 3.8 percent exceeded the goal of 2.5 percent. Agrarian reform did not improve, housing shortages continued, unemployment worsened because of high birth rates, and the international trade outlook remained bleak. Between 1962 and 1971 the U.S. contributed $11 billion in financial and technical aid. Additional aid was extended by several international agencies.

By the early 1970s, the alliance was being criticized by all parties. Some critics considered it an example of Yankee imperialism in Latin America. A reduction in loans further limited the possibilities of success, and the program slowly ceased to function.

**ALLIGATOR** (Span. *el largato,* "the lizard"), common name for two carnivorous reptiles in the crocodile order. Alligators have broad, flat, and rounded snouts, as opposed to the longer, sharper snouts of other crocodilians; also unlike other crocodilians, their lower teeth cannot be seen when their mouths are closed. Alligators feed on fish, frogs, snakes, turtles, birds, mammals, and carrion. They are also known to attack humans. Because alligators can survive a wider range of temperatures than other crocodilians, they are often found in more temperate regions, and their breeding season is generally restricted to spring. When alligators search for a mate they bellow often, perhaps to announce their presence. Unwanted intruders are confronted with ritual gaping, lunging, and hissing, but courtship behavior is sedate. After mating, the male seeks his own territory while the female builds a nest of mud and plants nearby, above flood level. The eggs, from 30 to 60 in a clutch, are covered with mud and incubated in the heat of the sun while the female stands guard. When the eggs hatch, in about 60 days, the female cares for the young, carrying them by mouth or leading them about, until the following spring.

Only two species of alligator exist: the American alligator and the Chinese alligator. The Chinese alligator makes its home in the Yangtze River basin of China. It is more timid and much smaller than the American alligator, seldom exceeding 1.5 m (5 ft) in length, and is considered little threat to humans.

The American alligator lives mainly in freshwater swamps, lakes, and bayous in the southeastern U.S., but ranges as far west as the Rio Grande in Texas. It is a large (anywhere from 2 to 6 m/6 to 20 ft long) and fierce species considered dangerous to humans. Hunted for generations both for sport and for its hide, the American alligator dwindled until, in 1967, it was declared an endangered species. Under this protection it made a strong comeback and became bolder in the presence of humans. Little more

*American alligator,* Alligator mississipiensis

than a decade later, hunting was again allowed in some states.

See CROCODILE.

| COMMON NAME | FAMILY | GENUS AND SPECIES |
|---|---|---|
| American alligator | Alligatoridae | *Alligator mississipiensis* |
| Chinese alligator | Alligatoridae | *A. sinensis* |

**ALLIGATOR LIZARD,** common name for solitary, slow-moving lizards, so named for their shape and heavy, protective scales. Their bony armor makes them so stiff that they could not breathe without the long, flexible grooves of soft scales along their sides. Five species live in the U.S., mostly in moist, hilly areas. The northern alligator lizard has the widest range, south from British Columbia to central California and east into Montana.

| COMMON NAME | FAMILY | GENUS AND SPECIES |
|---|---|---|
| Northern alligator lizard | Anguidae | *Gerrhonotus coeruleus* |

**ALLITERATION,** repetition of the initial letter (generally a consonant) or first sound of several words, marking the stressed syllables in a line of poetry or prose. A simple example is the phrase "through thick and thin." It is used to emphasize meaning and thus can be effectively used in oratory. Alliteration is a characteristic of Anglo-Saxon poetry, notably the epic *Beowulf;* it is still used, with modifications, by modern poets.

**ALLOBROGES,** Celtic tribe of ancient Gaul, whose territory lay between the Rhône and Isère rivers and Lake Geneva in the vicinity of the present-day French-Swiss border. Their chief town was Vienna (now Vienne, France), on the Rhône River, and their frontier outpost against their enemies the Helvetii was Geneva. After they were defeated by the Romans in 121 BC, their territory was incorporated into Transalpine Gaul. In 63 BC envoys of the Allobroges were invited to take part in a conspiracy led by the Roman statesman Catiline, but, preferring to perform a service for the Roman government, they informed the statesman and orator Marcus Tullius Cicero of the plot and procured for him proof of the conspiracy.                                      G.E.D.

**ALLOSAURUS,** genus of large, carnivorous dinosaurs (*see* DINOSAUR), of the suborder Theropoda, that flourished approximately 150 million years ago during the Late Jurassic period. These saurischian (lizard-hipped) dinosaurs reached 12 m (40 ft) in length, stood more than 4.5 m (15 ft) tall, and weighed up to 3.6 metric tons. Like other members of the suborder Theropoda, *Allosaurus* was an obligatory biped; it walked on stout hindlegs with large birdlike feet, while using its heavy tail for balance. The digits of the feet and the hands of the shorter forelimbs were equipped with sharp, grasping claws. The jaws of its huge head (1 m/3 ft long) were filled with long, serrated teeth that enabled *Allosaurus* to bolt enormous chunks of flesh. Fossil remains have been found in Wyoming and Colorado.

**ALLOTROPY,** the manifestation by a chemical element of two or more distinct physical forms. Carbon, for example, displays allotropy in the forms of graphite and diamond. Because of differing arrangements of atoms in their crystalline structures (*see* CRYSTAL), allotropic forms of an element may exhibit greatly differing values for such physical properties as color, luster, density, hardness, odor, and electrical and thermal conductivity. Other elements displaying allotropy include phosphorus, sulfur, and tin (qq.v.).

**ALLOY,** substance composed of two or more metals. Alloys, like pure metals, possess metallic luster and conduct heat and electricity well, although not generally as well as do the pure metals of which they are formed. Compounds that contain both a metal or metals and certain nonmetals, particularly those containing carbon, are also called alloys. The most important of these is steel. Simple carbon steels consist of about 0.5 percent manganese and up to 0.8 percent carbon, with the remaining material being iron.

An alloy may consist of an intermetallic compound, a solid solution, an intimate mixture of minute crystals of the constituent metallic elements, or any combination of solutions or mixtures of the foregoing. Intermetallic compounds, such as $NaAu_2$, $CuSn$, and $CuAl_2$, do not follow the ordinary rules of valency. They are generally hard and brittle; although they have not been important in the past where strength is required, many new developments have made such compounds increasingly important. Alloys consisting of solutions or mixtures of two metals generally have lower melting points than do the pure constituents. A mixture with a melting point lower than that of any other mixture of the same constituents is called a eutectic. The eutectoid, the solid-phase analog of the eutectic, frequently has better physical characteristics than do alloys of different proportions.

The properties of alloys are frequently far different from those of their constituent elements, and such properties as strength and corrosion resistance may be considerably greater for an alloy than for any of the separate metals. For this reason, alloys are more generally used than pure metals. Steel is stronger and harder than wrought iron, which is approximately pure iron, and is used in far greater quantities. The alloy steels, mixtures of steel with such metals as chromium, manganese, molybdenum, nickel, tungsten, and vanadium, are stronger and harder than steel itself, and many of them are also more corrosion-resistant than iron or steel. An alloy can often be made to match a predetermined set of characteristics. An important case in which particular characteristics are necessary is the design of rockets, spacecraft, and supersonic aircraft. The materials used in these vehicles and their engines must be light in weight, very strong, and able to sustain very high temperatures. To withstand these high temperatures and reduce the overall weight, lightweight, high-strength alloys of aluminum, beryllium, and titanium have been developed. To resist the heat generated during reentry into the atmosphere of the earth, alloys containing heat-resistant metals such as tantalum, niobium, tungsten, cobalt, and nickel are being used in space vehicles.

A wide variety of special alloys containing metals such as beryllium, boron, niobium, hafnium, and zirconium, which have particular nuclear absorption characteristics, are used in nuclear reactors. Niobium-tin alloys are used as superconductors at extremely low temperatures. Special copper, nickel, and titanium alloys, designed to resist the corrosive effects of boiling salt water, are used in desalination plants.

Historically, most alloys have been prepared by mixing the molten materials. More recently, powder metallurgy has become important in the preparation of alloys with special characteristics. In this process, the alloys are prepared by mixing dry powders of the materials, squeezing them together under high pressure, and then heating them to temperatures just below their melting points. The result is a solid, homogeneous alloy. Mass-produced products may be prepared by this technique at great savings in cost. Among the alloys made possible by powder metallurgy are the cermets. These alloys of metal and carbon (carbides), boron (borides), oxygen (oxides), silicon (silicides), and nitrogen (nitrides) combine the advantages of the high-temperature strength, stability, and oxidation resistance of the ceramic compound with the ductility and shock resistance of the metal. Another alloying technique is ion implantation, which has been adapted from the processes used to produce computer chips; beams of ions of carbon, nitrogen, and other elements are fired into selected metals in a vacuum chamber to produce a strong, thin layer of alloy on the metal surface. Bombarding titanium with nitrogen, for example, can produce a superior alloy for prosthetic implants.

Sterling silver, 14-karat gold, white gold, and plantinum-iridium are precious metal alloys. Babbitt metal, brass, bronze (qq.v.), Dow-metal, German silver, gunmetal, Monel metal, pewter, and solder are alloys of less precious metals. Commercial aluminum is, because of impurities, actually an alloy. Alloys of mercury with other metals are called amalgams.

*See also* IRON AND STEEL MANUFACTURE; METALWORK.

**ALL SAINTS' DAY,** also Allhallows or Hallowmas, festival celebrated on November 1 in the Roman Catholic and Anglican churches in honor of God and all his saints, known and unknown. It became established as a church festival early in the 7th century when the Pantheon in Rome was consecrated as the Church of the Blessed Virgin and All Martyrs. Pope Gregory IV (d. 844) gave the custom official authorization in 835. November 1 may have been chosen because it was the day of one of the four great festivals of the pagan nations of the north, and it was church policy to supplant pagan with Christian observances.

**ALL SOULS' DAY,** in the Roman Catholic church, a festival falling on November 2, the object of which is, by prayers and almsgiving, to assist souls in purgatory (q.v.). First instituted in the monasteries of Cluny, France, in 998, the observance soon became general, without any ordinance at large on the subject. Among European peasants, All Souls' Day is a time for reviving many pre-Christian folk customs. Roman Catholic priests are permitted to say three masses for the dead on this day.

**ALLSPICE.** See PIMENTO.

**ALLSTON, Washington** (1779–1843), American painter, the country's first major landscapist, who introduced the romantic painting style to the U.S. and foreshadowed the Hudson River school of artists. Born near Georgetown, S.C., Allston was educated at Harvard University, at London's Royal Academy, and in Paris and Italy. His paintings, from the vividly dramatic *Rising of a Thunderstorm at Sea* (1804) to the luminous serenity of *Moonlit Landscape* (1819), both in the Museum of Fine Arts, Boston, reveal his subjective interpretation of nature and his skill in conveying that vision. His historical scenes, such as *The Deluge* (1804, Metropolitan Museum, New York City) and the vast, unfinished *Belshazzar's Feast* (1817–43, Detroit Institute of Arts), are charged with fantasy.

**ALLUVIUM,** silt, sand, clay, gravel, or similar loose material deposited by flowing water. Alluvium usually occurs at any point where the velocity of fast-running water is abruptly slowed and the carrying capacity of the flow reduced to a point where transport of the sediment is no longer possible. Alluvial deposits are found on the floodplains of river valleys, through river deltas, and where steep mountain streams enter quiet lakes or flow out onto a comparatively flat surface. When the deposit, in the course of its accumulation, takes the shape of a fan or cone, as at the base of a mountain, it is called an alluvial fan. Among the great alluvial deposits of the world are the deltas of the Nile in Egypt, the Ganges in India, and the Huang He (Yellow River) in China and the floodplain of the Mississippi in North America. *See also* DEPOSIT.

**ALMA,** city, Lac-Saint-Jean-Est Co., S Québec Province, on Alma Island and both banks of the Saguenay R., near Lac St.-Jean (Lake St. John); inc. as a city 1958. The site of a large hydroelectric facility (built 1923), it has granite quarries and industries producing aluminum and paper. The community, founded in 1867, was known as Saint-Joseph-d'Alma until 1954. Several nearby towns were annexed in 1962. Pop. (1986) 25,923; (1991) 25,910.

**ALMA-ATA.** See ALMATY.

**ALMAGEST.** See PTOLEMY.

**ALMAGRO, Diego de** (1475–1538), Spanish soldier and adventurer, born in Almagro, near Ciudad Real. He went to the New World in 1514, and settled in the new town of Panama five years later. In 1524 he formed a partnership with the Spanish explorer Francisco Pizarro to explore and conquer the region on the coast of the Pacific Ocean south of Panama, which was reported to hold deposits of gold. In their first two expeditions (1524–25 and 1526–28), although beset by great hardships, they learned of the wealth of the Incan Empire. In 1529 Pizarro was granted authority by the Holy Roman emperor Charles V to conquer and rule Peru, and in 1533 the partners completed the conquest of the country. In 1535 Charles V appointed Almagro governor of New Toledo, an area lying south of Pizarro's grant and including the northern portion of present-day Chile. After invading and subjugating his lands in 1535–36, Almagro claimed that Cuzco, the ancient Incan capital, lay within his region and entered the city as the legitimate governor. Consequently, a civil war broke out between the followers of Almagro and those of Pizarro. Attempts to negotiate a peaceful settlement were unsuccessful, and in 1538 Almagro was defeated and executed on Pizarro's orders.

**ALMANAC** (Span. Arab. *al manākh,* roughly translated "a calendar of the heavens"), book or table containing a calendar, together with astronomical and navigational data and, often, religious holidays, historical notes, proverbs, and astrological and agricultural forecasts. Almanacs in various forms date from antiquity and were probably the first publications of most countries in the world. Ancient almanacs were carved on wooden sticks—Egyptian priests called these "fingers of the sun"—as well as on stone slabs; medieval almanacs, from as early as the 12th century, were recorded on parchment. The earliest existing printed almanac is that of the German mathematician and astronomer Johann Müller, known as Regiomontanus (1436–76), whose illustrated, 12-leaf *Kalendarium Novum* was printed (1476) in both red (for lucky days) and black, in Venice, Italy.

**Almanacs and Astrology.** From their beginning, almanacs contained predictions of the future based on the position of heavenly bodies, and during the 15th and 16th centuries astrological prognosticating became their dominant feature. Some of the predictions became so frightening (foretelling the deaths of kings, for example) that Henry III of France forbade (1579) almanac makers by law to make prophecies.

Sixteenth-century "Philomath" almanacs, known as such because their editors affixed this word, meaning "lover of learning," to their names, served as calendars, atlases, agricultural and medical advisers, and textbooks. Although astrology was then included among the sciences, almanac editors emphasized increasingly that "astrological predictions serve only to delude and amuse the Vulgar."

**Early American Almanacs.** The first American almanac was *An Almanack for . . . 1639 . . . for New England,* compiled by "William Pierce, Mariner" (1590–1641), in Cambridge, Mass. During the 17th and 18th centuries almanacs outnumbered all other books published in America. American farmer's almanacs were started by John Tulley (1638–1701), from Saybrook, Conn. In 1687 he compiled an almanac that included, for the first time, a weather forecast. As the 18th century progressed, and competition among almanacs became intense, anecdotes, proverbs, riddles, poems, essays, artwork, and humorous items were added to their contents.

Distributed in bookshops, by the printers themselves, or by peddlers, almanacs were widely circulated. From 1726 to 1764 Nathanael Ames, Sr. (1708–64), of Dedham, Mass., sold 50,000 to 60,000 copies annually of his *Astronomical Diary and Almanac.* The most famous of early American almanacs, renowned for its aphorisms, was Benjamin Franklin's *Poor Richard's Almanack,* published under the pseudonym "Richard Saunders, Philom." Franklin issued the almanac from 1732 to 1757; long after his connection with it was in name only, *Poor Richard's* still had enormous circulation. In 1766, for example, 141,257 copies were sold.

The leader in the almanac field, however, was Robert Bailey Thomas (1766–1846), of West Boylston, Mass., who began his 54 years of compiling *The Farmer's Almanac* in 1792. From 1848, as *The Old Farmer's Almanac,* it has been published annually in the same format, providing information on agriculture and giving long-range weather forecasts, with humorous anecdotes, homespun verses, and moral tales interspersed. With a circulation in the millions, it also has the distinction of being the oldest continuously published periodical in the U.S.

Besides *The Old Farmer's Almanac* a few other modern almanacs survive from the past. *Old Moore's Almanac,* started (1680) in England and revived (1966) in the U.S., continues the 15th-century tradition of predicting catastrophic events.

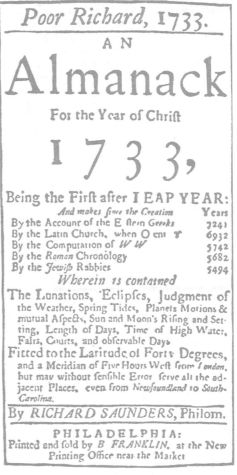

The title page of the first edition of Poor Richard's Almanack, *published (1732) by Benjamin Franklin under the pseudonym Richard Saunders.*

*Baer's Agricultural Almanac,* published in Lancaster, Pa., has existed since 1826.

**Modern Almanacs.** During the 19th century a great variety of topical almanacs were published: temperance, political, health, antislavery, anti-Masonic, and comic almanacs, among others. Almanacs are still published in fairly large numbers, but in general have returned to the serious information concept of the Philomath almanacs. The first publisher of *The World Almanac and Book of Facts* (1868) proclaimed it a "compendium of universal knowledge." Similar compilations of facts and figures include the *Corpus Almanac of Canada* (1965–  ), the British *Whitaker's Almanack* (1869–  ), and such American publications as the *Information Please Almanac* (1947–  ) and *The Universal Alamanac* (1990–  ). Several recent publications that call themselves almanacs do not include any astronomical information. Thus, "almanacs" such as *The Almanac of American Politics* (1972–   ), the *Places Rated Almanac* (1981), *The Vermont Almanac* (1989–   ), and the *Top Ten Almanac* (1991), all published in the U.S., are simply compendiums of information on, respectively, U.S. elected officials, places to live, the state of Vermont, and, as explained by the book's subtitle, "the best of everything according to the numbers."

*The Planetary Ephemeris Program,* developed (1961) at the Lincoln Laboratory in Lexington, Mass., for the use of scientists, is one of the most advanced astronomical almanacs, or ephemerides. It is an enormous corpus of computer-generated data giving highly detailed astronomical observations from 1750 to the present. Perhaps a modern almanac such as this is, after 8000 years of almanac evolution, the ultimate "calendar of the heavens."                    J.D.H.

*For further information on this topic, see the Bibliography in volume 28, section 11.*

**ALMANDITE.**  *See* GARNET.

**ALMA-TADEMA, Sir Lawrence** (1836–1912), British painter in the academic tradition. Born in Dronrijp, the Netherlands, and trained at the Academy of Antwerp, Belgium, he settled in England in 1869. Alma-Tadema's paintings are noted for fine detail, smooth finish, and realistic textures. The majority of his works, such as *A Roman Emperor* (1871), depict idealized settings of ancient civilizations or medieval France. He joined the Royal Academy in 1879 and was knighted in 1899.

**ALMATY** (Kazakh, "apple place"), formerly ALMA-ATA, city, SE Kazakhstan, capital of the country and of Almaty Oblast, on the Great and Little Almaatinka rivers. Located in the foothills of the Tien Shan Mts. near China, the city is the processing center of a fertile fruit-producing region. Besides processed food, manufactures include mining machinery, electrical equipment, textiles, motion pictures, and tobacco products. Known as one of the loveliest cities of the former USSR, Almaty has opera and ballet houses, a symphony orchestra, a state university, and an academy of sciences.

Founded (1854) around the Russian fort Zailiyskoe, the city was known as Verny from 1855 to 1921. Earthquakes (1887, 1911) and a flood (1921) badly damaged the city. In the 1920s it developed into a major economic center as a terminus on the newly built Turkestan-Siberian Railroad. In 1929 the city became the capital of the Kazakh SSR. Pop. (1991 est.) 1,156,200.

**ALMEIDA, Francisco de** (c. 1450–1510), Portuguese soldier. Almeida first distinguished himself in the conquest of Granada in 1492. In 1505 Emanuel, king of Portugal, appointed him the first Portuguese viceroy of Portuguese India, where he strove to exclude the Muslims and Venetians from all commerce with the East. In 1507 he ravaged the Muslim port of Goa and other seaports on the coast of India and completely destroyed the Muslim fleet at Diu, India. He was slain in battle with the Khoikhoi (Hottentots) at Cape Saldanha, South Africa.

**ALMEIDA GARRETT, João Baptista da Silva Leitão, Visconde de** (1799–1854), Portuguese poet, dramatist, and statesman, the founder of the romantic movement in Portuguese literature, born in Oporto. As a political exile in England and France between 1823 and 1832, he came under the influence of the Scottish novelist and poet Sir Walter Scott and the French romanticists. This influence is reflected in his epics *Camões* (1825), the theme of which is the poet's longing for home, and *Dona Branca* (1826), a long satire on monastic life. In 1832 Almeida Garrett returned to Portugal and became active in political life. In 1833 he was made minister of the interior, and he subsequently became a member of the legislature. He interested himself especially in the founding of a national theater and a conservatory of dramatic art and wrote several plays on national characters, one of the greatest of which is *Brother Luiz de Sousa* (1844; trans. 1909). *Viagens na minha terra* (Journeys in My Native Land, 1846) is a freewheeling commentary on his own life and age. One of his most important contributions to literature is his *Romanceiro* (1851–53), a collection of early Portuguese ballads and romances. His last work, published in 1853, was a collection of sensual, melancholy love poems, *Fólhas cíadas* (Fallen Leaves).

**ALMERÍA** (anc. *Unci* and *Portus Magnus*), city, S Spain, capital of Almería Province in Andalusia, and a seaport and tourist center on the Mediterranean. Iron, lead, white Almería grapes, esparto grass, and oranges are exported. Almería was an important trading center in Roman times, and it was used as an arsenal by the Moors. In May 1937, during the Spanish civil war, the city was severely bombarded by five German warships in retaliation for an attack by Loyalist airplanes on the German warship *Deutschland* and the Italian warship *Barletta.* Pop. (1991) 153,288.

**ALMOHADS** (Arab. *al-muwahhid,* "who proclaim the unity of God"), Berber Muslim reform movement and dynasty established in North Africa and Spain during the 12th and 13th centuries. Because of their belief in the unity of God, the Almohads were known as Unitarians. The origin of the movement is traced to Muhammad ibn Tumart (c. 1080–1130), an Arab reformer in

Morocco who preached moral reform and the doctrine of the unity of divine being. He gathered a large following of Arabs and Berbers and in 1121 was proclaimed Al Mahdi ("The Rightly Guided"). The founder of the dynasty was the Berber Abd al-Mumin (1094?–1163), who succeeded Ibn Tumart and took the title of caliph. He conquered (1140–47) Morocco and other parts of North Africa, thus putting an end to the previous dynasty of the Almoravids. By 1154 he also ruled Islamic Spain and part of Portugal. Notable among successive Almohad rulers was Yakub al-Mansur (c. 1160–99), who ruled in Spain from 1184 until his death. He aided the sultan Saladin against the Crusaders and was responsible for the construction of numerous architectural monuments. The Almohad dynasty flourished until 1212, when the united kings of Castile, Aragón, and Navarre defeated the Almohad forces in the Battle of Navas de Tolosa. After that defeat, the power of the Almohads declined and finally came to an end in Spain in 1232 and in Africa in 1269.

**ALMOND,** common name for a small tree, *Prunus amygdalus,* of the family Rosaceae (*see* ROSE), and for the kernel of its fruit. The tree is characterized by the coarsely furrowed and wrinkled shell of the drupe and by the young leaves that have their sides folded along the central vein. It grows up to 9 m (30 ft) high. A native of western Asia, it now grows wild throughout southern Europe and is cultivated in the U.S. The wood is hard, of reddish color, and is used by cabinetmakers. The almond is valued chiefly for its nut, which is an important article of commerce. Varieties are classified as either sweet or bitter. Sweet almonds contain a large quantity of a bland, fixed oil and emulsin, gum, and mucilage sugar; they have an agreeable taste and are nutritious. Bitter almonds contain the same substances and, in addition, a crystalline glucoside called amygdalin. The long almonds of Málaga, Spain, known as Jordan almonds, and the broad almonds of Valencia, Spain, are the most valued.

The dwarf almond tree (*Amygdalus nana*), a low shrub, is similar to the common almond, with smaller fruit. It is common in the plains of Central Asia and is frequently planted as an ornamental shrub in England. Flowering almonds, shrubs or small trees, are cultivated extensively in the U.S. for their profusion of showy, white to rose blossoms.

**ALMORAVIDS,** Berber dynasty that ruled in Africa and Spain in the 11th and 12th centuries. Between 1053 and 1061, a large part of northwestern Africa was subjugated by the Muslim religious military brotherhood known as the hermits (Arab. *al-murabit*). Leadership of the movement passed in 1061 to Yusuf ibn Tashfin (d. 1106), a Berber chieftain who had previously conquered the region constituting present-day Morocco. In 1062 he assumed the title of king. After enlarging their domain in northwestern Africa, the Almoravids invaded Spain in 1086; during the next four years, they conquered the area between the Tagus and Ebro rivers. In 1147 the dynasty was overthrown by the Almohads, another Muslim reform movement.

**ALMQVIST, Carl Jonas Love** (1793–1866), Swedish writer, born in Stockholm, and educated at the University of Uppsala. His novels, short stories, poems, and verse dramas were collected in *Törnrosens Bok* (The Book of the Thorn Rose, 14 vol., 1832–51). Almqvist's work marks the transition from romanticism to realism in Swedish literature. His most important single work is *Sara Videbeck* (1839; trans. 1919), a realistic story dealing with love and marriage. In 1851 Almqvist was charged with forgery and murder. He fled first to the U.S. and later to Bremen, Germany, where he lived under the name of Professor Westermann.

***ALOE,*** genus of plants of the family Aloaceae (*see* LILY). More than 150 species are known, most native to South Africa; they usually have short stems, fleshy, lanceolate leaves crowded in rosettes at the end of the stem, and red or yellow tubular flowers in dense clusters. Species of *Aloe* vary in height from several centimeters to more than 9 m (30 ft); they are widely cultivated as garden and tub plants. Several species are commercially important as the source of the aloes used in medicine. The name aloe also denotes plants in the genus *Agave*.

**ALONSO, Alicia,** *née* MARTINEZ (1917– ), Cuban ballerina and teacher, founder and director of an important ballet company in Latin America. Born in Havana, she studied there and in New York City and London and began her career in Broadway musicals. From 1941 to 1960, although plagued by serious eyesight problems, she was one of the principal stars of the American Ballet Theatre; she was particularly noted in the role of Giselle. In 1948 she formed the Ballet Alicia Alonso (renamed Ballet de Cuba in 1955 and, after the Cuban Revolution of 1959, Ballet Nacional de Cuba). Its ballet school is admired for the quality of its training and recruiting system.

**ALOYSIUS, Saint.** *See* GONZAGA, SAINT ALOYSIUS.

**ALPACA,** common name for a South American mammal, *Lama pacos,* of the family Camelidae (*see* CAMEL). Partially domesticated, the alpaca possibly was derived from the wild guanaco

*Alpaca,* Lama pacos          © 1988 F. Erize–Bruce Coleman, Inc.

(q.v.) and is closely related to the llama and vicuña. The natural habitat of the alpaca is the Andes in South America. It is most commonly kept in flocks by the Indians in the highlands of Peru and Chile.

The alpaca, a surefooted animal, is smaller than the llama, has longer, softer wool, and ordinarily is not used as a beast of burden. Like the llama and camel, it spits when angry. After 11 months' gestation the female gives birth to one offspring. The young have short wool until they mature.

Flocks of alpacas graze almost wild on high plateaus, 4267 to 4877 m (14,000 to 16,000 ft) above sea level. At shearing time the Indians drive them to the villages and clip off about 20 cm (about 8 in) of the wool. The alpaca provides white, gray, or yellow wool, although the black and dark brown fibers are especially valued. The fiber is elastic and strong and is straighter and silkier than sheep's wool. Although the flesh of the alpaca is palatable, the animal is generally kept primarily for its wool, from which a fine cloth is made.

**ALPHABET** (from *alpha* and *beta,* the first two letters of the Greek alphabet), set of written symbols, each representing a given sound or sounds, which can be variously combined to form all the words of a language.

An alphabet attempts ideally to indicate each separate sound by a separate symbol, although this end is seldom attained, except in the Korean alphabet (the most perfect phonetic system known) and, to a lesser degree, in the Japanese

syllabaries. Alphabets are distinguished from syllabaries and from pictographic and ideographic systems. A syllabary represents each separate syllable (usually a sequence of from one to four spoken sounds pronounced as an uninterrupted unit) by a single symbol. Japanese, for example, has two complete syllabaries—the *hiragana* and the *katakana*—devised to supplement the characters originally taken over from Chinese. A pictographic system represents picturable objects, for example, a drawing of the sun stands for the spoken word *sun.* An ideographic system combines various pictographs for the purpose of indicating nonpicturable ideas. Thus, the Chinese pictographs for *sun* and *tree* are combined to represent the Chinese spoken word for *east.*

Early systems of writing were of the pictographic-ideographic variety; among them are the cuneiform (q.v.) of the ancient Babylonians and Assyrians, Egyptian hieroglyphs (q.v.), the written symbols still used by the Chinese and Japanese (*see* CHINESE LANGUAGE; JAPANESE LANGUAGE), and Mayan picture writing (*see* AMERICAN INDIAN LANGUAGES; MAYA). What converts such a system into an alphabet or syllabary is the use of a pictograph or ideograph to represent a sound rather than an object or an idea. The sound is usually the initial sound of the spoken word denoted by the original pictograph. Thus, in early Semitic, a pictograph representing a house, for which the Semitic spoken word was *beth,* eventually came to symbolize the initial *b* sound of *beth.* This Semitic symbol, standing originally for the entire word *beth* and later for the sound of *b,* ultimately became the *b* of the English alphabet.

**North Semitic Alphabet.** The general supposition is that the first known alphabet developed along the eastern Mediterranean littoral between 1700 and 1500 BC. This alphabet, known as North Semitic, evolved from a combination of cuneiform and hieroglyphic symbols; some symbols might have been taken from kindred systems, such as the Cretan and Hittite. The North Semitic alphabet consisted exclusively of consonants. The vowel sounds of a word had to be supplied by the speaker or reader. The present-day Hebrew and Arabic alphabets still consist of consonantal letters only, the former having 22 and the latter 28. Some of these, however, may be used to represent long vowels, and vowels may also be indicated in writing by optional vowel points and dashes placed below, above, or to the side of the consonant. Writing is from the right to the left. *See* ARABIC LANGUAGE; SEMITIC LANGUAGES.

Many scholars believe that about 1000 BC four branches developed from the original Semitic alphabet: South Semitic, Canaanite, Aramaic, and

# TABLE OF ALPHABETIC DEVELOPMENT

| Semitic name of letters | North Semitic | square Hebrew | Greek name of letters | Greek | Cyrillic | Roman |
|---|---|---|---|---|---|---|
| ALEF | | א | ALPHA | A | А, Я, Ⱥ | A |
| BETH | | ב | BETA | B | В, Б | B |
| GIMEL | | ג | GAMMA | Γ | Г, Ґ | C, G |
| DALETH | | ד | DELTA | Δ | Д | D |
| HE | | ה | EPSILON | E | Е, Є, Э | E |
| | | | DIGAMMA | F | | F |
| VAV | | ו | UPSILON | Y | У, Ү | V, U, Y, W |
| ZAYIN | | ז | ZETA | Z | З | Z |
| CHETH | | ח | ETA | H | И, Й | H |
| TETH | | ט | THETA | Θ | Θ | |
| YOD | | י | IOTA | I | І, Ј | I, J |
| KAF | | כ | KAPPA | K | К | K |
| LAMED | | ל | LAMBDA | Λ | Л, Љ | L |
| MEM | | מ | MU | M | М | M |
| NUN | | נ | NU | N | Н, Њ | N |
| SAMEKH | | ס | XI | Ξ | | |
| AYIN | | ע | OMICRON | O | О, Ю | O |
| PE | | פ | PI | Π | П | P |
| TSADE | | צ | | | Ч, Ц, Ц | |
| QUF | | ק | KOPPA | Ϙ | | Q |
| RESH | | ר | RHO | P | Р | R |
| SHIN | | ש | SIGMA | Σ | С, Ш, Щ | S |
| TAU | | ת | TAU | T | Т | T |
| | | | PHI | Φ | Ф | |
| | | | CHI | X | Х | X |
| | | | PSI | Ψ | Ж, Ѧ | |
| | | | OMEGA | Ω | | |

*Additional Cyrillic characters:* Ъ, ь, ы, Ѣ, Ћ, Ҍ

From *Language for Everybody* by Mario Pei. Published by Devin-Adair. Copyright © 1956

Greek. (Other scholars, however, believe that South Semitic developed independently from North Semitic or that both developed from a common ancestor.) The South Semitic branch was the ancestor of the alphabets of extinct lan- guages used in the Arabian Peninsula and in the modern languages of Ethiopia. Canaanite was subdivided into Early Hebrew and Phoenician, and the extremely important Aramaic branch be- came the basis of Semitic and non-Semitic scripts throughout western Asia. The non-Semitic group was the basis of the alphabets of nearly all Indian scripts; the Semitic subbranch includes Square Hebrew, which superseded Early Hebrew to become the prototype of modern Hebrew writing.

**Greek and Roman Alphabets.** The Greeks adapted the Phoenician variant of the Semitic alphabet, expanding its 22 consonant symbols to 24 (even more in some dialects), and setting apart some of the original consonant symbols to serve exclusively as vowels (*see* GREEK LANGUAGE). After about 500 BC, Greek was regularly written from left to right. The Greek alphabet spread throughout the Mediterranean world, giving rise to various modified forms, including the Etruscan, Oscan, Umbrian, and Roman alphabets. Because of Roman conquests and the spread of the Latin language (q.v.), that language's Roman alphabet became the basic alphabet of all the languages of western Europe.

**Cyrillic Alphabet.** About AD 860 Greek missionaries from Constantinople converted the Slavs to Christianity and devised for them a system of writing known as Cyrillic (*see* CYRILLIC ALPHABET) from the name of one of its inventors, the apostle to the South Slavs, Saint Cyril. The Cyrillic alphabet, like the Roman, stems from the Greek; it is based on a 9th-century writing style. Additional characters, however, were devised to represent Slavic sounds that had no Greek equivalents. The Cyrillic alphabet, in various forms, is used currently in Russian, Ukrainian, Serbian, and Bulgarian, but not in Polish, Czech, Slovak, or Slovenian, which are written in modified Roman alphabets. An interesting division exists in the Balkans where the Roman Catholic Croats use the Roman alphabet, but the Greek Orthodox Serbs employ Cyrillic for the same language.

**Arabic Alphabet.** The Arabic alphabet, another offshoot of the early Semitic one, probably originated about the 4th century AD. It has spread to such languages as Persian and Urdu and is generally used by the Islamic world: throughout the Near and Middle East, in parts of Asia and Africa, and in southern Europe. Arabic is written in either of two forms: Kufic, a heavy, bold, formal script, was devised at the end of the 7th century; Naskhi, a cursive form, is the parent of modern Arabic writing. The question arises whether the various alphabets of India and Southeast Asia are indigenous developments or offshoots of early Semitic. One of the most important Indian alphabets, the Devanagari alphabet used in the Sanskrit language (q.v.; *see also* INDIAN LANGUAGES), is an ingenious combination of syllabic and true alphabetic principles. The progenitors, whether Semitic or Indian, of the Devanagari alphabet seem also to have given rise to the written alphabets of Bengali, Tamil, Telugu, Sinhalese, Burmese, and Siamese, or Thai.

**Artificial Alphabets.** Most of the alphabets considered in this article evolved gradually or were adapted from older prototypes. Some alphabets, however, have been created artificially for peoples previously illiterate, or for nations hitherto using alphabets of foreign origin. An outstanding example is the Armenian alphabet invented by Saint Mesrob (350–439) in 405 and still in use today. Also of great interest is the Mongolian hP'ags-Pa script (written from top to bottom), invented in China about 1269. In modern times, the Cherokee syllabary was invented soon after 1820 by the American Indian leader Sequoya. Later in the 19th century, missionaries and others created syllabaries and alphabets for American Indian languages, based on the Roman and, in the northwest, Russian Cyrillic scripts.

**Alphabet Modifications.** Any alphabet used by peoples speaking different languages undergoes modifications. Such is the case with respect both to the number and form of letters used and to the subscripts and superscripts, or diacritical marks (accents, cedillas, tildes, dots, and others), used with the basic symbols to indicate modifications of sound. The letter *c* with a cedilla, for instance, appears regularly in French, Portuguese, and Turkish, but rarely, except in borrowed words, in English. The value of ç in French, Portuguese, and English is that of *s*, but in Turkish it represents the *ch* sound in *church*. It used to represent *ts* in Spanish, but that sound no longer exists in standard Spanish. So, too, letters have different sound values in different languages. The letter *j*, for example, as in English *jam*, has a *y* sound in German.

Although alphabets develop as attempts to establish a correspondence between sound and symbol, most alphabetically written languages are highly unphonetic, largely because the system of writing remains static while the spoken language evolves. Thus, the spelling of the English word *knight* reflects the pronunciation of an earlier period of the language, when the initial *k* was pronounced and the *gh* represented a sound, since lost, similar to the German *ch* in *Wacht*. The divergence between the written and spoken forms of certain languages, particularly English, has prompted movements for spelling (q.v.) reform. *See also* LANGUAGE; RUNES; SHORTHAND; WRITING; and articles on the individual letters and languages. M.P. & D.M.La.

*For further information on this topic, see the Bibliography in volume 28, sections 354–55.*

**ALTAIC LANGUAGES,** family of languages spoken by about 75,000,000 people in a vast area of Eurasia extending from Turkey in the west to the Sea of Okhotsk in the east. It consists of three main subfamilies or groups: Turkic, Mongolic, and Manchu-Tungus.

Foremost among the Turkic languages is Turkish or Osmanli (Turkey, the Balkans). Other Turkic languages include Azerbaijani (Azerbaijan and northwestern Iran), Kazak, Uzbek, Turkoman, and Kirghiz (Central Asia), Tatar (Turkey, the Balkans, the former USSR, and China), Uighur (Sinkiang-Uighur Autonomous Region, China), and Yakut (mainly northeastern Siberia). The Mongolic languages include Buryat (eastern Siberia), Kalmuck (chiefly the Kalmuck autonomous region), and the most widely spoken of the group, Mongolian (Mongolian republic and the Inner Mongolian Autonomous Region of China). Among the Manchu-Tungus group, Manchu (Manchuria in China) has the greatest number of speakers. Other languages of this group include Evenki (China and the former USSR), Lamut (near the Sea of Okhotsk), and Tungus (eastern Siberia).

Altaic languages are generally characterized by an agglutinative type of suffixation, and by vowel harmony (that is, only vowels of the same coloring can occur in the same word); the vowels of the suffixes are altered so that they agree with the color of the root vowel. Altaic languages lack grammatical gender. They have a rich variety of vowels, but a relatively meager selection of consonants. Some scholars group the Altaic languages together with the Uralic languages (q.v.) in a larger Ural-Altaic grouping; recent researchers, however, increasingly believe that too little evidence exists to support such a grouping.

Certain Altaic-speaking peoples are important historically, for example, the nomadic Huns and Mongols, who invaded Europe between the 4th and 13th centuries AD, and the Manchus of the Ch'ing dynasty who ruled China from 1644 to 1912. Turkish has been written with various scripts since the 8th century; the Mongolian script was in use by the 12th century.                                    M.P.

**ALTAI MOUNTAINS,** also Altay Mountains, mountain range, Central Asia, extending from the headwaters of the Ob and Irtysh rivers in S Siberian Russia into Xinjiang Uygur (Sinkiang Uighur) Autonomous Region of China and into Mongolia. The highest peak is Mt. Belukha (4506 m/14,783 ft). Below about 1830 m (about 6000 ft) the mountain slopes are thickly covered with trees, including cedar, pine, larch, fir, and birch. Between the forests and the snow line, from about 2440 to 3050 m (about 8000 to 10,000 ft), are alpine pastures. The mountains are rich in minerals, especially coal, zinc, and lead, with some gold, iron ore, copper, silver, and tin.

**ALTAR,** surface or structure upon which a religious sacrifice (q.v.) is offered. Although the term is sometimes used simply to designate a center for religious ritual or for the worship of the gods, and although in many nonliterate societies sacrifices are offered without an altar, altar and sacrifice are generally connected in the religious history of humanity.

The earliest and most reliable evidence of an altar, dating from about 2000 BC, is a horned limestone altar excavated at the ancient Palestinian city of Megiddo. Although common in many cultures, the altar is not universal. It is rarely found in indigenous religions of South America and Africa, and Islam seems to be the only world religion that does not use it. Altars vary in size, shape, and construction. A mound of earth; a heap of stones; one large slab of stone, wood, or metal; or a trench dug into the ground, like the *vedi* (altar) of ancient India, have all served as places of offering or sacrifice.

The altar has been ascribed deep religious and symbolic significance. It has been considered a holy and revered object, a place hallowed by the divine presence, where contact and communication with deities and other spirits could be achieved. So sacred was its power, often protected by taboos (see TABOO), that it served, at times, as an asylum for those seeking refuge. At the heart of all altar symbolism lies the idea that it is the center or image of the universe. The Greeks regarded it as the navel of the earth, out of which all life emerged. Particularly in India, the cosmic significance of the altar was fully explored. The ancient sages saw its different parts as representing the various sections of the universe and concluded that its construction was a repetition of creation. The altar, as a heaped-up mound of earth, also symbolized the sacred mother; its very shape could be compared with the body of a woman.

In Christianity the altar held far-reaching religious meaning. Starting from a simple communion table, it became a symbol of Christ and was marked with five symbolic wounds at its consecration. By the Middle Ages, the Christian altar had become a richly decorated throne on which lay the consecrated host (bread and wine) for the purpose of adoration (see EUCHARIST). As in many other religions, the altar table in Christianity has been the focal point of unity, reverence, prayer, and worship.                              J.A.Sa.

**ALTAY MOUNTAINS.** See ALTAI MOUNTAINS.

**ALTDORF,** town, central Switzerland, capital of Uri Canton. According to legend, it was the

**ALPHA CENTAURI,** triple star system, also called Rigil Kent, in the constellation Centaurus (q.v.). To the unaided eye, Alpha Centauri appears as a single star with an apparent magnitude (q.v.) of −0.1, making it the third brightest in the sky. The two bright stars (Alpha Centauri A and B) have apparent magnitudes of −0.01 and 1.33 and orbit each other with a period of 80 years. The faint star Alpha Centauri C has an apparent magnitude of 11.05 and orbits Alpha Centauri A and B with a period of perhaps 1 million years. Alpha Centauri C is also called Proxima Centauri because, at a distance of 4.3 light-years, it is the closest star to the earth.

**ALPHA PARTICLE,** positively charged nuclear particle, symbol a, consisting of two protons bound to two neutrons. Alpha particles are emitted spontaneously in some types of radioactive decay (see RADIOACTIVITY). They are also produced when helium-4 atoms are completely ionized (see ION; IONIZATION). Alpha particles are also notated $_2^4He_2^{2+}$.

**ALPHONSO.**  See ALFONSO.

**ALPHONSUS, Saint.** See LIGUORI, SAINT ALPHONSUS.

**ALPHORN,** Swiss long wooden horn with a cupped mouthpiece and a conical bore ending in a bell, or flare. The tubing is about 1.5 to 3 m (about 5 to 10 ft) long and is typically straight with an upturned bell; the tubing may also be completely straight, S-shaped, or coiled like a trumpet. The notes are the natural harmonics of the tube's fundamental pitch (like the notes of a bugle). Known since antiquity, the alphorn is primarily used for signaling, although Swiss cowherders' songs (*ranz des vaches*) and other music can be played on alphorns in three- and four-part harmonies. Instruments that are similar to the alphorn can be found in the Carpathians and the Pyrenees.

**ALPINE LIFE.** See ALPS; TUNDRA.

**ALPS,** great mountain system, S central Europe, forming an arc some 1200 km (750 mi) long from the Gulf of Genoa to the Danube R. at Vienna. The Alps are the highest and most densely settled mountain belt of Europe, occupying an area of about 240,000 sq km (about 92,700 sq mi) and inhabited by some 20 million people. The valleys of the Alps are areas of year-round settlement; the flatter upland tracts comprise pastures and seasonally inhabited settlements, and the zone above the timberline serves as pasture and for recreation. Important economic activities of the Alps region include tourism, dairy farming, forestry, the production of hydroelectric power, and the extraction of salt and iron ore. With its important pass routes between central and S Europe, the Alps have been an area of transit trade dating from ancient times.

**Geologic Structure and Formation.** The Alps are a complex fold-mountain system. Sedimentary deposits of vast thickness, mainly limestone and dolomite, were laid down in the ancestral Tethys Sea during the Triassic and Jurassic periods (qq.v.). Subsequently, enormous pressure generated by a collision between the African and Eurasian plates (see PLATE TECTONICS) thrust these rock strata upward and northward to form recumbent folds (nappes), which in the process of movement were detached from their roots. The four glaciations of the Quaternary period (beginning about 2.5 million years ago) were of great importance in the sculpturing of the Alps. Vast ice masses moved through the valleys, transforming them into deep troughs with steep walls; the overflow of ice across the mountain divides shaped the passes. Glacial deposits in the form of moraines dammed the streams and rivers and produced the region's many lakes, the two largest of which are Lake Geneva and Lake Constance.

**The Alpine System.** Structurally, the Alpine mountain system is divided into the Western and Eastern Alps by a furrow that leads from the Rhine Valley in N Switzerland, across Splügen Pass to Lake Como in N Italy. The Western Alps average about 1000 m (about 3300 ft) higher and are narrower and more rugged than the Eastern Alps. The highest peak of the Alps, Mont Blanc (4807 m/15,771 ft), is on the Franco-Italian border. Among the principal ranges are the Maritime, Ligurian, Cottian, and Graian Alps in France and Italy and the Bernese, Glarus, and Pennine (or Valais) Alps in Switzerland. The Jura Mts. are a NW outlier of the French Alps. From Lake Geneva the Alpine ranges curve NE and become more widely separated, attaining a width of 250 km (155 mi) in the center of the arc. The ranges of the Eastern Alps diverge, finally to plunge to the Danubian Basin near Vienna. Well-known mountain chains of the Eastern Alps are the Bavarian Alps, Allgäu Alps, Hohe Tauern, and Niedere Tauern in the N and the Dolomite and Carnic Alps in the S.

Summit regions above 3000 m (about 9800 ft) are glaciated. Peaks and crests, however, rise above the ice, displaying jagged shapes (toothlike horns, needles, and knife-edged ridges). About 2% of the total area of the Alps is covered by ice. The longest valley glacier, the Aletsch Glacier in the Bernese Alps, is 18 km (11 mi) long.

Broad and deep longitudinal valleys, which hold the courses of the upper Rhône, upper Rhine, Inn, Salzach, Mur, and Drau rivers, separate the structural units of the Alps, and contain the main permanent settlements and the principal arteries

*Mt. Doldenhorn, a peak of the Bernese Alps in Switzerland. The principal chain of the Bernese Alps is some 110 km (some 68 mi) long and contains the largest number of Alpine glaciers.*
Swiss National Tourist Office

for traffic. Deeply incised, transverse tributary valleys lead up to the pass regions. Passes at elevations above 2000 m (about 6600 ft) are blocked with snow during the winter months; these include the Mt. Cenis, Great Saint Bernard, Simplon, and Saint Gotthard passes. Brenner Pass, at 1370 m (4495 ft), and Reschen Pass, at 1508 m (4948 ft), provide the easiest crossings. Engineering feats, such as tunneling of the higher passes for highways and railroads, have lessened the barrier effect of the Alps.

**The Physical Environment.** The Alps receive high precipitation on the windward (N) side of about 3000 mm (about 120 in) annually. This precipitation sustains the forests, and the runoff feeds many of the large rivers of Western Europe, such as the Rhine, Rhône, and Po rivers and the tributaries of the Danube (Inn and Drau rivers).

Elevation and exposure to maritime air masses and to the sun's rays are the prime variables influencing vegetation. Oak, hornbeam, and pine trees dominate the warm foothill zones, and sheltered valleys opening onto the Upper Italian Lakes abound with subtropical vegetation. A region of beech forests encompasses the cooler zone and grades at higher elevations into the fir and spruce belt. Mountain maple, spruce, and larch extend to the timberline. Above 1800 m (about 5900 ft) is the treeless zone, a realm of Alpine tundra and Alpine flora that extends to the permanent snow line and includes rhododendron, edelweiss, rock flora, sedges, rowan, creeping pine, and dwarf shrubs. This is a strikingly colorful zone during the short summer growing season of three to four months. Alpine fauna occupies the solitary heights below the snow line. The dominant species are the ibex, chamois, woodchuck, snow grouse, snow mouse, and Alpine daw.                                              E.T.S.

*For further information on this topic, see the Bibliography in volume 28, sections 795, 867, 997.*

**ALSACE,** administrative region and former province, NE France, now comprising the departments of Haut-Rhin, Bas-Rhin, and Territoire de Belfort. After the partitions (817 and 843) of the empire of Charlemagne, Alsace became part of Lotharingia, the kingdom of Lothair. In 925 Alsace became part of the German duchy of Swabia or Alamannia and was absorbed into the Holy Roman Empire, of which it remained a part for some 800 years. It remained a German possession until the 17th century, and during this period strong feudal principalities, controlled largely by the Habsburg rulers of Austria, emerged. A number of rich and powerful towns, such as Strassburg (Strasbourg) and Kolmar, developed in the late

Middle Ages and won status as free towns or miniature republics. By the terms of the Peace of Westphalia in 1648, which concluded the Thirty Years' War, Alsace was placed under the sovereignty of France. Alsace constituted a province of the kingdom of France until the French Revolution, when it was split into the departments of Bas-Rhin and Haut-Rhin. These departments, together with part of Lorraine, were incorporated into the German Empire after the Franco-Prussian War of 1870–71. (For subsequent history see ALSACE-LORRAINE.)

**ALSACE-LORRAINE** (Ger. *Elsass-Lothringen*), historic frontier area, NE France, separated from Germany on the E by the Rhine R. and drained by the Moselle R. The Vosges Mts. are in the E. Today it consists of three departments: Bas-Rhin and Haut-Rhin, in the French administrative region of Alsace (q.v.), and Moselle, part of the region of Lorraine (q.v.). The chief cities are Strasbourg, Mulhouse, and Metz.

After the breakup of Charlemagne's empire in the 9th century, the region became the object of disputes between French and Germanic rulers, passing from the control of one to the other. The term Alsace-Lorraine was first used in 1871, when, by the terms of the Peace Treaty of Frankfurt concluding the Franco-Prussian War, the former provinces of Alsace and Lorraine, which had been under French rule since the middle of the 17th century, were annexed by Germany. They were returned to France in 1919, after World War I, by the terms of the Treaty of Versailles. During World War II, under terms of the armistice of 1940 between France and Germany, the territory was ceded to Germany, but France regained it after Germany's defeat in 1945.

The German-speaking population is centered chiefly in Alsace; the French-speaking, chiefly in Lorraine. In many respects, however, the culture of the whole region is uniform, containing both French and German elements. At various times autonomy movements have been initiated, directed against Germany between 1871 and World War I and against France after World War I. The sentiment of the region during both world wars, however, was markedly pro-French.     G.W.H.

**ALTADENA,** unincorporated urban community, Los Angeles Co., SW California, on the lower slopes of the San Gabriel Mts., near Pasadena. It is a residential community situated in a region producing avocados and citrus fruit. Founded in the 1880s, Altadena is noted for its Christmas Tree Lane, an avenue flanked by 150 tall deodars (cedars native to the Himalayas), which are decorated with colored lights in December. Pop. (1980) 40,510; (1990) 42,658.

home of the Swiss patriot William Tell. The spot on which his son stood when Tell shot an apple off his head is marked by a bronze statue. Pop. (1992 est.) 8060.

**ALTDORFER, Albrecht** (c. 1480–1538), German painter, architect, and engraver, considered the first landscape painter in Western art. Although his birthplace is unknown, he spent most of his life in Regensburg as city architect and life member of the city council.

Altdorfer is important to the history of painting as a founder and leading master of the group of 16th-century German artists known as the Danube school. His pictures are characterized by an evocative imagination, ranging from the playful to the grandiose and from the picturesque to the fantastic. One of his best works is a great altarpiece (1518) in the monastery of Saint Florian in Enns, Austria, in which he used a number of night scenes, unusual for that time. In his huge painting called *Battle of Alexander at Issus* (1529) thousands of tiny figures in a wild, craggy landscape are seen from high in the air against a fiery sunset. It and a number of his other major works, such as the exquisite little *St. George in a Landscape* (1510), are in Munich's Alte Pinakothek. Paintings by Altdorfer in the Berlin Museum include *Repose on the Flight to Egypt* (1510), *Beggary Sitting on the Train of Pride* (1531), and a *Nativity* (1512).

Altdorfer's skill as a graphic artist entitles him to a place among the so-called Little Masters, a group of 16th-century German engravers noted for their expert execution of designs on a small scale. His graphic style was influenced by the great master of his day the German painter and engraver Albrecht Dürer. Altdorfer's prints include an outstanding series of 9 etched landscapes and a set of 40 engravings collectively called *The Fall and Redemption of Man*.

**ALTERNATION OF GENERATIONS,** occurrence of two or more alternating forms in the life cycle of plants. All plants take two generations to complete one life cycle. Among some algae, the two generations are similar in structure and appearance. In other plants, the two generations are fundamentally different.

In all cases, the alternating generations are a sexual one, called the gametophyte, and an asexual one, called the sporophyte. The gametophyte generation produces gametes (eggs and sperm) that fuse, giving rise to the sporophyte generation. The essential characteristic of the sporophyte is that its reproductive cells or spores are asexual and each spore germinates to produce a gametophyte.

Among the mosses and liverworts, the game-

tophytic generation is the conspicuous form; the sporophyte cannot exist independently. The sporophyte of the moss is composed of a capsule, which is the center of spore formation; a stalk; and a foot that attaches the sporophyte body to the tip of the gametophyte.

The gametophyte and the gametes that it produces are haploid, that is, they contain half the number of chromosomes that is characteristic of the species. When the egg and sperm fuse, they form a sporophyte that is diploid, that is, it has the complete number of chromosomes. When cell division occurs within the spore-bearing structures (sporangia) of the sporophyte, the diploid chromosome number is reduced again to the haploid state.

Among plants more advanced in evolutionary development than the ferns, the gametophyte does not occur as an independent plant. The sporophyte is the conspicuous generation, and the vestigial gametophytes are reduced to a few nuclei that can be seen only with a microscope. Among the flowering plants, the pollen grain is the microspore, within which are produced male gametophytes that contain the sperm. The egg sac, or female gametophyte, is produced by germination of a megaspore within the ovary or pistil of the flower. Microspores and megaspores are produced inside of the anther sacs of stamens and inside of the ovulary tissues of the pistil, respectively.

For some years scientists have known that some sporophytes spontaneously give rise to gametophytes, which are therefore diploid. Experimentally disturbed gametophytes may also give rise to sporophytes, which may then be haploid. These unusual conditions have caused scientists to question the validity of earlier conclusions about the significance of the life cycle of plants. Animals do not undergo alternation of generations that differ in chromosome number. Among the coelenterates, however, is found a kind of alternation of generations between a colonial polyp form and a free-swimming medusa or other jellyfish form. Both forms are diploid. This cycle is known as metagenesis and is not really comparable to the alternation of generations among plants.

**ALTGELD, John Peter** (1847–1902), American political leader, born in Germany. He was taken to the U.S. as an infant by his parents, who settled near Mansfield, Ohio. At the age of 16 he joined the Union army and fought until the end of the American Civil War. Altgeld studied law and became an attorney. He was elected a judge of the Cook Co., Ill., Superior Court in 1886. A member of the Democratic party, he was governor of Illinois from 1893 to 1897. During his administration, he aroused bitter criticism throughout the country because he pardoned the anarchists involved in the bomb throwing that took place in the Haymarket Square Riot in Chicago in 1886; Altgeld considered the conviction of the men unjust.

In 1895, during the Pullman strike, when the American Railway Union tied up all rail transportation in Illinois, Richard Olney (1835–1917), federal attorney general, sent troops to keep the trains running. Altgeld protested vigorously to President Grover Cleveland against the use of federal troops in a case in which the state militia was in control of the situation. This action of the governor was also widely condemned as being dangerously radical. In the presidential campaigns of 1896 and 1900, Altgeld actively supported the candidate of his party, William Jennings Bryan. In keeping with his liberal political and economic ideas, Altgeld was an advocate of prison reform. He wrote *Our Penal Machinery and Its Victims* (1884).

**ALTHING** (Icel., "general assembly"), parliament of Iceland, the oldest functioning legislature in the world. It was established in 930 and met yearly in the summer at Thingvellir, northeast of Reykjavík. The supreme governing body of the country during the old commonwealth (930–1262), it served as both legislature and court. Following Iceland's loss of independence in 1262, the Althing's powers were gradually dissipated as royal authority grew more assertive; by the end of the 17th century, when absolutism had become the norm, it was stripped of its judicial powers and reduced to a token existence. Suspended in 1800, the Althing was reconvened in 1843 and has since met in Reykjavík.

**ALTIMETER,** mechanical or electronic device commonly used in aircraft to measure vertical height above the surface of the earth. Two main types of altimeter exist: pressure and radio. The more common pressure altimeter operates on the principle that atmospheric pressure decreases with an increase in altitude. Pointers on the graduated face of the altimeter dial connect through a system of gears and levers to an aneroid capsule, a hollow, metallic disk partially evacuated of air that expands and contracts slightly with changes in atmospheric pressure, that is, with altitude (*see* BAROMETER). Radio altimeters, radar devices modified to measure vertical distance only, beam a pulse of electromagnetic radiation (q.v.) downward from the aircraft. A receiving antenna on the craft then detects the radio waves reflected by the surface of the earth. By measuring the time difference (*t*) between sending and receiving the pulse, the altitude (*h*) can be computed in the equation

$$h = \frac{tc}{2}$$

where *c* is the speed of light (q.v.).

**ALTIPLANO,** high plateau region, SW Bolivia and S Peru, in the Andes. It comprises a series of intermontane basins located at an altitude of about 3650 m (about 12,000 ft) between the Eastern and Western cordilleras, or ranges, of the Andes. The Altiplano is a heavily populated region, even though it has a cold, dry, and windy climate. Potatoes and barley are grown, and llamas are raised. Lakes Titicaca and Poopó are located in the Altiplano.

**ALTITUDE,** in astronomy, the angle in degrees of a heavenly body above the horizon. An altitude measurement is not a linear distance, but rather the angle between the plane of the horizon and a line drawn from the eye to the heavenly body, or the arc of a vertical circle intercepted between the heavenly body and the horizon.

In physical geography, altitude refers to elevation above mean sea level. This measurement is determined most accurately by triangulation with optical instruments. The altitude of an airplane, however, is measured most accurately by means of a radio altimeter.

**ALTMAN, Benjamin** (1840–1913), American merchant, art collector, and philanthropist, born in New York City. After a public school education, he worked in the small store established by his father on the Lower East Side. Altman worked in small stores after the death of his father, but in 1865 he opened a dry goods store of his own in New York City. His business steadily increased in scale and became one of the largest department store enterprises in the world; in 1913 it was incorporated under the name of B. Altman & Co. Altman's art collection, valued by experts at $15 million at the time of his death, was bequeathed to the Metropolitan Museum of Art in New York City.

**ALTO** *or* **CONTRALTO,** lowest of the three principal ranges of voice found in women or young boys, the other two ranges being the soprano and mezzosoprano. The contralto voice has a range of about two octaves upward from E or F below middle C. Originally the term also was applied in choral music to designate the highest male voice, the countertenor, or male alto. In modern times it generally refers to the vocal part below the soprano part of a musical composition; contralto is the term for the voice or the performer. Today women who have a rich, weighty quality in the lower register are called contraltos. In combination with the name of an instrument (alto trombone, alto saxophone), the word *alto* denotes an instrument with a range just below the highest range reached by that family of instruments. The alto clef is the C clef, so placed as to indicate that middle C is on the third line of the staff.

**ALTON,** city, Madison Co., SW Illinois, on the Mississippi R., near its confluence with the Missouri R.; inc. 1837. Flour has been milled here since 1831, and the city's huge glassmaking industry dates from 1873. Other manufactures include ammunition, refined oil, and steel products. Rufus Easton (1774–1834), a judge and politician, platted the city in 1817 near the site of the first camp of the Lewis and Clark expedition; he named it for his son Alton. The abolitionist Elijah P. Lovejoy was murdered in Alton in 1837, and in 1858 the city was the site of the last Lincoln-Douglas debate. The state's first penitentiary (partly preserved as a museum) was in Alton; during the American Civil War it housed thousands of Confederate prisoners. Pop. (1980) 34,171; (1990) 32,905.

**ALTOONA,** city, Blair Co., central Pennsylvania, at the E escarpment of the Allegheny Mts.; inc. as a city 1868. Manufactures include railroad equipment, electronic components, clothing, electrical appliances, and processed food. Large railroad repair shops are here. A campus (1929) of Pennsylvania State University is in Altoona. The community was founded (1849) by the Pennsylvania Railroad (later merged into the Penn Central) as a base for constructing a rail line across the Alleghenies. A spectacular railroad horseshoe curve nearby is a tourist attraction. The origin of the city's name is unclear; it may be derived from the Indian word *allatoona* ("high valuable lands"), from the Latin *altus* ("high"), or from the German community of Altona (now a district of Hamburg, Germany). Pop. (1980) 57,078; (1990) 51,881.

**ALTRUISM,** devotion to the welfare of others. It is the English form of the French word *altruisme* created by the 19th-century French philosopher and sociologist Auguste Comte from the Italian *aitrui,* "of or to others." Introduced into English by the translators and followers of Comte, the word has gradually come into more general use. In philosophy altruism describes a theory of conduct that aspires to the good of others as the ultimate end for any moral action. Egoism and selfishness are antonyms of the word.

**ALTUS,** city, seat of Jackson Co., SW Oklahoma; inc. 1919. It is the center of an irrigated cotton- and wheat-growing area. Cattle, horses, and racing greyhounds are also raised here. Altus Air Force Base and a junior college are here. The commu-

nity, founded nearby as Frazer about 1887, was flooded in 1891, prompting its relocation to its present higher ground—hence its current name, Latin for "high." Pop. (1980) 23,101; (1990) 21,910.

**ALUM,** colorless mixed salt, $KAl(SO_4)_2 \cdot 12H_2O$, also called potassium alum, that forms large octahedral or cubic crystals (*see* CRYSTAL) when potassium sulfate and aluminum sulfate are dissolved together and the solution is cooled. Solutions of alum are acidic.

Alum is soluble in seven times its weight of water at room temperature and is very soluble in hot water. When dry crystalline alum is heated, some of the water of hydration becomes chemically separated, and the partly dehydrated salt dissolves in this water, so that the alum appears to melt at about 90° C (about 194° F). When heated to about 200° C (about 392° F), alum swells up, loses all the water and some sulfur trioxide, and becomes a basic salt called burnt alum. Alum has a density (q.v.) of 1.725.

Alum was probably known in pre-Christian times. Until about 1600 it was made by heating a mineral, alunite, and extracting the product with water, yielding a solution of alum and a residue of alumina (q.v.). In later times more common minerals were used, which required treatment with sulfuric acid or potash to produce alum. Alum and related substances are now prepared from aluminum sulfate, which is made from bauxite and sulfuric acid (qq.v.). *See also* SULFUR.

Alum is used in the flameproofing of textiles; in baking powders; in mordants for delicate dyeing operations; and in medicines. It is a powerful astringent and styptic; the ordinary styptic pencil used by shavers to stop bleeding from small cuts is usually made entirely of alum.

**ALUMINA** or **ALUMINUM OXIDE,** $Al_2O_3$, the only oxide formed by the metal aluminum. It is found in nature as the minerals corundum, $Al_2O_3$; diaspore (qq.v.), $Al_2O_3 \cdot H_2O$; gibbsite, $Al_2O_3 \cdot 3H_2O$; and most commonly, bauxite (q.v.), an impure form of gibbsite. The precious stones ruby and sapphire (qq.v.) are composed of corundum colored by small amounts of impurities.

Fused alumina, alumina that has been melted and recrystallized, is identical in chemical and physical properties with natural corundum. It is exceeded in hardness only by diamond and by a few synthetic substances, notably carborundum, or silicon carbide. Both impure natural corundum (emery) and pure synthetic corundum (Alundum) are used as abrasives (*see* ABRASIVE). At room temperature alumina is insoluble in all ordinary chemical reagents. Its melting point is high, slightly above 2000° C (3632° F), and so

A hot solution of alumina in sodium hydroxide is cooled in a precipitation tank to form hydrated crystals of alumina.
**ALCOA**

alumina is useful as a refractory, for example, for the linings of special furnaces.

Alumina can be purified by fusing it with sodium carbonate. The resulting sodium aluminate is dissolved in water, leaving impurities, such as iron, as an insoluble residue. Hydrated alumina is reprecipitated from the solution by carbon dioxide. Because the alumina contained in bauxite is soluble in sodium hydroxide solution, a less expensive method may be used. By alternately concentrating and diluting the solution, hydrated alumina is precipitated, and the sodium hydroxide may be reused without neutralization. Hydrated alumina, also called aluminum hydroxide or aluminum hydrate, has a composition approximating the formula $Al(OH)_3$, also written $Al_2O_3 \cdot 3H_2O$, which may include more or less water. Hydrated alumina is readily soluble in acids or alkalies and is used as a raw material in the manufacturing process of all aluminum compounds.

**ALUMINUM** (in Canada and Europe, aluminium), trivalent metallic element, symbol Al, in group 13 (or IIIa) of the periodic table (*see* PERIODIC LAW); at.no. 13, at.wt. 26.9815. Aluminum melts at 660° C (1220° F), boils at 2467° C (4473° F), and has a sp.gr. of 2.7.

Hans Christian Oersted, a Danish chemist, first isolated aluminum in 1825, using a chemical process involving potassium amalgam. Between 1827 and 1845 Friedrich Wöhler, a German chemist, improved Oersted's process by using metallic potassium. He was the first to measure the specific gravity of aluminum and show its lightness. In 1854 Henri Sainte-Claire Deville (1818–81), in France, obtained the metal by reducing aluminum chloride with sodium. Aided by the financial backing of Napoleon III, Deville established a large-scale experimental plant and displayed pure aluminum at the Paris Exposition of 1855.

**Properties.** Aluminum is a strongly electropositive metal and extremely reactive. In contact with air, aluminum rapidly becomes covered with a tough, transparent layer of aluminum oxide that resists further corrosive action. For this reason, materials made of aluminum do not tarnish or rust. The metal reduces many other metallic compounds to their base metals. For example, when thermite, a mixture of powdered iron oxide and aluminum is heated, the aluminum rapidly removes the oxygen from the iron; the heat of the reaction is sufficient to melt the iron. This phenomenon is used in the thermite process for welding iron (*see* WELDING).

The oxide of aluminum is amphoteric, showing both acidic and basic properties. The most important compounds include the oxide, hydroxide, sulfate, and mixed sulfate compounds (*see* ALUM). Anhydrous aluminum chloride is important in the oil and synthetic-chemical industries. Many gemstones (q.v.), ruby and sapphire, for example, consist mainly of crystalline aluminum oxide.

**Occurrence.** Aluminum is the most abundant metallic constituent in the crust of the earth; only the nonmetals oxygen and silicon are more abundant. Aluminum is never found as a free metal; it occurs most commonly as aluminum silicate or as a silicate of aluminum mixed with other metals such as sodium, potassium, iron, calcium, and magnesium. These silicates are not useful ores, for it is chemically difficult, and therefore an expensive process, to extract aluminum from them. Bauxite (q.v.), an impure hydrated aluminum oxide, is the commercial source of aluminum and its compounds.

In 1886 Charles Martin Hall (1863–1914) in the U.S. and Paul L. T. Héroult (1863–1914) in France independently and almost simultaneously discovered that alumina (q.v.), or aluminum oxide, would dissolve in fused cryolite ($Na_3AlF_6$) and could then be decomposed electrolytically to a crude molten metal. A low-cost technique, the Hall-Héroult process, is still the major method used for the commercial production of aluminum, although new methods are under study. The purity of the product has been increased until a commercially pure ingot is 99.5% pure aluminum; it may be further refined to 99.99%.

High-strength aluminum alloy is rolled into a thin sheet for use on an aircraft fuselage. Aluminum may make up 80 percent of a plane's weight.   General Dynamics

Sections of preshaped aluminum are joined together to form the skin of each of the several large transport planes, shown in the final assembly area of an aircraft manufacturer.   Douglas Aircraft Co.

*A mixture of alumina and cryolite is placed in electrolytic cells (left), in which it is smelted to form aluminum. A worker watches the molten metal being tapped from one of the cells. The next step is for the molten aluminum to be poured into casting molds. Automated lifts (right) pull the cooled ingots from the molds. The resulting ingots are more than 99 percent pure aluminum.* ALCOA

**Uses.** A given volume of aluminum weighs less than one-third as much as the same volume of steel. The only lighter metals are lithium, beryllium, and magnesium. Its high strength-to-weight ratio makes aluminum useful in the construction of aircraft, railroad cars, and automobiles and for other applications in which mobility and energy conservation are important. Because of its high heat conductivity, aluminum is used in cooking utensils and the pistons of internal-combustion engines. Aluminum has only 63% of the electrical conductivity of copper for wire of a given size, but it weighs less than half as much. Weight is particularly important in long-distance, high-voltage power transmission, and aluminum conductors are now used to transmit electricity at 700,000 V or more.

The metal is becoming increasingly important architecturally, for both structural and ornamental purposes. Aluminum siding, storm windows, and foil are widely used. The metal is also used as a material in low-temperature nuclear reactors because it absorbs relatively few neutrons. Aluminum becomes stronger and retains its toughness as it gets colder and is therefore used at cryogenic temperatures. Aluminum foil 0.018 cm (0.007 in) thick, now a common household convenience, protects food and other perishable items from spoilage. Because of its light weight,

ease of formation, and compatibility with foods and beverages, aluminum is widely used for containers, flexible packages, and easy-to-open bottles and cans. The recycling of such containers is an increasingly important energy-conservation measure. Aluminum's resistance to corrosion in salt water also makes it useful in boat hulls and various aquatic devices.

A wide variety of coating alloys and wrought alloys can be prepared that give the metal greater strength, castability, or resistance to corrosion or high temperatures. Some new alloys can be used as armor plate for tanks, personnel carriers, and other military vehicles.

**Production.** In 1886 the world production of aluminum was less than 45 kg (less than 100 lb), and its price was more than $11 per kg (more than $5 per lb). In 1989, by contrast, the estimated world production of primary aluminum was 18 million metric tons and an estimated 4 million metric tons was produced in the U.S. alone, whereas the price of aluminum was less than $2 per kg. U.S. consumption, by major markets, consisted of containers and packaging, 31%; building and construction, 20%; transportation, 24%; electric equipment, 10%; consumer durables, 9%; and miscellaneous, 6%. The U.S. recycled 2.2 million tons of aluminum in 1989, and aluminum recovered from discarded aluminum products accounted for about 20% of total consumption.     S.Z.L.

*For further information on this topic, see the Bibliography in volume 28, section 629.*

**ALUMINUM OXIDE.**  *See* ALUMINA.

**ALVA, Fernando Álvarez de Toledo, Duke of** (1507–82), Spanish general of noble family. He rose to prominence as commander of the armies of Charles V, Holy Roman emperor, and gained a brilliant victory for Charles over Elector John Frederick (1503–54) of Saxony at Mühlberg in 1547. In Charles's Italian campaign against the French and papal forces, Alva overran the Papal States, but after the abdication of Charles V, Philip II, king of Spain, relinquished them. Alva was appointed captain general of the Netherlands in 1567, with authority to repress the Dutch revolt against Spain. He set up a tribunal, the Blood Council, which condemned and executed some 18,000 people and confiscated their property. Among the victims was the Flemish statesman Lamoral Egmont. Alva's troops defeated the Flemish forces and, on Dec. 22, 1568, entered Brussels. His tyranny intensified Dutch resistance, and he was recalled in 1573. In 1580 King Philip dispatched Alva to conquer Portugal, which he did with characteristic cruelty.

**ALVARADO, Pedro de** (1486–1541), Spanish explorer, born in Badajoz. In 1518 he accompanied the Spanish explorer Juan de Grijalva (1489?–1527) on his voyage along the coast of Mexico. In 1519 he was second in command to the Spanish adventurer Hernán Cortés on their voyage from Havana and took an active part in the conquest of Mexico. He conquered and settled Guatemala in 1523–24 and in 1534 headed an expedition to claim the territory of Quito, maintaining it had not been included in the grant made to the Spanish conqueror of Peru, Francisco Pizarro. Met by Pizarro's troops, he agreed to turn back upon the payment of a large indemnity. Alvarado was killed during an Indian rebellion in Mexico.

**ALVAREZ, Luis Walter** (1911–88), American scientist and Nobel laureate, born in San Francisco and educated at the University of Chicago. He won the 1968 Nobel Prize in physics for developing the liquid hydrogen bubble chamber, with which he found atomic particles produced by high-energy nuclear events. He also developed the proton linear accelerator known as LINEAC. Alvarez had wide-ranging interests in science. In 1981 he and his son Walter (1940–    ), after studying geological strata, published a controversial theory that a giant meteor striking the earth had caused the extinction of the dinosaurs.

**ALWAR,** city, N India, in Rajasthan State, capital of Alwar District. Alwar, which is circled by a wall and moat, has several fine palaces and temples and a library containing rare Oriental manuscripts. Before the partition of India in 1947, the city served as the capital of Alwar, a princely state. Pop. (1991, greater city) 211,162.

**ALYATTES,** (d. about 560 BC), king of Lydia (c. 619–560 BC), and founder of the ancient Lydian Empire. Under Alyattes, the Lydians fought against many nations. After a war with the Medes, which ended after a solar eclipse in 585 BC, Alyattes' power extended to the river Halys (modern Kızıl Irmak) in Asian Turkey. He also conquered the Ionian cities of Smyrna (now İzmir) and Colophon. His tomb, one of the wonders of antiquity, near the river Hermus (modern Gediz), north of Sardis, was excavated in 1854. His son, Croesus, was the last king of Lydia.

*ALYSSUM,* genus of low-growing, mostly perennial plants of the family Brassicaceae (*see* MUSTARD), also called madwort. *Alyssum saxatile,* golden tuft or rock madwort, and *A. argenteum,* yellow tuft, are spring-flowering perennials often cultivated in rock gardens. A related plant of the same family, *Lobularia maritima,* is commonly called sweet alyssum. It is a European perennial, cultivated in the U.S. as an annual. Clusters of white flowers bloom throughout the spring and summer and have a pleasant fragrance. Blue and purple varieties have been introduced.

**ALZHEIMER'S DISEASE,** progressive degenerative disease of the brain now considered a leading cause of dementia (*see* SENILE DEMENTIA) among the old. First described by the German neuropathologist Alois Alzheimer (1864–1915) in 1906, it affects an estimated 4 million persons in the U.S. The incidence of the disease increases with advancing age, but there is no evidence that it is caused by the aging process.

The average life expectancy of persons with the disease is between five and ten years, although many patients now survive 15 years or more due to improvements in care and medical treatment. The cause of this disease has not been discovered, although palliative therapy is available. The ability of doctors to diagnose the disease has improved over the last ten years, but this remains a process of elimination, and final diagnosis can be confirmed only at autopsy.

At autopsy, Alzheimer's patients show nerve cell loss in the parts of the brain associated with cognitive functioning. The hallmark lesions of Alzheimer's disease include the formation of abnormal proteins known as neurofibrillary tangles and neuritic plaques. The nature of these abnormal proteins and the location of the gene for producing the precursor protein has been identified. Alzheimer's disease is also characterized by profound deficits in the brain's neurotransmitters, chemicals that transmit nerve impulses, particularly acetylcholine, which has been linked with memory function. The important scientific issue concerning Alzheimer's disease revolves around the question of why particular classes of nerve cells are vulnerable and subject to cell death. To answer this question researchers examine the potential effects of genetic factors, toxins, infectious agents, metabolic abnormalities, and a combination of these factors. Recent findings indicate that a small percentage of Alzheimer's cases may be inherited.

**AM.** See FREQUENCY MODULATION; RADIO.

***AMADIS OF GAUL,*** title of a medieval romance of chivalry, written in prose and relating the adventures of a legendary hero of the same name. Its authorship is sometimes credited to the Portuguese knight Vasco de Lobeira (1360?–1403). The story was published (1508) in four books by Garcia Ordóñez de Montalvo (c. 1450–1510), who claimed that he revised the first three books from 14th-century versions and wrote the fourth himself. *Amadis of Gaul* has been translated into numerous languages.

**AMADO, Jorge** (1912– ), Brazilian novelist, noted for works based on life in his native state of Bahia. Starkly realistic, often ironic, and displaying deep psychological insight, his novels reflect a continuing sense of social injustice. *The Violent Land* (1944; trans. 1945), often considered his masterpiece, depicts the harsh life of workers on the cacao plantations. Other works include *Gabriela, Clove and Cinnamon* (1958; trans. 1962), about urban social and political transition; *Home Is the Sailor* (1960; trans. 1964); *Shepherds of the Night* (1964; trans. 1967); *Dona Flor and Her Two Husbands* (1966; trans. 1969), which was later made into a film; and *Showdown* (1984; trans. 1988). Many of these mix naturalistic themes and ribald humor.

**AMADORA,** city, W Portugal. It is a residential suburb located on the outskirts of Lisbon, NW of the city center. Pop. (1991) 122,106.

**AMAGASAKI,** city, Japan, S Honshu Island, in Hyogo Prefecture, a seaport on the Yodo R. and Osaka Bay, near Osaka. It is an industrial center with plants producing iron and steel products, chemicals, textiles, glass, pottery, drugs, dyes, and woodwork. Other industrial installations are breweries, machine shops, and shipyards. The principal exports include drugs, dyes, metal products, and pottery. An important part of the Osaka-Kobe industrial complex, the city was raided by U.S. bombers late in World War II. Pop. (1993 est.) 488,600.

**AMALEKITES,** warlike, nomadic tribe in the southwestern part of ancient Palestine. A long-standing hostility existed between the tribe and the Israelites, whose King Saul had nearly annihilated the Amalekites in the 11th century BC. David, king of Israel, later defeated them in a dreadful slaughter. He crushed a later uprising, and the descendants of the survivors were exterminated in the days of Hezekiah, king of Judah.

**AMALFI,** town, S Italy, in Campania Region, near Naples. Beautifully situated on limestone cliffs, the picturesque town overlooks the Gulf of Salerno. Amalfi is a small fishing port and tourist resort and the seat of an archbishopric. Of note is the 11th-century cathedral. In the 9th century Amalfi was a powerful maritime republic. Its maritime code, one of the earliest known, was widely recognized around the Mediterranean Basin well into the 16th century. After the 12th century, when Amalfi was annexed (1131) by King Roger II of Sicily and then sacked (1135 and 1137) by the Pisans, it gradually declined as a commercial and naval power. Pop. (1991) 6121.

**AMALGAM.** See MERCURY (metallic element).

**AMANA,** unincorporated village, Iowa Co., E central Iowa, near the Iowa R. It is an agricultural trade center with manufacturing industries producing household appliances, furniture, woolen goods, wine, and processed food (especially meat). Amana is the oldest of seven adjacent villages established in 1855 by a communal band of Pietists led by Christian Metz (1794–1867). In search of religious freedom, they had emigrated (1843) from Germany and settled in Ebenezer, N.Y. (near Buffalo). The communities, which flourished during the late 19th century, suffered during the depression of the 1930s and were reorganized in 1932, when private enterprise was adopted and religious and civil government were separated. The Museum of Amana History, the Amana Heim Museum, and the Amana Society Barn Museum are here.

**AMANA SOCIETY.** See COMMUNAL LIVING.

**AMANITA.** See MUSHROOM.

**AMARANTH,** common name for any flowering plants with blossoms that do not readily fade when picked, and especially for plants of the genus *Amaranthus,* of the family Amaranthaceae, in the order Caryophyllales (*see* PINK). The genus contains about 50 species, most of which are found in the Tropics. They are herbs or shrubs, with simple leaves, and flowers in heads or spikes. The spikes are sometimes several centimeters long. Because the dry red bracts that surround the flower retain their freshness for some time, the plant is considered a symbol of immortality. The annual weeds pigweed (*A. retroflexus*) and tumbleweed (*A. graecizans*) of the U.S. belong to this genus. The globe amaranth, *Gomphrena* *globosa,* of the same family, has purple flowers that retain their beauty for years. *See also* EVERLASTINGS.

**AMARILLO,** city, seat of Potter Co. and extending into Randall Co., NW Texas, in a mineral-rich area of vast cattle ranches and irrigated grain farms; inc. 1892. The economic heart of the Texas Panhandle, Amarillo is an industrial and educational center noted for its mineral research and production (petroleum, natural gas, copper, zinc). Its other industries include medical services, aircraft and machinery manufacturing, and food processing. Local attractions include cattle auctions, annual rodeos, and the Amarillo Art Center. Amarillo College (1897) and Texas State Technical College-Amarillo (1970) are in the city; and West Texas State University (1910) is nearby. The community was founded (1887) as a cattle-shipping point at a rail junction. Its economic growth was fostered by the discovery of natural gas (1918) and petroleum (1921). The city's name, Spanish for "yellow," refers to the color of the banks of a nearby stream. Pop. (1980) 149,230; (1990) 157,615.

**AMARYLLIS,** common name applied to any of several plants of the genus *Hippeastrum,* of the family Liliaceae (*see* LILY), especially to certain hybrids cultivated as ornamentals and sold as dried bulbs for growing as houseplants. A related plant, the belladonna lily or naked lily, *Amaryllis belladonna,* is the only member of its genus.

The name was formerly applied to a family containing about 65 genera and 900 species in the order Liliales. Members of the order with inferior ovaries (ovaries fused to the floral tube) were placed in the Amaryllidaceae, while those with superior ovaries (free from the tube) were assigned to the Liliaceae. Division on this basis is now considered unnatural. In addition to the members of the genus *Hippeastrum,* familiar plants formerly placed in the Amaryllidaceae include the daffodils of the genus *Narcissus,* the snowdrops of the genus *Galanthus,* and the common houseplant, *Clivia.*

**AMATEUR ATHLETIC UNION OF THE UNITED STATES** (AAU), national nonprofit organization founded in 1888 and comprising 60 associations and thousands of volunteers interested in fostering amateur sports and physical fitness. The AAU defines an amateur athlete as "one who engages in sport for pleasure . . . and to whom sport is nothing more than an avocation."

The AAU administers the AAU/USA Junior Olympics, an annual nationwide athletic program open to all girls and boys between the ages of 8 and 18. Competition is offered in 22 sports. Divisions include baseball, basketball, boxing, cross-country running, decathlon, diving, field hockey, gymnastics, heptathlon, judo, soccer, swimming, synchronized swimming, table tennis, track and field, trampoline and tumbling, volleyball, water polo, weight lifting, winter sports, and wrestling. The annual Junior Olympic Games help to identify candidates for international Olympic competition.

Each year the AAU gives physical fitness tests to millions of U.S. students between 6 and 17 years of age, in order to develop a fitness profile of American youth. For adults aged 25 and over, the AAU maintains the Masters Sports and Fitness Program. Senior sports programs are also sponsored. The AAU annually presents its James E. Sullivan Award to the outstanding U.S. amateur athlete. National AAU headquarters is in Indianapolis, Ind.

**AMATI,** family of celebrated Italian violin makers of Cremona.

**Andrea Amati** (c. 1520–78), founder of the Cremona school of violin makers. His model was a small violin with high back and belly, amber varnish, and a clear although weak tone.

**Antonio Amati** (c. 1550–c. 1638) and **Girolamo Amati** (c. 1556–c. 1630), sons of Andrea Amati. They worked together and followed their father's style. Girolamo also developed a larger violin with an altered sound hole.

**Nicolò Amati** (1596–1684), son of Girolamo Amati. He became the most eminent craftsman of the family. His model is extremely elegant, with the backs and bellies arched and made of beautiful grained wood. The sound holes are graceful and bold, the scroll is exquisitely cut, and the varnish is transparent and of a deep, rich hue. As a rule, he used a small pattern, although he produced some large violins, which are now called grand Amatis and are highly valued. He also made numerous beautiful violas and cellos. The great Italian violin makers Antonio Stradivari and Andrea Guarneri were his pupils.

**Girolamo Amati** (1649–1740), son of Nicolò Amati, ended the leadership of the Amati name in the craft of violin making.

**AMAZIAH** (Heb., "whom Yahweh strengthens"), king of Judah (800–783 BC). He fought against the kingdoms of Edom and Israel. He defeated the Edomites in 798 BC but was himself overcome and taken prisoner about 795 BC by Jehoash, king of Israel. Amaziah was killed by conspirators several years later at Lachish.

**AMAZON** (Port. and Span. *Amazonas*), river, N South America, largely in Brazil, ranked as the largest in the world in terms of watershed area, number of tributaries, and volume of water discharged. Measuring about 6275 km (about 3900 mi) from source to mouth, it is second in length

© GeoSystems Global Corp.

only to the Nile among the rivers of the world. With its hundreds of tributaries, the Amazon drains a territory of more than 6 million sq km (2.3 million sq mi), roughly half of which is in Brazil; the rest is in Peru, Ecuador, Bolivia, and Venezuela. It is estimated that the Amazon discharges between 34 and 121 million liters (9 and 32 million gal) of water per second and deposits a daily average of 3 million tons of sediment near its mouth. The annual outflow from the river accounts for one-fifth of all the fresh water that drains into the oceans of the world. The outpouring of water and sediment is so vast that the salinity and color of the Atlantic Ocean are altered for a distance of about 320 km (about 200 mi) from the mouth of the river.

**Course and Physical Environment.** The major headstreams of the Amazon are the Ucayali and Marañón rivers, both of which rise in the permanent snows and glaciers of the high Andes Mts. and follow parallel courses N before joining near Nauta, Peru. From this confluence the main trunk of the Amazon flows in a generally E direction to the Atlantic Ocean. The Amazon enters the Atlantic through a broad estuary, roughly estimated at 240 km (about 150 mi) in width. Here delta deposits have formed a maze of islands that separate the river into branches. The mouth of the main stream is 80 km (50 mi) wide. This branch, known as the Pará, is separated from a smaller branch by Marajó Island, which has an area of more than 36,000 sq km (14,000 sq mi). During new and full moon a tidal bore, or wave front from the ocean, sweeps some 650 km (more than 400 mi) upstream at speeds in excess of 65 km/hr (40 mph). This phenomenon, known as *pororoca*, often causes waves up to 5 m (16 ft) in height.

A hot, humid climate characterizes the Amazon watershed, which encompasses the largest and wettest tropical plain in the world. Heavy rains drench much of the densely forested lowland region throughout the year but especially between January and June. Broad areas traversed by the Amazon are subject to severe floods. In Brazil the width of the river ranges between 1.6 and 10 km (1 and 6 mi) at low stage but expands to 48 km (30 mi) or more during the annual floods. To drain the mass of water, the Amazon has carved a deep bed in the plain through which it flows. Near Óbidos, Brazil, the bed is more than 91 m (300 ft) below the average surface level.

Because of its vastness, annual floods, and navigability, the Amazon is often called the Ocean R. The total number of its tributaries is as yet uncounted, but more than 200 are in Brazil alone. Seventeen of the largest known tributaries are more than 1600 km (1000 mi) in length. The Amazon proper is navigable to ocean liners of virtually any tonnage for two-thirds of its course. Transatlantic ships call regularly at Manaus, nearly 1600 km (1000 mi) upstream; and ships of 3000 tons can reach Iquitos, Peru, 3700 km (2300 mi) from the river's mouth, the farthest point from sea of any port serving ocean traffic. River steamers of more modest tonnage can navigate on more than 100 of the larger tributaries.

**Exploration and Development.** The first European to enter the Amazon delta may have been Vicente Yáñez Pinzón in 1500. Exploration did not begin until 1541, when an expedition led by the Spanish explorer Francisco de Orellana started down the Napo R., in what is now Ecuador, and reached the Atlantic Ocean. Some authorities believe that the river's name came from Orellana's tales of having seen on his journey women warriors he likened to the Amazons of Greek mythology; others insist that the name is derived from the Indian word *amassona* ("boat destroyer"). The first Europeans to undertake an upstream voyage were led by the Portuguese navigator Pedro Teixeira (1575?–1640). In modern times the river has been explored by many scientific expeditions, including that led (1914) by Theodore Roosevelt.

For centuries people made little impact on the Amazon Basin. In recent decades, however, the activities of loggers, farmers, ranchers, miners, and road builders have destroyed vast stretches of forestland. Nevertheless, much of the region remains a wilderness. One may fly for hours over tropical rain forests and see no sign of human settlement. Indians hostile to strangers continue to live much as they did before the arrival of the Europeans. By some estimates slavery, disease, and slaughter have decreased their numbers from close to 7 million in 1500 to less than 1 million today.

The river and its tributaries are home to more than 1500 species of fish, including the pirarucu, which weighs as much as 225 kg (500 lb). A wide variety of animals and plants, many of which are found nowhere else in the world, flourishes in the Amazon Basin. Mineral deposits are also plentiful. Although mining and lumbering are increasingly important to the economy, the principal occupations are still primitive agriculture, hunting and fishing, and the gathering of forest products. Under pressure from international conservation groups, Brazil has begun to take control of exploitation and development of the Amazon Basin to ensure that the area's natural resources, especially the rain forests, are not destroyed.     J.P.A.

*For further information on this topic, see the Bibliography in volume 28, sections 426, 1235.*

**AMAZON PARROT.** *See* PARROT.

**AMAZONS,** in Greek mythology, a race of warlike women who excluded men from their society. The Amazons occasionally had sexual relations with men of neighboring states, and all male children born to them were sent to their fathers or killed. The girls were trained as archers for war, and the custom of burning off the right breast was practiced to facilitate bending the bow—hence the name Amazon, derived from the Greek word for breastless. In art, however, they are depicted as beautiful with no apparent mutilation. Ancient art, such as that on temple friezes, vases, and sarcophagi, usually presents them in battle scenes. According to legend, they were almost constantly at war with Greece and fought other nations as well. According to one version, they were allied with the Trojans, and during the siege of Troy their queen was slain by the Greek warrior Achilles. Some scholars who attribute a historical foundation to the legends identify the country of the Amazons with Scythia or Asia Minor on the shores of the Black Sea.

**AMBASSADOR.** *See* DIPLOMACY.

**AMBATO,** city, central Ecuador, capital of Tungurahua Province, on the Ambato R. A leading commercial and transportation center and a mountain resort, the city is in a fertile region near the N foot of Mt. Chimborazo. Ambato has frequently been damaged by earthquakes. Called the Garden City of Ecuador, Ambato is known for the production of peaches, apples, grapes, pears, oranges, and strawberries. Grain, sugarcane, and vegetables are also grown. Local industries produce textiles, flour, canned fruit, leather goods, rubber, wine, and furniture. The poet Juan Montalvo (1832–89) was born here. Nearby, Gen. Antonio José de Sucre won an important battle during the war for independence against Spain. Pop. (1990) 124,166.

**AMBER,** fossil resin that, in prehistoric times, exuded from various now-extinct coniferous trees. It is usually yellow or yellow-brown in color. Found in either round, irregular lumps, grains, or drops, it is slightly brittle and emits an agreeable odor when rubbed. Amber burns with a bright flame and pleasant smell and becomes negatively electric by friction. Extinct and extant species of insects are sometimes found encased in samples of amber. It was obtained in antiquity from the southern coast of the Baltic Sea, where it is still found. It is also found in small quantities in Sicily, Romania, Siberia, Greenland, Burma, Australia, and the U.S. Amber is used in the arts and in the manufacture of jewelry, cigarette holders, and pipestems.

**AMBERGRIS** (Fr. *ambre gris*, "gray amber"), fatty or pitchlike substance, black or gray in color, with yellow or red striae. Sperm whales produce it in their intestines, apparently when sick. The horny, parrotlike beak of the cuttlefish, the main food of the sperm whale, is often found embedded in ambergris. Ambergris probably forms around the irritating, indigestible beak.

Occasionally ambergris is taken from the bowels of the sperm whale. More frequently, however, it is found floating in tropical waters, or cast upon the seashore, in lumps of from 14 g (0.5 oz) to 91 kg (200 lb). The harder, more valuable gray ambergris accumulates in the intestine of the whale, obstructing it and eventually causing the animal's death. The softer, black variety is that which the whale has been able to eject soon after its formation. When fresh, ambergris smells strong and unpleasant. After exposure to the air it hardens and develops a sweet, musty odor.

At one time ambergris was used as a medicinal cure-all in the Orient and in Europe and as a flavoring for food in Asia. Its value now is as the best fixative in making costly perfumes; it prevents the volatile oils from evaporating too quickly. Because the demand for ambergris far exceeds the uncertain supply, the value is high.

*An ambulance used in New York City in 1899.*
Museum of the City of New York

In 1955 the Yugoslav-Swiss chemist Leopold Ružička developed synthetic ambergris, which is far less expensive than the natural substance.

**AMBIDEXTERITY.** *See* HANDEDNESS.

**AMBLYOPIA.** *See* VISION.

**AMBOISE, Georges d'** (1460–1510), French prelate and statesman, born in Chaumont-sur-Loire. From 1493 to 1498, he was archbishop of Rouen, France. In 1498 he was appointed cardinal and chief minister by Louis XII. As such, he became the most important figure in the political affairs of France. He introduced reforms in the judicial system, reduced taxation, and from 1499 to 1503 was active in military campaigns in northern Italy against Milan. After Pope Alexander VI's death in 1503, Amboise made unsuccessful efforts to gain the papacy. He served as papal legate to France from 1503 until his death.

**AMBON** *or* **AMBOINA,** island, E Indonesia, one of the Moluccas Islands, in the Banda Sea. It is mountainous but has a fertile and well-watered coastal plain. The chief products are cloves, nutmeg, rice, sugar, and copra, which are shipped from the port city of Ambon (pop., 1990, 206,260). It was discovered by the Portuguese in 1512, but was captured by the Dutch in 1605 and held by them until 1949, when Indonesia gained independence. Ambon led a brief revolt against Indonesia in 1950. Area, about 813 sq km (about 314 sq mi).

**AMBRIDGE,** borough, Beaver Co., W Pennsylvania, on the Ohio R.; inc. as a borough 1905. It is an industrial community founded by the American Bridge Co. (hence its name) in 1901. The steel mills, closed in 1983, now house small man-ufacturing companies. Located in Ambridge is Old Economy Village, a collection of buildings preserved from a communal settlement maintained by members of the Harmony Society from 1825 to 1905. Pop. (1980) 9575; (1990) 8113.

**AMBROSE, Saint (340?–97),** one of the most celebrated Fathers of the Church (q.v.) and one of the four original Doctors of the Church (q.v.), born in Trier (now in Germany), and educated in Rome. His father was prefect of Gaul. Ambrose studied law, entered the civil service, and about 370 was appointed a consular magistrate in Upper Italy, with his headquarters at Milan. In this office his kindness and wisdom won the esteem and love of the people, who called him to be bishop of Milan in 374. As bishop, he defended the churches of Milan against the introduction of Arian doctrines and brought Theodosius I, emperor of Rome, to repentance and public penance for ordering the massacre of the rebellious Thessalonians.

Ambrose is best known as the friend of Monica (332?–87), mother of St. Augustine, and as the one who received Augustine into the church. He is the patron saint of Milan, and the Ambrosian Library in Milan is named for him. His writings include exegetical treatises and a manual of Christian morality. He also composed hymns, many of which are extant. His feast day is December 7.

**AMBROSIAN LIBRARY.** *See* MILAN.

**AMBULANCE,** vehicle designed for the transportation of the sick or injured. In addition to cots mounted on a resilient base to prevent jarring the patients, modern ambulances are equipped with blood-transfusion apparatus, oxygen-inhalation devices, and in some cases incubators for the newborn. The two main types of ambulances are the civilian and the military. Modern civilian ambulances are built for speed and smooth riding. As a rule they have facilities for one or two patients and an attending physician, nurse, or paramedic. Community hospitals, most voluntary and private hospitals and clinics, and, in the larger urban areas, many private firms provide ambulance service. Because of the rugged conditions in the field, military ambulances are designed for sturdiness rather than for speed and are equipped for emergency treatment of the wounded on the way to collection stations. The military ambulance usually has a load capacity of six ambulatory or four stretcher patients.

Animal-drawn ambulances were first used in the 1850s in the Crimean War. Standardized horse-drawn military ambulances were introduced in the U.S. during the American Civil War. The first U.S. motorized ambulance unit operated in Mexico in 1916 during the American punitive expedition against the Mexican revolutionary general Pancho Villa. Since the signing of the Geneva Convention in 1864, ambulance units and the wounded in their care have been considered neutrals on the field of battle.

**AMEBIASIS,** widespread human disease in tropical regions, resulting from infection by the amoeba (q.v.) *Entamoeba histolytica.* The parasite most commonly is acquired in its encysted form in tainted food or drink. When it infects only the intestines it can cause dysentery (q.v.), but it may also spread to other organs. Amebiasis is easily dealt with by drugs, but if untreated it can lead to abscesses of the liver, the lungs and, less frequently, the heart; rarely, it may even reach and damage the brain.

**AMENDMENT,** in legislation, the alteration of an existing statute. Although the U.S. Congress has no power to alter the Constitution, it does have the power to repeal and alter laws. The method of amending the Constitution is provided by Article V. According to this article, an amendment passes after a two-thirds vote of both houses of Congress or after the petition of two-thirds of the state legislatures. Amendments are ratified by either the legislatures of three-fourths of the states or by conventions in three-fourths of the states. The Constitution contains no provision directly limiting the power of the state legislatures to repeal the statutes of the several states, but Article I, Section 10, limits the power of a state legislature to repeal statutes that are in effect contracts with the citizens of the state. For details on specific amendments to the Constitution, *see* CONSTITUTION OF THE UNITED STATES.

In parliamentary procedure, an amendment may be a motion, bill, or resolution. When adopted in accordance with the rules of parliamentary procedure, an amendment becomes a part of the original motion or bill.

In the law of pleading and practice, an amendment corrects an error or defect in a pleading or judicial proceeding in the progress of an action or other proceeding.

**AMENEMHET I,** king of Egypt (1991–1962 BC), the first of the 12th Dynasty; his last ten years were spent in coregency with his son Sesostris I (c. 1980–1930 BC). Amenemhet limited the power of the nobles, reorganized the government (moving the capital to Faiyum), and restored prosperity to the country.

**AMENEMHET III,** king of Egypt (1842–1797 BC), of the 12th Dynasty. He removed the last threat of the provincial nobles to the central government and during his long reign focused his efforts on economic expansion. He constructed vast irrigation and reclamation projects, notably one at Lake Moeris in the Faiyum district, and greatly increased mineral production. His trading fleets plied the Red Sea and traversed the Mediterranean as far as Cyprus and Crete.

**AMENHOTEP III,** king of Egypt (1386–1349 BC), of the 18th Dynasty, builder of extensive architectural works, including portions of the Temple of Luxor and the so-called Colossi of Memnon. His reign was one of peace and prosperity, when Egyptian power was at its height. Amenhotep's diplomatic correspondence is preserved in the Amarna Letters, a collection of some 400 clay tablets found in Tell el-Amarna in 1887. Ikhnaton, Egypt's great religious reformer, was his son.

**AMENHOTEP IV.** *See* IKHNATON.

**AMERICA,** second largest isolated landmass of the earth, comprising the two continents of the western hemisphere. America is a common designation for either or both North America and South America, for the western hemisphere as a whole, and for the United States of America. The entire western hemisphere is often called the Americas. The word first appeared in *Cosmographiae Introductio* (Introduction to Cosmography), edited and published in 1507 by the German cartographer Martin Waldseemüller. The name was derived from Americus, the Latinized given name of the Italian navigator Amerigo Vespucci, whose expeditions to the New World are described in the work. As used by Waldseemüller, the term America specifically referred to the lands that were explored by Christopher Columbus, Vespucci, and other early explorers of the West Indies and the NE coast of the southern continent. The Flemish geographer Gerardus Mercator first used the word to indicate all the western hemisphere on a map of the world published in 1538.

**AMERICAN,** river, N central California, about 48 km (about 30 mi) long. It has its source in the Sierra Nevada Mts. and flows in a generally SW direction, emptying into the Sacramento R., near Sacramento.

**AMERICAN ACADEMY OF ARTS AND SCIENCES,** institution that sponsors projects designed to relate the intellectual resources of the learned professions to problems of science and of social and technical change. It was founded in 1780 in Boston; its headquarters is now in Cambridge, Mass. Included in its membership are more than 3000 fellows and more than 500 foreign honorary members, elected for eminence in scholarship and professional attainments. The academy publishes a quarterly journal, *Daedalus;* an annual, *Records;* and a number of books, articles, and papers. The academy also awards prizes for achievements in arts and sciences.

**AMERICAN ACADEMY AND INSTITUTE OF ARTS AND LETTERS,** honorary association founded (as the American Academy of Arts and Letters) in 1904 by the National Institute of Arts and Letters to encourage literature, music, and the fine arts. In 1976 the institute and the academy, headquartered in New York City, officially merged. Only institute members are eligible for election to the 50-member academy. The academy–institute awards monetary prizes and medals for distinguished work in the arts.

**AMERICAN ANTI-SLAVERY SOCIETY,** association organized in December 1833 in Philadelphia to advance the abolition of slavery in the U.S. It was established by delegates from similar state and local societies, including the Boston organization, which had been founded in January 1832 under the leadership of the abolitionist William Lloyd Garrison and was the first such society in America. The three abolitionist leaders responsible for establishing the American Anti-Slavery Society were Theodore Dwight Weld (1803–95), Arthur Tappan (1786–1865), and Lewis Tappan (1788–1873). Militant in the fight against slavery, the organizers were regarded in the South as fanatics; members of the society were denounced, and meetings were broken up. In 1839 some less-militant members broke away from the society and formed the Liberty party. The society operated until 1870, when the adoption of the 15th Amendment to the U.S. Constitution granted citizenship to blacks.

**AMERICAN ARBITRATION ASSOCIATION,** private nonprofit organization founded in 1926 to administer arbitration in voluntary agreement with the disputants. The association has about 50,000 qualified arbitrators who resolve labor, commercial, and contractual disputes and the claims of uninsured motorists. When requested by the parties in dispute, the association presents a list of arbitrators to be selected by the disputants. Membership in the association is open to labor unions, trade associations, civic groups, law firms, and private parties. *See* ARBITRATION; LABOR RELATIONS.

**AMERICAN ART AND ARCHITECTURE,** the fine arts of painting, sculpture, and architecture as developed in European colonies in North America and subsequently in the U.S.

As a frontier land, and later as a developing nation, the U.S. was heavily influenced by the styles in art and architecture already developed to a high point in the mature societies of Europe. In the course of the 19th century, however, the country developed distinctive variations on the European models. Finally, at the end of the 19th century in architecture, and by the middle of the 20th century in painting and sculpture, U.S. masters and schools of art were exerting a powerful worldwide influence over art and architecture. This period of artistic leadership coincided with the country's increasing degree of international political and financial leadership, and reflected the nation's prosperity. Because of the great size of the country, stylistic variations developed within this main line of artistic growth. Regions that had been settled by different European nations reflected their early colonial heritage in artistic forms, particularly in architecture, to a decreasing degree through the middle of the 19th century. Climatic variations across the extent of the country also shaped distinctive regional architectural traditions. In addition, differences persisted between the art produced in the city and that produced in the country within the various regions; rural artists, trained or untrained, were isolated from current trends and competitive pressures and produced highly individual modes of expression that were imaginative and direct, independent of prevailing formal conventions. Known collectively as folk art, or naive art, this type of American art is discussed elsewhere (*see* FOLK ART).

The decorative arts, in particular metalwork and furniture (qq.v.), also represented an important form of artistic expression during the colonial period. Silver, in the 17th century, and furniture, in the 18th century, were perhaps the most significant American forms of artistic creation and represented the most sophisticated and lively traditions.

*THE COLONIAL ERA*

Colonial art and architecture reflects that of the

*San Xavier del Bac, 18th-century Spanish mission near Tucson, Ariz. Its bell towers, balustrades, and carved facade show baroque style successfully transported to the New World.* Gene Ahrens–Bruce Coleman, Inc.

European colonizing nations, adapted to the dangers and harsh conditions of a vast wilderness. Spanish influences prevailed in the West, while English styles, with a leaven of Dutch and French, predominated in the East.

**Colonial Architecture.** In the 17th and 18th centuries the Spanish colonists of the Southwest encountered a developed native building tradition in adobe, which employed readily available materials suited to the region's climate. Spanish colonial churches in Arizona and New Mexico, and the chain of missions from San Diego to San Francisco in California, represent an accommodation with American Indian traditions of building and design. In New Mexico, the Pueblo Indians reshaped the colonial style in terms of their adobe tradition to create the most striking and freshest form of early architecture in what was to become part of the U.S. Outside the Southwest, native styles did not exert a lasting influence on colonial art and architecture.

The history of architecture in the rest of the U.S. reflects the development of European architecture, in particular English architecture. A considerable lag, however, occurred in the introduction of English styles, so periods often do not correspond. Seventeenth-century English colonial architecture most resembles the late medieval forms that survived in rural England. Houses were built in a range of sizes, although only more modest dwellings have survived. The Parson Capen House (1683), in Topsfield, Mass., is typical of the two-story New England house of overlapping weatherboards. Its gables, overhangs, and lack of symmetry lend it a late medieval flavor. In Virginia and Maryland, brick construction was preferred for the typically story-and-a-half homes with chimneys at both ends and a more nearly symmetrical facade, as in the Thomas Rolfe House (1652), in Surry Co., Va. The architectural style of the Senate House (built c. 1676), in Kingston, N.Y., and the manor house, Fort Crailo (1642), in Rensselaer, N.Y., reflect the Dutch influence on the colony of New York.

Aside from fortifications, the principal nondomestic structures in the 17th-century colonies were places of worship. Because the meeting house in Puritan New England was often the only public building in the community, and served as church, school, and gathering place for social and governmental functions, the colonists developed a less ecclesiastical style for them, similar in appearance to their private houses.

**17th-Century Painting and Sculpture.** Like colonial architecture, 17th-century colonial painting reflects English styles of at least a century earlier, which had been perpetuated in the rural areas from which the colonists came. The earliest paintings, all portraits, date from the 1660s in New England, a long generation after the founding of the colony. The most notable are the pair *John Freake* and *Mrs. Elizabeth Freake and Baby Mary* (c. 1674, Worcester, Mass., Art Museum). The relatively flat figures are arranged decoratively,

433

*Stanley-Whitman House (c. 1660), Farmington, Conn. Overhanging story recalls Jacobean English houses. Central chimney (and its two fireplaces), clapboards, and small windows are for warmth.*
Conn. Department of Commerce

with attention to firm line and areas of patterning, the subjects stiffly posed in their finery. Evidence indicates that portraiture began in the Hudson Valley area about the same time. Religious paintings and church decoration were carried out in the Southwest during the century.

Sculpture in the 17th century on the East Coast was limited to applications of the decorative arts, in the carving of furniture and the shaping of metalwork in silver and iron. The religious figures carved in the Southwest remain at the level of inspired folk sculpture.

**The 18th Century.** With the turn of the 18th century, the colonies began to take on a more permanent and established character, as the hardships of the wilderness were overcome, and increasing commerce and production permitted the growth of prosperous cities. Although the expansion of most cities at this time was chaotic, some newly founded cities, such as Williamsburg, Va., and Annapolis, Md., were laid out on a regular grid, with public squares—similar to Philadelphia's design a few decades earlier.

*Architecture before the Revolution.* Architects also began to employ more current styles, following contemporaneous English practice in larger and much more ambitious buildings. The so-called Wren Building (begun 1695) at William and Mary College, in Williamsburg, with its symmetry and central pediment; the Capitol (1699–1705), in Williamsburg; and the Philadelphia Courthouse (1709) are modest versions of London's early baroque styles. The publication of the work of leading English architects such as James Gibbs made it possible for colonial builders and architects to design such sophisticated churches as Christ Church (1727–44), in Philadelphia, and Saint Michael's (1751–53), in Charleston, S.C., with its distinctive portico.

The first quarter of the 18th century is represented in domestic architecture by the McPhedris-Warner House (1718–23), in Portsmouth, N.H., two rooms deep with a central-stair hall. Around midcentury, country houses were designed in the English Palladian style, featuring compact two-story or three-story buildings dominated by a central portico, with the principal rooms often raised to the second floor. An early example is Drayton Hall (1738) near Charleston. Important public buildings were also treated in the Palladian style, as was the Pennsylvania Hospital (begun 1754) in Philadelphia.

*Painting before the Revolution.* As the 18th century began, artists were active in several parts of the colonies. Henrietta Johnston (1670?–1729), the first American woman artist, worked in Charleston, executing the earliest pastel portraits. But the most active school of painting was in the Hudson River valley, where the major landholders, or patroons, required portraits for their Dutch-style manor houses. The semitrained artists produced relatively flat images with little control of modeling, basing their compositions, including the elaborate backgrounds, on English prints. The school culminated in the monumental full-length portraits *Pieter Schuyler* (c. 1719, City Hall, Albany, N.Y.) and *Ariandtje Schoomans* (c. 1717, Albany Institute of History and Art), imposing in their almost iconic quality.

As the century advanced, artists with more training began to immigrate to the colonies. The most important was John Smibert (1688–1751), a successful London portraitist working in the school of the English portraitists Sir Godfrey Kneller and Thomas Hudson (1701–79). Smibert settled in Boston in 1729.

By 1750 the pace of artistic activity had picked up considerably, with many more artists working than before. The talented native-born portraitist Robert Feke was Smibert's principal successor in New England, modifying Smibert's bulky manner with a heightened sense of line and surface design. Other leading artists were Joseph Blackburn (c. 1700–65) in New England, John Wollaston (d. 1770?) in New York and the mid-Atlantic colonies, and Jeremiah Theus (c. 1719–74) in Charleston.

Two major artists of international significance emerged shortly after midcentury, Benjamin West and John Singleton Copley. Trained in Philadelphia, West left for Italy and England in late 1759, becoming dean of the English neoclassical school, president of the Royal Academy, and historical painter to King George III of England, in which role he painted his masterpiece *The Death of General Wolfe* (1770, National Gallery of Canada, Ottawa). To his studio in London he welcomed a generation of American art students, among them the portraitist Gilbert Stuart.

Copley was reared in Boston. His talents developed rapidly in the early 1760s, and he brought colonial portraiture to entirely new levels of realism and psychological depth. His finest American works are marked by an almost obsessive literalness, supported by a mastery in the rendering of light and textures. His work in the decade before his departure (1774) for England represents the apex of colonial painting.

## THE NEW NATION: FROM 1776 TO 1865

The social and economic dislocations of the American Revolution brought building virtually to a halt. Painting also languished. After Copley's departure, the new nation was not home to a painter of his talent and abilities until Gilbert Stuart returned in 1792. The commissions of the Continental Congress went to the Philadelphian Charles Willson Peale, creator of the first monumental portraits of George Washington.

**Architectural Styles.** A resurgence in art and architecture, as well as the establishment of a new national style, occurred from 1785 to about 1810. In the 1790s the postwar prosperity of such cities as Boston and Salem, Mass., New York, Baltimore, Md., and Savannah, Ga., produced much building activity in a distinctive style termed Federal, which reflects the delayed acceptance of the British architect Robert Adam's version of English neoclassical architecture. The large flat surfaces,

*McPhedris-Warner House (1718-23), Portsmouth, N.H. The dignified brick box with symmetrical facade and classical pediments is a New England adaptation of English Georgian style.*

simple columns, and refined classical detail of the Federal style can be seen in its purest form in the stuccoed homes of Savannah, such as the Richardson-Owens-Thomas House (1817–19). In the northeast, this style is exemplified by the many remaining examples—both domestic and civic in purpose—of the architecture of Charles Bulfinch. His Massachusetts State House in Boston (completed in 1798) was the most outstanding building in the new nation for many decades and was a model for numerous structures in other states, some of which Bulfinch designed.

The nation's leaders associated their young republic with those of the ancient world. Thomas Jefferson, a leader in introducing to the colonies a more advanced neoclassical design in his home, Monticello (completed 1809), designed the new state capitol at Richmond directly after a Roman temple, the Maison Carrée at Nîmes, France. The neoclassical, based primarily on Roman sources and the work of Adam and the English architect Sir John Soane, became the official and popular style of the new nation, filling the new city of Washington, D.C. Benjamin Latrobe, born and schooled in England, was the first fully trained architect to work in the U.S., where he produced the country's finest neoclassical buildings, such as the Cathedral of the Assumption of the Blessed Virgin Mary (1806–18) in Baltimore.

The neoclassical style was followed by the Greek Revival, which reflected the heavier taste of the late Regency in England and became (1820–50) what might be called the national style. The pedimented and colonnaded Greek-temple form was preferred for public and domestic structures alike; among the best-known examples are the Custis-Lee Mansion in Arlington, Va., the

Mrs. James Warren *(c. 1763), by John Singleton Copley, oil on canvas.*

Fairmount Water Works in Philadelphia, and several surviving southern plantation houses. About 1850 a wider range of romantic revival styles was being employed as well; Gothic and Tuscan revivals, which display asymmetrical floor plans and picturesque groupings of architectural components, were favored. The financial panic of 1857 and the disruptions of the American Civil War, however, brought to a close this building phase.

**Painting After the Revolution.** The prosperity that followed the Revolution likewise supported a

*Thomas Jefferson designed his own home, Monticello (completed 1809), near Charlottesville, Va., in the neoclassical Palladian style, which became highly popular in the U.S. for both domestic and public buildings.*

Desolation *(1836), by Thomas Cole, last in the five-part allegorical series* The Course of Empire.

New-York Historical Society, New York City

flowering of semitrained or folk portraiture in New England, headed by Ralph Earl (1751–1801). The leading artists who returned from England after the Revolution had been trained by Benjamin West in the neoclassical school of painting. Gilbert Stuart was the finest portraitist of the generation, his skillful brushwork capturing the likenesses of many chief figures of the Federal period, including Washington, immortalized in Stuart's so-called "Athenaeum" portrayal (1796, Museum of Fine Arts, Boston). John Trumbull returned to become the first artist to paint events in the history of the new nation, depicting such milestones as *The Declaration of Independence* (1794, Yale University Art Gallery, New Haven, Conn.), later versions (1817–24) of which may be seen in the Rotunda of the U.S. Capitol, in Washington, D.C.

An outstanding American romantic painter was Washington Allston, who worked in Boston most of his life, except for two lengthy sojourns in England. He produced landscapes and history paintings of great imaginative force.

**Romantic portraiture and genre painting.** Until at least 1840 painting continued to be dominated by portraiture in the romantic manner. Thomas Sully created idealized images in the English manner of the portrait painter Sir Thomas Lawrence. Another leading romantic portraitist was Samuel F. B. Morse, perhaps the most talented artist of his generation before he turned his full attention to the development of telegraphy.

Among the most outstanding painters of the genre school that arose were William Sidney Mount, who recorded the daily lives of Long Island farmers in such paintings as *Bargaining for a Horse* (1835, New-York Historical Society, New York City), and George Caleb Bingham, who lived in the far west of the day and painted scenes from the lives of the fur traders and flatboatmen along the Mississippi River.

**The Hudson River school.** Landscape painting emerged about 1835 as the strongest and most original current in American art, and remained dominant during much of the 19th century. The early leaders of what is called the Hudson River school (q.v.) were Thomas Cole, Asher B. Durand, and Thomas Doughty (1793–1856). In the 1820s Cole began to paint highly dramatic, romantic landscapes, a departure from the prevailing classical style based on the 17th-century tradition of the French landscapist Claude Lorrain. Cole's distinctive contribution was his vision of the awesome majesty of the American wilderness, especially along the banks of the Hudson River, which he deftly captured in his vigorous brushwork.

The second generation of the Hudson River school, working between about 1850 and 1870, approached landscape with the midcentury's clear realism. Concentrating on effects of light and atmosphere (in a manner known as luminism), they produced extremely detailed paintings in a precise technique that left hardly any trace of brushwork. The leading figure of this generation was Cole's only pupil, Frederick E. Church. With his thorough knowledge of natural history and his in-exhaustible technical facility, he painted such natural spectacles as *Niagara Falls* (1857, Corcoran Gallery, Washington, D.C.) and South American wonders such as *Cotopaxi* (1863, Reading, Pa., Public Museum and Art Gallery) on immense canvases that toured the country to crowds and acclaim. The German-trained Albert Bierstadt had a similar success with large, theatrical paintings of Rocky Mountain scenery. Fitz Hugh Lane (1804–65) painted crystalline views of New England harbors. John F. Kensett (c. 1816–72) and Martin J. Heade (1819–1904) painted modest-size landscapes in the luminist manner.

At the same time, still-life painting flourished as the second most important genre. History painting also flourished between about 1845 and 1860, mainly in the manner learned by Americans at the art academy in Düsseldorf, Germany, and exemplified in *Washington Crossing the Delaware* (1848, Metropolitan Museum, New York City), by Emanuel Leutze (1816–68). Events of the Revolution again served as a chief source of themes.

**Sculpture Before the Civil War.** American sculpture in a formal sense began with William Rush (1756–1833), who evolved from a leading carver of ship figureheads to creator of the first monumental American sculptures, *Comedy* and *Tragedy* (1808, Edwin Forrest Home, Philadelphia). Although Rush carved his neoclassical figures in wood, the preferred medium until 1865 was white marble, also favored in the idealized Greek Revival architecture of the young republic. Hiram Powers made his reputation with what became the most widely admired of all American marble sculptures, his nude *Greek Slave* (1843, six replicas). This first generation produced relatively severe, compact, idealized Greek sculptures in the cool spirit of the Italian sculptor Antonio Canova and the Danish sculptor Bertel Thorvaldsen. The more literal sensibility and baroque taste of the mid-19th century asserted itself in detailed, sentimental, and dramatic sculptures, beginning with the innovative *Cleopatra* (1858, three versions) by William W. Story (1819–95). Among the many American artists who spent much of their careers studying and working in Italy was Harriet Hosmer (1830–1908). Her sculpture often derived its theme from the antique and was worked mainly in marble. Although most of her sculpture was completed after the Civil War, her style reflects that of her pre–Civil War male colleagues.

## FROM THE AMERICAN CIVIL WAR TO THE ARMORY SHOW: 1865 TO 1913

The two major developments of post–Civil War architecture were the polychromed "muscular" High Victorian Gothic and the mansarded Second Empire style. The popularity of these styles signaled a shift toward French influence and away from English styles that had dominated American architecture, painting, and sculpture until then. At the end of the century, study abroad became more accessible and was even considered a prerequisite for acceptance in some circles. Study in Italy continued to be popular, and the high-quality art instruction in Paris drew young American artists.

**Architecture After the Civil War.** Superior training and increasing sophistication were particularly evident among the architects who returned from the École des Beaux-Arts in Paris with a command of more extensive planning and correct detailing in a range of styles. The first to return was Richard Morris Hunt, best known for his mansions for the Vanderbilt family, such as Biltmore in Asheville, N.C., and others in New York, in the style of 16th-century French châteaus; and The Breakers in Newport, R.I., an Italian Renaissance palazzo. The partners of the firm of McKim, Mead, and White preferred Italian Renaissance styles for their major commissions, such as New York City's palatial Henry Villard Houses (1882–85) and the Boston Public Library (1888–95). Perhaps the greatest talent of the generation was Henry H. Richardson, whose bold sense of mass and control of detail is evident in his Trinity Church (1872–77, Boston), carried out in the Romanesque style, which became immensely popular in the U.S. during the 1880s.

In the late 19th century Americans led the way in two architectural forms: the country house and the skyscraper. The American shingle style was developed out of the Queen Anne revivals of the English architects Norman Shaw (1831–1912) and William Burges (1827–81). Organized in an informal, rambling fashion around a large living hall, these houses show the development of the open plan and easy transitions between indoors and outdoors that were to become hallmarks of the best modern architecture of the early 20th century. The vertical development of office buildings was made possible by the introduction of the elevator, which was put into operation in New York City office buildings in the 1850s. With the introduction of internal metal-frame construction in William Le Baron Jenney's Home Insurance Company Building (1885, demolished 1931) in Chicago, the stage was set for the innovations of the Chicago school (q.v.) of architects, led by Louis Sullivan. Sullivan's Guaranty Building (1894–95, Buffalo, N.Y.) expresses in its cladding (sheathing) the internal structure, achieving lightness with its emphatic verticality and unity with its bold cornice.

The works of the early 20th century provided the basis for later exciting architectural styles, but this

*Carson Pirie Scott Building (1899–1904), Chicago, Ill. Louis Sullivan's spacious, clean-lined structure with its horizontal bands of windows was the forerunner of modern architecture.*
Hedrich–Blessing

period was also the culmination of late-19th-century ideas. A skyscraper such as Cass Gilbert's graceful Woolworth Building (1910–13, New York City) could only have been built using new technology, but its sheath of Gothic detail hearkens back to an earlier time.

**Painting After the Civil War.** The development of American painting after the Civil War became more complex as the number of artists greatly increased, as their communication with Europe and awareness of a wider range of current styles grew, and as they expanded their interests to include new subjects and a wider range of media.

*Late 19th-century painters.* Landscape painting culminated in the mature work of George Inness.

Drawing on the example of the French Barbizon school, Inness added to his American naturalism a taste for the moods of nature. Using increasingly rich color, he developed a poetic manner.

A fascination with technique was characteristic of the academically better trained artists of the late 19th century. During the 1870s a group of Americans, including Frank Duveneck, William Merritt Chase (1849–1916), and J. Frank Currier (1843–1909), studied painting at the Munich Academy, where they acquired a bold and brilliant alla prima (rapid completion) technique. Another master who emerged during the 1870s was the facile John Singer Sargent, the most popular Anglo-American portraitist of his time.

# AMERICAN ART AND ARCHITECTURE

The two foremost painters of 19th-century American life were Winslow Homer and Thomas Eakins. Starting his career as an illustrator, Homer began to paint the life of rural America, particularly the world of children, as in *Snap the Whip* (1872, Butler Institute, Youngstown, Ohio). In the 1880s he turned his attention primarily to the dangerous life of deep-sea fishermen, finding in the struggle against the treacherous sea a metaphor for the helplessness of humans before their fate. His vision became even blacker in such austere late works as *The Fox Hunt* (1893, Pennsylvania Academy of the Fine Arts) and *The Gulf Stream* (1899, Metropolitan Museum). His finest works achieve a depth of vision and mastery of design that has seldom been surpassed in American art. Eakins's realism began with a highly scientific naturalism, as in his series of boating pictures done in the 1870s. In the 1880s and '90s he brought this realist vision to bear mainly in portraiture. His greatest achievement was his portrait of Dr. Samuel Gross (1805–84) demonstrating a surgical procedure to a class, known as *The Gross Clinic* (1875, Jefferson Medical College, Philadelphia). Audiences were shocked by the unflinching realism of the large portrait, particularly by the blood on the hand of the lecturing surgeon. In his other portraits Eakins achieved a penetrating insight and clear understanding of form.

A less profound realism was perfected in the illusionistic still-life painting of William M. Harnett (1848–92) and his followers in the last two decades of the century. Their control of textures and lighting gave the objects in their paintings a sense of solidity and actuality that was meant to fool the eye.

At the same time, the romantic current in American art, strong since the time of Washington Allston, found expression in the new landscape school, in the poetic works of William Morris Hunt and John La Farge, and in the brooding expressionistic creations of Ralph Blakelock, best known for his moonlit nocturnes, and Albert Pinkham Ryder, whose imaginary subjects reveal an inner vision of great intensity. The American landscape painter perhaps most closely allied to the French impressionists was John Henry Twachtman, whose cool, shimmering color evoked the experience of nature in his canvases.

Perhaps the most admired and influential artist throughout the Western world at the turn of the century was James Abbott McNeill Whistler, who worked abroad most of his career, developing advanced principles of nearly abstract surface design and unified color. Another important expatriate artist was Mary Cassatt, who was closely associated with the French impressionists, in particular with Edgar Degas; her admiration for Japanese prints is reflected in many of her paintings (after

Max Schmitt in a Single Scull *(1871, Metropolitan Museum of Art, New York City), by Thomas Eakins, one of the most influential painters of the 19th-century realist tradition in America.* Alfred N. Punnett Fund and Gift of George D. Pratt, 1934

Backyards, Greenwich Village *(1914, Whitney Museum, New York City), by John Sloan, one of the leading members of the group called The Eight, also known as the Ashcan school.*
Whitney Museum of American Art

1890) of her favorite theme, the mother and child. Partly through the influence of Cassatt on American collectors, American artists who painted in the impressionist style found support, and they formed the most vigorous school of impressionism outside France.

*Early 20th-century painters.* The two reigning styles at the turn of the century—the academic style, with its ideal subjects, and impressionism, with its focus on patrician country life—both ignored the urban scene. In the early years of the century Robert Henri advocated more contemporary subjects to his students, including George Luks, William Glackens, John Sloan, and Everett Shinn (1876–1953). These artists drew on their earlier experience as newspaper illustrators to capture the vitality, variety, and color of urban life. The sketchy appearance and frank realism of their paintings brought official rejection; in 1908 these artists exhibited together as part of a group called The Eight. Although not part of this exhibition, George W. Bellows also used his vigorous brushwork to express the vitality of the urban scene, as in his *Cliff Dwellers* (1913, Los Angeles County

Museum of Art), depicting street life among the immigrants in New York City. As an avant-garde movement, The Eight (or the Ashcan school) had a relatively short life, being supplanted by the wave of modernism after the Armory Show, the epochal exhibition of modern European art held in a New York City armory in 1913.

**Late 19th- and Early 20th-Century Sculpture.** French influence dominated American sculpture after the Civil War, when most leading sculptors studied in Paris. Marble sculpture became more pictorial, as the simple volumes of the neoclassical school gave way to more open and detailed forms, in which the play of light created patterns across space. Bronze, more romantic and potentially more realistic, became a substitute for the favored white marble of the earlier period.

Despite the material or actual size, most sculpture of these years strove for a monumentality seldom seen before in American sculpture. The works of Augustus Saint-Gaudens (e.g. *Robert Gould Shaw Memorial*, 1897, Boston Common) and Daniel Chester French (*Abraham Lincoln*, 1922, Lincoln Memorial, Washington, D.C.), as well as

441

The Bronco Buster, *a bronze statuette by Frederic Remington, noted for his paintings, drawings, and sculpture of the American West.*

Thomas Gilcrease Institute of American History & Art, Tulsa, Okla.

Frederic Remington's small bronzes of the Old West, reflected the new American attitude of dominance and strength.

## MODERN AMERICAN ART AND ARCHITECTURE

Following World War I, American art achieved international stature and worldwide influence as architects, painters, and sculptors continued to devise new forms, new styles, and even new means of artistic expression.

**Architecture Since World War I.** Beaux-arts styles continued until the stock market crash ended the building boom of the 1920s. In both civic and domestic buildings, Georgian and Roman styles predominated, adapted with a refinement of detail to 20th-century needs.

At the same time, certain pioneers struck out in individual directions that were part of the progression toward modern design. California, in particular, proved to be fertile ground for innovative architects. Charles Greene (1868–1957) and his brother Henry (1870–1954) incorporated the quiet beauty of the Arts and Crafts movement into their meticulously designed and constructed residences, among them the David B. Gamble house (1908) in Pasadena. Beaux-arts-trained Julia Morgan (1872–1957) created William Randolph Hearst's spectacular castle (1919–39) at San Simeon, among other projects, each of which attested to her originality.

**Frank Lloyd Wright.** The most notable innovator was Frank Lloyd Wright, who began his career in the Chicago office of Louis Sullivan. Before World War I, Wright set new directions with the development of his prairie houses, suburban dwellings mainly in the vicinity of Chicago. He experimented freely with the organization of plans to develop articulated yet unified and simplified spaces. Space was made to flow between interior and exterior, and the long horizontal lines of eaves further served to unify the design and to suggest the wide prairie expanses of the Midwest. The publication (1910) of these advanced designs in Germany influenced the development of architecture in Europe during the 1920s. In 1936 Wright developed these ideas further in Fallingwater, a country house near Pittsburgh, Pa. It is boldly cantilevered over a waterfall, its glass walls permitting interior and exterior to mingle without detracting from the emphatically horizontal composition of the suspended concrete slabs. In his later work Wright used concrete in inventive structural systems and in bold geometric forms, usually planned on a dominant geometric principle, as in the spiral Guggenheim Museum (1956–59) in New York City.

**The International Style and recent trends.** An important change of direction in American architecture occurred with the arrival (c. 1930) in the U.S. of a number of German and Austrian architects who left Europe partly as a result of the Nazi suppression of avant-garde architecture. Rudolph Schindler (1887–1953) and Richard Neutra, in Los Angeles, Walter Gropius and Marcel Breuer, in Cambridge, Mass., and Ludwig Mies van der Rohe, in Chicago, brought to the U.S. the forthright expression of function and structure and the sense of abstract composition that was first associated with the German-based art school, the Bauhaus (q.v.), and later became known as the International Style. They continued teaching in America, developing schools of architecture that were the most advanced of their day.

Mies was to be the most influential, with his development of the steel structure, around which was stretched the nonbearing curtain wall, often mostly of glass. This system was the basis of the ubiquitous glass-box skyscraper.

One of Gropius's pupils, Philip Johnson, played a prominent role in introducing the International Style to the U.S. In collaboration with Mies, he designed one of the greatest triumphs of the style, the Seagram Building (1958) in New York City. In the 1980s Johnson became a leading exponent of the eclectic postmodern style, notably in the AT&T (now Sony) building (1984) in New York, which incorporated Renaissance elements and a baroque pediment.

*Robie House (1909), Chicago. Frank Lloyd Wright's influential design used low, sweeping lines, squat chimneys, sheltering overhangs, and warm-hued bricks to express a Midwest prairie setting.*

Hedrich–Blessing

In reaction to the stark, compact slabs of office buildings that embodied (less and less creatively) the International Style, a movement arose in the 1950s toward more fluid expression through conspicuous engineering, as in the work of Eero Saarinen. Seeking bolder composition and more aggressive expression of the materials (notably concrete), Paul Rudolph led a trend derived from the English New Brutalism. In the 1950s and '60s some of the finest work of Louis I. Kahn was built, ingeniously combining monumental elegance of form with utility, as in his Salk Institute (1965, La Jolla, Calif.). I. M. Pei has designed buildings of eloquent simplicity all over the world, including the East Building wing (1978) of the National Gallery of Art in Washington, D.C., the Jacob K. Javits Convention Center (1986) in New York City, and the pyramid-shaped glass entrance (1989) to the Louvre in Paris.

In the 1970s and '80s postmodern architecture emerged as a reaction against the Bauhaus austerities dominant in the U.S. after World War II. Postmodernism is characterized by individuality, the incorporation of stylistic elements from earlier periods, and sometimes playfulness and eccentricity. Among its leading practitioners were Robert Venturi (1925– ), Michael Graves (1934– ), Charles Gwathmey (1938– ), Robert A. M. Stern (1939– ), and Richard Meier (1934– ). Outstanding examples of the style include public structures, such as Graves's Portland Building (1982) in Portland, Oreg., and Meier's High Museum of Art (1985) in Atlanta. Gwathmey's Cogan Residence (1972) in East Hampton, N.Y., is a fine example of postmodern domestic design. Somewhat independent of postmodernism are Frank O. Gehry (1929– ) and Helmut Jahn (1940– ). Gehry, conceiving of buildings as sculpture, deliberately utilized low-budget chain-link fencing and corrugated metal in maverick designs for residences, shopping malls, and public buildings such as the mini-campus of Loyola Marymount University's Law School (1984) in Los Angeles. Jahn sought to modify Mies van der Rohe's influence by employing circular shapes and facades enlivened by receding bays, colored glass, and metal strips. An example of his "user-oriented" public buildings is the State of Illinois Center (1985), Chicago.

**Painting Since World War I.** American students in Paris in the early 1900s experienced directly the work of Paul Cézanne, the Fauves, and Pablo Picasso, as well as other early forms of abstraction. In 1908, the photographer Alfred Stieglitz began to show in his Photo-Secession Gallery in New York City the work of John Marin, Arthur Dove, Max Weber, and other innovative American artists, including many photographers. Photography's recognition as a fine art was just in its early stages, but its creative potential continued to develop and its importance as art grew as the century progressed. *See* PHOTOGRAPHY.

For a brief period after World War I, American painters participated in variations on the cubist movement. Joseph Stella took up Italian futurism, celebrating motion and industrial forms in his monumental *Brooklyn Bridge* (1919, Yale University Art Gallery). Georgia O'Keeffe turned to nearly abstract composition, based on the bold forms and flowing lines of flowers and southwestern artifacts.

*Regionalism.* The influence of the Stieglitz group lessened during the course of the 1920s, as more traditional forms were again reasserted. The most widespread movement of representational painting was regionalism, which rejected the internationalism of abstract art and took as its subject matter the daily life of the American farm or

*Rockefeller Center (1930s), New York City. The slablike stone skyscrapers (center) grouped around a pedestrian mall show effective city planning. Glass towers behind (1960s) adapt the International Style.* Ezra Stoller–ESTO

small town. Thomas Hart Benton, the leading figure of the movement, developed a monumental, highly plastic style, the bulging forms and abrupt spatial transitions of which were directly inspired by baroque art. Grant Wood worked in a painstaking, highly detailed manner, combining the precision of 16th-century Flemish and German painting with the large, simple forms and naive presentation of American folk painting, as in his famous *American Gothic* (1930, Art Institute of Chicago). Both artists treated their anecdotal, rustic subjects with elements of caricature and the mock-heroic. Regionalism flourished in most parts of the country, and during the Great Depression of the 1930s it was the dominant style in such relief programs as the Work Projects Administration (WPA), through which the federal government put artists to work painting murals for post offices and other public buildings.

**Realism.** The best-known American realist painter of the 20th century is Edward Hopper, an independent who stood apart from contemporary movements. His work conveys the loneliness of the city and its inhabitants. His formal purity and depth of vision rank him, along with Homer and Eakins,

among the most profound of American realists. Another well-known independent realist, Andrew Wyeth, drew upon rural subject matter to create haunting, wistful images rendered with meticulous draftsmanship and subdued coloring.

Another type of realism grew out of the experience of the Great Depression and characterized the work of many artists involved in the WPA programs. The social realists—so called because of their passionate concern with the effects of poverty and injustice in the U.S.—include such artists as Ben Shahn and Jacob Lawrence (1917– ), the first prominent modern black artist.

**Painting Since World War II.** During World War II, the U.S. emerged as the world's most powerful nation, militarily and economically. This prosperity supported the nation's growing leadership in art, as New York City, the home of the most significant development in abstract art since cubism, replaced Paris as world art capital.

*Abstract expressionism.* The school of abstract expressionism (or New York school) sought to reinterpret abstract painting in terms of the strong color and broad, "gestural" brushstrokes of expressionism. A key element was the surrealist theory that through automatic, undirected processes the artist could draw upon subconscious creative forces.

Jackson Pollock developed a technique that involved dripping paint from cans and brushes on outsize canvases, creating patterns through rhythmic, semiautomatic motions. During the process he would respond to the accidental quality of the drips to develop or balance what had occurred previously. Other artists, while sharing the free, energetic brushwork and large scale characteristic of the movement, achieved quite distinct styles and expressive qualities. Willem de Kooning, never a truly abstract painter, is perhaps best known for his violently intense depictions of women. A much more serene feeling is conveyed by the meditative paintings of Robert Motherwell and by the stark canvases of Franz Kline, whose bold black brushwork suggests calligraphy. The related movement of color-field painting, characterized by broad, subtly varied expanses of pure color, reached its highest distinction in the work of Clyfford Still, Mark Rothko, and Barnett Newman.

Still others employed images of things seen or imagined. Armenian-born Arshile Gorky was among the earliest painters to be called an abstract expressionist. His canvases are filled with organic forms that defy identification but bring to mind objects from nature, as do the titles he chose for them. William Baziotes (1912–63) also populated his bold canvases with unidentifiable "characters," seemingly drawn from myths or dreams. The painting of Philip Guston (1913–80) was never wholly abstract, even in his work from the 1940s and '50s. Later, he introduced into his work numerous objects—shoes, hooded figures, clocks, bottles—which invited immersion into the painter's confusing, often threatening world. Abstract expressionism is not confined to those artists at work in the 1940s and '50s; its adherents in the 1980s and '90s have developed eloquent, sometimes disturbing, works. Among these painters are Elizabeth Murray (1940–  ) and Katherine Porter (1941–  ).

**Pop and Minimalism.** By 1960, two separate reactions against abstract expressionism had emerged. Jasper Johns, with his cool, deadpan depictions of flags and other ordinary objects, and Robert Rauschenberg, incorporating mass media material into his collages, set the stage for pop art, in which Andy Warhol and Roy Lichtenstein, among others, reproduced images drawn from advertisements, comic books, and other products of popular culture.

At the same time, minimalist artists, seeking to emphasize the purely formal, surface qualities of painting, confined their work to flat, precisely rendered geometric forms. Geometric abstraction was adopted by a number of artists in the 1960s and continued to be developed through the '90s. Frank Stella's early monochromatic works gave way in the '70s to his enormous, brilliantly colored "protractor" series. Often washing huge shaped canvases with only a single, uniform hue, Ellsworth Kelly carried these ideas to their ex-

*Interior, TWA Terminal (1962), Kennedy Airport, New York City. Through the swooping sculptural quality of reinforced concrete shell construction, Eero Saarinen creates a sense of flight.* **Trans World Airlines**

tremes. Starting in the late 1980s and continuing into the '90s, the Canadian painter Dorothea Rockburne (1921–   ) also worked in this form.

**Pluralism.** During the 1970s and '80s there was no dominant movement in American painting. It was a period of pluralism, encompassing a bewildering variety of styles and methods. Nevertheless, a few distinct tendencies did emerge. Conceptual art, concerned chiefly with calling attention to ideas, inherited the analytical impulse of minimalism. Installation art, often in the form of mixed media assemblages, as in the playful, large-scale work of Jonathan Borofsky (1942–   ), was also important. The emphasis on personal and political content found in the work of many women artists of the '70s led to a revival of expressive and socially conscious tendencies in art.

While often political by implication, a number of graffiti artists came to prominence in the 1980s. Keith Haring (1958–90) and Haitian-born Jean-Michel Basquiat (1960–88) began painting on city walls and streets, before taking to canvas and other mobile media. Highly charged works inspired by political issues continued to be important in art into the 1990s. The conceptual and mixed-media work of Jenny Holzer (1950–   ) and Barbara Kruger (1945–   ) combined text and image to comment on various social issues. The often horrific images of Leon Golub (1922–   )

brought to the fore human rights abuses, and David Wojnarowicz (1955–92) used his painting and collages to deal with the issue of acquired immune deficiency syndrome (AIDS).

Figurative or realistic painting, kept alive in the postwar period by such influential artists as Milton Avery and Fairfield Porter (1907–75), underwent a revival after 1970. Like Avery and Porter, younger figurative painters assimilated many of the aesthetic concerns of abstract painters in their work, as in the formally rigorous nude figure studies of Philip Pearlstein (1924–   ) and the flatly composed, elegantly simplified landscapes and portraits of Alex Katz (1927–   ). Janet Fish (1938–   ) used colors of extreme brilliance for her landscapes and still lifes. The ironically humorous works of Robert Colescott (1925–   ) use famous works of art and comic-book format to comment on the roles of blacks in American art and society. An ironical stance toward the art establishment is also evident in the multimedia works of Mike and Doug Starn (1961–   ), and in the mammoth canvases painted by Mark Tansey (1949–   ), who brings to bear a technique akin to the best of the academic artists of the last century as well as a keen interest in philosophy and psychology. The influence of pop art was apparent in photo-realism, exemplified by the meticulous cityscapes of Richard Estes (1936–   ) and the large-scale portraits of Chuck Close (1940–   ).

Three Flags *(1958, Whitney Museum, New York City), by Jasper Johns, one of the pioneer artists of the post–World War II pop art movement.*

The "new image" painters who emerged in the mid-1970s, such as Jennifer Bartlett (1941– ), Susan Rothenberg (1945– ), and Neil Jenney (1945– ), played a crucial role in the transition from abstraction to figurative work. They were the predecessors of the neoexpressionist movement of the early '80s, in which painters used lurid color, ambiguous imagery, and often crude, cartoonlike drawing to convey provocative, personal visions. Artists associated with the movement were Julian Schnabel (1951– ), David Salle (1952– ), Robert Longo (1953– ), and Eric Fischl (1948– ). A more sober realism, mixing modernist sensibility with such traditional forms as still life and allegory, flourished in the work of William Bailey (1930– ), Jack Beal (1931– ), and Alfred Leslie (1927– ).

**20th-Century American Sculpture.** Although academic sculptural styles, as modified by the French sculptor Auguste Rodin, dominated American sculpture in the first decade of the century, artists such as Paul Manship and Gaston Lachaise introduced a degree of simplification and stylization. In 1916 Elie Nadelman returned from Paris with a personal cubist sculptural style, which he later abandoned for elegant stylized figures inspired by folk sculpture. John Storrs (1885–1956), Jacques Lipchitz, Chaim Gross, and William Zorach were other early abstract sculptors.

Isamu Noguchi's work was first seen in the late 1920s; he studied with the Romanian-French sculptor Constantin Brancusi and derived lasting inspiration from the older master's simple volumes and smoothly flowing surfaces. Alexander Calder, influenced by the biomorphic surrealism of Joan Miró, a Spaniard, invented a new form of sculpture, the mobile, which brought to sculpture movement and spontaneous change.

Constructivism, the building of sculptures from different manufactured elements, was introduced to the U.S. by émigrés from Germany in the late 1930s and 40s, in particular by the brilliantly inventive sculptor Naum Gabo. Constructivism became the basis for the new American sculpture of the 1940s and '50s, through which Americans established world preeminence. Like abstract expressionist painting, American abstract sculpture possessed a heroic expressive energy. David Smith, the leading force in the movement, welded together sheets of industrial metal, found objects, even tractor parts, into brutally direct compositions of compelling force. Other abstract sculptural styles range from Richard Lippold's delicate yet complex wire hangings to Mark di Suvero's playful, gigantic outdoor forms, and the foreboding architectonic "structures" of Vito Acconci (1940– ) and Alice Aycock (1946– ).

After 1970, American sculpture, like painting, entered into a period of pluralism. Pop sculpture encompassed the polychrome plastic figures, bordering on caricature, by Duane Hanson

*David Smith's Cubi XVII (1963, left) and Cubi XVIII (1964), made of burnished stainless steel, at Smith's farm, Bolton Landing, N.Y. (now in the Dallas Museum of Fine Arts and the Museum of Fine Arts, Boston, respectively).*  Estate of David Smith

(1925– ), and the painted plaster representations and the so-called soft sculptures of fast food items and other mundane objects created by Claes Oldenburg; the sculptor George Segal is sometimes classified as a pop artist, but his life-like white plaster figures go beyond the impersonality of pop art. The enormous metal structures of Richard Serra (1939– ) were devised to articulate outdoor spaces, as opposed to the more intimately scaled wooden wall environments of Louise Nevelson. Other important works of the 1970s ranged from earthworks covering vast expanses of land to the precise, symmetrical minimalist sculpture of Donald Judd and Sol LeWitt (1928– ). The 1980s and '90s saw the emergence of many important sculptors who looked to organic forms for their inspiration. Louise Bourgeois (1911– ), whose work spans four decades, came into greatest prominence. Also of note are Martin Puryear (1941– ), Nancy Graves (1940– ), and Kiki Smith (1954– ). These artists are sometimes referred to as postmodern or post-minimalist sculptors.　　　　　　　M.A.Q.

See also AMERICAN INDIANS; ARCHITECTURE; GLASS; MODERN ART AND ARCHITECTURE; PAINTING; PORTRAITURE; PRINTS AND PRINTMAKING; SCULPTURE; WOOD CARVING. For additional information on individual artists, see biographies of those whose names are not followed by dates.

For further information on this topic, see the Bibliography in volume 28, sections 662–63, 677.

**AMERICAN ASSOCIATION FOR THE ADVANCEMENT OF SCIENCE** (AAAS), society of scientists, founded in 1848 for the purpose of advancing science in the New World in every feasible way. The association emphasizes the unity of interest of workers in all branches of science, which it promotes through the publication of reports and the organization of meetings. One of the largest associations of scientists in the world, it has some 285 affiliated and associated societies, covering the entire field of pure and applied science. It is grouped in 19 sections: mathematics; physics; chemistry; astronomy; geology and geography; biological sciences; anthropology; psychology; social, economic, and political sciences; history and philosophy of science; engineering; medical sciences; dentistry; pharmaceutical sciences; agriculture; industrial science; information, computing, and communication; atmospheric and hydrospheric sciences; and social impacts of science and engineering. The association publishes the weekly magazine Science, as well as various symposium volumes. It has produced new materials for the teaching of science from kindergarten through the elementary grades.

AAAS headquarters is in Washington, D.C.

Similar organizations have been founded in many other countries, including the British Association for the Advancement of Science and the Institut de France.

**AMERICAN BAR ASSOCIATION,** national organization of the legal profession, founded in 1878. Its activities include maintenance of high ethical standards for which a comprehensive Code of Professional Responsibility for lawyers was adopted in 1969; support of legal education and approval of law schools that meet the standards of the association; extension of legal services; and legal research through the American Bar Foundation. Its policies are determined by a house of delegates representing the legal profession and administered by a board of governors. Headquarters is in Chicago and Washington, D.C.

**AMERICAN BIBLE SOCIETY,** society for the promotion of worldwide circulation of the Bible, without regard to race or creed. Founded in 1816 in New York City and headquartered there, it distributes various versions of the Bible, in many languages, and also in forms printed and recorded for the blind. The official publication of the society is the Bible Society Record.

**AMERICAN CIVIL LIBERTIES UNION** (ACLU), national nonprofit and nonpartisan association founded in 1920 by a group of liberals, including the social reformer Jane Addams, the writers Helen Keller and James Weldon Johnson, the socialist leaders Eugene V. Debs and Norman Thomas, and the jurist Felix Frankfurter. Chapters are located throughout the U.S. The ACLU conducts its business through staff and cooperating attorneys; it maintains a national staff in New York City, a legislative office in Washington, D.C., and a regional office in Atlanta, Ga.

Organized to defend the civil liberties of all citizens, it follows a liberal interpretation of U.S. constitutional law in defense of freedom of speech, press, assembly, and religion. It is active before national, state, and local legislative bodies, in courts of all jurisdictions, and in the preparation of educational materials. Since 1920 it has acted directly or by intervention in almost all cases involving civil liberty in the U.S., including the Sacco and Vanzetti, Scopes, and Scottsboro trials, and cases involving freedom of expression in the arts, the rights of religious groups, the unconstitutionality of white primaries, and the prosecution of citizens under so-called loyalty acts. It also took a leading part in the legal fight that resulted in the abolition by the U.S. Supreme Court of segregation in public schools under the doctrine of separate but equal facilities.

**AMERICAN ELK.** See WAPITI.